HUMAN RIGHTS IN INTERNATIONAL LAW: LEGAL AND POLICY ISSUES

Edited by
THEODOR MERON

CLARENDON PRESS · OXFORD

Oxford University Press, Walton Street, Oxford OX2 6DP

Oxford New York Toronto
Delhi Bombay Calcutta Madras Karachi
Petaling Jaya Singapore Hong Kong Tokyo
Nairobi Dar es Salaam Cape Town
Melbourne Auckland
and associated companies in
Berlin Ibadan

Oxford is a trade mark of Oxford University Press

Published in the United States
by Oxford University Press, New York

First published 1984
First issued as a paperback 1985
Reprinted 1988, 1989

British Library Cataloguing in Publication Data
Meron, Theodor
Human rights in International law.
Vol. 1
1. Civil rights (International law)
I. Title
341.4'81   K3240
ISBN 0–19–825540–3 (pbk.)

Library of Congress Cataloguing in Publication Data
Human rights in international law.
Includes biographies and index.
1. Civil rights (International law)   I. Meron, Theodor, 1930–
K3240.4.H835   1984   341.4'84   83–4214
ISBN 0–19–825540–3 (pbk.)

0163233

Printed in Great Britain
at the University Printing House, Oxford
by David Stanford
Printer to the University

I dedicate this book to
Professor Louis B. Sohn,
a great human rights scholar and teacher,
my friend and mentor

T.M.

Preface

The object of this book—which has been funded by a major grant from the Rockefeller Foundation, by financial aid provided by the New York University School of Law Research Program, and by Mr. Harold Robbins—is to provide teachers and students not only with a textbook covering the principal human rights areas, but also with pedagogical suggestions, syllabi, bibliographies, and case studies. The volume offers teachers an opportunity to choose topics either for an entire course on international human rights or for a few hours devoted to the subject within a course on constitutional law, international relations, political science, international organizations, etc. The work is equally suitable for use as a reference book by persons engaged in research or practice. A detailed introduction to the volume is contained in *Teaching Human Rights: An Overview* (chapter 1).

I wish to record my gratitude to the Rockefeller Foundation, both for its grant and for enabling me to work on the book as scholar-in-residence in the Foundation's Villa Serbelloni, to my research assistants, Martha Schweitz, Anna M. Pappas, Linda L. Hazou, and, in particular, James J. Busuttil, and to my secretary, Madelon Blavatnik.

Theodor Meron

Contributors

Thomas Buergenthal: Judge, Inter-American Court of Human Rights; Dean and Professor of Law, Washington College of Law, American University.

Yoram Dinstein: Rector and Yanowicz Professor of Human Rights, Tel Aviv University.

Jack Greenberg: Director Counsel, NAACP Legal Defense and Educational Fund; Adjunct Professor of Law, Columbia University

Louis Henkin: University Professor, Columbia University.

Rosalyn Higgins: Professor of Law, London School of Economics.

John P. Humphrey: Gale Professor of Law, Emeritus, McGill University School of Law; Canadian Human Rights Foundation.

Richard B. Lillich: Howard W. Smith Professor of Law, University of Virginia School of Law.

Theodor Meron: Professor of Law, New York University School of Law.

Jerome J. Shestack: Attorney; past United States Representative to the United Nations Commission on Human Rights.

Louis B. Sohn: Woodruff Professor of International Law, University of Georgia School of Law.

David M. Trubek: Professor of Law, University of Wisconsin-Madison Law School.

David Weissbrodt: Professor of Law, University of Minnesota Law School.

Francis Wolf: Legal Adviser and Assistant Director-General, International Labour Office.

INTERNATIONAL LAW OF HUMAN RIGHTS

Summary of Contents

Table of Contents

Part I: The Setting

Chapter 1
Teaching Human Rights: An Overview*

Theodor Meron

A. Teaching Human Rights: State of the Art

1. REASONS FOR TEACHING HUMAN RIGHTS

The reasons for teaching and learning human rights were described as early as 1948 in the Universal Declaration of Human Rights (Universal Declaration),[1] the basic statement of human rights which continues to be the inspiration of all other human rights instruments and activities. Article 26(2) of the Universal Declaration provides that education should be directed to the 'strengthening of respect for human rights and fundamental freedoms'. Education should promote understanding, tolerance, and friendship among all nations and racial or religious groups, and further the maintenance of peace. Article 26(2) thus contains the essential reasons which continue to guide the teaching of human rights today.

The 1978 UNESCO International Congress on Teaching of Human Rights, which convened in Vienna, further developed the reasons for teaching human rights.[2] The Final Act of the Vienna Congress recognized that '[w]hile education should make the individual aware of his or her own rights, it should at the same time instill respect for the rights of others'.[3] Human rights must, moreover, 'be seen as an aspect of professional, ethical and social responsibility in all fields of research, study, teaching and work'.[4] The International Congress also recognized that the teaching of human rights should have among its goals securing the observance of human rights in cases of armed conflict and that therefore it should include the teaching of international humanitarian law.[5] Indeed, the dissemination of the applicable rules of humanitarian law to the armed forces constitutes a legal duty of the parties to the instruments governing the conduct of armed conflicts.[6] Unless soldiers know the human rights applicable in

---

* © Theodor Meron 1983.

[1] G.A. Res. 217A, U.N. Doc. A/810, at 71 (1948).

[2] *See* Part I(3), Final Document of the International Congress on the Teaching of Human Rights, *contained in* The Teaching of Human Rights Proceedings of the International Congress on the Teaching of Human Rights 40 (UNESCO 1980) [hereinafter cited as Vienna Final Document].

[3] *Id*. Part I(4).   [4] *Id*. Part I(6).

[5] *Id*. Preamble, *in fine* at 39.

[6] *See, e.g.,* art. 1. [Hague] Convention No. IV Respecting the Laws and Customs of War on

time of armed conflict, their compliance with those binding rules cannot realistically be expected. This is particularly important with the emergence of many newly independent states which do not have armed forces with established military traditions and military manuals.[7]

Knowledge and awareness of human rights is equally important in time of peace. There has been progress in the observance of human rights because of the pressure of public opinion exerted by peoples on their own governments and on the governments of other countries. Only peoples educated about and aware of their human rights can demand that their governments observe those rights. Human rights education, which is essential for the formation of public opinion and the generation of public pressure for compliance with human rights, is thus a *sine qua non* for the observance and the advancement of human rights.[8] Most importantly, knowledge of human rights is essential as a tool for the observance and the promotion of human rights and for the creation of a climate of public opinion in which gross violations of human rights are unacceptable. In the past, massive violations of human rights brought about an atmosphere which was conducive to war. While education alone cannot prevent the occurrence of gross violations of human rights, it can create moral and mental inhibitions and a sense of shame on the part of diplomats, leaders, and the military and can thus contribute to the prevention of war. The importance of the creation of a sense of shame on the part of violators or potential violators of human rights, long recognized and employed with effective leverage by the International Labour Organization (ILO), should be recognized as potentially a major factor which could contribute to the observance of human rights in areas outside the concern of the ILO.[9]

Given the multiplicity of available procedures and substantive rights and the potential for their domestic implementation, protection of human rights is now a subject to be taught not only as an academic or intellectual exercise, but, increasingly, as a skill for practitioners. It may be unethical, indeed, to practice law without having some

Land, 36 Stat. 2277, T.S. No. 539; art. 144, [Geneva] Convention Relative to the Protection of Civilian Persons in Time of War, 6 U.S.T. 3516, T.I.A.S. No. 3365, 75 U.N.T.S. 287; art. 83, Protocol Additional to the Geneva Conventions of August 12, 1949, and Relating to the Protection of Victims of International Armed Conflicts (Protocol I), U.N. Doc. A/32/144 (1977).

[7] *See* remarks by Dinstein, in Meron, *A Report on the N.Y.U. Conference on Teaching International Protection of Human Rights*, 13 N.Y.U. J. Int'l L. & Pol. 881, 918–19 (1981) [hereinafter cited as Meron Report].

[8] *See* remarks by Dinstein, *id.* at 888.

[9] *See* remarks by Wolf on the 'mobilization of shame' by the ILO on a tripartite basis, *id.* at 932.

knowledge of human rights.[10] Human rights should therefore be taught as a practical skill and to show law as a process. Moreover, students would be educated as 'citizens of the world'.[11]

Professor Sohn has suggested that human rights must be taught not only because for some it is an important theoretical and philosophical issue which goes to the essence of the law, or because for others it is a very practical issue which students ought to know because they might have use for it in practice, but because it is a part of a general education which people ought to have.[12] International protection of human rights has, as a subject, both a great potential and 'a great intellectual appeal because it is a topic of universal concern that cuts across major ideological, political and cultural boundaries'.[13]

2. PRESENT STATE OF THE TEACHING OF HUMAN RIGHTS AND THE AVAILABLE RESOURCES

Despite the many cogent reasons for teaching human rights, international human rights as a subject has not yet entered the mainstream of university education. The realization that human rights are of worldwide concern has increased interest in the subject, but the scarcity of teaching materials and teaching tools such as casebooks and textbooks has been an obstacle which has made it difficult for human rights to become part of the standard university curriculum.[14] The paucity of teaching materials and the marginal increase in the number of universities where human rights are taught[15] are also related to the scarcity of qualified teachers. The inadequacy of syllabi, bibliographies, reading lists, hypotheticals and examples for class discussion, role-playing and problem solving situations, etc., which could be useful not only for law teachers but for social scientists, have all contributed to the reluctance of university teachers to start teaching international protection of human rights. This is not to suggest that

[10] *See* remarks by Lillich, *id.* at 894; remarks by Weissbrodt, *id.* at 939.

[11] *See* remarks by Trubek, *id.* at 902.

[12] *See* remarks by Sohn, *id.* at 949. Sohn cited Chancellor Kent who said at the beginning of his Commentary on International Law (at 45, J.T. Abdy ed. 1866) that international law is something that everybody—not only a lawyer, but every gentleman—ought to know something about.

[13] Buergenthal, *A Challenge for the Universities*, UNESCO Courier, Oct. 1978, at 25, 26 [hereinafter cited as Buergenthal]. *See also* Buergenthal & Torney, *Expanding the International Human Rights Research Agenda*, 23 Int'l Studies Q. 321 (1979) [hereinafter cited as Buergenthal & Torney].

[14] *See* remarks by Redlich, in Meron Report, *supra* note 7, at 885-86.

[15] *See* remarks by Lillich, *id.* at 893. *See generally* Claude, *The ABA National Survey on Human Rights Teaching*, (unpublished) (presented to the Subcomm. on Human Rights Education of the American Bar Association and the Center for the Study of Human Rights of Columbia University) (Dec. 10, 1979); Claude, Krechevsky & Love, *Teaching International Human Rights: The State of the Art*, Pol. Sci. Teaching News, (Nov. 1980). For reports on the teaching of human rights in universities, *see* Vienna Final Document, *supra* note 2, at 49-90.

there are no important teaching resources in existence now. Apart from collections of documents,[16] the volumes by Sohn and Buergenthal,[17] Lillich and Newman,[18] and McDougal, Lasswell, and Chen[19] are of major importance. Another valuable book is the UNESCO Teaching Manual, edited by Vasak.[20] Reference should also be made to books which, while not primarily designed for teaching, can be useful for teaching purposes. One such book consists of essays on the International Covenant on Civil and Political Rights (Political Covenant),[21] edited by Henkin;[22] another is the comparatively short introduction to human rights by Robertson.[23] There has been a considerable increase in bibliographies, documentation, and collection of syllabi and curricula.[24]

Given the existing difficulties, the present volumes have been prepared with the aim of providing teachers and students not only with a textbook covering the principal human rights areas, but also with pedagogical suggestions, syllabi, bibliographies, case studies, hypotheticals, and examples.

[16] Basic documents on Human Rights (2d ed. I. Brownlie 1981) [hereinafter cited as Brownlie] is particularly useful. *See also* P. Sieghart, The International Law of Human Rights (1983).

[17] International Protection of Human Rights (1973) (and its documentary supplement: Basic Documents on International Protection of Human Rights) [hereinafter cited as Sohn & Buergenthal].

[18] International Human Rights: Problems of Law and Policy (1979) [hereinafter cited as Lillich & Newman].

[19] Human Rights and World Public Order (1980).

[20] Les Dimensions internationales des droits de l'homme (1979). The English translation of this Manual has appeared under the title: The International Dimensions of Human Rights (P. Alston ed. 1982).

[21] G.A. Res. 2200, 21 U.N. GAOR, Supp. (No. 16) 52, U.N. Doc. A/6316 (1966).

[22] The International Bill of Rights: The Covenant on Civil and Political Rights (L. Henkin ed. 1981).

[23] A. Robertson, Human Rights in the World: An Introduction to the Study of the International Protection of Human Rights (2d ed. 1982).

[24] Of particular interest is the bibliographic essay *Human Rights Law: A Research Guide to the Literature* by Diana Vincent-Daviss. It appears in three installments in N.Y.U. J. Int'l L. & Pol.: Part I discusses the literature and methods necessary for research into world-wide human rights programs, emphasizing rights formally recognized by the United Nations, 14 N.Y.U. J. Int'l L. & Pol. 209 (1981); Part II surveys materials dealing with refugees, nationality, and statelessness, and humanitarian law, 14 N.Y.U. J Int'l L. & Pol. 487 (1981); and Part III covers the human rights activities of the ILO, 15 N.Y.U. J. Int'l L. & Pol. 211 (1982). *See also* Friedman, *Human Rights Teaching and Research Instruments*, in l Universal Human Rights 77 (1979). The Columbia University Center for the Study of Human Rights has been compiling and keeps available for consultation a collection of syllabi and curricula. Important bibliographies are contained in Sohn & Buergenthal, *supra* note 17, and Lillich & Newman, *supra* note 18. Also see the material listed in Buergenthal & Torney, *supra* note 13. Attention should also be drawn to a number of human rights teaching institutes. Of particular importance are programs offered by the International Institute of Human Rights, Strasbourg, France, and the Human Rights Teaching Institute, co-sponsored by the American Bar Association's Subcommittee on Human Rights Education, the Columbia University Center for the Study of Human Rights, and Catholic and Cincinnati Universities. *See also* International Committee of the Red Cross & Henry Dunant Institute, Bibliography of International Humanitarian Law Applicable in Armed Conflicts (1980). Extensive bibliographies appear, of course, in the present volume.

B. Introducing the Book

1. THE PLAN AND THE CHAPTERS

No course on human rights could attempt to cover all the questions which are dealt with, sometimes in great detail, in this book. However, by providing a rich menu, the volume offers teachers the opportunity to choose topics either for an entire course on the international protection of human rights (primary concentration on human rights), or for a few hours devoted to the subject within a course on civil rights, constitutional law, international relations, political science, international organizations, etc. (secondary concentration on human rights). To this end, each chapter is subdivided as follows: I. Legal and Policy Considerations; II. Teaching Suggestions; III. Syllabus; IV. Minisyllabus; V. Bibliography; and VI. Minibibliography.

The Legal and Policy Considerations portions, without purporting to offer an exhaustive analysis of any of the topics (each of which comprises an extensive range of legal, political, and social issues), provide an overview and broad clarification of the principal concepts involved in the main human rights areas. They form the core of the book; indeed, several of the authors include their chapter in their minibibliography so that teachers using the shortened list would gain some familiarity with the area before focusing attention on a single issue. The book can also be useful as a reference work. The creative diversity evidenced in the Legal and Policy Considerations is matched only by the variety of methods proposed in the Teaching Suggestions, filling the spectrum from the most concrete to the most abstract, from the analytical to the process oriented.

The chapters were written by international lawyers specializing in the human rights field. They are particularly suitable for law teachers but could be used as well by teachers of other disciplines. The Editor is painfully aware of the difficulties involved in finding a common language for lawyers and other social scientists. This book can certainly help in the further cross-fertilization between law and the other social sciences.

Before addressing pedagogical tactics and making certain introductory observations about the chapters, the logic and purpose in the order of the chapters deserve mention. By proceeding from the jurisprudence of human rights through global protection to regional systems—and within the latter from the Inter-American system to the European—the sequence progresses not only from the global toward the more specific and more regional, but also towards the more settled, defined, or 'hard' law of international human rights.

Of course, for any given area, the more broad the consensus that exists on the standards of protection, the more readily do mechanisms of implementation take hold. Mere geographic scope is not the only variable here. While the practice that has developed under the European Convention on Human Rights[25] is highly advanced as compared to other efforts, other regions, particularly the Organization of African Unity and the League of Arab States, are just beginning a similar evolution.[26] Separate chapters have not been devoted to those regional developments because they are in their early stages and their outcome is still uncertain.

Henkin's chapter[27] comparing U.S. and international human rights is placed immediately after this overview not to suggest in any way that international protection of rights is merely U.S. constitutionalism projected around the world, but rather to provide a philosophical and comparative approach to the subject that is crucial to effectively understand and teach it. International human rights have developed from many separate strands in international relations and international law but most directly from domestic systems of rights protection. Students of the subject often approach the field from the domestic perspective. The fact that they approach it at all indicates that they are farsighted enough to recognize that the frequent absence of domestic-type enforcement mechanisms does not negate human rights as legal norms. The comparative jurisprudential perspective offered by Henkin provides a sound foundation on which to build. The U.S. constitutional system, which is a principal human rights system, is compared to the international system. In broad strokes, Henkin traces the different notions of the concept of rights, their place in U.S. national political theory, the advantages and disadvantages of the U.S. conception of rights, and the role of judicial review.

Shestack's chapter[28] on jurisprudence reveals and deepens our understanding through philosophical inquiry. This chapter is particularly valuable in directing attention not only to the definition of 'rights' but to sources and theories which have generated the multitude of claims considered in various quarters to be 'rights'. These philosophical underpinnings promote deeper insight into the norm-making process and the transformation of claims and 'weak' rights into 'hard' rights.

2.   EMPHASIS ON IMPLEMENTATION

Implementation, the heart of international protection of human rights, pervades the entire book. The range of mechanisms discussed is impressive: the 'mobilization of shame' in Wolf's chapter,[29] the

[25] [European] Convention for the Protection of Human Rights and Fundamental Freedoms, *reprinted in* Brownlie, *supra* note 16, at 242.
[26] The Organization of African Unity recently adopted the African Charter on Human and

influence and the role of nongovernmental organizations in Weissbrodt's,[30] the Human Rights Committee and other U.N. organs in Sohn's,[31] courts and commissions in Buergenthal's[32] and Higgins',[33] and outright military reprisal in Dinstein's.[34] Throughout this array, the recurring theme is that progress comes only as quickly as attitudes change and consensus is approached, whatever the procedures available. At the same time, procedures of implementation contribute to changed attitudes.

Emphasis is placed on the fundamental idea that in the long run an educated public opinion is essential to protect rights and develop further means of implementation. Humphrey points out in this regard that the protection of certain rights, particularly freedom of expression, is a condition precedent to the protection and development of others since it is a vehicle for educating the public.[35] Greenberg indicates that perhaps the most valuable fruit to come of a realistic appreciation of the limited utility of present international standards is the resolve 'to devise remedies and better develop political consensus'.[36] Practical efforts to implement rights advance certain conceptual approaches, and through this process rights are actually protected 'by the way in which human thinking about rights shifts over a period of time'.[37] This process is at work domestically as well. As Greenberg notes in the civil rights context, human rights law developed in the United States as underlying political, economic, and social relations changed; the institutionalization of change via the new rules in turn helped bring about further growth.

The push for teaching international protection of human rights cannot properly be viewed as a parochial or theoretical concern. As Sohn has pointed out, the effectiveness of the procedures now being developed to protect rights internationally will depend largely on the generation of students presently being taught. 'If in the United States today most of the leaders of the country, most of the congressmen and

---

Peoples' Rights, *approved* July 1981, *reprinted in* 21 Int'l Legal Materials 58 (1982), at 76. *See also* ch. 10 *infra*.

[27] Ch. 2 *infra*.
[28] Ch. 3 *infra*.
[29] Ch. 7 *infra*.

---

[30] Ch. 11 *infra*.
[31] Ch. 10 *infra*.
[32] Ch. 12 *infra*.
[33] Ch. 13 *infra*.
[34] Ch. 9 *infra*.
[35] Ch. 5 *infra*.
[36] Ch. 8 *infra*.
[37] *Id*.

senators, had been trained not even in human rights law but at least in international law, our situation would be quite different.'[38]

Lillich's approach[39] is largely analytical, rather than historical. In his consideration of basic civil rights he follows closely the pattern of the Universal Declaration and emphasizes those rights which cannot be derogated from under the Political Covenant.

In a chapter[40] which stresses the historical context of the development of the norms, Humphrey considers the basic political rights and clarifies the relationship of the rights of the individual to group rights.

Trubek's chapter[41] deals with the question of teaching certain rights covered by the International Covenant on Economic, Social, and Cultural Rights (Economic Covenant).[42] Of these, Trubek focuses on 'social welfare rights'. The chapter reflects the effect of political and social circumstances in shaping law, and the role of law in shaping political and social circumstances. The instruments refer implicitly at least to processes of implementation which give the broader goals of the instruments a certain normative content and, at the same time, increase the likelihood of realization of these goals. The question of implementation led Trubek to focus on the behavior of institutions, because implementation in this area is largely the role of the specialized agencies of the United Nations. The meaning of the substantive norms and their implementation thus turns on the behavior of institutions. Trubek was cognizant of the fact that while the Economic Covenant speaks in the language of rights, it refers to the realities of programs. He attempted to determine the meaning of the rights protected by that Covenant in the Third World context by examining certain programs of certain specialized agencies.[43] The rights under the Economic Covenant apply also to the developed states, including Western Europe and the United States, but Trubek suggests that 'social welfare rights' arise in the West in a different institutional structure. By concentrating on the Third World, he focuses on the development activity of the various specialized agencies which reflects a priority recognized by the U.N. system of organizations.[44]

Wolf's chapter [45] focuses on the protection and the implementation of those human rights which are protected by the ILO. Wolf analyzes the functioning of the independent international machinery for the

[38] Remarks by Sohn, in Meron Report, *supra* note 7, at 957.
[39] Ch. 4 *infra*.
[40] Ch. 5 *infra*.
[41] Ch. 6 *infra*.
[42] G.A. Res. 2200, 21 U.N. GAOR, Supp. (No. 16) 49, U.N. Doc. A/6316 (1966).
[43] Remarks by Trubek, in Meron Report, *supra* note 7, at 904.
[44] *Id.* at 908.
[45] Ch. 7 *infra*.

supervision of the application of international labour conventions which was established as early as 1927 and thus performed an important pioneering role as a model[46] for universal and regional human rights conventions. The idea that the ILO is concerned with the right to work does not adequately reflect the broad social and economic dimensions and diversity of its activities, which include the adoption of no less than 156 international labour conventions and 165 recommendations covering a wide variety of social and labour matters.[47] The key element in the work of the ILO is its tripartite character. Instruments are developed not only by governments but also by employers and workers, acting together in the organs of the ILO.[48] Wolf emphasizes the role of the ILO in the 'mobilization of shame on the tripartite basis'[49] and discusses the sophisticated and effective ILO procedures of investigation of violations and consideration of complaints, which include impartial consideration by quasi-judicial bodies. The basic principle of due process has attained a central role among the ILO principles of supervision.

Greenberg's chapter[50] deals with the prohibition of discrimination on grounds of race, sex, or religion. These subjects of discrimination have been selected because the international community has placed the notion of equality on a special priority level.[51] The chapter reflects the perspective of a U.S. practitioner of civil rights. Greenberg makes clear that while the international rules concerning racial discrimination are clear enough, those that deal with sex discrimination and, to an even greater extent, with religious discrimination,[52] are still in an inchoate form. In his view, the international status of such rules is not drastically different from the situation that existed in the United States some thirty years ago. Greenberg highlights the fact that virtually all the international instruments on human rights deal with the subject of affirmative action, which has been so crucial to the advancement of human rights in the United States. He focuses on the significance of the 'purpose or effect' clause in article 1(1) of the International Convention on the Elimination of All Forms of Racial Discrimination,[53]

---

[46] *See* Jenks, *Human Rights, Social Justice and Peace: The Broader Significance of the I.L.O. Experience*, in International Protection of Human Rights 227 (A. Eide & A. Schou eds. 1968) [hereinafter cited as Jenks].

[47] *See* remarks by Wolf, in Meron Report, *supra* note 7, at 909.

[48] See *id.* at 931.

[49] See *id.* at 932.

[50] Ch. 8 *infra*.

[51] *See* remarks by Alice Henkin, in Meron Report, *supra* note 7, at 955.

[52] On 25 Nov. 1981, the U.N. General Assembly adopted by Resolution 36/55 a Declaration on the Elimination of All Forms of Intolerance and of Discrimination Based on Religion or Belief, U.N. Doc. A/RES/36/55 (1981).

[53] 660 U.N.T.S. 195, *reprinted in* Brownlie, *supra* note 16, at 150.

i.e., the action proscribed is that which has the purpose or the effect of bringing about racial discrimination. Greenberg discusses also the intriguing question of how certain important U.S. cases could have been resolved under the relevant international instruments rather than under the U.S. Constitution or statutes.[54]

As has been mentioned, humanitarian law, which is discussed in Dinstein's chapter,[55] is one of the principal historic sources of human rights. Dinstein discusses not only the essence of human rights in armed conflict and the interplay of human rights in peacetime and wartime, but also the problems of enforceability and supervision and, in this context, the role of reciprocity. He points out that certain crucial human rights provisions included in instruments pertaining to armed conflict are more advanced, specific, and elaborate than those of the general instruments such as the Political Covenant.

Sohn focuses on implementation of human rights in the U.N. context.[56] An understanding of the U.N. system of implementation and supervision of the observance of human rights is crucial to the understanding of the functioning of the global system of protection of human rights. Sohn discusses many of these developments, some of which are still in an inchoate form, such as the increased resort to the good offices of the U.N. Secretary-General,[57] the more frequent use of working groups of independent experts,[58] and the use of fact-finding groups.[59] Sohn also discusses the crucial problem of domestic implementation of human rights. Sohn considers the great range of international measures of implementation, starting with reporting by states, through inter-state complaints, and ending with the role of private communications, emphasizing the growing rights of individuals to complain to international courts and commissions.[60] In recognizing the difficulties involved in enforcement of human rights law, Sohn notes the role of public opinion and public pressures.[61]

Nongovernmental organizations have played an extremely important role in assisting the implementation of human rights and in focusing public opinion on violations. Weissbrodt's chapter on non-

---

[54] *See* remarks by Greenberg, in Meron Report, *supra* note 7, at 953–55.

[55] Ch. 9 *infra*.

[56] Ch. 10 *infra*.

[57] *See, e.g.*, Comm'n on Human Rights Res. 27(XXXVI), 1980 U.N. ESCOR, Supp. (No. 3) 187, U.N. Doc. E/CN.4/1408 (1980). *See also* Ramcharan, *The Good Offices of the United Nations Secretary-General in the Field of Human Rights*, 76 Am. J. Int'l L. 130 (1982).

[58] *See, e.g.*, Comm'n on Human Rights Res. 20(XXXVI), 1980 U.N. ESCOR, Supp. (No. 3) 180, U.N. Doc. E/CN.4/1408 (1980).

[59] *See generally* suggestions by The Netherlands presented to the Commission on Human Rights during its thirty-seventh session, U.N. Doc. E/CN.4/L.1560/Add. 17, at 10-11 (1981).

[60] *See* remarks by Sohn, in Meron Report, *supra* note 7, at 923–26.

[61] *Id.*

governmental organizations[62] (NGOs) introduces the reader to the use by NGOs of international fora. Weissbrodt highlights the relevant work techniques of the NGOs and encourages the involvement of students in their human rights activities. His chapter includes problems suitable for class discussion and role-playing by students.

Turning to regional problems, Buergenthal[63] discusses in detail the inter-American system for the protection of human rights. He focuses on problems of implementation, on the roles of the Inter-American Commission on Human Rights and of the Inter-American Court of Human Rights. Buergenthal clarifies the difficult issues involved in the relationship between the regime established under the Charter of the Organization of American States[64] and the regime established by the American Convention on Human Rights.[65] He illustrates the role of country studies, on-site inspections, and individual communications.

Dealing with another region, Higgins[66] discusses the European Convention on Human Rights. She starts with an important conceptual discussion, stressing the cultural, political, and philosophical context in which human rights jurisprudence is rooted,[67] and then moves on to the implementation machinery. Higgins' discussion benefits from the availability of the rich body of jurisprudence of the European Commission of Human Rights and the European Court of Human Rights. Out of the various human rights protected by the European Convention and the Protocols,[68] Higgins selects for detailed discussion a number of rights, such as the freedom from torture, which are crucial to an understanding of the European Convention. These rights are discussed through case studies.

3. PEDAGOGICAL TACTICS

Many choices in substance, purpose, and method must be made when deciding how to teach the international protection of human rights. In substance, the authors have generally provided a broad overview of the area, narrowing it to one or more segments for purposes of the minisyllabus. The Universal Declaration has often served as a convenient point of departure for both the substantive discussion and for pedagogical purposes. In a field as new and relatively undefined as international human rights, however, even such overviews imply choices and priorities which may contribute to the further

---

[62] Ch. 11 *infra.*
[63] Ch. 12 *infra.*
[64] 2 U.S.T. 2394, T.I.A.S. No. 2361, 119 U.N.T.S. 3.
[65] O.A.S. T.S. No. 36, *reprinted in* Brownlie, *supra* note 16, at 391.
[66] Ch. 13 *infra.*
[67] *See* remarks by Kommers, in Meron Report, *supra* note 7, at 912.
[68] For Protocols 1-5, *see* Brownlie, *supra* note 16, at 257-65.

definition of the field. For instance, Lillich focuses on the nonderogable rights in the Political Covenant. His chapter is based on the premise that civil rights, and especially the nonderogable ones, should be emphasized in an international human rights course. In the area of economic and social rights, Trubek focuses on the Third World, not because the Western and Socialist nations have no difficulties to overcome in the implementation of such rights, but because the United Nations has made economic and social rights in the Third World context an area of priority concern and action.

The method of teaching turns largely on the purpose to be achieved and naturally will vary with whether the students are aspiring political scientists, lawyers, or philosophers. Is the purpose to show a law student that he or she would be unethical to go out and practice without being knowledgeable in the field? Or is the purpose to broaden perception of 'the law'? Does teaching the international law of human rights have the more fundamental purpose of promoting a more educated public opinion as a means of furthering those rights? The practical approach may well be useless without incorporating, to some extent, elements of a conceptual approach.[69] A teacher may start at either end but must finally cover both.

Certain approaches, however, seem particularly well-suited to a given area. As the title of Trubek's chapter suggests, implementation of economic and social rights is largely programmatic, and a process oriented approach can be most fruitful when teaching that area. Lillich's method is largely analytical, but he stresses process over substance in his Teaching Suggestions. Humphrey examines the relative advantages and disadvantages of the 'historical-structural' (dynamic) and 'analytical-exegetical' (static) methods. In his discussion of certain basic political rights, particularly in the historical perspective, he focuses on the difference between the rights of the individual and the rights of the group. Greenberg, Weissbrodt, and Higgins each place great emphasis on the case method and case studies. This rich variety allows the teacher to tailor the approach to suit his or her needs and talents. A great advantage of teaching a new field is this opportunity to experiment and create. No method can as yet be deemed superior to the exclusion of others.

Human rights as a subject can and should be taught so that it is integrated into appropriate disciplines, such as philosophy, political science, and law.[70] In order to facilitate the task of teachers who

[69] *See* remarks by Neier, in Meron Report, *supra* note 7, at 946-47.
[70] Part I(9), Vienna Final Document, *supra* note 2, at 40-41. Human rights are relevant to the teaching of medicine, history, philosophy, education, sociology, political science, law, international relations, international development, regional studies, international organization, and other subjects. *See* Buergenthal, *supra* note 13, at 26. In law, human rights are particularly

cannot devote an entire course or seminar to human rights in general or to a particular area of human rights, mini-syllabi and mini-reading lists have been included in each chapter. Any human rights course should cover, in an appropriate proportion, substantive, procedural, and historical issues. It is particularly important that teachers point out the philosophical, jurisprudential, and historical sources of human rights, including the influence of the law of international responsibility of states for injuries to aliens.[71]

There are many possible approaches to the methodology of teaching human rights. The subject can be taught in an analytical, issue oriented manner. It can be taught in a historical, dynamic perspective. It can be taught in a comparative manner, *e.g.*, by comparing certain concepts in international human rights law to concepts of the constitutional law or criminal law of a certain country or countries. A comparison of various norms in an analytical and historical perspective, as they are reflected in the various human rights instruments, both universal and regional, may be of particular interest. Human rights can be taught in a clinical method by encouraging students to do research and write memoranda for various human rights organizations.

All teachers, whether of law or of other social sciences, should contribute to the clarification of the processes through which international human rights are elaborated, focusing on the norm-making process and the transformation of moral claims and 'soft' rights into firm or 'hard' rights. Teachers should consider the relationship of international human rights norms to national legal systems and the specific techniques for the implementation of human rights not only on the international but also on the domestic plane.[72]

In some areas, such as the observance of rules of humanitarian law, the teacher should emphasize the role of reciprocity. Teachers should explain the transformation that the international protection of human rights has undergone and is still undergoing, particularly in the context of the diminishing scope of matters which are essentially within the domestic jurisdiction of states, the internationalization of human rights, and the increasing role of the individual as a subject of international human rights.[73] Tremendous progress has taken place in the elaboration of human rights norms through the many international

appropriate for inclusion in courses in international law, United Nations law, European law, inter-American law, constitutional law, comparative constitutional law, and civil rights law.

---

[71] Regarding the contribution of certain judgments of U.S. courts to the development of human rights, *see* remarks by Sohn, in Meron Report, *supra* note 7, at 950.

[72] *See* remarks by Ramcharan, *id.* at 906.

[73] *See* Buergenthal, *supra* note 13, at 26; Henkin, *Human Rights and Domestic Jurisdiction*, in Human Rights, International Law and the Helsinki Accord 21 (T. Buergenthal & J. Hall eds. 1977); Sohn, *The Human Rights Law of the Charter*, 12 Tex. Int'l L.J. 129 (1977).

agreements and other instruments, some of which are widely accepted. While the process of norm-making will no doubt continue, especially with regard to the prohibition of torture and cruel, inhuman, or degrading treatment or punishment,[74] freedom of religion,[75] rights of the child,[76] and such rights as the right to socio-economic development,[77] it has been observed that 'new norm setting and development is not the principal challenge of the present',[78] and that the principal challenges of today are the wider acceptance of human rights treaties and improvement of the domestic and the international implementation of human rights. Indeed, teachers of human rights might wish to emphasize that domestic implementation of human rights is the ultimate test of the effectiveness of human rights norms. The international implementation of human rights is, of course, closely related to this question. The utilization and the improvement of international implementation procedures must therefore also continue to be the focus of the teaching of international protection of human rights.[79]

4. SUBSTANTIVE CONVERGENCE

The chapters in this book, in terms of their substantive scope, are not mutually exclusive. In numerous instances the authors make cross-references to each other's chapters. To derive the benefit of this convergence the reader should be alert to the different contexts in which a single subject is addressed and the perspectives from which it is viewed. Often a comparison of the approaches used will be instructive in itself.

For example, freedom of thought, conscience, and religion (article 18 of the Universal Declaration) is discussed in some detail in Humphrey's chapter on political and related rights, and more briefly in Lillich's on civil rights. The former uses a historical/developmental approach; the latter an analytical/comparative approach. The con-

[74] Regarding the proposed convention against torture and other cruel, inhuman, or degrading treatment or punishment, *see* G.A. Res. 36/60, U.N. Doc. A/RES/36/60 (1981); Report of the Working Group on a Draft Convention against Torture and Other Cruel, Inhuman or Degrading Treatment or Punishment, U.N. Doc. E/CN.4/L.1576 (1981).

[75] The recent Declaration, *supra* note 52, does not eliminate the need for a convention on this subject.

[76] Regarding the proposed convention on the rights of the child, *see* G.A. Res. 36/57, U.N. Doc. A/RES/36/57 (1981); Report of the Working Group on a Draft Convention on the Rights of the Child, U.N. Doc. E/CN.4/L.1575 (1981).

[77] *See* Comm'n on Human Rights Res. 36(XXXVII), 1981 U.N. ESCOR, Supp. (No. 5) 237, U.N. Doc. E/CN.4/1475 (1981).

[78] Written Statement submitted by the International League for Human Rights to the U.N. Commission on Human Rights, U.N. Doc. E/CN.4/NGO/318, at 2 (1981).

[79] Commission to Study the Organization of Peace, New Aspects of the International Protection of Human Rights (1977), lists implementation of human rights instruments as its first recommendation. The other recommendations of the Commission concern: science, technology, and human rights; freedom from torture; freedom from terrorism; international protection of women's rights; the rights of indigenous peoples; and measures to protect religious freedom.

tribution of the International Labour Organization to the protection of human rights, particularly in the context of the supervisory techniques employed, is the subject of Wolf's chapter, while implementation by the ILO of the right to work serves as one of the two major examples given in Trubek's chapter on programmatic protection of economic, social, and cultural rights. The Inter-American and European systems are addressed primarily in Buergenthal's and Higgins' chapters, respectively, but the other authors, most prominently Lillich, consistently refer to provisions in the American and European Conventions.

Race, sex, and religious discrimination, as dealt with in a variety of international instruments, is the subject of Greenberg's chapter, while it also receives treatment by Humphrey in the context of freedom of religion. As already mentioned, Henkin's chapter necessarily cuts across most of the instruments and institutions analyzed elsewhere in the volumes. Another fruitful comparison may be made concerning American constitutional issues, utilizing primarily the chapters of Henkin, Shestack, Lillich, and Greenberg.

5. TO SPEAK OF 'RIGHTS'

The term 'rights' has a broad spectrum of meanings in this book. It is used in all contexts from the most traditional 'right to freedom of religion' through the 'rights to work and to health'. To some, such a wide spectrum of definition is worse than conflicting; it is dangerous because it devalues the concept of 'rights' until it is meaningless.

Shestack's chapter on the jurisprudence of human rights offers the theoretical framework which makes sense of this spectrum. Common law lawyers may not necessarily be unsettled by the fact that the term does not have a concise and definitive meaning; if they are, it is likely to be due to the practical difficulty of advocating protection of something as a human right when the term may have been overused to the point of meaninglessness. The training received by civil law lawyers may give rise to a search for a coherent concept of rights. Whatever the source of this urge for a definition, there seems to be a common sentiment that one should not be allowed to call anything one pleases a right.[80] But at the same time a warning is needed: sharpness of definition must not be confused with narrowness of definition; an effort to sharpen could lead to taking the narrow category of traditional political and civil rights as the paradigm.[81]

The age of a human right, in terms of when effective legal and political action began to protect it, may have a bearing on its specificity and the possibility of its enforcement. For example, protection of

---

[80] *See* remarks by Strong, in Meron Report, *supra* note 7, at 936.
[81] Remarks by Shue, *id.* at 937.

certain human rights in time of armed conflict (humanitarian law) was known well before international protection of human rights in peace-time was generally recognized as a possible function of the international community. However, the age of the instrument or right provides no assurance of specificity or enforcement. Thus, while freedom of religion is one of the most ancient concepts, as a 'right' it is still relatively soft. Beyond the general statements in the Universal Declaration and the Political Covenant and other instruments of a general character, it has so far proved impossible to reach a consensus on a convention governing exclusively religious freedoms, although a Declaration has been adopted.[82] On the other hand, rights recognized fairly recently by the relatively homogenous European states have obtained an advanced measure of enforceability. And some 'new' rights, such as freedom from discrimination, have received wide support and a modicum of successful implementation.

Different rights are in various stages of the law-creating process—whether or not one accepts the theory that there are separate generations of rights—and the further the process has developed, the greater is the consensus that a 'right' exists. Of course, this statement is equally true if it is inverted, since consensus as to the existence of a right furthers the law-creating process. But the point here for teaching purposes is that to advocate a body of knowledge and experience as worthy of inclusion in a curriculum requires substantial delineation (not to say definition) of the subject area and proof that the subject has significant intellectual and/or practical merit. It is the work of those who would teach human rights to demonstrate that these requirements are met, and simultaneously to further such delineation and work toward increasing such merit.

Implicit in the notion of defining rights is the idea that some rights are more important than others. Difficult choices must be made as to what to teach out of the panorama presented in this book, and relative importance would seem at first glance to be as good a means for choosing alternatives as any. But this is an exceedingly difficult question, fraught with personal and cultural bias, and, to make matters worse, one which the international community as a whole has not addressed. The category of nonderogable rights[83] has been established in, for example, article 4 of the Political Covenant, but this ranks rights only in a circuitous and inconclusive manner at best because states' parties are expressly permitted to derogate from their obligations under the Political Covenant in time of public emergency

---

[82] *See* note 52 *supra*.

[83] *See generally* Higgins, *Derogations Under Human Rights Treaties*, 48 Brit. Y.B. Int'l L. 281 (1979).

except with respect to certain enumerated rights. Does this mean that the exigencies of a public emergency are more important than some rights but not as important as the nonderogable ones? Or rather that there is no rational way in which invading the nonderogable rights can be considered necessary as a response to an emergency—implying a conclusive presumption that in such cases the emergency could only be an unsupportable excuse, not a justification, for derogation? If the former is true, then the Political Covenant ranks the nonderogable rights ahead of all derogable rights. If it is the latter, it cannot be concluded that all derogable rights are necessarily subordinate to other rights, only that they are subordinate to certain inconsistent emergency measures a state may conceivably have to take.

In recent years, much has been made of the distinction between civil/political and economic/social rights. Part of the reason for this debate has been merely a desire to score rhetorical points; part has been a sincere effort to discover the historical reasons for which states put emphasis on one set of rights instead of another; and part has been a desire for reconciliation and mutual understanding. This distinction between rights is an issue which necessarily arises repeatedly in this book and is addressed from various angles. In practice, either both groups of rights or neither are given protection.[84] In their actions, states do not give the priority their words would imply to one set of rights over another; rights are indivisible.[85]

6.   POLITICS: THE ART OF THE POSSIBLE

The major international human rights instruments have been widely signed and ratified, yet serious rights violations persist. What is it about the international arena that causes countries to participate actively in the drafting and adoption of instruments without then reforming their practices? Do the rights embodied in these instruments 'have their roots in many different nations and cultures'[86] or were they rather adopted by 'a small clique of lawyers, bureaucrats and intellectuals who are highly westernized and most of whom have absolutely nothing to do with the cultures in which . . . their fellow nationals live'?[87]

Political realities set the parameters for the legal action possible to protect human rights but those realities are also altered in the process, as the way people think about rights changes over time. It is the sign of our time that states are finding it harder to assert unlimited sovereignty and that an international community is evolving. Individual human

---

[84] *See* Trubek, ch. 6 *infra*.
[85] *See* remarks by Dinstein, in Meron Report, *supra* note 7, at 891.
[86] Remarks by Young–Anawaty, *id.* at 901.
[87] Remarks by Berger, *id.*

beings are now frequently deemed to be subjects of international law and to have certain rights independent of the will of their governments.

C. Status of Acceptance of Human Rights

Teachers of human rights should take into account the status of acceptance of the principal human rights instruments, which reflects the growing consensus among countries with regard to various areas of international 'legislation' in the human rights area. In certain situations, the status of acceptance may constitute one of the indicators of whether a human right contained in an instrument reflects customary international law on the subject. The status of acceptance is indicative of the narrowing scope of the exclusive domestic jurisdiction with regard to various human rights questions. It is crucial to the study of various regional aspects of human rights.

It is essential that teachers and students consult the relevant documentation in order to ascertain which states parties have made reservations and to assess the scope of the reservations and their true legal significance. It should be made clear that certain reservations may greatly diminish or even render meaningless the legal significance of a ratification of a human rights instrument.[88] It should also be made clear that the nomenclature used by the reserving states is not conclusive as to the true nature of the action taken. A 'declaration', an 'interpretative statement', or other title attached to a statement made by a state may be tantamount to a reservation.[89]

D. Geography of Human Rights

A person who would judge the state of human rights which prevails in a particular country solely, or even primarily, by the number of human rights instruments which that country has ratified or acceded to would be living in a realm of unreality. Students must be introduced to the real world and made to understand something about the geography of human rights.[90] It is wrong to assume that 'the acid test of observance of international human rights is the number of international conventions relating to human rights which a given state has signed and ratified'.[91] For example, the United States has a very poor

[88] *See* Schachter, *The Obligation of the Parties to Give Effect to the Covenant on Civil and Political Rights*, 73 Am. J. Int'l L. 462 (1979). *But see* Jenks, *supra* note 46, at 246, who observes that '[b]oth substantive and procedural reservations to the provisions of the Covenants appear to be freely admissible and the effect on the obligations resulting from the Covenants of any reservation or objection thereto remains somewhat indeterminate . . .'

[89] *See* art. 2(1)(d) of the Vienna Convention on the Law of Treaties, *done* 22 May 1969, *entered into force* Jan. 27, 1980, U.N. Doc. A/CONF.39/27 (1969), *reprinted in* 8 Int'l Legal Materials 679 (1969).

[90] *See* remarks by Gastil, in Meron Report, *supra* note 7, at 905.

[91] Remarks by Dinstein, *id.* at 892.

record of ratification of human rights instruments, but its record in the observance of human rights cannot be gauged solely on that basis.[92] As Dinstein has observed, often the most blatant transgressors of human rights have the best record in terms of acceptances of human rights instruments.[93]

One of the principal objectives of education in the field of human rights should be to analyze impartially a particular country's implementation of international human rights. Every country violates some human rights some of the time. Violations of human rights by a given country may, however, be so pervasive that they may set that country apart from the international community. Education, by focusing attention on massive human rights violations in a particular country, may create a sense of shame on the part of its leaders, and, through moral and mental inhibitions, may contribute to the advancement of human rights.[94] Study of the geography of human rights is not, therefore, merely a contribution to the state of knowledge with regard to particular countries and to particular regions. It is also, and more importantly, a vital factor in the promotion of human rights.[95]

The evaluation of a country's performance in the field of human rights is, of course, a function of the organs of the United Nations, the specialized agencies, and the regional organizations, which are competent to consider reports and complaints of violations of human rights . . .'.[96] In addition, fact-finding processes in international or under special conventions. Unfortunately, owing to the politicization of the United Nations and certain other organizations, the United Nations 'has not yet proved capable of adopting a genuinely non-selective and impartial position towards violation of human rights . . .'[96] In addition, fact-finding processes in international organizations have suffered from various weaknesses, including lack of due process.[97] In view of these circumstances, it is not surprising that assessment of country performance in human rights has become, to a large extent, a function of individual governments and NGOs. Objective evaluations of each country's record of observance of international human rights is not an easy undertaking. It raises, *inter alia*, the question of standards and criteria. Out of the great number of

---

[92] *Id.*

[93] *Id.*

[94] *Id.* at 889.

[95] For a discussion by former U.S. Pres. Carter of public opinion as a factor in improving state behaviour in human rights, *see* N.Y. Times, 18 May 1981, at A1, col. 5, *But cf.* statement by former U.S. Sec'y of State Haig, N.Y. Times, Apr. 21, 1981, at A6, col. 1.

[96] Ministry of Foreign Affairs of The Netherlands, Human Rights and Foreign Policy 26 (1979); *see* remarks by Dinstein, in Meron Report, *supra* note 7, at 890.

[97] *See* Franck & Fairley, *Procedural Due Process in Human Rights Fact-Finding by International Agencies*, 74 Am. J. Int'l L. 308 (1980) [hereinafter cited as Franck & Fairley].

human rights stated in the principal human rights instruments, which should be selected as the principal yardstick of compliance? How can we ensure that the evaluators will be guided by objective considerations and not by partisan or national interests?

The country reports on human rights prepared annually by the U.S. Department of State[98] groups internationally recognized rights into two broad categories:

—first, the right to be free from governmental violations of the integrity of the person—violations such as torture, cruel, inhuman or degrading treatment or punishment; arbitrary arrest or imprisonment; denial of fair public trial; and invasion of the home;

—second, the right to enjoy civil and political liberties, including freedom of speech, press, religion and assembly; the right to participate in government; the right to travel freely within and outside one's own country; the right to be free from discrimination based on race or sex.[99]

These reports benefit from information furnished by U.S. missions abroad, congressional studies, NGOs, and human rights organs of international organizations.[100] The wealth of the data used must be balanced, however, against the fact that the reports were prepared by the U.S. Department of State and that conclusions may be suspected by some as self-serving.

The 1980 Report indicated that there has been a continuing decrease in violations of the integrity of the person in countries whose human rights records have been subject to intense international scrutiny but that in countries not under scrutiny torture and cruel punishment continue to be practiced. The Report also pointed to the limited capability of most less developed countries to fulfill the basic human needs of the population and the obstacles faced by them in the achievement of economic rights, but observed that economic rights continued to rank higher than political and civil liberties on the agenda of many countries, especially in the Third World. Regarding the status of political and civil freedoms in the world, the Report noticed few

[98] *See, e.g.,* Country Reports on Human Rights Practices for 1981, Report Submitted to the House Comm. on Foreign Affairs and the Senate Comm. on Foreign Relations by the Dep't of State in Accordance with Sections 116(d) and 502B(b) of the Foreign Assistance Act of 1961, as Amended, 97th Cong., 2d Sess. (Joint Comm. Print 1982) [hereinafter cited as 1981 Report].

[99] *Id.* at 2. In a Report submitted by the Carter Administration, another category—'the right to the fulfillment of vital needs such as food, shelter, health care and education'—was recognized. *See* Country Reports on Human Rights Practices for 1980, Report Submitted to the Senate Comm. on Foreign Relations and the House Comm. on Foreign Affairs by the Dep't of State in Accordance with Sections 116(d) and 502B(b) of the Foreign Assistance Act of 1961, as Amended, 97th Cong., 1st Sess., at 2 (Joint Comm. Print 1981) [hereinafter cited as 1980 Report].

[100] *See* 1981 Report, *supra* note 98, at 1.

changes.[101] A study of the success of U.S. human rights policy noted that the record on direct and explicit use of foreign assistance as leverage to bring about specific improvements in human rights conditions was hardly encouraging, but that there had been improvements in the fifteen countries on which the study focused and that it was 'reasonably clear that U.S. policy has sensitized foreign governments to human rights issues and has been a contributing factor in many situations where conditions have improved'.[102]

Another attempt to provide a reference point for evaluating the status of civil and political rights in various countries has been made by a private organization, Freedom House of New York, which has been publishing since 1973 an annual 'Comparative Survey of Freedom'.[103] The criteria employed by Freedom House are different from those applied by the U.S. Department of State. 'Freedom' is defined in terms of political rights which allow people to participate freely and effectively in choosing their leaders or in voting directly on legislation, and in terms of civil liberties that guarantee speech, privacy, and a fair trial, especially those making it possible to criticize the political, economic, and religious systems under which people live. This definition excludes welfare interests.

The method used has been explained as follows:

The rating a nation received for political freedom is determined by factors such as the existence of two or more competing political parties or the independence of opposition candidates from government control. For a nation to achieve a high rating in the Survey, elections and legislatures have to demonstrate a significant opposition, and those elected have to be given real power. Civil freedoms include freedom of the press, the openness of public discussion, the existence of organizations separate from the government, an independent judiciary, and the absence of political imprisonment.[104]

Having placed countries on scales for political rights and civil liberties, the Survey divides them into categories of free, partly free, or not free. At the beginning of 1980, there were, according to Freedom House, 56

[101] *See* 1980 Report, *supra* note 99, at 2. For an important assessment of U.S. human rights policy, *see* Human Rights and U.S. Foreign Assistance, Experiences and Issues in Policy Implementation (1977-1978), A Report Prepared for the Senate Comm. on Foreign Relations by the Foreign Affairs and National Defense Div., Congressional Research Service, Library of Congress, 96th Cong., 1st Sess. (Comm. Print 1979).

[102] *Id.* at 5. Regarding the problems faced in the preparation of country reports by the Dep't of State, *see id.* at 96-98. *See also* Human Rights in the International Community and in U.S. Foreign Policy, 1945-76, A Report Prepared for the Subcomm. on Int'l Organizations of the House Comm. on Int'l Relations by the Foreign Affairs and National Defense Div., Congressional Research Service, Library of Congress, 96th Cong., 1st Sess. (Comm. Print 1977); American Association for the International Commission of Jurists, Human Rights in United States & United Kingdom Foreign Policy: A Colloquium (1979).

[103] R. Gastil, Freedom in the World, 1980 (1980).

[104] *Id.* at 5.

independent states in the world classified as not free, 51 classified as free, and 54 classified as partly free. It may be of interest for students of human rights to compare the Freedom House lists to the tabulation of parties to the principal human rights instruments. At the same time, however, it should be made clear to students that the Survey's definition of freedom has been criticized as reflecting the values of Western constitutional democracies, as being culturally ethnocentric, and as being 'right wing'.[105] The geography of human rights is also important in regional studies.[106]

E. Conflicts

One of the characteristic phenomena of contemporary international life is the proliferation of human rights instruments and systems of supervision. In addition to the U.N. Charter and to comprehensive global conventions such as the Political Covenant and the Economic Covenant, instruments have been adopted within the United Nations or the specialized agencies to govern particular aspects of human rights, such as racial discrimination, rights of women, labour, education, or health and, within regional organizations such as the Council of Europe and the Organization of American States, to govern general and particular aspects of human rights.[107] In the context of the United Nations, the general practice has been that whenever systems of supervision have been established, each normative instrument has created its own supervision system.[108] Typically, each organ of supervision applies only the norms adopted in the specific 'founding' instrument rather than the entire *corpus juris* of international human rights, or at least all of the instruments comprising the International Bill of Human Rights.[109]

[105] For the replies of Freedom House to such criticisms, *see id.* at 6.

[106] Regarding developments in Africa and other areas, *see* Commission to Study the Organization of Peace, Regional Promotion and Protection of Human Rights (1980).

[107] *See* Human Rights: A Compilation of International Instruments, U.N. Doc. ST/HR/1/Rev. 1 (1978), which lists 50 human rights instruments; Brownlie, *supra* note 16. These compilations are necessarily selective. The ILO alone has adopted at least 156 international labour conventions.

[108] *E.g.*, International Convention on the Elimination of All Forms of Racial Discrimination, 660 U.N.T.S. 195 (which established the Committee on the Elimination of Racial Discrimination), *discussed in* Buergenthal, *Implementing the UN Racial Convention*, 12 Tex. Int'l L.J. 187 (1977); Political Covenant (which established the Human Rights Committee), *discussed in* Robertson, *The Implementation System: International Measures*, in The International Bill of Rights: The Covenant on Civil and Political Rights 332 (L. Henkin ed. 1981). *See generally* Van Boven, *Human Rights Fora at the United Nations. How to Select and to Approach the Most Appropriate Forum. What Procedural Rules Govern?*, in International Human Rights: Law and Practice 83 (J. Tuttle ed. 1978).

[109] *Compare* this trend *with* the unified system of implementation and supervision followed by ILO, *discussed in* Wolf, ch. 7 *infra*; Wolf, *Aspects Judiciaires de la Protection Internationale des Droits de l'Homme par L'O.I.T.*, 4 Revue des Droits de l'Homme 773 (1971); the incorpora-

This proliferation of normative instruments and systems of supervision, which is similar to the proliferation which has given rise to difficult questions of coordination within and between international organizations in the budget, program, and administration fields,[110] has led to problems of overlapping jurisdiction and even of conflicts between the 'legislative' and supervisory competence, or claims of competence, of various international bodies.[111] The object here is to draw the attention of the teacher and the student to these questions.[112] The development of an integrated system of international treaty law governing human rights has a number of goals, which merit mention. Such a system would prevent unnecessary duplication, prevent conflicts between instruments, avoid differences in the interpretation and implementation of instruments adopted by different organizations, and ensure that statutory provisions concerning complex technical subjects are established and supervised by the most competent organizations.[113]

tion by reference in art. 15 of the European Convention on Human Rights of norms originating in human rights instruments established outside the framework of the Council of Europe, *discussed in* Buergenthal, *International and Regional Human Rights Law and Institutions: Some Examples of Their Interaction*, 12 Tex. Int'l L.J. 321, 324-25 [hereinafter cited as Buergenthal]; and the broad principles which are applicable before the future African Commission on Human and Peoples' Rights, arts. 60 & 61, African Charter on Human and Peoples' Rights. It should be observed, however, that fact-finding bodies established by resolutions of international organs invoke 'broadly recognized normative standards'. Franck & Fairley, *supra* note 97, at 308.

110 *See, e.g.*, Sharp, *Program Coordination and the Economic and Social Council*, in UN Administration of Economic and Social Programs 102 (G. Mangone ed. 1966); Meron, *Administrative and Budgetary Coordination by the General Assembly, id.* at 37; Meron, *Budget Approval by the General Assembly of the United Nations: Duty or Discretion?*, 42 Brit. Y.B. Int'l L. 91 (1967).
111 *See* Report of the Committee of Experts on Human Rights to the Committee of Ministers of the Council of Europe on Problems Arising from the Co-Existence of the United Nations Covenants on Human Rights and the European Convention on Human Rights, Council of Europe Doc. H. (70) 7 (1970); Directorate of Human Rights, Council of Europe, Proceedings of the Colloquy about the European Convention on Human Rights in Relation to other International Instruments for the Protection of Human Rights, Athens, Sept. 21-22, 1978 (Strasbourg 1979); M. Tardu, Human Rights: The International Petition System (1980); Buergenthal, *supra* note 109; Eissen, *The European Convention on Human Rights and the United Nations Covenant on Civil and Political Rights: Problems of Coexistence*, 22 Buffalo L. Rev. 181 (1972); Tardu, *The Protocol to the United Nations Covenant on Civil and Political Rights and the Inter-American System: A Study of Co-Existing Petition Procedures*, 70 Am. J. Int'l L. 778 (1976).
112 *See generally* Meron, *Norm-making and Supervision in International Human Rights: Reflections on Institutional Order*,76 Am. J. Int'l L. 754 (1982); International Complaint Systems, Council of Europe Doc. CAHMP (80) 2 (1980), a Secretariat Information Memorandum prepared by the Directorate of Human Rights for the Ad Hoc Committee on the Multiplication of Complaint Procedures at the International Level of the Council of Europe.
113 *See* Annual Report of the Administrative Committee on Co-ordination for 1973-1974, U.N. Doc. E/5488, at 51-52 (1974); Report of the *Ad Hoc* Inter-Agency Meeting of Legal Experts on Co-ordination of Legislative Work of Organizations, U.N. Doc. Co-Ordination/R. 1003, at 1 (1973).

F. A Final Remark

In conclusion, this book provides the teacher, the student, and the practitioner with a wealth of materials which they can adapt to their particular needs or interests. It is up to them to pick and choose among the materials given in this book. It is my ardent hope that in their future work they will find them useful.

Chapter 2

International Human Rights and Rights in the United States*

Louis Henkin

To understand international human rights and the international law of human rights one must understand their relation to rights 'systems' in national societies. American students, in particular, should appreciate the relation of international human rights to constitutional and other rights under American law.[1] American conceptions and practices have additional relevance since the United States was one of the principal spiritual ancestors of the international human rights movement, an important political midwife at its creation, and attentive kin to its development.

Strictly, there are no 'international human rights'.[2] The international human rights movement did not invent the concept of human rights. In the prevailing perspective, international law has not created legal human rights or indeed any legal rights for individuals. Human rights are 'rights' in some moral order or perhaps under some natural law. In our international system of nation-states, human rights are to be enjoyed in national societies as rights under national law. The purpose of international law is to influence states to recognize and accept human rights, to reflect these rights in their national constitutions and laws, to respect and ensure their enjoyment through national institutions, and to incorporate them into national ways of life.

The international law of human rights builds and depends on national law. One cannot appeal to international law or institutions until domestic laws have been invoked and domestic remedies

---

* © Louis Henkin 1983.
[1] The essay that is the core of this chapter is the University Lecture given at Columbia University on Apr. 2, 1979, and published as Henkin, *Rights: American and Human*, 79 Colum. L. Rev. 404 (1979). An earlier version was delivered as the Third Francis Biddle Memorial Lecture at the Harvard Law School on Apr. 6, 1978, and was published under the title *Constitutional Rights and Human Rights*, 13 Harv. C.R.-C.L. L. Rev. 593 (1978).

I use the adjective 'American' with apologies to inhabitants of other American Republics because it is often awkward to use 'United States' as an adjective. In the present context, moreover, I often use it to describe persons and ideas before the creation of the United States. It is more appropriate also when the reference is not, or not only, to national or federal law and practice, but includes the law and practice of the states of the United States.

[2] *See* Henkin, *International Human Rights as 'Rights'*, 1 Cardozo L. Rev. 425 (1979).

exhausted.[3] When a state is deficient in respecting or ensuring human rights, the international law of human rights does not supersede national laws and institutions, but seeks to induce the state to improve them and make them more effective.

The obligations assumed by the United States under international human rights law, then, would depend heavily on U.S. law and institutions. Insofar as human rights recognized by the United States as international obligations are congruent with the rights of individuals under U.S. law, the United States would be required to do as a matter of international obligation only what it is already required to do by the U.S. Constitution and laws. Where the United States assumes obligations to recognize rights beyond those already required by domestic law, the United States would have to adopt any necessary laws and take other measures to assure the additional rights.

Since the United States has taken steps towards adhering to the principal international human rights covenants and conventions, comparison of the rights recognized by those instruments with those already enjoyed by individuals in the United States under domestic law would highlight the consequences of U.S. adherence. That comparison will indicate what new rights would be accorded, what new laws or other measures might be required. But there is an additional interest in such comparison in view of the U.S. contribution to international human rights. Americans can properly claim an important part in launching the modern concept of human rights in the eighteenth century, out of older materials and under Anglo-European influences. In our time, American constitutionalism became one leading model for, and principal strand in, international human rights. American scholars, political persons, and citizens were prominent in the process of translating American rights for an international screen and context.[4] Students of human rights, then, will be concerned to understand the great similarities and the important differences between

---

[3] *See, e.g.*, International Covenant on Civil and Political Rights, art. 41 (1) (c), G.A. Res. 2200, 21 U.N. GAOR, Supp. (No. 16) 52, U.N. Doc. A/6316 (1966); Optional Protocol to the International Covenant on Civil and Political Rights, *id.* at 59, art. 2. *See generally* Schachter, *The Obligation to Implement the Covenant in Domestic Law*, in The International Bills of Rights: The Covenant on Civil and Political Rights 311 (L. Henkin ed. 1981); Robertson, *The Implementation System: International Measures*, in *id.* at 332.

[4] In addition to general contributions by the United States and by individual Americans to political theory and constitutional jurisprudence, statesmen and judges have contributed to the growth of human rights by their contribution to human rights ideas in international law. For example, in 1825 John Marshall found that, although the slave trade did not violate the law of nations, 'That it is contrary to the law of nature will scarcely be denied.' The Antelope, 23 U.S. (10 Wheat.) 66, 120 (1825); *see* The Plattsburgh, 23 U.S. (10 Wheat.) 133, 142 (1825) (Story, J.). The United States has been a leading exponent of the principle that international law holds a state responsible for 'denial of justice' to a foreign national. *See, e.g.*, E. Root, 1910 Proc. Am. Soc'y Int'l L. 20-21, 22; 5 Hackworth, Digest of International Law 471-72 (1943).

international human rights and American rights—in their conceptions, assumptions, content, and scope. They will wish to compare also the different institutions and remedies contemplated by the two rights systems and their respective import and impact.

What follows is not a structured comparative study. Designed for other purposes, it compares U.S. and international human rights in spirit and jurisprudential perspective rather than in fine detail, in order to contribute to understanding the attitudes and policies of the United States towards the international human rights movement generally and towards the principal international human rights agreements in particular. For these purposes it considers principally constitutional rights which are binding on the government of the United States (and on the States) just as rights recognized by international agreement would be. Only secondarily does it take note of a vast array of other 'rights' granted by Congress or State legislatures or developed by the courts. This chapter, I believe, can be taught interestingly on its own terms. It also provides a framework and an outline, and strikes key notes, for a structured comparison of rights in the United States—or in other national societies—with 'international human rights'.

I. Legal and Policy Considerations

In considering American constitutional rights and American constitutionalism, I shall initially quote not from the U.S. Constitution but from the Declaration of Independence, a document now reserved for ceremonial occasions; and I shall draw, rather, on early state constitutions—notably those of Virginia and Massachusetts—now known only to students of history. In fact, for some of what I say there is little evidence in the U.S. Constitution itself; in particular, it barely hints at the concept of rights, only in one phrase in the preamble[5] and in another in one of the early amendments.[6] That is because, at its conception and at birth, the U.S. Constitution was not an authentic, full-blown, expression of American constitutionalism.

Let me explain this heresy.[7] It contributes to understanding the U.S. Constitution to keep in mind its genealogy. In 1776, with independence, the thirteen colonies became thirteen states, each with a state constitution and a state government. These constitutions and govern-

---

[5] I refer to the implications of individual autonomy and popular sovereignty in the words 'We the People . . . ordain and establish this Constitution . . .'

[6] 'The enumeration in the Constitution, of certain rights, shall not be construed to deny or disparage others retained by the people.' U.S. Const. amend. IX. *Cf. id.* amend. X ('The powers not delegated to the United States by the Constitution, nor prohibited by it to the States, are reserved to the States respectively, or to the people.').

[7] *See* Henkin, *Constitutional Fathers, Constitutional Sons*, 60 Minn. L. Rev. 1113, 1115–18 (1976).

ments were the direct descendants of the Declaration of Independence, realizing its political theory, carrying out its political promises.

The U.S. Constitution came thirteen years later. It had not only 'come-lately', but was at best only a collateral heir of the Declaration of Independence, derived not from it, but from a concurrent and parallel development. At the time the colonies moved to independence and self-government, they also moved to union: on the same day in June 1776 that a committee was appointed to draft a declaration of independence, another committee was appointed to draft articles of union. The Articles of Confederation were also conceived in 1776, although they did not come into effect until a few years later. In 1787 those wise men now called the Constitutional Fathers came to Philadelphia under instructions to improve the Articles of Confederation. But they went beyond their instructions, abandoned the Articles, and produced in their stead the U.S. Constitution.

It is not only historically, but spiritually and conceptually, too, that the U.S. Constitution descended not from the Declaration but from the Articles. At the Constitutional Convention, the focus was not on principles of government and the relation of individuals to society—to which the Declaration had spoken—but on the needs and uses of union, which the Articles had addressed. The new Constitution did not replace, subsume, or modify the state constitutions and the state governments; only the *links between* states were transformed into a small superstructure of government over and above the state governments, to form a 'more perfect Union'.[8]

And so, one may say, while the state constitutions descended from the Declaration and its principles of self-government, the U.S. Constitution descended from the Articles and its concerns with union. American principles of government, American constitutionalism, were alive and well-formed before confederation, and they remained largely unaffected by it. In principle, and perhaps in fact, constitutional government would have remained alive and well had the new-born states abandoned the effort to confederate and gone thirteen separate ways, had they become two or three confederacies instead of one, or had confederation survived and succeeded under the Articles, without the Constitution ever being born.

This brief genealogical excursion will explain why, unlike the Declaration and the state constitutions, the U.S. Constitution articulates no political theory and contains little political rhetoric. All the political theory in the Constitution is that implied in the fact of a written constitution, and in the words 'We the people . . . ordain . . . this Constitution. . . .' All the rhetoric is in a few borrowed, undefined references to 'Justice' and the 'Blessings of Liberty'. There was no bill

[8] U.S. Const. preamble.

of rights because individual rights were n⟨
union that were the concern of the new sup⟨
Powers were allocated to different, more-or-⟨
the new government, but there is no articulat⟨
the philosophy of separation-of-powers, as t⟨
Virginia and Massachusetts constitutions. Even⟨
was, of course, original, is not articulated or justifie⟨
owed less to Locke and Montesquieu than to the limit⟨
Americans, to their fears and needs, and to ⟨
compromises, emerging—in Charles and Mary Beard⟨ ⟩—as
'the mosaic of their second choices'.

During the process of ratification a bill of rights was promised and one was added shortly after the new government was formed. Even with the Bill of Rights, however, the U.S. Constitution lacked much of what is identified with American constitutionalism. It took nationalizing influences in American life, legitimized by nationalistic interpretations of the Constitution; it took the Civil War and the constitutional amendments that constituted the peace treaty ending it; it took the Supreme Court, another American contribution, to establish the United States government, the Constitution, and especially American constitutional rights, as they are today. Perhaps the genetic defects of the Constitution, including a less-than-clear theory of government and of rights, provided room for growth and development without the forbidding difficulties of formal amendment.[9]

A.   CONCEPTIONS OF RIGHTS

American constitutional rights were born in the eighteenth century out of European ideas and antecedents. International human rights, born during World War II from revulsion at the horrors of Hitler, drew heavily on American constitutionalism (and on related constitutional developments in Europe and Latin America), but took also from a different ideology, *i.e.*, from socialism and other commitments to the welfare state. American constitutionalism developed in its own national climate and was nurtured and maintained by home-grown institutions. International human rights were developed by representatives of many nations, in a complex, unorganized, political process; they are designed for diverse national societies, maintained by diverse national institutions, and monitored in uncertain, small ways by primitive international procedures in a loose international political system.

The theory of American rights is nowhere fully articulated and is rarely expressed. Many Americans may be hardly aware that there is

[9] C. Beard & M. Beard, The Rise of American Capitalism 317 (1935).

...heory, and some may question the conception here set forth.
...wever, I believe that this theory was held by the principal framers of
early American constitutions and institutions and underlies individual
rights in the United States to this day.

American rights were proclaimed by Americans in 1776 for themselves, but they were not claimed only for themselves. Declared by way
of justifying independence from British rule—what today would be
called 'self-determination'—they reflect a political theory applicable
to every human being, in relation to every political society, in every
age.

Consider the words we all know: [10]

> We hold these truths to be self-evident, that all men are created equal,
> that they are endowed by their Creator with certain unalienable Rights, that
> among these are Life, Liberty and the pursuit of Happiness. That to secure
> these rights, Governments are instituted among Men, deriving their just
> powers from the consent of the governed. That whenever any Form of
> Government becomes destructive of these ends, it is the Right of the People to
> alter or to abolish it, and to institute new Government, laying its foundation
> on such principles and organizing its powers in such form, as to them shall
> seem most likely to effect their Safety and Happiness.

Words that are familiar are not necessarily clear, and even self-
evident truths may profit from translation. I shall distill and restate,
perhaps amplify somewhat, the theory of rights implied in these lines.

Individual rights derive from and depend on a larger political
conception. Originally—in some hypothetical, conceptual, state of
nature—the individual is autonomous, his/her own master. In principle, the original decision of individuals to form a society was
voluntary, though perhaps inevitable; in principle, surely, the form of
political society established is voluntary. Upon entering society, the
autonomy of each individual is combined with that of other individuals,
and transformed into sovereignty of the people. Sovereignty of the
people implies self-government by the people directly or through
chosen representatives. But every individual retains some of his or her
original autonomy as 'rights' which are protected even against the
people and their representatives. Autonomy, self-government, is the
basic right, the foundation of all others.

American constitutionalism, then, has two elements; representative
government and individual rights. Both are confirmed by constitutional compact. The Constitution was a contract among all the people to
create, and to submit to, representative government; it was—it is—
also a contract between the people and their representatives as to the
terms and conditions of government; and high among these is respect

[10] U.S. Declaration of Independence.

for individual rights. The government's responsibility to the people, and its respect for individual rights, are the condition of the people's submission, and the basis of the government's legitimacy.

The individual rights of Americans, then, are 'natural', inherent; they are not a gift from society or from any government. They do not derive from the Constitution: they antecede it. When the people of the United States adopted the Constitution creating their new government, they retained substantial autonomy and freedoms for themselves and for their descendants as individual rights against that government.

The Constitution, the Declaration of Independence, and the early state constitutions and bills of rights do not describe explicitly and fully the rights which the people retained. The Bill of Rights does cite several important freedoms which government must respect. These rights and freedoms are not granted by the Constitution; the people would have had them had the Constitution never mentioned them. Expressed were some rights which, it was believed, needed articulation and emphasis. The Bill of Rights, moreover, refers in addition to 'liberty' generally, and expressly provides that other rights not enumerated are 'retained by the people'.[11]

Of course, what the people retained is determined also by what they gave up. The people ceded to their representatives the authority necessary for governing. That grant is also not particularized, but its scope is defined by the purposes for which government was formed, purposes which were commonly understood. And they were distinctly limited purposes. Expressing the common view, Thomas Jefferson, in his first Inaugural Address,[12] described these purposes as follows:

> Still one thing more, fellow-citizens—a wise and frugal Government, which shall restrain men from injuring one another; shall leave them otherwise free to regulate their own pursuits of industry and improvement, and shall not take from the mouth of labor the bread it has earned. This is the sum of good government, and this is necessary to close the circle of our felicities.

Government was to be a watchman, a policeman. That would leave the individual free to pursue his happiness. While the Constitution was ordained, as the preamble tells us, to 'establish Justice' and to 'promote the general welfare', those phrases are not to be read with twentieth-century preconceptions nurtured in a 'welfare state'. For the framers, justice, and the general welfare, would be the result of the kind of government to be established, a government committed to the accepted, limited purposes. Notably, the business of government was

11 U.S. Const. amends. V, IX.
12 1 Messages and Papers of the Presidents 309, 311 (J. Richardson ed. 1897).

not to provide the people with a 'welfare-state' kind of welfare; government was to leave the individual free to pursue such welfare himself.

Such was the theory of government as it was conceived; in constitutional principle that is the theory of government still. It was not a hypothetical construct: the early Americans saw their polity in fact as the result of a social compact, although 'the people' making that compact were not all the inhabitants, but only white, male, freemen attached to the community by ties of commitment and property.[13] The concept of individual rights inherent in that theory of government has also been intrinsic to American democracy since the beginning. It has never been challenged or doubted, and early became recognized as part of the law, as supreme law. Unlike what happened in some other countries, in American democracy the philosophy of individual rights precluded notions of absolute legislative supremacy or large executive prerogative at the expense of individual rights, and contributed rather to the rise of judicial authority and its eventual supremacy. The principle of original autonomy has remained ever-available as a basis for unexpressed rights—in the ninth amendment, later in substantive due process, recently in the new 'privacy' of the contraception and abortion cases.[14]

Compare international human rights. The product of the decades following World War II, international human rights reflect no single, comprehensive theory of the relation of the individual to society. That there are 'fundamental human rights' was a declared article of faith, 'reaffirmed' by 'the Peoples of the United Nations' in the U.N. Charter.[15]

The Universal Declaration of Human Rights,[16] striving for a pronouncement that would appeal to diverse peoples governed by diverse political systems, built on that faith and shunned philosophical exploration. Because of that faith—and because of political and

---

[13] '[A]ll men having sufficient evidence of permanent common interest with, and attachment to, the community, have the right of suffrage. . . .' Va. Bill of Rights, art. 6.

[14] *See, e.g.,* Roe v. Wade, 410 U.S. 113 (1973); Henkin, *Privacy and Autonomy,* 74 Colum. L. Rev. 1410 (1974).

The U.S. conception is reflected, too, in the judicial jurisprudence of rights: constitutional issues are raised in court by individuals, not by other branches of government or by opposition parties. This system may be compared with the system of review in France. *See* Henkin, *Rights: Here and There,* 81 Colum. L. Rev. 1582, 1590-97 (1981).

The U.S. conception of rights has been complicated, however, by federalism. The national government has remained in principle a government of enumerated, delegated powers even though those powers have grown tremendously. Rights are implicated principally in relations between the individual and the states, only secondarily and later—after the Civil War and especially after World War II—between the individual and the federal government.

[15] U.N. Charter, preamble.

[16] G.A. Res. 217A, U.N. Doc. A/777, at 71 (1948).

ideological forces—governments accepted the concept of human rights, agreed that they were appropriate for international concern, cooperated to define them, assumed international obligations to respect them, and submitted to some international scrutiny of their compliance with those obligations.[17]

Those who built international human rights perhaps also saw them as 'natural', but in a contemporary sense: human rights correspond to the nature of man and of human society, to his psychology and its sociology. That is evident in the language of the principal international instruments: '[R]ights derive from the inherent dignity of the human person, . . . '[18] '[R]ecognition . . . of the equal and inalienable rights of all members of the human family is the foundation of freedom, justice and peace in the world, . . . '[19] '[R]espect for, and observance of, human rights' will help create 'conditions of stability and well-being which are necessary for peaceful and friendly relations among nations . . . '[20] We are not told what theory justifies 'human dignity' as the source of rights, or how the needs of human dignity are determined. We are not told what conception of justice is reflected in human rights, or how preserving human rights will promote peace in the world.

International human rights are recognized as inherent, but it is not necessarily assumed that the human individual is in principle autonomous or that rights antecede government. The international instruments nod to popular sovereignty, but there is no hint of social compact, and the continuing consent of the governed is at best faintly hinted at. Respect for retained rights is not a condition of government or a basis of its legitimacy; violation of rights does not warrant undoing government by revolution.

Like American rights, international human rights inevitably implicate the purposes for which government is created. But—unlike American rights originally—international rights surely do *not* reflect a commitment to government-for-limited-purposes-only. On the contrary, born after various socialisms were established and spreading, and after commitment to welfare economics and the welfare state was nearly universal, international human rights imply rather a conception of government as designed for many purposes and seasons. The rights deemed to be fundamental include not only freedoms which government must not invade, but also rights to what is

---

[17] Submission to scrutiny is limited and its extent is disputed. *Compare* Henkin, *Human Rights and 'Domestic Jurisdiction' with* Frowein, *The Interrelationship Between the Helsinki Final Act, the International Covenants on Human Rights and the European Convention on Human Rights,* in Human Rights, International Law and the Helsinki Accord (T. Buergenthal ed. 1977).

[18] Political Covenant, preamble.

[19] Universal Declaration, preamble.

[20] U.N. Charter, art. 55.

essential for human well-being, which government must actively provide or promote. They imply a government that is activist, intervening, committed to economic-social planning for the society, so as to satisfy economic-social rights of the individual.

B. RESPECTING, PROTECTING, AND ENSURING RIGHTS

Since American rights, in their theory, antecede the Constitution and are above government, they have the highest status and significance. They do not derive from official grant; they are not enjoyed by official grace. They cannot be taken away, or even suspended, without the people's consent; some of them may be 'inalienable' so that the people—or any one of them—could not give them away even if they wished to.

International human rights are less exalted in principle. Although denominating them 'rights' implies that individuals have a claim to them under some conception of natural law or some agreed moral order, international human rights have been declared by governments, and depend on the continued willingness of governments to accept and honor them. Subject to developing and uncertain notions of *jus cogens*, rights based in international law or agreement, presumably, can be abolished or modified by new law or agreement, or can lose their vitality by erosive interpretations or by desuetude.

The higher status of American rights, however, has had consequences that are not wholly favorable to them. First, if individual rights antecede the Constitution, they are not strictly constitutional rights. The U.S. Constitution, I have stressed, does not create, establish, or grant rights. Perhaps because rights were not the concern of the framers of the U.S. Constitution, it does not exalt, celebrate, or proclaim rights. In fact, the original Constitution virtually did not mention rights at all. The Bill of Rights was a postscript if not an afterthought, the price of getting the Constitution approved. With the Bill of Rights added, the Constitution explicitly declares the antecedent rights and provides that they shall be respected by government. But there was no thought of imbuing the Constitution with rights, of giving individual rights constitutional stature and status. And no one thought to require, or even to authorize, the new federal government to secure and protect individual rights, or to nurture, promote, or encourage their exercise and enjoyment.

And so, for example, it is ordained that Congress shall make no law abridging the freedom of speech or of the press[21]—*the* freedom, known and pre-existing. But neither, apparently, was Congress to make any law to promote or protect the freedom of speech or of the

[21] U.S. Const. amend. I.

press, for Congress has only the legislative powers 'herein granted', and no authority to protect freedom was given to Congress by the Constitution. Later, general powers of Congress were interpreted as permitting the enactment of some such law. Today, under its power to regulate commerce between states,[22] for example, Congress can promote the freedom of speech or press in activities that are in, or that affect, interstate commerce, *e.g.*, radio and television. Or, Congress probably has authority to spend money to promote the freedom of speech because it has power to spend money for the general welfare,[23] and promoting such freedom is presumably for the general welfare. But it is still not certain that Congress can protect or enhance rights directly and completely.[24] For example, although a complicated argument could be made and would probably prevail, it is not obvious that Congress could mandate the study of the Bill of Rights in the nation's schools. The very idea of legislating to protect rights against official invasion, as by civil rights statutes, was foreign to our original conceptions. It required major constitutional amendment following the Civil War to make national civil rights legislation permissible and thinkable. After the first such program to implement the emancipation of the slaves, a hundred years elapsed before Congress embarked on another serious civil rights program. And even the states, which might have done so from the beginning without any constitutional hindrance, did not learn to shore up individual rights by legislation until our day.

A related consequence of the American conception of rights as antecedent freedoms is that the protection provided them by the Constitution is limited. The Constitution does not protect individual autonomy and freedom against all invaders; it bars only their violation by government and its officials. Consequently, when the Civil War Amendments finally gave Congress authority to enforce respect for some rights, that authority suffered similar limitations; it extended only to protecting rights against official state violation or where the state is otherwise involved. Congress was given no authority to protect rights against strictly private interference, and a series of Supreme Court cases later declared efforts to provide such protection unconstitutional. To this day, national legislation to protect individual rights must take account of that constraint (except where interstate commerce is involved).[25]

---

[22] *Id.* art. I. § 8, cl. 3.

[23] *Id.* cl. 1.

[24] The power later given to Congress to implement the Civil War Amendments (XIII-XV) supports only legislation to safeguard the rights protected by those amendments and then only against violations by the states. *But see* note 25 *infra*.

[25] The exception is the thirteenth amendment abolishing slavery which is not written as a

I have emphasized the constitutional limitations on what Congress can do for individual rights. But even what Congress *may* do, Congress is not constitutionally *required* to do. Congress is not required to do anything to protect or promote individual rights, or to make them effective or more effective.

International human rights have less exalted status than American Constitutional rights and depend on uncertain national and international forces. But they aim farther. While authoritative interpretation of these rights is just beginning to develop, these rights are apparently independent, affirmative values, not merely limitations on government. In the International Covenant on Civil and Political Rights, states undertake not only to respect but also 'to ensure' those rights, apparently against private as well as governmental interference.[26] A state is obligated to adopt such measures as may be necessary to give effect to these rights. For one example, the Political Covenant provides that the inherent right to life 'shall be protected by law'.[27] The U.S. Constitution, on the other hand, requires only that government itself should not deprive a person of life without due process of law.

C.   RIGHTS AND REMEDIES

The pre- and supra-constitutional character of American rights may also be responsible for another handicap they suffer. While the Bill of Rights confirms that individual rights are not to be abridged by government, the framers did not deem it necessary or proper to say *how* these rights were to be secured against such violation, or what remedies should be provided to anyone whose rights had been violated.

The framers doubtless expected that the system of government—the separation of powers, an array of checks and balances, and the division of authority between federal and state governments—would protect against invasion of rights by preventing concentration of power. Periodically, the people could vote to replace their representatives with others who would do better by the people's rights. Between elections, individual officials could be impeached and removed from office for invasions of rights that resulted from treason, bribery, or other high crimes and misdemeanors. In extreme circumstances, there would

prohibition addressed to government; the powers of Congress to implement that amendment are not limited to state action. Jones v. Alfred H. Mayer Co., 392 U.S. 409 (1968).

[26] Art. 2(1). *See* Buergenthal, *To Respect and to Ensure: State Obligations and Permissive Derogations*, in The International Bill of Rights: The Covenant on Civil and Political Rights 72 (L. Henkin ed. 1981).
[27] Art. 6(1).

presumably be another remedy, not articulated or even implied in the Constitution, but which the revolutionary ancestors could hardly deny. Since, as the Declaration of Independence affirms, 'to secure these rights' was the purpose for which government was instituted, the people had the right to 'alter or abolish' their government whenever it 'became destructive' of those rights.

Americans know—indeed the world knows—that American rights are protected by the courts. That too is not obvious from the Constitution. Since safeguards against invasion of rights, or remedies for their abridgment, did not appear to the framers appropriate for inclusion in the Constitution, it is perhaps not surprising that judicial review—going to court to vindicate rights—also is not explicitly provided for in the Constitution. Most scholars accept, however, that judicial review was contemplated by the framers, although without any clear view as to its scope and form. In any event, Chief Justice John Marshall established judicial review at the beginning of the nineteenth century. It is interesting to speculate on what the constitutional history of the United States might have been had Marshall not dared, or had he recanted (as apparently he later considered doing in order to escape the the threat of impeachment by political opponents).[28] If the courts had not been available to protect individual rights, would these rights have survived nibbling, or battering, by Congresses and Presidents, by state legislatures and governors and generations of lesser officials? Would the particular characteristics of American government—federalism, separation of powers, and checks and balances—themselves have survived, and would they have prevented tyranny, as the framers expected? Would there have developed other institutions—human rights commissioners, ombudsmen or procurators-general—or other ways to protect rights? Would the United States have done as well as Great Britain, its mother-in-law and in rights? Or would Americans have been less fortunate, like many peoples today, living under noble constitutions that are proclaimed, heralded, and often disregarded?

After 180 years the judicial remedy against governmental violation of individual rights is strong and effective, honored by heady Congresses and powerful Presidents, by proud state legislatures and governors, and by the expanding federal and state bureaucracies. From the Constitution, the Supreme Court has also inferred some particular remedies whereby the courts can give special effect to some rights, and deter future violations. For example: the courts invalidate a criminal conviction if the trial was not fair or did not satisfy other constitutional requirements; the courts exclude evidence obtained by unreasonable search and seizure.

[28] *See* 3 A. Beveridge, Life of John Marshall 177-78 (1919).

Judicial review is a powerful remedy. It is an American hallmark and pride, imitated by some countries and envied in many others. But judicial review is a limited remedy. It is limited in one sense because the courts have developed an elaborate jurisprudence of reasons for not deciding cases, even though a violation of rights may have occurred: courts decide only authentic cases or controversies, when the claimant has standing, when the case is ripe and not moot, when the issue is justiciable not political, and when other, sometimes technical, requirements are satisfied.

But judicial review is a limited remedy in a larger sense, for it essentially provides protection only against the future; it cannot undo or remedy past violations. For past violations there is no constitutional remedy; and there is no constitutional obligation upon Congress, or upon the states, to provide remedies, or to compensate victims for violations of their rights. A person improperly convicted of crime, a person unlawfully detained, a person whose freedom of speech or religion has been abridged, often has no remedy at all, and if he/she has any it is only by legislative favor.[29] The Civil War Amendments to the Constitution *permit* Congress to provide remedies for some violations, and other clauses *permit* remedies for some others. But nothing in those Amendments, or elsewhere, obligates Congress to provide them. Congress has in fact provided some remedies for some violations of individual rights—making some violations a crime, authorizing monetary compensation to some victims and sometimes injunctions against future violations,[30] and the courts have interpreted—some say misinterpreted—those provisions to expand the relief they apparently offer.[31] State legislatures have also provided some remedies for some violations. But many violations of rights remain unrepaired and unremedied.

In contrast, the obligation of countries to 'ensure' international human rights includes an obligation 'to adopt such legislative or other measures as may be necessary to give effect to the rights . . .'[32] A party undertakes to ensure that any victim shall have an effective remedy for any violation.[33] In two respects there is an express, additional requirement: 'Anyone who has been the victim of unlawful arrest or detention

[29] In some cases, however, the courts have provided a remedy for constitutional violations on their own authority. *E.g.*, Bivens v. Six Unknown Fed. Narcotics Agents, 403 U.S. 388 (1971). *See also* Davis v. Passman, 442 U.S. 228 (1979); Carlson v. Green, 446 U.S. 14 (1980).

[30] *E.g.*, 18 U.S.C. §§ 241-42 (1976); 42 U.S.C. §§ 1981-83, 1985 (1976).

[31] *E.g.*, Jones v. Alfred H. Mayer Co., 392 U.S. 409 (1968). But courts have also found in the Civil Rights Acts immunities from suit for various officials. *See, e.g.*, Tenney v. Brandhove, 341 U.S. 367 (1951) (state legislators); Pierson v. Ray, 386 U.S. 547 (1967) (judges); Imbler v. Pachtman, 424 U.S. 409 (1976) (state prosecutors).

[32] Political Covenant, art. 2(2).

[33] *Id.* art. 2(3).

shall have an enforceable right to compensation.'[34] Persons wh
been convicted and have suffered punishment as a result of
carriage of justice 'shall be compensated according to law'.[35]

D. CONTENT OF RIGHTS

And now to the rights themselves. There are large, intrinsic
similarities between American and human rights; there are also
important differences.

Americans were prominent among the architects and builders of
international human rights, and American constitutionalism was a
principal inspiration and model for them. As a result, most of the
provisions of the Universal Declaration of Human Rights, and later of
the International Covenant on Civil and Political Rights, are in their
essence American constitutional rights projected around the world.
But there are differences—some small, some large, some uncertain.
American rights are still contained largely in delphic, eighteenth-
century instruments, and much that is now part of American Constitutional jurisprudence, found in those texts by exegesis and
development in the intervening centuries, has to be distilled from a
confusion of Supreme Court opinions. Inevitably, some differences
developed in the course of translating American and kindred ideas for
universal use by diverse procedures in a complex political process.

American constitutional rights include, and are part of, a comprehensive theory of representative democracy, while international
human rights, although they provide for universal and equal suffrage,
were designed to be acceptable in political systems that differ from that
of the United States in important respects. Within the American as
within the international system of rights there are conflicts of values,
which each system may resolve differently: for example, the Political
Covenant requires countries to prohibit propaganda advocating war
or racial or religious hatred;[36] in the United States such prohibition
would probably violate the freedom of speech or press. Some American
rights—for example, the right to a jury trial or freedom from established religion—are peculiar to the political climate and history of the
United States and do not commend themselves as universal necessity.
Some American rights were adopted in essence, but not in detail, if
only because American rights are not wholly clear in scope and
definition even to Americans; and there is continuing disagreement
among Supreme Court Justices and other citizens as to what those
rights are or should be in particular respects.

[34] *Id*. art. 9(5).
[35] *Id*. art. 14(6).
[36] *Id*. art. 20.

Thus, international human rights include also rights that are not plain on the face of the U.S. Constitution, but which U.S. courts have found to be constitutionally protected. Some of the most precious and confirmed rights—for example, the presumption of innocence, freedom of travel, the right to marry and found a family, the rights of parents to ensure the moral-religious education of their children, even the right to vote—are not visibly in the U.S. Constitution,[37] but they are explicit in the international instruments. On the other hand, protection for property, explicit in the Bill of Rights, was omitted from the international covenants, largely because of continuing controversy between developed and developing states as to whether a state that nationalizes an alien's property must provide just compensation. Such protection is included in the Universal Declaration,[38] however, and it is commonly assumed that to own property and not to be arbitrarily deprived of property are human rights.

Particular civil-political rights have wider scope in international human rights than under the U.S. Constitution. The Political Covenant forbids torture and cruel, inhuman, or degrading treatment or punishment;[39] the Constitution forbids only 'cruel and unusual punishments' upon conviction for crime.[40] The Political Covenant bars capital punishment for pregnant women;[41] that was forbidden at common law, but might not be held to be barred by the Constitution. Double jeopardy—being tried twice for the same offense—is forbidden by both the Political Covenant[42] and the Constitution,[43] but in 1959, five Justices of the Supreme Court held that the Constitution is not violated if a person is tried by both the Federal Government and a state where the same act is both a state and a federal crime.[44] The Political Covenant requires that persons accused of crime be confined

[37] The Supreme Court has found these rights principally in the due process clauses, U.S. Const. amends. V and XIV. *See* Zablocki v. Redhail, 434 U.S. 374 (1978) ('fundamental right to marry'); Wisconsin v. Yoder, 406 U.S. 205 (1972) (religious education of children); *In re* Winship, 397 U.S. 358 (1970) (guilt beyond reasonable doubt); Reynolds v. Sims, 377 U.S. 533 (1964) (right to vote); Kent v. Dulles, 357 U.S. 116 (1958) (right to travel abroad); Skinner v. Oklahoma, 316 U.S. 535 (1942) (right to procreate); Pierce v. Society of Sisters, 268 U.S. 510 (1925) (right to send children to private school).

[38] Art. 17.   [39] Art. 7.

[40] Amend. VIII; *see* Furman v. Georgia, 408 U.S. 238 (1972) (amend. VIII applies to the states). *But see* Ingraham v. Wright, 430 U.S. 651 (1977) (amend. VIII does not apply to corporal punishment in schools).

[41] Art. 6(5).

[42] Art. 14(7).

[43] U.S. Const. amend. V; *see* Benton v. Maryland, 395 U.S. 784 (1969) (amend. V applies to the states).

[44] Bartkus v. Illinois, 359 U.S. 121 (1959); Abbate v. United States, 359 U.S. 187 (1959). The Executive Branch, however, has adopted the 'Petite' policy under which U.S. Attorneys are forbidden to prosecute any person for allegedly criminal behavior that was an ingredient of a previous state prosecution against that person. *See* Thompson v. United States, 444 U.S. 248 (1980); Petite v. United States, 361 U.S. 529, 531 (1960).

separately from those already convicted, and juveniles accused of crime separately from adults;[45] the Constitution has not been held to require that. The Political Covenant provides that the 'penitentiary system shall comprise treatment of prisoners the essential aim of which shall be their reformation and social rehabilitation'.[46] That has not been deemed a constitutional requirement and in the United States today reformation and social rehabilitation seem to be dismissed as hopeless, unsophisticated, and outdated motivations. Criminal process apart, the Political Covenant requires respect and protection for a person's honor and reputation;[47] in the United States, the Supreme Court has told us, reputation is neither 'liberty' nor 'property' and therefore not protected by the Constitution.[48] On the other hand, there is no international counterpart to the provision in the Bill of Rights denying to government the authority to quarter troops in a private home in time of peace.[49] The Political Covenant has nothing comparable to the special constitutional safeguards in trials for treason.[50]

I have mentioned small differences. But on the face of the instruments, at least, there is a major difference between the U.S. Constitution and international human rights documents as regards equality. While the Declaration of Independence asserts that all men are created equal and while de Tocqueville and others have seen equality as a leading idea in American democracy, equality was missing from the original Constitution and even from its Bill of Rights; it is difficult now to believe that the word 'equality' is not to be found there. Even later, after slavery ended and the fourteenth amendment established the 'Second constitution', the constitutional commitment to equality was less than complete. While under that amendment '[n]o *State* shall . . . deny to any persons . . . the equal protection of the laws' (emphasis added), there is no such prohibition in the Constitution with respect to the federal government. That had to be inferred, much later, by historically and intellectually questionable constitutional interpretation, intoning 'due process of law',[51] the same clause which one hundred years earlier had been invoked to maintain Dred Scott in slavery.[52] Today, as a result of these judicial readings, equal protection is probably required of the federal government quite as fully as of state governments, but the Constitution hardly rings with it. And the

---

[45] Art. 10(2).
[46] Art. 10(3).
[47] Art. 17.
[48] Paul v. Davis, 424 U.S. 693 (1976).
[49] U.S. Const. amend. III.
[50] *See*, *id*. art. III, § 3, cl. 1.
[51] Bolling v. Sharpe, 347 U.S. 497 (1954).
[52] Scott v. Sandford, 60 U.S. (19 How.) 393 (1857).

ordinary reader in the United States and especially elsewhere might find the absence of a provision forbidding the government of the United States to deny the equal protection of the laws, or to discriminate on account of race, or religion, or sex, an incomprehensible and embarrassing lacuna.

The American conception of equality is limited. Both in constitutional principle and in fact, the American commitment is only to equal protection of the laws and equality of opportunity. For many, however, while such equality is necessary, it is hardly sufficient. We know Anatole France's biting characterization of the majestic equality of the law which forbids rich and poor alike to beg, to steal, and to sleep under bridges at night. More recently, poor and disadvantaged Americans have questioned the adequacy, and reality, of such equality and have pressed the claim for less inequality in fact. No such notions are in American constitutional jurisprudence. There is no constitutional obligation to distribute the great national wealth more equitably. Even to equalize a little, by taxing according to ability to pay, required the sixteenth amendment. There is no constitutional requirement that equal amounts be spent for the education of each child even in the same state, or that welfare payments be the same for every needy individual.[53] Since *Bakke*,[54] the Constitution permits some equalization by some kinds of 'affirmative action' programs, but no one suggests that the Constitution requires such measures.

For international human rights, equality is a principal theme.[55] The major U.N. covenants are permeated with the commitment to equality. Discrimination on grounds of race, color, sex, language, religion, and other such characteristics is prohibited again and again, even in times of public emergency.[56]

Different conceptions of equality may underlie the major difference between American and international human rights. While international human rights are as consistent with varieties of capitalism as with various socialisms, the Universal Declaration and the International Covenant on Economic, Social and Cultural Rights[57] advance a few small, important steps toward an equality of enjoyment, declaring that all individuals are entitled to have society supply their basic human needs and other economic-social benefits if the individual

[53] San Antonio Independent School Dist. v. Rodriguez, 411 U.S. 1 (1973); Dandridge v. Williams, 397 U.S. 471 (1970). *See also* Lavine v. Milne, 424 U.S. 577, 584 n.9 (1976).

[54] Regents of the Univ. of California v. Bakke, 438 U.S. 265 (1978).

[55] Lord Acton noted that in Revolutionary France 'Liberty was the watchword of the middle-class, equality of the lower'. History of Freedom and Other Essays 88 (J. Figgs & R. Laurence eds. 1922). Americans today are one of a few middle class peoples in a world of economically lower class peoples.

[56] *See, e.g.*, Political Covenant, art. 4(1).

[57] G.A. Res. 2200, 21 U.N. GAOR, Supp. (No. 16) 49, U.N. Doc. A/6316 (1966).

cannot do so. That Covenant adds a galaxy of rights, most of them unknown to American constitutionalism—rights to food, clothing, housing, and education: rights to work, leisure, fair wages, decent working conditions, and social security; rights to physical and mental health, protection for the family, and for mothers and children; a right to participate in cultural life.[58] Although states adhering to the Economic Covenant undertake only to realize these rights 'progressively' and 'to the maximum of [their] available resources',[59] the Covenant uses the language of right, not merely of hope; of undertaking and commitment by governments, not merely of aspiration and goal. Some have asked whether it is meaningful to call what is promised there 'rights', since the undertakings are vague and long-term; they are unenforceable, if only because they require major governmental planning and programs and are conditioned upon availability of resources. But in international law and rhetoric, they are legal rights, and in many societies, including the United States, the language of rights is increasingly used and the sense of entitlement to such benefits is becoming pervasive.

The division between civil-political and economic-social rights is not sharp; a few of the rights in the Economic Covenant are American constitutional rights as well. The right to join a trade union, for example, is protected in American constitutional law as an aspect of the freedom of association.[60] The right to choose one's work is an aspect of constitutionally protected liberty.[61] If the government decides to make available economic or social benefits, invidious discrimination in providing them would be a denial of the equal protection of the laws. But, in the main, the rights in the Economic Covenant are not constitutional rights in the United States. The Constitution tells government what not to do, not what it must do. The framers saw the purposes of government as being to police and safeguard, not to feed and clothe and house. Of the Four Freedoms which Franklin Roosevelt proclaimed to the world, the Constitution guarantees three against abridgment by government—Freedom of Expression, Freedom of Religion, and Freedom from Fear. But there is no constitutional right to Freedom from Want.

Let there be no doubt. The United States is now a welfare state. But the United States is not a welfare state by constitutional compulsion.

---

[58] *Id.* arts. 6-15. *See also* Universal Declaration, arts. 22-27.

[59] Economic Covenant, art. 2(1).

[60] *Compare id.* art. 8(1)(a) *with* Brotherhood of Railroad Trainmen v. Virginia, 377 U.S. 1 (1964); NAACP v. Alabama *ex rel.* Patterson, 357 U.S. 449 (1958).

[61] *Compare* Economic Covenant, art. 6(1) *with* Greene v. McElroy, 360 U.S. 474, 492, 507 (1959); Allgeyer v. Louisiana, 165 U.S. 578, 589 (1897). *See also* Baird v. State Bar, 401 U.S. 1, 8 (1971) (Black J.); Henkin, *What of the Right to Practice a Profession?*, 67 Calif. L. Rev. 131 (1979).

44 *Louis Henkin*

Indeed, it became a welfare state in the face of powerful constitutional resistance: federalism and, ironically, notions of individual rights— economic liberty and freedom of contract—held the welfare state back for half a century; and a constitutional amendment was required to permit the progressive income tax which was essential to make the welfare state possible. Jurisprudentially, the United States is a welfare state by grace of Congress and of the states. In constitutional principle, probably, Congress could abolish the welfare program; the states could end free public education without violating the Constitution. Surely the level of subsistence and the quality of education which Congress and the states provide are limited by political forces and budgetary choices, not merely—as under the Economic Covenant—by available economic resources. To the world, whatever the United States does in fact, it does not proclaim a national commitment in principle to meeting basic human needs. Americans are frequently reminded that their eighteenth-century philosophy, their kind of democracy, their national hagiography, show the United States committed to protecting property, but not to alleviating hunger, even of their own people.

There is another, different, happier, 'lacuna' in the U.S. Constitution, which Americans looking around the world today might note with pleasure and pride. It is a happy fruit of the ancestral political theory. In a Constitution ordained by the sovereign people, constituting its social compact and its instructions to its official trustees and servants, there is no provision for suspending the Constitution or even the laws, and no provision for government other than by the people's representatives, for government by decree. There is no provision for suspending any rights; only the privilege of the writ of *habeas corpus* can be suspended, and this can be done only by the people's representatives in Congress, only in cases of rebellion or invasion, only if the public safety requires it.[62] Contrast the Political Covenant which permits a state to derogate from its obligations as regards many rights to the extent strictly required in time of declared public emergency which threatens the life of the nation[63]—a condition which, alas, is frequently declared in many countries. Also, unlike some other contemporary constitutions, the U.S. Constitution does not mention the people's duties. The framers knew they had duties—to God, to each other, and to their posterity—but these were not included in the U.S. Constitution. The Universal Declaration asserts that an individual owes duties to his community, though it does not spell out what those duties are, and it does not fairly imply—as some constitutions do—

[62] U.S. Const. art. I, § 9, cl. 2.
[63] Art. 4(1).

that performing one's duties is somehow a condition of enjoying one's rights.[64]

E.   NON-CONSTITUTIONAL RIGHTS IN THE UNITED STATES

I have described American constitutional rights and compared them to contemporary international standards. The comparison is seriously misleading in one respect. International human rights law and ideology do not require that human rights have superior, constitutional status, only that they be respected and that societies use law and institutions to ensure their enjoyment. American constitutional rights in fact satisfy international requirements as regards the bulk of civil and political rights, and these have the special character and protection enjoyed by supreme law. But the American version of human rights also includes a whole array of rights that are provided by law and which Americans enjoy in fact although these do not have the status of supreme law and are therefore not protected as constitutional rights.

I cannot pretend to know and summarize all the relevant laws of the United States, but some of the discrepancies between American constitutional rights and international human rights which have been mentioned are in fact supplied by federal or state legislation. If the Constitution protects against torture or mistreatment only when used as criminal punishment, or by denying the use of evidence obtained by these means, there are few if any circumstances in which such torture or mistreatment would not be subject to important civil or criminal statutory penalties.[65] In the overwhelming majority of states, capital punishment is not imposed upon persons under 18 years of age or upon pregnant women. Many states value honor and reputation as highly as do the covenants. Although human rights are generally seen as rights against the state, not against individuals, Congress and many state legislatures have enacted laws against private discrimination on account of race, religion, or gender, in employment, housing, and public accommodation.[66] Federal and state agencies play an active part in implementing such laws and there are civil rights divisions in various agencies of government to help achieve such non-discrimination by government itself and by many in the private sector who deal with government.

The courts and the legislatures have been alert to prevent 'ingenious

[64] *See* U.S.S.R. Const. art. 59; Henkin, The Rights of Man Today, at ch. 2 (1978).

[65] *E.g.*, under the legislation cited in note 30 *supra*.

[66] *E.g.*, Jones v. Alfred H. Mayer Co., 392 U.S. 409 (1968); South Carolina v. Katzenbach, 383 U.S. 301 (1966); Heart of Atlanta Motel, Inc. v. United States, 379 U.S. 241 (1964); Civil Rights Act of 1968; Voting Rights Act of 1965; Civil Rights Acts of 1957, 1960, and 1964; Civil Rights Act of 1866.

as well as ingenuous' violations of rights.[67] Most important, Congress and the states have in fact provided important remedies for many violations of individual rights, and the courts have inferred some from the Constitution itself. It is a federal crime to violate, or to conspire to violate, many of the individual rights protected by the Constitution, a law which is increasingly enforced against state and local officials and which serves to deter violations. Pursuant to an act of Congress, courts will award a victim money damages against state or local officials, and for some violations the courts have awarded damages against federal officials on the basis of the Constitution itself (without reference to any statute).[68] Recently, the courts have interpreted federal statutes as affording a remedy against a municipality in some cases[69] (not only against the individual official or policeman who might not be able to pay and who might not be deterred by the threat of a suit), which should make the remedy more meaningful and effective. State law sometimes gives additional remedies for violations of rights by state or local officials. Legal counsel helps make these remedies more effective. The right to be represented by counsel in a criminal case has been recognized as a constitutional right and, if the accused cannot obtain counsel, government must provide him with counsel at the public's expense.[70] In civil contexts, too, there have been facilities, many of them publicly financed, for legal services to help individuals vindicate their various rights.

Still, many violations of rights remain unrepaired or unremedied. Neither federal nor state remedies apply to all violations or all violators. Judges and some other officials enjoy broad immunity from liability.[71] And being largely dependent on legislative grace, remedies and remedial services may decline when legislatures are unsympathetic or are inclined to reducing expenditures.[72]

By contemporary international standards, I have said, the greatest deficiency in American constitutional rights is their restricted, negative character. They provide protections against abuse by government; they impose no affirmative obligation on government to guarantee to every individual basic human needs. In the language of international human rights, the U.S. Constitution assures only civil and political rights, not economic, social, and cultural rights.

[67] *See* Smith v. Texas, 311 U.S. 128, 132 (1940).
[68] *See* notes 29-31 *supra*. *See generally* R. Spurrier, To Preserve These Rights (1977).
[69] Monell v. New York City Dept. of Social Services, 436 U.S. 658 (1978); Owen v. Independence, 445 U.S. 622 (1980).
[70] Gideon v. Wainwright, 372 U.S. 335 (1963).
[71] *See* note 31 *supra*.
[72] *E.g.*, someone who has spent substantial time in prison as a result of a mistake or other miscarriage of justice will be compensated only if, as a matter of 'grace', the legislature decides to provide it. Contrast Political Covenant, arts. 9(5), 14(6).

That, however, is less than half the story. For whatever the text and the theory of the U.S. Constitution, the impression common around the world that Americans care for and enjoy only civil-political rights not economic-social rights is essentially mistaken.

The United States, I repeat, is a welfare state. Public education has long been provided by every state. Social security, welfare assistance, and health-aid are provided by combined federal-state authority. There is the right to work in the sense contemplated by international documents, *i.e.*, the freedom to seek and choose employment. There is unemployment insurance. There are minimum wage and maximum hours laws and a host of other safeguards for labour. The constitutional right to join a trade union is further safeguarded by federal and state legislation. Surely the United States has moved far from 'negative' government, from thinking that the poor are a special and natural category of people and are not the responsibility of society and government but only of church and charity. In theory, Congress could probably abolish the welfare system at will, and the states could probably end public education. But that is a theoretical theory. The welfare system and other rights granted by legislation (for example, laws against private racial discrimination) are so deeply imbedded as to have near-constitutional sturdiness. It was President Franklin Roosevelt who proclaimed 'The Four Freedoms' to the world, equating freedom from want with political freedoms. Some will insist that every American's basic human needs are satisfied far better than the needs of inhabitants of countries where those needs are labeled rights and whose governments have assumed international obligations to realize them.[73] And Americans have begun to think and speak of social security and other benefits as matters of entitlement and right.

Individual rights in the United States, it need hardly be said, are far from perfect. Past American sins are grievous and notorious: genocide and lesser violations of Native Americans; slavery, racial segregation and other badges of servitude for blacks; other racial, ethnic, and religious discrimination, including relocations and concentrations of citizens of Japanese ancestry during World War II; Chinese exclusion and other racist immigration laws; post-war anti-Communist hunts, invading and chilling political freedom; and many more.

If these are for the largest part happily past, other offenses are still with us. There are still racial discriminations and inequalities, at least *de facto*. Immigration, exclusion, and deportation laws are built on outdated conceptions, including the absolute right to exclude and deport an alien. Many object in principle to balancing away rights in

[73] Many Americans have claimed that the United States was well-along to realizing its own version of what communism promised but abandoned: 'From each according to his ability, to each according to his need.'

favor of some alleged public good, or to the balance struck in particular instances, for example the preference for the right to publish
over the right of privacy.[74] Some see violations of freedom in laws
against obscenity, in limitations on newspapers and journalists, in
regulations of the telecommunications media, in laws against group
libel. While many applaud 'affirmative action' programs for minorities
and women, some see them as violations of the equal protection of the
laws. From a different perspective, some see failure of rights in
excessive toleration, in maintaining freedom for those who abuse it, in
too much 'legalism' at the expense of order and the administration of
justice, and in failing to provide freedom from fear.

Economic and social benefits are inadequate and unequal: so long as
any part of the U.S. population has less than 'adequate food, clothing
and housing',[75] a country as wealthy as the United States cannot fairly
claim to be taking steps 'to the maximum of its available resources,
with a view to achieving . . . the full realization' of those rights, even
with a view to achieving them 'progressively'.[76] Much is left to the
states, and different states have different conceptions of basic human
needs. Even in the same state there is often less than equality in
education or in welfare support.[77] Especially in austere, 'conservative'
times—as under the Reagan Administration—the responsibility of
society tends to be seen as residual, to help only those who really
cannot help themselves, and then only to the extent of providing
minimum necessities at poverty levels. It is at these times that the
commitment of the United States to welfare-state principles comes into
question.

Even where American principles are unexceptionable, there are
ever-present instances where practice deviates from principle and is
not readily remedied. There have been accusations of 'political
justice'—of denials of due process and equal protection to Communists
and 'leftists', to the deviant, the stranger. Police abuses are too
frequent, prison conditions often unspeakable, and ubiquitous
government and ever-advancing technology threaten essential privacy.
Valued freedoms are sometimes empty for those unable or afraid to
exercise them, or for those denied access to media that will make those
freedoms effective. There is poverty, unemployment (which falls
particularly heavily on blacks and other minorities), inadequate

---

[74] *See, e.g.*, Cox Broadcasting Corp. v. Cohn, 420 U.S. 469 (1975); Time, Inc. v. Hill, 385 U.S.
374 (1967).
[75] *See* Economic Covenant, art. 11.   [76] Id. art. 2(1).
[77] A state may leave the funding of education to local financing even if the result is that there
will not be an equal amount spent for the education of each child in the state. *See* Rodriguez, 411
U.S. 1. A state may impose a maximum limit on welfare payments per family, with the result that
children in larger families will receive less support than others. *See* Dandridge, 397 U.S. 471.

housing and health care, even hunger, and wider economic inequities and inequalities. The United States is not doing all it could to eliminate *de facto* segregation and private discrimination. Traditional Marxists might see in the American system as a whole basic inequity and the alienation of the 'working classes', denying them essential dignity, and rendering so-called human rights immaterial.

Some of these weaknesses reflect the original conception. In particular, the welfare state in the United States is less than perfect. It meets continuing resistance from traditional conceptions. Notions of free enterprise operate to leave many welfare services to private sources, *e.g.*, to insurance. Some rights related to employment or social services, which in other countries are provided by government, are left to collective bargaining between employers and unions, but as much as seventy percent of American labour is not covered by collective-labour agreements. Even the subjects of legislation are not covered as well as might be: *e.g.*, laws fixing maximum hours usually do not in fact limit the hours which a person may work, but only provide extra payment for overtime. In general, social security does not assure an adequate standard of living, by American standards, for all. Notions of federalism, and of limited federal government, also tend to discourage mandatory centralized programs and to compel reliance exclusively on spending and regulation incidental to spending, leading to lower and unequal standards. 'Localism' impels leaving much implementation to the states even when the cost is borne by the federal government. Financing and regulating education, which has long been the responsibility of the states, is in fact often left by the states to local option.[78] Planning is still uncongenial and Americans are reluctant to sacrifice—or even act with restraint—now for future generations.

Rights in the United States still depend too heavily on courts. Rights fare better when Congress and courts both strive to increase them, as in the kind of *pas de deux* of the 1960s. Courts are effective for protecting civil and political rights, but they need congressional mandate and support, especially as regards private and *de facto* discrimination. Economic and social rights need legislative planning and spending, and the courts can only monitor them to assure against invidious discrimination.

But in all, I conclude, human rights—economic-social as well as civil-political—are deeply imbedded in the American political system in principle and are alive and rather well in the United States in fact. American society would in general satisfy international human rights standards if those standards were honestly and impartially interpreted and applied.

---

[78] *See* Rodriguez, 411 U.S. 1.

F. THE UNITED STATES AND THE INTERNATIONAL LAW OF HUMAN RIGHTS

I have compared American constitutional rights with international human rights, stressing—and thus exaggerating—the differences. The similarities are impressive, and the affinities are deep. Many of the differences, moreover, have been bridged by legislation. And yet, it is not only of intellectual interest but of considerable contemporary significance that American commitments, as proclaimed in the national Constitution, are below contemporary international standards, particularly in respect of equality and economic-social rights.

There is little likelihood that the U.S. Constitution will be amended to correct what might be called its genetic defects. The Constitution is difficult to amend. Surely, there has never been any disposition to amend it merely to illuminate it, so that all will see what is already there to the eye of a Supreme Court Justice. Nor is there any felt need to have the face of the Constitution 'lifted' so as to modernize its statement to the world, as others have done with their national documents—if only because Americans see their Constitution as a living, work-a-day law, rather than as a manifesto.[79] In any event, an attempt to amend the Constitution to include an obligation that government provide every person's basic human needs, or to improve the articulation of its commitment to equality, would surely and quickly drown in controversy.

The United States could, of course, express its contemporary national commitment by adhering to the principal international human rights covenants and conventions. Assuming international obligations to provide its citizens with basic human needs and declaring them to be human rights might even serve indirectly to elevate them in the constitutional conception.[80] Adherence would make explicit the requirement that the federal government must not deny the equal protection of the laws. It would express a national commitment to economic-social rights and dispel international misconceptions. It would give Americans a few rights which the Supreme Court has not found in the Constitution, and it would obligate Congress (or the states) to provide full remedies for violations of rights.

The United States has not adhered to the principal human rights conventions.[81] There is no assurance that it will, and if it does it will

---

[79] *See* the comparison of different constitutions in L. Henkin, The Rights of Man Today, at ch. 2 (1978).

[80] For example: the Supreme Court has held that because education and welfare are not fundamental rights state regulations and classifications of them are not subject to strict judicial scrutiny, *see* Rodriguez, 411 U.S. 1. Might the Court hold otherwise if the United States adheres to international agreements that recognize these to be fundamental rights?

[81] Although the United States has not adhered to the principal conventions, some violations of

probably adhere with substantial reservations. To understand why requires incursion into United States human rights policy which is beyond the scope of this chapter. But it is relevant to note that these reasons are political, not constitutional.

Once, some lawyers questioned the constitutional authority of the treaty makers to adhere to such agreements: it was said that the agreements dealt with matters that under the Constitution were reserved to the states; or were delegated exclusively to Congress; or were not a proper subject for a treaty because they were of exclusively 'domestic concern'. Each of these objections was long ago refuted.[82] Some thirty years ago some feared that United States adherence to international human rights agreements would threaten then-existing institutions and practices, such as racial segregation; now, happily, those practices are outlawed, independently of international agreements. Some thirty years ago Senator Bricker pressed a constitutional amendment designed to prevent the use of treaties to 'nationalize' human rights matters and give Congress authority to deal with them. Today, as a result of new constitutional interpretations, individual rights are already national and Congress already has ample power to legislate about them.

And yet, resistance to United States adherence remains strong. In some measure, that resistance builds on the differences between constitutional rights and international human rights which I have described. Contemporary international human rights, while espousing popular sovereignty, do not imply any particular system of government; individual participation in government is recognized but is only one right among others, and the form of participation is not defined.[83] The Communist states insist that their form of government satisfies the international norm and indeed is the only one that is authentically democratic. Many Third World countries, too, are single-party states and claim a need for strong government to build a nation and promote political, social, and economic development; these countries also insist

human rights, *e.g.*, torture, have been held to be violations of the U.N. Charter or of customary international law. *See* Filartiga v. Peña-Irala, 630 F.2d 876 (2d Cir. 1980) (torture is violation of 'law of nations' within meaning of federal jurisdictional act); United States v. Toscanino, 500 F.2d 267, *rehearing denied*, 504 F.2d 1380 (2d Cir. 1974) (forcible abduction of accused from territory of another state violates U.N. Charter and precludes jurisdiction to try him in United States). *But cf.* United States *ex rel.* Lujan v. Gengler, 510 F.2d 62 (2d Cir.), *cert. denied*, 421 U.S. 1001 (1975) (no violation of international law and federal jurisdiction not precluded in absence of objection by foreign state from whose territory individual was abducted).

---

[82] *See* L. Henkin, Foreign Affairs and the Constitution 140-56 (1972); Henkin, *The Constitution, Treaties, and International Human Rights*, 116 U. Pa. L. Rev. 1012 (1968); Henkin, *The Treaty Makers and the Law Makers—The Law of the Land and Foreign Relations*, 107 U. Pa. L. Rev. 903, 930-36 (1959).

[83] *See* Political Covenant, art. 25.

that they are democratic and are based on popular sovereignty, even if this support is expressed only in periodic plebiscites. American constitutional rights, on the other hand, are individualistic and deeply democratic in their eighteenth-century conception. Self-government is the basic right on which all others depend: *'representative government is freedom'*, Thomas Paine said.[84] Many Americans believe that societies that are not democratic violate the basic human right on which all others depend; they are reluctant to adhere to an agreement which reflects a conception of human rights that does not include that commitment to authentic political democracy.

But the resistance is deeper. There is resistance to imposing national standards on matters that have long been deemed 'local'; even more, there is resistance to accepting international standards and international scrutiny on matters that have been for Americans to decide. A deep isolationism continues to motivate many Americans, even some who are eager to judge others and to intercede on behalf of human rights in other countries. Human rights in the United States, they believe, are alive and well. The United States has nothing to learn, and does not need scrutiny from others, surely not from the many countries where human rights fare so badly. Moreover, they say, the United States would take human rights obligations seriously, as other governments do not; in the United States the courts and other institutions would give them effect, as does not happen in most other countries. They argue that the United States ought not join in a human rights enterprise with countries that do not share American ideals, that will dilute American standards, and that will use United States adherence to international covenants as a pretext to distort and criticize the human rights record of the United States.

Americans who favor United States participation in international human rights believe that the United States should join, not abandon, the arena of ideological competition. Even if authentic democracy cannot at present be the linchpin of international human rights, other rights are still worth striving for. Human rights are not 'all-or-nothing'. Without granting that single-party states satisfy the individual's right to self-government, we can insist that single-party states, and even totalitarian regimes, refrain from torture, lawless detentions, 'disappearances', fake trials; that they accord due process of law; that they respect freedom of conscience and freedom of movement; and that they afford substantial freedom of expression. They should establish Freedom from Fear.

Lawyers generally have been convinced that United States adherence to the covenants would be permissible, proper, desirable. American

[84] T. Paine, The Rights of Man 278 (A. Caulden-Marshall ed. 1970) (emphasis in original).

Presidents have been persuaded that it is in the national interest. In October 1977, finally, President Carter signed the principal conventions, and in 1978 sent them to the Senate for its consent to ratification.[85] But perhaps because he believed that many Senators are still 'unreconstructed', or perhaps because the executive branch itself is not wholly reconstructed, the President proposed that the United States enter several reservations, apparently designed to meet every possible kind of resistance to ratification.

One of these reservations is probably necessary: the United States should not, of course, undertake any obligation which it could not carry out under the Constitution. For one instance—perhaps the only instance—the United States would have to enter a reservation or understanding to the article requiring it to prohibit any 'propaganda for war', or any 'advocacy of national, racial or religious hatred that constitutes incitement to discrimination, hostility or violence . . .'[86] Such a prohibition would presumably violate freedom of speech or press, unless the prohibition were limited to circumstances where advocacy amounts to incitement to unlawful action.

The other reservations, however, are not constitutionally necessary. One of them would declare all the provisions 'non-self-executing' so that the courts would not apply any provision in the covenants until there has been legislation to implement it. There is an ambiguous, confusing—and confused—statement designed to leave some implementation to the states. There is a series of reservations, understandings, and declarations designed 'to harmonize the treaties with existing provisions of domestic law':[87] the United States will agree to do only what it already does but will not undertake any obligation that would require any change in American law and practice. The notion that the United States would adhere to an international human rights agreement only insofar as it would require no change in the way we do things seems—to put it mildly—anomalous. The principal purpose of undertaking obligations is to promise to do what one is not yet doing, in this instance, to improve—if only in small ways—where necessary to conform to common international standards. Some have suggested

---

[85] President Carter sent to the Senate the International Convention on the Elimination of All Forms of Racial Discrimination, the Economic Covenant, the Political Covenant, and the American Convention on Human Rights. He did not transmit the Optional Protocol to the Political Covenant whereby the United States would agree that the Human Rights Committee, established pursuant to the Political Covenant, could receive communications from individuals alleging violations of human rights by the United States. *See* Message of the President Transmitting Four Treaties Pertaining to Human Rights, S. Exec. Doc. No. 95-C, D, E and F, 95th Cong., 2d Sess. (1978) [hereinafter cited as Message].

[86] Political Covenant, art. 20.

[87] Message, *supra* note 85, at vi.

that such a reservation is invalid because it is incompatible with the object and purpose of the agreement.[88]

Full United States participation in the international human rights movement is long overdue. Needless to say, this will not assure human rights for all everywhere and at all times. It will not even assure the sovereignty of American ideas. But it will give American ideals important support in a continuing struggle in the world arena. American adherence to the principal conventions would help maintain the universal standards of political and civil rights which the United States has sought to establish. Adherence would give the United States a voice in the institutions that are applying and monitoring those standards, would enable it to resist those who would distort or dilute them. Adherence would support the political efforts of Congress and the Executive to disassociate the United States from, and to deter, gross violations of human rights in the world. It would help remove the ambiguities that mar the present national posture, making clear the commitment of the United States to equality and to the welfare rights which Americans also value, and which are paramount in the eyes of others.

Human rights began as constitutional rights, and American constitutionalism can proudly claim an important part in their development and in their dissemination to every continent and corner of the world. Europe has followed the constitutional lead of the United States; the United States' ancestor in law and in rights, the United Kingdom, and our closest neighbor, Canada, are seriously discussing the desirability of an effective Bill of Rights and judicial review.[89] The American kinds of rights are now in more than 150 constitutions. Even the Communist states pay them at least the homage of lip service, and consequently must pay them some heed in fact.

Universal acceptance of American ideas and American words is a

[88] *See* Vienna Convention on the Law of Treaties, *opened for signature* 23 May 1969, U.N. Doc. A/CONF. 39/27 (1969), *reprinted in* 8 Int'l Legal Materials 679 (1969), art. 19; Schachter, *The Obligation of the Parties to Give Effect to the Covenant on Civil and Political Rights*, 73 Am. J. Int'l L. 462, 465 (1979). For the suggestion that the proposed U.S. reservation which would render the Political Covenant non-self-executing may be invalid, *see* Note, *The Domestic Legal Effect of Declarations That Treaty Provisions Are Not Self-Executing*, 57 Tex. L. Rev. 233 (1979). *See generally* Weissbrodt, *United States Ratification of Human Rights Covenants*, 63 Minn. L. Rev. 35 (1978); U.S. Ratification of the Human Rights Treaties With or Without Reservations? (R. Lillich ed. 1981).

[89] *See, e.g.*, Q. Hailsham, The Dilemma of Democracy (1978); L. Scarman, English Law—The New Dimension (1974); Scarman, *Fundamental Rights: The British Scene*, 78 Colum. L. Rev. 1575 (1978). On Canada, *see* Parl. Bill C-60, proposed Constitution of Canada Act §§ 5-29; Tarnapolsky, *A Bill of Rights and Future Constitutional Change*, 57 Can. B. Rev. 626 (1979); Tarnapolsky, *A New Bill of Rights* 161 (Law Soc'y of Upper Can., Special Lectures 1978); Schmeiser, *The Entrenchment of a Bill of Rights*, 19 Alta. L. Rev. 375 (1981); comments by Green and Remillard, *id.* at 384-90.

compliment, but it brings the danger that others will seek to distort them to other meanings and other ends. Although American rights are for living, individual men and women, some will render them collective, rather than individual; future rather than present; sacrificing individual rights and even basic needs today for economic development, for a larger gross national product, for a new international economic order tomorrow. Vigilance and participation is the price of maintaining the American kind of liberty.

Americans have done very well under their eighteenth-century constitution but they have also come a long way from their early years. The rights of gentlemen have now, finally, become the rights of man, of all men and women and children; for Americans, too, freedom now means freedom from want as well as other freedoms. We achieved this by learning from other peoples, other ideas. We still have some things to learn. We will learn better, I believe—and we will teach and maintain our way more effectively—if we join the international human rights movement. As we are part of mankind, our constitutional rights are part of the human rights of all.

II. Teaching Suggestions

There is, of course, no single way to teach national and international human rights comparatively. The best way would be to teach it as one would teach comparative constitutional law, but there, too, there is no agreed best way, or even agreed good ways. In general, one is compelled to choose between the 'vertical' and the 'horizontal', between presenting the two systems successively or comparing their approaches to particular issues. I find it more congenial and more effective to combine the two methods, but even that permits a variety of combinations. As in comparative legal studies generally, it is important here, too, to emphasize the purpose of the study, the methods and modes of study, and the materials to be used. (*See, e.g., Introduction to Comparative Law*, in Comparative Law: Western European and Latin American Legal Systems—Cases and Materials (J. Merryman & D. Clark eds. 1978).)

One might consider two different ways of teaching the subject. One can compare national (*e.g.*, United States) and international human rights as implied in this chapter; that would be a single comparison in as much depth as circumstances permit. One can also complicate—and enrich—the study by comparing two or more national human rights systems in the light of the international standards. Thus, for example, one can pair countries, *e.g.*, the United States and France (two

'Western' rights systems),[90] the USSR and China, two Latin American or two African countries, and compare the members of each pair as well as the different pairings with each other, with each comparison looking also to the international standard. This method would inevitably sacrifice depth as to any particular national system but national differentiation would add enlightenment.

Comparing national systems adds—and requires—an important dimension of reality and context. National societies are real, their rights systems have historical roots and are based in a framework of political, social, and economic institutions, data, and events. A meaningful comparison must examine not only constitutions, laws, and institutions but the cultural and societal factors which produced them, which continually shape them, and which give effect and form to what they seem to promise. One should ask why a particular society has produced a particular ideology and commitment and particular laws and institutions bearing on rights and how the society gives effect to them in fact. And one must ask the same questions about every other society to be compared, gaining insights into why societies differ as they do in regard to rights.

Comparing national and international human rights is different from comparing national legal systems, although the two kinds of comparison are related in important respects which reflect the relation between international and national human rights. The international system, I have noted above, sees human rights as rights within national societies. International human rights derive from conceptions born and developed within national legal systems. Terms used in international instruments derive from, and incorporate developments in, national rights systems—'freedom of the press', 'national security', 'public order'. International rights therefore are inevitably shaped by national conceptions and by the national institutions that implement them. The international political system, however, is not a society and individual rights do not operate within it in the same sense, way, or degree. The forces that produced the international human rights movement are largely inter-state forces. The decision to promote rights, the rights selected (and those not selected), the remedies and machinery provided for their implementation, the successes and failures, reflect international politics, with internal domestic forces in particular countries only peripherally influential.

International human rights, intended for application in different national societies, are inevitably couched in more general terms, leaving room for different interpretations and forms of application. A

---

[90] I have attempted that lightly in Henkin, *Rights: Here and There*, 81 Colum. L. Rev. 1582 (1981).

comparison of a national rights system with international human rights compares a living system with a model (not an ideal), and a model reflecting forces in a loose inter-state system in the last half of the twentieth century. A comparison of national rights systems, on the other hand, compares realities in particular, and often very different, national societies, influenced only marginally by the international political system and by its human rights program (which the particular states themselves may have helped shape).

These differences underscore what would be involved in the two kinds of study here proposed. Each has advantages and makes different demands. One can also pursue a third study, or series of studies, by combining the two general plans, using the simpler comparison, *e.g.*, United States—international, but stopping along the way—or moving on at the end—to compare particular elements in different national rights systems, for example: 'Criminal procedure in the United States and France in the light of article 14 of the Political Covenant', or 'American democracy and the single-party state under article 25 of the Political Covenant'.

III. Syllabus

This chapter comparing individual rights under American and international law reflects in its outline a syllabus for how that subject might be taught to American students. It can be taught in shorter or longer compass.

If taught as a complete, self-contained course, the following is a possible syllabus for a comparison of U.S. and international rights:

    I. *History and Development*
        A. Individual Rights in the United States.
            1. Antecedents.
                a. Natural law and natural rights.
                b. The Levellers, Locke, Rousseau, and Kant.
            2. American Constitutionalism.
                a. The ideas of the American Revolution.
                b. Thomas Paine and others.
                c. The Declaration of Independence.
                d. Early state declarations and constitutions.
                e. The drafting of the U.S. Constitution, the Federalist Papers, the ratification of the Constitution, the adoption of the Bill of Rights, the ninth and tenth amendments.
                f. Comparison with the French Declaration on the Rights of Man and of the Citizen.

3. Development.
   a. The Bill of Rights.
   b. Barron v. Baltimore, 32 U.S. (7 Pet.) 243 (1833); Dred Scott v. Sandford, 60 U.S. (19 How.) 393 (1857).
   c. The Civil War Amendments.
   d. Intimations of natural law and substantive due process; Calder v. Bull, 3 U.S. (3 Dall.) 386 (1798); Slaughterhouse Cases, 83 U.S. (16 Wall.) 36 (1873); Loan Ass'n v. Topeka, 87 U.S. (20 Wall.) 655 (1875).
   e. From Lochner v. New York, 198 U.S. 45 (1905), to Nebbia v. New York, 299 U.S. 502 (1934), and West Coast Hotel Co. v. Parrish, 300 U.S. 379 (1937); the *Social Security* cases (Steward Machine Co. v. Davis, 301 U.S. 1 (1948); Helvering v. Davis, 301 U.S. 619 (1937)); United States v. Darby, 312 U.S. 100 (1941).
   f. The new privacy-autonomy, Roe v. Wade, 410 U.S. 113 (1973).
   g. 'Ordered liberty' and 'incorporation' of the Bill of Rights: Adamson v. California, 332 U.S. 46 (1947); Mapp v. Ohio, 367 U.S. 643 (1961); Rochin v. California, 342 U.S. 165 (1952).
   h. Equality: From Plessy v. Ferguson, 163 U.S. 537 (1896), to Brown v. Board of Education, 349 U.S. 294 (1955); Gender equality: Reed v. Reed, 404 U.S. 71 (1971); Frontiero v. Richardson, 411 U.S. 677 (1973).
   i. Separation of church and state: Everson v. Board of Education, 330 U.S. 1 (1947).
4. Remedies.
   a. Judicial enforcement and supremacy: Marbury v. Madison, 5 U.S. (1 Cranch) 137 (1803); Cooper v. Aaron, 358 U.S. 1 (1958).
   b. Constitutional remedies: Mapp v. Ohio, 367 U.S. 643 (1961); Monroe v. Pape, 365 U.S. 167 (1960); Bivens v. Six Unknown Fed. Narcotics Agents, 403 U.S. 388 (1971); Davis v. Passman, 442 U.S. 228 (1979); Carlson v. Green, 446 U.S. 14 (1980).
   c. The Civil Rights Acts 1866-75, 1964-68; Heart of Atlanta Motel v. United States, 379 U.S. 241 (1964); South Carolina v. Katzenbach, 383 U.S. 301 (1966); Jones v. Alfred H. Mayer Co., 392 U.S. 409 (1968).

B. International Human Rights.
   1. Antecedents.
      a. Natural law in international law.
      b. 'Justice' and 'equity' in international law.
      c. 'Justice' for aliens.
      d. Rights of individuals in treaties of friendship, commerce, and navigation.
      e. Minorities treaties.
      f. League of Nations mandates.
      g. Humanitarian intervention.
      h. The ILO and its conventions.
      i. The humanitarian laws of war
   2. Development.
      a. The U.N. Charter.
      b. The United Nations and human rights.
      c. The Universal Declaration.
      d. Regional conventions.
      e. The Covenants.
      f. Specialized conventions.
   3. Remedies.
      a. U.N. organs.
      b. ECOSOC Resolution 1503.
      c. The Optional Protocol.
      d. Special committees under conventions.
      e. NGOs and the media.
      f. Bilateral enforcement (Congress; the Carter program; the Reagan Administration).

II. *Content of Rights*
   A. Rights in the United States.
      1. Civil and Political Rights: The Bill of Rights; liberty and substantive due process; equal protection of the laws; the right to vote; the Civil Rights Acts, federal and state.
      2. Economic and Social Rights: the Four Freedoms; the right to work; minimum wages and maximum hours; welfare and social security, unemployment compensation; trade union rights.
      3. Limitations on rights: public good and private right; balancing, fundamental rights and compelling state interests.
   B. International Rights.
      1. The Charter, the Universal Declaration, and the Covenants.

2. Civil and political rights.
3. Economic and social rights.
4. The nature of the obligations.
5. Derogations and limitations.
6. Humanitarian law: the Geneva Conventions of 1949.
7. The Helsinki 'baskets'.
8. Third and fourth generation rights: development; environment peace.

C. Particular Rights and Limitations under U.S. and International Law.
1. Participation in government and the right to vote.
2. Freedom of conscience or religion.
3. Freedom of expression.
4. Right to life.
5. Physical integrity.
6. Due criminal process.
7. Private property.
8. Protection of honor and reputation.
9. Freedom of residence and movement.
10. Family, parents, children.
11. Personhood and nationality.
12. Basic human needs, education, health and welfare.
13. Equality and non-discrimination.
14. Limitations on rights; limitations on particular rights; national security, 'public order' and due process.

III. *Remedies*

A. Remedies in the United States.
1. Separation of powers, federalism.
2. Judicial review.
3. Declaratory judgments, injunctions, compensation for violations.
4. Limitations on remedies.
5. Societal forces for and against respect for rights.

B. International Remedies.
1. Inter-state complaints.
2. The Security Council, the General Assembly, and human rights.
3. ECOSOC; the Human Rights Commission; Resolution 1503.
4. Special inter-state complaints before convention-created bodies.
5. Private and NGO complaints.
6. Public opinion and scrutiny—NGO's and the media.
7. Regional commissions and courts.

8. 'Bilateral international enforcement'—Congress; the Carter program; the Reagan Administration.
9. National enforcement of international standards.
   a. *Filartiga, et al.*
10. Implementing Helsinki.
11. Limitations on international remedies.
   a. State sovereignty in the international system.
   b. International politics and human rights—'Friendly relations'.
   c. Politicization of human rights in international bodies —bilateral or multilateral remedies.

The alternative method suggested above of comparing national rights systems and holding them to the light of international standards requires a more generalized syllabus. One outline might be as follows:

A. Dominant conceptions of rights in each society; political theory and ideology (*e.g.*, individual autonomy, popular sovereignty; constitutionalism, limited government, retained rights, purposes of government), or the corporate state; or socialism.
B. Economic-social assumptions; free enterprise, modified free enterprise; degrees of socialism.
C. Place and character of rights in law and institutions: constitutionalism; prescriptive or descriptive constitution; the constitution as law or as manifesto.
D. Content of rights: those recognized or not recognized; hierarchies and preferences among rights; the status of particular rights, *e.g.*, the integrity of the person, individual autonomy and privacy, the rule of law and due process of law, equality, 'basic human needs' (right to food, clothing, shelter, education), self-government, political freedom, freedom of religion, property, group rights—study of selected rights.
E. Derogations, suspensions or exceptions; emergency government by decree; detention, national security, and public order.
F. Enforcement and remedies: system of government (separation of powers? federalism?); judicial review, ombudsman, procurator general.
G. Relevance of societal forces: stage of development and stability; demography (class, ethnic, and other divisions); education and literacy; political styles and traditions; other institutions (*e.g.*, church, press, lawyers); susceptibility to external influence.

Into this general outline the materials on the United States in the previous syllabus can be fed in with as much detail as feasible. The international materials there will serve as the common standard.

IV. Minisyllabus

For the teacher who would devote two or three hours to a comparison of rights in the United States with international human rights, this chapter itself provides the framework, and notes for the major themes. It can be taught under an outline provided by the subheadings of this chapter, *i.e.*:

A. Conceptions of rights compared.
B. Respecting or protecting and ensuring rights.
C. Rights and remedies in each system.
D. The content of rights compared.
E. Non-Constitutional Rights in the United States.
F. The United States and the international law of human rights.

The scope of such a minicourse can be extended as one likes by selecting one or more of the themes for more detailed coverage. *e.g.*:

Remedies in national (U.S.) law and under the international Covenants.

The rights of persons accused of a crime under national (U.S.) law and under the international Covenants.

The concept and practice of equality compared.

V. Bibliography

The choice of materials for background and for particular assignments presents special problems. As the rights systems of the United States and of the international community differ sharply in age, political context, and effective application, they differ sharply in the amount and quality of their literature. For the United States, every word in the massive literature on the Constitution is relevant, by hypothesis. But that literature is not rich in over-all perspective or in conceptualization lending itself readily to comparative study. The literature on international human rights is young, thin, light and some of it in languages other than English. Writing on comparative human rights is just beginning.

It is desirable to begin with an introduction to comparative method generally. Then the human rights bibliography may be divided into two categories: a bibliography introducing the subject generally with background bibliographies for particular sections, where available; and particular writings relevant to particular issues.

In addition, a teacher of human rights would wish to be at least modestly acquainted with several strands in political theory and moral philosophy. The natural law and natural rights tradition; the 'liberal' tradition—Locke, Kant—and their modern 'followers', *e.g.*, Nozick, Rawls; the Utilitarians—Bentham, Mill; Marx and Marxism; various theories of 'Justice' and the 'Good Society' from Aristotle to Rawls; the 'rights' literature; emerging human rights theory. Excerpts from the relevant literature are available in the anthologies listed in the first part of the bibliography that follows. (Since the original sources for each reading is indicated, one can go back to them, as desired.)

1. Political Theory
   V. Held (ed.), Property, Profits and Economic Justice (1980).
   D. Lyons (ed.), Rights (1979).
   A. Melden (ed.), Human Rights (1970).
   J. Sterba (ed.), Justice: Alternative Political Perspectives (1980).
   Also see the section on Theory and History in the general human rights list.

2. Comparative Law
   Comparative study of two or more countries requires a bibliography pertaining to those countries. Teachers not experienced in comparative law study may also wish to refer to the general comparative law literature. For example:

   Study of Comparative Law, 4 Encyclopedia Britannica 1035 (1975).
   R. David & J. Brierley, Major Legal Systems of the World Today: An Introduction to the Comparative Study of Law (1978).
   H. Gutteridge, Comparative Law (2d ed. 1949).
   G. Glos, Comparative Law (1949).
   J. Merryman & D. Clark (eds.), Comparative Law: Western Europe and Latin American Legal Systems—Cases and Materials (1978).
   E. Stein, *Uses, Misuses and Nonuses of Comparative Law*, 72 Nw. L. Rev. 198 (1977).
   C. Szladits, Bibliography on Foreign and Comparative Law (1955–75).
   M. Cappelletti, Judicial Review in the Contemporary World (1971).
   M. Cappelletti & W. Cohen, Comparative Constitutional Law: Cases and Materials (1979).
   W. Murphy & J. Tanenhaus, Comparative Constitutional Law (1977).

3. Human Rights
   General
      L. Henkin, The Rights of Man Today (1978).

Theory and History

C. Beitz, *Human Rights and Social Justice*, in Human Rights and U.S. Foreign Policy (Brown and MacLean eds. 1979).

S. Benn & R. Peters, The Principles of Political Thought (1959).

M. Cranston, What are Human Rights? (1973).

R. Dworkin, Taking Rights Seriously (1977).

J. Feinberg, Social Philosophy (1973).

M. Golding, *Towards a Theory of Human Rights*, 52 The Monist 521 (1965).

J. Halasz (ed.), Socialist Concept of Human Rights (1966).

Institut International de Philosophie, Le Fondement des droits de l'homme (Actes des Entretiens de l'Aquila Institut International de Philosophie) (1964) (1966).

E. Kamenka & A. Tay (eds.), Human Rights: Ideas and Ideologies (1978).

M. Konvitz, Judaism and Human Rights (1976).

A. Mawdudi, Human Rights in Islam (1976).

A. Melden (ed.), Human Rights (1970).

J. Pennock & J. Chapman (eds.), Human Rights (Nomos XXIII 1981).

E. Pollack (ed.), Human Rights (1971).

D. Raphael (ed.), Political Theory and the Rights of Man (1967).

A. Rosenbaum (ed.), Philosophy of Human Rights: International Perspectives (1981).

D. Sidorsky, *Contemporary Reinterpretation of the Concept of Human Rights*, in Essays on Human Rights (D. Sidorsky ed. 1979).

P. Singer, Practical Ethics (1979).

A. Verdoodt, *Naissance et Signification de la Déclaration Universelle des Droits de l'Homme* (1964).

UNESCO, Human Rights: Comments and Interpretations (1949).

USSR Academy of Sciences, Socialism and Human Rights (1979).

Symposium, *Jurisprudence Symposium*, 11 Ga. L. Rev. 969 (1977).

—— *Perspective on Rights*, 13 Ga. L. Rev. 1117 (1979).

Human Rights in the United States

N. Dorsen, The Rights of Americans (1970).

G. Gunther, Constitutional Law—Cases and Materials (10th ed. 1980).

L. Henkin, *Constitutional Fathers, Constitutional Sons*, 60 Minn. L. Rev. 113 (1976).

—— *Privacy and Autonomy,* 74 Colum. L. Rev. 1140 (1974).
—— *Rights, American and Human,* 79 Colum. L. Rev. 405 (1979).
L. Tribe, American Constitutional Law (1978).

Comparative Human Rights

L. Adegbite, *African Attitudes to the International Protection of Human Rights,* in International Protection of Human Rights (A. Eide & A. Schou eds. 1968).
D. Bayley, Public Liberties in the New States (1964).
L. Beer (ed.), Constitutionalism in Asia: Asian Views of the American Influence (1979).
R. Claude, Comparative Human Rights (1976).
I. Duchacek, Rights and Liberties in the World Today (1973).
R. Emerson, *The Fate of Human Rights in the Third World,* World Politics (January 1975).
R. Falk, *Comparative Protection of Human Rights in Capitalist and Socialist Third World Countries,* 1 Universal Human Rights 2: 3-30 (1979).
T. Franck, Human Rights in Third World Perspective (1982).
R. Gastil, Freedom in the World: Political Rights and Civil Liberties (annual).
K. Glaser & S. Posony, Victims of Politics: The State of Human Rights (1979).
S. Haider, Islamic Concept of Human Rights (1978).
L. Henkin, The Rights of Man Today, chapter 2 (1978).
—— *Rights: Here and There,* 81 Colum. L. Rev. 1582 (1981).
International Commission of Jurists, Human Rights in a One Party State (1978).
R. Macdonald & J. Humphrey (eds.), The Practice of Freedom: Canadian Essays on Human Rights and Fundamental Freedoms (1979).
A. Mawdudi, Human Rights in Islam (1976).
A. Mower, *Human Rights in Black Africa: A Double Standard?,* 9 Revue des Droits de l'Homme 39 (1976).
V. Nanda, J. Scarrett, & G. Shepard (eds.), Global Human Rights (1981).
J. Nelson & N. Green (eds.), International Human Rights: Contemporary Issues (1980).
J. Paul, *Some Observations on Constitutionalism, Judicial Review, and Rule of Law in Africa,* 35 Ohio St. L.J. 851 (1974).
A. Pollis & P. Schwab, Human Rights: Ideological and Cultural Perspectives (1979).

A. Robertson (ed.), Human Rights in National and International Law (1968).

C. Stolber, *Rights to Liberty: A Comparison of the European Convention on Human Rights with United States Practice*, 5 Human Rights 333 (1976).

W. Veenhoven (ed.), Case Studies on Human Rights and Fundamental Freedoms (1975).

Symposium, 11 How. L.J. 257 (1965).

International Human Rights

P. Brown & D. MacLean, Human Rights and U.S. Foreign Policy (1979).

T. Buergenthal (ed.), Human Rights, International Law and the Helsinki Accord (1977).

J. Carey, UN Protection of Civil and Political Rights (1970).

Commission to Study Organization of the Peace, The U.N. and Human Rights (1968).

J. Dominguez, N. Rodley, B. Wood & R. Falk, Enhancing Global Human Rights (1979).

J. Fawcett, *Human Rights in International Relations*, in The Study of International Affairs (R. Morgan ed. 1972).

E. Haas, Human Rights and International Action (1970).

L. Henkin, *International Human Rights as 'Rights'*, 1Cardozo L. Rev. 425 (1979).

—— The International Bill of Rights: The Covenant on Civil and Political Rights (L. Henkin ed. 1981).

W. Korey, *The Key to Human Rights—Implementation*, Int'l Conciliation No. 570 (1968).

H. Lauterpacht, International Law and Human Rights (1973).

R. Lillich (ed.), Humanitarian Intervention and the United Nations (1973).

—— U.S. Ratification of the Human Rights Treaties With or Without Reservations? (1981).

—— & F. Newman, International Human Rights: Problems of Law and Policy (1979).

M. McDougal, H. Lasswell, & L. Chen, Human Rights and World Public Order (1979).

B. Ramcharan (ed.), Human Rights: Thirty Years After the Universal Declaration (1978).

A. Robertson, Human Rights in the World (1982).

—— Human Rights in Europe (1977).

E. Schwelb, Human Rights in the International Community (1964).

L. Sohn & T. Buergenthal (eds.), International Protection of Human Rights: Cases and Materials (1973).

United Nations Action in the Field of Human Rights, U.N. Doc. ST/HR/2/Rev. 1 (1980).

K. Vasak (ed.), Les Dimensions internationales des droits de l'homme (UNESCO Manual 1976).

—— The International Dimensions of Human Rights, English edition (P. Alston ed. 1982).

Symposium, *Social Welfare and Human Rights*, Proceedings of XVIth International Conference on Social Welfare, Helsinki (1968).

Collected Documents

I. Brownlie (ed.), Basic Documents in Human Rights (2d. ed. 1980).

Z. Chafee (ed.), Documents on Fundamental Human Rights (1951).

J. Joyce (ed.), Human Rights: International Documents (1978).

W. Laqueur & B. Rubin (eds.), The Human Rights Reader (1980).

R. MacIver (ed.), Great Expressions of Human Rights (1950).

United Nations, Human Rights: A Compilation of International Instruments, U.N. Doc. ST/HR/1/Rev. 1 (1978).

Readings on particular rights, or rights in particular countries or regions, are numerous and can be located through normal sources.

VI. Minibibliography

The Declaration of Independence.
The Virginia Bill of Rights.
The Massachusetts Bill of Rights.
The U.S. Constitution.
The Universal Declaration of Human Rights.
The International Covenant on Civil and Political Rights.
The International Covenant on Economic, Social, and Cultural Rights.
For the international system, one might refer to a guide to the interpretation of the International Covenant on Civil and Political Rights, such as L. Henkin (ed.), The International Bill of Rights: The Covenant on Civil and Political Rights (1981).

Reference Sources

The annotated Constitution of the United States (Library of Congress).

A standard constitutional law case book (*e.g.*, Gunther's 10th ed. 1980).

L. Tribe, American Constitutional Law (1978).

Chapter 3
The Jurisprudence of Human Rights*

Jerome J. Shestack

I. Legal and Philosophical Considerations

A. INTRODUCTION

This book surveys the world of human rights and quickly immerses the reader into the sea of covenants, declarations, and documents that record the small victories and large frustrations in this area.

Yet, at the outset it may be prudent to confess a deficiency in the process, one which offers a challenge to serious students. Moses Moskowitz has put it in these words:

> International human rights is still waiting for its theoretician to systemize the thoughts and speculations on the subject and to define desirable goals. Intelligent truisms do not necessarily add up to a theory. No one has yet arisen to draw together into a positive synthesis the facts and fancies which emerge daily from events of bewildering complexity and to carry on an authentic debate. . . . In the absence of a definite body of doctrine, as well as of deeply rooted convictions, international human rights have been dealt with on the basis of the shifts and vagaries of daily affairs and of evocations of daily events. . . .[1]

Despite the force of this observation on the tattered condition of contemporary philosophy, there are benefits from discussing the jurisprudential theories of human rights. Indeed, our own attitudes toward the subject are likely to remain obscure unless we try to understand the philosophies that shape them. The essential task of philosophic inquiry is to deepen our understanding of the issues, not necessarily by providing answers, but by illuminating the concepts and logic with which we address the issues. Perhaps our goal should be no more than to identify the relevant questions. A pertinent anecdote is that of Gertrude Stein, who, on her deathbed, asked of her friends:

---

* © Jerome J. Shestack 1983.

[1] M. Moskowitz, The Politics and Dynamics of Human Rights, 98–99 (1968). The problem remains. As McDougal, Lasswell, and Chen recently put it: 'One of the most important of the many conditions affecting the transnational community's failure in securing the protection of human rights may be described as that of simple intellectual confusion.' M. McDougal, H. Lasswell, & L. Chen, Human Rights and World Public Order 63-68 (1980) [hereinafter cited as McDougal, Lasswell & Chen]. *See also* Hart, *Between Utility and Rights*, 79 Colum. L. Rev. 828, 846 (1979) [hereinafter cited as Hart].

'What is the answer? What is the answer?' A philosopher friend leaned over and spoke gently in her ear. Gertrude Stein closed her eyes and whispered: 'Then, what is the question? What is the question?' In this chapter we shall concentrate on the questions.

B. THE NATURE OF RIGHTS

One of the initial questions is what is meant by human rights. The question is not trivial. Particularly in the international sphere, where diverse cultures are involved, where positivist underpinnings are shaky, and where implementation mechanisms are nonexistent or fragile, the issue of definition can be crucial. Human beings, as Sartre said, are 'stalkers of meaning'. Meaning tells us 'why'. How we understand the meaning of human rights will influence our judgments on such issues as which rights are regarded as absolute, which are universal, which should be given priority, which can be overruled by other interests, which call for international pressures, which can demand programs for implementation, and which will be fought for.[2]

The definitional process is not easy. Consider first the term 'rights', a chameleon-hued word as Professor Hohefeld has taught us. Certainly, as we examine the various rights dealt with in this volume, we will observe that 'rights' is an ambiguous term used to describe a variety of

[2] The jurisprudential theories discussed in this chapter generally developed in the framework of domestic legal systems. Obviously, under our present system of world organization, the chief protection for human rights must come from domestic systems. Our discussion, however, encompasses the application of rights theory to the international context where there is a central question as to the status of the individual in international law. The traditional view is that international law is applicable between states and while individuals may be the *objects* of international law, they are not *subjects*, *i.e.*, bearers of duties and responsibilities. Others disagree, citing examples of access of individuals to international fora and other indicia. The issue is important. Professor Lauterpacht has pointed out that 'The evolution of an international law in which the individual is the subject of duties imposed by it is in some respects a corollary of the attribution of rights grounded in international law. It is difficult to urge and justify the existence of the former without admitting the validity of the latter.' Further, 'the full and effective acceptance of the principle that individuals are subjects of international duties has a direct bearing on the evolution of international morality.' H. Lauterpacht, International Law and Human Rights 45-47 (1973). Various approaches to this issue are dealt with in Higgins, *Conceptual Thinking About the Individual in International Law*, 24 N.Y.L.S. L. Rev. 13 (1978). From a philosophic view, a succinct, cogent argument for recognizing the status of the individual is made by D. O'Connell, 1 International Law 118 (1965):

Is it true to say that the end of legal action is a philosophical one in which the lawyer can pretend to be disinterested? Does it suffice to admit that the individual's good is the ultimate end of law but refuse the individual any capacity in the realisation of that good? Is the good in fact attained by treating the individual as an instrumentality of law and not as an actor? Philosophy and practice demonstrates that the answer to all these questions must be in the negative. The individual as the end of community is a *member* of the community, and a member has status; he is not an object. It is not a sufficient answer to assert that the State is the medium between international law and its own nationals, for the law has often fractured this link when it failed in its purpose.

legal relationships.[3] According to Hohefeldian analysis, 'right' sometimes is used in its strict sense of the right-holder being *entitled* to
something with a correlative duty in another. Sometimes, 'right' is used
to indicate an *immunity* from having a legal status altered. Sometimes
it indicates a *privilege* to do something. Sometimes it refers to a *power*
to create a legal relationship.[4]

Although all of these terms have sometimes been identified as rights,
each concept invokes different protections and produces variant
results. Consider, for example, the human rights dealt with in the
International Covenant on Civil and Political Rights[5] and discussed in
chapter 4. Some of these rights are in the nature of immunities,
meaning that governments cannot derogate from them. But are there
any absolute rights? Surely, the right to life guaranteed by article 6(1)
of that Covenant would seem to be so basic as to be considered
absolute. Yet, article 6(1) only offers protection against 'arbitrary'
deprivation of life. What is the effect of this qualification on the nature
of the right involved?

When we speak of inalienable rights, what do we mean? Do we
mean a right to which no exceptions or limitations are valid? Or do we
mean a 'prima facie' right with a special burden on the proponent of
any defeasance? Or do we mean a principle[6] which must be followed
unless some other principle weighty enough to allow abridgment
arises? Must the considerations which justify an exception be of the
same moral category as those that underlie the right?[7] These will be
recurring problems as we study the human rights dealt with in this
volume.

If we classify a right as a *claim* against a government to refrain from
certain acts, such as not to torture its citizens or deny them freedom of
speech, religion, or emigration, then other complexities arise. Again,
we need to understand the basis for asserting such claims. If a particular claim stems from a metaphysical concept such as the nature of
humanity, or from a religious concept such as the divine will, or from
some other *a priori* concept, then the claim may really be an immunity
to which normative judgments should not apply. If, however, the claim

---

[3] *See* Hohefeld, *Fundamental Legal Conceptions as Applied in Judicial Reasoning*, 23 Yale
L.J. 16 (1913); Allen & Laymen, *Right₁, Right₂, Right₃, Right₄, And How About Right*, in
Human Rights 106 (E. Pollack ed. 1971). [hereinafter cited as Pollack].

[4] The words are used here in the sense ascribed to them in Hohefeldian analysis. In international law, privileges and immunities are words of art applicable to special contexts and often
used without differentiation.

[5] G.A. Res. 2200, 21 U.N. GAOR, Supp. (No. 16) 52, U.N. Doc A/6316 (1966).

[6] For an excellent discussion of the distinction between rule and principle, *see* R. Dworkin,
Taking Rights Seriously 22-31 (1977) [hereinafter cited as Dworkin].

[7] *See* Human Rights (A. Melden ed. 1970) [hereinafter cited as Melden] Melden, *Introduction*,
in *id.* at 1; Vlastos, *Justice and Equality*, in *id.* at 76.

is based on certain interests such as the common good, other problems arise such as the need to determine the common good, which may allow a wide variety of moral interpretations,[8] many of which are not supportive of individual human rights demands. We may also have to balance any particular claim against other societal interests such as national security or public morality or whatever else may be juxtaposed as a limitation.

If we are speaking of *privileges*, there are other concerns: if the privileges are granted by the state, then presumably the state is entitled to condition them. This, indeed, is the approach in the Soviet Constitution in which rights are viewed as privileges conditioned on furthering Communist ideology.[9] Does the right of a state to derogate from rights given in an international covenant mean that the rights are only privileges? For example, the International Covenant on Civil and Political Rights does not permit a state to derogate from the right set forth in article 8 not to be held in slavery or servitude. The same article also prohibits a state from requiring an individual to perform forced labour; yet, that right is subject to derogation in time of public emergency under article 4. Is the right not to be enslaved an *immunity* or an *absolute right*, and the right not to perform forced labour merely a *privilege*, since there are times when the latter right is not available? How do you determine what kind of 'right' you are dealing with?

An example of the confusion that can arise from the definitional problem is the designation of 'rights' in the International Covenant on Economic, Social and Cultural Rights.[10] The 'rights' there include such matters as the right to favorable conditions of work, to social security, to health, to education, to fair wages, to a decent standard of living, and even to holidays with pay. Unlike the case of civil and political rights, this Covenant does not provide specifically for derogation from such rights.[11] Are these 'rights' claims which individuals may assert; if so, on whom are the correlative duties? If they are privileges, under

---

[8] This has always been a difficult problem as the discussion later bears out. For example, Thomas Aquinas, while agreeing generally with the Aristotelian concept that the common good of the state extended above the private good, added the qualification that the subordination of the individual to the common well-being of the state ceases at the point where spiritual values are involved which only a soul-bearing human, not a juridical organization, can have. But which are those values? And are all human beings considered soul-bearing or only those who have accepted the faith?

[9] Thus, the Constitution of the U.S.S.R. declares that various freedoms of speech, press, and assembly are granted '[i]n accordance with the interests of the people and in order to strengthen and develop the socialist system'. *See* arts. 39, 50. Of course, other constitutions contain other ideologies. For example, the Bonn Constitution of 1949 provides: 'Man's dignity is inviolable. . . . For this reason the German people accept the inviolable and immutable human rights as the basis of every human society, of peace and justice in the world.' Art. 1, paras. 1, 2.

[10] G.A. Res. 2200, 21 U.N. GAOR, Supp. (No. 16) 49, U.N. Doc. A/6316 (1966).

[11] *See id.* art. 4.

what conditions can they be denied? Professor Trubek, in chapter 6 of this volume, refers to such 'rights' as ones that are 'recognized' rather than declared or ensured. And he says that they involve the principle of 'progressive realization', apparently meaning that they are aspirations or goals. If so, is it erroneous and even misleading to hold out such goals as rights? Who is subject to a duty to provide the rights?

Some scholars classify civil and political rights as types of immunities since they protect against encroachments of government. They are restraints on government in the nature of a command: 'Thou shalt not.' Generally, such negative restraints can be secured by fairly simple legislation. Economic, social, and cultural rights, on the other hand, are 'rights' in which affirmative action by the government is necessary. Therefore, they are viewed as claims upon the governments which may or may not be realized depending on such matters as availability of resources and other conditions.[12]

If it were that simple, the logical conclusion would seem to be that civil and political rights (in the nature of immunities) deserve a hierarchical preference over contingent claims or expectations. But as we discuss later, Communist states and some Third World states often assert the reverse: that economic or social claims have a priority among the classes of rights. Indeed, it is frequently argued that achievement of economic and social rights is a pre-condition for other rights, that is, until the economic and social rights are realized a state is not in a condition to provide civil and political rights. Many assign an equal and interdependent status to civil and political rights and economic and social rights even if they have a different jural status.[13] The authority for and the priorities to be assigned these two sets of rights involve issues of *real-politik* which have often sharply divided East and West, North and South. But the issues also involve conflicts between utilitarian and anti-utilitarian philosophy, conflicts between values of equality and liberty, and other issues of contemporary philosophy which shall be discussed shortly.

Finally, in the case of international human rights one is always faced with the question of what are rights worth where the type of enforce-

---

[12] *See* M. Cranston, What Are Human Rights ch. VIII (1973) [hereinafter cited as Cranston]. *Compare* Cranston's view, *id., with* Gewirth's view that economic and social rights must be considered human rights even if they do not quite meet the tests of universality and practicability, A. Gewirth, Reason & Morality (1978) [hereinafter cited as Gewirth]. *See also* Gewirth, *The Basis and Content of Human Rights*, 13 Ga. L. Rev. 1143, 1168-70 (1979); Watson, *Welfare Rights and Human Rights*, 6 J. Soc. Pol'y 31-46 (1977).

[13] A succinct plea for the interdependence of civil and political rights and economic and social rights is found in the observation of Andre Amalrik that a man who is hungry is not free, but a slave with a full belly is still a slave. Daniel Patrick Moynihan has argued that economic and social rights are likely to prosper more in societies which promote civil and political rights. Does this test out? Consider under which circumstances civil and political rights may be pre-conditions to the achievement of economic and social rights. *See* Gewirth, *supra* note 12.

ment procedures we find in a domestic system do not exist. It has often been said that there cannot be a right without a remedy. But is that so where there are various alternative forms of redress achieved through non-legal processes such as quiet diplomacy, threats of linkage, public opinion pressures, and other measures? This is a question of particular pertinence to the discussion in this volume of the role of non-governmental organizations in chapter 11.[14]

To summarize at this point, jurisprudential analysis of the nature of rights is not just an academic exercise. It is misleading and perhaps also futile to treat all of the rights discussed in this volume as of one class. Understanding the nature of the 'right' involved helps clarify our consideration of the degree of protection available, the nature of the derogations or exceptions, the priorities to be afforded to various rights, the question of whether a series of rights will be treated in hierarchical relationships, and similar problems. A central task of developing a human rights system is to invest rights with a legal status that protects them from limitation or derogation. One obviously cannot go about the task without understanding the jural relationships created by a rights system—a problem which will confront the reader throughout this book. We turn next to issues generally viewed as being principally within the province of moral philosophy.

C. WHICH RIGHTS ARE HUMAN RIGHTS?

Let us turn next to the question what are *human* rights? Once the question is asked the complexities are apparent. To speak of human rights requires a conception of what rights one possesses by virtue of being human. Of course, we are not speaking here of human rights in the self-evident sense that those who have them are human but in the sense that in order to have them one need *only* be human. Put another way, are there rights that human beings have simply because they are human beings and independent of their varying social circumstances and degrees of merit? The answers that individuals and states provide to this question have great bearing on their attitudes and their vigor with respect to protecting human rights.

Some scholars have identified human rights as those which are important, moral, and universal.[15] It is obviously comforting to adorn human rights with those characteristics. But, these terms, if they are not to be considered mere truisms, contain certain ambiguities. For example, when we say a right is 'important', we may be speaking of

---

[14] Elsewhere, I have discussed the capability of nongovernmental human rights organizations to effect redress of abuses. *See* Shestack, *Sisyphus Endures: The International Human Rights NGO*, 24 N.Y.L.S. L. Rev. 89 (1978).

[15] *See, e.g.*, Edel, *Some Reflections on the Concept of Human Rights*, in Pollack, *supra* note 3, at 1. *See also* Cranston, *supra* note 12, at 1.

one or more of the following qualities: (1) its intrinsic value; (2) its instrumental value; (3) its value to a scheme of rights; (4) its importance in not being outweighed by other considerations; or (5) its importance as structural support for the system of the good life.[16] 'Universal' and 'moral' are perhaps even more complicated words.[17] What makes certain rights universal, moral, and important, and who decides? This is another way, perhaps, of getting at the question of what is the source of authority for human rights, or how can they be established or justified.

Approaches to this question vary widely.[18] The more one delves into this subject the more one is tempted to go along with those intuitive moral philosophers who claim that definitions of human rights are futile because they involve moral judgments which must be self-evident and are not further explicable.[19] Other moral philosophers, faced with the instability of meaning, focus on the effect of human rights, or what they are *for*.[20] A refinement on this process advanced by the prescriptivist school says that we should not be concerned with what is sought to be achieved *by* issuing a moral (human rights) utterance but with what is actually done *in* issuing it, *i.e.*, what act is accomplished; what facts are brought into existence.[21]

However useful these approaches may be, the justificatory questions remain: what are the sources, if any, of moral (human rights) claims? How compelling are the justifications that can be urged for or against them? What is their scope or content and how do they relate to one another? Such questions have been a concern for virtually every school of jurisprudential thought—theological, natural law, positivist, historical, utilitarian, social science, realist—and variants thereof. Each theory contributes insights; in this chapter we have only space to note those particularly pertinent to the development of a human rights structure.

D. SOURCES OF HUMAN RIGHTS

1. *Religion*

The term 'human rights' as such is not found in traditional religions.

[16] *See* Edel, in Pollack, *supra* note 3, at 4-6.

[17] For a discussion of the difficulties in determining the universality of a proposition, see R. Hare, Freedom and Reason 10–13, 30 (1963).

[18] *See* Weyrauch, *On Definitions, Tautologies and Ethnocentivism in Regard to Universal Human Rights*, in Pollack, *supra* note 3, at 198–202.

[19] *See* H. Prichard, Moral Obligations (1949); W. Ross, The Right and The Good (1930). *Compare* this view *with* the U.S. Declaration of Independence, 'We hold these truths to be *self-evident*, that all men are created equal, that they are endowed by their Creator with certain unalienable Rights . . .' (emphasis supplied).

[20] *See* C. Stevenson, Ethics & Language (1944); cf. Aiken, *Rights, Human and Otherwise*, 52 The Monist 515 (1968).

[21] *See, e.g.*, Gewirth, *supra* note 12; Hare, *supra*, note 17.

Nonetheless, theology presents the basis for a human rights theory stemming from a law higher than the state and whose source is the Supreme Being. Of course, this theory presupposes an acceptance of revealed doctrine as the source of such rights.

If one accepts the premise of the Old Testament that Adam was created in the image of God, this implies that the divine stamp gives human beings a high value of worth.[22] Further, a universal common father gives rise to a common humanity and from this flows a universality of certain rights.[23] Since the rights stem from a divine source, they are inalienable by mortal authority.[24] This concept is found not only in the Judeo-Christian tradition, but in other religions with a deistic base.

Even if one accepts the revealed truth of the fatherhood of God and the brotherhood of man, the problem remains as to which human rights flow therefrom. Equality of all human beings in the eyes of God would seem a necessary development from the common creation by God, but freedom to live as one prefers is not. Indeed, religions generally impose severe limitations on individual freedom. Moreover, revelation is capable of differing interpretations even as to equality and some religions have been quite restrictive toward slaves, women, and non-believers, even though all are God's creations.

Despite the problems in the theological approach, religious doctrine offers the possibility, as Professor Pagels has pointed out, of selecting elements of various religious traditions to construct a broad inter-cultural rationale which supports the various principles of equality and justice which underlie international human rights.[25] Indeed, once the leap to belief has been made, religion may be the most attractive of

[22] An appealing expression of this comes from the Talmud:
>   A man may coin several coins with the same matrix and all will be similar, but the King of Kings, the Almighty, has coined every man with the same matrix of Adam and no one is similar to the other. Therefore, every man ought to say the whole world has been created for me. Sanhedrin 38:1.

[23] *See, e.g.,* S. Greenberg, Foundations of a Faith (1967); M. Konvitz, Judaism and Human Rights (1972). For example, the Bible prescribed various human rights concepts far advanced for that time such as: limitations on slavery (*Exodus* 21:2); justice to the poor (*Isaiah* 1:16-17); fair treatment of strangers (*Leviticus* 23:22); racial equality (*Amos* 9:7); and protection of labour (*Deuteronomy* 23:25-26, 24:6, 10, 12-13, 15), etc.

[24] There is a positivist aspect to divine orders since obedience derives from one's duty to God, not from one's inherent nature. Still, the fact remains that once the duties are ordered by God, those duties accrue to the individual's benefit and may be inviolate from denigration by the state, which is an important objective of any human rights system. The Bible, for example, is full of examples of prophets denouncing rulers for departing from the divine law to the detriment of individuals. *See* Greenberg, Foundations of a Faith ch. IV (1967). *See also* Nasr, *The Concept and Reality of Freedom in Islam & Islamic Civilization*, in The Philosophy of Human Rights 96-101. (A. Rosenbaum ed. 1980) [hereinafter cited as Rosenbaum].

[25] Pagels, The Internationalization of Human Rights, paper delivered at Aspen Institute, Aspen, Colo., Aug. 14-19, 1977. But the usefulness of this approach should not be over-emphasized because some religions espouse conceptions of the nature of humanity that are

the theoretical approaches.[26] When human beings are not visualized in God's image then their basic rights may well lose their metaphysical raison d'être. The concept of human beings created in the image of God certainly endows men and women with a worth and dignity from which there can logically flow the components of a comprehensive human rights system.[27]

2. *Natural Law: The Autonomous Individual*

Philosophers and jurists did not leave human rights solely to theologians. In their search for a law which was higher than positive law, they developed the theory of natural law. Natural law theory has underpinnings in Sophocles and Aristotle, but it was first elaborated by the stoics of the Hellenistic period and later of the Roman period. Natural law, they believed, embodied those elementary principles of justice which were right reason, *i.e.*, in accordance with nature, unalterable and eternal.[28]

Medieval Christian philosophers, such as Thomas Aquinas, put great stress on natural law, which conferred certain immutable rights upon individuals; they viewed it, however, as part of the law of God.[29] The modern secular theories of natural law, particularly as enunciated by Grotius and Pufendorf, detached natural law from religion, laying the groundwork for the secular, rationalistic version of modern natural law. According to Grotius, a natural characteristic of human beings is the social impulse to live peacefully and in harmony with others; whatever conformed to the nature of men and women as rational, social beings was right and just; whatever opposed it by disturbing the social harmony was wrong and unjust. Grotius defined natural law as a 'dictate of right reason which points out that an act, according as it is or is not in conformity with rational nature, has in it a quality of moral baseness or moral necessity'.[30]

fundamentally different from those in Jewish and Christian doctrine. *See* A. Donegan, The Theory of Morality 32–36 (1977).

[26] *See* Cassin, *From the Ten Commandments To The Rights of Man*, Essays in Honor of Haim Cohen 13 (S. Shoham ed. 1971).

[27] While the discussion here has been based on theological considerations, it is possible to construct a system of moral rights from the moral values of the Hebrew–Christian tradition without relying on the deistic base. Prof. A. Donegan has done so in his book, The Theory of Morality (1977).

[28] For a short exposition of the theory of natural law, *see* Sidorsky, in Essays on Human Rights—Contemporary Issues and Jewish Perspectives 92–98 (D. Sidorsky, S. Liskofsky & J. Shestack eds. 1979) [hereinafter cited as Sidorsky].

[29] St. Thomas Aquinas, Summa Theologis, pt. II, 1st pt.; L. Strauss, Natural Right and History (1953); Henle, *A Catholic View of Human Rights: A Thomistic Reflection*, in Rosenbaum, *supra* note 24, at 87-97.

[30] H. Grotius, De Jure Belli ac Pacis, Bk. I, ch. 1. *See also* International Protection of Human Rights (A. Eide & A. Schou eds. 1968); H. Rommen, The Natural Law: A Study in Legal and Social History and Philosophy (1948).

Grotius, it should be noted, was also a father of modern international law. He saw the law of nations as embodying both laws which had as their source the will of man (as distinguished from immutable principles) and laws derived from the principles of the law of nature. This theory, of course, has immense importance for the status and legitimacy of human rights as part of a system of international law.[31]

Natural law theory led to natural rights theory—the theory most closely associated with modern human rights. The chief exponent of this theory was John Locke, who developed his philosophy within the framework of seventeenth-century humanism and political activity. Locke imagined the existence of human beings in a state of nature. In that state men and women were in a state of freedom, able to determine their actions, and also in a state of equality in the sense that no one was subjected to the will or authority of another. To end the certain hazards and inconveniences of the state of nature, men and women entered into a contract by which they mutually agreed to form a community and set up a body politic. However, in setting up that political authority they retained the natural rights of life, liberty, and property which were their own.[32] Government was obliged to protect the natural rights of its subjects and if government neglected this obligation it would forfeit its validity and office.

Natural rights theory makes an important contribution to human rights. It affords an appeal from the realities of naked power to a higher authority which is asserted for the protection of human rights. It identifies with human freedom and equality from which other human rights easily flow. And it provides properties of dependability, security, and support for a human rights system both domestically and internationally.[33]

The critical problem facing natural rights doctrine now is how to determine the norms that are to be considered as part of the law of nature and therefore inalienable, or at least prima facie inalienable.[34]

Under Locke's view of human beings, in the state of nature, all that was needed was the opportunity to be self-dependent; life, liberty, and

[31] Lauterpacht has been a principal advocate for the rule of natural rights in a system of international law. *See* H. Lauterpacht, International Law and Human Rights (1973).

[32] J. Locke, The Second Treatise of Civil Government. Locke's theory of natural law combined with Montesquieu's doctrine of separation of powers is seen in American constitutionalism, as Henkin points out in Henkin, *Rights: American and Human*, 79 Colum. L. Rev. 405 (1979); E. Corwin, The Higher Law Background of American Constitutional Law (1955).

[33] *See* Edel, in Pollack, *supra* note 3, at 14-15.

[34] The need to delineate the scope of natural rights perhaps was not pressing for the early natural law philosophers. Life, liberty, property, trial by jury, the right to assembly and to petition appeared to represent such self-evident values that they seemed to require little elaboration. Hence, the doctrine of natural rights was less concerned with the content of the rights than with the rationale, such as the inherent nature of man, the divine will, or historic tradition. Of course, in substantial measure, the rationale determined the content.

property were the inherent rights that met this demand. But what of a world unlike the times of Locke, in which there are not ample resources to satisfy human needs? Opportunity in such a world may be less important than an assured outcome. Does natural law theory have the flexibility to satisfy new claims based on contemporary conditions and modern human understanding? Perhaps it does, but that very potential for flexibility has been the basis for the chief criticism of natural rights theory. Critics point out that most of the norm-setting of natural rights theories contain *a priori* elements deduced by the norm-setter. In short, the principal problem with natural law is that the rights considered to be natural differ from theorist to theorist, depending upon their conceptions of nature.

Because of this and other difficulties, natural rights theory became unpopular with legal scholars and philosophers.[35] However, in revised form natural rights philosophy had a renaissance in the aftermath of World War II, as we shall discuss shortly.

3. *Positivism: The Authority of the State*

Another approach to human rights study is that of legal positivism. This philosophy came to dominate legal theory during most of the nineteenth century and commands considerable allegiance in the twentieth. Classical positivists deny an *a priori* source of rights and assume that all authority stems from what the state and officials have prescribed. This approach rejects any attempt to discern and articulate an idea of law transcending the empirical realities of existing legal systems. Under positivist theory, the source of human rights is to be found only in the enactments of a system of law with sanctions attached to it. Views on what the law *ought* to be have no place in law and are cognitively worthless. The need to distinguish with maximum clarity law as it *is* from what it *ought to be* is the theme that haunts positivist philosophers, and they condemned natural law thinkers because they had blurred this vital distinction.[36]

The positivist contribution is significant. If the state's processes can be brought to bear in the protection of human rights, it becomes easier to focus upon concrete deprivations and upon the specific implemen-

[35] Jeremy Bentham, for example, considered natural rights as so much 'bawling on paper'. Oft-quoted is his colorful attack: 'Right is a child of law; from real laws come real rights, but from imaginary law, from "laws of nature," come imaginary rights. . . . Natural rights is simple nonsense: natural and imprescriptible rights, rhetorical nonsense,—nonsense upon stilts.' Bentham, Anarchical Fallacies. For a summary of Bentham's critique of natural rights theory, *see* Hart, *Utilitarianism and Natural Rights*, 53 Tul. L. Rev. 663 (1979); McDougal, Lasswell & Chen, *supra* note 1, at 68-71; M. Cohen, Reason and Nature, Bk. III, ch. 4 (1931).

[36] *See, e.g.*, J. Austin, The Province of Jurisprudence Determined and the Uses of Jursiprudence (1954); H. Kelsen, Principles of International Law (1952). *See generally* Hart, *Positivism and the Separation of Law and Morals*, 71 Harv. L. Rev. 593 (1955).

tation that is necessary for the protection of particular rights. Indeed, positivist thinkers such as Bentham and Austin were often in the vanguard of those who sought to bring about reform in the law. A positivist system also offers flexibility to meet changing needs since it is always under human control.

The *methodology* of the positivist jurists in the technical building of legal conceptions is also pragmatically useful in developing a system of rights in international law. For example, the human rights treaties dealt with in this volume reflect a positive set of rights, *i.e.*, rules developed by the sovereign states themselves, and then made part of a system of international law. While states differ on the theoretical basis of these rules, the rules themselves remain to provide a legal grounding for human rights protection. On the other hand, in theory, positivism tends to determine an international basis for human rights because of the emphasis positivists place on the supremacy of national sovereignty without accepting the restraining influence of an inherent right above the state. Under this view, rules of international law are not law but merely rules of positive morality set or imposed by opinion. Furthermore, by emphasizing the role of the nation-state the positivist approach produces the view that the individual has no status in international law.

The positivist theory has been widely criticized and we can deal here with only a few of its deficiencies. One is that such law is no better than the source of its authority—an authority whose tradition may embody concepts which do not further human rights and which are, indeed, anti-human rights. Positive legal theory with its emphasis on the 'is' in the law also tends to discourage thought of what the law 'ought' to be. By philosophically divorcing a legal system from the ethical and moral foundations of society, the system lacks any motive for action or goals for future development.[37] What is worse, if positive law is the only law, then it encourages the belief that that law *must* be obeyed, no matter how immoral it may be. The anti-Semitic edicts of the Nazis, although abhorrent to moral law, were obeyed as positive law. The same is true of the immoral *apartheid* practices contained in South African law today. The fact that positivist philosophy has been used to justify obedience to iniquitous laws has been a central focus for much of the modern criticism of that doctrine.

An influential moral philosopher, Professor H.L.A. Hart, has done

[37] *Cf.* L. Fuller, The Morality of Law (1964) and Fuller, *Positivism and Fidelity to Law—A Reply to Professor Hart*, 71 Harv. L. Rev. 630 (1950), where Fuller seeks to establish that lawmaking (positivism) necessarily involves compliance with certain substantive moral standards. For a criticism of Fuller's thesis, *see* Dworkin, *Philosophy, Morality and Law—Observations Prompted by Professor Fuller's Novel Claim*, 113 U. Pa. L. Rev. 668 (1965). For a midpoint between the natural law and positivist views based on a criteria of reasonableness, *see* Perelman, *Can the Rights of Man Be Founded*, in Rosenbaum, *supra* note 24, at 46-51.

much to refine positivist philosophy and to free it from some of its mistakes. Hart finds the authority for the rules of law in the background of legal standards against which the government acts, standards that have been recognized and accepted by the community for that government. This legitimizes the decisions of the government and gives them the warp and woof of obligation that the naked commands of classical positivism lacked. Accordingly, positivism becomes a good bit more palatable. Still, when Hart applies his theory to iniquitous law (*e.g.*, Nazi purification laws), Hart does not say, 'This is not law', but rather, 'This is law, but it is too iniquitous to obey.'[38] In short, he continues to argue for a concept of law which allows the invalidity of law to be distinguished from its morality. And this remains a basic difference between natural rights philosophy and positivist philosophy.

4. *Marxism: Man as a Specie Being*

We have dealt so far with two major theories of the source of human rights. One source is the autonomous nature of human beings (natural rights theory). The other source is the will of the sovereign (positivist law). We come now to Marxist theory, an approach which is also concerned with the nature of human beings. However, here the view of men and women is not of individuals with rights developed from either a divine or inherent nature, but of men and women as 'specie beings'.[39]

Marx regarded 'the law of nature' approach to human rights as 'idealistic' and 'ahistorical'.[40] He saw nothing 'natural' or 'inalienable' about human rights. In a society in which capitalists monopolize the means of production, he regarded the notion of individual rights as a bourgeois illusion. Concepts such as law, justice, morality, democracy, freedom, etc., are considered historical categories, whose content is determined by the material conditions of the life of a people and by their social circumstances. As the conditions of life change, so the content of notions and ideas may change.

Marxism sees a person's essence as the potential to use one's abilities

---

[38] Hart's argument is that by withholding legal recognition from iniquitous rules, we may grossly oversimplify the variety of moral issues to which they give rise. There is not only the moral question of obedience: Am I to do this evil thing?; there is also Socrates' question of submission: Am I to submit to punishment for disobedience or make my escape? Hart argues that a concept of law which allows the invalidity of law to be distinguished from its immorality enables us to identify more clearly the complexities and variety of the different problems. H. L. A. Hart, The Concept of Law 206–07 (1971); Hart, *supra* note 36. *See generally The Symposium in Honor of A. D. Woosky: Law and Obedience*, 67 Va L. Rev. 1 (1981).

[39] I. Berlin, Two Concepts of Liberty (1958) [hereinafter cited as Berlin].

[40] According to Engels, the pre-civilized state was not that of autonomous individuals but a primitive communalism. F. Engels, The Origin of the Family, Private Property and the State (1972).

to the fullest and to satisfy one's needs.[41] Since in capitalist society production is controlled by a few, such a society cannot satisfy those individual needs. An actualization of potential is contingent on the return of men and women to themselves as social beings which occurs in a communist society devoid of class conflict. However, until that stage is reached, the state is a social collectivity and the vehicle for the transformation of society. As modern communist doctrine has developed this theory, the current system in Eastern Europe and the Soviet Union represents the transitional state of socialism under which the state and ruling party must play a key role in transforming society. As Professor Pollis has neatly summarized:

> Such a conceptualization of the nature of society precludes the existence of individual rights rooted in the state of nature which are prior to the state. Only legal rights exist, rights which are granted by the state and whose exercise is contingent on the fulfillment of obligations to society and to the Soviet state. Furthermore since capitalism is exploitive, and individual rights, inclusive of the right to private property, are bourgeois rights, socialist rights, which satisfy the basic needs of survival and security, constitute the substance of human rights. . . .[42]

The inclusion of economic and social rights in U.N. declarations and covenants owes much, though not all, to the impetus of Communist states. Today, there can be little doubt of the value of expanding the definition of human rights to include basic economic and social needs. Western philosophical thought today certainly recognizes the importance of economic and social rights as part of a value system having justice (including the component of equality) as an objective. But there is a sharp difference between Communist and Western theory which goes beyond the question of merely broadening the base of rights and deciding upon their priorities. Western recognition of rights stems from its view of the autonomous nature of human beings and the need to satisfy the claims of individuals, which include various economic and social needs. Marxist recognition of rights stems from its view of persons as indivisible from the social whole; only by meeting the will of the whole can the higher freedom of individuals be achieved. Under this view, even satisfaction of basic needs can become contingent on realization of societal goals such as industrialization or the building of communism.

The Communist system of rights has often been referred to as 'parental', with the political body providing the guidance in value choice. Of course, the theory that an elite class or ruling political party

---

[41] K. Marx, The Economic and Philosophic Manuscripts of 1944, at 135 (D. Struch ed. 1964).
[42] A. Pollis, Culture, Ideology, Economics and Human Rights (1981) [hereinafter cited as Pollis].

knows what is best for the people is not new, at least since Plato. Even for those who reject such a notion as a general proposition, it may be sometimes justifiable, or at least reasonable, to coerce persons in the name of a goal, *e.g.*, vaccination or compulsory child education, which they would pursue if they were more enlightened. But what modern Communist doctrine says further is that no matter what the actual wishes of men and women may be, their 'true choice' is to choose the goals the state has set.[43] With that premise, coercing people into accepting those goals becomes a matter of fulfilling their real selves in furtherance of true freedom. The creation of a 'specie being' is a type of paternalism that not only ignores transcendental reason but negates individuality. In practice, pursuit of the prior claims of society as reflected by the interests of the Communist state has resulted in systematic suppression of individual civil and political rights. While it does not follow that such suppression is compelled by Marxist theory, that is the way it has generally worked out.

On an international level, Marxist theory does not appear compatible with a functioning universal system of human rights. The prior claims of a communist society do not recognize any overruling by international norms.[44] While Communist governments may admit a theoretical recognition of the competence of the international community to establish transnational norms, the *application* of those norms is held to be a matter of exclusive domestic jurisdiction. The constant assertion by Communist states in international fora that their alleged abuse of human rights is a matter of exclusive domestic jurisdiction is not just a matter of protecting sovereignty or avoiding the embarrassment of international examination. It may be such, but it also reflects communist theory on the unlimited role of the state to decide what is good for the specie beings.

5. *The Sociological Approach: Process and Interests*

To many scholars, each of the theories of rights discussed so far is deficient. Moreover, the twentieth century is quite a different place

[43] *See* Berlin, *supra* note 39. No attempt has been made here to deal with some of the substantial reinterpretation and modification of Marxist theory made by various Third World Socialist countries. *See* G. Senghor, On African Socialism (1964); J. Nyerere, Essays on Socialism (1968). For a perceptive analysis on these points, *see* Pollis, *supra* note 42.

[44] Contemporary Soviet writers and diplomats often express commitment to civil and political rights as well as to the interdependence of rights. *See, e.g.*, S. Zivs, Human Rights: Continuing the Discussion (1980) (an articulate discussion of Soviet human rights philosophy). It is clear that however much the various individual rights are lauded in writings or public fora, the interests of the 'people' as defined by the state prevail over individual freedom. In practice, Soviet abuses of international human rights norms have been systematic and continuous. *See, e.g.*, V. Chalidze, To Defend These Rights: Human Rights and the Soviet Union (1974); Annual Reports of the International League for Human Rights 1977-1982.

from the nineteenth. Natural and social sciences have developed and begun to increase understanding about people and their cultures, their conflicts, and their interests. Other disciplines have lent their insights. These developments have inspired what has been called the sociological school of jurisprudence. 'School' is perhaps a misnomer since what has evolved is a number of disparate theories which have the common denominator of trying to line up the law with the facts of human life in society. Sociological jurisprudence tends to move away from both *a priori* theories and analytical types of jurisprudence. This approach, insofar as it relates to human rights, sometimes directs attention to the questions of institutional development; sometimes focuses on specific problems of public policy that have a bearing on human rights; sometimes aims at classifying behavioral dimensions of law and society. In a human rights context the approach is useful in that it identifies the empirical components of a human rights system in the context of the social process.[45]

For human rights theory, a primary contribution of the sociological school is its emphasis on obtaining a just equilibrium of interests among prevailing moral sentiments and the social and economic conditions of time and place. In many ways this approach can be said to build on William James' pragmatic principle that 'the essence of good is simply to satisfy demand'. This approach also was related to the development in twentieth-century society of increased demands for a variety of wants beyond classical civil and political liberties— such matters as help for the unemployed, the handicapped, the under-privileged, minorities, and other elements of society.

It is not possible here to outline the particular approaches of the leading sociological thinkers, but Roscoe Pound's analysis merits a special reference. Pound pointed out that during the nineteenth century, the history of the law was written largely as a record of an increasing recognition of individual rights. In the twentieth century, he continued, 'this history should be written in terms of a continually wider recognition of human wants, human demands and social interests'. Pound catalogued the interests as individual, public, and social. He did not try to give value preferences to these interests. His guiding principle was one of 'social engineering', that is, the ordering of human relations through politically organized society so as to secure all interests insofar as possible with the least sacrifice of the totality of interests.[46]

[45] *See* K. Llewellyn, Jurisprudence (1962). *See generally* Comparative Human Rights (R. Claude ed. 1976), particularly chs. 1 & 2.

[46] R. Pound, Jurisprudence (1959). Pound's individual interests include personality (physical integrity, liberty, reputation, freedom of opinion, etc.) and domestic relations and substance (property, contracts, etc.). Public interests include interests of the state as a juristic person and as a guardian of social interests. Social interests include general security, security of social institutions, general morals, conservation of social resources, general progress, and individual life.

Pound's approach usefully enlarges our understanding of the scope of human rights and their correlation with demands. His identification of the interests involved takes into account the realities of the social process; he shows us how to focus on rights in terms of what people are concerned about and what they want. He makes us 'result-minded, cause-minded and process-minded'. However, a problem with an approach which merely catalogues human demands is a lack of focus on how rights are interrelated or what the priorities should be. As Llewellyn has said, 'A descriptive science in the social field is not enough.'[47] That seems equally true in the human rights field. Interests theorists, in general, suffer from a certain lack of goal identification. They do not answer the logical question of how a normative conclusion about rights can be empirically derived from factual premises such as the having of interests. Their approach thus provides a useful method, but a method in need of a philosophy. Nonetheless, by providing a quantitative survey of the interests which demand satisfaction, this school sharpens perceptions of the values involved and the policies necessary to achieve them.

E. MODERN HUMAN RIGHTS THEORIES

Modern rights theorists display a number of common characteristics. First, they are eclectic, benefiting from each other's insights so that it is imprecise to characterize their theories as simply utilitarian, natural rights, intuitive, behavioral, etc. Second, modern theorists recognize and try to address, using various approaches, the tension between liberty and equality. Some do so through theories of resolution which try to show that those goals are reconcilable and achievable within the same social order. Some find the tension irreconcilable and seek to resolve the dilemma by ranking goals hierarchically. Others evolve refining theories which accept a relationship between liberty and equality characterized by shifting readjustment.[48] Third, most theorists acknowledge the need to construct an entire system of rights. But so far the prevailing theories have failed to satisfy fully *a posteriori* inquiry on whether the principles advanced are adequate for explaining and evaluating all morally relevant actions and institutions in consistent and conflict-resolving ways. In the discussion that follows, only the more influential modern theories can be addressed and then only in a bare-bones outline.

1. *Theories Based on Natural Rights: Core Rights*

A revival of natural rights theory emerged in the aftermath of World

[47] Llewellyn, Book Review, 28 U. Chi. L. Rev. 174 (1960). *See also* Stone, *Roscoe Pound and Sociological Jurisprudence*, 78 Harv. L. Rev. 1578 (1965).

[48] Michelman calls such readjustment 'an endlessly dialectical sort of "progress" toward ultimate settlement.' Michelman, *In Pursuit of Constitutional Welfare Rights: One View of Rawls' Theory of Justice*, 121 U. Pa. L. Rev. 962, 970 (1973).

War II. Certainly, this was due in part to the revulsion against Nazism which revealed the horrors that could emanate from a positivist system in which the individual counted for nothing. It was not surprising that there should emerge a renewed search for immutable principles which would protect humanity against such brutality. As Professor Sidorsky explained, 'To find logical faults in the theory of the equality of persons in a society where human worth is respected is one thing; to intellectually undermine the theory when human dignity is systematically denied is another thing.'[49]

While the new rights philosophers do not wear the same metaphysical dress as the early expounders of the Rights of Man, they do adopt what may be called a qualified natural law approach in that they try to identify the values which have an eternal aspect. They also have in common the concept that only a positive law which meets those values can function as an effective legal system. In a larger sense, the object of much of revived natural rights thought can be viewed as attempts to work out the principles which might reconcile the 'is' and the 'ought'.

There is, of course, a large variety of presentations and analyses among neo-scholastic and other rights oriented scholars, *e.g.*, Del Vecchio, Radbruch, Rommen, Le Fur, Maritain, Dabin, Northrup, Siches, Coing, Raz, Fuller, etc.[50] But all appear to conclude that a minimum absolute or core postulate of any just system of rights must include some recognition of the value of individual freedom or autonomy.

Even most positivist philosophers seem now to have conceded that unless the idea of a moral non-legal right is admitted, no account of justice as a distinct segment of morality can be given. Professor Hart, for example, while continuing to defend positivist theory, has evolved the initial dimension of a rights theory along the following lines. Starting with the modest *a priori* proposition that survival is the central indisputable element which gives empirical good sense to the theory of natural law, he argues that in any moral system there is at least one natural right—the equal right of all people to be free.[51] Hart sees that right as one which is logically presupposed when other types of rights are invoked. Put simply, any society which uses the vocabulary

[49] Sidorsky, *supra* note 28, at 98.
[50] *See, e.g.*, J. Finnis, Natural Law and Natural Rights (1980); E. Bodenheimer, Jurisprudence, ch. IX (1974); The Legal Philosophies of Lask, Radbruch and Dabin (1950).
[51] By this Hart means that any human being capable of choice (1) has the right to forebearance on the part of all others from the use of coercion and restraint against him except to hinder coercion or restraint, and (2) is at liberty to do any action which is not coercing or restraining or designed to injure other persons. *See* Hart, *Are There Any Natural Rights in Human Rights*, in Melden, *supra* note 7.

of rights presupposes that some justification is required to interfere with a person's freedom. Without that minimal right of freedom, an important segment of our moral schema (but not all of it) would have to be relinquished and the various political rights and responsibilities which we talk about could not exist. But Hart himself recognizes that this bare dimension of a rights theory does not identify the features that can be constituted from the theory or the way in which that dimension of morality relates to other values pursued through government.

Some modern philosophers, such as John Rawls and Alan Gewirth, build on Kant's intuition that the central focus of morality is personhood, namely the capacity to take responsibility as a free and rational agent for one's system of ends. Another way of putting it is that rights flow from the autonomy of the individual in choosing his or her ends.

In variant forms these core theories seem to be settling for concepts of natural necessity, *i.e.*, necessity in the sense of prescribing a minimum definition of what it means to be human in society.[52] The concept of what we take human beings to be is a profound one. Still, as shall be discussed, agreement on the minimum or core is far from agreement on the scope or emphasis to be given to the rights that flow therefrom.

Finally, there is a certain 'vindication' aspect to some of the new theories. They seem to be saying that if we adopt certain human rights as norms, *e.g.*, freedom, we can produce a certain kind of society; and if one finds that kind of society desirable one should adopt the norms and call them absolute principles. This, of course, is a type of tautology. Then, again, tautologies can be significant if society is willing to accept them.

Despite its shortcomings, the renaissance of rights theory has had a beneficial influence on international human rights norms. A reflection of that influence is found in the Universal Declaration of Human Rights itself, which begins with the following concept: '*Whereas* recognition of the inherent dignity and of the equal and inalienable rights of all members of the human family is the foundation of freedom, justice and peace in the world . . .' In a similar vein, article 1 provides: 'All human beings are born free and equal in dignity. They are endowed with reason and conscience and should act toward one another in a spirit of brotherhood.'

Whatever the gap between principle and practice, such articulations

---

[52] As Oldfrom put it, some modes of treatment of human beings are 'so fundamental to the existence of anything we would be willing to call a society that it makes better sense to treat an acceptance of them as constitutive of a nature of man as a social being than as an artificial convention'. Oldfrom, *Essence and Concept in Natural Law Theory*, in Law and Philosophy 239 (1964).

reflect the philosophy that in any morally tolerable form of social life there must be certain protections for individual rights. However, affirming that principle is one thing; working out all the elements of a system of rights is something else. In the next sections, we shall discuss some of the leading theorists who have sought to develop an overall system of rights.

2. *Theories Based on the Value of Utility*

The approach to the problem of rights through theories of values has an obvious attraction. An ontological commitment may not be necessary here (or at least is not so evident) since values (equality, happiness, liberty, dignity, respect, etc.) concern behavior and are not known in a metaphysical sense but rather, are accepted and acted upon.

We start with the value of utility because utilitarian theory has played such a commanding role in nineteenth- and twentieth-century philosophy and political theory. The family of theories called utilitarianism must therefore be taken into account and either refuted, reformed, or accepted by any philosopher taking a position in normative ethics.

Utilitarian theories have a teleological structure, that is, they seek to define notions of right solely in terms of tendencies to promote certain specified ends, *e.g.*, common good. Jeremy Bentham, who expounded classical utilitarianism, believed that every human decision was motivated by some calculation of pleasure and pain. He thought that every political decision should be made on the same calculation, that is, to maximize the net produce of pleasure over pain. Hence, both governments and the limits of governments were to be judged not by reference to individual rights but in terms of their tendency to promote the greatest happiness of the greatest number. Under utilitarian doctrine everyone counts and is counted equally; but this does not mean that everyone is treated equally, for distribution factors as such are irrelevant. Thus, two different distributions of good might yield the same total of happiness and have equal claims under utilitarian theory. In short, utilitarianism is a *maximizing* and *collectivizing* principle that requires governments to maximize the total net sum of the happiness of all their subjects. This principle is in contrast to natural rights theory which is a *distributive* and *individualizing* principle that assigns priority to specific basic interests of each individual subjects.

Bentham's happiness principle enjoyed enormous popularity and influence during the nineteenth century when most reformers spoke the language of utilitarianism.[53] Nonetheless, Bentham's principle met

---

[53] Even philosophers who accepted the idea of a moral non-legal right tried to do so within the letter of utilitarian theory. Thus, J.S. Mill claimed that the respect for individual liberty which justice requires does not conflict with utility but is part of it. He reached this conclusion by

with no shortage of criticism. His hedonic calculus, that is, adding and subtracting the pleasure and pain of different persons to determine what would produce the greatest net balance of happiness, has come to be viewed as a practical, if not theoretic, impossibility.

Later utilitarian thinkers have restated the doctrine in terms of 'revealed preferences'. Here, the guide for governmental conduct would not be pleasure or happiness but an economically focused value of general welfare, reflecting the maximum satisfaction and minimum frustration of wants and preferences. Even then there remain conceptual and practical problems with the process of identifying the consequences of an act and in estimating the value of the consequences.

Particularly relevant to our discussion is the modern criticism of utilitarianism on the ground that it fails to recognize individual autonomy. The criticism here is along the following lines: Utilitarianism, however refined, retains the central principle of maximizing the aggregate desires or general welfare as the ultimate criterion of value. While utilitarianism treats persons as equals it does so only in the sense of including them in the mathematical equation but not in the sense of attributing to each individual worth. Under the utilitarian equation, one individual's desires or welfare may be sacrificed as long as aggregate satisfaction or welfare is increased. As Professor Richards has written, 'Utilitarianism thus fails to treat persons as equals in that it literally dissolves moral personality into utilitarian aggregates.'[54] Moreover, the mere increase in aggregate happiness or welfare, if abstracted from questions of distribution and worth of the individual, is not a real value or true moral goal.

Thus, the critics have shown that despite the egalitarian pretentions of utilitarian doctrine, it has a sinister side in which the well being of the individual may be sacrificed. In an era characterized by man's inhumanity to man, the dark side of utilitarianism made it too suspect to be accepted as a prevailing philosophy. Thus, most modern theorists seem to have reached an anti-utilitarian consensus, at least in recognizing certain basic individual rights as constraints on any maximizing aggregative principle. In Ronald Dworkin's felicitous phrase, rights

---

arguing that justice and respect for fundamental rights represent a particular 'branch of general utility which men recognized as having a superior binding force to ordinary claims of utility'. Mill's attempt to reconcile justice and utility by redefining utility may be somewhat sophistic but the fact that he felt a *need* to make the reconciliation demonstrates the force of the central insight of utilitarianism that one ought to promote happiness and prevent unhappiness whenever possible.

[54] Richards, *Human Rights and the Moral Foundations of the Substantive Criminal Law*, 13 Ga. L. Rev. 1372, 1450 (1979). Also oft-quoted is the criticism by Rawls that '[u]tilitarianism does not take seriously the distinction between persons'. J. Rawls, A Theory of Justice 187 (1971) [hereinafter cited as Rawls]. *See also* Hart, *supra* note 1, at 829-31.

are 'trumps' over countervailing utilitarian calculations. But as we shall see, the consensus is narrow; there remains sharp disagreement on the scope of basic rights, on the treatment of substantive economic issues, and on the nature of the conflict between liberty, equality, and other competing values.

3. *Theories Based on Justice*

The monumental thesis of modern moral philosophy is John Rawls' *A Theory of Justice*.[55] 'Justice is the first virtue of social institutions', says Rawls. Human rights, of course, are an end of justice; consequently, the role of justice is crucial to understanding human rights. No theory of human rights can be advanced today without considering Rawls' thesis.

Principles of justice, according to Rawls, provide a way of assigning rights and duties in the basic institutions of society. Those principles define the appropriate distribution of the benefits and burdens of social cooperation. Rawls' thesis is that each person possesses 'an inviolability founded on justice' that even the welfare of society as a whole cannot override. 'Justice denies that the loss of freedom for some is made right by a greater good shared by others. Therefore, in a just society the liberties of equal citizenship are settled; the rights secured by justice are not subject to political bargaining or to the calculus of social interests.'[56]

What are the rights of justice? To define them, Rawls imagines a group of men and women who come together to form a social contract. He conceives of them in an 'original position' of equality with respect to power and freedom, and that each is equally encumbered by a 'veil of ignorance' about his own particular qualities. He claims that if they are rational and act in a condition of disinterestedness or ignorance of their own status and prospects, they will choose two principles of justice.[57] The First Principle is that each person is to have an equal right to the most extensive total system of equal basic liberties compatible

[55] Rawls, *supra* note 54. The essence of Rawls' theory is found in §§ 1-4, 9, 11-17, 20-30, 33-35, 39-40. Space prevents discussion of Gewirth, another influential neo-Kantian philosopher who merits reading. *See* note 12 *supra*. Both Rawls and Gewirth share a broad common ground, though they develop Kantian premises somewhat differently. For a succinct comparison of the two, *see* Richards, *Human Rights and the Moral Foundations of the Substantive Criminal Law*, 13 Ga. L. Rev. 1396 (1979) [hereinafter cited as Richards].

[56] Rawls, *supra* note 54, at 28.

[57] *Id.* Rawls' theory may be compared with that of Gewirth. Gewirth holds that in reasoning ethically, an agent abstracts from his or her particular ends and thinks in terms of what generic rights for rational autonomy the agent would demand on the condition of a like extension to all other agents. These rights are those of freedom and well being, which Gewirth calls generic rights. He frames his moral thesis on the Principle of Generic Consistency: 'Act in accord with the generic rights of your recipients as well as yourself.' From these generic rights, says Gewirth, flow an entire structure of civil, political, economic and social rights. *See* Gewirth, *supra* note 12.

with a similar system of liberty for others. The Second Principle is that social and economic inequalities are to be arranged so they are both (a) to the greatest benefit of the least advantaged, and (b) attached to positions and offices open to all (equal opportunity).

The general conception of justice behind these principles is one of fairness and provides that all social primary goods—liberty and opportunity, income and wealth, and the bases of self-respect—are to be distributed equally unless an unequal distribution of any or all of these goods is to the advantage of the least favored. (This latter aspect is important in Rawls' theory and is known as the Difference Principle.)

Rawls' principles of justice are arranged in a hierarchy in which the first, liberty, has a priority. Liberty can be restricted only for the sake of liberty. There are two such cases: (a) a less extensive liberty must strengthen the total system of liberty shared by all, and (b) a less than equal liberty must be acceptable to those citizens with the lesser liberties.

What are the basic liberties with which the First Principle is concerned? Rawls does not give a precise enumeration of the class but indicates 'roughly speaking' that it includes political liberty, freedom of speech and assembly, liberty of conscience and thought, freedom of the person (along with the right to hold personal property), and freedom from arbitrary arrest and seizure. These liberties are all required to be equal by the First Principle since citizens of a just society are to have the same basic rights.

Rawls recognizes that a person may be unable to take advantage of rights and opportunities as a result of poverty and ignorance and a general lack of means. These factors, however, are not considered to be constraints on liberty; rather, they are matters which affect the 'worth' or 'value' of liberty. 'Liberty' is represented by the complete system of the liberties of equal citizenship, while the 'worth of liberty' to persons and groups is proportional to their capacity to advance their ends within the framework the system defines.[58] The basic liberties must be held equally; hence, the question of compensating for less than equal liberty does not arise. But the 'worth' of liberty may vary, because of inequality in wealth, income, or authority allowed under the Second Principle. Therefore, some have greater means to achieve their aims than others. However, the lesser worth of liberty is compensated for by the Difference Principle discussed above. Rawls, in short, builds a two-part structure of liberty, which allows a reconciliation of liberty and equality.[59] This, of course, is highly abstract philosophy and not easily digested.

[58] That is, the capacity of less-fortunate persons to achieve their aims would be even less if they did not accept the existing inequalities whenever the Difference Principle is satisfied.

[59] Rawls, *supra* note 54, at 204.

When one tries to apply Rawls' principles to concrete cases, the answers are not always satisfactory. With respect to basic liberties, Rawls recognizes that there may be clashes between liberty and other interests, such as public order and security, or efficient measures for public health and safety. He suggests a Principle of Reconciliation under which basic liberties may be restricted only when methods of reasoning acceptable to all make it clear that unrestricted liberties will lead to consequences generally agreed to be harmful for all. This Principle of Reconciliation is that of the common interest. Put another way, a basic liberty may be limited only in cases where there would be an advantage to the total system of basic liberty.

An easy example of this theory is a limitation of liberty to further national defense in a just war. But there are more difficult cases: the Socialist countries, for example, frequently contend that the various limitations they place on specific basic liberties are on behalf of public order and therefore are for the benefit of the total system. Even within a democratic system, two persons could apply Rawls' standard and emerge with different conclusions.

Assuming the institutional framework required by equal liberty and fair equality of opportunity, Rawls' Difference Principle deals with distributive justice. This Principle is a strongly egalitarian conception in the sense that unless there is a distribution that makes both groups better off, an equal distribution is preferred. It holds that the higher expectations of those better situated are just only if they are part of a scheme which improves the expectations of the least advantaged.

In Rawls' theory, the Difference Principle is the most egalitarian principle that would be rational to adopt. In practice, of course, a difficult empirical question is how much inequality in income and wealth will the Difference Principle allow. It may be that in any particular social structure the inequalities allowed under the Difference Principle would turn out to be too great to satisfy the reasonable demands for a more egalitarian distribution of goods and benefits.

One cannot, of course, cover Rawls' highly abstract neo-Kantian theory or deal with the considerable critical analysis of it in a few pages.[60] But even this brief discussion will show the importance of his theory for any political system which seeks to further human rights. Rawls effects a reconciliation of the tensions between egalitarianism and noninterference, between demands for freedom by the advantaged and demands for equality by the less advantaged. His structure of

[60] The amount of literature dealing with Rawls' thesis is huge. For an analysis of his theory, *see* Scanlon, *Rawls' Theory of Justice*, 121 U. Pa. L. Rev. 1020 (1973). The leading critical analysis of Rawls is R. Wolff, Understanding Rawls (1977). *See also* Chattopadhyaya, *Human Rights, Justice & Social Context*, in Rosenbaum, *supra* note 24, at 170-93.

social justice maximizes liberty and the worth of liberty to both groups. The theory is obviously comforting for the institutions and arrangements of constitutional democracy. Indeed, Rawls has been criticized for having designed his theory to support the institutions of modern democracy. But the fact that Rawls' thesis supports Western economic and social structures is not a refutation of his thesis. His critics still must show that his theory is wrong. Whether one agrees or disagrees with him, the theory of justice which Rawls describes commands a pre-eminent position in moral and political philosophy and furthers understanding of the elusive concept of social justice.

Before going on to other current theories, brief mention should be made of Professor Edmund Cahn's theory of justice. While Cahn's theory no longer has the influence it once enjoyed, it has a particular appeal to human rights activists. Cahn asserts that although there may be universal *a priori* truths concerning justice from which rights or norms may be deduced, it is better to approach justice from its negative rather than its affirmative side.[61] In other words, it is much easier to identify *injustice* from experience and observation than it is to identify *justice*. Furthermore, says Cahn, 'where justice is thought of in the customary manner as an ideal mode or condition, the human response will be contemplative and contemplation bakes no loaves. But the response to a real or imagined instance of injustice is alive with movement and warmth', producing outrage and anger.[62] Therefore, he concludes, justice is the active process of remedying or preventing what arouses the sense of injustice. An examination of the instances that will be considered injustice thereby allows a positive formulation of justice.

This concept of the need to right wrong has the capacity to produce action. The practical starting point may well be the strongly felt response to words that move one with 'emotional force and practical urgency' to press for the satisfaction or repair of some need, deprivation, threat, or insecurity.[63] Such an approach obviously will find a response in human rights advocates anxious to focus public attention at the injustice of disappearances in Argentina, repression of religion and emigration in the Soviet Union, or other current human rights abuses.[64]

---

[61] E. Cahn, The Sense of Injustice (1949).

[62] *Id.* at 13. One of the advantages of Cahn's approach is that it deals with the condition of justice in an actually functioning society. By contrast, Rawls deals with persons in the 'original position' behind the veil of ignorance. In that condition, the risk takers may see Rawls' proposition as a fair (hence, universally acceptable) gamble. However, the standards of justice and the risks one is prepared to accept may be perceived quite differently in a functioning society.

[63] Parker, *From Sensed Injustice to Natural Legal and Human Rights*, in Pollack, *supra* note 3, at 257-61.

[64] *See, e.g.*, annual reports of the International League for Human Rights, Amnesty International, and the International Commission of Jurists.

When we get to the more sophisticated kinds of entitlements arising from considerations of social justice, there is less agreement on what constitutes injustice and Cahn's insight offers less help. Here we need an overall structure of the type presented by Rawls, Gewirth, or Ackerman.[65] Still, Cahn's insight is useful; in the end it may well be that we will secure only those rights for which we are aroused to fight.

4. *Theory Based on a Revisited State of Nature and the Minimalist State*

An anarchistic resolution of the tension between liberty and equality is proposed by Professor Robert Nozick.[66] Starting with the state of nature in natural law philosophy, Nozick develops the concept of a minimal state, a state which he regards as inspiring, indeed utopian. Nozick's foundation of morality consists of the enforcement of a limited set of individual rights. These are the right not to be killed, robbed, assaulted, or defrauded; the right to acquire, retain and transfer property; the right to the performance of contracts; and, most importantly, the right to do as one chooses, so long as one does not violate the same right of others. To Professor Nozick, moral wrong-doing has one form—violation of these rights.

Under Nozick's view, the role of the state is minimal; it is to protect citizens against force, fraud, theft, and breach of contract, to settle disputes, and to punish violations. The state should *not* relieve poverty, provide for general welfare, or produce distributive justice among its citizens. In short, the state may not impose burdens or restrictions upon some citizens to meet the needs of others, however great those needs may be. In Nozick's moral landscape, the role of the state is that of the watchdog. Anything more extensive than this minimal state is unjustified because it deprives citizens of their liberty in violation of their natural rights.

Nozick's system, which he calls 'libertarian capitalism', is a radical extension of classical laissez-faire theory *ad absurdem*. His views may be attractive to extreme conservatives who already have a large share of worldly goods and need only watchdogs to protect their wealth. But, as a political perspective for the twentieth century, it is untenable and need not be taken seriously.

From an abstract philosophic view, Nozick's theory is more interesting. Normally, laissez-faire doctrine is justified by arguments that non-intervention by the state would yield a desirable or equitable market distribution. The arguments are buttressed by economic and

---

[65] There is not space to deal with B. Ackerman, Social Justice in the Liberal State (1980). However, it is a persuasive and innovative exposition of the liberal ideal, and merits study along with Rawls, Gewirth, and Dworkin.

[66] Nozick, Anarchy, State and Utopia (1974) [hereinafter cited as Nozick].

social analysis, predictions on performance, comparisons with alternative systems, and evaluations of outcomes or consequences. Nozick avoids all this by claiming a natural rights justification for his minimal non-interventionist state. He spins a complex metaphysical theory to show that if a state goes beyond its minimal role, it immorally deprives citizens of their liberty.[67] This is because interventions by the state sacrifice and use a person for the sake of others and do not sufficiently respect the fact that each person is separate and 'that his is the only life he has'.[68]

This is a rather barren morality. It may satisfy Nozick's moral view of human beings but there are many who believe that a moral concept of what it means to be human also includes freedom from discrimination, hunger, and homelessness, since such rights also go to the essence of living.

There are other conceptual problems with Nozick's theory. He effectively criticizes utilitarianism for ignoring individuality, but then falls into similar error by postulating that individuals in the aggregate have no interest in contributing to the welfare of the less advantaged. He holds that in a minimalist state those with privileges will not use their power to disadvantage others, which is a historically incorrect view of power.[69] He distorts personal egoism into the Kantian intuition of moral personality. And he equates individual freedom with individual choice, glossing over the fact that the choices under his system are quite limited, such as the poor choosing the bridges under which they may sleep.

Critics have exposed these and other deficiencies in Nozick's theory.[70] Still, it must be troublesome for natural rights philosophers to find such a narrow moral mold constructed out of the metaphysical mode of natural rights theory. That seems to reinforce the old criticism that natural rights philosophy is no better than the philosopher who delineates it. Be that as it may, from a human rights viewpoint, Nozick's theory seems neither just nor inspiring.

5. *Theories Based on Dignity*

A heroic effort at constructing a comprehensive system of human rights comes from Professors McDougal, Lasswell, and Chen who

---

[67] There is a circular aspect to Nozick's theory. He postulates the watchdog's role for the state; then he argues that any departure from that role violates the proper role of the state. But that, of course, is one of the questions at issue.

[68] Nozick, *supra* note 66, at 33. *See also* G. Gilder, Wealth & Poverty (1980).

[69] Nozick claims his minimalist state is utopian. But, in circular fashion, his conception of utopia is that of the minimalist state.

[70] *See, e.g.,* Teitelman, Book Review, 77 Colum. L. Rev. 495 (1977); Hart, *supra* note 1, at 831–36 (1979); Nagel, *Libertarianism Without Foundations*, 85 Yale L.J. 136 (1975).

follow what they call a value-policy oriented approach based on the protection of human dignity.[71]

McDougal, Lasswell, and Chen proceed on the premise that demands for human rights are demands for wide sharing in all the values upon which human rights depend and for effective participation in all community value processes. The interdependent values they specify are the demands relating to (1) respect, (2) power, (3) enlightenment, (4) well-being, (5) health, (6) skill, (7) affection, and (8) rectitude. They assemble a huge catalogue of the demands which satisfy those eight values, as well as all of the ways in which they are denigrated.

McDougal, Lasswell, and Chen find a great disparity between the rising common demands of people for human dignity values and the achievement of them. This disparity is due to 'environment' factors, such as population, resources, and institutional arrangements, and also to 'predispositional factors', *i.e.*, special interests seeking 'short term payoffs' in defiance of the common interests that would further human rights values. The ultimate goal, as they see it, is a world community in which a democratic distribution of values is encouraged and promoted; all available resources are utilized to the maximum; and the protection of human dignity is regarded as a paramount objective of social policy. While they call their approach a policy-oriented perspective, their choice of *human dignity* as the 'super-value' in the shaping and sharing of all other values has a natural right ring to it.[72]

Their approach has been criticized as having a Western bias, which it does, but that does not mean it is wrong. A more telling criticism is the difficulty in making use of their system. Their list of demands is huge; there is no hierarchical order; both trivial and serious claims are intertwined; and the whole is presented in a complex prose that is sometimes impenetrable. Still, McDougal, Lasswell, and Chen have shown how a basic value such as dignity—a value on which most people would agree—can be a springboard for structuring a rights

[71] McDougal, Lasswell & Chen, *supra* note 1.

[72] It is not entirely clear why human dignity is the super-value. The authors offer this explanation:

Our recommended postulate of human dignity is much easier to accept and to explicate today than ever before. The contemporary image of man as capable of respecting himself and others, and of constructively participating in the shaping and sharing of all human dignity values, is the culmination of many different trends in thought, secular as well as religious, with origins extending far back into antiquity and coming down through the centuries with vast cultural and geographic reach. The postulate of human dignity can no longer be regarded as the eccentric doctrine of lonely philosophers and peculiar sects. This postulate, as we have defined it in terms of demands for the greater production and wider sharing of all values and preference for persuasion over coercion, has been incorporated, as our study of constitutive process demonstrates, with many varying degrees of completeness and precision into a great cluster of global prescriptions, both conventional and customary, and into the constitutional and legislative codes of many different national communities.

Id. at 376-78.

system. Even if one disagrees with their formulation, they have opened the door to a more simple and useful construction built on their insights.

6. *Theory Based on Equality of Respect and Concern*

Finally, in our discussion of modern theories we must consider the work of Professor Ronald Dworkin who has advanced his own theory for reconciling the tension between liberty and equality.[73] Professor Dworkin proceeds from the postulate of political morality, *i.e.*, that governments must treat all their citizens with equal concern and respect. So far so good. In the absence of such a premise there lacks a basis for any valid discourse on rights and claims.

Dworkin next endorses the egalitarian character of the utilitarian principle that 'everybody can count for one, nobody for more than one'. (A practical political application of this principle is participatory democracy). Under this principle he believes that the state may exercise wide interventionist functions in order to advance social welfare.

Dworkin believes that a right to liberty in general is too vague to be meaningful. However, certain specific liberties, such as freedom of speech, freedom of worship, rights of association and personal and sexual relations, do require special protection against government interference. This is so not because these preferred liberties have some special substantive or inherent value (as most rights philosophers hold) but because of a kind of procedural impediment that these preferred liberties might face. The impediment is that if those liberties were left to a utilitarian calculation, that is, an unrestricted calculation of the general interest, the balance would be tipped in favor of restrictions.

Why is there such an impediment? Dworkin says that if a vote were truly utilitarian then all voters would desire the liberties for themselves and the liberties would be protected under a utilitarian calculation. But a vote on these liberties would not be truly utilitarian nor would it afford equal concern about and respect for liberties solely by reflecting personal wants or satisfactions of individuals and affording equal concerns to others. This is because external preferences, such as prejudice and discrimination against other individuals deriving from the failure to generally treat other persons as equals, would enter into the picture. These external preferences would corrupt utilitarianism by causing the individual to vote against assigning liberties to others.

Accordingly, the liberties that must be protected against such

---

[73] Dworkin, *supra* note 6. Dworkin is extraordinarily lucid and his book clears up a great deal of confusion in the contemporary philosophy of rights, even apart from whether one is convinced by the theory he expounds.

external preferences must be given a preferred status. By doing so we can protect 'the fundamental right of citizens to equal concern and respect' because we prohibit 'decisions that seem, antecedently, likely to have been reached by virtue of the external components of the preferences democracy reveals.'[74]

The argument is attractive because Dworkin (like Rawls, but in a different way) has minimized the tension between liberty and equality. Dworkin does so without conceding a general right to liberty (which might exacerbate the tension) but by specifying particular basic liberties that must be protected to prevent corruption of a government's duty to treat persons as equals.

Dworkin's theory seems to retain both the benefits of rights theory without the need for an ontological commitment, and the benefits of utilitarian theory without the need to sacrifice basic individual rights. Dworkin's resplendent universe thus seems to accommodate the two major planets of philosophic thought.

A troublesome aspect of Dworkin's argument is that it seems to rest on the fragility of his connection between denials of preferred liberties and denials of equal respect and concern. It is possible to have the first without the other. For example, the majority may deny individuals the right to emigrate not because of any lack of concern or respect but precisely because they feel the would-be emigrants are of value to their society and they do not want to lose them. Dworkin may be able to reply to this point by a particular definition of respect and concern, but the connection remains fragile.

Professor Hart has raised a series of objections to Dworkin's theory[75] but the chief criticism is that Dworkin fails to identify the true evils in the denial of liberty. The true evil, says Hart, is not the denial of *equal freedom* but the denial of *freedom*. What is deplorable, Hart points out, 'is the ill treatment of the victims and not the relational matter of the unfairness of their treatment compared with others'.[76] While there may be certain question-begging aspects to the criticism, it seems a fair point.

Nonetheless, Dworkin's theory is valuable in focusing on the relational rather than the conflicting aspects of liberty and equality. Even if one is not fully convinced at this stage by Dworkin's analysis, one has the feeling that he may yet evoke a reconciling theory that would work for the institutions of political democracy.

---

[74] *Id.* at 277.

[74] Hart, *supra*, note 1. Some of the objections seem to be semantic quibbles; others are more substantial.

[76] *Id.* at 845.

7. *Undeveloped Theories: New Generations of Rights*

Civil and political rights, and economic and social rights, have been called respectively the first and second generation of rights. In recent years, claims have been made for recognition of a third generation: rights of peace, rights of development, and rights of solidarity.[77] The increasing clamor for consideration of these rights requires attention.

These new rights pose some difficult theoretical questions. They are said to be collective rights as well as individual rights. The question of whether collective rights can be treated as human rights is unclear. One could argue in Kantian terms that *a priori* rights apply not only to individuals but to all rational beings, which include collectives.[78] But what would flow from this? If men and women collectively had rights, these might be taken to be more important than individual rights and used to sacrifice individual rights. Collective claims often turn out to be society's counter-claims to individual rights and may therefore have an anti-individual right consequence. The problems are not unlike the ones encountered in the earlier discussion of Marxist treatment of man as a specie being.

Another problem in this area is the need to define meaning and assess motive. Communist states have been asserting the right to live in peace as a new individual right. No one can deny the overriding importance of living in peace. And one can define a peaceful society as encompassing the various human rights proclaimed in the international convenants. But, as Tacitus taught, one can also create a desert and call it peace. In practice, the right to live in peace is often viewed by Communist states as a collective right and used to denigrate various individual liberties in the name of collective security and order. When a state's definition of the right to live in peace enables it to rationalize suppression of free speech, then it takes on anti-individual right qualities. What status do we accord to a new 'right' which seems to be desirable as such, but is used by its proponents to by-pass or violate established rights?

The right to development is also complex. Development itself has not been adequately defined. On the surface it seems to encompass no

[77] These rights have been the subject of extended discussions at the Armand Hammer Conferences on Peace and Human Rights which took place in Oslo in 1978, Campobello in 1979, Warsaw in 1980, Aix-en-Provence in 1981, and Hyde Park in 1982. The proceedings of those conferences, and particularly the paper by Karel Vasak, are useful compendiums on this subject.

[78] *See* Axinn, *Kant on Collective Human Rights*, in Pollack, *supra* note 4, at 321; Bayles, Axinn, *Kant and Rights of Collective Persons*, in *id.* at 411. For a plea on the collective rights of ethnic communities, *see* Van Dyke, *The Individual, the State and Ethnic Communities in Political Theory*, in Human Rights and American Foreign Policy (D. Kommers & N. Loescher eds. 1979); Shmudi, *The Right to Self-Realization & Its Predicaments*, in Rosenbaum, *supra* note 24, at 151–63.

more than the civil, political, economic, and social rights found in the existing covenants. But it has potential beyond that. It could encompass, for example, the Difference Principle of Rawls' theory discussed earlier. It could also encompass values not covered by the covenants, such as enhancement of respect, promotion of individual self-reliance, recognition of the interdependence of rights, and other measures.

The definition process, moreover, has been impeded because the right to development has become a potpourri of propaganda at the United Nations. It is used by some of the major violators of human rights to assert radical Third World claims against Western democracies. Thus, it has been used as a vehicle to claim a share of world resources, to bless the New International Economic Order, to call for reparations for past exploitations, and to generally condemn Western ideology.

Further, too often, the purpose of the proponents of the right to development is to deprecate the value of traditional human rights principles by mixing in a 'plethora of ambiguous and controversial priorities, so that little room is left for the non-priority area of individual rights.'[79] That is too bad, because the concept of development to enhance the human personality merits attention. One frequently faces the troublesome question of whether the constant misuse of a legitimate thesis voids its legitimacy.

The right to solidarity has its own gestalt. It appears to have particular relevance to the values of status and recognition and freedom from control by outside authority. These values are obviously attractive to Third World peoples whose lives were long directed by colonial rulers. The freedom sought is initially related not so much to the usual catalogue of negative or positive liberties as to integration of efforts and common dependence within the group, *i.e.*, solidarity.

The relationship of solidarity and fraternity to communist views of the social whole appears to be one factor that has attracted some Third World nations to Marxist philosophy. But it is also significant that Third World models of socialism seem to have made a basic reinterpretation of Marxist theory. Their emphasis is not so much on an atomized individual who is part of a social whole determined by the state, but on a social being whose basic human needs are best able to be fulfilled within a collectivity. Solidarity may be a good description for this type of political approach; it is not necessarily antithetical to individual human rights and merits sensitive analysis and understanding.

[79] Liskofsky, *The United Nations and Human Rights: Alternative Approaches*, in Sidorsky, *supra* note 28, at 63. *See also* M. Moskowitz, The Roots and Reaches of United Nations Actions and Decisions 154-70 (1980).

The new generation of rights requires considerable definition and theoretical analysis. Despite their present murky nature, they do offer a potential for expanding the family of rights in ways beneficial to the individual. But they also have a potential for mischief. As always, vigilance is needed so as not to confuse right and anti-right.

This brief description of modern theories does not, of course, exhaust the subject. The development of rights will certainly benefit from new philosophic and scientific exploration. For example, students of linguistics have developed theories of linguistics which indicate that deep principles of grammar are inherited as part of our cognitive knowledge. The same type of theory may yet show that various human rights principles and claims have a cognitive legitimacy that has not yet been perceived. Professor B.F. Skinner has suggested the use of behavioral reinforcement techniques as means to achieve human rights. And scholars such as Rawls, Ackerman, Donegan, Dworkin, Nozick, Nagel, Richards, etc., are still developing or refining their theories. The field is stirring and the potential for new discovery remains large.

F. FROM THEORY TO PRACTICE: EXERCISES RELATING TO EQUALITY

Long ago, Hume asked 'what authority any moral reasoning can have which leads into opinions so wide of the general practice of mankind'. It is a fair point which continues to nag us as we view the huge gap between principle and contemporary practice. But a more pertinent question may be whether moral reasoning can narrow the gap betwen principle and practice. There is no doubt that philosophers have difficulty in demonstrating how their theories, often derived from postulated choices in an imaginary state of affairs, can be usefully applied to the real world. We are entitled to ask whether philosophic theory is merely abstract, in which case it is trivial, or whether it serves as a heuristic device for the resolution of real problems.

The latter is certainly the case, as Professors Michelman, Richards, and Fletcher have shown so well in applying theory to the substantive areas of welfare law and criminal law. Their incisive analyses are highly sensitive and sophisticated, and should set an example for others.[80] In the space available here, we shall try to show in a much simplified form some of the ways in which philosophic theory may be helpful in approaching human rights issues. Because demands for equality are central to the human rights movement, we shall focus on that area.

[80] See Michelman, *In Pursuit of Constitutional Welfare Rights: One View of Rawls' Theory of Justice*, 121 U. Pa. L. Rev. 962 (1973); Richards, *supra* note 55; Fletcher, Rethinking Criminal Law (1978).

Obviously, there are different types of equality which can be pursued in a system of human rights and our practical problem is to decide how far to pursue each kind. [81] One type of equality which we have identified is equality with respect to 'basic liberties', as distinguished from allocation of resources. This involves recognition of individual autonomy as translated into such basic freedoms as speech, liberty, religion, assembly, fair trial, etc. The demands made are of a negative sort; they principally involve certain restraints upon government in recognition of the importance of individual autonomy.

Here, the respective positions of modern utilitarian, egalitarian, and natural rights philosophy seem to be in general agreement. Moreover, groupings are not so difficult: the inclusion of all persons does not negate or reduce the share of any; hence, there is probably the least chance of a clash with other values. The greater the universality of a claim, the easier it is to insist on equality for that claim. In constructing a rights system, it would therefore seem reasonable to impose a heavy burden on those who would treat persons unequally by denying any of them basic liberties. One begins to see how philosophy can help decide the correct response to claims.

Another claim for equality relates to opportunity. Opportunity stated as a principle of nondiscrimination is easy to put into legal precept and in fact the international human rights covenants and many domestic constitutions provide that there should be no discrimination by virtue of a person being of a particular sex, race, religion, or national origin. However, our empirical knowledge tells us that equality of opportunity is not enough because it is pursued within a society which orders the conditions of the pursuit thereby affecting the outcome. For example, a person who grows up under conditions of discrimination and deprivation does not have the same opportunity of getting into a college as someone who comes from the mainstream of society and has had a good elementary and secondary education.[82] Hence, to provide equality of opportunity it is necessary to compensate for unequal starting points. But the opportunities of others also should be protected. Our object, therefore, is to give those who have had an unequal start the necessary handicap points and yet not tamper with the liberties and opportunities of others. Here there may be substantial differences between strict rights philosophers and utilitarian and egalitarian theorists. It is not easy to resolve the differences but under-

[81] In identifying the functional problems, I have drawn from the analysis of Freund, *The Philosophy of Equality*, 25 Wash. Univ. L. Q. 11 (1979), and on the commentary thereon by Nagel, *id.* at 25. Particularly useful is T. Nagel, Mortal Questions 106-21 (1979).

[82] *See, e.g., De Funis Symposium*, 75 Colum. L. Rev. 483 (1975); Ely, *The Constitutionality of Reverse Racial Discrimination*, 41 U. Chi. L. Rev. 487 (1974).

standing the various moral conceptions at least enables us to focus on reconciliation.

Finally, another type of equality deals with a more equal apportionment of benefits of all kinds, especially economic benefits. In this area we find considerably more conflict among the philosophic views we have discussed regarding both the need to make broad economic redistribution and the ways in which it should be carried out. These problems become particularly complicated because of the enormous difficulties in arriving at a consensus on the underlying causes for the conditions of inequality and on determining where prime responsibility for redress lies. One's moral theory affects what one is willing to accept as relevant facts, as well as what one is willing to accept as reasonable solutions.

Changing the perspective a bit, we know that if rights are to mean anything, they must be translated into demands which have a reasonable chance of being met. Obviously, the pursuit of these various types of equality involves different demands on society. Which is hardest to achieve? Which easiest? The theories we have discussed surely have convinced us that the least difficult demands are to ask the government to enforce the equalities involved in basic liberties but not to enforce redistribution. The greater demands are to ask society to provide protection to basic rights plus economic benefits. These benefits, we know empirically, may range from modest ones such as free education, aid to the elderly, aid to the handicapped, social security, etc., to major redistributions of wealth. But obviously these benefits are not achieved by merely a negative restraint on government; tinkering with distribution is required. Is there a moral reason for not doing so? Here, our analysis might show that inequalities in society are due less to personal 'merit' than to factors beyond individual control such as class, environmental, education, and even genetic factors. The fact that such factors are to a large extent arbitrary perhaps will convince us that there is nothing wrong with tinkering with distribution if that will help to achieve desirable ends.

This brings us to the question of *how much* tinkering with the distribution system is suitable and to *what* desirable ends. The answer may depend on whether we regard economic needs as individualized claims or aggregative claims (the general welfare). How do we resolve this? As reasonable persons interested in the common good, we might recognize that certain economic needs of those at the bottom strata of society present so imperative a claim for relief that it is fair that they outweigh a larger aggregate of benefits to those higher on the economic scale. For example, we would hardly dispute that some taxation of the general population is desirable in order to provide for the needs of those at the lower end. With the possible exception of an extreme libertarian view (*e.g.*, Nozick) most modern theorists would agree up to this point. But to what extent can those aggregate benefits be taken?

How much of a moral claim does an individual have to economic benefits? At what point do we say we will no longer sacrifice the general allocation of benefits in order to meet the claims of those at the bottom?

The question of the degree of sacrifice the majority of society will accept in order to pursue egalitarian goals is, of course, not an easy question, philosophically, politically, or practically. Having identified the issue, we have to evaluate the moral relevance and strength of claims on a spectrum from most urgent to least urgent. Even if we acknowledge the claims for more equitable distribution of economic benefits, we still have to decide at what point on the spectrum we draw the line and say that the claims for equality do not outweigh the competing values of liberty or the utilitarian aggregate benefits that will be decreased by meeting the claims. Again, understanding the philosophic issues clarifies the decision-making process. And the answer will in large measure determine how egalitarian our society will be.

The philosophic issues are likewise pertinent in the quest for equality in the international context. Consider, for example, some of the basic conflicts involved in the New International Economic Order (NIEO). NIEO, which is advocated by Third World states as a program to achieve international economic justice, is premised on the assumptions that the developing states have been economically disadvantaged, that conditions in their societies make it impossible for them to overcome the disadvantages by self-help, and that those disadvantages can only be overcome by substantial transfer to them of resources and other benefits enjoyed by the developed countries. The moral basis put forward for this claim is that the disadvantages are the result of exploitation by the developed countries through colonialism, imperialism, racism, acts of multinational companies based in the developed countries, etc.

The moral response to this claim is important. If developed states accept the moral basis of such accusations, what follows? The perception would then be that the developed countries caused harm to the less developed ones and owe them a remedy. If, however, the accusation is rejected (as unfair, too old, inaccurate, etc.,) the developed countries may still be willing to help redress international economic inequality, but the approach would be altogether different. If that task is undertaken not out of guilt or the need to make reparations but out of the desire to achieve a more just world order, then as a pre-condition the developed donor states may ask the donees to observe certain civil and political liberties that the donors cherish. In other words, since such liberties fit into the donors' concept of justice, they may ask the donees to accommodate that concept as the price for more egalitarian international economics. Another condition for transfer of resources from developed to less developed states might be that the receiving states use the resources to increase distributive justice among their own citizens and thereby benefit the poor in those states, *e.g.*, along the lines of Rawls' theory.[83]

These issues are obviously quite complicated, with numerous considerations of *real-politik* intersecting. But even this short discussion shows that the questions of economic and social rights which are currently high on the international agenda cannot be divorced from the moral questions which swirl around contemporary moral and political philosophy. The contribution of moral theories to solutions of problems in the legal and political order may be impeded by lack of comprehension or inept articulation, but the interlacing is not barred by triviality or irrelevance. This much surely can be claimed for studying the jurisprudence of human rights: that it is often easier to bring something about if we understand clearly what it is we are trying to do.

* * *

Because of the constraints of space, the discussion in this chapter is barely an introduction to human rights theory. Its purpose has been to alert the reader to some of the principal issues in the area and to encourage further intellectual exploration. It is the natural bent of theory analysis to raise queries and articulate doubts. However, I hope that the philosophic difficulties expressed will not be taken to indicate any doubt on my part about the meaningfulness of the quest for a humane society. The objectives are good in themselves and so is the exercise; in Walt Whitman's apt phrase, 'strength it makes and lessons it teaches'.

II. Teaching Suggestions

Teaching jurisprudence recalls Karl Llewellyn's precocious quotation from The Bramble Bush:

> There was a man in our town
> and he was wondrous wise:
> he jumped into a Bramble Bush
> and scratched out both his eyes—

---

[83] The point has been made that unless such distribution takes place, the New International Economic Order would merely be taxing the poor of rich nations to benefit the rich of poor nations.

and when he saw that he was blind
with all his might and main
he jumped into another one
and scratched them in again.

It is especially difficult to teach the jurisprudence or philosophy of international human rights because most moral and legal philosophers deal with rights in the context of domestic systems without applying their theories to the international context. Indeed, the term 'human rights' does not even appear in the index of the books by such prestigious modern theorists as Rawls, Hart, Dworkin, Nozick, Donegan, and Ackerman. That does not mean that the various philosophic theories are not relevant to considerations of international human rights, only that the teacher will have to make the necessary connections.

The discussion in this chapter is pitched to the level of the first year law school or post-graduate student. My preferred approach to teaching this material would be to raise the philosophic issues as appropriate throughout a course rather than as a whole at the beginning.

The subject matter fits well into the other chapters. The discussion of meaning, universality, sources of rights, theories of freedom, equality, etc., fit particularly well into the chapters by Henkin,[84] Lillich,[85] Humphrey,[86] Greenberg,[87] and Trubek.[88] For example, Professor Henkin's syllabus overlaps the natural rights discussion in this chapter. My discussion of economic and social rights fits handily into Trubek's syllabus. Professor Higgins, in discussing a regional convention on human rights, devotes a substantial portion to jurisprudential issues; the part of her syllabus on conceptual issues readily could be incorporated into the teaching of this chapter and vice versa.

On the assumption that the jurisprudence of human rights may be taught as a separate course, I have outlined a fairly full syllabus which goes beyond the material in the chapter and also suggests a somewhat different progression for pedagogical purposes. I have also prepared a short syllabus on the assumption that this chapter will be covered in two to four hours at the beginning of a course. But I re-emphasize my preference for discussing theory throughout a course rather than in isolation.

I recommend that this chapter be read initially without footnotes and the second time with footnotes. If the reader is not familiar with the matters dealt with in footnote 2, that should be taken up quite early. Depending on the time available, there should be supplementary reading, which is identified in the syllabus.

[84] Ch. 2 *supra.*
[85] Ch. 4 *infra.*
[86] Ch. 5 *infra.*
[87] Ch. 8 *infra.*
[88] Ch. 6 *infra.*

On the whole, I have tried to avoid the jargon of moral philosophy but there are key words which theorists use repeatedly even though simpler words might do. The student should understand the meanings of these words at the outset and I suggest an initial assignment to define the following:

a posteriori	empirical	normative
a priori	hedonic	ontological
anarchical	heuristic	positivist
deontological	intuitionist	prescriptive
dialectic	lexical	teleological

A central problem in teaching moral philosophy is the lack of intercultural communications. As Felix Cohen observed, we need to devise 'a translation formulae that will permit men to speak to each other across all the gulphs of creed and to understand each other through all the curtains of dogma'. A fruitful assignment might be to analyze the applicability of the theories presented here to various states, religions, and systems with cultures different from our own.

Because of restraints of space, I have not used specific cases to relate the theoretical discussion to the realities of controversy in human rights. But the teacher should constantly make the tie. Moral theories are not removed from contemporary relevance. In Piaget's simple phrase, 'morality is the logic of action'. Perhaps Heinrich Heine put it best when he said that 'proud men of action' are 'unconscious instruments of the men of thought'.

III. Syllabus*

  I. *Reasons for Studying the Philosophy of Human Rights*
    A. Objectives.
      1. The need to know why we are doing something.
      2. The need to overcome dogma within one's own system.
      3. The need for a cultural interface; the ability to view a problem from different perspectives.
      4. The need for ordering in order to deal with heterogeneous behavior (Llewellyn).
      5. Other reasons.
        A good introduction to why study philosophy at all is Dworkin's first chapter in Taking Rights Seriously. Llewellyn's Bramble Bush provides valuable insights for any study of legal philosophy.
    B. Identify principal sources and terminology.

*The references herein appear in the chapter footnotes and the bibliography.

II. *The Difference between Human Rights Theory in a Domestic System and in an International System*
   A. The individual as a subject of international rights and duties.
   B. Criteria of validity for international rules.
      The need to deal with Section II depends upon the student's familiarity with international law. The analysis in Section II(A) can follow that of Lauterpacht in chapter II of International Law and Human Rights and the discussion in Section II(B) can stem from Hart's discussion of international law in chapter 4 of The Concept of Law.

III. *What Are Rights?*
   A. Jural relationships.
      The purpose here is to alert the student to the confusion in use of rights terminology, not to delve into substantive international law. I suggest that the student become familiar with the different meanings ascribed to: rights, privileges, immunities, claims, entitlements, powers, expectations (Hohefeldian analysis).
   B. The problem in international law of rights without remedies; alternatives to sanctions.

IV. *Diverse Meanings of Human Rights—General Discussion*
   A. Meaning derived from scope.
      How to determine which human rights are (1) important; (2) general; (3) universal.
   B. Meaning derived from values.
      Consider values which are (1) protective; (2) humanizing; (3) community building; (4) distributive.
   C. Meaning derived from functions.
      Consider (1) relational functions; (2) restraining functions; (3) legitimizing functions; (4) distributive functions.
   D. Other ways of ascertaining meaning.

V. *Justificatory Theories: Where do human rights come from?*
   A. Theology.
      1. The concept of common creation by God and family of humanity.
         Chapters IV and V of Greenberg's Fundamentals of a Faith is recommended.
      2. Rights that flow from the theistic concept; rights that do not flow from the concept.
      3. Intercultural generality of religious concepts.
      4. Non-theistic doctrine.
         Here, the teacher may want to cover the non-theological

theory of morality derived from a religious moral tradition. Donegan does this in The Theory of Morality.

B. Natural law and natural rights.
    1. Classical theory.
    2. Separation from theological roots: Grotius, Vattel, Pufendorf.
    3. From natural law to natural rights: Locke, Montesquieu. Chapter 1 of Nozick's Anarchy, State and Utopia is recommended.
    4. From natural rights to human rights. Consider here the six elements of relationship described by Sidorsky in Essays on Human Rights, at 92-95. Cranston's volume, What is Human Rights, is also good.
    5. Importance of natural rights theory. To human rights (dependability, security, inalienability, universality, etc.). To international law (consider Lauterpacht's analysis).
C. Positivist Theory.
    1. From Austin to Hart.
    2. Kelsen and positivist theory of international law.
    3. Criticism of positivist theory. For a short outline of positivist theory and criticism of it, see chapters 2 and 3 of Dworkin's book, Taking Rights Seriously.
D. Marxist Theory.
    1. Marxist views of natural rights.
    2. Effect of class struggle on rights.
    3. Role of the state in protecting rights.
    4. Emphasis on social and economic rights.
    5. Consequences of treating man as a specie being. Isaiah Berlin's analysis in Two Concepts of Liberty is useful here.
    6. Comparison of Marxist theory and current practice.
    7. Modified Marxist theory as found in various Third World systems.
E. Utilitarian Theory.
    1. From Bentham to Mill to modern utilitarianism.
    2. Modifications of the hedonic calculus to aggregate welfare.
    3. The basis of anti-utilitarian criticism (*e.g.*, Rawls, Gewirth).
F. Sociological Process.
    1. Usefulness of sociological process to identify interests.

2. Identifying interests (*e.g.*, consider how Pound's categories of interests fit into the international covenants).

3. Identifying interests through empirical comparative rights study.
Although not dealt with in the chapter, I suggest the approach of Claude in Comparative Human Rights.

4. Inadequacies of the interests approach to structure a human rights system.

5. Analysis of interests to identify values such as justice, morality, utility, equality, security, etc.

VI. *Modern Theories of Human Rights*
A. Principal problem areas.
  1. The need to structure a complete system.
  2. The need to resolve tension or conflict between liberty, equality, and utility.
  3. The need to relate to real problems.
B. Modern approaches.
Discuss the methodology of *a priori* approaches (Gewirth, Nozick); the universal prescriptivist approaches (Hare); the ideal observer approach (Ackerman, Firth and Brandt); rational contract approach (Rawls), etc.
C. Revived natural rights theory.
  1. Reasons for revival and contemporary force of natural rights theory.
  See Sidorsky's analysis referred to above.
  2. Minimalist and qualified approaches, *e.g.*, Hart, Fuller.
  3. Neo-scholastic approaches.
  4. Approaches based on modern conceptions of man, *e.g.*, Northrup, Hall, Gewirth.
  5. Approaches based on various presupposed conditions for moral discourse.
  6. Approaches based on cognitive knowledge, *e.g.*, Chomsky, Piaget.
  7. Approaches based on behaviorism.
D. Theories based on distributive justice.
  1. *Rawls' theory*—emphasis on social justice
  Cover (a) the original position—the social contract; (b) the two principles of justice; (c) the priority of liberty; (d) the application of the Difference Principle.
  Examine critiques of Rawls.
  Test application of Rawls to issues of distribution in a constitutional democracy.
  2. *Ackerman's theory*—egalitarianism pursued.

Review Ackerman's principles of rationality, consistency, and neutrality and apply them to current human rights issues.
3. *Cahn's approach*—identifying injustice.
E. Theories based on autonomy.
1. *Gewirth's theory*—a liberal approach.
The principle of generic rights and rights that flow from it. Compare Gewirth's extension of Kantian doctrine with that of Rawls.
2. *Nozick's theory*—libertarianism.
F. Theories based on equal respect.
1. *Dworkin's theory*.
How Dworkin reconciles equality and liberty.
2. *McDougal, Lasswell, & Chen approach*.
Claims that flow from human dignity.
G. Application of various theories to key values.
How would theorists such as Rawls, Gewirth, Dworkin, etc. differ in handling:
the problem of equal grouping;
the problem of equal opportunity;
the problem of distributive justice.
VII. *Collective Rights*
A. Are collective rights human rights?
B. Analysis of solidarity, development, peace.
C. How to reconcile conflicts between collective rights and individual human rights.
VIII. *Case Studies Applying Theory to Current Issues*

IV. Minisyllabus

The assumption here is that the material in this chapter will be dealt with briefly by way of introduction and then used subsequently as appropriate. The following syllabus is suggested for two sessions of one to two hours each.
First Session:
A. What are human rights?
Here the student should be exposed to the difficulties of the definitional and justificatory process. The following questions could be the focus for this discussion.
1. Is it needless to determine what is morally right.
2. Is it impossible to justify a supreme moral principle.
3. How should one determine which rights are universal and inalienable.
B. Justificatory theories for human rights. Discuss briefly

natural rights, positivism, and Marxist theory, and lead into modern theories.

Second Session:
- A. Utilitarian doctrine and its inadequacies from a human rights perspective.
- B. Minimalist theories of human rights.
- C. Efforts to build a system structure of rights.
  1. Rawls' theory (this deserves the most discussion).
  2. How Dworkin differs from Rawls.
  3. How Gewirth differs from Rawls.
  4. Approaches to resolving the tension between values of liberty, equality, utility, security, etc.
  5. What are the philosophic theories that underlie conflicts between civil and political rights and economic and social rights? How are these conflicts reconcilable?

V. Bibliography

If the course schedule lends itself to a fair amount of supplementary reading, I particularly recommend the following:

Human Rights, edited by Ervin H. Pollack, contains essays by philosophers, political scientists and law professors dealing with definition and justification of human rights and the relationship between human rights and legal rights. Especially useful are the essays by Edel, Pollack, Blackstone, & Jenkins.

What Are Human Rights, by Maurice Cranston, is a lucid account of natural rights theory, relating it to contemporary problems and practice.

A Theory of Justice, by John Rawls. This is required reading for any student of rights; almost anyone writing in the field refers to it. One can get the essence of the theory in §§ 1-4 and 11-17, but, of course, more is better. Wolff's book, *Understanding Rawls*, gives the gist of Rawls at 3-85.

Two Concepts of Liberty, by Isaiah Berlin, is only 57 pages long. In elegant style, Professor Berlin contrasts Western and Marxist concepts of freedom. The book is a gem.

The Philosophy of Human Rights—International Perspectives, edited by Alan S. Rosenbaum, is useful in presenting the approach of various philosophic traditions to international human rights. The introduction by Professor Rosenbaum is particularly good.

Relevant law review articles are cited in the footnotes and will not be repeated. Of course, the bibliographies in some of the other chapters, particularly those of Professors Henkin and Higgins, are also useful for this chapter.

Books*

B. Ackerman, Social Justice in the Liberal State (1980).
E. Bodenheimer, Jurisprudence (1974).
E. Cahn, The Sense of Injustice (1949).
V. Chalidze, To Defend These Rights: Human Rights and the Soviet Union (1974).
L. Claude, Comparative Human Rights (1976).
M. Cranston, What Are Human Rights (1973).
A. Donegan, The Theory of Morality (1977).
R. Dworkin, Taking Rights Seriously (1977).
J. Finnis, Natural Law and Natural Rights (1980).
A. Gewirth, Reason and Morality (1978).
S. Greenberg, Foundation Of A Faith (1967).
L. Henkin, The Rights of Man Today (1978).
H. Jolowicz, Lectures on Jurisprudence (1963).
D. Kommers & G. Loescher, (eds.), Human Rights and American Foreign Policy (1979).
M. Konvitz, Judaism and Human Rights (1972).
H. Lauterpacht, International Law and Human Rights (1973).
K. Llewellyn, Jurisprudence (1962).
A. Maadudi, Human Rights in Islam (1976).
M. McDougal, H. Lasswell & L. Chen, Human Rights and World Public Order (1980) (a mine of citations).
A. Melden, (ed.), Human Rights (1970).
T. Nagel, Mortal Questions (1979).
E. Pollack, (ed.), Human Rights (1971).
A. Rosenbaum, (ed.), The Philosophy of Human Rights, International Perspectives (1980).
D. Sidorsky, S. Liskofsky & J. Shestack, (eds.), Essays on Human Rights (1979).
B. Skinner, Beyond Freedom & Dignity (1971).
R. Wolff, Understanding Rawls (1977).

VI. Minibibliography

I. Berlin, Two Concepts of Liberty (1958).
J. Shestack, *The Jurisprudence of Human Rights* in this volume.
R. Wolff, Understanding Rawls 3-85 (1977).

---

* Many are available in paperback editions.

Part II: Global Protection of Human Rights

Chapter 4

Civil Rights*

Richard B. Lillich[1]

A decade ago this writer, surveying the development of international human rights law subsequent to the adoption of the U.N. Charter, observed that 'the progress in the area of human rights has been almost exclusively in the direction of clarifying and codifying the substantive law norms . . .'.[1] During the intervening years, which have seen considerable progress in the implementation area,[2] this trend has continued apace, as exemplified by the recent adoption by the United Nations of the Convention on the Elimination of All Forms of Discrimination Against Women.[3] Yet, upon reflection, one may conclude that perhaps more codification than clarification has occurred. As Professors McDougal, Lasswell, and Chen conclude in their *magnum opus*, '[i]t is in the substantive definition of human rights that the greatest confusion and inadequacy prevail. Little effort has been made to create a comprehensive map of the totality of human rights, and there has been little discussion of the detailed content of particular rights.'[4]

This chapter, as its title indicates, is not intended to be a comprehensive map of all international human rights norms. Rather, as befits a contribution to a volume whose principal purpose is to encourage the teaching of human rights in law and graduate schools, it is basically a description *cum* commentary of those international norms which purport to guarantee and protect one bundle of rights: the civil rights of individuals. These rights, commonly considered the most basic and fundamental of all human rights, will be familiar to readers versed in

*© Richard B. Lillich 1983.

[1] Lillich, *Editor's Foreword*, in J. Carey, UN Protection of Civil and Political Rights vii (1970).

The author wrote this chapter during the fall of 1980 while a Sesquicentennial Associate of the Center for Advanced Studies of the University of Virginia and Thomas Jefferson Visiting Fellow, Downing College, Cambridge. Grateful acknowledgment also should be made to the Ford Foundation for its support of the author's work through a grant to the Procedural Aspects of International Law Institute to study 'The Treatment of Aliens in International Law'.

[2] *See* Sohn, ch. 10 *infra*.

[3] Convention on the Elimination of All Forms of Discrimination Against Women, *adopted* Dec. 18, 1979, G.A. Res. 34/180, U.N. Doc. A/RES/34/180 (1980), *reprinted in* 19 Int'l Legal Materials 33 (1980).

[4] M. McDougal, H. Lasswell & L. Chen, Human Rights and World Public Order 64 (1980) [hereinafter cited as McDougal].

Richard B. Lillich

.tes constitutional law, for, as Professor Henkin has recalled:

ns were prominent among the architects and builders of international
rights, and American constitutionalism was a principal inspiration
.odel for them. As a result, most of the Universal Declaration of Human
.ts, and later the International Covenant on Civil and Political Rights, are
.heir essence American constitutional rights projected around the world.[5]

Since these rights find their expression in articles 3–18 of the
Universal Declaration of Human Rights[6]—restated, supplemented,
and occasionally modified by companion articles in the International
Covenant on Civil and Political Rights[7]—for the sake of convenience
they will be considered in the order they appear in the Universal
Declaration.

Before beginning this survey, however, the human rights to be
reviewed must be placed in proper juridical perspective. Specifically,
what is their status under contemporary international law, and what
restrictions may states impose upon their enjoyment? Unless these
questions can be answered satisfactorily, human rights, no matter how
nicely phrased, can have little real meaning in or effect upon the lives of
individuals.

As to the first question, it now may be argued persuasively that
substantial parts of the Universal Declaration, a U.N. General
Assembly resolution adopted in 1948 without dissent and originally
thought not to give rise to international legal obligations,[8] have
become, over the past third of a century, part of customary international law binding upon all states.[9] This view, first advanced solely

[5] Henkin, *Rights: American and Human*, 79 Colum. L. Rev. 405, 415 (1979). Numerous
witnesses at the Senate hearings in 1979 on U.S. ratification of four human rights treaties made
the same point. Thus, Professor Schachter noted that '[t]he Covenant on Civil and Political
Rights . . . is perhaps the central piece in the set of human rights treaties. It is the treaty which
most closely reflects American constitutional rights and the classic individual rights of Western
Europe'. *International Human Rights Treaties: Hearings Before the Senate Comm. on Foreign
Relations*, 96th Cong., 1st Sess. 85 (1979) (statement of Oscar Schachter). *See also* Message of
the President Transmitting Four Treaties Pertaining to Human Rights, S. Exec. Doc. No. 95-C,
D, E, and F, 95th Cong., 2d Sess. XI (1978) [hereinafter cited as *President's Message*]:
    The International Covenant on Civil and Political Rights is, of the [four] treaties sub-
    mitted, the most similar in conception to the United States Constitution and Bill of Rights.
    The rights guaranteed are those civil and political rights with which the United States and
    the western liberal democratic tradition have always been associated. The rights are primarily
    limitations upon the power of the State to impose its will upon the people under its
    jurisdiction.
[6] Universal Declaration of Human Rights, G.A. Res. 217A, U.N. Doc. A/810, at 71 (1948).
[7] International Covenant on Civil and Political Rights, *adopted* Dec. 16, 1966, *entered into
force* Mar. 23, 1976, G.A. Res. 2200, 21 U.N. GAOR, Supp. (No. 16) 52, U.N. Doc. A/6316
(1966).
[8] According to a contemporaneous commentator, the Universal Declaration 'implements the
Charter by defining human rights in a maximum program of a legally non-binding character'.
Kunz, *The United Nations Declaration of Human Rights*, 43 Am. J. Int'l L. 316, 322 (1949).
[9] Professor Humphrey, who was one of the Universal Declaration's drafters, now believes
that it is 'part of the customary law of nations and therefore is binding on all states'. Humphrey,

by legal scholars but subsequently supported by the statements of international conferences,[10] by state practice,[11] and even by court decisions,[12] now appears to have achieved widespread acceptance. Indeed the suggestion has even been made that the Universal Declaration has 'the attributes of *jus cogens*',[13] a statement that, in the opinion of this writer, goes too far if intended to imply that all rights enumerated in it have this character.[14] There is little doubt, however, that many of the human rights to be discussed in the following section— the prohibition of slavery being just one example—not only reflect

The International Bill of Rights: Scope and Implementation, 17 Wlm. & Mary L. Rev. 527, 529 (1976) [hereinafter cited as Humphrey]. *Accord,* McDougal, *supra* note 4, at 274, 325, 338; Sohn, *The Human Rights Law of the Charter,* 12 Tex. Int'l L.J. 129, 133 (1977); Waldock, *Human Rights in Contemporary International Law and the Significance of the European Convention,* in The European Convention on Human Rights, Int'l & Comp. L.Q. Supp. No. 11, at 1, 15 (1965).

[10] In 1968, the Assembly for Human Rights, a meeting of nongovernmental organizations, adopted the Montreal Statement, which included the assertion that the 'Universal Declaration of Human Rights . . . has over the years become part of customary international law'. Montreal Statement of the Assembly for Human Rights 2 (1968), *reprinted in* 9 J. Int'l Comm'n Jurists 94, 95 (1968). Also in 1968, a United Nations sponsored International Conference on Human Rights adopted the Proclamation of Teheran, which stated that '[t]he Universal Declaration of Human Rights . . . constitutes an obligation for the members of the international community'. Declaration of Teheran, Final Act of the International Conference on Human Rights 3, at 4, para. 2, 23 U.N. GAOR, U.N. Doc.A/CONF. 32/41 (1968).

[11] *See, e.g.,* statements by members of the U.S. Executive Branch suggesting that the Universal Declaration sets forth internationally recognized human rights in R. Lillich, The Use of International Human Rights Norms in U.S. Courts 18-19 (1980), a study prepared for the Civil Rights Div. of the U.S. Dep't of Justice.

(Perhaps the most explicit recognition by the United States that at least parts of the Universal Declaration have been received into customary international law is found in its Memorial to the International Court of Justice in the *Hostages Case* which invokes no less than six articles of the Universal Declaration in an attempt to establish that certain minimum standards governing the treatment of aliens exist as a matter of customary international law. Memorial of the Government of United States of America, Case Concerning United States Diplomatic and Consular Staff in Tehran at 71 n. 3 (Jan. 1980) [hereinafter cited as Memorial].]

[12] *See, e.g.,* Filartiga v. Peña-Irala, 630 F.2d 876, 882 (2d Cir. 1980), where the Court of Appeals for the Second Circuit held that 'the right to be free from torture . . . has become part of customary international law, *as evidenced and defined by the Universal Declaration of Human Rights* . . .' (Emphasis added.) *See* text at and accompanying notes 69–70 *infra.*

[13] McDougal, *supra* note 4, at 274.

[14] Higgins, writing about human rights treaties but reasoning along lines applicable to the Universal Declaration as well, makes a similar point.

[T]he suggestion has been made that human rights treaties have the character of *jus cogens.* There certainly exists a consensus that certain rights—the right to life, to freedom from slavery or torture—are so fundamental that no derogation may be made. And international human rights treaties undoubtedly contain elements that are binding as principles which are recognized by civilized States, and not only as mutual treaty commitments. Some treaties may focus almost exclusively on such elements—such as the Genocide Convention—while others may cover a wider range of rights, not all of which may have for the present a status which is more than treaty-based. This being said, neither the wording of the various human rights instruments nor the practice thereunder leads to the view that all human rights are *jus cogens.*

Higgins, *Derogations Under Human Rights Treaties,* 48 Brit. Y.B. Int'l L. 281, 282 (1976-1977) [hereinafter cited as Higgins].

customary international law but also partake of the character of *jus cogens*.[15] This conclusion is particularly valid when the right in question appears in both the Universal Declaration and the Political Covenant. The latter, of course, is binding conventional law only between states parties to it,[16] but many of its provisions now can be said to have helped create norms of customary international law— including ones having *jus cogens* status[17]—binding even states which have yet to ratify it.[18] Dramatic evidence of this process at work may be found in the U.S. Memorial to the International Court of Justice in the *Case Concerning United States Diplomatic and Consular Staff in Tehran,* [19] where, after citing four articles of the Political Covenant (to which, ironically, Iran is a party but the United States is merely a signatory), the United States argued that Iran had violated not only conventional law but also 'fundamental principles . . . of customary international law . . .'[20]

---

[15] Whiteman, Jus Cogens *in International Law, With a Projected List*, 7 Ga. J. Int'l & Comp. L. 609, 625 (1977). *Accord*, Domb, Jus Cogens *and Human Rights*, 6 Israel Y.B. Human Rights 104, 116-21 (1976), who in addition to the prohibition of slavery lists only the prohibition of genocide and the protection of persons in time of war as customary international law norms having *jus cogens* status. Despite this exceedingly conservative estimate, the author manages to end on an upbeat note: '[T]here can be little question that further conventional and customary developments in [international] law will produce additional aspirants to the rank of *jus cogens* among international human rights.' *Id.* at 121.

The American Law Institute's Revised Restatement of Foreign Relations Law suggests as examples of *jus cogens* 'genocide, slave-trading and slavery, apartheid and other gross violations of human rights, and perhaps colonialism and attacks on diplomats. The United States has not indicated whether it accepts any of these as constituting *jus cogens*.' Restatement of the Foreign Relations Law of the United States (Revised) § 339, Comment *a* at 164 (Tent. Draft No. 1, 1980) [hereinafter cited as Restatement]. *See generally* McDougal, *supra* note 4, at 338-50.

[16] There were 70 states parties to the Political Covenant as of Mar. 10, 1982.

[17] In seeking to determine what human rights protected by the Political Covenant have achieved *jus cogens* status, a good starting point is the list of rights which art. 4(2) makes nonderogable, *i.e.*, rights which a state may not suspend even in time of war or national emergency. *See* text at and accompanying notes 27-28 *infra*.

[18] There is ample language in the decisions of the International Court of Justice to support the late Judge (then Professor) Baxter's conclusion that '[t]reaties that do not purport to be declaratory of customary international law at the time they enter into force may nevertheless with the passage of time pass into customary international law'. Baxter, *Treaties and Custom*, 129 Recueil des Cours 25, 57 (1970-II). *Accord*, Restatement, *supra* note 15, § 102, Reporters' Note 5 at 34. For the application of this principle to international human rights treaties, *see* Lillich, *Duties of States Regarding the Civil Rights of Aliens*, 161 Recueil des Cours 329, 397-99 (1978-III). *Nota bene*: 'If an international agreement is declaratory, or contributes to customary law, its termination [*quaere*: or, in the case of an international human rights treaty, a state party's derogation from one or more of its provisions?] by the parties does not of itself affect the continuing force of those rules as international law.' Restatement, *supra* note 15, § 102, Comment *i* at 28.

[19] [1980] I.C.J. 3.

[20] Memorial, *supra* note 11, at 71. *See also* Memorandum for the United States as *Amicus Curiae, Filartiga v. Peña-Irala*, 630 F.2d 876, where, after surveying the various multilateral treaties proscribing torture, the United States concluded that '[t]his uniform treaty condemnation of torture provides a strong indication that the proscription of torture has entered into customary

With respect to the second question, the restrictions which a state may impose upon an individual's internationally protected human rights come in two tiers, both of which must be kept in mind in determining the protection afforded by particular guarantees. On the first tier of restrictions, both the Universal Declaration and the Political Covenant contain provisions limiting the rights guaranteed therein.[21] The former contains a general limitations clause, article 29(2), which provides that:

In the exercise of his rights and freedoms, everyone shall be subject only to such limitations as are determined by law solely for the purpose of securing due recognition and respect for the rights and freedoms of others and of meeting the just requirements of morality, public order and the general welfare in a democratic society.

In the Political Covenant, as Professor Higgins has pointed out, '[t]he references to the need for rights to be exercised in conformity with morality, public order, general welfare, etc., appear not as a general clause but as qualifications to specific freedoms.'[22] The specific limitations (or, as she aptly terms them, 'clawback' clauses[23]) in the Political Covenant relating to civil rights are contained in articles 12(3), 14(1), and 18(3).[24] One can only endorse Professor Humphrey's warning that such limitations can be 'highly dangerous (from the point of view of human rights) . . .'[25]

On the second tier of restrictions which is relevant to the Political Covenant alone, article 4(1) thereof permits states parties to derogate from, *i.e.*, suspend or breach, certain obligations '[i]n time of public emergency which threatens the life of the nation and the existence of which is officially proclaimed . . .'[26] No derogation may be made,

international law.' Memorandum at 13. It furthermore contended that '[t]hese treaty provisions, in conjunction with other evidence, are persuasive of the existence of an international norm that is binding as a matter of customary law on all nations, not merely those that are parties to the treaties'. *Id.* at 13 n. 28, *citing* A. D'Amato, The Concept of Custom in International Law 103, 124-28 (1971).

[21] *See generally* Garibaldi, *General Limitations on Human Rights: The Principle of Legality*, 17 Harv. Int'l L.J. 503 (1976).
[22] Higgins, *supra* note 14, at 283.
[23] 'By a "clawback" clause is meant one that permits, in normal circumstances, breach of an obligation for a specified number of public reasons.' *Id.* at 281. It thus differs from a derogation clause, *e.g.*, art. 4(1) of the Political Covenant, 'which allows suspension or breach of certain obligations in circumstances of war or public emergency.' *Id. See* text at notes 26-28 *infra*.
[24] *See* text at notes 150, 194, & 246 *infra*.
[25] Humphrey, *Political and Related Rights*, ch. 5 *infra*, at 185; *see* text at note 29 *infra*.
[26] *See generally* Higgins, note 14 *supra*. *See also* Hartman, *Derogation from Human Rights Treaties in Public Emergencies*, 22 Harv. Int'l L.J. 1 (1981). The various writings on the problems of derogation are marshalled in McDougal, *supra* note 4, at 814 n.50. *Quaere*: what is the effect of a derogation with respect to rights that have ripened into customary international law? *See* text at and accompanying note 18 *supra*.

however, from the human rights contained in articles 6, 7, 8(1), 8(2), 11, 15, 16, and 18,[27] evidence that at least some of these rights may have 'attributes' of *jus cogens*.[28] Nevertheless, as in the case of the limitation clauses discussed in the preceding paragraph, the fact that a wide variety of important rights—for example, the right to liberty and security of person guaranteed by article 9(1)—may be rendered temporarily 'inoperative' by means of derogation is extremely trouble-some from the human rights viewpoint.[29] Certainly the existence of both tiers of restrictions—limitations and derogations—must be kept in mind when assessing the degree of protection actually afforded individuals by the language of articles 3–18 of the Universal Declaration.[30]

I. Legal and Policy Considerations

A. RIGHTS TO LIFE, LIBERTY, AND SECURITY OF PERSON (ARTICLE 3)

Undoubtedly the essential core rights, from which numerous other rights flow, are contained in article 3 of the Universal Declaration, which provides that '[e]veryone has the right to life, liberty, and security of person'.[31] Language guaranteeing these rights is found in two separate provisions of the Political Covenant. Article 6(1) states: 'Every human being has the inherent right to life. This right shall be protected by law. No one shall be arbitrarily deprived of his life.'[32]

---

[27] Art. 4(2).

[28] Reservations to the Political Covenant, to the extent that they are directed to the rights guaranteed in these seven articles, presumably have no force or effect if these rights actually have acquired *jus cogens* status. *Cf.* Restatement, *supra* note 15, § 102, Comment *k* at 28: 'There are rules of international law accepted and recognized by the international community of states as peremptory, permitting no derogation. Such a peremptory norm is subject to modification only by a subsequent norm of international law having the same character.' An analysis of the reservations to the Political Covenant, which are gathered in R. Lillich, International Human Rights Instruments 170.15-170.30 (1983), is much needed for this and other reasons.

[29] *Compare* text at note 25 *supra*.

[30] Superficially analogous to the problems presented by the restrictions discussed in the last two paragraphs of the test is the issue raised by the use of the words 'arbitrary' or 'arbitrarily' throughout the Universal Declaration and the Political Covenant. *See* text at notes 36-40 and especially accompanying note 40 *infra*. These words, it now seems clear, should be construed to prohibit not only 'illegal' but also 'unjust' acts. Thus, despite the fears of some observers, a state cannot impinge upon an individual's internationally protected human rights simply by enacting legislation making its acts legal on the domestic plane.

[31] 'A basic human right is the right to life, from which all other human rights stem. This right is a basic human right, because only through it can a human being enjoy other rights. The enjoyment of the right to life is a necessary consideration of the enjoyment of all other human rights, for a person who is deprived of his right to life is automatically also deprived of all other human rights.' Przetacznik, *The Right to Life as a Basic Human Right*, 9 Revue des Droits de l'Homme 585, 589 (1976).

[32] Article 6(2), (4), & (5), containing several provisions limiting the circumstances in which capital punishment may be imposed or carried out, goes beyond current U.S. law. In keeping with

Article 9(1), its complement, reads: 'Everyone has the right to liberty and security of person. No one shall be subjected to arbitrary arrest or detention. No one shall be deprived of his liberty except on such grounds and in accordance with such procedures as are established by law.' Similar language is found in articles 2(1) and 5(1) of the European Convention on Human Rights[33] and in articles 4 and 7(1) and 7(2) of the American Convention on Human Rights.[34] Indeed, one cannot but agree with Rector Dinstein that at a minimum 'the human right to life is entrenched in customary international law . . .'[35]

As is the case with many international human rights norms, the right to life is pitched at such a high level of abstraction that its application to concrete cases presents numerous problems, only three of which—capital punishment, voluntary euthanasia, and abortion—space limitations permit mentioning here. All that seems clear is that states have an affirmative obligation to enact laws guaranteeing this right, and that such laws may not be applied in a way that arbitrarily deprives an individual of his life. Even here, however, absolute clarity is lacking: just what constitutes an arbitrary deprivation of life? Does it mean 'unjust' or merely 'illegal'? If only the latter, as a commentator

his general approach to U.S. ratification of the human rights treaties, President Carter recommended that the Senate, in giving its advice and consent to the Political Covenant, attach the following reservation: 'The United States reserves the right to impose capital punishment on any person duly convicted under existing or future laws permitting the imposition of capital punishment.' *President's Message, supra* note 5, at XII.

---

[33] [European] Convention for the Protection of Human Rights and Fundamental Freedoms, *opened for signature* Nov. 4, 1950, *entered into force* Sept. 3, 1953, 213 U.N.T.S. 221. For a brief comparison of the similarities and differences between these articles and the parallel articles of the Political Covenant set out in the text, *see* Robertson, *The United Nations Covenant on Civil and Political Rights and the European Convention on Human Rights*, 43 Brit. Y.B. Int'l L. 21, 28-31 *passim* (1968-69) [hereinafter cited as Robertson], *revised and reprinted in* A. Robertson, Human Rights and the World 80, 86-90 *passim* (1972) [hereinafter cited as Robertson, Human Rights]. *See also* Trechsel, *The Right to Liberty and Security of the Person: Article 5 of the European Convention on Human Rights in the Strasbourg Case-Law*, 1 Human Rights L.J. 88 (1980).

[34] American Convention on Human Rights, *opened for signature* Nov. 22, 1969, *entered into force* July 18, 1978, O.A.S. T.S. No. 36, *reprinted in* Inter-American Commission on Human Rights, Handbook of Existing Rules Pertaining to Human Rights, O.A.S. Doc. OEA/Ser.L/V/II.50, doc. 6, at 27 (1980). For a brief comment on the U.S. constitutional law problems created by art. 4, *see* R. Goldman, The Protection of Human Rights in the Americas: Past, Present and Future 22 (5 N.Y.U. Center for Int'l Studies Policy Papers No. 2, 1972) [hereinafter cited as Goldman]. President Carter, noting that '[m]any of the provisions of Article 4 are not in accord with United States law and policy, or deal with matters in which the law is unsettled', indicated that the Senate may wish to attach the following reservation: 'United States adherence to Article 4 is subject to the Constitution and other law of the United States.' *President's Message, supra* note 5, at XVIII.

[35] Dinstein, *The Right to Life, Physical Integrity and Liberty*, in The International Bill of Rights: The Covenant on Civil and Political Rights 114, 115 (L. Henkin ed. 1981) [hereinafter cited as Dinstein]. Furthermore, the essential core 'right to life' probably has achieved the status of *jus cogens*. Recall in this regard that art. 4(2) of the Political Covenant forbids derogation from this right.

has pointed out, 'then all despotic and oppressive acts of a government would be unassailable so long as they were in accordance with municipal laws.'[36] Since, as demonstrated by comprehensive studies of the *travaux préparatoires* of both the Universal Declaration[37] and the Political Covenant,[38] the drafters of these instruments—with fresh memories of the 'legal' atrocities of the Nazi régime—intended them to limit the 'legal' discretion of states, 'arbitrarily' should not be considered synonymous with 'illegality'. In short, 'the reason for the use of the words "arbitrary" or "arbitrarily" was to protect individuals from both "illegal" and "unjust" acts'.[39] Even if one accepts this view, however, the question of what constitutes an 'unjust' deprivation of life remains.[40]

Turning to the three specific problems mentioned above, the right to life guarantee contained in article 3 of the Universal Declaration surely cannot be construed to proscribe capital punishment, since nearly all the states voting for the Universal Declaration in 1948 countenanced it, as most states still do. Moreover, article 6 of the Political Covenant clearly contemplates the continued use by states of the death penalty, laying down six limitations on its imposition and stating specifically that nothing therein 'shall be invoked to delay or to prevent the abolition of capital punishment . . .'[41] The Political Covenant thus 'reflects a more liberal spirit than the European Convention',[42] although it is not as 'progressive' as the American Convention which, in addition to setting forth several limitations on the death penalty's imposition, specifically provides that capital punishment 'shall not be extended to crimes to which it does not presently apply' and, furthermore, 'shall not be reestablished in states that have abolished it'.[43] At

---

[36] Hassan, *The Word 'Arbitrary' As Used in the Universal Declaration of Human Rights: 'Illegal' Or 'Unjust'?* 10 Harv. Int'l L.J. 225, 228 (1969) [hereinafter cited as Hassan].

[37] *See id. passim.*

[38] *See* Hassan, *The International Covenants on Human Rights: An Approach to Interpretation,* 19 Buffalo L. Rev. 35 (1969). *See also* Hassan, *The International Covenant on Civil and Political Rights: Background and Perspective on Article 9(1),* 3 Denver J. Int'l L. & Pol'y 153 (1973).

[39] Hassan, *supra* note 36, at 254.

[40] The problem discussed in this paragraph is not limited to the right to life since the words 'arbitrary' or 'arbitrarily' appear in arts. 9, 12, 15(2), and 17(2) of the Universal Declaration, and (in addition to arts. 6(1) and 9(1) mentioned in the text above) in arts. 12(4) and 17(1) of the Political Covenant. Commentators interpreting the words in other contexts agree with Hassan's assessment, namely, that they proscribe 'unjust' as well as merely 'illegal' state acts. *See e.g.,* Robertson, *supra* note 33, at 29 ('arbitrary' as used in art. 9(1) of the Political Covenant 'is intended to mean "unlawful and unjust" and . . . would thus prohibit arrest or detention which might be permitted under some systems of law but which, by international standards, would not be considered "just"'.); Aréchaga, *The Background to Article 17 of the Universal Declaration,* 8 J. Int'l Comm'n Jurists 34, 35 (No. 2, 1967) ('There may be deprivation of property unchallengeable in law, but which is clearly arbitrary when the law is not in accord with certain standards of equity and justice.')

[41] Art. 6(6).

[42] Robertson, *supra* note 33, at 31.

[43] Art. 4(2) & (3). *See* text accompanying note 34 *supra.*

present, therefore, one can do no more than note a trend toward the abolition of capital punishment.

As to voluntary euthanasia and abortion, the relevant international human rights instruments offer meager guidance indeed. The right to life, it can be argued, does not require an individual to go on living; hence, voluntary euthanasia—either by the administration of drugs or the withdrawal of life support systems—should be allowed.[44] On the other hand, it has been argued that the consent of the individual involved should not legitimize what otherwise would be a violation of the right to life norm.[45] The legality of abortion also is a much-debated question, turning as it does upon the determination of when the life that is to be protected commences;[46] the prevalent view is that, if there is not already an absolute right to abortion,[47] such a right at least exists during most of a woman's pregnancy and is not incompatible with the norm governing the right to life.[48] Since both voluntary euthanasia and

---

[44] *Cf.* J. Fawcett, The Application of the European Convention on Human Rights 30 (1969) [hereinafter cited as Fawcett] ('The [European Commission of Human Rights] has not had to consider the effect under Article 2 of the consent of the individual to his life being taken as in forms of euthanasia, although [a German court] has held that the giving of fatal doses of drugs by a doctor to sick persons, whose death was certain, was not contrary to Article 2.')

[45] 'The legalization of euthanasia, which would seem *prima facie* contrary to the express terms of the first sentence of Article 2 as well as falling outside the exceptions permitted by that Article, might raise the difficult question how far the consent of a victim may negate what would otherwise be a violation of the Convention. In principle, it would seem that the fundamental character of the rights guaranteed by the Convention, and the element of public interest, would exclude the possibility of any form of waiver of those rights.' F. Jacobs, The European Convention on Human Rights 22 (1975) [hereinafter cited as Jacobs].

[46] *Cf.* Z. Nedjati, Human Rights Under the European Convention 61 (1978) [hereinafter cited as Nedjati] ('The question from which moment onwards life is protected is left open in the text of the European Convention [as it also is by the Universal Declaration and the Political Covenant]. The beneficiaries of the protection of the right of life are described in the Convention text as "everyone" . . . It is not possible to say whether and if so, to what extent, abortion . . . would constitute interference with life in contravention of the above provisions.').

But see art. 4(1) of the American Convention, which specifically states, *inter alia*, that the right to life shall be protected, 'in general, from the moment of conception.' This provision 'clearly conflicts with the public policy of many U.S. states which permit abortions under varying circumstances.' Goldman, *supra* note 34.

[47] Dinstein finds that 'at least during most of pregnancy—until "the point at which the fetus becomes 'viable', that is, potentially able to live outside the mother's womb, albeit with artificial aid"—the only human rights that have to be taken into account are those of the woman. If the right of the fetus to life is not recognized, one may even speak about the human right of the woman to abortion.' Dinstein, *supra* note 35, at 122, *quoting* Roe v. Wade, 410 U.S. 113, 160 (1973) (Blackmun, J.).

[48] 'This human right [to life] cannot be interpreted as implying a general prohibition of legalised abortion. However, the question may arise as to how far a law on the right to abortion may go. It would hardly be accepted as compatible with Art. 2(1) if a law gave full freedom of abortion right up to the time of delivery. However, in their laws States must be free to consider the risks of endangering the life and health of the future mother in a critical situation.' F. Castberg, The European Convention on Human Rights 81 (1974) [hereinafter cited as Castberg]. An Austrian court has held that a law permitting abortion does not violate art. 2. *See* 106 Journal du Droit International 144 (1979).

abortion are matters of 'legitimate diversity',[49] it would seem preferable to interpret the right to life norm to permit states, at their option, to sanction their limited use.

As set out at the beginning of this subsection, in addition to the right to life, article 3 of the Universal Declaration guarantees the rights to 'liberty and security' as well. These rights are given more concrete meaning by the guarantees against arbitrary arrest and detention and against interference with one's privacy, family, home, or correspondence spelled out in articles 9 and 12 respectively; accordingly, they will be considered at the appropriate subsections below.

B. PROHIBITION OF SLAVERY AND SERVITUDE (ARTICLE 4)

This article, after stating that '[n]o one shall be held in slavery or servitude', provides that 'slavery and the slave trade shall be prohibited in all their forms'. This right, called 'the cornerstone of all human rights',[50] is also found in article 8(1) and (2) of the Political Covenant, with article 8(3)(a) thereof adding a prohibition against 'forced or compulsory labour . . .' Article 4 of the European Convention and article 6 of the American Convention contain the same comprehensive prohibition. Other international instruments manifesting widespread concern with slavery and servitude are the Slavery Convention of 1926,[51] augmented by the Supplementary Convention on the Abolition of Slavery of 1956,[52] and two International Labour Organisation conventions—the Convention concerning Forced or Compulsory Labour of 1930[53] and the Convention concerning the Abolition of Forced Labour of 1957.[54] In view of this universal condemnation of the practice, coupled with the fact that article 4(2) of the Political Covenant prohibits derogation from the provisions of article 8(1) and

---

[49] '"Legitimate diversity" is a phrase used to suggest that there is no global consensus in favor of making universal a single substantive standard. Therefore, states are at liberty to adopt diverse national standards. Such diversity is legitimate, in this sense, with respect to the practice of either socialism or capitalism, but not for the choice between upholding civil liberties or practicing genocide.' R. Falk, The Role of Domestic Courts in the International Legal Order 127 n.29 (1964).

[50] N. Robinson, Universal Declaration of Human Rights 41 (1950) [hereinafter cited as Robinson].

[51] Convention to Suppress Slave Trade and Slavery, *adopted* Sept. 25, 1926, *entered into force* Mar. 9, 1927, 46 Stat. 2183, T.S. No. 778, 60 L.N.T.S. 253.

[52] Supplementary Convention on the Abolition of Slavery, the Slave Trade, and Institutions and Practices Similar to Slavery, *done* Sept. 7, 1956, *entered into force* Apr. 30, 1957, 18 U.S.T. 3201. T.I.A.S. No. 6418, 266 U.N.T.S. 3.

[53] Convention concerning Forced or Compulsory Labour (ILO No. 29), *adopted* June 28, 1930, *entered into force* May 1, 1932, 60 L.N.T.S. 55.

[54] Convention concerning the Abolition of Forced Labour (ILO No. 105), *adopted* June 25, 1957, *entered into force* Jan. 17, 1959, 320 U.N.T.S. 291.

(2) proscribing slavery and servitude, there seems no doubt that customary international law now prohibits those practices.[55] Indeed, this writer believes that the prohibition against slavery and servitude now constitutes *jus cogens*.[56]

Forced or compulsory labour, however, which is not mentioned in the Universal Declaration but is partially proscribed by the Political Covenant (subject to possible derogation under article 4(2)), is not so uniformly condemned. Indeed, according to the Political Covenant, the term expressly does not preclude: (a) the performance of hard labour as punishment for a crime;[57] and (b):

(i) Any work or service, not referred to in [(a) above], normally required of a person who is under detention in consequence of a lawful order of a court, or of a person during conditional release from such detention; (ii) Any service of a military character and, in countries where conscientious objection is recognized, any national service required by law of conscientious objectors; (iii) Any service exacted in cases of emergency or calamity threatening the life or well-being of the community; (iv) Any work or service which forms part of normal civil obligations.[58]

Exemptions almost identical to the four immediately above are found in articles 4(3) and 6(3) of the European and American Conventions respectively. Thus, in contrast to slavery and servitude, forced or compulsory labour is not absolutely prohibited by the major international human rights instruments, much less by customary international law.

The above exemptions appear to be relatively self-explanatory, although some questions have been raised about what constitutes an 'emergency or calamity' and what are 'normal civil obligations'. In the *Iversen Case*,[59] where the European Commission on Human Rights held that a Norwegian dentist's compulsory assignment to perform public dental service in the northern portion of Norway was not forced or compulsory labour, two members relied upon the former exemption, contending 'that the service of Iversen at Moskenes was service reasonably required of him in an emergency threatening the well-being of the community . . .'[60] As for the latter exemption—work or service

---

[55] *Cf.* McDougal, *supra* note 4, at 505. This treatise contains an excellent description and analysis of the evolution of the international norm prohibiting slavery and servitude. *Id.* at 473-508. *See also* Nanda & Bassiouni, *Slavery and the Slave Trade: Steps Toward Eradication*, 12 Santa Clara Law. 424 (1972), *reprinted in part in* 1 M. Bassiouni & V. Nanda, Treatise on International Criminal Law 504-22 (1973).

[56] *See* text at and accompanying note 15 *supra*.

[57] Art. 8(3)(b).

[58] Art. 8(3)(c).

[59] 'Iversen' Case [1963] Y.B. Eur. Conv. on Human Rights 278 (Eur. Comm. on Human Rights).

[60] *Id.* at 330.

forming part of normal civil obligations—'[w]hat is meant here is presumably primarily the obligation of citizens to undertake joint efforts in the common interest on a local level, such as taking part in fire brigades or similar measures against other calamities.'[61] Thus it cannot, according to Professor Fawcett, 'be translated into a general subjection to direction of labour for economic purposes.'[62] Nor should it be read to sanction a state imposing an obligation to work through enactment of an 'antiparasite' law,[63] since such legislation, to quote Rector Dinstein, 'collides head-on with the prohibition of forced labor.'[64]

C. PROHIBITION OF TORTURE AND CRUEL, INHUMAN, OR DEGRADING TREATMENT OR PUNISHMENT (ARTICLE 5)

This article also states a very basic human right: 'No one shall be subjected to torture or to cruel, inhuman or degrading treatment or punishment.' Article 7 of the Political Covenant repeats this language *in haec verba* and adds this sentence: 'In particular, no one shall be subjected without his free consent to medical or scientific experimentation.'[65] Nearly identical language, minus the reference to scientific experimentation, is also found in articles 3 and 5(2) of the European Convention and American Convention respectively. Moreover, by General Assembly Resolution 3452, adopted without dissent on 9

[61] Castberg, *supra* note 48, at 92.

[62] Fawcett, *supra* note 44, at 56.

[63] The Soviet Constitution of 1977 imposes the duty upon every able-bodied Soviet citizen to engage in socially useful labour. Konstitutsiia (Constitution) art. 60 (USSR). Pursuant to this article's predecessor, art. 209-01 of the Soviet Criminal Code had made it an offense for an adult able-bodied citizen *not* to work. For a discussion of this antiparasite law, *see* H. Berman, Soviet Criminal Law and Procedure 77-81 (2d ed. 1972) *Cf.* J. Hazard, W. Butler & P. Maggs, The Soviet Legal System 327 (3d ed. 1977), indicating that in 1975 the Soviet Union repealed art. 209-01. Other antiparasite laws, however, remain on the books. *See also* text accompanying note 64 *infra*.

[64] Dinstein, *supra* note 35, at 128. His view finds weighty support in the ILO's recent determination that the Soviet Union's antiparasite 'laws making work a moral obligation violate the international convention prohibiting forced labor.' N.Y. Times, May 13, 1980, § A, at 7, col. 1.

[65] 'When this latter provision was incorporated in the Covenant text, it clearly aimed at the cruelties inflicted in concentration camps during the Second World War in the guise of medical and scientific experiments. The question arises, however, whether the text, as it is now worded, should be interpreted as also prohibiting acts which are not reprehensible, such as genuine medical experiments, medical operations which might have to be performed on unconscious people, fluoridation of water, etc. Having regard to the *travaux préparatoires* of the U.N. Covenant text, however, it would appear that there was no intention in Article 7 of the Covenant to exclude genuine medical experiments or to prohibit practices which might be permitted in European Member States, such as experiments with the fluoridation of water.' Nedjati, *supra* note 46, at 63.

December 1975,[66] the United Nations not only condemned but for the
first time authoritatively defined both 'torture'[67] and 'cruel, inhuman
or degrading treatment or punishment'.[68] Thus it would be difficult
today to contend that torture, at the very least, does not constitute a
violation of customary international law.[69] Indeed, in a splendid
opinion that should contribute markedly to the development of international human rights law, the U.S. Court of Appeals for the Second
Circuit in *Filartiga v. Peña-Irala* broke new ground for a domestic
court by holding that 'official torture is now prohibited by the law of
nations'.[70]

In determining just what conduct is prohibited by the various

[66] Declaration on the Protection of All Persons from Being Subjected to Torture and Other
Cruel, Inhuman or Degrading Treatment or Punishment, *adopted* Dec. 9, 1975, G.A. Res. 3452,
30 U.N. GAOR, Supp. (No. 34) 91, U.N. Doc. A/10034 (1975). The U.N. Commission on
Human Rights currently is drafting a convention against torture, thus codifying the norms of
customary international law expressed in the Universal Declaration and providing for procedures
to implement its prohibition of torture. *See* G.A. Res. 36/60, U.N. Doc. A/RES/36/60 (1982);
Report of the Working Group on a Draft Convention against Torture and Other Cruel, Inhuman
or Degrading Treatment or Punishment, U.N. Doc. E/CN.4/1982/L.40 (1982).

[67] [T]orture means any act by which severe pain or suffering, whether physical or mental, is
intentionally inflicted by or at the instigation of a public official on a person for such
purposes as obtaining from him or a third person information or confession, punishing him
for an act he has committed or is suspected of having committed, or intimidating him or
other persons. It does not include pain or suffering arising only from, inherent in or
incidental to, lawful sanctions to the extent consistent with the Standard Minimum Rules
for the Treatment of Prisoners.
Art 1(1), G.A. Res. 3452.

[68] 'Torture constitutes an aggravated and deliberate form of cruel, inhuman or degrading
treatment or punishment.' Art. 1(2), *id.*

[69] 'The prohibition of torture may be regarded as an integral part of customary international
law, and it may even have acquired the lineament of a peremptory norm of general international
law, i.e., *jus cogens*.' Dinstein, *supra* note 35, at 122. Note that art. 4(2) of the Political Covenant
does not permit derogation from this right. For an examination of the status of torture under
contemporary international law, *see* Bassiouni & Derby, *An Appraisal of Torture in International Law and Practice: The Need for an International Convention for the Prevention and
Suppression of Torture*, 48 Revue International de Droit Penal 17, 67-88 (1977). *See also* text
accompanying note 70 *infra*.

[70] Filartiga v. Peña-Irala, 630 F.2d at 884. While the court nowhere specifically addresses the
question of whether the prohibition of torture constitutes *jus cogens*, *see* text accompanying note
69 *supra*, its language points in that direction. 'Among the rights universally proclaimed by all
nations . . . is the right to be free of physical torture. Indeed, for purposes of civil liability, the
torturer has become—like the pirate and slave trader before him—*hostis humani generis*, an
enemy of all mankind.' 630 F.2d at 890.
For arguments in *Filartiga* that torture violates customary international law but which do not
raise the *jus cogens* issue, *see* Brief of the International Human Rights Law Group, the Council on
Hemispheric Affairs and the Washington Office on Latin America as *Amicus Curiae* Urging
Reversal; Brief for Amnesty International-U.S.A., International League for Human Rights, and
the Lawyers' Committee for International Human Rights as *Amicus Curiae*; and (most significantly) Memorandum for the United States as *Amicus Curiae*. This writer, in an affidavit
submitted to the court, 630 F.2d at 879 n.4, also averred that, 'like piracy, slavery and genocide
before it, the prohibition against torture is now a peremptory norm of international law', *i.e.*, jus
cogens.

categories of article 5 of the Universal Declaration and article 7 of the Political Covenant, guidance may be had from European Convention practice.[71] In the *Greek Case*,[72] the European Commission of Human Rights rendered the following interpretation of analogous article 3:

It is plain that there may be treatment to which all these descriptions [in article 3] apply, for all torture must be inhuman and degrading treatment, and inhuman treatment also degrading. The notion of inhuman treatment covers at least such treatment as deliberately causes severe suffering, mental or physical, which, in the particular situation, is unjustifiable.

The word 'torture' is often used to describe inhuman treatment, which has a purpose, such as the obtaining of information or confessions, or the infliction of punishment, and *it is generally an aggravated form of inhuman treatment.* Treatment or punishment of an individual may be said to be degrading if it grossly humiliates him before others or drives him to act against his will or conscience.[73]

As the italicized phrase in the above quotation indicates, then, it is the degree of maltreatment that distinguishes torture from inhuman treatment.[74]

This distinction and the inherent difficulty in applying it to concrete cases is well illustrated by the contrasting decisions of the European Commission and the European Court of Human Rights in the case of *Ireland v. United Kingdom*, where Ireland claimed that the United Kingdom's application to Irish Republican Army suspects of five techniques of 'interrogation in depth' constituted torture or inhuman or degrading treatment or punishment.[75] The Commission unanimous-

---

[71] *See* Spjut, *Torture Under the European Convention on Human Rights*, 73 Am. J. Int'l L. 267 (1979). As Humphrey notes, the jurisprudence under the European Convention, if one takes into account the terminological differences between the parallel articles in it and the Political Covenant, is 'persuasive authority' in interpreting the latter. Humphrey, *Political and Related Rights*, ch. 5 *infra*, at 179. The U.N. Human Rights Committee has just begun to construe art. 7 of the Political Covenant. *See* Communication No. R.1/5 (Uruguay), Third Report of the Human Rights Committee, 34 U.N. GAOR, Supp. (No. 40), Annex VII at 124, U.N. Doc. A/34/40 (1979) [hereinafter cited as Third Report]; Communication No. R.2/8 (Uruguay), Fourth Report of the Human Rights Committee, 35 U.N. GAOR, Supp. (No. 40), Annex VI at 111, U.N. Doc. A/35/40 (1980) [hereinafter cited as Fourth Report]; Communication No. R.1/4 (Uruguay), Fourth Report, *id.*, Annex VIII at 121; and Communication No. R.2/11 (Uruguay), Fourth Report, *id.*, Annex X at 132.

[72] 'Greek' Case, [1969] 1 Y.B. Eur. Conv. on Human Rights 1 (Eur. Comm. on Human Rights).

[73] *Id.* at 186 (emphasis added).

[74] *See* text at and accompanying notes 67 & 68 *supra*. And, of course, it is the degree of maltreatment that distinguishes inhuman treatment from harsh but permissible treatment. *See* Nedjati, *supra* note 46, at 63: 'Ill treatment must attain a minimum level of severity if it is to fall within the scope of Article 3. The assessment of this minimum is, in the nature of things, relative; it depends on all the circumstances of a given case . . .' *See also* text at and accompanying notes 78-80 *infra*.

[75] The five techniques consisted of hooding, wall-standing, noise, deprivation of sleep, and bread and water diet.

ly determined that the five techniques, applied together,[76] amounted to inhuman and degrading treatment. It also, again unanimously, found them to constitute torture. '[T]he systematic application of the techniques for the purpose of inducing a person to give information', concluded the Commission,

shows a clear resemblance to those methods of systematic torture which have been known over the ages. Although the five techniques—also called 'disorientation' or 'sensory deprivation' techniques—might not necessarily cause any severe after-effects the Commission sees in them a modern system of torture falling into the same category as those systems which have been applied in previous times as a means of obtaining information and confessions.[77]

However, when the case came before the European Court of Human Rights, the Court, while agreeing with the Commission's view that the five techniques constituted inhuman and degrading treatment,[78] held that 'they did not occasion suffering of the particular intensity and cruelty implied by the word torture as so understood'.[79] The standard used by the European Court in reaching this judgment thus mirrored the one the Commission had adopted in the *Greek Case*.[80]

In addition to the above two cases, numerous other decisions have been rendered delimiting inhuman or degrading treatment or punishment in the European context.[81] As Professor Jacobs has noted, '[i]t is possible to group these cases in two main categories, according to whether the allegations are of physical ill-treatment or brutality by prison officers or police officers, or of inadequate conditions of detention, lack of medical treatment, and so forth'.[82] Many of these

[76] Concerning the five techniques in the present case, the Commission considers that it should express an opinion only as to whether or not the way in which they were applied here, *namely in combination with each other*, was in breach of Art. 3. It observes that, if they were considered separately, deprivation of sleep or restrictions on diet might not as such be regarded as constituting treatment prohibited by Art. 3. It would rather depend on the circumstances and the purpose and would largely be a question of degree.
Ireland v. United Kingdom, [1976] Y.B. Eur. Conv. on Human Rights 512, 792 (Eur. Comm. on Human Rights) (emphasis added).

[77] *Id.* at 794.

[78] The five techniques were applied in combination, with premeditation and for hours at a stretch; they caused, if not actual bodily injury, at least intense physical and mental suffering to the persons subjected thereto and also led to acute psychiatric disturbances during interrogation. They accordingly fell within the category of inhuman treatment within the meaning of Article 3. The techniques were also degrading since they were such as to arouse in their victims feelings of fear, anguish and inferiority capable of humiliating and debasing them and possibly breaking their physical or moral resistance.
Ireland v. United Kingdom (18 Jan. 1978, Eur. Ct. of Human Rights), *reprinted in* 17 Int'l Legal Materials 680, 702 (1978).

[79] *Id.*

[80] *See* text at notes 72-74 *supra*.

[81] *See* Castberg, *supra* note 48, at 83-87; Fawcett, *supra* note 44, at 34-41; Jacobs, *supra* note 45, at 26–36; Nedjati, *supra* note 46, at 62–69. *See also* Higgins, ch. 13 *infra*.

[82] Jacobs, *supra* note 45, at 28.

cases concern what constitutes degrading treatment as distinguished from punishment, *e.g.*, discrimination based upon race is degrading treatment,[83] and 'birching' is degrading punishment.[84] In the future, the term 'treatment', which has received little separate consideration to date,[85] most likely will be read to expand the thrust of article 3's proscription well beyond the field of the criminal law and prisons into many areas of the civil law where state-sponsored facilities, *e.g.*, hospitals, mental treatment centers, foster homes, and the like, are involved.[86] This jurisprudence cannot help but have great impact upon the U.N. Human Rights Committee's construction of article 7 of the Political Covenant and on the Inter-American Commission on Human Rights' interpretation of article 5(2) of the American Convention. Together, the three systems undoubtedly will develop a body of law going well beyond the traditional prohibition of torture.

D. RIGHT TO LEGAL RECOGNITION (ARTICLE 6)

This article of the Universal Declaration states that '[e]veryone has the right to recognition everywhere as a person before the law'. With minor changes, the right is guaranteed by article 16 of the Political Covenant and article 3 of the American Convention; no corresponding provision appears in the European Convention.[87] The right has been cited as an example of rights 'so general or imprecise that the texts

---

[83] 'East African Asians' Case, [1970] Y.B. Eur. Conv. on Human Rights 928, 944 (Eur. Comm. on Human Rights).

> [T]he Commission's decision on the interpretation of "degrading" treatment in Article 3 is important as showing that the Convention is not a static instrument, but must be interpreted in the light of developments in social and political attitudes. Racial discrimination may not have been in the minds of the drafters of Article 3 but can clearly be regarded as degrading treatment by the standards of 1970.

Jacobs, *supra* note 45, at 36.

[84] 'Tyrer' Case, [1978] Y.B. Eur. Conv. on Human Rights 612 (Eur. Ct. of Human Rights). Comment from various quarters is collected in R. Lillich & F. Newman, International Human Rights: Problems of Law and Policy 621-27 (1979) [hereinafter cited as Lillich & Newman]. *Quaere*: if 'birching' is degrading, what about other forms of corporal punishment? *See* N.Y. Times, May 25, 1980, at 37, cols. 1-2, reporting that a British surgeon and his wife had been sentenced to public floggings in Saudi Arabia. *Cf.* Jacobs, *supra* note 45, at 31: 'Article 3 should be considered as imposing an absolute prohibition of certain forms of punishment such as, perhaps, flogging, which are by their very nature inhuman and degrading.' *But see* The Times (London), Feb. 26, 1982, at 2, col. 4, reporting that the European Court of Human Rights unanimously had held that the use of the tawse (a leather strap applied to the palm) in Scottish schools did not constitute a violation of art. 3.

[85] '[L]ittle significance can be attached to the distinction between "treatment" and "punishment".' Jacobs, *supra* note 45, at 30.

[86] *See* Castberg, *supra* note 48, at 83.

[87] *See* Robertson, Human Rights, *supra* note 33, at 123. Note that derogation from this right is prohibited by art. 4(2) of the Political Covenant.

appear to be more statements of political principle or policy than of legally enforceable rights'.[88] An examination of the *travaux prépara-toires*, however, reveals that the formulators of the right had certain definite objectives in mind.

The phrase 'person before the law', hardly a term of art in the common law, is the English translation of the phrase *personalité juridique*, which has definite legal connotations in the civil law, *i.e.*, it guarantees 'to every human being the right to exercise rights, to enter into contractual obligations, and to be represented in actions at law'.[89] Thus, explains one commentator, 'it covers those fundamental rights relating to the "legal capacity" (legal status) of a person, which are not explicitly mentioned in the subsequent articles of the Declaration'.[90]

At the time of the Universal Declaration's adoption, the right to recognition as a person before the law was thought to be just as important as those rights safeguarding the physical integrity of the individual. The prohibition of slavery and servitude, René Cassin noted, prevented 'the abasement of the human being from the physical point of view, while article [6] was intended to combat and to deny the possibility of his abasement from the legal point of view.'[91] Given the fact that Nazi Germany had arbitrarily deprived many persons of their juridical personality before subjecting them to assaults on their physical integrity, article 6 was viewed by its drafters as a key right through which individuals might assure themselves of their 'fundamental civil rights' embodied elsewhere in the Universal Declaration.[92] While it could have considerable importance in the future in the context of countries like South Africa where many individuals still are not accorded full recognition as persons before the law, its very general nature, coupled with the failure of states to apply it in practice, militates against its being regarded as part of customary international law.

---

[88] Jacobs, *supra* note 45, at 38; *see* Robertson, *supra* note 33, at 39 ('Once more we are confronted with provisions which are excellent statements of political principles but lack the precision necessary for legal texts.')

[89] 3 U.N. GAOR, C.3 (111th mtg.) 224 (1948) (Mr. Cruz). '[O]ne of the basic rights included in [the right to recognition] was precisely the right to enter into contracts, which meant the right to make a purchase, to enter into negotiations for employment, in short, to satisfy the material needs of life.' *Id.* at 226 (M. Cassin).

The right to recognition, in contrast to certain other rights discussed in this chapter, *e.g.*, the prohibition of torture, is not an absolute one. 'As a general rule, everyone has the right to recognition as a person before the law, but there are certain exceptions which are quite compatible with the rule of law and with the proper respect for fundamental rights in a democratic society, as in the case of minors and persons of unsound mind.' Robertson, *supra* note 33, at 39.

[90] Robinson, *supra* note 50, at 43; *see* text at note 92 *infra*.

[91] 3 U.N. GAOR, C.3 (111th mtg.) 226 (1948).

[92] *Id.* (M. Cassin); *see* text at note 90 *supra*.

E. RIGHTS TO EQUALITY BEFORE THE LAW AND TO NONDISCRIMINATION IN ITS APPLICATION (ARTICLE 7)

Equality before the law and nondiscrimination in its application are provided for by this article, which reads: 'All are equal before the law and are entitled without any discrimination to equal protection of the law. All are entitled to equal protection against any discrimination in violation of this Declaration and against any incitement to such discrimination.' Language almost identical with the first sentence of article 7 is found in the first sentence of article 26 of the Political Covenant; the second sentence of article 26, however, contains the following variation: '*In this respect*, the law shall prohibit any discrimination and guarantee to all persons equal and effective protection against discrimination on any ground . . .'[93] Language paralleling the first sentence of article 7 is found in article 24 of the American Convention,[94] while the European Convention contains no directly corresponding provision.[95]

Almost from the beginning, the words 'equal protection of the law' caused confusion. According to one member of the Third Committee during debates on the draft Declaration, 'it was not clear whether they meant that there should be laws which should be applied equally or that all were equally entitled to the protection of whatever laws existed'.[96] This lack of clarity, in the view of some observers, persists under the Political Covenant. Professor Robertson analyzes and evaluates the alternative interpretations as follows:

Broadly speaking, two quite different meanings seem possible: that the substantive provisions of the law should be the same for everyone; or that the application of the law should be equal for all without discrimination. The former interpretation would seem unreasonable; for example, in most countries women are not required to perform military service, while it is unnecessary that the law should prescribe maternity benefits for men. It would seem, therefore, that the meaning rather is to secure equality, without discrimination, in the application of the law, and this interpretation is borne out by the *travaux préparatoires*.[97]

[93] Emphasis added. For the importance of the three italicized words, see text at note 99 *infra*. The sentence concludes: 'such as race, colour, sex, language, religion, political or other opinion, national or social origin, property, birth or other status'.

[94] 'All persons are equal before the law. Consequently, they are entitled, without discrimination, to equal protection of the law.'

[95] Robertson, Human Rights, *supra* note 33, at 124. *Cf.* art. 14 of the European Convention, which states that '[t]he enjoyment of rights and freedoms set forth in this Convention shall be secured without discrimination on any ground . . .'

[96] 3 U.N. GAOR, C.3 (112th mtg.) 234 (1948) (Mr. Aquino).

[97] Robertson, *supra* note 33, at 39, *citing* Annotation on the Text of the Draft International Covenants on Human Rights, 10 U.N. GAOR, Annexes (Agenda Item 28, pt. II) 1, 61, U.N. Doc. A/2929 (1955) [hereinafter cited as Annotation]: 'The provision was intended to ensure equality, not identity, of treatment, and would not preclude reasonable differentiations between individuals or groups of individuals.'

He acknowledges that the second sentence of article 26,[98] 'if it stood alone, would constitute an important and far-reaching commitment and a general protection against discrimination', but points out that 'in the Third Committee the words "in this respect" were added at the beginning of this sentence . . . so that its scope is now limited to the general statement of equality and equal protection contained in the preceding sentence'.[99]

This interpretation is consistent with the approach taken in article 2 of the Universal Declaration and article 2(1) of the Political Covenant, both of which mandate nondiscriminatory treatment, but only insofar as the rights set out in the respective human rights instrument are concerned.[100] Articles 7 and 26, therefore, while specifically guaranteeing one important civil right to all persons on a non-discriminatory basis,[101] surely cannot be read to constitute a general norm of nondiscrimination invocable in other contexts.[102] Properly limited, however, the right considered in this subsection probably now has become customary international law.

F. RIGHT TO A REMEDY (ARTICLE 8)

This unique article, added at the last minute by the Third Committee to fill a supposed lacuna in the draft Declaration,[103] guarantees all persons 'the right to an effective remedy by the competent national tribunals for acts violating the fundamental rights granted him *by the constitution or by law*'.[104] Although, as one commentator has observed

[98] *See* text at note 93 *supra*.

[99] *Id*. 'As a result, the phrase is, in the view of one expert, largely tautologous.' *Id*., *citing* Schwelb, *The International Convention on the Elimination of All Forms of Racial Discrimination*, 15 Int'l & Comp. L.Q. 996, 1019 (1966):

> The second sentence as amended . . . makes the article an accumulation of tautologies. It now says, *inter alia*, that the law shall prohibit any discrimination in respect of the entitlement not to be discriminated against. It says further that the law shall guarantee to all persons equal and effective protection against discrimination in respect of their entitlement to equal protection of the law. In other words: the second sentence has no normative content at all and the prohibition of 'any discrimination' has, in fact, disappeared from the provision.

[100] 'It is to be noted that Art. 2 [of the Universal Declaration] does not lay down a *general* rule of equality but only of equality in regard to the rights and freedoms set forth in the Declaration. In other words, Art. 2 cannot be considered as having established the right to equal treatment as a human right, but only as a *principle of the Declaration*. Therefore inequality in anything which does not specifically represent a human right under the Declaration (for instance, in cohabitation out of wedlock) could not be considered a violation of Art. 2.' Robinson, *supra* note 50, at 39; *see id*. at 45-46.

[101] Other articles of the Universal Declaration and Political Covenant similarly guarantee specific civil rights on a nondiscriminatory basis. *See, e.g.*, arts. 10 and 14(1) respectively, by which individuals are guaranteed equality before the courts.

[102] On the emergence of a general norm of nondiscrimination, *see* McDougal, *supra* note 4, ch. 8.

[103] 3 U.N. GAOR, C.3 (113th mtg.) 242 (1948).

[104] Emphasis added.

in an analogous context, 'there is a certain anomaly in the right to a remedy itself being classed among the rights guaranteed',[105] that fact has not prevented the inclusion of roughly similar provisions in article 2(3) of the Political Covenant, article 13 of the European Convention, and article 25 of the American Convention.

Since, as Professor Humphrey has remarked, 'human rights without effective implementation are shadows without substance',[106] there is no doubt that the right to a remedy is an extremely important one. For this reason, despite assertions that such a right was superfluous or would prove of little value,[107] it has been included not only in the Universal Declaration and the Political Covenant, but, as indicated above, in the European Convention and American Convention as well. Its importance, however, depends greatly upon the scope of the 'substantive' rights it is designed to protect. Here there is considerable variation in the language of the relevant articles.

The Universal Declaration, quoted above,[108] guarantees an effective domestic remedy for acts which violate rights granted by the constitutions or laws of the various states. Thus, in contrast with article 7, whose reach extends only to acts in violation of the Universal Declaration,[109] article 8's scope is potentially much broader. 'It relates not to the rights granted under the Declaration', as Dr. Robinson notes, 'but to those granted by the domestic constitution and domestic law . . .'[110] Since the ambit of the rights granted by the latter generally is larger (at least on paper) than that of the rights enunciated in the Universal Declaration, the right to a remedy contemplated by article 8 may be regarded as a broad one indeed.

Unfortunately, both the Political Covenant and the European Convention are more restrictive in this regard. Effective remedies are guaranteed by article 2(3)(a) of the Political Covenant only to vindicate

---

[105] Jacobs, *supra* note 45, at 215.

[106] Humphrey, *Report of the Rapporteur of the International Committee on Human Rights*, in Int'l Law Assoc., Report of the Fifty-Third Conference 437, 457 (Buenos Aires 1968). His remarks echo the more poetic words of Justice Holmes: 'Legal obligations that exist but cannot be enforced are ghosts that are seen in the law but are elusive to the grasp.' The Western Maid, 257 U.S. 419, 433 (1922).

[107] 'An opinion was expressed that there was no need to specify the obligations of States parties in the event of a violation of the covenant, since it was obvious that if the States undertook to abide by the covenant, they would have to provide for effective remedies against infringements. It was also likely that provisions of that kind might be too broad and sweeping to be of much value. The view was accepted, however, that the proper enforcement of the provisions of the covenant depended on guarantees of the individual's rights against abuse, which comprised the following elements: the possession of a legal remedy, the granting of this remedy by national authorities and the enforcement of the remedy by the competent authorities.' Annotation, *supra* note 97, at 18.

[108] *See* text at note 104 *supra*.

[109] *See* text at notes 99–102 *supra*.

[110] Robinson, *supra* note 50, at 47.

'rights or freedoms as herein recognized', *i.e.*, recognized by the Political Covenant. Similarly, article 13 of the European Convention guarantees an effective remedy only for 'rights and freedoms as set forth in this Convention . . .'[111] The American Convention, on the other hand, provides the person seeking relief the best of all possible worlds: article 25(1) combines the approaches of the Universal Declaration, Political Covenant, and European Convention, requiring states to accord prompt and effective relief 'against acts that violate . . . fundamental rights recognized by the constitution or laws of the state concerned *or by this Convention* . . .'[112]

To date only article 13 of the European Convention has been interpreted and, in Professor Fawcett's words, its interpretation has revealed 'a basic confusion of thought as to the real purpose and function of the Article'.[113] Is article 13, he asks, 'concerned with the international or the domestic implementation of the Convention, with the collective guarantee, or with internal remedies'?[114] Does the article, from the claimant's perspective, mandate that an effective domestic remedy be in place ready to consider any alleged violation of the European Convention, or does it become applicable only after there has been a determination (by the Committee of Ministers, the European Court of Human Rights, or a domestic court applying the Convention as part of domestic law) that another, 'substantive' article of the Convention actually has been violated?[115] For textual and other reasons, Professor Fawcett leans away from the former ('domestic' or 'internal') and toward the latter ('international' or 'collective') view of the article.[116] This view, which greatly minimizes the importance of

[111] 'This right relates exclusively to a remedy in respect of a violation of one of the rights and freedoms set forth in the Convention.' Nedjati, *supra* note 46, at 10.

[112] Emphasis added.

[113] Fawcett, *supra* note 44, at 232.

[114] *Id.* at 229.

[115] *Id.*

[116] '[I]t may be said that if the drafters of Article 13 had wished to base the entitlement to a remedy upon a claim or allegation of a breach of the Convention, as opposed to an actual breach, they could easily have done so, and have not. A textual approach then leads away from the "domestic" view of the Article.' *Id.* at 230. *Accord*, Castberg, *supra* note 48, at 158:

It might be tempting to disregard the wording of Art. 13 and construe the provision as an independent right. This would mean that everyone is entitled to an effective remedy under Art. 13, when he claims that one of his rights according to the Convention is violated. However, this would undoubtedly be going too far in disregarding a text whose wording is unambiguous. [*Quaere?*] Art. 13 says that everyone whose 'rights and freedoms' as set forth in the Convention *are* violated shall have an effective remedy before a national authority. It does not say that everyone who *alleges* such a violation shall have this right.

He adds by way of footnote that 'Art. 13 of the Convention concurs largely on this point with the formulation in Art. 8 of the Universal Declaration of Human Rights of 1948.' *Id.* at 174 n.1. So too, assuming the author's 'unambiguous' construction, do art. 2(3) of the Political Covenant and art. 25(1) of the American Convention.

the right to a remedy,[117] has not been explicitly adopted by the European Court of Human Rights and hopefully will be rejected by the U.N. Human Rights Committee and the American Commission and Court of Human Rights when the issue arises under the Political Covenant and the American Convention respectively. In any event, so much confusion exists about the scope of this right that it can be said with reasonable assurance that it is not part of customary international law.

G. PROHIBITION OF ARBITRARY ARREST, DETENTION OR EXILE (ARTICLE 9)

Article 3, it will be recalled, establishes not only the right to life, but also the right to liberty and security of person. The Political Covenant handles these rights in two articles, 6(1) and 9(1), the latter of which, in addition to guaranteeing 'the right to liberty and security of person', provides, *inter alia*, '[n]o one shall be subjected to arbitrary arrest or detention'.[118] 'Protection against arbitrary arrest and detention', Professor Jacobs rightly notes, 'is clearly the central feature of any system of guarantees of the liberty of the individual'.[119] Indeed, the drafters of the Universal Declaration considered the prohibition of arbitrary arrest and detention so important that rather than treating it as just one liberty interest, they devoted a separate article to it, demonstrating their intention to establish it as an independent human right.[120] Thus, article 9 of the Universal Declaration provides that '[n]o one shall be subjected to arbitrary arrest, detention or exile'.

The *travaux préparatoires*, revealing an understandable reluctance to define 'arbitrary'[121] and an enthusiastic endorsement of an amendment adding 'exile' to the draft Declaration's proscription against

[117] 'The conclusion thus reached confirms that the importance of Art. 13 is very limited, but it does not, as already observed, become superfluous. It might, of course, be said that to establish a violation of Art. 13 will then merely be to reinforce the finding of a violation of another Article. However, it may be noted that, after all, it is a genuine additional violation of the Convention when not only is it a case of one of Arts. 2-12 having been violated, but the State responsible has further not given the victim of the violation the possibility to have the wrong redressed by an effective remedy in his own country.' *Id.* at 158-59. *Accord,* Jacobs, *supra* note 45, at 215-16.

[118] It concludes: 'No one shall be deprived of his liberty except on such grounds and in accordance with such procedure as are established by law.' *See generally* the first paragraph of subsection A *supra*.

[119] Jacobs, *supra* note 45, at 75.

[120] 'Article 9 of the Universal Declaration deals with freedom from arbitrary arrest, detention or exile as an independent human right, separate from the right to liberty in Article 3. Article 9 of the Covenant, however, brings the freedom from arbitrary arrest or detention (though not the freedom from arbitrary exile) within the bounds of the right to liberty, as do Article 5 of the European Convention and Article 7 of the American Convention.' Dinstein, *supra* note 35, at 129 (footnotes omitted).

[121] *See, e.g.,* 3 U.N. GAOR, C.3 (113th mtg.) 245 (1948) (Mr. Aquino). *See* text at notes 36-39 and especially accompanying note 40 *supra*.

'arbitrary arrest or detention',[122] indicate that most members of the Third Committee were pleased with the article's 'eloquent brevity'[123] and content to leave it to the Political Covenant to spell out its general terms. The Political Covenant, in article 9, fulfills their expectations by elaborating in considerable detail the rights to be accorded a person who has been arrested or detained.[124] Most of these rights also are protected by article 5 of the European Convention[125] and article 7 of the American Convention[126] in 'substantially similar terms'.[127]

[122] *See id.* at 244 (Mr. Andrade); *id.* at 244-45 (Mr. Matienzo); *id.* at 245 (Mr. Aquino); *id.* at 246 (Mr. Cruz); *id.* at 247 (Mr. Azkoul); *id.* (Mr. de Athayde); *id.* at 248 (Mr. Davies); *id.* at 249 (Mr. Cisneros); *id.* at 251 (Mr. Change); *id.* (Miss Klompé); *id.* 255 (Count de Wiart); *id.* at 256 (Mr. de Aréchaga); and *id.* (Mr. Pavlov). The prohibition of exile is an interesting one that has received relatively little scholarly attention. According to Robinson, '[i]t is obvious that this motion [*sic*] must cover not only "exile" in the sense of physical expulsion but also the creation of conditions as created by the Nazis during the years 1933-1939, which forced a part of the population to seek refuge abroad'. Robinson, *supra* note 50, at 49. Questions about the scope of the right are less important, however, than the question of whether such a right actually exists today, given its unfortunate omission from the Political Covenant. Robertson, *supra* note 33, at 40-41. (Note, in this regard, that art. 12(1) of the Political Covenant prohibits 'internal exile', a practice common in the Soviet Union.) Since art. 3(1) of Protocol No. 4 to the European Convention and art. 22(5) of the American Convention enjoin states from expelling their nationals, considerable normative support, in the opinion of this writer, continues to exist for the prohibition of exile contained in art. 9 of the Universal Declaration. Whether the right has attained the status of customary international law, however, is questionable.
[123] 3 U.N. GAOR, C.3 (113th mtg.) 244 (1948) (M. Cassin).
[124] For a survey of the rights guaranteed by art. 9, *see* Noor Muhammad, *Due Process of Law for Persons Accused of Crimes*, in The International Bill of Rights: The Covenant on Civil and Political Rights 138 (L. Henkin ed. 1981). *See also* Dinstein, *supra* note 35, at 128-35.
[125] *Cf.* Fawcett, *supra* note 44, at 57: 'The First U.N. Covenant, Articles 9-13, goes far beyond Article 5 and establishes a code governing arrest and detention, the conditions of detention, and residence in and departure from a country, and the expulsion of aliens.' European practice under art. 5 is voluminous. *See id.* at 57-120; Castberg, *supra* note 48, at 92–106; Jacobs, *supra* note 45, at 45-76; Nedjati, *supra* note 46, at 83-99.
[126] 'Article 7, Right to Personal Liberty, sets forth essential due process guarantees long recognized in Anglo-American jurisprudence, such as the proscription of arbitrary arrest and imprisonment (Section 3), and prompt notification to the accused of charges against him (Section 4).' Goldman, *supra* note 34, at 22-23. A constitutional difficulty in connection with U.S. ratification of the American Convention is thought to arise under art. 7(7), which provides that '[n]o one shall be detained for debt. This principle shall not limit the orders of a competent judicial authority issued for nonfulfillment of duties of support.' President Carter, believing that the qualification contained in the second sentence is not broad enough to bring the provision into line with U.S. constitutional law, suggested that '[t]he Senate may wish to record its understanding that the second sentence of paragraph (7) of Article 7 applies to orders of any competent judicial authority, whether or not issued for fulfillment of duties of support'. *President's Message, supra* note 5, at XIX.
[127] When it is said that these rights are defined in substantially similar terms, this is not meant to conceal the fact that in some cases there are differences in the definitions which may have some importance. Thus, as regards the right to liberty and security of person, Article 9 of the United Nations Covenant prohibits 'arbitrary arrest or detention', while Article 5 of the European Convention prohibits arrest or detention except in six sets of circumstances which are specifically defined (after conviction by a competent court, for non-compliance with the lawful order of a court, etc.). The question thus arises whether there is a correspondence between the prohibition of 'arbitrary arrest or detention' and the more carefully defined European formula. . .

After the language quoted above,[128] article 9(1) of the Political
Covenant concludes with the following sentence: 'No one shall be
deprived of his liberty except on such grounds and in accordance with
such procedure as are established by law.' The purpose of this provision
is to require states to spell out in legislation the grounds on which an
individual may be deprived of his liberty and the procedures to be used.
With the freedom of action of the executive branch of government thus
restricted, Rector Dinstein observes, '[n]ot every policeman (or other
state functionary) is entitled to decide at his discretion, and on his own
responsibility, who can be arrested, why and how'.[129] Nor is any
detention allowed by law permissible, as a literal interpretation of the
provision might suggest. Just as an arrest may not be arbitrary—
defined as 'unjust' and not merely 'illegal'[130]—so too must a detention
not be arbitrary. The deprivation of liberty therefore must be not only
in accordance with law, but also in conformity to the principles of
justice.[131]

The balance of article 9 defines certain guarantees applicable in case
of any arrest or detention, plus certain special guarantees applicable
when a person is arrested or detained on a criminal charge. Space
dictates that these guarantees be listed rather than fully evaluated
here.[132] In the first, general category are the following:

Article 9(2). 'Anyone who is arrested shall be informed, at the time of
arrest, of the reasons for his arrest and shall be promptly informed of any
charges against him.'

Article 9(4). 'Anyone who is deprived of his liberty by arrest or detention

> As another example, the United Nations text (Article 9, paragraph 2) requires that a
> person arrested shall be informed of the reasons 'at the time of his arrest', while the
> European requirement is that he should be informed 'promptly'. The requirement of the
> Covenant may be considered as imposing a stricter obligation; nevertheless, it appears
> that the intention—and the consequential obligation—is much the same, so that the
> conclusion seems justified that these rights are defined in 'substantially similar terms'.
> Robertson, *supra* note 33, at 29.

---

[128] *See* text at note 118 *supra*.
[129] Dinstein, *supra* note 35, at 130.
[130] *See* text accompanying note 40 *supra*.
[131] Annotation, *supra* note 97, at 35.
[132] The U.N. Human Rights Committee has recently begun to construe the various provisions
of art. 9 of the Political Covenant. *See, e.g.*, Communication No. R.1/5 (Uruguay), Third Report,
supra note 71, Annex VII at 124 (art. 9(1), (2), (3), & (4)); Communication No. R.2/9
(Uruguay), Fourth Report, *supra* note 71, Annex V at 107 (art. (4)); Communication No. R.2/8
(Uruguay), Fourth Report, *supra* note 71, Annex VI at 111 (art. 9(1), (3), & (4));
Communication No. R.1/4 (Uruguay), Fourth Report, *supra* note 71, Annex VIII at 101 (art.
9(1) & (4)); Communication No. R.1/6 (Uruguay), Fourth Report, *supra* note 71, Annex IX at
127 (art. 9(3) & (4)); Communication No. R.2/11 (Uruguay), Fourth Report, *supra* note 71,
Annex X at 132 (art. 9(3) & (4)). Hence any extended discussion of this article would be far less
authoritative today than 10 years hence. For European practice in regard to similar guarantees,
see the authorities cited in note 125 *supra*.

shall be entitled to take proceedings before a court, in order that court may decide without delay on the lawfulness of his detention and order his release if the detention is not lawful.'

Article 9(5). 'Anyone who has been the victim of unlawful arrest or detention shall have an enforceable right to compensation.'[133]

In the second category—special guarantees applicable to persons arrested or detained on criminal charges—article 9(3) provides that such persons 'be brought promptly before a judge' and thereafter 'be entitled to trial within a reasonable time or to release'. Additionally, it establishes a presumption that persons awaiting trial shall not be detained in custody; their release, however, may be made subject to guarantees of appearance, the most common of which presumably would be bail.[134]

Interpretative guidance as to the meaning of most of the above provisions can be obtained from the nascent practice of the U.N. Human Rights Committee[135] as well as the more developed practice of the European Court of Human Rights under article 5 of the European Convention.[136] Given the differences in wording, however, the latter must be used with care.[137] In any event, taking into account uncertainties about the contours and content of the prohibition of arbitrary arrest and detention, plus the fact that states may derogate therefrom under article 4(2) of the Political Covenant, it seems unlikely that little more than the basic core prohibition can be said to constitute part of customary international law at present.

H.   RIGHT TO A FAIR TRIAL (ARTICLE 10)

This article, which along with its companion, article 11, guarantees individuals 'the basic right to a fair trial [in] both civil and criminal matters',[138] enunciates a very important right, for the implementation

---

[133] Art. 9(5) 'grants a right to compensation for unlawful arrest or detention which goes beyond current federal law'. *President's Message, supra* note 5, at XII. *Accord*, Henkin, ch. 2 *supra*, at 38 & 39. Hence, President Carter recommended that the Senate, in giving its advice and consent to the Political Covenant, attach the following reservation: 'The United States does not adhere to paragraph (5) of Article 9. . . . '

[134] 'The guarantees that may be required for release from custody (when granted) may vary from one country to another, and they do not necessarily have to be "of a purely financial character". Yet bail is probably the most common guarantee. The forms of bail are manifold, but the common purpose is to secure the presence of the accused at his trial "by the threat that non-appearance will entail the forfeiture by the accused or some other person of a specified sum of money".' Dinstein, *supra* note 35, at 134 (footnotes omitted).

[135] *See* note 132 *supra*.

[136] *See* the authorities cited in note 125 *supra*. *See also* Daintith & Wilkinson, *Bail and the Convention: British Reflections on the Wemhoff and Neumeister Cases*, 18 Am. J. Comp. L. 326 (1970); Harris, *Recent Cases on Pre-Trial Detention and Delay in Criminal Proceedings in the European Court of Human Rights*, 44 Brit. Y.B. Int'l L. 87 (1970).

[137] *See* Robertson, *supra* note 33, at 28-30 *passim*.

[138] Robinson, *supra* note 50, at 50.

of all other rights depends upon the proper administration of justice.[139] In its entirety article 10 reads as follows: 'Everyone is entitled in full equality to a fair and public hearing by an independent and impartial tribunal, in the determination of his rights and obligations and of any criminal charge against him.' Two preliminary points should be made with respect to this language. First, it lumps together both criminal and civil proceedings, despite cogent arguments for their being treated separately, the potential for abuse of state power obviously being greater where the rights of an accused—as opposed to a mere party in civil lawsuit—are concerned.[140] Second, it is so terse that it offers little help when applied to the facts of particular cases.[141] Hence, here more than elsewhere, guidance as to the meaning of the right must be obtained from parallel provisions in subsequent international human rights instruments and the decisions of competent bodies interpreting them.[142]

The requirements of a fair trial in criminal proceedings, the sole concern of this subsection, can be divided somewhat arbitrarily into four general categories: the character of the tribunal, the public nature of the hearing, the rights of the accused in the conduct of his defense and, lastly, a miscellaneous collection of other prescriptions.[143]

The first category, the character of the tribunal, obviously is of prime importance. Article 10 requires tribunals to be 'independent and

[139] *See* Annotation, *supra* note 97, at 42.

[140] 'The right to a fair trial in criminal proceedings is concerned with the additional element of protection of the accused against an abuse of power by the State which plays comparatively little part in civil proceedings in which the primary and often only consideration is to ensure adequate and equal facilities for two private parties. In consequence it seems desirable to separate the two.' Harris, *The Right to a Fair Trial in Criminal Proceedings as a Human Right*, 16 Int'l & Comp. L.Q. 352, 353 n.9 (1967) [hereinafter cited as Harris]. Nonetheless, the Political Covenant in art. 14(1), the European Convention in art. 6(1), and the American Convention in art. 8(1) all mention civil and criminal proceedings in the same context before specifying, in subsequent provisions, additional guarantees applying only to persons charged with a criminal offence. For example, art. 14(2) of the Political Covenant contains the all-important safeguard that '[e]veryone charged with a criminal offense shall have the right to be presumed innocent until proved guilty according to law'. *Accord*, arts. 6(2) and 8(2) of the European Convention and American Convention respectively. *See* text at note 159 *infra*.

[141] *Cf.* Robinson, *supra* note 50, at 50:
 It is obvious that the notions of 'fair' hearing, 'independent' and 'impartial' tribunal must differ from country to country, depending on the general progress of justice there. However, as the Declaration enunciates basic principles only, these general concepts are appropriate and a detailed description would introduce undesired differentiations.

[142] *See, e.g.*, art. 14 of the Political Covenant and recent decisions of the Human Rights Committee construing it. Communication No. R.1/5 (Uruguay), Third Report, *supra*, note 71, Annex VII at 124 (art. 14(1), (2), & (3)); Communication No. R.2/8 (Uruguay), Fourth Report, *supra* note 71, Annex VI at 111 (art. 14(1), (2), & (3)); Communication No. R.1/4 (Uruguay), Fourth Report, *supra* note 71, Annex VIII at 121 (art. 14(3)); and Communication No. R.1/6 (Uruguay), Fourth Report, *supra* note 71, Annex IX at 127 (art. 14(1) & (3)).

[143] This writer has taken these four categories from Harris, *supra* note 140, at 354, to whom he records his indebtedness.

impartial', as does article 14(1) of the Political Covenant and articles 6(1) and 8(1) of the European Convention and American Convention respectively. As Professor Harris has put it,

[t]hese are obvious and overlapping requirements. The primary meaning of 'independent' is independence of other organs of government in the sense of the doctrine of the separation of powers: in particular, a judge must not be subject to the control or influence of the executive or the legislature. . . The requirement that the court must be 'impartial' needs little amplification. It is reflected in the 'universally accepted doctrine' that no man may be a judge in his own cause and is an obvious characteristic for a court to possess.[144]

Whether such independence and impartiality can be assured when a state resorts to *ad hoc* or special tribunals, as frequently occurs after revolutions or in national emergencies, is a doubtful proposition: for this reason, it is disappointing that article 10 does not speak directly to this point. In contrast, article 14(1) of the Political Covenant and article 8(1) of the American Convention add the requirement that the tribunal be 'competent', a word which, according to the *travaux préparatoires* of the former, 'was intended to ensure that all persons should be tried in courts whose jurisdiction had been previously estab-lished by law, and arbitrary action so avoided'.[145] Article 8(1) of the American Convention goes one step further, specifically stating that a trial must be conducted by a tribunal 'previously established by law . . .'[146] Arguably, this requirement can be read into the 'independent and impartial' language of the Universal Declaration.[147]

The second category, the public nature of the hearing, also is of importance in protecting individuals from arbitrary proceedings. The drafters of article 10 of the Universal Declaration inserted the words 'and public' between the words 'fair' and 'hearing' to insure the openness of trials, a procedure conducive to their fairness.[148]

[144] *Id.* at 354–56. *Accord*, Fawcett, *supra* note 44, at 156:
> The often fine distinction between independence and impartiality turns mainly, it seems, on that between the status of the tribunal determinable largely by objective tests and the subjective attitudes of its members, lay or legal. Independence is primarily freedom from control by, or subordination to, the executive power in the State; impartiality is rather absence in the members of the tribunal of personal interest in the issues to be determined by it, or some form of prejudice.

[145] *See* note 139 *supra. Compare* Robertson, *supra* note 33, at 32, who after paraphrasing this definition of 'competent' concludes that 'this notion is already included or implied in "independ-ent . . . tribunal established by law"' and hence 'appears [to be] of minor importance'.

[146] For background data suggesting that the Latin American states want the norm contained in art. 8(1) to be part of the 'universally understood minimum content to a guarantee of a fair criminal trial', *see* Harris, *supra* note 140, at 356.

[147] *See* text at and accompanying note 141 *supra. But see* 3 U.N. GAOR, C.3 (115th mtg.) 263-64 (1948), where an amendment to the draft Declaration which would have added the words 'previously established' before 'tribunal' was rejected by an 18-15-9 vote.

[148] *Id.* at 263.

Moreover, despite language in the *travaux préparatoires* that '[t]here were circumstances in which a secret trial might be acceptable',[149] article 10 itself acknowledges no such exception. Article 14(1) of the Political Covenant, however, closely tracked by article 6(1) of the European Convention, contains a wide range of exceptions 'so large and loosely expressed as to cover almost any denial of public hearing'.[150] Article 14(1) reads, *inter alia*, as follows: 'The Press and the public may be excluded from all or part of a trial for reasons of morals, public order (*ordre public*) or national security in a democratic society, or when the interest of the private lives of the parties so requires, or to the extent strictly necessary in the opinion of the court in special circumstances where publicity would prejudice the interests of justice . . .' Such language, as Professor Fawcett remarks with respect to article 6(1) of the European Convention, is so broad that 'it is doubtful whether the requirement of public hearing under the Convention is likely in practice to yield much protection'.[151]

The rights of the accused in the conduct of his defense, the third category, presents the converse of the above. Rather than the Political Covenant undercutting a broad and unqualified right found in the Universal Declaration, here the Political Covenant spells out at length in article 14(3) just what rights an accused has in a criminal proceeding. In brief, they are the right to be informed promptly of the charge against him; the right to have adequate time and facilities to prepare a defense and to communicate with counsel; the right to be tried without undue delay; the right to be tried in his presence and to defend himself in person or through counsel; the right to cross-examine witnesses against him and to summon witnesses on his own behalf; the right to an interpreter; and the right not to be compelled to testify against himself. Roughly similar guarantees are found in article 6(3) of the European Convention and article 8(2) of the American Convention. As is apparent, they generally reflect the procedural due process rights developed by the U.S. Supreme Court from the fifth and fourteenth amendments to the U.S. Constitution.[152]

[149] *Id.* at 260.
[150] Fawcett, *supra* note 44, at 150. Article 8(5) of the American Convention, although far briefer, is subject to much the same criticism in that it sanctions non-public criminal proceedings when 'necessary to protect the interests of justice'.
[151] Fawcett, *supra* note 44, at 150. *See* Nedjati, *supra* note 46, at 116, who uses nearly identical language.
[152] *See generally* Lillich, *Procedural Human Rights*, in Human Rights: The Cape Town Conference 124 (C. Forsyth & J. Schiller eds. 1979). Although '[i]t is possible to read all the requirements contained in Article 14 as consistent with United States law, policy and practice', President Carter nevertheless recommended that the Senate, in giving its advice and consent to the Political Covenant's ratification, consider recording its understanding, *inter alia*,

> that subparagraphs (3)(b) and (d) of Article 14 do not require the provision of court-appointed counsel when the defendant is financially able to retain counsel or for petty

The fourth and final category comprises a number of miscellaneous rights, none of which are set out in the Universal Declaration, which generally are thought to contribute to a fair trial in criminal proceedings. In the order in which they appear in article 14 of the Political Covenant, they are: the right of juveniles to be tried under special procedures;[153] the right to appeal one's conviction and sentence;[154] the right to compensation when one is convicted through a miscarriage of justice;[155] and the right not to be subjected to double jeopardy.[156] The fact that none of these rights is mentioned in the European Convention (and only three are guaranteed by the American Convention) suggests that they are part of conventional rather than customary international law, a status they are likely to retain until the Political Covenant becomes so widely accepted as to be generally norm-creating.[157] Moreover, without the interpretative assistance of the Political Covenant, the right to a fair trial provided for in article 10 of the Universal Declaration seems too generally phrased to constitute

offenses for which imprisonment will not be imposed. The United States further understands that [sub]paragraph (3)(e) does not forbid requiring an indigent defendant to make a showing that the witness is necessary for his attendance to be compelled by the court. *President's Message, supra* note 5, at XIII. He recommended that a similar understanding as to art. 8 of the American Convention be attached to U.S. ratification thereof. *Id.* at XIX.

---

[153] Art. 14(4). Neither the European nor the American Conventions recognize this right.

[154] Art. 14(5). While the European Convention does not recognize the right of appeal, art. 8(2)(h) of the American Convention guarantees 'the right to appeal the judgment to a higher court'.

[155] Art. 14(6). While the European Convention does not recognize the right to compensation, art. 10 of the American Convention provides that '[e]very person has the right to be compensated in accordance with the law in the event he has been sentenced by a final judgment through a miscarriage of justice'.

It is worth noting that there is some doubt as to whether U.S. law as it now stands complies with art. 14(6). Henkin, ch. 2 *supra*, at 38 & 39. In an abundance of precaution, President Carter suggested that the Senate, in giving its advice and consent to the Political Covenant's ratification, record its understanding, *inter alia*, that '[t]he United States considers that provisions of United States law currently in force constitute compliance with paragraph (6)'. *See President's Message, supra* note 5, at XIII. He suggested that a similar understanding in regard to art. 10 of the American Convention be attached to U.S. ratification thereof. *Id.* at XIX.

[156] Art. 14(7). In view of federal-state problems, President Carter suggested that the Senate, in giving its advice and consent to the Political Covenant's ratification, consider recording its understanding, *inter alia*, 'that the prohibition on double jeopardy contained in paragraph (7) is applicable only when the judgment of acquittal has been rendered by a court of the same governmental unit, whether the Federal Government or a constitutional unit, which is seeking a new trial for the same cause'. *President's Message, supra* note 5, at XIII.

While the European Convention does not recognize the right not to be subjected to double jeopardy, art. 8(4) of the American Convention provides that '[a]n accused person acquitted by a nonappealable judgment shall not be subjected to a new trial for the same cause'. For the reasons given in the preceding paragraph in connection with the proposed understanding to art. 14(7) of the Political Covenant, President Carter recommended a similar understanding with respect to art. 8(4). *Id.* at XIX.

[157] *See* note 18 *supra*.

a customary international law rule capable of application in concrete cases.[158]

I. PRESUMPTION OF INNOCENCE AND PROHIBITION OF EX POST FACTO LAWS (ARTICLE II)

This article, closely related to article 10 of the Universal Declaration, also is concerned with the rights of the accused in criminal proceedings. It establishes the presumption of innocence and proscribes *ex post facto* offences. These important and distinct guarantees will be discussed separately.

Article 11(1) provides that '[e]veryone charged with a penal offence has the right to be presumed innocent until proved guilty according to law in a public trial at which he has had all the guarantees necessary for his defence'. Since the latter part of this sentence is redundant, in view of the rights accorded accuseds by article 10, it was omitted when the language of article 11(1) was adopted, almost *in haec verba*, as article 14(2) of the Political Covenant. Language almost identical to article 11(1) is contained in articles 6(2) and 8(2) of the European Convention and American Convention respectively. Thus, there is a unanimous consensus supporting the presumption of innocence in criminal proceedings;[159] surely therefore it has become part of customary international law.

Little difficulty has been encountered so far in applying the principle under the European Convention,[160] although, as Professor Jacobs cautions, it has a slightly different meaning in the civil law than it has at common law.

The principle of the presumption of innocence is reflected in English law in the rule placing the burden of proof on the prosecution. But it cannot be equated with that rule, to which there are in any event numerous exceptions. Under the inquisitorial system of criminal procedure found in many of the Contracting Parties [to the European Convention], it is for the court to elicit the truth in all cases. What the principle of the presumption of innocence requires here is first that the court should not be predisposed to find the accused guilty, and second that it should at all times give the accused the benefit of the doubt, on the rule *in dubio pro reo*.[161]

[158] For application of art. 14 of the Political Covenant by the U.N. Human Rights Committee, *see* note 142 *supra*. Once again, the fact that under art. 4(2) of the Political Covenant a state may derogate from the right to a fair trial guaranteed by art. 14 cuts against the right's acceptance into customary international law at present.

[159] *See* note 140 *supra*. Note, however, that art. 4(2) of the Political Covenant permits derogation from the presumption of innocence found in art. 14(2).

[160] *See generally* Castberg, *supra* note 48, at 127; Fawcett, *supra* note 44, at 161-63; Jacobs, *supra* note 45, at 111-14; Nedjati, *supra* note 46, at 125-27.

[161] Jacobs, *supra* note 45, at 113.

While the principle thus concerns primarily the behavior of judges,[162] the admissibility in evidence of prior convictions[163] and the effect of pre-trial publicity[164] have been alleged, so far unsuccessfully, to violate the right to be presumed innocent. Other such allegations can be anticipated as this right is tested under the Political Covenant and the American Convention.

Article 11(2), which proscribes *ex post facto* offenses, requires quoting in full. It states:

No one shall be held guilty of any penal offence on account of any act or omission which did not constitute a penal offence, under national or international law, at the time when it was committed. Nor shall a heavier penalty be imposed than the one that was applicable at the time the penal offence was committed.

Two points here are worth noting: first, the reference to international law, inserted 'to exclude doubts as to the Nuremberg and Tokyo trials'[165] and 'to ensure that no one shall escape punishment for a criminal offence under international law by pleading that his act was legal under his own national law';[166] and, second, the extension, in the second sentence, of the nonretroactivity principle to increased penalties.[167]

Article 15(1) of the Political Covenant, from which there may be no derogation according to article 4(2), closely follows article 11(2); thus it may be argued convincingly that customary international law now prohibits both *ex post facto* offenses and penalties. Moreover, article 15(1) adds a sentence designed to guarantee an accused the benefits of *ex post facto* legal reforms: 'If, subsequent to the commission of the offence, provision is made by law for the imposition of a lighter penalty, the offender shall benefit thereby.'[168] Article 15(2) of the

---

[162] *See, e.g.*, Boeckmans v. Belgium, [1965] Y.B. Eur. Conv. on Human Rights 410, 422 (Report of the Sub-Commission).

[163] X v. Austria, [1966] Y.B. Eur. Conv. on Human Rights 550, 554 (Eur. Comm. of Human Rights).

[164] Austria v. Italy, [1963] Y.B. Eur. Conv. on Human Rights 740, 788 (Eur. Commn. of Human Rights).

[165] Robinson, *supra* note 50, at 51. *Cf.* 3 U.N. GAOR, C.3 (116th mtg.) 271 (1948) (M. Cassin): '[I]t was not a question of securing approval for those judgments, but of making sure that there was no repudiation of the very principles which had presided over the creation of a community of nations born of the victory of freedom over war-crimes.'

[166] Annotation, *supra* note 97, at 45.

[167] An amendment to the draft Declaration added this sentence. 3 U.N. GAOR, C.3 (115th mtg.) 265, (116th mtg.) 273 (1948).

[168] A similar sentence appears in art. 9 of the American Convention. The European Convention, however, contains no such provision. '[T]he offender has no right under the Convention to be sentenced in accordance with a law being passed after the offence was committed and being more lenient than the law then in force.' Castberg, *supra* note 48, at 129.

It should be noted that, while U.S. law often grants this right in practice, it is not required by law. For this reason President Carter, in urging the Senate to give its advice and consent to the

Political Covenant also adds an entirely new and arguably superfluous provision[169] justifying past and authorizing future international war crimes trials: 'Nothing in this article shall prejudice the trial and punishment of any person for any act or omission which, at the time when it was committed, was criminal according to the general principles of law recognized by the community of nations.'[170] Articles 7 and 9 of the European Convention and American Convention respectively are based upon article 11(2) of the Universal Declaration and article 15 of the Political Covenant, albeit both contain one or more variations.[171]

While the primary purpose of such *ex post facto* provisions is to prohibit retrospective penal legislation, a secondary purpose is to preclude 'the courts from extending the scope of the criminal law by interpretation'.[172] Thus the European Commission, construing article 7 of the European Convention, noted that it 'does not merely prohibit—except as provided in paragraph (2)—retroactive application of the criminal law to the detriment of the accused', but 'also confirms, in a more general way, the principle of the statutory nature of offences and punishment . . . and prohibits, in particular, extension of the application of the criminal law "*in malam partem*" by analogy . . .'[173] It further added that,

although it is not normally for the Commission to ascertain the proper interpretation of municipal law by national courts . . . , the case is otherwise in matters where the Convention expressly refers to municipal law, as it does in Article 7 . . . [U]nder Article 7 the application of a provision of municipal penal law to an act not covered by the provision in question directly results in a conflict with the Convention, so that the Commission can and must take cognisance of allegations and of such false interpretation of municipal law . . . [174]

The above remarks, according to Castberg, 'clearly keep the door open for preventing under Article 7 not only the application of criminal law by analogy, but also extensive interpretations'.[175] Whether the U.N. Human Rights Committee, construing article 15 of the Political Covenant, or the Inter-American Commission on Human Rights,

ratification of the Political Covenant and the American Convention, recommended the adoption of reservations indicating that the United States does not adhere to the third clause of art. 15(1) and the third sentence of art. 9 respectively. *President's Message, supra* note 5, at XII, XIX.

[169] *See* note 166 *supra*.
[170] Art. 7(2) of the European Convention contains a similar provision. None is found, however, in the American Convention.
[171] *See* text accompanying notes 168 & 170 *supra*.
[172] Jacobs, *supra* note 45, at 120.
[173] X v. Austria, [1965] Y.B. Eur. Conv. on Human Rights 190, 198 (Eur. Comm. of Human Rights).
[174] *Id.*
[175] Castberg, *supra* note 48, at 130.

interpreting article 9 of the American Convention, take this approach too remains to be seen. The various proscriptions against *ex post facto* offenses certainly offer the three systems an opportunity to develop a similar body of restraints against retroactive judicial as well as legislative action.

J. RIGHT TO PRIVACY (ARTICLE 12)

Article 3, it will be recalled once again, protects not only the right to life, but also the right to 'liberty and security'. The latter right is spelled out in article 9, which prohibits arbitrary arrest, detention or exile, and in article 12, which, while commonly thought to protect only the 'right to privacy', actually protects a number of 'somewhat disparate' rights.[176] *In toto* the latter reads: 'No one shall be subjected to arbitrary interference with his privacy, family, home or correspondence, nor to attacks upon his honour and reputation. Everyone has the right to the protection of the law against such interference or attacks.' The Political Covenant, in article 17, inserts the words 'or unlawful' before 'interference', and 'unlawful' before 'attacks', in the first sentence[177] and upgrades the second sentence into a separate paragraph,[178] but

[176] *Cf.* Jacobs, *supra* note 45, at 126 ('However, the fact that they are grouped together in the same Article strengthens the protection given by that Article, since each right is reinforced by its context. Thus, the right to respect for family life, the right to privacy, and the right to respect for the home may be read together as guaranteeing collectively more than the sum of their parts.')

It is interesting to contrast other opinions expressed during the debates on the draft Declaration. One member of the Third Committee, for instance, 'doubted whether article [12] was necessary at all; its substance had already been covered by article 3. If the liberty and security of the person had already been guaranteed, there was no need for detailed qualifications.' 3 U.N. GAOR, C.3 (119th mtg.) 309 (1948) (Mr. Macdonnell). 'However, it was rightly held that Art. 12 followed from Art. 3, but extended its scope and concretized its underlying ideas.' Robinson, *supra* note 50, at 53. On the other hand, another member

recommended that the article should be divided into three separate articles. The first article would ensure man's moral inviolability, which was based on two factors: a subjective factor, honour, and an objective factor, reputation. The second article would be expressly concerned with the principle of the inviolability of the home. The third article would guarantee not only inviolability of correspondence but would supplement that concept by the concept of free circulation of correspondence.

3 U.N. GAOR (116th mtg.) 275 (1948) (Mr. Cisneros). He subsequently withdrew his amendment to this effect and accepted the text of art. 12 that was adopted. 'He would have liked, however, to see the right to unhampered transmission of correspondence explicitly included. In the view of his delegation, that was implied in the text.' *Id.* at 310.

[177] While there is some doubt about the purpose and meaning of the first insertion, '[t]he insertion of "unlawful" before "attacks" was intended to meet the objection that, unless qualified, the clause might be construed in such a way as to stifle free expression of public opinion'. Annotation, *supra* note 97, at 47.

[178] The need for such a clause was questioned since article 2 of the draft covenant [*cf.* art. 8 of the Universal Declaration] already provided that each State party would undertake 'to take the necessary steps . . . to adopt such legislative or other measures as may be necessary to give effect to the rights recognized in this Covenant'. On the other hand, it was contended that the addition of the clause would not be superfluous. It was not enough to

otherwise it follows article 12 of the Universal Declaration *in haec verba*. While article 8 of the European Convention and article 11 of the American Convention substitute 'private life' in place of 'privacy', they both, especially the latter, reaffirm the general norms found in the Universal Declaration and the Political Covenant.[179]

In determining the meaning of privacy *strictu sensu*, a concept to date so amorphous as to preclude its acceptance into customary international law, limited help can be obtained from European Convention practice.[180] The European Convention, it has been suggested, should protect the individual from:

1. Attacks on physical or mental integrity or moral or intellectual freedom.

2. Attacks on honor and reputation and similar torts.

3. The use of name, identity, or likeness.

4. Being spied upon, watched, or harassed.

5. The disclosure of information protected by the duty of professional secrecy.[181]

Yet the practice by the European institutions thereunder—perhaps because article 8, unlike the other international human rights instruments, contains a paragraph legitimizing interference with the exercise of the right 'in accordance with the law and . . . in the interests of national security, public safety or the economic well-being of the country, for the prevention of disorder or crime, for the protection of health or morals, or for the protection of the rights and freedoms of others'[182]—has tended, in the opinion of this writer, to restrict rather

> recognize the right of everyone not to be subjected to arbitrary or unlawful attacks on his honour and reputation; his right to be protected by the law against such interferences or attacks must also be expressly recognized.   *Id.*

---

[179] Art. 8(1) of the European Convention omits protection of one's 'honour and reputation' while art. 8(2) specifically legitimizes certain 'interference by a public authority with the exercise of this right . . . ' *See* text at and accompanying note 182 *infra*. Art. 11 of the American Convention closely parallels art. 12 of the Universal Declaration and art. 17 of the Political Covenant.

[180] 'The scope of the protection of privacy under the Convention remains largely unexplored in the case-law . . . [T]hose applications which have raised the issue have often been treated on other grounds.' Jacobs, *supra* note 45, at 126. *See* Privacy and Human Rights (A. Robertson ed. 1973) [hereinafter cited as Privacy and Human Rights].

[181] Jacobs, *supra* note 45, at 126. *Quaere*: does the European Convention actually protect one against attacks on his honor or reputation? *See* text accompanying note 179 *supra*. *See also* Fawcett, *supra* note 44, at 186.

[182] Art. 8(2). No such provision appears in the Universal Declaration, the Political Covenant, or the American Convention. It has been argued, however, that the Universal Declaration (and, by analogy, the other two human rights instruments) should be interpreted as if it included such a provision. 'Art. 12 thus does not prohibit all interference with the privacy, etc. of the individual, but only prohibits "arbitrary" interference in the sense given in Art. 9 above. The reason is that interference was considered justifiable in the interests of national security, public health, and public morality.' Robinson, *supra* note 50, at 54.

than enlarge the scope of this right.[183] Many of these restrictive interpretations undoubtedly will be challenged[184] and other new issues involving the right to privacy raised in the future.[185]

While the potential scope of the right to privacy is thus still problematic, '[a] number of official and nonofficial clarificatory efforts suggest that "privacy" and "private life" may admit of considerable expansion of their historic references'.[186] Moreover, when one examines the interrelated proscriptions of article 12 of the Universal Declaration, 'which is broader than the technical concept of privacy and pregnant with potentiality for further expansion',[187] additional possibilities present themselves. It is to be hoped that the European Commission and the European Court of Human Rights will take a fresh look at old problems and exhibit a progressive attitude toward new ones. The U.N. Human Rights Committee and the Inter-American Commission, too, have an excellent opportunity to develop the cluster of interrelated norms found in article 17 of the Political Covenant and article 11 of the American Convention, for, as Professor McDougal has demonstrated at length, 'existing transnational prescriptions concerning privacy or private life are undergoing an expansion in general community expectation that will permit their application to many important emerging threats to civic order'.[188] Thus this area surely will be one of the frontiers of international human rights law in the foreseeable future.

K. RIGHT TO FREEDOM OF MOVEMENT (ARTICLE 13)

Although in the past freedom of movement was regarded in some quarters as not a fundamental, but rather a secondary, right, in the contemporary world there is no question but that it constitutes 'an important human right and one which [is] an essential part of the right

---

[183] For example, despite the fact that laws making homosexuality a criminal offence patently violate the right to respect for private life guaranteed by art. 8(1), '[t]he Commission has always declared these applications inadmissible as manifestly unfounded. It has ruled that Article 8(2) permits a high contracting party to legislate to make homosexuality a punishable offence and that the right to respect for private and family life may in a democratic society be made subject to interference in accordance with the law of the party in question for the protection of health or morals.' Privacy and Human Rights, *supra* note 180, at 85.

[184] 'It is merely a question of time before the Commission must take the new and more humane approach into consideration. Sooner or later punishment for homosexual relations will presumably be held contrary to the respect for private life required by Art. 8.' Castberg, *supra* note 48, at 145.

[185] *See generally* McDougal, *supra* note 4, at 840–56 *passim*.

[186] *Id.* at 841.

[187] *Id.* at 840.

[188] *Id.* at 844.

to personal liberty'.[189] Accordingly, the right finds a prominent place in article 13 of the Universal Declaration, which provides:

(1) Everyone has the right to freedom of movement within the borders of each State.

(2) Everyone has the right to leave any country, including his own, and to return to his country.

This article, along with article 12 of the Political Covenant, article 2 of Protocol No. 4 to the European Convention, and article 22(1)–(5) of the American Convention, thus speaks both to internal movement within a state and to transnational movement from and to a state. To date only the latter appears to have received much attention either at the United Nations[190] or in the literature.[191]

Turning first to internal movement, despite an attempt by the Soviet Union to restrict this right,[192] the Universal Declaration guarantees free internal movement in absolute terms to citizens and aliens alike.[193] Article 12(1) of the Political Covenant contains similar language, unfortunately qualified by article 12(3), permitting restrictions 'which are provided by law, are necessary to protect national security, public order (*ordre public*), public health or morals or the rights and freedoms of others . . . '[194] The European Convention and the American Convention take the same restrictive approach.[195] Although

---

[189] Annotation, *supra* note 97, at 38. *Accord*, Nanda, *The Right to Movement and Travel Abroad: Some Observations on the U.N. Deliberation*, 1 Denver J. Int'l L. & Pol'y 109 (1971) [hereinafter cited as Nanda] ('[I]t is one of those basic human rights, the universal recognition of which is likely to be a major accomplishment in accepting the importance of the individual as a subject of international law.')

[190] *See* Ingles, *Study of Discrimination in Respect of the Right of Everyone to Leave Any Country, Including His Own, and to Return to His Country*, U.N. Doc. E/CN.4/Sub. 2/220/Rev. 1 (1963).

[191] *See, e.g.*, The Right to Leave and to Return (K. Vasak & S. Liskofsky eds. 1976).

[192] 'An amendment was introduced by the USSR which provided for the granting of freedom of movement within the country and the right to leave the country only in accordance with the laws of the state. This amendment was rejected because the majority felt that this would mean the adaptation of the Declaration to the existing laws of every country instead of inducing the states to make their laws conform to the spirit of the Declaration, which, in other words, would permit the state to introduce any restriction of these rights it considers fit.' Robinson, *supra* note 50, at 55.

[193] *Id.* This right is subject, of course, to the general limitations of art. 29(2). *See* text at and following note 21 *supra*.

[194] *Cf.* Humphrey, *supra* note 9, at 534-35: 'The limitations permitted by the Covenant on Civil and Political Rights are much more far-reaching than those permitted by the Declaration . . . ; there are therefore greater possibilities of abuse and the legal problems involved in their interpretation are more difficult.' To support this view, the author calls attention to the fact that '[a]rticles that appeared in the Soviet press after the Soviet Union ratified the Covenants in September 1973 interpret the limitation clauses to permit the restrictions imposed on the enjoyment of human rights in that country'. *Id.* at 536, *citing* N.Y. Times, Sept. 28, 1973, § 1, at 1, col. 4. *See also* note 192 *supra*.

[195] *See* art. 2(1), (3), & (4) of Protocol No. 4 to the European Convention and art. 22(1), (3), & (4) of the American Convention. *See also* Castberg, *supra* note 48, at 184-85.

'internal exile' in the Soviet Union and similar practices in other states clearly run afoul of the Universal Declaration and probably of the other international human rights instruments as well, neither these nor other violations of the right to internal movement have attracted significant international condemnation. It would therefore be difficult to establish that such a right was recognized by customary international law.

Insofar as transnational movement—the right to leave and to return to a country—is concerned, once again the Universal Declaration is relatively straightforward, granting both citizens and aliens the right to leave any country, but limiting the right to return (obviously) to citizens of that country.[196] Article 12(2) and (3) of the Political Covenant also allows both citizens and aliens the right to leave, but subjects the right to the above-mentioned restrictions.[197] Both article 2(2) and (3) of Protocol No. 4 to the European Convention and article 22(2) and (3) of the American Convention take the Political Covenant's approach. Like the Universal Declaration, all three human rights instruments state that citizens shall not be deprived of the right to 'enter' their country.[198] Moreover, they make no provision for any restrictions on this right.[199] Thus, both the right to leave and the right to return seem well-established in conventional and perhaps even customary international human rights law. However, as Professor Nanda has noted, it is equally clear that they are rights that are 'difficult if not impossible to implement.'[200] *

In recent years, enforcement efforts in this area have been directed primarily at the Soviet Union and other Communist countries that deny or restrict the right of their citizens to emigrate.[201] Unhappily, the U.N. bodies charged with developing and enforcing this right have shown little enthusiasm when the question of its violation has been raised. The United States, through the Jackson–Vanik Amendment to the Trade Reform Act of 1974, which prohibits, *inter alia*, the granting of most-favored-nation treatment to nonmarket economy countries that infringe upon this right,[202] has tried with mixed results to bring

[196] Since aliens have no right to enter a country in the first place, absent a treaty, it necessarily follows that they have no right to return to it.

[197] *See* text at and accompanying note 194 *supra*.

[198] Art. 12(4) of the Political Covenant; art. 3(2) of Protocol No. 4 to the European Convention; art. 22(5) of the American Convention.

[199] Art. 12(4) of the Political Covenant, however, which provides that '[n]o one should be *arbitrarily* deprived of the right to enter his own country' (emphasis added), carries with it the implication that some such deprivations might be permissible. *See generally* text accompanying note 30 and at notes 36-40 *supra*.

[200] Nanda, *supra* note 189, at 115.

[201] On the plight of Soviet citizens (primarily Jews) seeking to leave that country, *see* T. Taylor, Courts of Terror: Soviet Criminal Justice and Jewish Emigration (1976).

[202] Trade Reform Act of 1974 § 402, 19 U.S.C. § 2432 (1976).

economic as well as political pressure to bear upon such states to secure their compliance with article 13(2) of the Universal Declaration and article 12(2) of the Political Covenant.[203] Sadly, its initiative has received little support from other states. Indeed, current proposals before UNCTAD, for a 'brain drain' tax, cut, indirectly if not directly, against the right to leave one's country.[204] Given these recent trends, one cannot be overly optimistic about the future status of this or any of the freedom of movement rights.

L.　RIGHT TO ASYLUM (ARTICLE 14)*

Traditionally, the 'right to asylum' meant the right of a state to grant asylum; only since World War II has it come to be thought of, at least in some quarters, as a right to be claimed by the individual.[205] Thus, article 14(1) of the Universal Declaration advances the proposition that '[e]veryone has the right to seek and to enjoy in other countries asylum from persecution'.[206] As Professor Humphrey points out, however, this approach to the problem is 'unsatisfactory',[207] since giving individuals the right to claim asylum has little meaning unless states are under some sort of obligation to grant it.[208] Clearly the drafters of the Universal Declaration had no intention of creating any

---

[203] The amendment intitially was relatively successful in the case of Rumania. *See* Note, *An Interim Analysis of the Effects of the Jackson-Vanik Amendment on Trade and Human Rights: The Romanian Example*, 8 J.L. & Pol'y Int'l Bus. 193 (1976). Subsequently, it appears to have had an impact upon Soviet emigration patterns as well. *See* N.Y. Times, Apr. 4, 1979, § 1, at 1, col. 1.

[204] *See* Pomp & Oldman, *Tax Measures in Response to the Brain Drain*, 20 Harv. Int'l L.J. 1 (1979).

[205] *See* A. Grahl-Madsen, Territorial Asylum 2 (1980); G. Goodwin-Gill, International Law and the Movement of Persons Between States 138 (1978):
> [T]he right of asylum is the right of the State to grant protection, which in turn is founded on the 'undisputed rule of international law' that every State has exclusive control over the individuals within its territory. Today, this exclusively jurisdictional approach has been mitigated somewhat by increased recognition of protection as a humanitarian duty. Progressive development in the laws of extradition, in the concept of political offence, in the notion of persecution, and in the principle of non-discrimination have all tended to improve the over-all lot of the individual. Nevertheless, it is still to be doubted whether there is any rule which obliges States to admit those fleeing from persecution . . .

[206] Art. 14(2) qualifies this right somewhat by adding that it 'may not be invoked in the case of prosecutions genuinely arising from non-political crimes or from acts contrary to the purposes and principles of the United Nations'.

[207] Humphrey, *supra* note 9, at 528. *Cf.* Robinson, *supra* note 50, at 58:
> Persecutees have the right to seek asylum in other countries. There is however no corollary to this human right in the form of an obligation on the part of the state; i.e., every state decides, at its own discretion, whether it will or will not admit a persecutee seeking asylum.

[208] Under customary international law, states are not required to grant asylum. *See* text accompanying note 205 *supra*. *See also* Morgenstern, *The Right of Asylum*, 26 Brit. Y.B. Int'l L. 327 (1949).

such obligation.[209] Moreover, the fact that neither the Political Covenant nor the European Convention mention the right to asylum indicates that the trend is against the acceptance, much less the strengthening, of even this limited right. Additionally, the American Convention, which in article 22(7) replicates the Universal Declaration by granting individuals 'the right to seek' asylum, underscores the limited nature of the right by providing explicitly that a state need grant asylum only 'in accordance with the legislation of the state and international conventions . . .' Thus it can be said, unhappily but without hesitation, that the right to asylum—if, indeed, it actually can be classified as a right[210]—is among the weakest of the rights considered in this chapter. Certainly it is not part of customary international law.

M. RIGHT TO A NATIONALITY (ARTICLE 15)

This article, after stating that '[e]veryone has the right to a nationality', provides that '[n]o one shall be arbitrarily deprived of his nationality nor denied the right to change his nationality'. Like article 14, it is 'a total innovation in the history of international law'.[211] It proclaims the right of everyone to have, retain, or change his nationality, 'without indicating or entailing action to implement it, except insofar as this follows from the relevance of the Declaration'.[212] Unfortunately, like article 14, the right protected in this article has received very little subsequent support from states and thus can be regarded as one of the weaker rights surveyed in this chapter.

Initially, it bears remembering, the draft Declaration did not provide for the right to a nationality; only the right to retain or change one's nationality was protected. As explained by Mrs. Roosevelt during the debates of the Third Committee, the draft article

was designed to make clear first, that individuals should not be subjected to action such as was taken during the Nazi régime in Germany when thousands had been stripped of their nationality by arbitrary government action; and, secondly, that no one should be forced to keep a nationality which he did not

---

[209] [E]very persecuted person should be able to enjoy the right of asylum. That right was indisputable, both from the humanitarian point of view and because to deny it would mean the abandonment of the essential principles of the declaration. That did not mean, however, that everyone had the right to obtain asylum in the country of his choice, although that country might not be prepared to receive him. Such a principle would be a flagrant violation of the sovereignty of the State concerned.
3 U.N. GAOR, C.3, (121st mtg.) 331 (1948) (Mr. Baroody).

[210] '[T]he principle concerned was not a right but a humanitarian practice which the State concerned was free to accept or to reject.' *Id.* at 332 (Mr. Plaza).

[211] Robinson, *supra* note 50, at 60.

[212] *Id.*

want and that he should not therefore be denied the right to change his nationality.[213]

In view of the existence of hundreds of thousands of stateless persons, it was urged that the draft article 'did not cover sufficient ground',[214] so an amendment was adopted inserting the first clause guaranteeing everyone a nationality.[215] Since numerous rights under international as well as national law depend upon one's having a nationality,[216] article 15 can only be viewed as a commendable first step in the effort to eradicate statelessness and thus offer all individuals access to such rights.

Article 15 appears to have been the highwater mark in this international effort, for the Political Covenant, while providing in article 24(3) that '[e]very child has the right to acquire a nationality', contains no general nationality provision. Moreover, on the regional level, the European Convention offers even less protection on this score, since it 'confers no right to a nationality as such . . .'[217] The American Convention, however, basically adopts article 15 of the Universal Declaration in its article 20(1) and (3), adding for good measure in article 20(2) a 'safety net' provision to the effect that '[e]very person has the right to the nationality of the state in whose territory he was born if he does not have the right to any other nationality'. This provision is modeled after article 1(1) of the Convention on the Reduction of Statelessness[218] which was drafted in the 1950s when the problem of statelessness was felt more acutely. It is an indication of the unwillingness of states to come to grips with the problem of statelessness that by 1983 only a handful had ratified it.[219] Until more do, and until the prescriptions of article 15 receive wider and stronger support, the 'right to a nationality' will remain a relatively meaningless right and certainly not one recognized by customary international law.

[213] 3 U.N. GAOR, C.3 (123d mtg.) 352 (1948).

[214] *Id*. at 348 (M. Cassin).

[215] *Id*. at 359.

[216] *See generally* McDougal, Lasswell & Chen, *Nationality and Human Rights: The Protection of the Individual in External Arenas*, 83 Yale L.J. 900 (1974), *revised and reprinted in* McDougal, *supra* note 4, at 861.

[217] Jacobs, *supra* note 45, at 186.

[218] Convention on the Reduction of Statelessness, *adopted* Aug. 30, 1961, *entered into force* Dec. 13, 1975, U.N. Doc. A/CONF. 9/15 (1961).

[219] As of Mar. 10, 1982, only 10 states are parties to the convention. They are Australia, Austria, Canada, Costa Rica, Denmark, the Federal Republic of Germany, Ireland, Norway, Sweden, and the United Kingdom. 'It is especially important that wider acceptance be accorded to the Convention on the Reduction of Statelessness so that it can command wide application.' McDougal, *supra* note 4, at 941 n. 416.

N.   RIGHT TO MARRY AND FOUND A FAMILY
(ARTICLE 16)

This article, dealing with the right to marry and to found a family, provides that:

(1) Men and women of full age, without any limitation due to race, nationality or religion, have the right to marry and to found a family. They are entitled to equal rights as to marriage, during marriage and at its dissolution.

(2) Marriage shall be entered into only with the free and full consent of the intending spouses.

(3) The family is the natural and fundamental group unit of society and is entitled to protection by society and the State.

All of article 16's provisions find their counterparts in article 23 of the Political Covenant, which adds a clause to the effect that, in case of dissolution of a marriage, 'provision shall be made for the necessary protection of any children'.[220]

As the *travaux préparatoires* of the Universal Declaration make clear, the key provisions of article 16 are the ones mandating that marriages be entered into voluntarily[221] and that the partners thereto be treated on the basis of absolute equality.[222] Similar concerns were expressed during the drafting of article 23 of the Political Covenant.[223] Surprisingly, neither concern is reflected in article 12 of the European Convention, a crabbed and retrogressive provision blandly stating that '[m]en and women of marriageable age have the right to marry and to found a family, according to the national laws governing the exercise of this right'.[224] The American Convention, on the other hand, not only guarantees all the rights found in the Universal Declaration and the Political Covenant, but in article 17(5) also requires that '[t]he law

---

[220] Art. 23(4).

[221] The reason for specifying that marriage might be contracted only with the full consent of the intending spouses was that the custom still existed whereby parents, guardians or others arranged marriages without the consent of the spouses. Marriage was a basic right; it should not be negotiated like a treaty or a business deal.
3 U.N. GAOR, C.3 (124th mtg.) 363 (1948) (M. Cassin).

[222] [T]he idea of absolute equality between men and women as to marriage which had been accepted by all delegations, [should] be specifically expressed, for the nations and individuals should be able to rely not only on the spirit but also on the letter of the declaration. There were countries which had not yet granted women absolute equality from the legal point of view. The ultimate goal of article [16] should therefore be to influence governments to revise their legislation, if necessary, in order to abolish any disability affecting women in connexion with marriage.
Id. at 369 (Miss Bernardino).

[223] Annotation, *supra* note 97, at 57-59 *passim*.

[224] For a comparison of the Political Covenant and the European Convention on this point in which the latter comes out a distant second, *see* Robertson, *supra* note 33, at 34-35. *See also* Castberg, *supra* note 48, at 139-41; Fawcett, *supra* note 44, at 224-27; Jacobs, *supra* note 45, at 161-64.

shall recognize equal rights for children born out of wedlock and those born in wedlock'.[225]

Here, even more than in the case of the right to a nationality,[226] special subject-matter treaties have been promulgated to reinforce the norms found in the Universal Declaration and the general international human rights instruments. The Convention on Consent to Marriage, Minimum Age for Marriage, and Registration of Marriages,[227] for instance, replicates article 16(2) of the Universal Declaration, article 23(3) of the Political Covenant, and article 17(3) of the American Convention by providing, in article 1(1), that '[n]o marriage shall be legally entered into without the full and free consent of both parties . . .' Article 16(1)(b) of the Convention on the Elimination of All Forms of Discrimination Against Women[228] also repeats this requirement. Article 16(1)(c) of this important Convention also embraces the principle of absolute equality in marriage found in article 16(1) of the Universal Declaration, article 23(4) of the Political Covenant, and article 17(4) of the American Convention. Thus the two key rights found in article 16 of the Universal Declaration have gained widespread general and special support over the years, at least on the normative level. Given the fact that this article touches upon some of the currently most sensitive areas in all societies, however, it remains to be seen whether and to what extent these rights, often perceived to be controversial, are widely implemented. Surely it would be difficult to establish that they reflect customary international law at this time.

O.   RIGHT TO OWN PROPERTY (ARTICLE 17)

Among the more important rights which individuals traditionally have enjoyed is the right to own property. This right is recognized in

[225] This provision, plus the provision in art. 17(4) (similar to provisions in art. 16(1) of the Universal Declaration and especially art. 23(4) of the Political Covenant) that '[t]he States Parties shall take appropriate steps to ensure the equality of rights and the adequate balancing of responsibilities of the spouses as to marriage, during marriage, and in the event of its dissolution', admittedly exceed the standards of U.S. law. 'Both paragraphs state goals towards which United States law is moving, but neither goal has been fully achieved.' *President's Message, supra* note 5, at XXI. Thus President Carter, in urging the Senate to give its advice and consent to the American Convention's ratification, recommended that it attach the following statement: 'The United States considers the provisions of paragraphs (4) and (5) of Article 17 as goals to be achieved progressively rather than through immediate implementation.' *Id.*

Surprisingly, the President recommended no such statement with respect to art. 23(4) of the Political Covenant (or, for that matter, to art. 24(1) of the Political Covenant), which presents the same 'problem' as art. 17(5) of the American Convention. *See id.* at XIII.

[226] *See* text at notes 211-19 *supra.*

[227] Convention on Consent to Marriage, Minimum Age for Marriage and Registration of Marriages, *opened for signature* Dec. 10, 1962, *entered into force* Dec. 9, 1964, 521 U.N.T.S. 231. As of Mar. 10, 1982, 32 states were parties to the Convention.

[228] *See* note 3 *supra.* As of Mar. 10, 1982, 35 states were parties to this Convention. For useful background information on the Convention and the problems at which it is aimed, *see* McDougal, *supra* note 4, at 633-43.

the Universal Declaration, article 17(1) of which states that '[e]veryone
has the right to own property alone as well as in association with
others'.[229] Article 17(2), aimed primarily at the question of
expropriation,[230] guarantees that '[n]o one shall be arbitrarily deprived of his property'.[231] These provisions, which reflect traditional
international law, find no counterpart in the Political Covenant,[232] an
omission that underscores the international community's decreasing
concern over the years with the protection of private property
rights.[233] Yet article 1 of Protocol No. 1 to the European Convention
accords protection to property rights, as does article 21(1) of the
American Convention. Moreover, article 21(2) of the latter
Convention specifically states that '[n]o one shall be deprived of his
property except upon payment of just compensation . . . ' Thus one
may conclude that the right to own property generally is recognized in
the major international human rights instruments; the silence of the
Political Covenant on this score, however, obviously weakens the
consensus underpinning the customary international norm.[234]

Although many speeches have been made and much ink spilt over
this question, the one principal fighting issue remains whether and to
what extent states must compensate foreign owners of nationalized
property.[235] Until relatively recently most commentators assumed that

[229] 'It was generally agreed that the ownership of property was subject to the laws of the
country concerned, but there seemed no need to include such a provision in the declaration.' 3
U.N. GAOR, C.3 (126th mtg.) 382 (1948) (Mrs. Corbett). *Cf.* text accompanying note 233 *infra.*

[230] 'The second paragraph deals with expropriation. It is as general as the first, and leaves as
much room for the application of national law.' Robinson, *supra* note 50, at 63.

[231] On just what constitutes an arbitrary deprivation of property, *see* text accompanying note
40 *supra.*

[232] Starr, *International Protection of Human Rights and the United Nations Covenants*, 1967
Wis. L. Rev. 863, 866. For the reasons leading to the omission of the right to own property from
the Political Covenant, *see* Annotation, *supra* note 97, at 65-67.

[233] One striking discrepancy between the original draft [Covenant] and the general law of
nations on the treatment of aliens is its failure to protect private ownership of property—
in contrast with Article 17 of the Universal Declaration of Human Rights, which expressly
recognizes such right of ownership. The general principles of international law do, or did,
contain principles protecting property interests, within certain limits [,] but international
law does not say that a state must allow aliens or anyone else to acquire property in the
first place.
Freeman, *Human Rights and the Rights of Aliens*, 45 Proc. Am. Soc'y Int'l L. 120, 124-25
(1951). *Cf.* text accompanying note 229 *supra.*

[234] It also has occasioned Senator Helms to propose an amendment to the Political Covenant
in the form of the text of art. 17 of the Universal Declaration. *See International Human Rights
Treaties, Hearings Before the Senate Comm. on Foreign Relations*, 96th Cong., 1st Sess. 6–10
(1979). President Carter already had recommended a similar declaration with respect to arts.
2(3) and 25 of the International Covenant on Economic, Social and Cultural Rights, *adopted*
Dec. 16, 1966, *entered into force* Jan. 3, 1976, G.A. Res. 2200, 21 U.N. GAOR, Supp. (No. 16)
49, U.N. Doc. A/6316 (1966). *See President's Message, supra* note 5, at IX.

[235] *See generally* 1-3 The Valuation of Nationalized Property in International Law (R. Lillich
ed. 1972-75). *See also* Dawson & Weston, '*Prompt, Adequate and Effective': A Universal
Standard of Compensation?*, 30 Fordham L. Rev. 727 (1962).

General Assembly Resolution 1803 on Permanent Sovereignty over Natural Resources,[236] which provides that in case of nationalization the foreign owner shall be paid 'appropriate compensation, in accordance with the rules in force in the state taking such measures in the exercise of its sovereignty and in accordance with international law', represented a reasonably accurate reflection of customary international law. After nearly a decade of claims to a 'New International Economic Order', manifested in numerous other General Assembly resolutions, especially the Charter of Economic Rights and Duties of States,[237] it now appears fairly certain that '[t]he principles so formulated [in Resolution 1803] cannot be relied on in a dispute between capital-importing and capital-exporting states'.[238] Just what norm governing compensation in such cases is emerging remains unclear. In the opinion of this writer, it should require—at a minimum— that foreign owners should not be deprived of their property arbitrarily,[239] and that when their property is taken appropriate compensation should be forthcoming.[240] One may argue, too, that this norm also should apply when the property involved is owned by a citizen of the nationalizing state.[241]

P. FREEDOM OF THOUGHT, CONSCIENCE, AND RELIGION (ARTICLE 18)

One of the oldest internationally recognized human rights,[242] the right

---

[236] G.A. Res. 1803, 17 U.N. GAOR, Supp. (No. 17) 15, U.N. Doc. A/5217 (1962). *See* Schwebel, *The Story of the U.N.'s Declaration on Permanent Sovereignty over Natural Resources,* 49 A.B.A.J. 463 (1963); Gess, *Permanent Sovereignty over Natural Resources,* 13 Int'l & Comp. L.Q. 398 (1964).

[237] G.A. Res. 3281, 29 U.N. GAOR, Supp. (No. 31) 50, U.N. Doc. A/9631 (1974). *See* Brower & Tepe, *The Charter of Economic Rights and Duties of States: A Reflection or Rejection of International Law?* 9 Int'l Law. 295 (1975); Rozental, *The Charter of Economic Rights and Duties of States and the New International Economic Order,* 16 Va. J. Int'l L. 309 (1976); White, *A New International Economic Order, id.* at 323.

[238] O'Keefe, *The United Nations and Permanent Sovereignty over Natural Resources,* 8 J. World Trade L. 239, 282 (1974); *see* Muller, *Compensation for Nationalization: A North-South Dialogue,* 19 Colum. J. Transnat'l L. 351 (1981).

[239] For an excellent analysis of the concept of arbitrariness in this area, *see* Murphy, *Limitations upon the Power of a State to Determine the Amount of Compensation Payable to an Alien upon Nationalization,* in 3 The Valuation of Nationalized Property in International Law 49, 56-62 (R. Lillich ed. 1975).

[240] *See* Lillich, *The Valuation of Nationalized Property in International Law: Toward a Consensus or More 'Rich Chaos'?,* in *id.* at 183, 195-204.

[241] *See* text accompanying note 234 *supra. But see* text accompanying notes 229 & 233 *supra.*

[242] 'Freedom of religion is indeed the oldest of the internationally recognized human freedoms, the one therefore with which the international community has had the longest experience.' Humphrey, ch. 5 *infra,* at 176. Although discussed at length in his chapter, Humphrey acknowledges that this right is more civil than political. *Id.* at 172. Whether the right—no matter how old or how characterized—is now part of customary international law is doubtful. *See* text at note 251 *infra.*

of religious freedom finds recognition in this article,[243] which provides:

Everyone has the right to freedom of thought, conscience and religion; this right includes freedom to change his religion or belief, and freedom, either alone or in community with others and in public or private, to manifest his religion or belief in teaching, practice, worship and observance.

While the *travaux préparatoires* reveal that little attention was paid to the protection of the freedom of nonbelievers, '[s]uch freedom seems to be implicit in the words "religion" or "belief" . . . '[244]

The gist of article 18 finds expression in article 18(1) of the Political Covenant, although the freedom 'to change' has been replaced by the freedom 'to have or to adopt a religion or belief', a shift which appears to be one more of verbiage than of substance.[245] Other provisions state that no one shall be subjected to coercion which would impair his freedom of religion, that religious freedoms may be subjected only to certain limitations prescribed by law, and that parents may ensure the religious education of their children in conformity with their own convictions.[246]

Articles 9 and 12 of the European and American Conventions respectively are an interesting pastiche of provisions found in the Universal Declaration and the Political Covenant. Article 9(1) of the former basically restates article 18 of the Universal Declaration, retain-

[243] Commentary upon this article focuses almost exclusively upon religious freedom. Freedom of 'thought' and 'conscience', closely connected with freedom of 'religion', are read as supporting the latter rather than as separate concepts worthy of independent analysis and development. Since freedom of thought is a very broad concept which actually includes freedom of conscience as well as freedom of religion, 3 U.N. GAOR, C.3 (127th mtg.) 397 (1948) (Mr. Chang), it would seem that most commentators have been viewing art. 18 from the wrong end of the telescope. *But see* Robinson, *supra* note 50, at 64, who rightly notes that '[t]his article deals not only with the religious but also with the philosophical, cultural, scientific, and political aspects of freedom of thought'. For purposes of this chapter the present writer will limit his analysis of article 18 (and corresponding provisions of other related international human rights instruments) to freedom of religion, reserving the right to treat freedom of thought and conscience as independent concepts in the future.

[244] Clark, *The United Nations and Religious Freedom*, 11 N.Y.U. J. Int'l L. & Pol. 197, 201 (1978) [hereinafter cited as Clark].

[245] The freedom to change one's religion or belief had been challenged, even during the debates on the Universal Declaration, by certain Islamic states who claimed that it 'unduly favored missionary activities'. *Id.* at 200. Its omission from the Political Covenant appears insignificant, however, in view of statements by representatives of such states that this freedom was implicit in the guarantee of religious freedom. 15 U.N. GAOR, C.3 (1023d mtg.) 206 (1960) (Mr. Baroody).

It is interesting to note that some states 'thought that, since the article as a whole dealt with freedom of "thought", "conscience" and "religion", any elaboration of freedom of "religion" without a corresponding elaboration of freedom of "thought" and "conscience" would make the article *somewhat unbalanced*'. Annotation, *supra* note 97, at 48 (emphasis added). *Cf.* Humphrey, ch. 5 *infra*, at 178; text accompanying note 243 *supra*.

[246] Art. 18(2), (3), & (4).

ing the right to change one's religion,[247] while article 9(2) contains a limitations clause similar to the one found in article 18(3) of the Political Covenant.[248] Article 12(1) of the American Convention also essentially reproduces article 18 of the Universal Declaration; article 12(2) restates a noncoercion clause similar to the one contained in article 18(2) of the Political Covenant; article 12(3), like article 18(3) of the Political Covenant and article 9(2) of the European Convention, contains a limitations provision; and article 12(4), like article 18(4) of the Political Covenant, guarantees parents the right to provide for the religious education of their children.

Here, as in the case of the right to a nationality under article 15 and the right to marry and found a family under article 16, the high level of generality in the relevant provisions of the international human rights instruments has made apparent the need for a special instrument designed to eliminate religious intolerance. The attempt by the United Nations to draft either a declaration or a convention, going back two decades, 'is a tale punctuated by hypocrisy, procedural jockeying, and false starts'.[249] Only in 1981 was the General Assembly able to adopt a Declaration on the Elimination of All Forms of Intolerance and of Discrimination based on Religion or Belief.[250] Whether a draft convention restating its norms and containing effective enforcement procedures can be completed by the end of this decade is problematical. Thus, while it is disappointing to have to end this section with a whimper rather than a bang, one is forced to acknowledge that the right of religious freedom, like the other two rights mentioned at the outset of this paragraph, is one of the weakest—from the point of view of its recognition and its enforcement—of all the rights contained in articles 3–18 of the Universal Declaration.[251]

[247] *See* Robertson, *supra* note 33, at 30.

[248] *Compare* art. 2 of Protocol No. 1 to the European Convention, which provides, *inter alia*, that 'the State shall respect the right of parents to ensure . . . education and teaching in conformity with their own religious and philosophical convictions', *with* art. 18(4) of the Political Covenant. For discussions of the small amount of practice under this provision of the European Convention, *see* Castberg, *supra* note 48, at 146-49; Fawcett, *supra* note 44, at 198-209, 352-54; Jacobs, *supra* note 45, at 143-50, 169-77. *But see* the recent decision of the European Court of Human Rights, *supra* note 84, which relied upon art. 2 of Protocol No. 1 rather than art. 3 of the European Convention to condemn the use of the tawse in Scottish schools.

[249] Clark, *supra* note 244, at 220. *See also* Claydon, *The Treaty Protection of Religious Rights: U.N. Draft Convention on the Elimination of All Forms of Intolerance and of Discrimination Based on Religion or Belief*, 12 Santa Clara Law. 403 (1972); Neff, *An Evolving International Norm of Religious Freedom: Problems and Prospects*, 7 Cal. W. Int'l L.J. 543 (1977). As usual, the most comprehensive study of the problem may be found in McDougal, *supra* note 4, at 653-89.

[250] G.A. Res. 36/55, U.N. Doc. A/RES/36/55 (1981).

[251] *See* note 242 *supra*.

II. Teaching Suggestions

To paraphrase the late Justice Frankfurter, pedagogical discussions always have left this writer cold.[252] Yet, given the range and complexity of the civil rights surveyed in the previous section, the author of a chapter in a volume intended to encourage the teaching of the international law of human rights has an obligation to offer some guidance as to what rights should be emphasized and how they should be taught. Accordingly, recognizing that there are as many ways to teach this subject matter as there are to skin the proverbial cat, this writer will offer his own highly personalized preferences in the section that follows.

Preliminarily, focusing on how the rights should be taught, the writer has a strong preference for a problem-oriented as opposed to a lecture approach.[253] Moreover, given the relatively nascent state of international human rights law and the inadequacies of existing procedures for enforcing it, he believes it more important to stress process—the implementation of such law—over substance. Thus, in his own international human rights course—a three hour, one semester offering comprising forty-two classroom hours—he takes up twelve separate but interrelated problems, primarily from the procedural perspective.[254] While most of these problems directly raise one or more issues of substantive human rights law, collectively they do not constitute a comprehensive map even of the civil rights guaranteed individuals, much less their political or economic, social, and cultural rights. Time constraints simply do not permit more than a brief mention of most of these rights even in a full semester course. How, then, should one choose the civil rights to be taken up and how should one single out those rights worthy of in-depth treatment? These questions will be considered first in the context of a course running a full semester; then brief mention will be made of how to introduce students to civil rights via a 'mini module' when only a few hours are available for their coverage.

A. CIVIL RIGHTS IN AN INTERNATIONAL HUMAN RIGHTS LAW COURSE

In determining which civil rights to cover in a full semester course, considerable help may be derived from the relevant international human rights instruments themselves. Although neither the Universal Declaration nor the Political Covenant directly rank human rights in

[252] 'I've always been left cold by curricular discussions. Oh yes, I know they are important, but not very.' Felix Frankfurter Reminisces 170 (H. Phillips ed. 1960).
[253] *See Preface* to Lillich & Newman, *supra* note 84, at ix-x.
[254] *Id.* at vii-viii.

any order of priority, some guidance as to the international community's ranking of civil rights may be gleaned indirectly from the list of rights which article 4(2) of the Political Covenant makes nonderogable, *i.e.*, which may not be suspended by a state even in time of public emergency.[255] They are as follows (article references are to the Political Covenant):

1. The right to life (article 6);
2. The prohibition of slavery and servitude (article 8(1)(2));
3. The prohibition of torture and cruel, inhuman, or degrading treatment or punishment (article 7);
4. The right to legal recognition (article 16);
5. The prohibition of *ex post facto* offenses (article 15(1)); and
6. The right to freedom of thought, conscience, and religion (article 18).[256]

Keeping the 'preferred' status of the above rights in mind, a brief survey of the rights mentioned in the previous section and the controversial issues they raise may suggest to the reader an order of priority for teaching them; at the very least, it will reveal the preferences of this writer.

The right to life, liberty, and security of person—found in article 3 of the Universal Declaration and replicated in articles 6(1) and 9(1) of the Political Covenant—certainly is the basic civil right and deserves extended consideration. Indeed, most civil rights fall within this rubric. Under the core right of life, which has achieved the status of *jus cogens*, the questions of capital punishment, voluntary euthanasia, and abortion may be discussed. Here as elsewhere the brevity of the Universal Declaration should be compared with the general expansiveness of the Political Covenant; moreover, here and throughout, both instruments should be contrasted with the American Convention and European Convention and with U.S. constitutional law.[257]

The right to liberty, a highly generalized right, is spelled out in many separate articles to be discussed below, *e.g.*, article 4 of the Universal Declaration and article 8(1)(2) of the Political Covenant, which proscribe slavery and servitude. The right to security is found primarily in article 5 of the Universal Declaration and article 7 of the Political Covenant, which forbid torture and cruel, inhuman, or degrading

---

[255] *See generally* text at and accompanying notes 26-30 *supra*.

[256] Also made non-derogable by article 4(2) is the prohibition against imprisonment for failure to fulfil a contractual obligation (article 11). This right, not mentioned in the Universal Declaration, is so much less important than the other non-derogable rights set out in the text that it can be omitted from all but the most comprehensive surveys of civil rights.

[257] For a somewhat outdated but still useful starting point in making the last contrast, *see* Bitker, *Application of the United Nations' Universal Declaration of Human Rights Within the United States*, 21 De Paul L. Rev. 337 (1971). *See also President's Message*, note 5 *supra*. *See generally* Henkin, ch. 2 *supra*.

treatment or punishment, plus article 9 of the Universal Declaration and article 9 of the Political Covenant, which prohibit arbitrary arrest or detention. These latter rights, from which states may derogate in time of emergency, nevertheless are very important ones and worthy of thorough examination. International practice, as exemplified by the decisions of the U.N. Human Rights Committee,[258] is slowly defining the guarantees available to persons arrested or detained on criminal charges: at any given moment a prominent political dissident is likely to be under arrest or detention in some state, whose plight will serve as a useful case study.

Slavery and servitude—forbidden by article 4 of the Universal Declaration and article 8(1) and (2) of the Political Covenant—are relatively well-defined concepts and their prohibition, here as well as in other international human rights instruments, now can be said to represent *jus cogens*. Forced or compulsory labour, not mentioned in the Universal Declaration but proscribed by article 8(3) of the Political Covenant, is another matter, as attested to by the fact that states may derogate from article 8(3) but not from article 8(1) and (2). To determine just what falls within this prohibition one should start with article 8(3), which actually permits both hard labour as punishment for a crime and four other types of work or service, and proceed to other situations where a state seeks to compel persons to work for general economic reasons. The questions of 'antiparasite' laws and whether they run afoul of the prohibition of forced labour should serve to generate a lively classroom debate.[259]

The prohibition against torture and cruel, inhuman, or degrading treatment or punishment—contained in article 5 of the Universal Declaration and repeated in article 7 of the Political Covenant—also is a basic civil right which has achieved at least the status of customary international law and probably that of *jus cogens*. Here one should consider what state-sanctioned conduct constitutes torture and what conduct falls within the balance of the prohibition. The practice under the European Convention is especially helpful in posing this question.[260] Also worth pointing out is the fact that the prohibition covers not only affirmative acts by state officials, but also their failure to provide minimal conditions of detention, adequate medical treatment, and the like. That the prohibition is not limited to situations involving actual physical abuse can be illustrated graphically by the decision of the European Commission to the effect that discrimination based upon race may constitute degrading treatment.[261] Also worthy of emphasis

[258] *See* notes 132 & 142 *supra*.
[259] *See* text at and accompanying notes 63 & 64 *supra*.
[260] *See* text at and accompanying notes 72-80 *supra*.
[261] *See* text at and accompanying note 83 *supra*.

is the fact that, contrary to popular belief, the prohibition extends well beyond the field of criminal law and prisons into areas of the civil law where state-sponsored facilities are involved. Thus it potentially has great impact in many cases where children, the sick, the old, or the handicapped are, at least figuratively speaking, wards of the state. In short, the study of this prohibition illustrates how the international community is attempting to cope with the evil of torture as it tradition-ally has been defined, while at the same time it shows how a body of law going well beyond the prohibition of torture is in the process of development.

The right to legal recognition, guaranteed by article 6 of the Universal Declaration and article 16 of the Political Covenant, origin-ally was thought to be an important civil right, as its status as a nonderogable one indicates. Its extreme generality, however, coupled with the fact that it rarely has been invoked in practice, makes it a difficult right to teach, although exploration of its meaning, scope, and potential uses should be encouraged. Eminently teachable, though, are the presumption of innocence and the prohibition of *ex post facto* criminal laws found in article 11 of the Universal Declaration and articles 14(2) and 15(1) of the Political Covenant respectively. In addition to discussing what actions may impinge upon the presumption of innocence and what the parameters of the *ex post facto* proscription are, attention should also be paid to why the Political Covenant makes only the latter right nonderogable: surely it will come as a surprise to persons being exposed to international human rights law for the first time to learn that states may sidestep the presumption of innocence norm in cases of public emergency, just the sort of situation where, one would have thought, it is most needed to protect individuals from governmental excesses. Lastly, the nonderogable right to freedom of thought, conscience, and religion—guaranteed by article 18 of the Universal Declaration and fleshed out by article 18 of the Political Covenant—deserves adequate treatment. Not only should the mean-ing of religious freedom be plumbed, but the inordinate delay of the international community in elaborating norms against religious dis-crimination—in contrast to its quick codifications in the area of racial discrimination—should be examined. Also worthy of mention are the heretofore overlooked possibilities for invoking the freedom of 'thought' and freedom of 'conscience' provisions in article 18.[262]

In addition to the above mentioned civil rights, many of which now reflect customary international law and some of which constitute *jus cogens*, other civil rights discussed in the previous section should be covered in any full semester international human rights law course,

[262] *See* text accompanying note 243 *supra*.

including especially (references are to the Universal Declaration): the right to a fair trial (article 10); the right to freedom of movement (article 13); and the right to own property (article 17). Other rights mentioned in the previous section which warrant briefer comment—either because they are ambiguous, meaningless, or couched in such generalized language as to be difficult of application—are the right to equality before the law and to nondiscrimination in its application (article 7); the right to a remedy (article 8); the right of asylum (article 14); the right to a nationality (article 15); and the right to marry and found a family (article 16). Depending upon time constraints and the interests of the instructor, these rights can even be omitted from coverage altogether.

B.   CIVIL RIGHTS AS A 'MINIMODULE'

If only a few hours are available to the instructor to introduce, cover, and assess the civil rights of individuals guaranteed by international human rights law, he or she is indeed on the horns of a dilemma: to consider even one right adequately would take up the available time, leaving all other rights uncovered; on the other hand, trying to cover all the rights surveyed in this chapter would necessitate treatment so superficial as to be almost pointless. The dilemma can be handled, practically if not entirely satisfactorily, by having the students read the first section of this chapter for coverage purposes, then devoting the available classroom time exclusively to one particular right. This right might vary, depending upon the interests of the instructor and the student composition of the class, as well as upon the significance of the right, the extent to which it currently is at issue, and whether its application and future development are viewed as matters of great importance. For his own part, this writer would select the prohibition of torture and cruel, inhuman, or degrading treatment or punishment.[263]

Using, as a case study, *Filartiga v. Peña-Irala*, he first would raise the question of how pre-Charter international law regarded torture. Basically, of course, traditional international law permitted a state to treat its nationals as it saw fit. While a body of law grew up regarding the treatment of aliens, which rendered a state responsible to an alien's state for any maltreatment (*e.g.*, torture) the alien received at the hands of agents or officials of the respondent state, international law afforded no similar protection to nationals of that state. There was the doctrine of humanitarian intervention, of course, which theoretically allowed states to intervene in a state when its treatment of its nationals

---

[263] The discussion and authorities relevant to this exceptionally important basic human right may be found at and accompanying notes 65-86 *supra*. More specific citations here or throughout the rest of this section are thought unnecessary.

'shocked the conscience of mankind', but the threshold of shock was so high and the willingness of states to invoke the doctrine so low that it offered little comfort to most victims of oppressive regimes.[264] Thus, before 1945, not only did most torturers go unpunished, but their acts generally did not even violate international law.

After establishing the above state of the law in 1945 for 'benchmark' purposes, the present writer would raise the extent to which the U.N. Charter, an international treaty binding on member states, removed the way states treated their own nationals (*e.g.*, whether they tortured them or not) from the area of 'domestic jurisdiction' to one of 'international concern'. The prohibition of torture found in article 5 of the Universal Declaration then would be explored, both for the light it sheds on a state's obligations under the Charter and for the extent to which it now reflects customary international law. Similar prohibitions of torture found in the Political Covenant and in the European Convention and American Convention—all raised by counsel in *Filartiga*—next would be examined, both for the legal effect they have on states parties thereto and for the contribution they have made to the development of a customary international law norm that most likely constitutes *jus cogens*. Here comparisons with the normative status of other civil rights guaranteed by the Universal Declaration would be made.

Since the acts that the defendant allegedly committed in *Filartiga* clearly constitute torture by anyone's definition, the case can be used only as a starting point in determining the extent of the prohibition. This writer thus would introduce the emerging practice of the U.N. Human Rights Committee with respect to article 7 of the Political Covenant, as well as the practice of the European Commission and Court and the Inter-American Commission under the European Convention and American Convention respectively. The European practice would be stressed heavily, since it not only is the most elaborate at present but it also explores the parameters of 'tortures' as well as providing the best guidance as to what is 'cruel, inhuman or degrading treatment or punishment'.

Finally, given the importance of the process aspects of the subject matter, the present writer would point out the atypical nature of the remedy invoked in *Filartiga*; survey the remedies available under 'customary international law' (*e.g.*, before the U.N. Sub-Commission on the Prevention of Discrimination and the Protection of Minorities and the U.N. Commission on Human Rights), the Political Covenant (*e.g.*, before the U.N. Human Rights Committee), the European Convention, and the American Convention; and stress the need for the

---

[264] *See generally* Humanitarian Intervention and the United Nations (R. Lillich ed. 1973).

inclusion of effective enforcement mechanisms in the convention proscribing torture now being drafted by the United Nations. This discussion also would be used to introduce the question of the enforcement of international human rights law generally. Ending the 'minimodule' on this note not only would provide some balance between the 'substantive' and the 'procedural' law, but also would underscore the fact that international human rights, like all rights, are relatively meaningless insofar as individuals are concerned unless backed by effective remedies.

III. Syllabus

The following brief syllabus, based upon the analysis contained in the first section and the teaching suggestions found in the first part of the above section, is designed to give the prospective instructor of a course on the international law of human rights an overview of the basic civil rights guaranteed by articles 3-18 of the Universal Declaration. It is grouped, somewhat artificially, under two headings entitled 'Substantive Rights' and 'Procedural Rights'. Since, as mentioned in the previous section,[265] time constraints preclude a comprehensive survey of all these rights—save perhaps in a special seminar focusing exclusively upon them—the syllabus should be regarded as more of a checklist for the instructor than an actual teaching tool. As such, though, it should have some useful value, even (or especially) for instructors like this writer who prefer to stress process over substance when teaching international human rights law.[266]

    I.   *Substantive Rights*
        A. The Right to Life.
            1. General Observations.
            2. Specific Issues.
                a. Capital Punishment.
                b. Voluntary Euthanasia.
                c. Abortion.
        B. The Right to Liberty.
            1. Prohibition of Slavery, Servitude, or Forced Labour.
            2. Right to Freedom of Thought, Conscience, and Religion.
            3. Right to Freedom of Movement and Residence.
            4. Right to Marry and to Found a Family.

---

[265] *See* text following note 254 *supra*.

[266] As a checklist it does not encompass such issues as the creation, application, and present status of the various international human rights norms listed. These and other *process* issues must always be kept in mind when considering each individual civil right contained in articles 3-18 of the Universal Declaration.

> 5. Right to Own Property.
> 6. Right to Leave and to Return.
> 7. Right to Seek Asylum.
> C. The Right to Security.
>> 1. Prohibition of Torture or Cruel, Inhuman, or Degrading Treatment or Punishment.
>> 2. Prohibition of Arbitrary Arrest, Detention, or Exile.
>> 3. Prohibition of Arbitrary Interference with Privacy, Family, Home, or Correspondence.
> II. *Procedural Rights*
>> A. Right to Recognition as a Person Before the Law.
>> B. Right to Equality Before the Law and to Nondiscrimination in Its Application.
>> C. Right to an Effective Remedy.
>> D. Right to a Fair and Public Hearing.
>> E. Right to be Presumed Innocent in Criminal Cases.
>> F. Prohibition of *Ex Post Facto* Criminal Laws.
>> G. Right to a Nationality.

IV. Minisyllabus

Prohibition of torture and cruel, inhuman, or degrading treatment or punishment: *Filartiga v. Peña-Irala.*

> A. Pre-Charter international law.
> B. U.N. Charter.
> C. International human rights instruments.
>> 1. Universal Declaration of Human Rights, art. 5.
>> 2. International Covenant on Civil and Political Rights, art. 7.
>> 3. [European] Convention for the Protection of Human Rights and Fundamental Freedoms, art. 3.
>> 4. American Convention on Human Rights, art. 5(2).
> D. International practice.
>> 1. U.N. Commission on Human Rights.
>> 2. U.N. Human Rights Committee.
>> 3. European Commission and Court of Human Rights.
>> 4. Inter-American Commission and Court of Human Rights.
> E. Remedies.

V. Bibliography

Books

J. Carey, UN Protection of Civil and Political Rights (1970).

F. Castberg, The European Convention on Human Rights (1974).

J. Fawcett, The Application of the European Convention on Human Rights (1969).

L. Henkin (ed.), The International Bill of Rights: The Covenant on Civil and Political Rights (1981).

International Human Rights Treaties: Hearings Before the Senate Comm. on Foreign Relations, 96th Cong., 1st Sess. (1979).

F. Jacobs, The European Convention on Human Rights (1975).

H. Lauterpacht, International Law and Human Rights 394-434 (1950).

R. Lillich & F. Newman, International Human Rights: Problems of Law and Policy (1979).

M. McDougal, H. Lasswell, & L. Chen, Human Rights and World Public Order (1980).

Message of the President Transmitting Four Treaties Pertaining to Human Rights, S. Exec. Doc. No. 95-C, D, E, and F, 95th Cong., 2d Sess. (1978).

Z. Nedjati, Human Rights Under the European Convention (1978).

A. Robertson, Human Rights in the World 28-48, 80-110 (1972).

N. Robinson, The Universal Declaration of Human Rights (1950).

L. Sohn & T. Buergenthal, International Protection of Human Rights (1973).

Articles

Aréchaga, *The Background to Article 17 of the Universal Declaration*, 8 J. Int'l Comm'n Jurists (No. 2, 1967).

Bitker, *Application of the United Nations' Universal Declaration of Human Rights Within the United States*, 21 De Paul L. Rev. 337 (1971).

Clark & Nevas, *The First Twenty-Five Years of the Universal Declaration of Human Rights—And the Next*, 48 Conn. B.J. 111 (1974).

Craig, *The International Covenant on Civil and Political Rights and United States Law: Department of State Proposals for Preserving the Status Quo*, 19 Harv. J. Int'l L. 845 (1978).

Garibaldi, *General Limitations on Human Rights: The Principle of Legality*, 17 Harv. Int'l L.J. 503 (1976).

Haight, *International Covenants on Human Rights* (1966), 1 Int'l L. 475 (1967).

Hassan, *The Word 'Arbitrary' As Used in the Universal Declaration of Human Rights: 'Illegal' Or 'Unjust'?* 10 Harv. Int'l L.J. 225 (1969).

Higgins, *Derogations Under Human Rights Treaties*, 48 Brit. Y.B. Int'l L. 281 (1976–1977).

Humphrey, *The International Bill of Rights: Scope and Implementation*, 17 Wm. & Mary L. Rev. 527 (1976).

——*The U.N. Charter and the Universal Declaration of Human Rights*, in The International Protection of Human Rights 39 (E. Luard ed. 1967).

Kunz, *The United Nations Declaration on Human Rights*, 43 Am. J. Int'l L. 316 (1949).

Report of the Secretary General, *Annotation on the Text of the Draft International Covenants on Human Rights*, 10 U.N. GAOR, Annexes (Agenda Item 28, part II) 1, U.N. Doc. A/2929 (1955).

Robertson, *The United Nations Covenant on Civil and Political Rights and the European Convention on Human Rights*, 45 Brit. Y.B. Int'l L. 21 (1968–1969).

Schwelb, *The Influence of the Universal Declaration of Human Rights on International and National Law*, 53 Proc. Am. Soc'y Int'l L. 106 (1959).

——*Entry Into Force of the International Covenants on Human Rights and the Optional Protocol to the International Covenant on Civil and Political Rights*, 70 Am. J. Int'l L. 511 (1976).

Starr, *International Protection of Human Rights and the United Nations Covenants*, 1967 Wis. L. Rev. 863.

Weissbrodt, *United States Ratification of the Human Rights Covenants*, 63 Minn. L. Rev. 35, 62-76 (1978).

VI. Minibibliography

Filartiga v. Peña-Irala, 360 F.2d 876 (2d Cir. 1980).

Bassiouni & Derby, *An Appraisal of Torture in International Law and Practice: The Need for an International Convention for the Prevention and Suppression of Torture*, 48 Revue International de Droit Penal 17 (1977).

Dinstein, *The Right to Life, Physical Integrity, and Liberty*, in The International Bill of Rights: The Covenant on Civil and Political Rights 114, 122-26 (L. Henkin ed. 1981).

Lillich, *Civil Rights*, in this volume.

MacDermot, *How to Enforce the Torture Convention: A Draft Optional Protocol*, Rev. Int'l Comm'n Jurists 31 (No. 22, June 1979).

Spjut, *Torture Under the European Convention on Human Rights*, 73 Am. J. Int'l L. 267 (1979).

Chapter 5
Political and Related Rights*

John P. Humphrey

This chapter is about the freedoms of thought, conscience, and religion, of opinion and expression, and of peaceful assembly and of association; the rights of everyone to take part in the government of his country and of equal access to public service; and the right of peoples to self-determination. With the exception of the collective right to self-determination, these rights and freedoms—all of them rights and freedoms of the individual—are enunciated and proclaimed by articles 18, 19, 20, and 21 of the Universal Declaration of Human Rights.[1] The corresponding provisions of the International Covenant on Civil and Political Rights[2] are articles 18, 19, 20, 21, 22, and 25. Article 1 of this Covenant and article 1 of the International Covenant on Economic, Social and Cultural Rights[3] set forth the right of 'all peoples' to self-determination. Most of these rights and freedoms, with the outstanding exception of the right to self-determination, are also proclaimed by the European Convention for the Protection of Human Rights and Fundamental Freedoms,[4] by the American Convention on Human Rights,[5] and by the American Declaration on the Rights and Duties of Man.[6]

Since a separate chapter is here devoted to these rights, the question may be asked whether, the collective right to self-determination apart, they constitute a separate category with common characteristics that distinguish them from the other rights and freedoms enunciated by the Universal Declaration. The U.N. General Assembly, it may be noted, did not treat them as such when it adopted the Political Covenant which groups them together with articles on the rights of the family and of children.

These rights and freedoms have been called group rights because, it

---

* © John P. Humphrey 1983.

[1] G.A. Res. 217A, U.N. Doc. A/810, at 71 (1948).

[2] G.A. Res. 2200, 21 U.N. GAOR, Supp. (No. 16) 52, U.N. Doc. A/6316 (1966).

[3] G.A. Res. 2200, 21 U.N. GAOR, Supp. (No. 16) 49, U.N. Doc. A/6316 (1966).

[4] Arts. 9, 10, 11, 213 U.N.T.S. 221. There is no article in the European Convention on Human Rights corresponding to art. 21 of the Universal Declaration.

[5] Arts. 13, 15, 16, 23, O.A.S. T.S. No. 36. Art. 14 of the American Convention, which has no counterpart in the Covenants or in the European Convention, is devoted to the right of reply. There is, however, a Convention on the International Right of Correction, 435 U.N.T.S. 191.

[6] Arts. 3, 4, 21, & 22, *reprinted in* Handbook of Existing Rules Pertaining to Human Rights, O.A.S. Doc. OEA/SER.L/V/II.50, doc. 6, at 17 (1980).

is said, they are not usually exercised by individuals acting alone or in isolation. None of them would have had very much meaning for Robinson Crusoe alone on his island. But who is to say that Crusoe did not possess these rights even though he had no occasion to use them? I do not use all my rights all the time although I do possess them. More specifically, for example, it is sometimes said that freedom of association is a group right and that organized groups therefore have a right to put pressure on individuals; but this proposition finds no support in article 20 of the Universal Declaration which proclaims freedom of association as an individual right.

To call these basic individual rights and freedoms group rights is especially questionable at a time and in a world when and where the chief ideological conflicts are between collectivities, including states, and between their collective rights on the one hand and individual men and women and their individual rights and freedoms on the other. To call these individual rights group rights is, in these circumstances, almost to contaminate them. It is especially farfetched to suggest that the interior and private freedoms of thought, conscience, and belief are group rights. The language of the Universal Declaration and the other instruments is in any event clear; they enunciate all these rights and freedoms as individual rights. The right to self-determination, however, is just as clearly a collective right.

All these rights are with better reason often called political rights, a category whose existence is recognized in the title of the International Covenant on Civil and Political Rights. However, that Covenant does not tell us which of the rights it enunciates are civil and which are political. Some of them, while essentially political, are not exclusively so. The right of everyone to take part in the government of his or her country is exclusively political.[7] The freedoms of opinion and expression are not exclusively political, and the freedoms of thought, conscience, and religion even less so if at all. The freedoms of expression, assembly, and association, though not exclusively political, are each in a special way part of the democratic process, in that they permit and encourage criticism of government. They are indeed political rights of a very special kind—for they can be recognized and enjoyed only in democracies and there can be no democracy in any real sense without them. Their recognition and enjoyment is therefore a test of whether the government of a country is democratic. Three out of the four basic

---

[7] R. Chakravarti, Human Rights and the United Nations 68 (1958) [hereinafter cited as Chakravarti] reserves the term 'political rights' for the rights enunciated in art. 21 of the Universal Declaration. The U.N. Secretariat, in Annotations on the Text of the Draft International Covenants on Human Rights, 10 U.N. GAOR, Annexes (Agenda Item 28, pt. II) 1, 59, U.N. Doc. A/2929 (1955) [hereinafter cited as Annotation], gives the title 'political rights' to the Comm'n on Human Rights' draft of the same article.

freedoms mentioned in the first amendment to the U.S. Constitution belong to this group. Some other human rights, including some collective rights and some economic and social rights, can be and often are recognized and enjoyed even in authoritarian countries where there may be no or very little individual freedom.

As for the collective right to self-determination, its recognition and enjoyment may also be a test of whether or not a country is democratic, if the right means only that 'the will of the people shall be the basis of the authority of government'.[8] It is not necessarily so if the right includes the right of part of the population of a country to secede from that country. All the peoples that have exercised that right (if right it be) have not become democracies, nor have parts of populations to which the exercise of this right has been refused (including the Confederate States of America) necessarily become any less democratic by reason of that refusal.

Although all of these rights are intimately associated with the idea and practice of democracy, it is well to remember that they have values of their own. Democracy is a means to certain ends and not an end in itself. Indeed, there is always a danger in a democracy that the majority will impose its will on a minority or minorities. There *is* such a thing as the tyranny of the majority. There is, moreover, a vast difference between democracy as a form of government—the democratic state— and democracy as a way of life. Democracy as a form of government provides no guarantee that all the rights and freedoms set forth in the Universal Declaration will be respected. That is why, when the U.N. Commission on Human Rights was drafting article 29 of the Universal Declaration, which provides that the exercise and enjoyment of the rights enunciated in the Universal Declaration may be legitimately limited by the 'requirements of morality, public order and the general welfare', the majority of the Commission's members insisted that those 'requirements' be 'just . . . in a democratic *society*' rather than accept the Soviet sponsored 'just . . . in a democratic *state*'.[9]

Most of the texts with which this chapter will be concerned use terms for which the relevant instruments provide little or no definition. Definitions are indeed rare in the international law of human rights. This becomes a major problem when, as in the case of the U.N. instruments relating to human rights, there is no judicial apparatus for their interpretation. In the case of freedom of assembly, for example, all article 20(1) of the Universal Declaration says is that the assembly

---

[8] Art. 21(3), Universal Declaration.
[9] Humphrey, *The Just Requirements of Morality, Public Order and the General Welfare in a Democratic Society* [hereinafter cited as Humphrey], in The Practice of Freedom 146-47 (MacDonald & Humphrey eds. 1979) [hereinafter cited as the Practice of Freedom].

must be peaceful. As for freedom of association, the Universal Declaration also says that no one may be compelled to belong to an association,[10] a rule that is not repeated in the Political Covenant, the Economic Covenant, or either of the regional conventions. The articles on self-determination contain no definition of the key word 'peoples'. The freedoms of religion and of expression, on the other hand, are defined in some detail.

This paucity of definitions is less serious in the case of the regional conventions (both of which are nevertheless based on the U.N. Covenants, the European Convention directly and the American Convention indirectly) because they create relatively elaborate systems, including judicial apparatuses, for their interpretation and international implementation. Because, however, the language of the European Convention is so often the same as that of the Political Covenant, the considerable jurisprudence that already exists under the European Convention is persuasive authority for the interpretation of the Political Covenant. An unnecessary difficulty was introduced by the frequent use in the American Convention of different language to express the same ideas.

The poverty of the international law of human rights in definitions and, in the case of the U.N. instruments, the practical non-existence of a jurisprudence interpreting the articles are two reasons why the historical and structural methods, and not the analytical or exegetical, are the best for teaching the discipline, except of course for that important part which relates to the European Convention.

I. Legal and Policy Considerations

A. THE FREEDOMS OF THOUGHT, CONSCIENCE, AND RELIGION

There are three freedoms, not only one, enunciated by article 18 of the Universal Declaration.[11] For most people, these freedoms are the most intimate if not the most sacred of all freedoms. In some countries they are, in this skeptical age, often taken for granted; but we know that in many countries it is still the state which decides what a man or a woman shall believe, that there is, as it were, an official conscience, that people are not allowed to manifest their religion, and that they may suffer discrimination because of their beliefs. Toleration in these

[10] Art. 20(2), Universal Declaration. Association must also be peaceful. Art. 20(1), *id. See* discussion in section I.C. *infra.*

[11] Art. 9(1) of the European Convention protects these same rights. Art. 12 of the American Convention does not mention freedom of thought. Since the European Convention was used as a model, one wonders why.

matters is a relatively new thing even in those countries where the freedoms are now taken for granted. '*Dans les vieux ages*', says Fustel de Coulanges in *La Cité antique*, '*la religion et l'Etat ne faisaient qu'un*'.[12] And for many years, the rule *cujus regio ejus religio* continued to govern. Even in England, it was only in 1828 that the Test Act was finally repealed and Catholics, Non-Conformists, and Jews were allowed to hold public office. Full political emancipation would come only much later.[13]

No one has put it better than Henry Hallam. There is, he wrote, a scale of restraints and penalties by which governments have at various times limited the religious freedoms of their subjects:

The first and slightest degree is the requirement of a test of conformity to the established religion, as the condition of exercising offices of civil trust. The next step is to restrain the free promulgation of opinions, especially through the press. All prohibitions of the open exercise of religious worship would appear to form a third, and more severe, class of restrictive laws. They become yet more rigorous, when they afford no indulgence to the most private and secret acts of devotion or expressions of opinion. Finally, the last stage of persecution is to enforce by legal penalties a conformity to the established church, or an abjuration of heterodox tenets.[14]

These freedoms—of thought, conscience, and religion—are, like most rights, most appreciated by people who do not enjoy them. But paradoxically it is often these very people who, once their own claims have been satisfied, are most apt to deny their enjoyment to others. Conviction very often goes hand in hand with intolerance. As Macaulay once put it:

I am in the right and you are in the wrong. When you are the stronger, you ought to tolerate me; for it is your duty to tolerate truth. But when I am the stronger, I shall persecute you; for it is my duty to persecute error.[15]

Such a spirit of intolerance animated the early pilgrims who had come to America in order to be able to practise their religion freely. Freedom of religion nevertheless became part of the U.S. tradition and was enshrined in the Constitution by the first amendment. In other parts of the continent the tradition was quite different. Except in the very early years, only Catholics were allowed to settle in the French colonies of Acadia and Quebec. However, when those colonies were ceded to the protestant British crown by the treaties of Ghent (1713)

[12] *Quoted in* Les Libertés Publiques 330 (4th ed. C. Colliard 1972) [hereinafter cited as Colliard].

[13] *See* G. Trevelyan, History of England 631 (1926).

[14] H. Hallam, Constitutional History of England 160.

[15] Macaulay's essay on Sir James MacKintosh. T. Macaulay, Critical and Historical Essays 336 (1870).

and Paris (1763), the religious rights of Catholics were guaranteed, and this at a time when there was no freedom of religion in Britain—at least for Catholics, Non-Conformists, and Jews.

These two treaties were by no means the first to stipulate respect for the religious rights of designated categories of persons. Such treaties have been fairly common ever since the Peace of Augsburg in 1555. As one writer has said, 'after the Reformation, a stage was reached in Europe when a mutual guarantee of religious liberty became the only alternative to religious conflicts'. 'Here', he points out, 'is the first important nucleus for possible development of human rights in international law. It was a regulation of one aspect of the relationship between the state and the individual through treaties and conventions.'[16] Freedom of religion is indeed the oldest of the internationally recognized human freedoms and therefore the one with which the international community has had the longest experience. This is why perhaps, as in this chapter, writers on human rights devote more attention to this freedom than to any other.[17]

One important precedent, referred to by Clemenceau in his letter to Paderewski forwarding the Polish minority treaty after World War I, was the condition attached to the recognition of Serbia, Montenegro, and Romania at the Congress of Berlin in 1878 that they accept 'the great principle of religious liberty'.[18] And if President Wilson had had his way, there would have been a provision in the Covenant of the League of Nations obliging member states not to interfere with the free exercise of any religious belief, as long as it did not conflict with public order or morals, nor to persecute anyone because of his religious beliefs. Such a provision was included in the early drafts of the Covenant of the League, but it was dropped when the French objected that religious freedom was not a proper matter for inclusion in the treaty and the Japanese suggested quite appropriately that if religious liberty were to be protected there should also be a provision protecting racial equality, a suggestion that frightened some countries whose immigration laws restricted Asiatic immigration.[19] One article of the League Covenant did mention the freedoms of conscience and religion: article 22 stated that one of the purposes of the mandates system was to guarantee freedom of conscience and religion in one category of mandated territories. But the most important work of the League for the protection of religious liberty is not mentioned in the Covenant.

[16] Chakravarti, *supra* note 7, at 7.

[17] *See, e.g.,* D. Schmeiser, Civil Liberties in Canada 54-191 (1964) [hereinafter cited as Schmeiser].

[18] The letter is reproduced in O. Janowsky, Nationalities and National Minorities app. III (1945) [hereinafter cited as Janowsky].

[19] F. Walters, 1 A History of the League of Nations 63 (1952) [hereinafter cited as Walters].

The Council of the League became the guarantor of the provisions relating to minorities in the so-called minorities treaties[20] by which certain countries undertook, as part of the peace settlement after World War I, to respect the rights of their racial, religious, and linguistic minorities.[21]

Although very much concerned with the prevention of discrimination, including discrimination on the ground of religion, the United Nations did not take over the responsibilities of the League under the minorities treaties;[22] but it did take over the mandates system under a different name and subject to different rules. The Charter says that one of the purposes of the trusteeship system is to 'encourage respect for human rights and for fundamental freedoms for all without distinction as to race, sex, language, or religion'.[23] This is a principle purpose of the United Nations as well, as stated in article 1(3) and 55(c) of the Charter. Provisions relating to freedom of religious worship were also included after World War II in the peace treaties with Bulgaria, Finland, Hungary, Italy, and Romania. The failure of Bulgaria, Hungary, and Romania to live up to their obligations under these treaties gave rise early in 1949 to a bitter debate in the General Assembly.[24]

In the meantime, on 10 December 1948, the General Assembly had adopted the Universal Declaration of Human Rights, article 18 of which proclaims the freedoms of thought, conscience, and religion. Other articles prohibit discrimination on the ground of religion.[25] Article 14 of the first draft of this Declaration—the so-called Secretariat Outline[26]—had said: 'There shall be freedom of conscience and belief and of private and public religious worship', concise language that probably included all the details in the article finally adopted by the General Assembly. The precision and detail, which were added by the Drafting Committee of the Commission on Human Rights, the Commission itself, and the Third Committee of the General

---

[20] These treaties did not only relate to minorities.

[21] *See* Macartney, *League of Nations Protection of Minority Rights*, in The International Protection of Human Rights (E. Luard ed. 1967).

[22] In 1950, the U.N. Secretariat advised the Economic and Social Council that the treaties were no longer in force having been terminated by the operation of the *clausula rebus sic stantibus*. U.N. Doc. E/CN.4/367. This use of a controversial doctrine by an international secretariat to confirm the demise of an important institution for the respect of human rights has been much criticized.

[23] U.N. Charter art. 76(c).

[24] [1948-1949] U.N.Y.B. 316-27.

[25] *See*, *e.g.*, art. 2. The list of grounds on which discrimination is prohibited is, it will be noted, open-ended.

[26] The Secretariat contribution was a draft declaration and not merely an outline. *See* [1947] Y.B. on Human Rights 485 (United Nations).

Assembly,[27] are nevertheless useful improvements. The fact that freedom of religion (but not of thought and conscience) is defined with greater precision than are most of the other rights and freedoms enunciated by the Universal Declaration reflects, amongst other things, the long experience of the international community with this freedom; the influence of Charles Malik, the representative of the Lebanon—a country where religious freedom was particularly important since the nation was almost equally divided between Christians and Muslims; and a well-organized lobby by the World Council of Churches.

Article 18 of the Universal Declaration has two parts. The first part proclaims the existence of certain freedoms: 'Everyone has the right to freedom of thought, conscience and religion.' The second part then goes on to enunciate certain consequences of this proclamation and to indicate some, but not necessarily all, of the things that one of these freedoms, the freedom of religion, encompasses. '[T]his right includes', says the article, 'freedom to change [one's] religion or belief, and freedom, either alone or in community with others and in public or private, to manifest [one's] religion or belief in teaching, practice, worship and observance.' Article 19 proclaims the freedoms of opinion and expression—freedoms that have very much in common with the freedoms of thought, conscience, and religion—and is drafted in much the same way. There too, as will be seen, special circumstances encouraged relatively precise drafting.

None of the international human rights instruments under discussion expressly mention either agnosticism or atheism, but there can be no doubt that both are included in the word 'belief'. This word is not, however, used in article III of the American Declaration of the Rights and Duties of Man, which does not in terms protect the right to profess any belief other than a religious faith. And article 12 of the American Convention does not mention freedom of thought. Finally, none of the texts call for the separation of church and state, a prescription that is dear to the U.S. tradition and enshrined in the first amendment to the U.S. Constitution.

The specific mention in article 18 of the Universal Declaration of the right of everyone 'to change his religion or belief'—again included on the initiative of the representative of Lebanon—gave rise to controversy. In fact, the presence of these words was the reason given by the representative of Saudi Arabia[28] for that country's abstention in the vote to adopt the Universal Declaration, although his contention that

---

[27] For the legislative history of the article, *see* A. Verdoodt, Naissance et signification de la declaration universelle des droits de l'homme 176 (1964) [hereinafter cited as Verdoodt].

[28] Mr. Jamil Baroody, a Christian Lebanese.

the provision was contrary to the Koran was challenged by the representative of Pakistan.[29] The rule is repeated in article 9 of the European Convention and article 12 of the American Convention, but is not mentioned in article 18 of the Political Covenant, an omission that can be attributed to the persuasive powers of the active representative of Saudi Arabia. But the language of the Political Covenant as adopted[30] certainly includes the right to change one's religion or belief, as would indeed the language of the Universal Declaration without the Lebanese addition.

Another difference between the Universal Declaration and the Political Covenant is that article 18 of the latter calls for 'respect for the liberty of parents and, when applicable, legal guardians to ensure the religious and moral education of their children in conformity with their own conviction', a matter that is dealt with more fully in article 13(3) of the Economic Covenant. The same matter is, however, fully covered by article 26 of the Universal Declaration which proclaims the right to education using language which, it can be argued, goes beyond that of the Political Covenant since it does not include the qualifying words 'religious and moral'.[31] The point is not without current interest. In the Canadian province of Quebec, for example, the law now restricts the right of parents to send their children to English language schools.

Other textual differences reflect different approaches toward permissible limitations on the exercise of the rights in question. As long as the freedoms of thought, conscience, and religion remain a personal and private matter, they might be thought to be absolute, in the sense that there should be no circumstances which could ever justify the state restricting or in any way interfering with thought or belief. Nor can what I think or believe prejudicially affect the rights of others as long as I keep my thoughts to myself. The fact is, however, that the state does play an ever increasing role in determining the way people think, not only by its control in many countries of the information media but in most countries through a public school system. There are problems here of the greatest difficulty. In any event, quite different problems arise when I begin to externalize my thoughts. For there can be no doubt that the state can in certain circumstances restrict my right to manifest my religion or beliefs, as is expressly recognized in article 18(3) of the Political Covenant. Similar provisions are found in the regional conventions.

[29] Sir Mohammed Zafrullah Khan, a future judge of the International Court of Justice.
[30] 'This right shall include freedom to have or to adopt a religion or belief of his choice.' Art. 18(1).
[31] Art. 26(3) states: 'Parents have a prior right to choose the kind of education that shall be given to their children.'

Unlike the Covenant and the regional conventions, where the permissible limitations on rights are indicated in the articles enunciating the rights, the Universal Declaration deals with limitations in one separate article (article 29) at the end of the instrument, the provisions of which apply to all the rights and freedoms proclaimed by the instrument, including those set forth in article 18. This article says, *inter alia*, that:

> In the exercise of his rights and freedoms, everyone shall be subject only to such limitations as are determined by law solely for the purpose of securing due recognition for the rights and freedoms of others and of meeting the just requirements of morality, public order and the general welfare in a democratic society.[32]

If article 18 of the Political Covenant permits limitations on the manifestation of religion only and not on the freedoms of thought and conscience themselves, the same cannot be said of the Universal Declaration which makes no distinction in this regard between the freedoms of thought, conscience, and religion, and the freedom to manifest one's religion. It seems unlikely, however, that 'the rights and freedoms of others' or 'the just requirements of morality, public order and the general welfare in a democratic society' could ever justify placing limitations on the exercise of the internal and private freedoms of thought and conscience, although such requirements might, as the Political Covenant recognizes in article 18(3), justify restraining the right to manifest one's religion. Any limitation put on the free exercise of religion or on the other rights and freedoms proclaimed by the Universal Declaration in the interest of morality, public order, or the general welfare is, in any case, suspect in the sense that the burden of proving the imperative necessity falls on the authority imposing the limitation.

It will be noted that unlike article 29 of the Universal Declaration, article 18 of the Political Covenant does not use the phrase 'just . . . in a democratic society' to qualify the highly abstract reasons for limitations in the interest of 'public safety, order, health, or morals'.[33] However, article 18 of the Political Covenant is more respectful of individual rights than are article 19 on freedom of opinion and expression, article 21 on freedom of assembly, and article 22 on freedom of association, because it makes no use of the civil law concept of *ordre public* which is included in brackets in the latter articles. Article 18 does not even use the expression 'public order' but only 'order', both of which expressions in English mean only the absence of

---

[32] Art. 29(2). On the meaning of this language, *see* Humphrey, *supra* note 9.

[33] *But cf.* art. 9, European Convention (which refers to limitations 'necessary in a democratic society').

disorder. The civil law concept of *ordre public*, on the other hand, is equivalent to public policy[34] and perhaps even *raison d'état*. 'Public order' is used in the English texts of both regional conventions without, however, the addition in brackets of the French expression. Indeed, whereas the English text of article 9 of the European Convention uses the expression, 'public order' the French text says simply *ordre*, which may well mean that the drafters were giving the expression its English meaning, the absence of disorder, and no more.

The international instruments which we have been analyzing not only set forth the freedoms of thought, conscience, and religion, they also prohibit discrimination because of religion and belief. There are also separate instruments that are directed towards the prevention of such discrimination. These and other provisions, including those of the Charter itself, are discussed in another chapter of this book.[35] Some mention should perhaps be made here, however, of the Declaration and still to be adopted Convention on the Elimination of All Forms of Intolerance and of Discrimination Based on Religion or Belief,[36] the preparation of which was recommended by the General Assembly as long ago as 1962 in response to certain manifestations of anti-semitism and other forms of religious intolerance. A Declaration and a Convention on the Elimination of All Forms of Racial Discrimination, the preparation of which the Assembly recommended on the same date, are now in force—the Declaration having been adopted in 1963, and the Convention opened for signature in 1965, coming into force in 1969. The different treatment which the United Nations has afforded to two parts of what was conceived as a single package may be attributed to 'a coalition of delegations seeking to downplay the issues of anti-semitism and other forms of religious intolerance'.[37] And, finally, a reference should be made to the study undertaken for the Sub-Commission on the Prevention of Discrimination and the Protection of Minorities and completed in 1960 by its Special Rapporteur, Mr. Arcot Krishnaswami of India, on Discrimination in the Matter of Religious Rights and Practices.[38]

B. THE FREEDOMS OF OPINION AND OF EXPRESSION (FREEDOM OF INFORMATION)

'I would not undertake to govern for three months with freedom of

[34] The drafters of the Political Covenant could have used the expression 'public policy' to translate *ordre public*. That they refrained from doing so notwithstanding the advice of the official translators that this would be a proper translation is highly significant.

[35] *See* Greenberg, ch. 8 *infra*.

[36] G.A. Res. 36/55, U.N. Doc. A/RES/36/55 (1981).

[37] M. McDougal, H. Lasswell, & L. Chen, Human Rights and World Public Order 677 (1980) [hereinafter cited as McDougal, Lasswell, & Chen].

[38] U.N. Doc. E/CN.4/Sub.2/200/Rev. 1 (1960). McDougal, Lasswell & Chen refer to this study as 'outstanding', *supra* note 37, at 665.

the press', Napoleon is reported to have said to Metternich.[39] Freedom of information—the right to seek, receive, and impart information and ideas—is indeed unique among all the freedoms. It is, as the General Assembly said at its first session, the touchstone of all the freedoms to which the United Nations is consecrated[40] or, in the words of Justice Cardozo, 'the matrix, the indispensable condition of nearly every other form of freedom'.[41] It also determines the content of other freedoms;[42] it is, said Mirabeau, 'the freedom without which the others cannot be conquered'.[43]

However we may classify human rights and freedoms and whatever names we may give to them, it will be agreed that freedom of information is a somewhat, although not exclusively, political right. It is a political right of a very special kind; for, among other things, its exercise makes possible the criticism of government and exchange of information without which there can be no democracy. The freedom is so basic to the idea and practice of democracy that in Canada the Supreme Court ruled at a time when there was no bill of rights entrenched in the constitution, that this freedom is included in an implied bill of rights, because the preamble to the British North America Act says that Canada is to have a constitution similar to that of the United Kingdom, that is to say, of a democracy.[44]

A free press and other information media are, like an independent judiciary, instruments for the realization of other rights and freedoms because in a country where there is freedom of information and the information media are free, the chances are better that other rights and freedoms will also be respected. Whatever lawyers may say, the ultimate sanction of human rights is the force of an educated public opinion and it is the press and other media of information which both inform and educate public opinion. Free information media, where they exist, are also powerful agents for the implementation of human rights at the international level, that is to say, of the international law of human rights. Even authoritarian governments are sensitive to the force of world public opinion.

Like freedom of religion, freedom of information was not respected in antiquity. The ancient cities of Greece did not permit the expression of opinions that were thought to be against religion, the city, or morality.[45] We know from Plato's account of the trial and death of

[39] Colliard, *supra* note 12, at 419.
[40] G.A. Res. 59, U.N. Doc. A/64/Add. 1, at 95 (1946).
[41] Palko v. Connecticut, 304 U.S. 319, 327 (1937).
[42] Sloan, *Freedom of Information*, in The Practice of Freedom, *supra* note 9, at 158.
[43] Colliard, *supra* note 12, at 419.
[44] For a discussion of the elevant jurisprudence, *see* Leavy, *The Structure of the Law of Human Rights*, in The Practice of Freedom, *supra* note 9, at 54; Schmeiser, *supra* note 17, at 198; W. Tarnopolsky, The Canadian Bill of Rights 122 (1966).
[45] J. Bourquin, La Liberté de la presse 66 (1950).

Socrates that freedom of opinion and expression was not respected in Greece. Paradoxically, it was Tiberius in imperial Rome who said: '*In civitate libera linguam mentemque liberas esse debere.*'[46] But that is not to say that Roman law ever recognized a right to freedom of opinion or expression.

It was only after the unlicensed publication in 1644 of John Milton's *Areopagitica* that these freedoms became part of the English tradition. One early victory for freedom of speech was the winning, under James I, of the freedom of parliamentary debate. Nearly one hundred and fifty years later, the French *Déclaration des Droits de l'Homme et du citoyen* proclaimed: '*La libre communication des pensées et des opinions est un des droits les plus précieux de l'homme; tout citoyen peut donc parler, écrire, imprimer librement, sauf à répondre de l'abus de cette liberté dans les cas déterminés par la loi.*'[47] Already in the United States, freedom of the press had been guaranteed by the constitutions of some of the states, and in 1791 the first amendment to the federal Constitution stipulated that 'Congress shall make no law . . . abridging the freedom of speech or of the press . . .' Applicable at first only to Congress, the U.S. Supreme Court extended the restraint in 1925 to the legislatures of the states.[48]

International recognition of these freedoms came much later. Although the League of Nations had shown some interest in the communications media,[49] only after World War II did freedom of information begin to be recognized as an international human right. At its very first session, the U.N. General Assembly requested the Economic and Social Council to convene a conference on freedom of information. The conference met in Geneva in the spring of 1948.

In the meantime, the Commission on Human Rights had set up its Sub-Commission on Freedom of Information and of the Press [50] and had begun to draft the instrument that became in 1948 the Universal Declaration of Human Rights. The Secretariat draft of this declaration had included four articles on freedom of information:

Article 15. Everyone has the right to form, to hold, to receive and to impart opinions.

---

[46] *Id.*

[47] It will be noted that the freedom belonged to citizens only and that there was no stated limitation on the extent to which it could be restricted by law.

[48] Gitlow v. New York, 268 U.S. 652.

[49] The International Convention concerning the Use of Broadcasting in the Cause of Peace of 1936 was adopted under the auspices of the League.

[50] This sub-commission was abolished in 1952. Although it had no powers of investigation and still less of condemnation, it did, in 1952, adopt a resolution condemning the closing down of *La Prensa* by the Peronista government of Argentina. In 1978 the General Assembly set up a new Committee of Information. G.A. Res. 33/115C, 33 U.N. GAOR, Supp. (No. 45) 74, U.N. Doc. A/33/45 (1978). For its report, *see* U.N. Doc. A/34/21 (1979).

Article 16. There shall be free and equal access to all sources of information both within and beyond the borders of the state.

Article 17. Subject only to the laws governing slander and libel, there shall be freedom of speech and of expression and by any means whatsoever, and there shall be reasonable access to all channels of communication. Censorship shall not be permitted.

Article 18. There exists a duty towards society to present information and news in a fair and impartial manner.[51]

These principles, with the notable exception of those contained in the last of the draft articles, were worked into a single text by the Commission's Drafting Committee which it sent to the Sub-Commission on Freedom of Information and the Geneva Conference on Freedom of Information for their views. It was on the basis of this expert advice that, after further discussion in its Third Committee, the General Assembly adopted article 19 of the Universal Declaration of Human Rights. The adoption of this text and the corresponding article of the Political Covenant, both of which state the applicable principles in a highly satisfactory manner, was a considerable achievement, particularly in light of the difficulties that later arose in connection with the three draft conventions prepared by the Geneva Conference (discussed *infra*), and compensates somewhat for the otherwise sorry and frustrating record of the United Nations in the matter of freedom of information.

Article 19 has, as already indicated, the same structure as article 18 in that it begins with the proclamation of a right and then sets forth some of the freedoms included in this right; the rights to freedom of opinion and expression include 'freedom to hold opinions without interference and to seek, receive and impart information and ideas through any media and regardless of frontiers'. As in the case of article 18, the right includes more than is indicated in the specific provisions of the second part of the article. In light of the success which attended the efforts of the representative of Saudi Arabia to substitute the milder word 'gather' in the still to be adopted Convention on Freedom of Information (one of the three draft conventions prepared by the Geneva Conference of 1948), special attention should perhaps be focused on the word 'seek'. That word is also used in article 19 of the Political Covenant and in article 13 of the American Convention, but not in the corresponding article 10 of the European Convention. Article IV of the American Declaration of the Rights and Duties of Man begins with a proclamation of the 'right to freedom of investigation'.

Freedom of information carries with it special duties and respons-

51 [1947] Y.B. on Human Rights 184 (United Nations).

ibilities, especially where information media are controlled by vast enterprises, including state and other monopolies or near monopolies. Special duties and responsibilities are recognized explicitly in both the Political Covenant and the European Convention, but while this principle was included in the Secretariat draft it does not appear in the Universal Declaration, unless it is included by implication in the first paragraph of article 29.[52] If I keep my opinions to myself there should be no interference with my right to hold them. It is a different matter when I begin to express them. No one, said Oliver Wendell Holmes, has the right falsely to cry 'fire' in a crowded theatre.[53] Nor have I any right to defame my neighbour.

Article 29 of the Universal Declaration sets forth the cases in which the exercise of the freedom of information may be legitimately restricted. As already mentioned when we were discussing the freedoms of thought, conscience, and religion, permissible limitations on the exercise of the rights enunciated by the Political Covenant and the two regional conventions are set forth in the articles enunciating the rights.[54] The third paragraph of article 19 of the Political Covenant merits special attention:

The exercise of the rights [of freedom of expression and opinion] carries with it special duties and responsibilities. It may therefore be subject to certain restrictions, but these shall only be such as are provided by law and are necessary: (*a*) For respect of the rights or reputations of others; (*b*) For the protection of national security or of public order (*ordre public*), or of public health or morals.

This is one of the five articles of the Political Covenant that use the highly dangerous (from the point of view of human rights) civil law concept of *ordre public*, a concept which, as we have seen, covers at least as much ground as public policy in English-American law and perhaps much more.[55] Another restriction on freedom of information provided by the Political Covenant is in article 20 which prohibits propaganda for war and stipulates that 'any advocacy of national, racial or religious hatred that constitutes incitement to discrimination, hostility or violence shall be prohibited by law'. The article as drafted by the Commission on Human Rights was quite different. 'Any advocacy', it said, 'of national, racial or religious hatred that constitutes an incitement to hatred *and* violence shall be prohibited by the law of the state'.[56] The Commission had rejected a text similar to the one adopted by the General Assembly on the ground that, while

---

[52] 'Everyone has duties to the community in which alone the free and full development of his personality is possible'.   [53] *See* Schenck v. United States, 249 U.S. 47, 52 (1919).

[54] *See* text accompanying note 32 *supra*.

[55] *See* Humphrey, *supra* note 9, at 137; text accompanying note 34 *supra*.

[56] Emphasis added.

incitement to violence is a definable legal concept, incitement to hatred is a subjective notion that does not lend itself easily to legal action.[57] Article 4 of the International Convention on the Elimination of All Forms of Racial Discrimination is even more explicit. It requires states parties to

declare an offence punishable by law all dissemination of ideas based on racial superiority or hatred, incitement to racial discrimination, as well as all acts of violence or incitement to such acts against any race or group of persons of another colour or ethnic origin, and also the provision of any assistance to racist activities, including the financing thereof . . .

Here, however, an effort was made to protect freedom of information by inserting a reference in the article to 'the principles embodied in the Universal Declaration of Human Rights . . .'

The United Nations Conference on Freedom of Information, to which reference has been made, was held in Geneva in the spring of 1948, at the very beginning of the Cold War.[57a] Notwithstanding that the role of the information media is at the heart of ideological conflict, the Conference was conducted in a spirit of optimism and at its conclusion there was a feeling that it had been a success. It prepared and sent to the U.N. Economic and Social Council three draft Conventions: on the Gathering and International Transmission of News; on the Institution of an International Right of Correction; and on Freedom of Information. It also adopted forty-three resolutions and, its most lasting achievement, certain draft articles for the Universal Declaration and the Political Covenant based on the work of the Sub-Commission on Freedom of Information and of the Press.

Had the participating delegations come to the Conference with the power to sign any conventions that it might prepare, it is probable that the three conventions would now be in force. The organizers of the Conference had felt, however, that it would add to the prestige and authority of the conventions if they were sent to the United Nations for final approval before they were opened for signature. Therefore, delegations came to the Conference with merely the power to sign the Final Act.[58] Since the Final Act and the texts of the three conventions were sent to the Economic and Social Council and the General Assembly, those governments which were opposed to the texts but which had been in a minority at the Conference were able to prevent the adoption of the Convention on Freedom of Information and the opening for signature of the Convention on the Gathering and International Transmission of News. Only the Convention on the Institution

[57] *See* Annotation, *supra* note 7, at 64.
[57a] Humphrey, *Human Rights and the United Nations* (Transnational, 1984), pp. 50 *et seq.*
[58] U.N. Doc. E/CONF.6/79 (1948).

of an International Right of Correction—by far the least important of the three—has come into force, and this between a very small number of states.[59] The great issue continues to be whether the press and other media of information should be instruments of freedom or of power. But also coming to the surface has been the resentment felt in many countries against the monopolistic practices of the great news-gathering agencies, and the simplistic concept of freedom of information current in the western democracies, particularly among professional journalists.

The Sub-Commission on Freedom of Information and of the Press was abolished in 1952, ostensibly as part of a retrenchment programme, with the result that there is now no body in the United Nations having expertise in this area. The Secretariat has, however, held two seminars on freedom of information under the advisory services programme.[60] An item on the matter appears regularly on the agenda of the Commission on Human Rights. In 1960 the Economic and Social Council sent a draft declaration on freedom of information to the General Assembly which, however, has not yet taken any action on it.[61] There is also a General Assembly Committee on Information,[62] composed of representatives of sixty-six states, but it is more concern-ed with the management of information than its freedom. Originally conceived as a Committee to Review United Nations Public Information Policies and Activities, its name was changed in 1979 when it was asked 'to promote the establishment of a new, more just and more effective world information and communication order intended to strengthen peace and international understanding based on the free circulation and wider and better balanced dissemination of information'. The Committee met three times in 1979.[63]

The United Nations Educational, Scientific and Cultural Organization (UNESCO) is now making great efforts to fill these gaps. UNESCO has a useful role to play at the technical level extending technical assistance to developing countries, but there is reason to fear that the highly political approach which it is now taking to information and com-munications questions is, like that of the General Assembly, more closely related to the management of information than to its freedom.

[59] On the history of the drafting process since the draft conventions were sent to the United Nations, *see* United Nations Action in the Field of Human Rights, U.N. Doc. ST/HR/2/Rev. 1, at 177–87 (1980) [hereinafter cited as U.N. Action].

[60] New Delhi (1962) and Rome (1964). For the reports of these seminars, *see* U.N. Doc. ST/TAO/HR/13; U.N. Doc. ST/TAO/HR/20.

[61] E.S.C. Res. 720, 27 U.N. ESCOR, Supp. (No. 1) 8, U.N. Doc. E/3262 (1959); E.S.C. Res. 732, 28 U.N. ESCOR, Supp. (No. 1) 20, U.N. Doc. E/3290 (1959); E.S.C. Res. 756, 29 U.N. ESCOR, Supp. (No. 1) 6, U.N. Doc. E/3373 (1960).

[62] *See* G.A. Res. 33/115C, 33 U.N. GAOR, Supp. (No. 45) 74, U.N. Doc. A/33/45 (1978).

[63] *See* U.N. Doc. A/34/21 (1979).

There is much talk about a 'new information and communications order' and 'a right to communication', but very little concern for the principles laid down in article 19 of the Universal Declaration.

Although international implementation of human rights law by the United Nations is discussed in chapter 10 *infra*, reference may be made here to the fact that, under resolutions of the Economic and Social Council, member states of the United Nations were requested to report every six years on the measures they have taken to realize freedom of information.[64]

C. THE FREEDOMS OF PEACEFUL ASSEMBLY AND ASSOCIATION

Article 20 of the Universal Declaration, which sets forth the 'right to freedom of peaceful assembly and association', enunciates two freedoms and not just one as its language might seem to indicate. The freedoms of peaceful assembly and of association are clearly treated as two separate freedoms in articles 21 and 22 of the Political Covenant[65] and in articles 15 and 16 of the American Convention; and, although both freedoms are set forth in article 11 of the European Convention, it clearly enunciates them as separate and distinct freedoms. One does not have to belong to an organization in order to exercise the right of peaceful assembly, and one can belong to an association without ever attending a meeting. In fact, there is a closer relationship between freedom of expression and freedom of assembly than there is between the freedoms of association and assembly, which are included in the same article of the Universal Declaration. There could hardly be freedom of assembly in any real sense without freedom of expression; assembly is indeed a form of expression. There is also, as history shows, a very close relationship between freedom of religion and the freedoms of assembly and association. One manifests one's religion 'either alone or in community with others', to borrow the language of article 18 of the Universal Declaration. When one manifests one's religion in community with others, one does so in assemblies and associations.

1. *Assembly*

All the texts speak of 'peaceful assembly', and the American Convention adds the further qualification 'without arms'. Just what is a

[64] E.S.C. Res. 1596, 50 U.N. ESCOR, Supp. (No. 1) 20, U.N. Doc. E/5044 (1971). On the periodic reporting system, *see* Humphrey, *The Implementation of International Human Rights Law*, 24 N.Y.L.S. L. Rev. 53 (1978).

[65] A proposal to include both freedoms in the same article was rejected. *See* Annotation, *supra* note 7, at 55.

peaceful assembly? There seems to be no international jurisprudence on the question.[66] Is an assembly which is otherwise peaceful a 'peaceful assembly' if one of its objects is to provoke violence by others? A march of Ku Klux Klansmen through the streets of Harlem, no matter how orderly, is hardly apt to be a peaceful occasion. What, moreover, is an assembly? Does it include a demonstration if the object is to achieve by intimidation something that it has not been possible to obtain through the ballot box? Is there a difference between simple protest and intimidation? Ambassador Vysshinsky apparently thought that freedom of assembly did not include the right to demonstrate when, in explaining the abstention of the Soviet Union in the vote on the adoption of the Universal Declaration, he complained that it did not include that right. And what if the demonstration includes the illegal occupation of premises?

Insofar as freedom of religion includes the right to manifest one's religion 'in community with others', freedom of assembly is as old as the former. In other respects, the right seems to have been a late arrival, at least at the international level. Its first international enunciation seems to have been in 1948 in article XXI of the American Declaration of the Rights and Duties of Man, which was, however, obviously inspired by the preparatory work that was being done on the Universal Declaration of Human Rights adopted later in the same year. The U.N. Secretariat draft of the latter Declaration devoted separate articles to the freedoms of assembly and of association,[67] the first of which said concisely: 'There shall be freedom of peaceful assembly.'[68] The language finally adopted says no more. The same concise language is used in article 21 of the Political Covenant, after a proposal that the article include the words 'freedom to hold assemblies, meetings, street processions and demonstrations' was rejected.[69]

The point has already been made that the Political Covenant and the regional conventions differ from the Universal Declaration in stating permissible limitations in the same articles which enunciate rights. The Political Covenant is the most restrictive with respect to the right of assembly, in that article 21 allows limitation based on the civil law concept of *ordre public*. Freedom of peaceful assembly can therefore be restricted if public policy so requires, the only qualification being that the limitations must be such as would be just and necessary in a 'democratic society'.

[66] On the discussion in the Third Committee, *see* Verdoodt, *supra* note 27, at 196; N. Robinson, The Universal Declaration of Human Rights 130 (1950) [hereinafter cited as Robinson].

[67] They were joined together on the initiative of the representative of France in the Commission on Human Rights' Drafting Committee. *See* Verdoodt, *supra* note 27, at 193.

[68] Art. 19 of the Secretariat draft.

[69] Annotation, *supra* note 7, at 54.

2. *Association*

Isolated and alone (if that were indeed possible in contemporary society) the individual is dangerously weak. It is a paradox that individuals must unite even to defend their individual rights. Democracy needs political parties, religion needs churches, and the worker needs his union. Associations of one form or another permeate our economic, scientific, artistic, religious, and educational lives. But freedom of association is, as we have already seen, enunciated as an individual right and not the right of any group. 'Everyone', says article 20 of the Universal Declaration 'has the right to freedom of . . . association.' The second paragraph of the article is even more explicit. 'No one may be compelled to belong to an association', an affirmation of the rights of individuals in the face of organized groups which has been challenged as not meaning what it says. Some writers, with the interests of trade unions in mind, have attempted to explain away one consequence of the right not to belong to an association, *i.e.*, the prohibition of the 'closed shop'.[70] There can be little doubt, however, that this prohibition is exactly what the Universal Declaration intends. It is true that this prohibition of mandatory association is not repeated in the other instruments and that a proposal to repeat the rule in the Political Covenant was rejected on the ground that it would not be in the interest of trade unions. But in a case before the European Commission of Human Rights, three employees of British Rail who were dismissed because they refused to join a trade union argued that the right to associate and the right not to associate were two sides of the same coin. The Commission decided that their rights under article 11 of the European Convention had been violated[71] and the European Court of Human Rights agreed.[72]

The trade union movement has a special interest in freedom of association. Indeed, there would be no trade union movement as it operates in democratic countries without freedom of association. The right to bargain collectively, the right to strike, and the very existence of the trade unions themselves all depend on it. Article 23 of the Universal Declaration and article 22 of the Political Covenant specifically mention the right to form and to join trade unions.[73] But as provided by article 22(2) of the Political Covenant there is no limit on the 'lawful restrictions' which may be placed on the right of members of the armed forces and of the police (categories to which article 11(2)

[70] *See* Robinson, *supra* note 66, at 131; Verdoodt, *supra* note 27, at 196.

[71] Young, James and Webster v. United Kingdom. *See* Minutes of the 139th sess., Eur. Comm'n of Human Rights 12 (July 2-13, 1979).

[72] Young, James, and Webster v. United Kingdom, 44 Judgments Eur. Ct. of Human Rights (Ser. A) (13 Aug. 1981).

[73] *See also* art. 8, Economic Covenant.

of the European Convention adds members of 'the administration of the State') to exercise the right to freedom of association. The right of public servants to form and to join trade unions, to bargain collectively, and even to strike is nevertheless one that is being claimed and even recognized more and more in democratic countries. But there is no basis in the international law of human rights for these controversial claims.

Reference has already been made to the close historical connection between religious freedom and freedom of assembly. Treaties providing for religious freedom were also providing for freedom of association; for whatever else they may be, churches are also associations. But the existence of this principle in the field of religious freedom did not mean that a person was free to join any kind of association. This highly selective approach continued until after World War II when, in 1948, the International Labour Organisation adopted its Convention on Freedom of Association and Protection of the Right to Organise (No. 87).[74]

The Universal Declaration provides for freedom of association for all purposes not expressly prohibited for acceptable reasons. The Secretariat draft had said: 'There shall be freedom to form associations for purposes not inconsistent with this Bill of Rights.' As already indicated, freedom of association was included, on the initiative of the representative of France, in the same article as freedom of assembly, with the result that in the Universal Declaration the qualification 'peaceful' applies to both freedoms.[75] There is no such qualification of freedom of association in any of the other instruments. However, the provisions relating to permissible limitations on the exercise of the freedom in articles 21 and 22 of the Political Covenant clearly permit the prohibition of associations for non-peaceful purposes. Article 22 of the Political Covenant is, it may be noted, another of the articles which makes use of the civil law concept of *ordre public*.

D. THE RIGHT OF EVERYONE TO TAKE PART IN THE GOVERNMENT OF HIS COUNTRY AND OF EQUAL ACCESS TO PUBLIC SERVICE; PERIODIC AND GENUINE ELECTIONS

Whatever hesitations one may have in calling political some of the other rights discussed in this chapter, that adjective can certainly be applied to the rights enunciated in article 21 of the Universal

[74] C. Jenks, The International Protection of Trade Union Freedom 14-16 (1957); U.N. Action, *supra* note 59, at 104.

[75] This appears most clearly from the French text: 'Toute personne a droit à la liberté de réunion et d'association pacifiques.'

Declaration.[76] They are, moreover, political rights of a very special kind in that they are inextricably part of the idea and practice of democracy. It would take us too far afield to attempt any discussion here of the meaning of democracy or the evolution of democratic institutions. It can be said, however, that the principle laid down in the third paragraph of article 21 that '[t]he will of the people shall be at the basis of the authority of government', is at the very heart of the concept. '[T]his will', the paragraph continues, 'shall be expressed in periodic and genuine elections which shall be by universal and equal suffrage and shall be held by secret vote or by equivalent free voting procedures.' That is as good a statement of the mechanics of representative democracy as can be found. Unlike the first two paragraphs of article 21 which proclaim the right to take part in government and the right to equal access to public services, this third paragraph does not by its terms enunciate any right of the citizen. Rather, it is in the nature of a constitutional prescription. Moreover, it is also an elaboration of the right to take part in government, for it explains one way, *e.g.*, by electing representatives, that everyone can take part in the government of his or her country. That is representative government. The other possibility contemplated by article 21 is direct participation, as in the ancient city states of Greece, or, for example, by referendum. Representative government, therefore, is not mandatory. The right of everyone to participate in the government of his country is also recognized by both the American Declaration on the Rights and Duties of Man[77] and the American Convention,[78] but it is not mentioned in the European Convention.

The U.N. Secretariat draft of the Universal Declaration devoted separate articles to the right to participate in government and the right of equal access to public services. Article 30 said: 'Everyone has the right to take an effective part of the government of the state of which he is a citizen. The state has a duty to conform to the wishes of the people as manifested by democratic elections. Elections shall be periodic, free, and fair.' Article 31 said: 'Everyone shall have equal opportunity of access to all public functions in the state of which he is a citizen. Appointments to the civil service shall be by competitive examination.' Although energetically defended by the representative of China, the reference to competitive examinations was dropped. Otherwise, as with so many other articles of the Universal Declaration, the text finally adopted was remarkably like the Secretariat draft, notwithstanding the protracted discussions and the amendments made

---

[76] Annotation, *supra* note 7, at 59; Chakravarti, *supra* note 7, at 68.
[77] Art. XX.
[78] Art. 23.

in the Commission on Human Rights' Drafting Committee, some of which were later rejected by the Commission as a whole and the General Assembly.

The rights set forth in article 21 belong to citizens only and not to all citizens. They can be denied to minors, lunatics, and others under legal disability. The justification for such restrictions must be found insofar as the Universal Declaration is concerned in article 29, while article XX of the American Declaration mentions citizens 'having legal capacity'; article 25 of the Political Covenant gives the relevant rights to every citizen 'without unreasonable restrictions'; and article 23 of the American Convention says that '[t]he law may regulate the exercise of [these] rights and opportunities . . . only on the basis of age, nationality, residence, language, education, civil and mental capacity, or sentencing by a competent court in criminal proceedings'—a formidable list that could permit significant restrictions. The question of limitations does not arise under the European Convention because it does not protect these rights.

E.   THE RIGHT OF PEOPLES TO SELF-DETERMINATION

The proposition (to begin by using a perfectly neutral word) that every people should freely determine its own political status and freely pursue its economic, social, and cultural development has long been one of which poets have sung and for which patriots have been ready to lay down their lives. We are interested here in the question of whether it reflects a legal right or simply a political principle which should be but rarely is followed.

To the extent that the peace treaties after World War I reflected the wishes of the populations concerned and not only the dictates of the victorious powers, the new map of Europe which resulted may have reflected in practice the principle of self-determination. The principle was dear to the heart of President Woodrow Wilson, the most influential of all the actors at the Versailles Peace Conference. The history of his country provided examples of both the realization of self-determination, when thirteen American colonies severed the ties that bound them to the British crown, and of its denial, when a bloody civil war was fought to prevent the Confederate States from leaving the Union.

It is significant that in both cases it was the fortunes of war that were responsible for the result. If numerous colonial peoples have been able, since the Second World War, to break the links that bound them to their imperial masters it was largely because the latter were unable to prevent it.

The principle of self-determination covers a wide variety of possible actions. In the cases mentioned above it was a matter of part of the population of a state attempting to separate, or being separated from that state, either to form a new state or to become part of some other existing state. But a people can manifest self-determination by deciding to associate with another people in, for example, a federation. Or they might simply decide to retain the status quo. It would even be a manifestation of self-determination if a colony were to decide to remain subject to the political domination of a metropolitan power—much as the colonies of Nova Scotia and Quebec decided to remain loyal to the British crown at the time of the American Revolution. If the principle meant anything less, the choice would not be free.

This principle of the self-determination of peoples, insofar as it envisages secession, has something in common with the more rigid doctrine of 'nationalities', which would have every nationality possess its own state and the citizens of each state be of one nationality only—a doctrine of which the national state, assuming that such a state anywhere exists, is the embodiment. The great liberal historian, Lord Acton, long since gave the lie to the claim that such states are more conducive to freedom than multinational states. 'The co-existence of several nations under the same state is', he wrote, 'a test as well as the best security of its freedom. . . . The presence of different nationalities under the same sovereignty provokes diversity and diversity preserves liberty.'[79] The assertion by the U.N. General Assembly that the right to self-determination is a prerequisite to the enjoyment of all fundamental rights[80] is, it is suggested, debatable if it includes a right to secede. There is indeed no evidence that the fundamental rights of the individual are better observed in some of the countries that have become independent since World War II than they were in those territories before they became independent. Nor does a denial of the right to secede necessarily mean a denial of individual rights. The inhabitants of the southern states of the United States were no less free because their right to secede was denied. Some of them, indeed, attained freedom for the first time. If, however, the right to self-determination means '[t]he will of the people shall be the basis of the authority of government'[81] that would be quite another matter.

It was only as a political principle that self-determination was used as a guide to practice in the peace settlement after World War I. That it was a political principle and not a legal right was very soon confirmed when, in 1920, Sweden, in her dispute with Finland over the future of the Swedish-speaking Aaland Islands, invoked the right of the islanders

[79] Lord Acton, Essays on Freedom and Power 185 (1948).
[80] *See, e.g.*, G.A. Res. 637, 7 U.N. GAOR, Supp. (No. 20) 26, U.N. Doc. A/2361 (1952).
[81] Art. 21, Universal Declaration.

to self-determination. Since the Permanent Court of International Justice had not yet come into existence, the Council of the League of Nations referred the dispute to a Commission of Jurists which reported back that the islanders had no right to separate themselves from Finnish sovereignty and become part of Sweden.[82]

It is as a political principle that the self-determination of peoples is mentioned in articles 1 and 55 of the U.N. Charter. But self-determination is now being claimed as a legal right and is indeed set forth as such in article 1 of both the Political Covenant and Economic Covenant. It is sometimes argued that the right is part of the customary law of nations, and at least one author goes so far as to say that it is part of *jus cogens*.[83] However, whether customary international law recognizes a right to self-determination is a controversial question; if it does, it is probable that the only beneficiaries of the right are colonial peoples, in which event it no longer has very much meaning since so few colonies still remain.

There can be no doubt, however, that now that the Political Covenant and Economic Covenant have entered into force there is, insofar as the parties to those instruments are concerned, a legal right to self-determination. 'All peoples', say these instruments, 'have the right of self-determination. By virtue of the right they freely determine their political status and freely pursue their economic, social and cultural development.' Two questions arise: what does the legal right include, and to whom does it belong? Does it, for example, include the right of part of the population of a state to secede from that state? It would seem that the content of the right is not necessarily the same as that of the political principle. And who are 'peoples' within the meaning of the Political and Economic Covenants?

It was at the initiative of the Soviet Union (the constitution of which country recognizes a highly theoretical right of secession) that the references to self-determination were included in the U.N. Charter. Molotov made it quite clear that he had the colonial and mandated peoples in mind.[84] That country also tried, but unsuccessfully, to have a reference to self-determination included in the Universal Declaration of Human Rights. Nor is there any mention of self-determination in the two regional conventions. In the Political and Economic Covenants, where it is enunciated as a legal right, it is given pride of place at the head of the list. Anyone who followed the debates on the matter

---

[82] League of Nations O.J., Spec. Supp. 3, at 5 (1920). For an account of the dispute, *see* Walters, *supra* note 19, at 103.

[83] I. Brownlie, Principles of Public International Law 515 (3d ed. 1979).

[84] *See* Green, *Self-Determination and Settlement of the Arab-Israeli Conflict*, 65 Proc. Am. Soc'y Int'l L. 43 (1971).

knows that the decision to include articles on self-determination was aimed at the administering and colonial powers, and that such articles were included notwithstanding the conviction that this could prevent those powers from ever ratifying the Covenants. If this obstacle to ratification has now been removed, it is because they no longer have any colonies. The decision to include these articles is only one example of the tendency in the United Nations to give priority to collective over individual rights. It was also evidence of a total lack of concern, in some delegations at least, about the future of the Covenants.

Already in 1960, some six years before the adoption of the Political and Economic Covenants, the General Assembly had adopted a Declaration on the Granting of Independence to Colonial Countries and Territories.[85] Article 2 of that Declaration based on the *travaux préparatoires* of the Covenants, contains language identical to that used in the latter. However, the penultimate paragraph of this Declaration says: 'Any attempt aimed at the partial or total disruption of the national unity and the territorial integrity of a country is incompatible with the purposes and principles of the Charter of the United Nations.' That would seem to mean that the self-determination this Declaration is concerned with is self-determination without the right of secession. But, as its title suggests, the secession of colonies and of other dependent territories is the Declaration's main concern. It seems to be saying that while a colony has the right to sever the ties that bind it to a metropolitan power, no right of secession is otherwise recognized; and from this it would follow logically that the right to secede can only be exercised once. This in any event is the prevailing view in the United Nations, notwithstanding the generality of the language used both in this Declaration and in the Political and Economic Covenants. 'All peoples' as used in the Declaration, and presumably also in the Covenants, therefore means colonial peoples only; and once a colony has exercised the right of self-determination it can never be exercised again. But if this view is correct—and for most governments it is a very convenient view—the right to self-determination no longer has very much meaning or value since most colonies have now become independent. There is, however, little support for this prevailing theory in the legislative history of the Political and Economic Covenants and it is clear that while they contain no definition of the word 'peoples', the General Assembly did not mean to include only colonial peoples in that term. But the question of who are 'peoples' for the purposes of self-determination remains open.

[85] G.A. Res. 1514, 15 U.N. GAOR, Supp. (No. 16) 66, U.N. Doc. A/4684 (1960). Prof. Tunkin, one time Legal Counsel to the Soviet Foreign Office, argues that this resolution has the force of customary international law. *See* G. Tunkin, *Droit International Public*, in Problèmes Théoriques 101 (1965).

II. Teaching Suggestions

There are two quite different approaches to teaching the international law of human rights: the historical-structural (the dynamic method) which is mainly concerned with the development of the whole of that part of international law which relates to human rights and the procedures and institutions for its implementation or enforcement, and the analytical-exegetical (static method) which is primarily concerned with the content and meaning of particular norms.

The first of these methods is the best for the teaching of the international law of human rights as a distinct system or discipline. Not only does the subject matter (*i.e.*, human rights in general) lend itself to this method but it is the one that is most likely to excite the interest of students, particularly when they see the role which the development of the international law of human rights has played in bringing about the radical developments which have taken place in the content and very character of international law after World War II from a system that was concerned only with the relations of states to a system which now imposes duties and confers rights on entities other than states, including individual men and women. The pedagogical advantages of the dynamic method are indeed many.

We are concerned here, however, not with human rights in general but with certain specific rights and norms. The most appropriate method for their study is the analytical-exegetical one. For apart from the right to religious freedom, which has a long history, the international recognition of these rights is a very recent phenomenon.

Unlike the historical-structural, the analytical-exegetical method examines the various texts in which human rights are enunciated and defined with a view to discovering their true meaning, and is not necessarily concerned with their history or possible future development—although the teacher would be advised because of the paucity of definitions in these texts and the relative lack of jurisprudence interpreting them to examine their legislative history much more closely than he ordinarily would a text of national law. Nor is the static method necessarily concerned with the evolution of the procedures and mechanisms, where they exist, for the implementation and enforcement of the rights. The approach is, it can be said, substantive rather than adjectival.

Before analyzing the pertinent texts however, the teacher will find it useful to look at the historical development—such as it is—of the rules and the nature of political rights taken as a group, if indeed they can be described as a distinctive group with characteristics that differentiate them from other human rights and freedoms. The teacher should also discuss the place that political rights occupy in the hierarchy of rights for they are of the very essence of the democratic tradition. There can be no democracy without them.

These rights are, as already indicated, sometimes called political rights. We have used this expression, for want of a better one, in a kind of shorthand in the title of this chapter. But what are political rights, and are all of the rights which have been discussed political? Political rights are, it might be said, rights that are related to the political process. But there is no agreement on what rights should be included under that caption. It has even been suggested that only those rights which are mentioned in article 21 of the Universal Declaration are, strictly speaking, political rights. Some of the rights discussed, including the freedoms of opinion, expression, assembly, and association, while certainly related to the political process at least in democratic countries, are not exclusively political. Artists, for example, want freedom of expression, but not necessarily for political reasons or purposes. And some of these rights, including religious freedom, may not be political at all.

Whatever we may call them, all of these rights are characteristic of and indeed peculiar to democratic societies. But, it must be stressed, they are also ends in themselves. Democracy itself is only a kind of government. The mention of democracy raises all kinds of subsidiary questions. What, in international law, is a democracy and what is meant by the expression 'democratic society' as used in article 29 of the Universal Declaration?[86]

While the term 'political rights' can be used as a convenient kind of shorthand, it will be better to discuss the rights not as a distinct category but as disparate concepts, always stressing their close relationship.

Having clarified the basic concepts that he will be using, the teacher may then want to turn to the history of the rights. If freedom of religion has a long history, this is also true of the freedoms of expression, assembly, and association insofar as they are included in the right to manifest one's religion. Treaties stipulating freedom of religion date back to the Peace of Augsburg in 1555. Freedom of religion is also mentioned in the minorities treaties (entered into by certain countries after World War I)[87] and in the Covenant of the League of Nations.[88] The other rights which have been discussed are not mentioned explicitly, although some of them might be subsumed as part of the undertaking in the minorities treaties to assure full and complete protection of 'life and liberty' to all inhabitants. The fact is that up until after World War II, most human rights and freedoms, including those with which we are

[86] On the meaning of 'democratic society', *see* Humphrey, *supra* note 9, at 153.
[87] *See* art. 2 of the Polish treaty. This is reproduced as app. II in Janowsky, *supra* note 18.
[88] Art. 22.

here concerned, were considered to fall within the domestic jurisdiction of states. Lacking a history for those rights at the international level, however, the teacher may wish to dwell, possibly at some length, on the history of the rights in various national legal systems. This will be useful and quite legitimate because the authors of the international texts were really transferring to the international level the fruits of some long national traditions.

The analytical method is one which lawyers rely upon when advising clients regarding their rights under national law. In countries where precedent is authoritative, these lawyers lean heavily on decided cases and the jurisprudence of the courts. But lawyers advising their clients on the meaning of a text of the international law of human rights must do so largely without benefit of jurisprudence. There are, especially in the matter of political and related rights, practically no decided cases which can be cited in support of this or that interpretation of a text. The International Court of Justice referred to the Universal Declaration in the Namibia case[89] but not in respect of any of the rights being studied here. As opportunities present themselves the International Court will undoubtedly build up a pertinent jurisprudence interpreting both the Universal Declaration and the Political and Economic Covenants, even though none of them confer compulsory jurisdiction on it. Not only does the Political Covenant not confer any compulsory jurisdiction on the Court, it does not, unlike the regional conventions, set up any special juridical apparatus for its application and interpretation. The possibility should not be dismissed, however, that a body of jurisprudence may be built up by the Human Rights Committee set up under Part IV of the Political Covenant. There is also the possibility that the United Nations will build up a kind of jurisprudence through some of its nonjudicial organs, including the General Assembly.[90]

The two regional conventions do set up special supranational courts for their application and interpretation, and the human rights commissions created by them have much wider powers than the U.N. Human Rights Committee. There already exists a considerable jurisprudence applying and interpreting the European Convention. This jurisprudence is of course the very best authority for interpreting the European Convention; it is also of persuasive authority for the interpretation of the Political Covenant insofar as the language of the two instruments is the same. But very little of this jurisprudence touches on political and related rights.

Even national jurisprudence may be persuasive. Not only did the

---

[89] [1971] I.C.J. 16, 76 (separate opinion by Fuad Ammoun, J.).

[90] *See* R. Higgins, The Development of International Law through the Political Organs of the United Nations 302 (1963).

authors of the international texts transfer, as it were, national concepts to the international level, but human rights and freedoms are, because of their very nature, essentially the same whether they are viewed in a national or an international perspective. Thus, the rules relating to religious freedom must be the same in both international and national law if that freedom is to be protected. It should be remembered, however, that if because of a lack of international jurisprudence we analyze national jurisprudence, the operation becomes one of the exegesis of national and not of international law.

State practice and the practice of international organizations can also be taken into consideration in the interpretation of norms of international law, because, failing the designation of any specific organ to apply that law (which is usually the case), the states which make the law can also interpret it.

An international court or an arbitral tribunal would not look at the *travaux préparatoires* if the meaning of a text were clear on its face. But the teacher will find it useful to refer to legislative history when discussing even the clearest of texts.

If political and related rights are treated as a part of a course on the international law of human rights, circumstances may not permit the teacher to devote more than two or three hours to the subject. There will be no great problem if he or she adopts the historical-structural method described above for he or she will deal with the historical development of rights and will examine the various institutions and conventions. There would, however, be no special emphasis on political rights.

There would obviously not be enough time, particularly if the course is a seminar, to deal at all adequately *seriatim* with all the rights in question if the teacher adopts the analytical method. Assuming, however, that this is the method adopted and that the course is a seminar, students should be required to familiarize themselves at least with the pertinent conventions—the Universal Declaration, the Political Covenant, the European Convention, and the American Convention—in order to participate intelligently in the discussion.

III. Syllabus

    I. *Concept of 'Political Rights'*
      A. Distinctive characteristics.
      B. Importance of political rights in the hierarchy of rights and in the democratic process.
      C. Political rights compared to programme rights.
      D. Individual rights compared to collective rights.

II. *History*
   A. International history of freedom of religion (and expression, assembly, and association).
   B. National histories of the more recent political rights.
III. *Substantive Analysis*
   A. Freedoms of Thought, Conscience, and Religion.
   B. Freedoms of Opinion and Expression.
   C. Freedoms of Peaceful Assembly and Association.
   D. Right to Take Part in Government and of Equal Access to Public Service.
   E. Right of Peoples to Self-Determination.
Sources for this Analysis:
   Texts of international instruments.
   Travaux préparatoires of international instruments.
   European jurisprudence.
   National jurisprudence.
   Practice of states and international organizations.

IV. **Minisyllabus**

   I. *Freedom of Information (Opinion and Expression) as a Political Right*
      A. Importance in the democratic process.
      B. Development in national legal systems.
   II. *Substance of the Freedom of Information*
      A. Provisions in international instruments.
      B. *Travaux préparatoires.*
      C. International Conference on Freedom of Information: Three draft conventions.
      D. Permissible limitations on the freedom.
   III. *Recent Developments*
      A. Third World objections to existing news-gathering agencies.
      B. UNESCO efforts.

V. **Bibliography**

M. Bates, Religious Liberty (1945).
J. Bourquin, La Liberté de la presse (1950).
L. Buckheit, Secession: The Legitimacy of Self-Determination (1978).
C. Colliard, Libertés Publiques (4th ed. 1972).
R. Chakravarti, Human Rights and the United Nations (1958).
B. Cox, Civil Liberties in Britain (1975).
H. Eek, Freedom of Information (A.L. Lundequistra Bokhandel Uppsala, 1953).

Emerson, *Self-Determination*, 65 Am. J. Int'l L. 459 (1971).

T. Emerson, D. Haber, & N. Dorsen, Political and Civil Rights in the United States (1967).

Humphrey, *The International Law of Human Rights in the Middle Twentieth Century*, in The Present State of International Law 75 (Boz ed. 1973).

——*The Universal Declaration of Human Rights: Its History, Impact and Juridical Character*, in Human Rights: Thirty Years After the Universal Declaration 21 (B. Ramcharan ed. 1979).

——*The Just Requirements of Morality, Public Order and the General Welfare in a Democratic Society*, in The Practice of Freedom 137 (MacDonald & Humphrey eds. 1979).

O. Janowsky, Nationalities and National Minorities (1945).

C. Jenks, The International Protection of Trade Union Freedom (1957).

——Human Rights and International Labour Standards (1960).

A. Krishnaswami, Study of Discrimination in the Matter of Religious Rights and Practices, U.N. Doc. E/CN.4/Sub.2/200/Rev.1 (1960).

M. McDougal, H. Lasswell, & L. Chen, Human Rights and World Public Order (1980).

Nanda, *Self-Determination in International Law: Tragic Tale of Two Cities*, 66 Am. J. Int'l L. 321 (1972).

A. Rigo Sureda, The Evolution of the Right of Self-Determination (1973).

A. Robertson, Human Rights in the World (1972).

N. Robinson, The Universal Declaration of Human Rights (1958).

D. Schmeiser, Civil Liberties in Canada (1964).

Schwelb, *The Teaching of the International Aspects of Human Rights*, 65 Proc. Am. Soc'y Int'l L. 342-46 (1971).

Sloan, *Freedom of Information*, in The Practice of Freedom 157 (MacDonald & Humphrey eds. 1979).

A. Stokes, Church and State in the United States (1950).

W. Tarnopolsky, The Canadian Bill of Rights (1966).

O. Umozoriki, Self-Determination in International Law (1978).

A. Verdoodt, Naissance et signification de la Déclaration Universelle des Droits de l'Homme (1964).

United Nations Documents

Annotations on the Draft Covenants on Human Rights, 10 U.N. GAOR, Annexes (Agenda Item 28, pt. II) 1, 61, U.N. Doc. A/2929 (1955).

Secretariat Draft of the Universal Declaration of Human Rights,
[1947] Y.B. of Human Rights 484 (United Nations).
Final Act of the Geneva Conference on Freedom of Information
(1948), U.N. Doc. E/CONF. 6/79 (1948).
López, Report on Freedom of Information, U.N. Doc. E/2426 (1953).
United Nations Action in the Field of Human Rights, U.N. Doc.
ST/HR/2/Rev. 1 (1980).
Study of the Right to Self-Determination (Implementation of United
Nations Resolutions) U.N. Doc. E/CN.4/Sub.2/405/Rev. 1 (1980).

VI. Minibibliography

Humphrey, *Political and Related Rights*, in this volume.
Universal Declaration of Human Rights, arts. 19, 29.
International Covenant on Civil and Political Rights, art. 19.
Declaration on the Elimination of All Forms of Racial Discrimination,
art. 4.
[European] Convention for the Protection of Human Rights and
Fundamental Freedoms, art. 10.
American Convention on Human Rights, arts. 13, 14.
American Declaration on the Rights and Duties of Man, art. IV.

Chapter 6

Economic, Social, and Cultural Rights in The Third World: Human Rights Law and Human Needs Programs*[1]

David M. Trubek

I. Legal and Policy Considerations

A. INTRODUCTION

International human rights law recognizes a distinction between political and civil rights, on the one hand, and economic, social, and cultural rights, on the other. This essay deals with rights classified as economic, social, and cultural. Its principal purpose is to explore the nature of such 'rights' and to determine how the international community seeks to 'protect' them.

I shall refer to this set of rights collectively, as 'social welfare rights'. This label is my own, and is not widely used in the literature. I adopt it not merely to avoid constant repetition of the phrase 'economic, social, and cultural rights', or the use of such barbarisms as 'ESC rights'. Rather, I employ this term because I think it evokes what is most basic and universal about this sphere of international law. Behind all the specific rights enshrined in international documents and supported by international activity lies a social view of individual welfare. That is, the idea of protecting these rights rests on the belief that individual welfare results in part from the economic, social, and cultural conditions in which all of us live, and the view that government has an obligation to ensure the adequacy of such conditions for all citizens. The idea that welfare is a social construct, and the conditions of welfare in part a governmental responsibility, lies behind the separate 'rights' articulated by numerous international instruments. It also expresses what is universal in this area. It is an idea held, at least at the

* © David M. Trubek 1983.

[1] Many people have helped me in this effort. I want to especially thank Oscar Schachter, who encouraged me to undertake it, whose work provided guidance and inspiration, and whose suggestions and comments were always helpful. K.T. Samson of the ILO provided detailed comments on relevant sections of the text. Richard Bilder, Jonathan Silverstone, Francis Wolf, Henry Shue, and Margaret Crahan were generous in their suggestions and assistance. Ted Meron was demanding yet patient—the perfect combination of editorial skills. Jeanette Holz as usual provided the support needed to get the manuscript finished. My greatest debt is to James Zorn of the Wisconsin Law School Class of 1981.

most general level, by all nations, even though there is great disagreement on the appropriate scope of governmental action and responsibility,
and the extent to which social welfare can be reached within particular
economic and political systems. It is because proponents of the liberal
welfare state and the socialist state, as well as variations and permuta-
tions of these structures, agree on the importance of state action for the
promotion of individual welfare that these rights have been accepted in
international law.

1. *Purpose of the Chapter*

Note that 'rights' and 'protection' have been placed in quotation
marks. I do this to stress that what is most problematic in this area is
the meaning of these two terms. What are we speaking of when we
describe an international 'right' to social welfare? What does 'international protection' of social welfare entail? The terms 'rights' and
'protection' are taken from municipal jurisprudence where there is,
relatively speaking, a common core of meaning that surrounds them.
In municipal parlance, we have some idea of what we refer to when we
speak of 'protecting rights'. But when we speak of the process by which
the international community engages in a collective effort to ensure
that individuals have a 'right to work', to 'fair wages', 'to form trade
unions', to 'social security', to an 'adequate standard of living', to
'health', and to 'education',—to mention a few dimensions of social
welfare that are covered by the principal U.N. documents—then terms
like 'rights' and 'protection' lose the core of meaning drawn from their
origins in municipal law and must be redefined. To speak, without
qualification and clarification, of the international protection of social
welfare rights, is to employ a metaphor whose power to evoke images
of law and law enforcement drawn from the municipal setting is,
unfortunately, matched by its capacity to obscure what is really at
stake. The goal of this chapter is to clarify what is obscured by the
metaphor, so that the quotation marks may be removed and the reader
will understand these terms in a new and more meaningful fashion.

The real topic of this chapter, therefore, is how to think about what I
shall call the international law of social welfare. It is my view that we
cannot teach in this area until we know better what we are talking
about when we refer to international 'rights' of this type. This chapter
shall put forth a concept of international social welfare law and
illustrate that concept with several concrete examples.

2. *The Approach Taken*

The central feature of the approach I take to this subject is the
concept of programmatic obligations. I believe that international law

is moving towards the creation of obligations which bind states to undertake programs to guarantee minimum levels of economic, social, and cultural well-being to all citizens of this planet, and progressively to increase such well-being.[2] These obligations affect all members of the United Nations. The International Bill of Rights[3] places duties on all member states to provide such programs for the benefit of their own citizens and to participate in international efforts to foster social welfare throughout the world. These obligations apply equally to all states, regardless of their economic systems, political arrangements, or level of economic development. The United Nations and its specialized agencies perform a key role in the system of elaborating and implementing such programs but international social welfare law must, perforce, deal with national as well as international programs and include all international efforts to promote individual well-being, whether through the United Nations or otherwise. While this concept gives the topic a scope that might seem audacious at best, and totally unbounded at worst, there is a core set of concepts, programs, and institutions which form the central subject matter and problematics of the area. This chapter seeks to identify that core.

Although the approach set forth here draws on the work of many scholars, to an extent I am proposing a new way to think about this subject. For this reason, this chapter is somewhat different from some of the others in this book. Unlike the field of economic, social, and cultural rights, substantial prior work has been done on other aspects of the international law of human rights, providing students and teachers with an overview of a set of norms in those areas. Part of my goal has been to indicate the aspects of economic, social, and cultural rights which need further consideration so that a synthesis equal in scope, power, and reality to that currently feasible in more 'well-worked' domains of human rights law may be achieved for international social welfare rights. My aim has been to provide some of the tools future teachers and students in this field will need to carry out the task of elaboration and synthesis.

---

[2] *See Basic Human Needs: The International Law Connection*, 72 Proc. Am. Soc'y Int'l L. 224, 227-32 (1978) [hereinafter cited as *Basic Human Needs*]; Schachter, *The Evolving International Law of Development*, 15 Colum. J. Transnat'l L. l, 9 (1976) [hereinafter cited as Schachter]; H. Shue, Basic Rights: Subsistence, Affluence, and U.S. Foreign Policy (1980) [hereinafter cited as Shue].

[3] The International Bill of Rights consists of three basic human rights documents: Universal Declaration of Human Rights, *adopted* Dec. 10, 1948, G.A. Res. 217A, U.N. Doc. A/810, at 71 (1948); International Covenant on Civil and Political Rights, *opened for signature* Dec. 19, 1966, *entered into force* Mar. 23, 1976, G.A. Res. 2200, 21 U.N. GAOR, Supp. (No. 16) 52, U.N. Doc. A/6316 (1966); International Covenant on Economic, Social and Cultural Rights, *opened for signature* Dec. 19, 1966, *entered into force* Jan. 3, 1976, G.A. Res. 2200, 21 U.N. GAOR, Supp. (No. 16) 49, U.N. Doc. A/6316 (1966). These documents clarify and define the human rights obligations of the U.N. Charter. *See* text accompanying notes 4, 5, & 6 *infra*.

3. The Scope of the Chapter

Because of the goals I set for this chapter, I have had to restrict its scope. I have focused exclusively on social welfare rights in the Third World. To illustrate the meaning of a 'programmatic obligation', one must examine details of actual welfare programs. While welfare obligations are universal, programs to realize welfare vary with the economic, social, and cultural conditions prevailing in specific states or group of states. The problems of realizing welfare obligations in the Third World are, therefore, different than those entailed in realizing welfare obligations in developed market economies or the Socialist bloc. I chose to focus on the Third World rather than other parts of the world because Third World development is a priority goal of the United Nations and its specialized agencies, and the current focus of U.N. social welfare rights work is on the Third World. While this choice precludes analysis of crucial aspects of the meaning and impact of international social welfare law, it allows me to develop and demonstrate an approach which ultimately can be adapted to problems in other parts of the world.

The second restriction in scope is the need to focus on a very limited number of the many economic, social, and cultural rights included in the International Bill of Rights. Once again, this restriction is imposed by my conceptions of the subject and the purpose of the chapter. The obligations which form the basis of international law in this area principally are state obligations to conduct programs at the national level, as well as possible obligations of other states to assist them. International efforts to 'implement' these obligations consist, largely, of international programs designed to support and complement national efforts, as well as international machinery to monitor national progress. Thus to understand how the international system works—or might come to work—in this area one must enter deeply into the details of specific programs. To do this requires selection of a few illustrative areas.

Therefore, while this chapter deals principally with the role of the international system in establishing and supporting programmatic welfare obligations for Third World countries in the areas of work and health, its real goal is to demonstrate, by detailed analysis of these specific areas, the general process by which an international law of social welfare is evolving.

B. THE CORE LEGAL DOCUMENTS AND THEIR MEANING

International social welfare law embraces a wide variety of materials ranging from U.N. General Assembly resolutions to programmatic documents issued by international conferences and specialized agencies.[4] To understand the assertion that there is an international law of social welfare, the student must be aware of the entire gamut of relevant materials and see how resolutions, covenants, declarations, and programs relate to one another. In addition, the student must grasp the overall social, economic, and political system within which these normative sources are embedded and through which they take on meaning.

1. *The Charter and the Universal Declaration*

The central core of this body of normative material is the International Bill of Human Rights. The U.N. Charter, the Universal Declaration of Human Rights, and the International Covenant on Economic, Social, and Cultural Rights are the fundamental sources of international social welfare law and the basis for the concept of programmatic obligations under international law. They provide the starting point for all analysis in this area and the framework within which the broader corpus of pertinent materials must be viewed.

The earliest and most basic of these documents is the U.N. Charter, specifically articles 55 and 56.[5] Article 55 commits the United Nations to promote:

higher standards of living, employment, and development; solutions to international economic, social, and health problems; international cultural and educational cooperation; and respect for human rights.

Article 56 constitutes a pledge by all members to achieve these purposes separately and jointly in cooperation with the United Nations.

These very general purposes and obligations were given more

---

[4] *See generally*, Schachter, *supra* note 2; The International Dimensions of the Right to Development as a Human Right, U.N. Doc. E/CN.4/1334, at 29-43 (1979) [hereinafter cited as Right to Development]. Historically, the sources and evidence of international law as such have included treaties and conventions, custom, general principles of law recognized by civilized nations, and, as subsidiary sources, judicial decisions and teachings of qualified publicists and academics. *See* art. 38, Statute of the International Court of Justice.
But:
> accelerating technological, economic and political changes in the world community require speedier means for developing the law than traditional processes can supply.
> There has resulted a search for new methods of making international law less uncertain and more responsive to new needs and conditions. A contributory cause of this search has been the desire of many new nations of Africa and Asia to find ways to participate effectively in shaping and changing a body of norms in the creation of which they had no voice. In recent years, the search for new methods of clarifying and developing international law has centered on the role of international organizations, and particularly of the United Nations General Assembly and its subsidiary organs.

International Law: Cases and Materials 91 (L. Henkin, R. Pugh, O. Schachter & H. Smit eds. 1980).
[5] *See* Sohn, *The Human Rights Law of the Charter*, 12 Tex. Int'l L.J. 129 (1977).

specificity in the Universal Declaration of Human Rights,[6] approved without dissent by the U.N. General Assembly in 1948. Article 22 of the Universal Declaration states that '[e]veryone . . . is entitled to realization, through national effort and international co-operation and in accordance with the organization and resources of each State, of the economic, social and cultural rights indispensible for his dignity and the free development of his personality'. Furthermore, the Universal Declaration states that everyone has rights to social security,[7] to work and to join trade unions,[8] to rest,[9] to an adequate standard of living (including medical care),[10] to education,[11] and to participate freely in cultural life.[12]

2. *The International Covenant on Economic, Social, and Cultural Rights*

The most detailed and specific document that deals with the entire field of international social welfare law is the Economic Covenant, which was adopted by the U.N. General Assembly in 1966 and came into effect in 1976. It is a principal source of international social welfare obligations for those states which have ratified it. For those which have yet to do so, it has value as a detailed interpretation of the Charter's obligations.[13] The Economic Covenant provides normative guidance for all states and provides an explicit system of international monitoring of progress toward its goals for those states which are parties to it. To understand the meaning of social welfare rights and to gain insight into actual and potential systems of international protection of such rights, three interrelated features of the Economic Covenant must be examined. These are: (i) the form of the rights which are specifically guaranteed by this convention; (ii) the principle of progressive realization; and (iii) the system of generic implementation.

(i) *Background.* The Universal Declaration sets forth a wide range of rights, including rights relating to political participation, individual liberty, and social welfare. In order to give greater specificity to the principles established by the Universal Declaration and to provide an instrument which individual states could ratify, the United Nations

[6] *See* arts. 22-27.
[7] Art. 22.
[8] Art. 23.
[9] Art. 24.
[10] Art. 25.
[11] Art. 26.
[12] Art. 27.
[13] *See* Sohn, *A Short History of United Nations Documents on Human Rights* [hereinafter cited as Sohn], in The United Nations and Human Rights 37, 169 (Commission to Study the Organization of Peace 1968) [hereinafter cited as the United Nations and Human Rights].

proceeded to develop a Covenant on Human Rights.[14] The original concept was a single covenant covering all the rights set forth in the Universal Declaration.[15] However, in the course of drafting the decision was made to divide the Human Rights Covenant into two separate instruments:[16] one covering political and civil rights—the Political Covenant; and one dealing with economic, social, and cultural rights—the Economic Covenant.

The reasons for this important decision were complex and have been little researched.[17] However, several factors seem to have been influential, among which was a belief that it was impossible to develop a single system of implementation for both the political-civil and the social welfare rights.[18] This problem itself had two aspects. It was obvious to some states that some rights, *e.g.*, the right to a fair trial, could be enacted into law immediately, while other rights, *e.g.*, the right to health, would require programs of action over time before they could be realized.[19] Appropriate national responses would vary with the 'nature' of the right. Protecting political and civil rights meant passing laws and revising constitutions, while guaranteeing social rights meant the establishment of programs as well. The second aspect of the objections to a single human rights implementation system was that the distinction between civil-political and social welfare rights suggested substantial differences in possible international measures to implement these rights.[20] It seemed that some form of international tribunal could and should be created to deal with alleged violations of political and civil rights, but that no court-like structure could be

---

[14] *See Eighteenth Report of the Commission to Study the Organization Peace* [hereinafter cited as Eighteenth Report], in The United Nations and Human Rights 11, *supra* note 13; Sohn, *supra* note 13, at 101.

[15] *See* Eighteenth Report, *supra* note 14, at 11.

[16] *See id.*; G.A. Res. 543, 6 U.N. GAOR, Supp. (No. 20) 36, U.N. Doc. A/2119 (1952).

[17] *See generally* Sohn, *supra* note 13, at 105, 106. The essential debate underlying this decision took place in the Third Committee of the General Assembly, which deals with social, humanitarian, and cultural questions. The Third Committee's debates are summarized in 6 U.N. GAOR, C.4 (358th-72d, 411th-17th mtgs.) 67, 67-150, 399-499, U.N. Docs. A/C.3/SR. 358-72, 411-17 (1951-1952). The decisions resulting from these debates are contained in the Report of the Third Committee, 6 U.N. GAOR, Annexes (Agenda Item 29) 37, U.N. Doc. A/2112 (1952) [hereinafter cited as Report of the Third Committee]. The General Assembly held brief debates on the Third Committee's Report before adopting Res. 543, *supra* note 16. These debates are summarized in 6 U.N. GAOR, (374th, 375th plen. mtgs.) 501, U.N. Doc. A/PV. 374-75 (1952) [hereinafter cited as Plenary Meetings].

[18] *See* Report of the Third Committee, *supra* note 17, at 40; Annotations on the Text of the Draft International Covenants on Human Rights, 10 U.N. GAOR, Annexes (Agenda Item 28, pt. II) 8, U.N. Doc. A/2929 (1955) [hereinafter cited as Annotations].

[19] *See* Memorandum submitted by Israel, 6 U.N. GAOR, Annexes (Agenda Item 29) 17, U.N. Doc. A/C.3/565 (1952); Plenary Meetings, *supra* note 18, at 504, 514; Annotations, *supra* note 18, at 8,

[20] *See* Report of the Third Committee, *supra* note 17 at 40; Plenary Meetings, *supra* note 17, at 504, 514; Annotations, *supra* note 18, at 8, 9.

created at the international level to supervise the rights to work, health, etc.[21] Whether these views are objectively correct or not, they seem to have influenced the decisions of the delegates considering a Human Rights Covenant.

The other factor which was influential in the division of the proposed Covenant was more political. There was substantial disagreement over the desirability of a covenant which dealt with social welfare at all. Some states which were prepared to support a covenant guaranteeing political and civil rights were not willing to agree to a document that would commit them to social welfare rights and thus to specific social welfare programs.[22] This led some states to suggest that the proposed covenant be limited to political and civil rights.[23] However, this option was blocked by a General Assembly resolution which directed the drafters to include both political-civil and social rights.[24]

Thus the decision to have two covenants avoided the dilemmas facing the drafters. It allowed them to comply with the General Assembly resolution and still establish different approaches for the implementation of the two categories of rights. At the same time, a state would now be able to ratify a covenant protecting one set of rights even if it was unwilling to specifically guarantee all the rights set forth in the Universal Declaration. This, it was thought, would increase the chances that the overall program would be accepted by the world community.[25]

(ii) *Rights Specific to the Economic Covenant.* The decision to divide the Human Rights Covenant into two documents[26] was not a decision to have two totally independent documents. There is substantial overlap between the substantive provisions of the two. Both proclaim the right of self-determination,[27] prohibit discrimination,[28] and protect the right to join trade unions.[29] However, there are rights which are dealt with only in one of the Covenants. The social welfare rights which are the subject of this chapter are included only in the Economic

---

[21] *See* Plenary Meetings, *supra* note 17, at 505; Annotations, *supra* note 18, at 4, 9.

[22] *See* Working Group on Economic, Social and Cultural Rights (2d mtg.), 7 Comm'n on Human Rights, U.N. Doc. E/CN.4/AC.14/SR.2, at 12 (1951) [hereinafter cited as Working Group]; 8 Comm'n on Human Rights (270th mtg.), U.N. Doc. E/CN.4/SR.270, at 11 (1952) [hereinafter cited as Comm'n on Human Rights (270th mtg.)]; 8 Comm'n on Human Rights (274th mtg.), U.N. Doc. E/CN.4/SR.274 (1952); Sohn, *supra* note 13, at 104.

[23] *See* Working Group, *supra* note 22, at 5, 23, 28; 8 Comm'n on Human Rights (271st mtg.), U.N. Doc. E/CN.4/SR.271, at 10 (1952) [hereinafter cited as Comm'n on Human Rights (271st mtg.)].

[24] G.A. Res. 421, 5 U.N. GAOR, Supp. (No. 20) 42, U.N. Doc. A/1775 (1950).

[25] *See* Sohn, *supra* note 13, at 107.

[26] *See* G.A. Res. 543, *supra* note 16; Sohn, *supra* note 14, at 106.

[27] Art. 1, Economic Covenant; art. 1, Political Covenant.

[28] Art. 2(2), Economic Covenant; art 2(1), Political Covenant.

[29] Art. 8, Economic Covenant; art. 22, Political Covenant.

Covenant. Those rights are stated in a specific form of language, and are subject only to the Economic Covenant's unique system of implementation.

There is a linguistic convention in the Economic and Political Covenants that warrants mention. In some cases, the parties 'recognize' a given right. In others, they 'undertake to ensure' a right. In most instances rights are simply declared. Most of the rights in the Political Covenant are declared. For instance, article 14 of the Political Covenant states, 'All persons shall be equal before the courts and tribunals . . . ' A few political and civil rights, *e.g.*, the right to non-discrimination, are 'ensured' by the parties.[30] On the other hand, most of the rights in the Economic Covenant are 'recognized'. When this language is used, the Economic Covenant then lists steps that will be taken 'to achieve full realization'. All of the 'recognized rights' are in the Economic Covenant and they are the social welfare rights with which I will deal. Specifically, the parties to the Economic Covenant *recognize* the rights:

1. to work; 2. to just and favorable conditions of work; 3. to social security; 4. to an adequate standard of living; 5. to health; 6. to education; and 7. to participate in and enjoy the fruits of culture and science.[31]

The Economic Covenant also recognizes the importance of protection for families and children, but does not refer to this as a 'right'.[32]

(iii) *Implementation: the Principle of Progressive Realization.* The Economic Covenant is oriented around the principle of 'progressive realization'.[33] This principle has several elements. First, the rights which are exclusively dealt with in the Economic Covenant are said to be 'recognized' rather than 'declared' or 'ensured'.[34] This implies that a party's obligations in the areas of work, education, health, etc., differ from its obligations in areas like the right to form trade unions, which right is 'ensured'.[35] Further, article 2(1) of the Economic Covenant, which states the principal obligation undertaken by parties in the social area, commits them 'to take steps' toward the realization of the rights that are 'recognized in the present covenant'.

[30] Art. 2(1), Political Covenant.
[31] These rights are recognized in arts. 6, 7, 9, 11, 12, 13 & 15, respectively, of the Economic Covenant.
[32] Art. 10.
[33] *See generally* 8 Comm'n on Human Rights (270th-275th mtgs.), U.N. Docs. E/CN.4/SR.270-75 (1952) [hereinafter Comm'n on Human Rights (270th-275th mtgs.)]; Report of the Comm'n on Human Rights, 14 U.N. ESCOR, Supp. (No. 4) 14, U.N. Doc. E/2256 (1952); Annotations, *supra* note 18, at 19-20.
[34] *See* text accompanying note 31 *supra*.
[35] Art. 8.

These 'steps' described in the Economic Covenant can be read as specifications of what the right means and as elements of the program to realize the right. For example, among the 'steps' contained in article 12, which establishes the right to health, is '[t]he creation of conditions which would assure to all medical service and medical attention in the event of sickness.[36] This 'step' is both a definition of what it might mean to realize a right to health and the outline of part of a health delivery strategy which stresses equal access to curative medical services.

Implementation of only the 'steps' mentioned in the various provisions of the Economic Covenant would not exhaust the states parties' obligations. In one instance, *i.e.*, social security, no steps at all are specifically listed, although the right is recognized.[37] All other articles setting out 'recognized' rights say that the specified measures are merely *included* in the steps that states must take. In addition, article 2 requires that a state use 'all appropriate means' to fully realize the recognized rights.

The language of article 2 that a state must take measures 'with a view to achieving progressively' the rights recognized 'to the maximum of its available resources' calls into question the binding nature of these obligations. These clauses are ambiguous, yet certain things are clear. The language of progressive realization in article 2 indicates that the rights must be implemented, if only over time, by a program of activities. The language in article 2 relating to available resources reflects awareness that the realization of these social welfare rights will require states to spend money on them and that resource constraints may affect the rate of progress towards the goals established.[38] The issue then becomes whether these clauses create obligations as to the priority to be given social welfare and the rate of progress that must be achieved.

Proponents of the position that the 'progressive realization' language creates an obligation to increased levels of commitment to social welfare argue that this language places 'upon signatories a duty to achieve ever higher and higher levels of fulfillment of rights'.[39] True, the 'available resources' clause qualifies any such obligation. But what is the nature of this qualification? It clearly says that a state cannot be expected to commit resources it does not have. But does it leave the allocation of resources between social welfare and other goals entirely to the individual state, so that state X can say: 'We have no available resources for social welfare because we have decided to spend all our

[36] Art. 12(2)(d).

[37] Art. 9.

[38] *See generally* Comm'n on Human Rights (270th–275th mtgs.), *supra* note 33.

[39] Annotations, *supra* note 18, at 20.

budget for defense (or industrial development?)' Or does the use of the phrase '*maximum* of its available resources'[40] suggest an obligation to give priority attention to the social welfare area?

I believe the available resources language should be read as establishing a priority for social welfare. Given the purpose of the Economic Covenant, it is hard to see how the alternative reading would make any sense. It is clear that the drafters of the Economic Covenant wished to impose obligations on states. Yet if the only obligation arising from the Economic Covenant was that a state could spend what it wanted on social welfare, then this would be no obligation at all and the drafters would have failed in their goal. This reasoning from purpose is supported by the legislative history. At one point, the United States tried to substitute a clause stating that the obligation would be to take steps 'to the maximum of the resources which may be used for the purpose'[41] This amendment, which would have clearly established the more restrictive reading of the 'available resources' clause, was rejected.[42] Supporting this rejection, one delegate said that the original (and final) version was preferable 'because it meant that without exceeding the possibilities open to them, States must do their utmost to implement economic, social and cultural rights'.[43] Another delegate, speaking to the same issue, noted that the protections of the Economic Covenant specify a bare minimum of those rights 'inherent in the human person', so that priority in favor of these over other demands on resources was both necessary and desirable.[44]

Assuming *arguendo* that the Economic Covenant can be read as imposing an obligation to give the social welfare area priority in resource allocation, it is nevertheless clear that resource constraints will be a factor in determining the appropriate level of activity in the area. Naturally, the problems of how to determine what resources are available and whether priorities are met do arise. There are many issues here that were clearly left open by the Economic Covenant. One issue, however, deserves special comment. When the Economic Covenant refers to 'resources', does it refer exclusively to *national* resources or does it include international aid within the meaning of that term? Specifically, in evaluating the performance of any state under the principle of progressive realization, would it be proper to take into account a decision not to use available international assist-

---

[40] Emphasis added.
[41] Comm'n on Human Rights (271st mtg.), *supra* note 24, at 3.
[42] The text of the draft Economic Covenant, as adopted by the Comm'n on Human Rights at its eighth session, did not include the substitute clause proposed by the United States. 8 Comm'n on Human Rights (275th mtg.), U.N. Doc. E/CN.4/SR.275, at 6 (1952).
[43] Comm'n on Human Rights (271st mtg.), *supra* note 23, at 6.
[44] *Id.* at 13.

ance to meet social needs? Assume, for example, that state X explains its failure to eradicate some disease on the basis of lack of national resources but that it had simultaneously failed to take advantage of an international program in this area. It is possible to argue that the availability of aid is irrelevant since article 2 speaks of 'its', meaning the state's, resources and, further, that issues of national sovereignty are raised by this reading. On the other hand, the legislative history of the Economic Covenant indicates that the broader meaning of 'available resources' was intended: the official history explicitly says that this clause was meant to include international aid.[45]

Another issue in interpretation of the Economic Covenant is the question of the obligation of developed countries to render assistance to less developed countries in the latter's efforts to promote economic, social, and cultural rights. It is clear that the Economic Covenant obligates all parties, developed or not, to promote the rights of their *own* citizens. But can it also be read as obligating the richer parties to aid poorer parties' economic, social, and cultural efforts? An argument along these lines can be maintained. Article 55 of the U.N. Charter specifies that one of the purposes of the United Nations is the promotion of 'higher standards of living, full employment, and conditions of economic and social progress and development'. Under article 56, member states pledge themselves 'to take joint and separate action in co-operation with the [United Nations]' to achieve these goals. Thus it could be argued that the Economic Covenant constitutes a more precise definition of the article 55 goals and that article 56 creates an obligation on all U.N. members to assist in these efforts. However, this very general argument finds no specific support in the text of the Economic Covenant or in its legislative history. Indeed, one could read articles 11 and 23 of the Economic Covenant as support for the argument that the drafters wished to leave the question of assistance from developed countries up to individual states, either through bilateral decisions or through future international agreements.[46] It is

---

[45] Annotations, *supra* note 18, at 20.

[46] Art. 11 of the Economic Covenant recognizes the right to an adequate standard of living for everyone and to continuous improvement of living conditions, thus seemingly incorporating many if not all of the other specifically enumerated rights in the Economic Covenant. Art. 11 requires all parties to take steps to realize the right to an adequate standard of living, including 'international co-operation based on *free consent*' (emphasis added). The addition of the term 'free consent' suggests an intent to encourage aid from rich to poorer parties, but not to require it by the terms of the Economic Covenant. Art. 23 contemplates that future action, including conventions, would be needed to secure the kind of international action needed to implement the Economic Covenant. The drafters may have thought that subsequent agreement could be the vehicle to create an aid-giving obligation. It is worth noting that the U.S. Executive Branch has adopted this construction of the Economic Covenant. Thus, in his letter of submission of the Economic Covenant to the U.S. Congress for its advice and consent to ratification, President Carter noted that the obligations under art. 2 do not include any obligation on the part of developed signatories to give economic aid to less developed states parties. *See* Weissbrodt, *United States Ratification of the Human Rights Covenants*, 63 Minn. L. Rev. 35, 53 (1978).

true that arguments have been made that international law is moving toward the recognition of a 'right to development' and that this right includes an obligation to provide development assistance.[47] The U.N. Secretary-General has indicated that it is time to consider whether the international community, through a series of actions concentrated in the past ten years, is moving toward the recognition of such an obligation.[48] But at the same time he concluded that no such obligation has yet been authoritatively established or accepted.[49] Thus it would seem inappropriate to try to ground such an obligation on the Economic Covenant alone. Of course, the lack of such an obligation on the part of developed countries does not affect the developing states parties' obligations under the Economic Covenant to use their own resources and such international assistance as is made available.[50]

The principle of progressive realization, therefore, really means that a state is obligated to undertake a program of activities, including but not limited to the specific measures listed in the Economic Covenant, and to realize those rights which are 'recognized' by the Economic Covenant. While the obligation of progressive realization is limited by resource constraints, the Economic Covenant indicates that priority should be given to social welfare and that the level of effort should increase over time. These obligations apply to any state that has ratified the Economic Covenant, regardless of that state's economic resources.

(iv) *Generic Implementation at the International Level.* The final important feature of the Economic Covenant is what I call the system of 'generic implementation'. This feature is best understood if we see what the implementation system of the Economic Covenant does *not* do. Even if a state is only obligated to progressively realize social welfare rights within available resources, a system could be created through which the United Nations would review the activities carried

---

[47] *See* Right to Development, *supra* note 4, at 29-43, 130-43; Schachter, *supra* note 2, at 9; *Basic Human Needs*, *supra* note 2, at 227-32 (comments by Oscar Schachter). *See also* Nayer, *Human Rights and Economic Development: The Legal Foundations*, 2 Universal Human Rights 55 (1980).

[48] *See* Right to Development, *supra* note 4, at 134-43.

[49] *Id.* at 141.

[50] The impact of the available resources clause on the obligation of *developed* countries to promote the social welfare of their citizens is also worth considering. One reason behind the introduction of the clause was the concern that less developed countries would lack resources to achieve welfare goals. Comm'n on Human Rights (270th mtg.), *supra* note 22, at 9; Comm'n on Human Rights (271st mtg.), *supra* note 23, at 4; 8 Comm'n on Human Rights (272d mtg.), U.N. Doc. E/CN.4/SR.272, at 7 (1952). The clause was designed in part to allow this lack of resources to be taken into account and to show the relationship between the obligations of less developed countries and the assistance programs that might be available. But the clause does not exclusively refer to less developed countries. To the extent that all countries face resource constraints, the Economic Covenant requires consideration of available resources in evaluating the absolute level of resources devoted to social welfare. In addition, to the extent that the clause says that priority should be given to social welfare, it affects all states.

out by state X in areas like health, work, etc., and determine whether the steps taken were adequate, given resources available and other appropriate factors. Although some drafters favored such a system for the Economic Covenant, it was not adopted.[51]

The implementation system of the Economic Covenant as adopted requires states to submit 'reports on the measures which they have adopted and the progress made in achieving the observance of the rights recognized herein'.[52] These reports are transmitted to the Economic and Social Council,[53] the relevant specialized agencies,[54] and the Commission on Human Rights.[55] All these bodies may make recommendations on matters related to the realization of social welfare rights.[56] However, the Economic Covenant makes clear that neither the Commission on Human Rights nor the Economic and Social Council can make specific observations, comments, or recommendations on the record of any specific country. The Commission on Human Rights is authorized to report its recommendations on the implementation of social rights and the Economic and Social Council can make similar recommendations to the General Assembly but this authorization is explicitly limited to 'general recommendations' in the case of the Commission[57] and 'recommendations of a general nature' in the case of the Council.[58]

The qualification that any recommendation be of a general nature was explicitly made by the drafters of the Economic Covenant in order to preclude specific comments by these two bodies on the activities of a particular state.[59] Indeed, the history of these clauses suggests that recommendations were to only concern positive steps which the *international community* might take to further the program of progressive realization set forth in the Economic Covenant.[60] Three factors can be distinguished which influenced the decision to limit recommendations to general and positive suggestions for programmatic efforts at the

[51] *See generally* Annotations, *supra* note 18, at 120; Report of the Comm'n of Human Rights, 18 U.N. ESCOR, Supp. (No. 7), 21, 22, U.N. Doc. E/2573 (1954) [hereinafter cited as Tenth Report of the Comm'n on Human Rights]; 10 Comm'n on Human Rights (420th-426th mtgs.), U.N. Docs. E/CN.4/SR.420-26 (1954) [hereinafter cited as Comm'n on Human Rights (420th-426th mtgs.)].
[52] Art. 16(1).
[53] Art. 16(2)(a).
[54] Art. 16(2)(b).
[55] Art. 19.
[56] Arts. 18-23.
[57] Art. 19
[58] Art. 21.
[59] *See* Sohn, *supra* note 13, at 163-64; Annotations, *supra* note 18, at 120. *See generally* Comm'n on Human Rights (420th-426th mtgs.), *supra* note 51.
[60] *See* 10 Comm'n on Human Rights (424th mtg.), U.N. Doc. E/CN.4/SR.424, at 7 (1954) [hereinafter cited as Comm'n on Human Rights (424th mtg.)]; Tenth Report of the Comm'n on Human Rights, *supra* note 51, at 14; Annotations, *supra* note 18, at 119.

international level. There was a desire on the part of some drafters to aid rather than embarrass states. One proponent of this view said that 'measures of implementation had been designed as a form of international cooperation to assist States by elucidating their real difficulties in giving effect to the rights rather than as a method of censoring them for failing to do so'.[61] There was also concern that any specific censure might trench on national sovereignty.[62] Finally, it was felt that social welfare issues were highly technical and that the general U.N. organs would lack necessary resources and expertise.[63] The principal international responsibility for implementation of social welfare rights would therefore better lie with specialized agencies such as the International Labour Organisation (ILO), the World Health Organization (WHO), the United Nations Educational, Scientific, and Cultural Organization (UNESCO), etc.[64]

The system of generic implementation, therefore, has three principal elements. First, reporting on implementation is done by the states parties themselves, who must analyze their own progress. Secondly, on the basis of these reports the Economic and Social Council and the Commission on Human Rights can make only general recommendations which deal with positive measures to increase international efforts to foster social welfare. Finally, the task of developing concrete programs to foster specific rights is left principally to the specialized agencies.

(v) *Role of Specialized Agencies.* The overall implementation system of the Economic Covenant is therefore oriented toward generic implementation, in the sense of programs of general and positive promotion of social welfare rights. But if this were the limit of the implementation procedure, the Economic Covenant would be a very weak instrument. Effective programs can be designed only after careful consideration of the experiences of specific states, with frank appraisals of the nature and causes of failures. Moreover, it seems unlikely that states themselves would be willing to fully reveal their shortcomings. It would be hard to imagine the implementation procedures of the Economic Covenant having much effect unless the progress of states parties toward the realization of social welfare rights was subject to some kind of impartial scrutiny.

Such external and specific appraisals can be injected into the implementation process by specialized agencies such as ILO, WHO,

---

[61] 10 Comm'n on Human Rights (420th mtg.), U.N. Doc. E/CN.4/SR.420, at 11 (1954).

[62] *See* Comm'n on Human Rights (424th mtg.), *supra* note 60, at 7, 8, 10; Tenth Report of the Comm'n on Human Rights, *supra* note 51, at 14.

[63] *See* Comm'n on Human Rights (424th mtg.), *supra* note 60, at 7-8.

[64] *See* Annotations, *supra* note 18, at 117; 10 Comm'n on Human Rights (425th mtg.), U.N. Doc. E/CN.4/SR.425, at 5 (1954) [hereinafter cited as Comm'n on Human Rights (425th mtg.)].

and UNESCO. One commentator on the role of the specialized agencies has concluded that the 'agencies have a fundamental responsibility to promote realization of human rights', and that 'the primary thrust of the [Economic Covenant's] implementation procedure is directed at the agencies'.[65] Moreover, the specialized agencies historically played a major role in designing the implementation procedures and as a result have a heavy responsibility to see that the procedures work effectively.[66]

The specialized agencies clearly have a role in the development of general positive programs to promote social welfare. They also have the power and ability to provide the specific analyses of country performances which are critical if the implementation procedure is to have 'bite'. This aspect of the specialized agencies' role, which is not well understood, is based on the text and purpose of the Economic Covenant and is supported by subsequent developments in the elaboration of the Covenant's implementation procedures.

The Economic Covenant requires that national reports be transmitted to the relevant specialized agencies,[67] which are authorized to report to the Economic and Social Council on progress in their respective fields.[68] The Economic Covenant does not state that these reports must be general in nature, as the recommendations of the Commission on Human Rights and the Economic and Social Council must be, and it allows the specialized agencies' reports to contain 'particulars'.[69] It is therefore possible to argue that the specialized agencies can specifically comment on whether appropriate steps toward implementation are being taken by specific countries. The drafters of the Economic Covenant explicitly inserted the qualifying language of generality elsewhere. Its omission in the provisions dealing with specialized agencies suggests an intent to allow specific reports. Moreover, such an interpretation would be consistent with the overall system of generic implementation. One of the reasons for limiting the Commission on Human Rights and the Economic and Social Council to making general recommendations was their lack of expertise in the area of social welfare. This concern does not apply to the specialized agencies. Also, as noted, it is hard to imagine how a system of general recommendations could function effectively unless it was at least

[65] Alston, *The United Nations' Specialized Agencies and Implementation of the International Covenant on Economic, Social and Cultural Rights*, 18 Colum. J. Transnat'l L. 79, 117 (1979) [hereinafter cited as Alston No. 1], *reprinted in* Alston, *Making and Breaking Human Rights: The U.N.'s Specialized Agencies and Implementation of Economic, Social and Cultural Rights* (Human Rights and Development Working Papers No. 1, Anti-Slavery Society, 1979) (mimeo).

[66] Alston No. 1, *supra* note 65, at 92.

[67] Art. 16(2)(b).

[68] Art. 18.

[69] *Id.*

informed by impartial evaluations of the progress of specific countries. The only sources of such evaluations are the specialized agencies.[70]

The practice that has evolved under the Economic Covenant's implementation procedures supports this view. Article 18 of the Economic Covenant and article 6 of the implementation procedures[71] allow the specialized agencies to make arrangements with the Economic and Social Council to submit reports on the progressive achievement of observance of social welfare rights and states that '[t]hese reports may include particulars of decisions and recommendations on such implementation adopted by [the specialized agencies'] competent organs'. Pursuant to the provision, the ILO has submitted reports to the Economic and Social Council which analyze in detail the performance of specific countries under the Economic Covenant.[72] Moreover, the ILO has given the task of preparing these reports to its Committee of Experts which has experience in monitoring country performance under ILO standards.[73] In its work pursuant to the Economic Covenant, the Committee of Experts has relied, in part, on ILO decisions on compliance with ILO standards relevant to the general areas covered by the Economic Covenant (*e.g.*, employment policy, trade union rights, social security) by these individual states.[74]

Besides their role in monitoring country performance, the specialized agencies must also help develop more specific standards and guidelines which facilitate accurate assessment of the progressive realization of social welfare rights.[75] The drafters of the Economic Covenant clearly contemplated that the specialized agencies would develop such standards in the areas within their competence. In article 23 of the Economic Covenant, the states parties explicitly agree that international action for the achievement of the recognized rights includes, *inter alia*, the 'conclusion of conventions' and the 'adoption of recommendations'. Furthermore, the official legislative history states that '[t]he Covenant . . . had been drafted so as to contain, in the main, general statements of obligations, on the understanding that it would in general be for the competent specialized agencies to elaborate *the detailed obligations required* for the realization of the rights . . .'[76]

Not only must the specialized agencies develop standards, they must

---

[70] For a persuasive and detailed analysis of this position, *see* Alston No. 1, *supra* note 65, at 112-14.

[71] E.S.C. Res. 1988, 60 U.N. ESCOR, Supp. (No. 1) 11, U.N. Doc. E/5850 (1976).

[72] *See, e.g.*, U.N. Doc. E/1978/27 (1978); U.N. Doc. E/1979/33 (1979); U.N. Doc. E/1980/35 (1980).

[73] *See* Alston No. 1, *supra* note 65, at 112.

[74] *See, e.g.*, U.N. Doc. E/1978/27, at 3-4 (1978).

[75] *See* Alston No. 1, *supra* note 65, at 114, 115.

[76] Annotations, *supra* note 18, at 117 (emphasis added); *see* Comm'n on Human Rights (425th mtg.), *supra* note 64, at 5.

also shape the positive programs of international cooperation and assistance which constitute the principal form of international implementation of the Economic Covenant. Seen as a whole, the generic implementation system is primarily designed to coordinate the efforts of the various specialized agencies and direct their energies to the issues which arise out of an overall assessment of national progress.[77]

The Economic Covenant has left to the specialized agencies the basic responsibility for clarifying norms and devising appropriate programs to promote the realization of social welfare rights. Therefore, the specialized agencies must deal with the manifold issues which are left unanswered by the text and the history of the Economic Covenant. The Covenant can be read as imposing on states parties an obligation to give some priority to social welfare. Even if this interpretation is accepted, it does not answer a myriad of other questions essential to the realization of the Economic Covenant's goals. These include:

What measures are likely to further social welfare? How, for example, does a nation ensure the right of all to employment or an adequate standard of living? To what degree is governmental action the appropriate way to foster social welfare?

How can one determine whether the allocation of resources to social welfare represents the 'maximum' consistent with available resources? Are there minimal standards of social welfare that should be met before other national priorities should be considered?

What priorities are appropriate within the social welfare area? Are some rights more important than others? Are some 'measures' specified in the Economic Covenant more crucial than others?

What implication do the social welfare goals have for other areas of national policy?

Several areas in which the specialized agencies have begun to grapple with questions like these are examined in the remainder of this chapter. For reasons explained at the beginning of the chapter, this examination focuses on the work of the specialized agencies in relation to the Third World. While the details of this analysis are specific to situations of development and industrialization, the analysis of process and institutions is general and can be applied to efforts to answer these questions and enforce these obligations in all parts of the world.

If the work of the specialized agencies in areas like employment policy, health, and similar substantive areas is examined, and if changes in the economic development strategy employed by the World Bank and similar agencies are considered, it is possible to see how the

[77] *See* Annotations, *supra* note 18, at 117-118. *See generally* Comm'n on Human Rights (420th-426th mtgs.), *supra* note 51.

principles of the Economic Covenant have oriented the evolution of an international program of social welfare for the Third World. Various international bodies have developed the content of this commitment to social welfare, maintaining the normative orientation of the Economic Covenant but increasingly refining the programmatic aspects so that they yield specific priorities, programs, and standards relevant to the realities of Third World states. The world community has supported this program—and thus the basic norms—through active efforts to promote social welfare goals. An examination of the development of an international program of social welfare for the Third World and the nature and impact of the international promotion of that program's goals shows how international social welfare rights may influence the behavior of states and how that behavior can affect individuals.

The answer to the question originally posed, *i.e.*, what does it mean to speak of international protection of social welfare rights, can now be considered. If one takes a very broad view of international law, *i.e.*, a set of norms which (a) is concrete enough to permit description of what compliance or non-compliance would mean; (b) is accepted by the world community; (c) has or is likely to have an influence on the behavior of states; and (d) ultimately will affect individual citizens, then international social welfare rights are law.[78] The balance of this chapter demonstrates that social welfare 'rights' are reasonably specific, are widely accepted, influence behavior, and will affect individuals.

C. THE CONTEXT OF INTERNATIONAL SOCIAL WELFARE LAW: WELFARE, RIGHTS, AND DEVELOPMENT DOCTRINE

International social welfare law includes a body of general norms, specific standards, and concrete programmatic efforts by which the international community creates standards, monitors progress, and assists states in their efforts to meet their obligation to progressively realize the rights specified in the Universal Declaration and the Economic Covenant. But one cannot read these normative texts or even analyze specific programs in isolation. These manifestations of an international and universal commitment to social welfare operate in the context of a complex series of national and international processes. These processes affect the concrete meaning of specific rights and condition efforts to 'implement' them.

A systematic study of the context of international social welfare law lies beyond the scope of this chapter. Such a study would have to

---

[78] *Compare Basic Human Needs, supra* note 2, *and* Schachter, *supra* note 2, *with* Watson, *Legal Theory, Efficacy and Validity in the Development of Human Rights Norms in International Law,* 1979 U. Ill. L.F. 609. *See also* note 4 *supra*.

include a wide range of ideas, processes, and institutions. It would examine the social, economic, and political structures of the states which are obligated to progressively realize these rights to see how the goals of international law affect and are affected by national resources, priorities, and development programs. The international institutions which directly seek to promote social welfare through various forms of assistance and monitoring would have to be understood, as well as how they relate—or fail to relate—to national programs and processes. In the Third World context, moreover, such a study would have to examine how the overall international economic order affects the prospects for social welfare.

One way to begin such an ambitious, but necessary, endeavor is through an examination of development doctrine. Development doctrine is a body of thought that orients national and international actors who design and conduct programs to improve the well-being of citizens of the Third World. It seeks both to identify the causes of underdevelopment and to direct the design of developmental strategies. If international social welfare law is to have an effect on the process of Third World development, it must be integrated into development doctrine. In the past, this has not been done. Development doctrine, at least as articulated by Western scholars and international agencies influenced by Western notions of development, has given little attention to social welfare rights either at the national or the international level. This has hampered the evolution of international social welfare law as well as limited the value of development doctrine itself. To understand why development doctrine has neglected social welfare and to see how changes in development thinking may make it possible to more closely relate international social welfare rights to the process of national development, we must look historically at Western development thinking in the post-World War II era with particular emphasis on the doctrine's treatment of social welfare rights.

1. *The Liberal View of Development*

Much of the theorizing about development has been indifferent to human rights in general and to social welfare rights in particular. Western thinking about development has focused on direct efforts to increase aggregate national income. It was thought that increased affluence would lead indirectly to increased political and civil freedom, and that a higher GNP would be translated directly into better jobs, a higher standard of living, improved medical care, and better education for all.

Unfortunately, we have learned that there is no necessary relationship between economic progress and increased protection for political and civil rights.[79] In the past ten years it has become clear that rapid economic growth in Third World countries is often accompanied by increasing resort to repression by authoritarian regimes which are fundamentally opposed to the ideals of the Universal Declaration and the standards of the Political Covenant. Much has been made of an alleged trade-off between political and civil rights, on the one hand, and economic progress on the other. Elsewhere I have commented on the dubious nature of the idea of trade-offs.[80] Here I wish to deal with another aspect of conventional Western development, thought—namely, the idea that social welfare is an automatic reflex of economic progress. This belief explains the relative lack of attention to social welfare in development thinking and underlies the general lack of concern in development doctrine for the establishment of social welfare rights as an integral part of the development process.

This point of view is still quite widespread. While few scholars and officials today believe the simplistic notion that economic progress automatically brings about political and civil freedom, many think that such progress will automatically enlarge the social welfare of all citizens. This theory, which is widely held in the West,[81] is an obstacle to the development of national or international social welfare law since it denies the need for *rights* to social welfare.[82]

The view that the establishment of social welfare rights—as opposed to social welfare—is secondary or unnecessary stems from normative and instrumental aspects of the liberal capitalist tradition of development doctrine. To understand how liberal development theory leads to

---

[79] *See* I. Adelman & C. Morris, Economic Growth and Social Equity in Developing Countries (1973); Alston, *Human Rights and Basic Needs: A Critical Assessment*, 12 Revue des Droits de l'Homme 19 (1979) [hereinafter cited as Alston No. 2], *reprinted in* Alston, *Human Rights and the Basic Needs Strategy for Development* (Human Rights and Development Working Papers No. 2, Anti-Slavery Society, 1979) (mimeo).

[80] *See* Trubek, *Unequal Protection: Thoughts on Legal Services, Social Welfare, and Income Distribution in Latin America*, 13 Tex. Int'l L.J. 243 (1978) [hereinafter cited as *Unequal Protection*].

[81] This section is based on the analysis of the role of law and development in liberal capitalism found in Kennedy, *Form and Substance in Private Law Adjudication*, 89 Harv. L. Rev. 1685 (1976); Trubek, *Complexity and Contradiction in the Legal Order: Balbus and the Challenge of Critical Social Thought about Law*, 11 L. & Soc. Rev. 529 (1977); Trubek & Galanter, *Scholars in Self-Estrangement: Some Reflections on the Crisis in Law and Development Studies in the United States*, 1974 Wis. L. Rev. 1062; R. Unger, Law in Modern Society (1976).

[82] This view is suggested in Shue, *supra* note 2. Shue argues that a certain set of economic and social rights, called 'subsistence rights', belong in a category of 'basic rights' which are everyone's minimum reasonable demands upon society. This category of rights has the highest priority of implementation because their protection is essential to the enjoyment of all other rights. The basic requirement for the fulfillment of the right to subsistence is the availability of what is needed for a decent chance at a reasonably healthy and active life of normal length. Components of the right to subsistence include at least adequate food, clothing, and shelter, and minimal preventive public health care. According to Shue, since subsistence rights are a subset of basic rights, all societies have a minimum affirmative obligation to provide subsistence at least for those who cannot provide it for themselves.

liberal dev theory: an obstacle for take attention to GSC

226   *David M. Trubek*

these conclusions, both its normative orientation and its views on the effective instrumentalities of social action must be critically examined.

Liberal development thought is not indifferent to social welfare—quite the contrary. But there are features of the liberal approach that focus attention away from social welfare *rights*. The liberal concept of society stresses individual action over collective action to achieve welfare; the liberal approach to the state places more emphasis on preserving rights by limiting state action than on affirmatively promoting rights; and the liberal idea of development stresses private economic growth as the major instrument to foster higher standards of living and increased general welfare. Each of these tenets of liberal thought admits of exceptions: liberalism recognizes that in some cases collective action is needed, affirmative state intervention justified, and market-directed growth inadequate. Otherwise, liberalism could not have accepted the modern welfare state, the national analogue of international social welfare law. But each of these aspects of the welfare state are treated as exceptions or qualifications to a general principle.

These tenets of liberal thought have influenced the shape of liberal attitudes toward development. Liberal development doctrine has been heavily influenced by the 'foreground' features of liberal thought—individualism, negative rights, and private market-led growth—with each reinforcing the others. This helps explain the relative lack of concern for social welfare rights in liberal development doctrine. Social welfare rights involve collective action and affirmative efforts by the state to intervene in or supersede the market. Full endorsement of social welfare rights would involve a threefold challenge to basic tenets of liberal, capitalist thought. The challenge can easily be avoided if it is assumed, *a priori*, that private market economic growth will lead directly to higher levels of employment, better health standards, more adequate nutrition, etc. If this is the case, then positive, collective action for social welfare is not necessary, except perhaps to care for certain especially vulnerable segments of the population.

To a great degree, this is how Western development theory dealt with issues of social welfare in the Third World in the 1950s and 1960s. Primary emphasis was given to measures thought to increase per capita GNP. Resources were allocated to expand infrastructures and increase industrial output. Foreign investment by multinational firms was encouraged. A substantial role was allocated to government, but principally because private markets were thought to be imperfect or underdeveloped. Whatever role was allocated to government, the purpose of public action was to foster private capital accumulation. Social welfare programs were not totally ignored, but were relegated to a secondary plane because it was believed that growth would generate jobs, raise real incomes, and thus ensure that the needs of the world's poor would be met.

2. *The Failure of Growth Strategy and the Emergence of Welfare-Oriented Development Policies*

Perhaps the most significant occurrence in Western development theory since World War II has been the recognition that economic growth does not necessarily lead to increased social welfare. As economists evaluated the records of the post-World War II economic development programs in Asia, Africa, and Latin America, they reached three basic conclusions about the effects on social welfare of economic growth in non-socialist countries:

1. Rapid growth did not necessarily reduce unemployment.
2. Rapid growth was usually associated with a widening gap between the incomes of the rich and poor, *i.e.*, even where the absolute position of the poor improved, their relative share of national income declined.
3. The resulting growth was not adequate to ensure that even the most basic needs of the growing number of poor people would be met.[83]

Recognition that unemployment, inequality, and even absolute poverty have increased despite several decades of growth caused a broad-reaching reappraisal by Western economists of the premises of the orthodox growth paradigm.[84] A variety of viewpoints and alternative strategies, some representing relatively moderate changes of approach, others leading to a radical re-orientation of development strategy, have emerged. Most of these new approaches, however, include more emphasis on direct measures to improve social welfare.[85]

Three of the new approaches to development which have emerged deserve special emphasis. These are (i) employment-orientation, (ii) redistribution with growth, and (iii) the Basic Needs Approach (BNA). Employment-orientation stresses the need for direct efforts to increase employment, which should be as important an investment priority as increased output, and suggests the importance of labour-intensive employment strategies.[86] Redistribution with growth underscores the

[83] *See* Wilber & Jameson, *Paradigms of Economic Development and Beyond* [hereinafter cited as Wilber & Jameson], in Directions in Economic Development 1 (K. Jameson & C. Wilber eds. 1978) [hereinafter cited as Directions in Economic Development].

[84] *See generally id.*; International Labour Office, Employment, Growth and Basic Needs: A One-World Problem (1976) [hereinafter cited as International Labour Office].

[85] *See id.* at chs. 1, 2; Wilber & Jameson, *supra* note 83, at 9.

[86] *See* International Labour Office, *supra* note 84; Declaration of Principles and Programme of Action Adopted by Tripartite World Conference on Employment, Income Distribution and Social Progress and the International Division of Labour, World Employment Conference, U.N. Doc. WEC/CW/E.1 (1976) [hereinafter cited as WEC Declaration]. These sources expressly advocate an employment-oriented Basic Needs Approach. *See also* Follow-up of the World Employment Conference: Basic Needs, 65 (No. 6) International Labour Office Report to the International Labour Conference 1 (1979) [hereinafter cited as WEC Follow-up].

need for affirmative state action to ensure that the fruits of growth are divided more equally than would occur under market conditions.[87] The Basic Needs Approach is really a supplement to the first two strategies:[88] proponents of BNA argue that in addition to promoting overall per capita growth, increasing total employment, and securing greater equality in income distribution, it is necessary to directly ensure that certain basic, minimum needs of the entire population are met.[89] BNA calls on governments to make available adequate levels of food, water, clothing, shelter, medical care, and education through direct action if necessary.[90] Moreover, BNA stresses the importance of broad-based local participation in meeting basic needs.[91]

These new approaches to development are all based on a belief that the success of a development policy must be determined by its impact on all members of society and particularly on the least well-off citizens. They agree in rejecting development policies that increase aggregate income without also increasing the share of that income which goes to the poor. They differ, however, in their views of the way this goal should be achieved. Thus there is a basic difference between the more indirect strategies, such as employment creation and redistribution with growth, and the Basic Needs Approach which calls, if necessary, for direct state provision of essential commodities and services.[92]

3. *The Welfare Approach to Development and the Role of Social Welfare Rights*

The critique of development policy focuses attention of social welfare. The new approach to development policy, especially the Basic Needs Approach, asserts that direct action is needed if development is to include improved social welfare for all citizens. Economic progress alone does not necessarily improve welfare and it may at times worsen

[87] *See* Wilber & Jameson, *supra* note 83, at 12.

[88] *See id.*, at 16; Streeten & Burki, *Basic Needs: Some Issues*, 6 World Dev. 411, 413 (1978) [hereinafter cited as Streeten & Burki]. For an understanding of the objectives and types of programs inherent in the Basic Needs Approach, *see generally* International Labour Office, *supra* note 84; WEC Declaration, *supra* note 86; Streeten, *A Basic-Needs Approach to Economic Development* [hereinafter cited as Streeten], in Directions in Economic Development 73, *supra* note 83; Alston No. 2, *supra* note 79.

[89] *See* International Labour Office, *supra* note 84, at 31; Streeten, *supra* note 88, at 73-74.

[90] *See* WEC Declaration, *supra* note 86, at 4; International Labour Office, *supra* note 84, at 54; Streeten & Burki, *supra* note 88, at 414.

[91] *See* Streeten & Burki, *supra* note 88, at 4; Streeten, *supra* note 88, at 74. *See also* Alston No. 2, *supra* note 79, at 48.

[92] *See* Wilber & Jameson, *supra* note 83, at 16-18; M. Haq, Basic Needs: A Progress Report 10 (World Bank Policy Planning and Program Review, Aug. 10, 1977) (mimeo) [hereinafter cited as Haq]; J. Weeks & E. Dore, Basic Needs: The Journey of a Concept (unpublished paper, Woodstock Theological Center, Apr. 1980).

the situation of significant numbers of people.[93] Therefore, if enhanced welfare for all is the real goal of national policy, states must pursue it in a direct, affirmative fashion. This means states must put social welfare at the top, not the bottom, of the list of national development priorities. They must have specific programs to ensure employment, meet basic needs, and redistribute income. They must also ensure that these programs are effectively carried out.

This last condition provides the nexus between a welfare-oriented development policy and social welfare *rights*. One of the great flaws in past development thinking has been its technocratic bias. However development has been conceived, there has been a tendency to see development efforts as technical manipulations of programs and policies by a neutral elite committed to 'universal' goals. This vision mocks the reality of life in Third World countries—or any country for that matter. The negative welfare effects of past development policy are not accidents or thoughtless omissions—they result because such development policies benefit powerful groups in society and the international environment in which these societies are embedded. To the extent that these policies have led to increased income, education, and wellbeing for the few, often at the cost of increased misery for the many, they also strengthen the power of the few and render efforts to reverse the situation all the harder.[94]

That is why social welfare *rights* are important if development policies are to be truly welfare-oriented. Under capitalist, neo-capitalist, and command economy growth policies, the accumulation of wealth and of power seem to go hand in hand.[95] Therefore, even if welfare-oriented *policies* are established, the inequalities of wealth, and consequently of power, generated by economic progress can undermine the effectiveness of welfare programs.[96] To offset these tendencies, it is necessary to establish rights to social welfare and ensure that they are effectively protected. The recognition of the importance of rights as a weapon against power and privilege has been the impetus of a long struggle in Western capitalist nations through which workers and others outside the status and property elites have sought to protect their welfare.[97] It underlies decades of work by the International Labour Office in the field of trade union rights and employment.[98] And it is crucial in the political and economic context

[93] *See, e.g.*, The World Bank, Brazil: Human Resources Special Report (A World Bank Country Study 1979) [hereinafter cited as Brazil: Special Report].
[94] *See Unequal Protection, supra* note 80.
[95] *See* C. Lindblom, Politics and Markets (1977).
[96] *See Unequal Protection, supra* note 80.
[97] *See* Goldthorpe, *The Current Inflation: Towards the Sociological Account*, in The Political Economy of Inflation (E. Hirsch & J. Goldthorpe eds. 1978).
[98] *See* text accompanying notes 103-46 *infra*.

of many Third World countries, where disparities of income and power are extreme and rooted in centuries-old structures.[99]

The development of social welfare rights, and the systems to enforce such rights, must therefore be an essential part of the new approach to development. Most of this work must go on at the national level, with the form of the protective systems varying substantially. Methods must be evolved to ensure that program goals are not distorted and that beneficiaries of social welfare policies participate in the formulation of those policies and the monitoring of their implementation. Protection of political and civil rights will therefore also be essential to the effective protection of social welfare rights, and the goal of greater participation in development policy—a main theme of the BNA—will have to be realized in practice.[100]

4. *The Effect of the New Approach to Development on International Social Welfare Law*

The new approach to development provides a framework within which the United Nations and other international bodies can develop concrete social welfare programs. It also offers a starting point for the establishment of specific standards through which the international community can evaluate the performance of countries which have pledged to progressively realize the rights recognized by the Universal Declaration and the Economic Covenant. The new approach therefore provides the basis for the evolution of an international law of social welfare.

The Economic Covenant leaves to the specialized agencies the task of defining the precise meaning of the rights to work, health, social security, an adequate standard of living, etc. It further delegates to them the job of determining what steps are desirable or necessary to realize these rights, of developing forms of international assistance to support states which wish to take these steps, and of monitoring the process of 'progressive realization'. But taken by itself, the Economic Covenant provides inadequate guidance for these tasks. It recognizes that social welfare will require affirmative state action, supported by the international community, and it makes clear that this action will involve the investment of resources, which will take time to accomplish. But it does not provide any key to how such programs should be developed, which aspects of investment should receive what priorities

---

[99] *See* Thome, *Legal and Social Structures and the Access of the Latin American Rural Poor to the States Allocation of Goods and Services*, 2 Research L. & Soc'y 251 (1979); S. Hewlett, The Cruel Dilemmas of Development: Twentieth Century Brazil (1980) [hereinafter cited as Hewlett].

[100] *See* Alston No. 2, *supra* note 79, at 48.

and what rate of progress can be reasonably expected. All of this is left to the specialized agencies.

The Economic Covenant speaks in the language of rights, but refers to the realities of programs. Programs require targets, priorities, and specific measures. The Economic Covenant sets maximum goals but does not specify minimum standards. As a result, it might become just one more set of pious and worthy aspirations.

The new development approach offers a way to overcome the weaknesses of the Economic Covenant. Because it stresses the importance of social welfare to development policy, it provides an opportunity to relate the general goals of the Economic Covenant to concrete issues of national and international decision-making. Since the new approach to development contains targets and priorities and incorporates minimum immediate goals as well as long-term aspirations, it could provide guidance to the specialized agencies which seek to define what is meant by the obligation to progressively realize rights to work, health, etc. This is not to say that the new development approach is a panacea or that it contains the answers to all the questions left unresolved by the Economic Covenant. The new approach is just a first step—the job of translating its broad strategies into detailed programs, guidelines, and standards has barely begun. Moreover, as noted above, there are contradictions within the new model and barriers to its acceptance by the international community and the countries of the Third World. To explore the potential—and the limits—of this new approach, specific areas of social welfare and the performance of specific specialized agencies must be more closely examined.

D.   A CASE STUDY OF THE EVOLUTION OF INTERNATIONAL SOCIAL WELFARE LAW: THE ILO, THE RIGHT TO WORK, AND BASIC NEEDS

Given the structure of the Economic Covenant, the general nature of the rights it recognizes, and the key role it gives to specialized agencies in implementation, the 'sources' of international social welfare law must go beyond the Universal Declaration and the Economic and Political Covenants and must include such material as declarations made by conferences, and resolutions, recommendations, and policies of international agencies such as the ILO, the World Bank, and the WHO.[101] Evidence that the international community is developing a coherent program for promotion of social welfare in the Third World and an effective strategy to carry out that program may be found in such standards and policies.

[101] *See* note 4 *supra*.

This section will examine in depth one of the Economic Covenant's social welfare rights, *i.e.*, the right to work, focusing on the work of the International Labour Organisation. The ILO is the key specialized agency concerned with the right to work established by the Economic Covenant. The ILO was active in this area long before the United Nations was founded and it played an influential role in the drafting of the social welfare portions of the International Bill of Rights.[102] Recently, the ILO has given increasing attention to the development of concrete programs to improve social welfare in the Third World and the establishment of standards to evaluate progress toward that goal. Its efforts in the area of employment demonstrate concretely how the international community has sought to refine the principles of the Economic Covenant, develop affirmative programs to assist states which seek to realize these rights, and develop methods to monitor progress. This brief study of the work of the ILO, when seen in the context of parallel work by other specialized agencies such as the World Bank and the WHO, suggests that progress has been made in this area, but also that the full promise of the Economic Covenant and of a truly effective international approach to social welfare has yet to be realized.

1. *The Right to Work*

One of the most important of the social welfare rights is the 'right to work', understood in the broad sense of the term. Creating a 'right to work' involves ensuring not only that all who seek and need work can find it but also that there exist:

   (i) the right to free choice of work;
  (ii) the right to a living wage;
 (iii) the right to decent working conditions;
 (iv) the right of freedom from discrimination in work; and
  (v) the right of workers to form trade unions.

The Economic Covenant protects all these aspects of the right to work. Article 6 recognizes 'the right to work, which includes the right of everyone to the opportunity to gain his living by work which he freely chooses or accepts . . . ' Article 7 recognizes fair wages, equal pay for equal work, a living wage, decent working conditions, and adequate leisure time. Article 8 protects the right to form trade unions, trade union freedom, and the right to strike. Article 11 supplements the guarantee of a living wage found in article 7 by recognizing 'the

---

[102] *See* Jenks, *Human Rights, Social Justice and Peace: The Broader Significance of the ILO Experience*, in International Protection of Human Rights 227 (A. Eide & A. Schou eds. 1968) [hereinafter cited as Jenks].

right of everyone to an adequate standard of living for himself and his family . . . '

2. *The ILO and the Economic Covenant*

The International Labour Organisation has played a major role in efforts to realize the right to work. At the time the Economic Covenant was adopted, it was clear that the specialized agencies would have an important role in giving specific content to the rights the Covenant protects.[103] Moreover, given the mandate of the ILO, which covers many of the social welfare rights from work to social security,[104] and its long record in this area, it was understood that the ILO would take the lead within the U.N. system in the implementation of the provisions of the Economic Covenant relating generally to work, employment, and trade unions.[105]

Immediately after the adoption of the Economic Covenant by the General Assembly, the ILO acknowledged its responsibilities under that Covenant. The Governing Body and the International Labour Conference pledged the full cooperation of the ILO in the task of implementing the Economic Covenant. Jenks has stated that the ILO could become 'the most effective executing agency of much of the Covenant'.[106] He argued that the ILO could provide a way to give specificity to the general provisions of the Economic Covenant and put teeth in its enforcement machinery.

Jenks' argument to demonstrate how the ILO could fill the gaps left by the drafters of the Economic Covenant highlights its weaknesses. He noted that while the language of the Economic Covenant is extremely general, the ILO had an established body of standards in the field of social welfare which could give content to the Covenant's general norms. Existing ILO conventions and recommendations (the 'International Labour Code') already dealt in detail with issues like fair wages, occupational health and safety, trade union rights, etc., and new international standards in specific areas not covered by the current Code could be added through appropriate ILO techniques. Unlike the Economic Covenant, ILO instruments provided for detailed reporting on compliance and established specific structures for international monitoring. Finally, Jenks pointed out that the ILO had the capacity to provide positive assistance to member states which sought to protect the right to work and other economic, social, and cultural

---

[103] *See* Jenks, *supra* note 102, at 250.

[104] *See* Constitution of the International Labour Organisation, 62 Stat. 3485, T.I.A.S. No. 1868, 15 U.N.T.S. 35.

[105] *See* Jenks, *supra* note 102, at 248-50.

[106] *Id.* at 251

rights. ILO advisory services and other forms of technical assistance were available and had been widely used.[107]

One of the first measures the ILO undertook following adoption of the Economic Covenant was a comparative analysis of the Economic and Political Covenants and the international labour conventions and recommendations.[108] This analysis was undertaken to permit the ILO to determine how it could make the most effective contribution to implementing the rights protected by the Economic and Political Covenants.[109] The report describes in detail all the standards that had been established by the ILO through 1968 as they relate to specific provisions of the two human rights Covenants. It contains a catalog of ILO instruments protecting social welfare,[110] and describes detailed conventions and recommendations covering a wide range of areas, including fair wages, equal pay, occupational safety and health, trade union rights, social security, and protection of the family.

In addition to indicating the areas in which the ILO had already developed international standards which could give greater specificity to rights guaranteed by the Economic Covenant, the report discusses the overall relationship between the activities of the ILO and the task of implementing social welfare rights.[111] One of the report's general observations in this area dealt with the relationship between the Economic Covenant's principle of progressive realization and the ILO's approach. While ILO instruments do not explicitly recognize the concept of progressive realization, they do contain sufficient flexibility so that there is no necessary conflict between the two approaches. The report concluded that since ILO instruments deal with very specific issues and since member states are not bound to adhere to all of them, the 'ILO system of individual conventions, each dealing with a clearly defined subject in itself, makes possible the gradual assumption of an ever-widening network of obligations'[112] and is therefore consistent with the principle of progressive realization.

The report's second general observation on the relationship of ILO activities and the implementation of social welfare rights confirmed Jenks' arguments. In many areas of social welfare, rights recognized in general terms in the Economic Covenant are already subject to a substantial body of precise and detailed ILO standards. Moreover, the report concluded, in many cases 'the guarantees called for by the ILO

---

[107] *See id.* at 245-57.
[108] *Comparative Analysis of the International Covenants on Human Rights and International Labour Conventions and Recommendations*, 52 ILO O. Bull. 181 (1969) [hereinafter cited as *Comparative Analysis*].
[109] *See id.* at 181; Jenks, *supra* note 102, at 250.
[110] *See Comparative Analysis, supra* note 108, at 181-214.
[111] *See id.* at 214-16.
[112] *Id.* at 214.

instruments go beyond the standards embodied in the Covenants'.[113] However, the report noted that there were areas covered by the Economic Covenant in which the ILO had not acted or in which existing ILO standards were incomplete, so that the Economic Covenant could serve as an impetus to further ILO actions in the social welfare area.

3. *The ILO, Employment Policy, and Development Strategy*

The overall work of the ILO in implementing human rights is covered elsewhere in this volume.[114] This section will focus on the work of the ILO in the area of employment policy. Employment policy is clearly a major aspect of any effective program to realize the right to work. Article 6 of the Economic Covenant explicitly lists a full employment policy as one of the 'steps' to be taken to realize the right to work. Moreover, employment policy is an area in which the effort to implement social welfare rights in the Third World has forced the international community in general, and the ILO in particular, to re-examine the conventional wisdom of development strategy and to articulate new approaches to development.

(i) *Unemployment and the Right to Work in the Third World.* The unemployment problem in the Third World is massive. According to a study prepared by the ILO in 1976, there were then 300 million persons in the Third World either unemployed or underemployed.[115] The ILO estimated that in the remaining quarter of the twentieth century, an additional 700 million people would enter the job markets of the developing countries.[116] In such a situation, the 'right to work' has a hollow sound. Legal protections are not likely to have much meaning if such conditions of massive unemployment prevail. In this context, employment policy becomes the central issue for any organization concerned with protecting the right to work.

But what constitutes an 'employment policy'? If the assumption is that rapid economic growth will, by itself, lead to increased levels of employment and growing real wages, then a growth policy is also an employment policy. As long as rapid growth is fostered, there is no need for specific affirmative efforts to foster employment. This was the approach taken by many institutions concerned with the development of the poorer countries. Apparently, this view was also held by the ILO in the years immediately following World War II.[117]

The ILO's special concern with employment, however, caused it to question the conventional wisdom of development economics even before other organizations had begun the reappraisal that marked the

---

[113] *Id.*
[114] *See* ch. 7 *infra.*
[115] *See* International Labour Office, *supra* note 84, at 3.
[116] *Id.* at 9.
[117] *See id.* at 1-3.

1970s. From these doubts emerged the belief that full employment requires active efforts by government and must be a priority goal in national planning.

(ii) *The Need for Affirmative Action: the Employment Policy Convention of 1964.* The ILO began its reappraisal of orthodox development doctrines in the 1960s. At that time, according to the ILO's Director General, 'the ILO began to question the conventional wisdom that higher levels of employment would automatically result from growth, irrespective of the pattern pursued'.[118]

This recognition of the need for affirmative action to ensure employment was reflected in the Employment Policy Convention (EPC) adopted by the General Conference of the ILO in 1964.[119] Although the EPC predates the Economic Covenant, it was explicitly designed to implement those provisions of the Universal Declaration which guarantee rights to work and to protection against unemployment.[120] The EPC requires ratifying states to declare and pursue a policy designed to promote full, productive, and freely chosen employment and to relate these goals to a coordinated economic and social policy. The EPC further specifies that such policies must be 'active' and must be a major goal of the ratifying state.[121]

While the 1964 Employment Policy Convention reflected an awareness by the ILO that affirmative state action would be needed to ensure realization of the right to work and that such action would have to be given priority, the EPC was silent on what types of measures should be taken or how priorities should be determined. Moreover, the EPC does not deal specifically with the problems of the Third World. Although it represented an important shift in approach, the EPC did not offer Third World governments and the international community the guidance needed if they were to shape an effective approach to employment policy in the context of development.[122]

Some of these deficiencies were remedied by the non-binding recommendations which were promulgated by the ILO to assist states which sought to implement the EPC.[123] But those recommendations fell short of articulating a comprehensive approach to the employment problems of the Third World.[124] In the 1970s, however, the ILO began

[118] *Id.* at 2.
[119] Employment Policy Convention (No. 122) *adopted* July 9, 1964.
[120] *Id.*
[121] *See id.*, arts. 1, 2.
[122] While its provisions are silent as to implementation measures and priorities, the EPC nevertheless must be viewed as a primary instrument establishing fundamental employment policy standards. *See* 48 Proc. International Labour Conference 773 (1964).
[123] Employment Policy Recommendations (No. 22), 48 Proc. International Labour Conference 908 (1964).
[124] *See id.* at 916-17, 925-26.

a new phase of its work on employment policy. From these activities emerged one of the most comprehensive international statements of the new approach to development.

(iii) *The World Employment Conference of 1976.* In 1969 the ILO initiated what it called an 'employment-oriented approach to development'.[125] Under its World Employment Programme, the ILO began to provide technical assistance in the employment policy area to countries which requested it and to conduct research on the relationship between development policy, income distribution, and employment.[126] In 1974, the Governing Body of the ILO convened a world conference on employment, income distribution, social progress, and the international division of labour. A reappraisal of conventional approaches to development, from the point of view of effective realization of the right to work was to be a key feature of this Conference.[127]

The preparatory material which the ILO produced for the Conference reflected a major shift in thinking about development in general and employment in particular.[128] Not only did the ILO reject the *laissez-faire* approach to employment policy and development strategy, it proposed a specific approach to development that would foster employment and articulated a new, comprehensive approach to development that went well beyond the issue of employment.

The key to the ILO's critique of past policies was the recognition that they did not reduce poverty. The ILO concluded that 'conventional development strategies have not succeeded in reducing the numbers of poor and inadequately employed people'.[129] Even though many less developed countries had experienced rapid growth, this growth had not significantly reduced unemployment, increased real wages, or lessened income inequality. Growth which was dependent on capital intensive investment did not provide enough jobs to allow employment to keep up with increases in population. Since growth strategies often compressed the real wages of industrial workers, they did not significantly contribute to better living conditions for the mass of the population. And since rapid growth led to increased profits for *elites*, income distribution in many Third World countries became less, not more, equal.[130]

To deal with this situation, the ILO proposed a new approach to

[125] International Labour Office, *supra* note 84, at 2.
[126] *See id.* at 2-3.
[127] *Id.* at 4-5.
[128] *See id.* at 4-7.
[129] *Id.* at 31.
[130] *See id.* at 15-30.

development. It would incorporate the lessons of the employment-oriented approach to development, but would include other elements as well. 'An employment-oriented strategy, by itself, will not suffice', the ILO concluded. 'The creation of more and better jobs is not enough; employment issues are intimately connected to the wider issues of poverty and inequality.[131] Therefore, the ILO proposed that development planning include as an explicit goal and high priority the satisfaction of an absolute minimum level of basic needs.

'Basic needs' are defined as minimum requirements for private consumption and essential community services. They include adequate food, shelter, and clothing, as well as safe water, sanitation, transport, health, and education. A basic needs strategy, moreover, implies the active participation in development decisions of the people affected.[132]

The basic needs approach differed from past development strategies in a number of ways. It involved making the satisfaction of basic needs a first priority, and rejected indirect, growth-based strategies as the exclusive mechanism for meeting this goal. It stressed redistribution of income, land reform, more labour-intensive technologies, productive mobilization of the unemployed, and techniques for improving the productivity of the working poor. It called for increased investment in the 'traditional' agricultural and 'informal' urban sectors, and for the establishment of institutions which would facilitate popular participation in the development process.[133]

The result of these efforts was the Tripartite World Conference on Employment, Income Distribution and Social Progress and the International Division of Labour, held in Geneva in 1976. This Conference issued a detailed Declaration of Principles and Programme of Action (WEC Declaration)[134] and requested the Governing Body of the ILO to implement the detailed program spelled out in the WEC Declaration.[135]

The WEC Declaration endorsed the ILO's critique of conventional development policy. It noted that:

the experience of the past two decades has shown that rapid growth of gross national product has not automatically reduced poverty and inequality in many countries, nor has it provided sufficient productive employment within acceptable periods of time; the growth of productive employment is one of the most effective means to ensure a just and equitable distribution of income and to raise the standard of living of the majority of the population; problems of underemployment, unemployment, and poverty must be attacked by

[131] *Id.* at 31.
[132] *Id.* at 32.
[133] *See id.* at 32-43.
[134] *See* note 86 *supra.*
[135] *See* WEC Declaration, *supra* note 86, at 8.

means of direct, well-coordinated measures at both national and international levels.[136]

The WEC Declaration also devised a Programme of Action covering Basic Needs, International Manpower Movements, Technologies for Productive Employment Creation in Developing Countries, Manpower Policies in Developing Countries, and the role of Multinational Enterprises in Employment Creation in the Developing Countries. A few features of this Programme of Action deserve special note. In dealing with strategies to create full employment and meet basic needs in developing countries, the WEC Declaration noted, *inter alia*, that:

these measures will often involve a transformation of social structures and income redistribution; systems to produce and distribute essential goods and services must be strengthened; employment creation must be a high priority; rural development and agrarian reform must be emphasized; and international as well as national action will be needed to meet basic needs.[137]

(iv) *From Labour Standards to a Comprehensive Development Strategy.* With the publication of the WEC Declaration, the ILO completed a long process by which its approach to the right to work had been extended to include not only standard setting but also an affirmative programmatic approach which included the whole range of development activity at the national and international level. Moreover, by proposing a basic needs strategy, which suggests in general terms the appropriate priorities for the allocation of available domestic and international resources, the ILO had produced at least a partial answer to the problem of defining the nature of a state's obligation under the Economic Covenant to progressively realize the right to work and other social welfare rights.

(v) *The Impact of the Basic Needs Approach on the Work of the ILO.* Two key questions remain to be answered: what effect has the WEC Declaration had on the work of the ILO, and to what extent has the ILO been able to influence development policy in the Third World? Full answers to these questions are beyond the scope of this chapter, but it is important to recognize that until they can be answered it will be impossible to evaluate Jenks' optimistic view that the ILO could become 'the most effective executing agency of much of the [Economic] Covenant'.[138]

The ILO has taken numerous actions designed to implement the principles of the WEC Declaration. In the area of standard setting, it has worked to secure implementation of several ILO conventions

[136] *See id.* at 2.
[137] *See id.* at 4-8.
[138] Jenks, *supra* note 102, at 251.

which relate directly to the basic needs and employment-orientation approaches. These include the Human Resources Development Convention (No. 142), which looks toward better utilization of labour resources,[139] and the Rural Workers' Organizations Convention (No. 141) which strengthens the capabilities of rural unions.[140] It has initiated action to revise the Employment Policy Convention (No. 122) to make it more consistent with the basic needs approach.[141] The ILO has also monitored progress by specific countries and the international community toward the goals of the WEC Declaration. In 1979 the International Labour Office produced a comprehensive report which assessed progress towards an international strategy for meeting basic needs, and included analyses of problems and results in a wide range of areas, from employment to health to local participation in development decision making.[142] As this report notes, the ILO has worked both with the member states of the United Nations and with other specialized agencies to foster the basic needs approach.[143] The report lists numerous technical assistance projects which the ILO has aided and missions it has sent to Third World states.[144] It points out that the ILO has helped other specialized agencies, such as the Food and Agriculture Organization (FAO)[145] and the WHO,[146] whose work is in areas into which ILO's concern for basic needs also extends.

It would be desirable to have a comprehensive and independent assessment of the extent and impact of these new directions in ILO activities. The 1979 report indicates that much has been done. It does not, however, permit an assessment of the priority which has been given to these activities within the ILO, nor to gauge the impact of these activities on other specialized agencies or on Third World states. If such an assessment confirms what a reading of the report suggests, then the ILO has made significant steps toward the goals outlined by Jenks.

(vi) *The ILO and Evaluation of Country Performance under the Economic Covenant.* Although insufficient data is available to allow an evaluation of the full impact of the ILO's programmatic efforts in social welfare, it is possible to examine a key feature of the ILO's work under the Economic Covenant. As indicated above, the ILO has assumed responsibility for commenting on the reports submitted by

[139] *See* WEC Follow-up, *supra* note 86, at 50.
[140] *See id.* at 113.
[141] *See id.* at 116; WEC Declaration, *supra* note 86, at 8.
[142] WEC Follow-up, *supra* note 86.
[143] *See id.* at 112-23.
[144] *See generally id.* at 39. *See also* International Labour Office, *supra* note 84.
[145] *See* WEC Follow-up, *supra* note 86, at 112.
[146] *See id.* at 53-55.

states parties on their progress under the Economic Covenant.[147] This responsibility offers an opportunity for the ILO to take the central role in implementation which it sought during the drafting of the Economic Covenant and which the debates over implementation procedures apparently indicate it was to have. It also offers an opportunity to relate all three aspects of the specialized agency implementation of the Economic Covenant—program development, standard setting, and country monitoring.

In its programmatic work the ILO has developed the idea of a basic needs approach which indicates the priorities which countries should set in their development policies and programs. These priorities offer at least a crude set of standards that can be used for evaluative purposes and are thus a starting point for the evolution of some of the specific norms which are needed in development policy.

In its observations on a country's progress, the ILO seeks to draw on a wide range of data including its own appraisal of that country's performance under existing ILO standards and the progress the country has made in implementing recommendations made by ILO advisory teams.[148] However, the observations fall short of what one might hope for, given the central role the ILO necessarily must play under the Economic Covenant. The observations on progress by Third World countries do reflect a desire to draw on available normative sources including the WEC Declaration and specific ILO instruments. Some effort is made to use these sources to develop guidelines and assess country performance in light of these principles. But the authors of the observations often lack essential information, do not try to reach any conclusions about the adequacy of specific efforts, and deal very cursorily with vital issues.[149]

It is clear that these 'deficiencies' in the observations in part reflect a conscious strategy on the part of the ILO. The Committee of Experts has signalled that it would begin its task of monitoring in a very general way, in part because of the technical problems involved in such evaluation and in part because of the resistance of some states to any critical evaluation. It is therefore too early to give a final assessment of the way the ILO will carry out these duties.[150]

This initial experience of the ILO underscores the potential of the approach in which the specialized agencies could combine program development, standard setting, and country monitoring, and in which programmatic ideas could be translated into standards for monitoring.

[147] *See* text accompanying note 74 *supra*.
[148] *See, e.g.,* U.N. Doc. E/1978/27, at 3-6 (1978); U.N. Doc. E/1979/33, at 10-11 (1979). *See also* WEC Follow-up, *supra* note 86, at 2.
[149] *See, e.g.,* U.N. Doc. E/1978/27, at 1, 3-6 (1978); U.N. Doc. E/1979/33, at 10-13 (1979).
[150] *See* U.N. Doc. E/1979/33, at 15, 16 (1979).

.lso underscores the difficulties of this approach. Among the
ns which have appeared are the lack of comprehensive data on
sues, the inadequacy of efforts to translate programmatic ideas
standards for evaluation, the failure to develop more specific
rnational instruments in the broad area covered by the Economic
Covenant, and the continuing resistance of some states to international monitoring. Perhaps as the ILO and the states parties gain
experience under the Economic Covenant and greater attention is
devoted to the task of translating programs into standards, these
problems will be resolved.

E.   THE WHO AND THE RIGHT TO HEALTH

The ILO is not the only specialized agency that has devoted attention
to the problem of developing programs, priorities, and standards for
improving social welfare in the Third World. This section very briefly
examines the parallel efforts of the World Health Organisation
(WHO). Its experience demonstrates that some of the concepts of the
new development approach are influencing work in the health field as
well as the employment field. But the WHO case also shows how far
some specialized agencies are from the goal of developing and applying
a body of normative principles based on the new approach.

1. *The WHO and the Economic Covenant*

Article 12 of the Economic Covenant guarantees the right to the
'highest attainable standard of physical and mental health'. Article
12(2) articulates the 'steps' necessary to achieve this right including
reduction of the stillbirth and infant mortality rates; provision for the
healthy development of children; improvement of all aspects of
environmental and industrial hygiene; the prevention, treatment, and
control of epidemic, endemic, occupational, and other diseases; and
provision to all of medical service and attention in the event of sickness.

The primary specialized agency responsible for implementing this
right to health is the World Health Organisation. The WHO has begun
to develop policies which could be used to evaluate whether countries
are taking reasonable efforts to progressively realize the right to health.
These policies, which have distinct similarities to the Basic Needs
Approach, suggest the possibility of identifying the minimal standards,
priority measures, and specific targets that are needed for effective
international implementation.[151]

[151] *See* Alternative Approaches to Meeting Basic Health Needs in Developing Countries (V.
Djukanovic & E. Mach eds. 1975) [hereinafter cited as Alternative Approaches]; World Health
Organisation, Primary Health Care (1978) [hereinafter cited as Primary Health Care]. Part IV of
Alternative Approaches, *supra*, at 109-12, is entitled 'Recommendations to WHO and
UNICEF'. The heart of the recommendations was incorporated in the conceptual and program-
matic aspects of primary health care as put forth by the WHO in Primary Health Care, *supra*.

The WHO's approach is called 'primary health care' (PHC).[152] The WHO has set the goal of health for all by the year 2000 and views primary health care as the strategy needed to achieve this goal.[153] In essence, PHC is an analogue to the Basic Needs Approach to development. PHC places the right to health in both the broader context of development and in the more narrow context of a specific health care system.

The fundamental concept of the WHO approach is as follows:

Primary Health Care is essential health care made universally accessible to individuals and families by means acceptable to them, through their full participation and at a cost that the community and country can afford. It forms an integral part both of the country's health system of which it is the nucleus and of the overall social and economic development of the community.[154]

The PHC strategy addresses fundamental health problems by providing promotive, preventive, curative, and rehabilitative services at community levels. The WHO report on PHC maintains that although PHC should reflect community needs and community social and economic conditions, certain essential elements are part of any country-specific PHC system. These elements include: (a) promotion of proper nutrition; (2) supply of adequate amounts of safe water; (3) provision of basic sanitation services; (4) provision of maternal and child care, including family planning; (5) immunization against major infectious diseases; (6) prevention and control of locally endemic disease; and (7) health education at the community level which addresses health problems, the methods of preventing and controlling them, and appropriate treatment for common diseases and injuries.[155]

Like the Basic Needs Approach, the Primary Health Care strategy rejects past and current trends in health care systems in both developed and developing countries. These trends have resulted in a high degree of urban centralization with curative medical specialization geared toward serving the rich and elite instead of meeting the health care needs of broader and needier segments of the population.[156] The PHC view is that the central issue is not a shortage of resources but the misallocation of health care and development resources.[157]

[152] *See* Primary Health Care, *supra* note 151.
[153] *See* The Work of WHO 1976-1977, 243 WHO O. Rec. x-xi (1978).
[154] Primary Health Care, *supra* note 151, at 2.
[155] *See id.*
[156] *See id.* at 7. *See also* Alternative Approaches, *supra* note 151, at 10-25; B. Hetzel, Basic Health Care in Developing Countries: An Epidemiological Perspective 1 (1978); Abel-Smith, Poverty, Development, and Health Policy 1, 13-20 (Public Health Papers No. 69, 1978).
[157] *See* Primary Health Care, *supra* note 151, at 7-10. *See also* Inter-relationships Between Health Programmes and Socio-Economic Development (Public Health Papers No. 49, 1973); Health Economics 1 (Public Health Papers No. 64, 1975).

Just as the WEC Declaration suggested that effective implementation of the right to work required measures in many areas, so the PHC goes beyond the confines of the health care system. The PHC calls for changes in agricultural policy to ensure more adequate and nutritious food, modification of water, housing, and transport policies, and reforms in education.[158]

The PHC can be seen as a detailed program for implementing article 12 of the Economic Covenant. It includes all elements of the 'steps' mentioned there but sets them forth in a more programmatic form, with due regard for the problems of health care in developing states. The PHC stresses giving priority attention to the most urgent needs and includes principles concerning the most efficient allocation of available resources. The PHC also stresses such features as appropriate technology, low-cost equipment, simple drugs, and local manufacture. Maximum use of local resources with community involvement in health care through the use of midwives, medical assistants, and 'barefoot doctors' is a major feature of the PHC approach.[159]

2. *The WHO and Implementation of the Economic Covenant*

While the Primary Health Care approach seems to provide a basis from which the WHO could evaluate progress toward realization of the right to health, the WHO has not sought to use these principles as standards to measure country progress under the Economic Covenant. Unlike the ILO, the WHO does not have a tradition of standard-setting through international agreements or of monitoring country progress through institutions like the ILO's Committee of Experts.[160] Perhaps for this reason, the WHO has construed its obligations under article 18 of the Economic Covenant very differently than has the ILO. The WHO has submitted one report[161] pursuant to Resolution 1988 (LX) of the Economic and Social Council, which calls on the specialized agencies to submit reports on progress toward achieving the goals of the Economic Covenant.[162] In contrast with the ILO's response, which focuses on individual country progress and comments on the extent to which specific standards have been met, the WHO report focuses exclusively 'on the implementation of Article 12 at the global, international level and on the relevant global policy decided collectively by the Organization's Member States'.[163] Thus the WHO's report merely covers those very issues of 'generic implementation' which the

---

[158] *See* Primary Health Care, *supra* note 151, at 16–18.
[159] *See id.* at 25–31.
[160] *See* Alston No. 1, *supra* note 65, at 111.
[161] U.N. Doc. E/1980/24 (1980).
[162] *See* text accompanying and note 71.
[163] U.N. Doc. E/1980/24, at 2 (1980).

Economic and Social Council is responsible for and ignores the kind of country-specific data which article 18 calls for from specialized agencies and which the ILO has provided.

One can only hope that the WHO will modify its approach in future reports. The ILO experience has shown that programmatic policies like the BNA or PHC can be used as sources of the standards needed for international monitoring of country progress. If the specialized agencies are to play the role assigned them by article 18, the WHO will have to find ways to follow the ILO lead and directly evaluate national efforts.[164]

F.   U.N. DEVELOPMENT POLICY AND SOCIAL WELFARE

This chapter has explored the nature of the international protection of social welfare rights. We have seen that within the U.N. system primary responsibility for this task lies with specialized agencies such as the ILO and WHO. These agencies have a triple role in the area of social welfare. They are responsible for developing positive programs to assist countries which seek to further the broad goals of the Economic Covenant, they are the source of more specific standards to measure progress toward those goals, and they are charged with monitoring country progress.

One of the major conclusions of this chapter is that the tasks of program development, standard setting, and country monitoring are complementary. The human rights standards of the Economic Covenant are too general to permit a simple comparison of national performance with the text of the Covenant. More precise standards must be developed before it is possible to determine if states are meeting the obligation under the Economic Covenant to progressively realize the rights they have recognized. But these 'standards' cannot be fixed except in the context of sensible programs to reach desired goals with limited resources.

This means that the first task is to design development policies which are oriented towards the social welfare goals of the Economic Covenant.[165] While the values articulated by the Economic Covenant provide a starting point for analysis, they must be related to specific measures and priorities. A development model oriented towards social welfare must take into account the overall national and international economic structure, recognize the need to generate resources as well as allocate them, identify linkages among goals, and specify barriers to the realization of those goals. Some of the specialized agencies

---

[164] *See* Alston No. 1, *supra* note 65, at 111.
[165] *See* Alston, *Human Rights and the New International Development Strategy*, 10 Bull. Peace Proposals 281 (1979) [hereinafter cited as Alston, *Human Rights*].

have begun to design such development policies. But these policies are far from forming a consistent and precise strategy. There are significant areas of debate and disagreement even among those who accept the new approach's basic principles. A great deal of work remains to be done.

It has only been possible to examine a few aspects of the work of the U.N. system in this area. The efforts canvassed in this chapter are part of the overall activity of the specialized agencies in the field of development policy. A more complete survey of the work of the United Nations in social welfare would have to examine the overall U.N. development effort. In such a canvass, special attention should be given to the work of the World Bank. Since the World Bank is the major international source of funds for development and since it has a significant impact on national development plans, its policies and programs are at the core of U.N. activity in the social welfare area. In recent years, the World Bank has given increased attention to problems of employment, health, education, and other aspects of social policy.[166] The Bank has endorsed the Basic Needs Approach,[167] and has made significant contributions to the new development model which underlies the approach taken by the ILO and the WHO.[168] It has made the eradication[169] of absolute poverty a priority goal[169] and has stressed the importance of more equitable distribution of the benefits of economic growth. The Bank has sought to allocate more money to the poorest countries and to the programs that aid the poorest segments of the population.[170] Moreover, it has conducted detailed studies to determine the resources needed to meet the basic needs goals in specific countries.[171]

If these trends continue, they hold promise for more effective implementation of the rights guaranteed by the Economic Covenant. Increased World Bank concern for social welfare will mean more detailed attention to the relationship between the goals of the Economic Covenant and national development policies. Since the Bank has substantial experience with development planning and policy, its technical staff has the capability to work out many of the

---

[166] *See* van de Laar, The World Bank and the World's Poor (ISS Occasional Papers No. 58, 1976).

[167] *See id. See also* Pres. Robert McNamara's 1970, 1973, & 1976 Addresses to the World Bank's Board of Governors.

[168] *See, e.g.,* Haq, *supra* note 92; Burki & Boorhoeve, Global Estimates for Meeting Basic Needs: Background Paper (World Bank Policy Planning and Program Review, Aug. 10, 1977); Brazil: Special Report, *supra* note 93.

[169] *See* World Bank Annual Report 3 (1978).

[170] *Id. See also* Pres. Robert McNamara's 1970, 1973, & 1976 Addresses to the World Bank's Board of Governors.

[171] *See, e.g.,* Brazil: Special Report, *supra* note 93.

complex problems presented by the challenge of the new development model. Moreover, the Bank can ensure that the level of international support for social welfare programs will increase. Thus the World Bank can at the same time help Third World states determine the best way to pursue the goal of progressive realization of social welfare, provide other specialized agencies with more specific ideas as to the policies which can be used to measure progress in this area, and provide resources needed to make these efforts effective.

G. SOCIAL WELFARE, BASIC NEEDS, AND THE NEW INTERNATIONAL ECONOMIC ORDER

This chapter has largely been concerned with analyzing relationships between international law and the national efforts to realize social welfare goals. The international law of human rights has established basic principles which should govern national endeavors. How specialized agencies can help set more precise standards, monitor progress, and provide direct assistance to Third World countries has already been demonstrated. It is, however, also important to see this process in the context of the broader effort now underway to transform the international economic order in ways that would substantially increase the resources available to Third World countries, thereby increasing their capability to enhance the welfare of their citizens. This effort has crystalized in the call for a New International Economic Order (NIEO). The struggle by Third World states to restructure what they consider to be an unjust international economic order will be one, if not the, dominant theme of the development debate in the 1980s.

1. *The NIEO*

The NIEO strikes at the heart of the economic relationships between developed and developing countries. Its fundamental goals are to close the resource gap between these countries and to enhance 'the capacity of developing countries for self-sustained as contrasted with dependent development'.[172] By their nature, the NIEO proposals represent comprehensive principles and programs of reform and restructuring which operate through a wide range of activities.

The NIEO can be seen as a continuation of the critique of past approaches to development policy. The new approach to development stresses the need to deal directly with the needs of the poor and to transform national structures that create and maintain poverty. The NIEO is based on the view that Third World poverty can only be

---

[172] U.N. Doc. A/S-11/5, at 12 (1980). *See generally* Declaration on the Establishment of a New International Economic Order, G.A. Res. 3201, S-VI U.N. GAOR, Supp. (No. 1) 3, U.N. Doc. A/9559 (1974).

understood in the context of the entire world economy. It asserts that the current international economic system is one of the causes of underdevelopment and that until it is reformed there is no way to make major progress toward greater global equality.

The basic NIEO principles are found in two General Assembly resolutions—the Declaration[173] and the Programme of Action[174] on the Establishment of a New International Economic Order. The Declaration sets forth the fundamental principles of the NIEO. Most importantly, they include:

(a) effective domestic control over natural resources; (b) regulation of the activities of multi-national corporations; (c) just and equitable prices for primary commodity and other exports of developing countries; (d) money and development finance reforms; (e) market access for products of developing countries; and (f) strengthening the science and technological capacity of developing countries.

These principles are promulgated within a framework of international cooperation and especially of mutual economic, trade, financial, and technical cooperation within the Third World.[175]

The Programme of Action elaborates upon the principles of the Declaration by both recognizing more targeted objectives and establishing specific modes of action. For example, the Programme of Action seeks strengthened Third World export earnings.[176] Moreover, it seeks greater real transfers of resources to the Third World through both official development assistance and international financial institutions.[177]

[173] *Id.*

[174] G.A. Res. 3202, S-VI U.N. GAOR, Supp. (No. 1) 5, U.N. Doc. A/9559 (1974).
Two other documents, the Charter of Economic Rights and Duties of States, G.A. Res. 3281, 29 U.N. GAOR, Supp. (No. 31) 50, U.N. Doc. A/9631 (1974), and G.A. Res. 3362 on Development and Economic Co-operation, S-VII U.N. GAOR, Supp. (No. 1) 3, U.N. Doc. A-10301 (1975), must be read *in pari materia* with the NIEO Declaration and Programme of Action. The Charter of Economic Rights and Duties of States reinforces the principles and programs of the NIEO by describing them with the judicial terms of 'rights', 'obligations', 'duties', and 'responsibilities'. This Charter might be viewed as the 'code of conduct for States in their economic relations'. Gosovic & Ruggie, *Origins and Evolution of the Concept*, 28 Int'l Soc. Sci. J. 639, 642 (1976) [hereinafter cited as Gosovic & Ruggie].
The Resolution on Development and Economic Co-operation was adopted at the General Assembly's Seventh Special Session in 1975. It elaborates upon both the NIEO Declaration and Programme of Action. In some respects, this Resolution is more programmatically specific than the foundational NIEO documents, especially with regard to measures of increasing real transfers of resources and levels of development assistance. *See* G.A. Res. 3362, *supra*, at sec. II (Transfer of real resources for financing the development of developing countries and international monetary reforms).

[175] The NIEO proposals contained in the Declaration and the Programme of Action are well summarized by the U.N. Secretary-General in his report to the General Assembly Eleventh Special Session. *See* U.N. Doc. A/S-11/5, at 6-18 (1980).

[176] *See* G.A. Res. 3202, *supra* note 174, at sec. I (Fundamental problems of raw materials and primary commodities).

[177] *See id.* at sec. II (International monetary system and financing of the development of developing countries), III (Industrialization).

The Programme calls for the progressive removal of tariff and other trade barriers in order to improve access to markets in developed countries[178] and for measures to promote the processing of raw materials within producer developing countries to help broaden the benefits of natural resource extraction.[179] In addition, the Programme seeks the reform of voting rights within international financial institutions such as the World Bank so as to afford the Third World greater participation in financial decision-making processes.[180] In order to make more funds available for development, the Programme calls for the renegotiation of Third World debts.[181]

2. *The Relationship between BNA and NIEO: Complementary or Conflicting Strategies?*

One might expect that proponents of the NIEO and the BNA would see these two policies as complementary aspects of a unified attack on Third World poverty.[182] Those who favor the Basic Needs Approach in place of past 'trickle-down' approaches to development should be the first to recognize the value of and need for complementary international reallocations of resources. The achievement of BNA goals requires the mobilization of substantial resources, and while some BNA adherents believe that the needed resources could be secured through domestic reallocations, most recognize that increasing the Third World's share of resources would facilitate the success of the BNA. This latter view was explicitly recognized by the WEC Declaration, which saw the emerging demands for a New International Economic Order as part of the strategy to implement the basic needs principles it articulated.[183] At the same time, the core of the NIEO is a belief that Third World poverty is caused in part by the conditions of economic dependency created by the current structure of international economic relations.[184] NIEO advocates should therefore support efforts to ensure that the real victims of such dependency—the poor of the Third World—should have a priority claim on resources generated by any international economic reforms. The complementarity of the BNA and the NIEO seems, at first blush, to be obvious.

---

[178] *See id.* at sec. I.3(a)(ii).

[179] *See id.* at sec. I.1.

[180] *See id.* at sec. II.2(c).

[181] *See id.* at sec. III.2(g).

[182] *See* WEC Follow-up, *supra* note 86, at 10, 11, 90; Galtung, *The New International Economic Order and the Basic Needs Approaches: Compatibility, Contradiction and/or Conflict?* 9 Annals Int'l Stud. 127, 143-48 (1978) [hereinafter cited as Galtung]; Streeten, *Basic Needs and the NIEO; Must There Be a Conflict?* 6 DEV. F. 1 (No. 5, 1979).

[183] *See* WEC Declaration, *supra* note 86, at 7, 8.

[184] *See* U.N. Doc. A/S-11/5, at 6-18 (1980); Gosovic & Ruggie, *supra* note 174; Marks, *Development and Human Rights*, 8 Bull. Peace Proposals 236 (1977) [hereinafter cited as Marks].

However, some see the policies as being in basic conflict.[185] Two very different types of conflict are noted. Some who favor the BNA think that the NIEO will not lead to the kind of people-oriented development strategy which they believe is necessary.[186] They agree that it is impossible to separate the international and the domestic effects of any changes in basic economic relationships and that each of the policies involved in the NIEO will affect the distribution of wealth and power within Third World states. However, they feel there is no guarantee that such redistribution will benefit the 'have-nots' of the Third World, and they have good reason to believe that the NIEO will principally benefit the 'haves'. If that were the case, then the NIEO would contain within it the flaws of prior orthodox development strategies.

Proponents of the NIEO who criticize the BNA take a rather different tack. They do not directly challenge the policies suggested by the BNA. Instead, they reject the principle that any external body should dictate to Third World governments the development strategy that they should follow.[187] The conflict here is not necessarily between the policies of the NIEO and the BNA. Rather, it is a conflict between the principle of the independence of sovereign states, one of the main aspects of the NIEO, and the perceived *imposition* of a particular development approach.[188] One of the main goals of the NIEO is to give the Third World more economic independence. If, however, any increase in resource transfer were conditioned on the existence of certain policies, even policies thought to benefit the poor of the Third World, the transfer would fail to meet one of the basic goals behind the drive for the NIEO.

Neither of these fears is groundless. There is no question that successful implementation of the NIEO could, under some circumstances, lead to resource transfers that would benefit Third World elites without significantly improving the lot of the poorest segments of society.[189] Nor is there any doubt that if the developed countries explicitly conditioned their agreement to some NIEO proposals on the acceptance of specific domestic policies by the Third World, Third World governments would have less freedom of maneuver than they desire.[190]

The NIEO probably cannot succeed without some sort of commitment to meeting basic needs, while it is doubtful that the BNA can

[185] *See generally* Galtung, *supra* note 182; WEC Follow-up, *supra* note 86, at 10,11.
[186] *See* Galtung, *supra* note 182, at 129-32.
[187] *See id.* at 135, 136.
[188] *See* WEC Follow-up, *supra* note 86, at 119.
[189] *See* Galtung, *supra* note 182, at 129-32.
[190] *See id.* at 136

succeed without reform of the international economic order.[191] It is not clear that the developed countries will accept the demands of the NIEO. But it is clear that the appeal of the NIEO to the developed states will be even further reduced if it does not contribute to alleviating real poverty within the Third World. The developed states will therefore seek assurances that resources allocated to the Third World by the NIEO will be used to meet priority problems and to deal with basic needs. The developed states will be reluctant to make the sacrifices the NIEO calls for under any circumstances, but they certainly will be unwilling if their sacrifices merely benefit already affluent elites in the Third World. On the other hand, the Third World will not accept or effectively administer a BNA if it is perceived as an alien imposition and is unaccompanied by the increased resource transfers which will make it possible to meet basic needs goals without sacrificing other vital national interests. Unless the Third World accepts the Basic Needs Approach as its own and has confidence that it will have enough resources to reach its goals, this approach will not work.

3. *International Social Welfare Law and a Global Compact*

International development is an area where effective legal institutions might help to overcome conflicts and reduce risks. Mechanisms are needed which can increase acceptance by developed and developing countries of their mutual responsibility to relieve world poverty and correct past injustices. Such mechanisms must perform two functions. First, they must contribute to building a normative consensus on the existence and nature of the mutual obligation to achieve development and social justice. Secondly, they must provide mutually satisfactory assurances that the developing and developed world will meet their respective obligations.

What is needed, therefore, is a sort of global compact through which agreement can be reached on methods to reallocate resources simultaneously at the international level and within the countries which will benefit from such a reallocation.[192] The question then arises: if the world community agreed to such a development strategy, could the international law of social welfare described in this chapter play a role in the establishment of the appropriate compact?

The answer to this question depends, in part, on what kind of arrangements such a compact would require. It would hardly call for a highly detailed and precise set of legal agreements with immediate and effective mutual sanctions—a sort of world-wide trust indenture, as it

---

[191] *See id.* at 143-48; Marks, *supra* note 183, at 243-46; WEC Follow-up, *supra* note 86, at 10-11, 89-90; Alston, *Human Rights supra* note 165, at 285.

[192] *See* Streeten & Burki, *supra* note 88, at 415.

were. Rather, a set of working principles, and institutions designed to develop these principles over time so that mutually conditioned performances are, by and large, accomplished, is needed. In this 'quasi-constitutional' as opposed to 'bond-indenture' model, the current international law of social welfare could provide a starting point.

Part of any global compact would be a commitment by developing countries to give priority to meeting basic human needs. We have seen that such priorities can be translated into relatively specific standards. Further, we have seen that the international community can agree on such standards and, to some degree, monitor progress toward them. The work done by the ILO illustrates how this can be done within the framework of existing human rights instruments. At the same time, the lack of comparable progress in areas such as health, and the general weakness of the system of international monitoring under the Economic Covenant, suggest the limits of the current mechanisms and the need for reform of the international social welfare system.

In any movement toward a global compact, such reform would be essential. Third World states would have to be assured of effective participation in the process of standard setting. This not only involves the framing of international agreements such as ILO conventions but also involves making detailed policy decisions in the specialized agencies. Thus to be sure that any emerging body of principles and policies really reflects an international consensus, it will be necessary to ensure—and accept—full Third World participation in the policy-making decisions of the specialized agencies.

A second weakness of the existing system—viewed in the perspective of the global compact suggested above—is the system's lack of mutuality of obligation. International monitoring of Third World progress toward social welfare goals should be part of a system that ensures international assistance. Thus it will be necessary to establish a principle that developed countries have an obligation to ensure that the Third World receives a greater share of global resources.[193]

Finally, any effective system which creates standards, renders assistance, and monitors progress must have more central direction than is currently available within the U.N. family. The strong point of the existing system is the specialized agencies, which have the capacity to monitor progress in their fields. But the absence of any central institution which can review country progress means that comprehensive reviews can not be conducted and thus a truly effective assessment of national efforts can not be made. While the ILO has construed its mandate to go well beyond the area of labour policy, its powers and expertise remain limited, so that even the most effective ILO appraisal

---

[193] *See, e.g.*, Right to Development, *supra* note 4, at 142, 143.

will fall short of the kind of country reviews that would be needed to make a global compact work.

The effort to secure the NIEO may provide the impetus for reform. For the NIEO to succeed, there will have to be more specific international commitments both to development assistance and to social justice in the Third World. The experience—both positive and negative—gained in the evolution of the international law of social welfare should be of immense value in the construction of such a reformed system, and the needs international social welfare law generates will help identify the flaws in the current structures. This is not to say that an improved international law of social welfare will effectively mediate all the conflicts between North and South or remove all the obstacles to social justice in the Third World. At best, it will provide partial gains and modest solutions to some of the conflicts.

H.   CONCLUSION: A NOTE OF CAUTION

Even if the goals are modest, caution is in order. There are positive trends in the social welfare area. But the effort to reorient development policy, develop more specific standards, and reallocate international resources faces substantial barriers. Perhaps the most important current development is the growing recognition of the existence of those barriers.

Neither the New International Economic Order nor the new development approach are neutral, technical concepts. They are rooted in certain general values which have been endorsed by the international community. But these values are not universally accepted. And the NIEO and the Basic Needs Approach cannot be realized without cost. These twin approaches to development require major and painful transformations in national social structures and international relations. In many countries, important and powerful groups have benefited from past development policies and from the existing structure of the world economy. Any effort to force a global compact comprising a new international economic order and a commitment to new domestic development policies will encounter strong resistance from such groups. Obviously, not everyone benefits from land reform or more labour-intensive growth strategies. The national elites of some developing countries are not the only potential losers from the BNA or the NIEO. The high-growth of development adopted by states such as Brazil has brought substantial benefits to multinational firms. Multinational firms are not likely to enthusiastically support policy changes which could substantially affect their profit margins and investment possibilities. The current system of international trade and monetary relations also benefits developed market economy countries in sigıficant ways. The developed states will not easily accede to the demands contained in the drive for a NIEO.

The effort to realize the economic, social, and cultural rights established by the International Bill of Human Rights therefore faces three basic barriers: the resistance of Third World elites, the unwillingness of developed countries to substantially alter the structure of the world economy, and the weakness of the international human rights machinery. The resistance of elites in some Third World nations is well documented. In a thoughtful essay on Brazilian economic history, Hewlett examines the reluctance of the Brazilian government to abandon its commitment to a growth strategy that has failed to benefit the poor, while enriching the top strata of the society. She notes that:

> A crucial cause of unequal development in Brazil is that vicious circle of wealth set up by capital intensive industrial structures producing sophisticated consumer good for an elite market. One way to break out of this circle and increase employment and income levels for a majority of the population would be by massively subsidizing the development of a more . . . labor intensive technology . . . [and] . . . substantial income distribution. . . . [194]

While such measures would foster the economic, social, and cultural goals, Hewlett concludes that:

> No Brazilian government enjoying the support of the contemporary power elite can make a significant dent on the social welfare problem, for a radical improvement in the condition of the poor would seriously threaten the very existence of the elite. [195]

Anyone who has followed the debate over the establishment of policies for the United Nations Third Development Decade and the unsuccessful effort to structure a negotiating process for the establishment of the NIEO will be aware of the reluctance of many developed countries to assume further obligations to the Third World. [196]

Finally, a principal purpose of this chapter has been to highlight the weaknesses of the existing machinery to implement international economic, social, and cultural rights. These weaknesses flow from many factors, including: (i) the obvious complexity of the task, which involves translating broad normative prescriptions into detailed standards and programs covering very different cultural, economic, and political conditions; and (ii) the novelty of developing international machinery to monitor *intranational* activities—a task inherent in the idea of international protection of social welfare but

---

[194] Hewlitt, *supra* note 99, at 207.
[195] *Id.*
[196] *See, e.g.*, U.N. Doc. A/S-11/1 (Part IV) (1980).

not well accepted either by national governments or international institutions.

When we understand the true meaning of the economic, social, and cultural rights that have been recognized by the international community, and especially when we understand the implications of these rights for citizens of the Third World, we see that the International Bill of Human Rights constitutes a challenge to existing systems of power and privilege in many parts of the world and to conventional approaches to international law. For some, this may mean that international economic, social, and cultural rights are pious aspirations incapable of realization. For others, this very challenge may be a spur to more comprehensive and effective international action to secure these rights.

II. Teaching Suggestions

A. INTRODUCTION—ONE COURSE OR MANY?

How should this subject be taught? I start from a disadvantage, as I have never tried to teach the material outlined in this chapter. While this may appear to disqualify me at the start, let me say that there are few in this country who have, so that my credentials are no worse than most who might otherwise be asked to comment on this matter. That is not to say that no attention has been paid to these subjects in various courses on human rights, international organization, or development policy. But an informal inquiry has failed to uncover any text, materials, or course devoted exclusively to the rights protected by the Economic Covenant.

One might see this as evidence of serious inattention to an area of major international importance. The creation of a new course devoted exclusively to these matters might be justified. Certainly the subject is important. Intellectually, the field is rich. It presents important issues about the nature of international law, the operations of international organizations, the problems of the Third World, and the evolution of the welfare state. International lawyers should know more about social welfare. Experts on development policy should be exposed to the normative content of the Economic Covenant and the role of specialized agencies in promoting and protecting rights to work, health, etc. Each of these groups will understand their roles and professions better if they are exposed to the issues I have sought to survey.

An increase in the understanding of the relationship between international law and social welfare is important for the realization of social welfare goals. This gist of this chapter is that effective implementation of what I have called 'social welfare rights' requires a combination of normative analysis and programmatic imagination. Teaching in this area could encourage the development and fusion of these two approaches.

But does that mean that such teaching should be incorporated in a special course on this subject? Perhaps in a few advanced centers of graduate study in human rights and international organization such a course might make sense. But in most university contexts, I suspect that another strategy would be preferable. Rather than trying merely to develop a specialized offering in economic, social, and cultural rights, I think we should devote our energies to increasing the coverage of these issues in more general courses on human rights, international organization, development policy, and substantive areas of welfare policy like labour, health, and social security.

I favor this approach for several reasons. The first is conceptual. My approach to the topic leads me to see international 'law' in this area as embedded in the policies and programs of specific agencies like the ILO, WHO, and World Bank. To fully understand what is involved in protecting these rights, the specific problems these specialized agencies deal with, the policies and programs they have developed, and the way they function, must be first understood. This approach requires a mastery of the details of complex areas and an understanding of the workings of complex institutions. In conducting the research for this chapter, I confronted this problem and barely began the task of developing the requisite kind of expertise in just a few of the areas covered by the Economic Covenant. There will be few teachers who will be able to master all the material needed to deal with the issues which would have to be included in a comprehensive survey of all the rights protected by the Economic Covenant. Yet without such mastery it is impossible to convey the essence of the message I think we should get across here.

To avoid this dilemma, I suggest that we try to build on existing expertise and explore the various issues in courses which will contain sufficient depth and background material that students and teachers can grapple with the core issues and dilemmas that are presented. This would suggest that a good way to fully explore the activities of the ILO in this area would be in a course on the ILO as an institution, or in a course on Employment Policy and Development. I would suggest that the best way to understand the special problems of implementing 'rights' of this nature may be in a general course on human rights, where various approaches to implementation could be examined. Further, one might want to examine the normative implications of the Economic Covenant in a variety of contexts, but especially in courses that deal with development policy and development strategy.

B.   LEARNING FROM THE BASIC NEEDS APPROACH— A STRATEGY FOR DEVELOPING THE FIELD

If there is a conceptual argument that supports the approach I suggest, there is also a very practical reason why it is best to start the teaching of this area in existing courses on human rights, international organizations, and development policy. As teachers, we can learn from some of the thinking that underlies the Basic Needs Approach and the Primary Health Care doctrine. One element of these approaches is to build on what is already there and improve the productivity of existing resources. That lesson applies to teaching as well as employment and health care. It is certainly desirable to increase the resources devoted to teaching students about the role of the international community in the social welfare area. But the resources currently available for this task are severely limited. I have not located one person teaching in U.S. universities who is really a specialist in this area. The literature in the field is sparse. If one defines the field broadly, as I have done, one can identify a wealth of primary material and libraries of relevant material that can be employed to illuminate the issues that are presented here. But I have found almost no comprehensive analyses of the overall topic, and very few detailed studies that focus on the specific questions I think should be covered. To continue the development analogy, there is a severe shortage of human resources and intellectual capital.

In such a situation, one must either invest massively in training teachers and producing detailed studies, or build gradually from the slender base that exists. The second of these options seems the most feasible. What exists, in this case, are teachers who are interested in human rights, international organization, and development policy. What we should do, then, is encourage people with this base of expertise to expand their focus to include international social welfare law in their current offerings. At the same time, it would be desirable to increase the resources devoted to research on this subject and to find ways to bring specialists from various areas together. In this fashion we can gradually expand our stock of human resources and intellectual capital.

C.   A TWO-PRONGED APPROACH

For the reasons outlined, I suggest that the development of this field be encouraged in two ways. First, specific courses on this subject should be added. Second, teachers of existing courses should add 'modules' on economic, social, and cultural rights to existing offerings. The syllabi for each of these approaches follow.

III. Syllabus

A specific course on 'Economic, Social, and Cultural Rights in the Third World' would have to be quite comprehensive and interdisciplinary. It might be best, where possible, to have such a course jointly taught by persons with backgrounds in international law and development policy. A substantial part of the course should be devoted to 'case studies' of the type set forth in the chapter, and to country-oriented studies which would give the student a clearer idea of the structures that affect social welfare and the barriers suggested in the last section of the discussion.

I. *Introduction*
   A. Brief history of international efforts to protect human rights.
   B. Principal U.N. human rights documents.
   C. Relation between civil/political and economic, social, and cultural rights.
II. *The International Covenant on Economic, Social and Cultural Rights*
   A. Drafting history and entry into force.
   B. Basic structure.
      1. Rights included.
      2. Principle of progressive realization.
      3. Implementation.
   C. Introduction to specific rights and 'steps' specified for their realization.
      1. Work.
      2. Just and favorable conditions of work.
      3. Social security.
      4. Adequate standard of living.
      5. Health.
      6. Education.
      7. Culture and science.
      8. Protection of families and children.
III. *The Third World and Development Policy*
   A. The challenge of development—description of economic, social, and cultural conditions in the Third World.
   B. Development models and development strategies.
      1. The post-war response.
      2. The first development decade.
      3. The debate over development strategies.
         a. Income distribution.
         b. Employment generation.

        c. Role of developed countries.
    4. The emergence of a new approach.
       a. Basic Needs Approach.
       b. Re-distribution with growth.
       c. Employment-orientation.
       d. New International Economic Order.
  C. The institutional structure of development.
    1. Domestic structures.
    2. Bilateral assistance.
    3. Specialized agencies.
IV. *Economic, Social, and Cultural Rights in the Third World*
  A. The basic approach—translating 'rights' into 'programs'.
  B. The specific role of the specialized agencies.
  C. Case studies.
    1. Employment.
    2. Health.
    3. Food.
  D. Country studies.
    1. Brazil.
    2. Sri Lanka.
V. *Issues and Problems*
  A. Barriers and obstacles.
    1. Third World social and political structures.
    2. International economic structures.
    3. Limits of U.N. machinery.
    4. Developed country attitudes.
  B. Relation of social welfare rights to civil and political rights.
  C. The New International Economic Order and the 'right to development'.
  D. Improving implementation machinery of the Economic Covenant.

IV. Minisyllabus

(1) MODULES FOR EXISTING COURSES

The second approach to teaching social welfare rights is to develop modules for existing course offerings. Detailed outlines are not possible here since they would have to be tailored to fit existing syllabi. Rather I shall merely suggest how the issues in this area might be approached from the viewpoint of separate courses on human rights law, international organizations, and development policy.

Any module in this area should cover at least three topics: (i) the normative content of the Economic Covenant and other relevant sources of international law; (ii) the operations of the specialized agencies that have programs in this area; and (iii) the national development policies that are needed to ensure social welfare and the international policies needed to support national efforts. However, teachers in different fields could emphasize different dimensions of this overall body of material. Thus one might imagine three modules with three different emphases:

Human Rights Law Emphasis

From the human rights lawyer's perspective, the problem appears most acutely as a question of 'implementation'. Much has been said about the alleged distinction between implementing political and civil rights on the one hand, and social welfare rights on the other. Much more is made of this distinction than I think is warranted, but it is a useful didactic starting point. The recognition that rights entail programs, and program specificity involves normative analysis, is a key insight, as is the role of the specialized agencies in the implementation task. The ILO is clearly the paradigmatic agency to evaluate in this area, but one should not stop with the ILO.

International Organization Emphasis

From this focus, I think the principal issue is: how do various specialized agencies determine policies, and how likely is it that they will take effective measures to implement the Economic Covenant? What do these specialized agencies actually do, and what effect do their activities have on national decision-making? What methods do the WHO, ILO, and World Bank use to get states to adopt the policies they endorse? What techniques work best? How do different organizational structures influence the social welfare rights work of the several specialized agencies?

Development Policy Emphasis

What is the argument for development policies that stress social welfare? Which countries have adopted such policies? Under what conditions have the elements of the new development model (BNA, employment-orientation, growth with redistribution) actually worked? What are the barriers to successful implementation of such policies? What implications does the new approach have for international economic relations? Do the current international economic policies of the developed states deter adoption of the new development model and encourage the growth and trickle-down approach that has been subjected to such criticism but still prevails in much of the Third World? What impact would the NIEO have on social welfare in the Third World?

(2) A BRIEF INTRODUCTION TO ECONOMIC, SOCIAL, AND CULTURAL RIGHTS

If a teacher of a general course on human rights wishes to include a short segment on 'International Economic, Social, and Cultural Rights', I suggest the following syllabus, which would require three class hours. Articles bearing on each subject are listed in the Mini-bibliography.

I. *Introduction—The Basic International Norms*

This class is devoted to introducing the basic texts and explaining how the Economic Covenant is designed. It is assumed that the student has already studied political and civil rights.

    A. Texts
        1. Articles 55 and 56 of the U.N. Charter.
        2. Article 22 of the Universal Declaration of Human Rights.
        3. The International Covenant on Economic, Social and Cultural Rights.
    B. Questions for Discussion.
        1. What are the differences between the rights protected by the Economic Covenant and those guaranteed by the International Covenant on Civil and Political Rights?
        2. Why did the drafters of the Economic Covenant include the principle of 'progressive realization' in the system of 'generic implementation'?
        3. What role did the authors of the Economic Covenant envision for the specialized agencies?
        4. What is the significance of article 23 of the Economic Covenant?

II. *The United Nations, Human Rights, and Development in the Third World*

This class places international economic, social, and cultural rights in the context of Third World development and the activities of the specialized agencies.

    A. Text.
        World Employment Conference, Declaration of Principles and Programme of Action Adopted by the Tripartite World Conference on Employment, Income Distribution and Social Progress and the International Division of Labor, U.N. Doc. WEC/CW/E.1 (1976).
    B. Questions for Discussion.
        1. What is the difference between a basic needs approach (BNA) and prior approaches to development?
        2. Is the BNA compatible with principles of the Economic Covenant?

3. Could the BNA be used to interpret the obligation to progressively realize rights like the right to work or health? How would this be done?

4. Could the WEC Declaration of Principles be used to interpret the meaning of the obligation to realize the right to work?

III. *Implementing Economic, Social, and Cultural Rights in the Third World*

This class uses the ILO comments on country progress under the Economic Covenant to elaborate the problems involved in implementing social welfare rights.

A. Texts

1. Economic and Social Council Resolution 1988. Procedures for the Implementation of the International Covenant on Economic, Social and Cultural Rights, U.N. Doc. E/RES/1988 (LX) (1976).

2. International Labour Organisation, Report by the Committee of Experts on the Application of Conventions and Recommendations of the International Labour Organisation on Progress in Achieving Observance of the Provisions of Articles 6 to 9 of the International Covenant on Economic, Social and Cultural Rights, U.N. Doc. E/1978/27, at 1-10 (1978) (introductory remarks on approach and methodology of the Report).

3. International Labour Organisation, Second Report by the Committee of Experts on the Application of Conventions and Recommendations of the International Labour Organisation on Progress in Achieving Observance of the Provisions of Articles 6 to 9 of the International Covenant on Economic, Social and Cultural Rights. U.N. Doc. E/1979/33, at 1-17 (1979) (introductory remarks on approach and methodology of the Report).

4. International Labour Organisation, Third Report by the Committee of Experts on the Application of Conventions and Recommendations of the International Labour Organisation on Progress in Achieving Observance of the Provisions of Articles 6 to 9 of the International Covenant on Economic, Social and Cultural Rights. U.N. Doc. E/1980/35, at 12-38 (1980) (analysis of and comments upon specific country reports).

5. Implementation of the International Covenant on Economic, Social, and Cultural Rights [World Health

Organization Report pursuant to article 18 of the International Covenant on Economic, Social, and Cultural Rights and to Economic Social Council Resolution 1988 (LX), U.N. Doc. E/1980/24 (1980).

B. Questions for Discussion

   1. Contrast the approaches taken by the WHO and the ILO in commenting on progress under the Economic Covenant. What explains the different approaches taken?

   2. Did the ILO Committee of Experts provide a very clear statement of the criteria used to evaluate country progress; of the extent of particular countries' compliance or non-compliance? Given the ILO's willingness to provide country-specific criticism, why did the ILO take the approach it adopted?

   3. What are the principal deficiencies of the implementation procedure? How could they be improved? Is there a role for NGOs in this procedure? What would it be?

V. Bibliography

I. General Background Materials

M. Adjala, Of Life and Hope: Toward Effective Witness in Human Rights (1979).

Bilder, *Rethinking International Human Rights: Some Basic Questions*, 1969 Wis. L. Rev. 171.

Van Boven, *Some Remarks and Special Problems Relating to Human Rights in Developing Countries*, 3 Revue des Droits de l'Homme 383 (1970).

J. Dominguez, *et al.*, Enhancing Global Human Rights (1980).

L. Henkin, The Rights of Man Today (1978).

J. Joyce, Human Rights: International Documents (3 vols.) (1978).

R. Lillich & F. Newman, International Human Rights: Problems of Law and Policy (1979).

E. Luard, The International Protection of Human Rights (1967).

A. Peaslee, International Governmental Organizations: Constitutional Documents (1961).

E. Schwelb, Human Rights and the International Community (1964).

L. Sohn & T. Buergenthal, Basic Documents on International Protection of Human Rights (1973).

——— International Protection of Human Rights (1973).

II. The International Covenant on Economic, Social and Cultural
Rights: Text and Drafting

A. *Books and Articles*
Alston, *The United Nation's Specialized Agencies and Implemen-
tation of the International Covenant on Economic, Social and
Cultural Rights*, 18 Colum. J. Transnat'l L. 79 (1979). [also
published as Alston, Philip, 'Making and Breaking Human
Rights: The U.N. Specialized Agencies and Implementation of
the International Covenant on Economic, Social and Cultural
Rights', Human Rights and Development Working Papers No.
1 (London: Anti-Slavery Society [180 Brixton Road, London
SW9 6AT] 1979)].
Capotorti, *The International Measures of Implementation In-
cluded in the Covenants on Human Rights*, in International
Protection of Human Rights (A. Eide & A. Schou eds. 1968).
Commission to Study the Organization of Peace, The United
Nations and Human Rights (1968).
A. Eide & A. Schou, eds. International Protection of Human
Rights (1968).
Jenks, *Human Rights, Social Justice and Peace: The Broader
Significance of the I.L.O. Experience*, in International
Protection of Human Rights (A. Eide & A. Schou eds. 1968).
Marks, *UNESCO and Human Rights: The Implementation of
Rights Relating to Education, Science, Culture and Com-
munication*, 13 Tex. Int'l L.J. 35 (1977).
Panel Discussion, *The United Nations Human Rights Covenants:
Problems of Ratification and Implementation*, 62 Proc. Am.
Soc'y Int'l L. 83 (1968).
B. Ramcharan, ed., Human Rights: Thirty Years After the
Universal Declaration (1979).
A. del Russo, International Protection of Human Rights (1971).
Schwelb, *Entry into Force of the International Covenants on
Human Rights and the Optional Protocol to the International
Covenant on Civil and Political Rights*, 70 Am. J. Int'l L. 511
(1976).
—— *Some Aspects of the International Covenants on Human
Rights of December 1966*, in International Protection of
Human Rights (A. Eide & A. Schou eds. 1968).
—— *Some Aspects of the Measures of Implementation of the
International Covenant on Economic, Social and Cultural
Rights*, 1 Revue des Droits de l'Homme 363 (1968).
Sohn, *A Short History of United Nations Documents on Human*

Rights, in Commission to Study the Organization of Peace, The United Nations and Human Rights (1968).

―――― *The Human Rights Law of the Charter,* 12 Tex. Int'l L.J. 129 (1977).

N. Valticos, The International Protection of Economic and Social Rights, *reprinted from* Rechten van de Mens in Mundial en Europees Perspectief (1978).

Vierdag, *The Legal Nature of the Rights Granted by the International Covenant on Economic, Social and Cultural Rights,* 10 Neth. Y.B. Int'l L. (1979).

Weissbrodt, *United States Ratification of the Human Rights Covenants,* 63 Minn. L. Rev. 35 (1978).

B. *U.N. Publications and Documents*

Economic and Social Council, Analytical Summary of Reports Submitted by States Parties in Accordance with Council Resolution 1988 (LX), Concerning Rights Covered by Articles 6 to 9 of the Covenant. U.N. Doc. E/1979/14 (1979).

―――― Resolution 1988, Procedures for the Implementation of the International Covenant on Economic, Social and Cultural Rights. 60 U.N. ESCOR, Supp. (No. 1) 11, U.N. Doc. E/5850 (1976).

―――― Commission on Human Rights, Report of the Sixth Session, 11 U.N. ESCOR, Supp. (No. 5), U.N. Doc. E/1681 (1950).

―――― Commission on Human Rights, Report of the Seventh Session, 13 U.N. ESCOR, Supp. (No. 9), U.N. Doc. E/1992 (1951).

―――― Commission on Human Rights, Report of the Eighth Session, 14 U.N. ESCOR, Supp. (No. 4), U.N. Doc. E/2256 (1952).

―――― Commission on Human Rights, Report of the Ninth Session, 16 U.N. ESCOR, Supp. (No. 8), U.N. Doc. E/2447 (1953).

―――― Commission on Human Rights, Report of the Tenth Session, 18 U.N. ESCOR, Supp. (No. 7), U.N. Doc. E/2573 (1954).

―――― Commission on Human Rights, Seventh Session, Resolution 384 (XIII), 13 U.N. ESCOR, Supp. (No. 1), U.N. Doc. E/2152 (1951).

―――― Commission on Human Rights, Seventh Session, Working Group on Economic, Social and Cultural Rights, Summary Records of 1st to 3d meetings, U.N. Docs. E/CN.4/SR.1-SR.3 (1951).

―――― Commission on Human Rights, Seventh Session, Working Group on Measures of Implementation of Economic, Social and Cultural Rights, Summary Records of 1st to 3d meetings,

U.N. Docs. E/CN.4/AC.15/SR.1-SR.3 (1951).

—— Commission on Human Rights, Eighth Session, Summary Records of the 270th meeting to the 275th meeting, U.N. Docs. E/CN.4/SR.270-SR.275 (1952).

—— Commission on Human Rights, Tenth Session, Summary Records of the 418th meeting to the 425th meeting, U.N. Docs. E/CN.4/SR.418-SR.425 (1954).

M. Ganji, The Realization of Economic, Social and Cultural Rights: Problems, Policies, Progress, U.N. Doc. E/CN.4/1108/ Rev. 1 (1975).

General Assembly, Annotations on the Text of the Draft International Covenants on Human Rights, 10 U.N. GAOR, Annexes (Agenda Item 28, pt. II), U.N. Doc. A/2929 (1955).

—— (Debates Prior to Adoption of Resolution 543 (VI) on the Question of One or Two Draft Covenants) 6 U.N. GAOR (374th, 375th plen. mtgs.), U.N. Docs. A/PV.374-375 (1952).

Resolution 543 (VI), Preparation of Two Draft International Covenants on Human Rights, 6 U.N. GAOR, Supp. (No. 20) 36, U.N. Doc. A/2119 (1952).

—— Third Committee, Draft International Covenant on Human Rights and Measures of Implementation (debate of question of one or two covenants), 6 U.N. GAOR, C.3 (358th to 372d mtgs., 411th to 417th mtgs.) U.N. Docs. A/C.3/SR.358-SR.372, U.N. Docs. A/C.3/SR.411-SR.417 (1951-1952).

—— Third Committee, Report of the Third Committee, 6 U.N. GAOR, Annexes (Agenda Item 29), U.N. Doc. A/2112 (1952).

—— Third Committee, Report of the Third Committee, 12 U.N. GAOR, Annexes (Agenda Item 33), U.N. Doc. A/3764 and Add. 1 (1957).

—— Third Committee, Report of the Third Committee, 21 U.N. GAOR, Annexes (Agenda Item 62), U.N. Doc. A/6546 (1966).

III. Human Rights, International Law, and Social Welfare

I. Adelman & C. Morris, Economic Growth and Social Equity in Developing Countries (1973).

Alston, *Human Rights and Basic Needs: A Critical Assessment*, 12 Revue des Droits de l'Homme 19 (1979) [also published as Alston, Philip, 'Human Rights and the Basic Needs Strategy for Development', Human Rights and Development Working Papers No. 2 (London: Anti-Slavery Society [180 Brixton Road, London SW9 6AT] 1979)].

—— *Human Rights and the New International Development Strategy*, 10 Bull. Peace Proposals 281 (1979).

L. Anell & B. Nygren, The Developing Countries and the World Economic Order (1980).

Basic Human Needs: The International Law Connection, 72 Proc. Am. Soc'y Int'l L. 224 (1978).

Claude & Strouse, *Human Rights Development Theory*, 1 Research L. & Soc. 45 (1978).

Ethical Dilemmas of Development: Analytical Frame of Reference, Asia Society Doc. M/72/INT/106/1 (1979).

Falk, *A New Paradigm for International Legal Studies: Prospects and Proposals*, 84 Yale L.J. 969 (1975).

Galtung, *The New International Economic Order and the Basic Needs Approaches: Compatibility, Contradiction and/or Conflict?* 9 Annals Int'l Stud. 127 (1978).

—— & Wirak, *Human Needs and Human Rights—A Theoretical Approach*, 8 Bull. Peace Proposals 251 (1977).

—— & Wirak, *Human Needs, Human Rights and the Theories of Development*, 37 UNESCO Rep. & Papers Soc. Sci. 7 (1976).

J. Garcia-Bouza, A Basic-Needs Analytical Bibliography (1980).

M. Haq, The Third World and the International Economic Order (Overseas Development Council Paper 22) (1976).

S. Hewlett, The Cruel Dilemmas of Development: Twentieth Century Brazil (1980).

—— *Human Rights and Economic Realities: Trade-offs in Historical Perspective*, 94 Pol. Sci. Q. 453 (1979).

Human Rights and Development [Report of a Seminar on Human Rights and Their Promotion in the Caribbean] (Bridgetown, Barbados, W.I.: The Cedar Press, 1978).

International Council on Social Welfare, Social Welfare and Human Rights (1969).

K. Jameson and C. Wilbur, eds., Directions in Economic Development (1979).

LeBlanc, *Economic, Social and Cultural Rights and the Inter-american System*, 19 J. Interamerican Stud. 61 (1977).

R. Macdonald, *et al.*, eds., The International Law and Policy of Human Welfare (1978).

Marks, *Development and Human Rights: Some Reflections on the Study of Development, Human Rights and Peace*, 8 Bull. Peace Proposals 236 (1977).

M. McDougal, *et al.*, Human Rights and World Public Order (1980).

—— *Human Rights and World Public Order: Human Rights in Comprehensive Context*, 72 Nw. U. L. Rev. 227 (1977).

Moving Toward Change: Some Thoughts on the New International

Economic Order (UNESCO 1976).

Nayar, *Human Rights and Economic Development: The Legal Foundations*, 2 Universal Human Rights 55 (1980).

M. Nerfin, ed., Another Development: Approaches and Strategies (1977).

Note, *The United Nations Seventh Special Session: Proposals for a New World Economic Order*, 9 Vand. J. Transnat'l L. 601 (1976).

C. Okolie, International Law Perspectives of the Developing Countries: The Relationship of Law and Economic Development to Basic Human Rights (1978).

Pyatt, *Economic Strategies for Growth with Equity*, 25 Econ. Dev. & Cultural Change 581 (1977).

Schachter, *The Evolving International Law of Development*, 15 Colum. J. Transnat'l L. 1 (1976).

H. Shue, Basic Rights: Subsistence, Affluence, and U.S. Foreign Policy (1980).

Streeten, *Basic Needs and the NIEO: Must There Be Conflict?* 6 (No. 5) Dev. F. 1 (1979).

—— *The Distinctive Features of a Basic Needs Approach to Development*, 19 Int'l Dev. Rev. 9 (1977).

—— & Burki, *Basic Needs: Some Issues*, 6 World Dev. 411 (1978).

The New International Economic Order: A Selective Bibliography (United Nations 1980).

Thome, *Legal and Social Structures and the Access of the Latin American Rural Poor to the State Allocation of Goods and Services*, 2 Research L. & Soc'y 251 (1979).

Towards a New International Economic and Social Order, 28 Int'l Soc. Sci. J. 640 (1976).

Trubek, *Complexity and Contradiction in the Legal Order: Balbus and the Challenge of Critical Social Thought about Law*, 11 L. & Soc'y Rev. 529 (1977).

—— Theories of Development as Obstacles to Implementing Human Rights in the Third World: The Latin American Case (unpublished paper, Madison, Wis.) (Jan. 30, 1975).

—— *Unequal Protection: Thoughts on Legal Services, Social Welfare, and Income Distribution in Latin America*, 13 Tex. Int'l L.J. 243 (1978).

—— & Galanter, *Scholars in Self-Estrangement: Some Reflections on the Crisis in Law and Development Studies in the United States*, 1974 Wis. L. Rev. 1062.

R. Unger, Law in Modern Society: Toward a Criticism of Social Theory (1976).

United Nations, Economic and Social Council, Commission on Human Rights, A Report by the Secretary-General on the Realization in All Countries of Economic and Social Rights and on a Human Right to Development in Relation to Peace and the Requirements of a New International Economic Order, U.N. Doc. E/CN.4/1334 (1979).

Watson, *Legal Theory, Efficacy and Validity in the Development of Human Rights Norms in International Law*, 1979 U. I. L.F. 609.

J. Weeks & E. Dore, Basic Needs: The Journey of a Concept (unpublished paper, Woodstock Theological Center) (Apr. 1980).

W. Verwey, Economic Development, Peace and International Law (1972).

IV. Specialized International Organizations and Economic, Social, and Cultural Rights

   A. *The International Labour Organisation*

      Comparative Analysis of the International Covenants on Human Rights and International Labour Conventions and Recommendations, 52 ILO O. Bull. 181 (1969).

      Follow-up of the World Employment Conference: Basic Needs, 65 (No. 6) International Labour Office Report to International Labour Conference (1976).

      International Labour Organisation, Constitution, 62 Stat. 3485, T.I.A.S. No. 1868, 15 U.N.T.S. 35.

      ILO, Report by the Committee of Experts on the Application of Conventions and Recommendations of the International Labour Organisation on Progress in Achieving Observance of the Provisions of Articles 6 to 9 of the International Covenant on Economic, Social, and Cultural Rights, U.N. Doc. E/1978/27 (1978).

      —— Second Report by the Committee of Experts on the Application of Conventions and Recommendations of the International Labour Organisation on Progress in Achieving Observance of the Provisions of Articles 6 to 9 of the International Covenant on Economic, Social and Cultural Rights, U.N. Doc. E/1979/33 (1979).

      —— Third Report by the Committee of Experts on the Application of Conventions and Recommendations of the International Labour Organisation on Progress in Achieving Observance of the Provisions of Articles 6 to 9 of the International Covenant on Economic, Social and Cultural Rights, U.N. Doc. E/1980/35 (1980).

—— International Labour Office, Bibliography of Published Research of the World Employment Programme (1979).

—— International Labour Office, Employment, Growth and Basic Needs (1977).

—— World Employment Conference, Declaration of Principles and Programme of Action Adopted by the Tripartite World Conference on Employment Income Distribution and Social Progress and the International Division of Labour, U.N. Doc. WEC/CW/E.1 (1976).

B. *The World Health Organisation*

B. Abel-Smith, Poverty, Development and Health Policy, World Health Organisation Public Health Papers No. 69 (1978).

V. Djukanovic and E. Mach, eds., Alternative Approaches to Meeting Basic Health Needs in Developing Countries (1975).

B. Hetzel, Basic Health Care in Developing Countries: An Epidemiological Perspective (1978).

K. Newell, ed., Health by the People (1975).

Primary Health Care (WHO 1978).

Report of the World Health Organisation under Article 18 of the International Covenant on Economic, Social and Cultural Rights, U.N. Doc. E/1980/24 (1980).

UNICEF, A Strategy for Basic Services (1977).

World Health Organisation, Health Economics, Pub. Pol'y Papers No. 64 (World Health Organisation 1975).

—— The World of WHO 1976-1977: Biennial Report of the Director General, WHO O. Rec. no. 243 (1978).

C. *The World Bank*

1979 Annual Meetings of the Board of Governors Summary Proceedings (1979).

Brazil: Human Resources Special Report [A World Bank Country Study] (1979).

S. Burki, & J. Voorhoeve, Global Estimates for Meeting Basic Needs: Background Paper, World Bank Basic Needs Paper No. 1 (Aug. 10, 1977).

Gordon, *The World Bank: New Directions in Africa*, 68 African Aff. 232 (1979).

M. Haq, Basic Needs: A Progress Report (World Bank Policy Planning and Program Review) (Aug. 10, 1977).

A. van de Laar, The World Bank and the World's Poor, Institute of Social Studies Occasional Papers 58 (1976).

R. McNamara, Address to the Board of Governors (1970).

—— Address to the Board of Governors (1973).

—— Address to the Board of Governors (1976).

Ringen, *Fruits of the United Nations: The Distribution of Development Aid*, 11 J. Peace Research 51 (1974).
World Bank and IDA Questions and Answers (1971).
World Bank Operations: Sectoral Programs and Policies (1972).

VI. Minibibliography

(To accompany Minisyllabus No. 2: 'A Brief Introduction to Economic, Social, and Cultural Rights')

Introduction—The Basic International Norms
  1. Alston, *The United Nations Specialized Agencies and Implementation of the International Covenant on Economic, Social and Cultural Rights*, 18 Colum. J. Transnat'l L. 79 (1979).
  2. Marks, *UNESCO and Human Rights: The Implementation of Rights Relating to Education, Science, Culture and Communication*, 13 Tex. Int'l L.J. 35 (1977).
  3. Trubek, *Economic, Social and Cultural Rights in the Third World: Human Rights Law and Human Needs Programs*, part I(2) in this volume.
  4. Watson, *Legal Theory, Efficacy and Validity of Human Rights Norms in International Law*, 1979 U. Ill. L.F. 609.

The United Nations, Human Rights, and Development in the Third World
  1. Alston, *Human Rights and Basic Needs, A Critical Assessment*, 12 Revue des Droits de l'Homme 19 (1979).
  2. Galtung & Wirak, *Human Needs, Human Rights and the Theories of Development*, 37 UNESCO Rep. & Papers Soc. Sci. 7 (1976).
  3. Thome, *Legal and Social Structures and the Access of the Latin American Rural Poor to the State Allocation of Goods and Services*, 2 Research L. & Soc'y 251 (1976).
  4. Trubek, *op. cit.*, part I(3).
  5. Wilber & Jameson, *Paradigms of Economic Development and Beyond*, in Directions in Economic Development (C. Wilber & K. Jameson eds. 1978).

Implementing Economic, Social, and Cultural Rights in the Third World
  1. Jenks, *Human Rights, Social Justice and Peace: The Broader Significance of the I.L.O. Experience*, in International Protection of Human Rights (A. Eide & A. Schou eds. 1968).
  2. Trubek, *op. cit.*, parts I(4) and (5).

Chapter 7

Human Rights and the International Labour Organisation*

Francis Wolf[1]

I. Legal and Policy Considerations

A. INTRODUCTION

Human rights are not a separate part of the activities of the International Labour Organisation (ILO), but lie at the very heart of its mission. According to the definition of the ILO's objectives, as contained in the Declaration of Philadelphia adopted in 1944 and subsequently incorporated in the ILO Constitution,[2] all national and international policies and measures should be based on the principle that all human beings, irrespective of race, creed, or sex, have the right to pursue both their material well-being and their spiritual development in conditions of freedom, dignity, economic security, and equal opportunity. The more detailed provisions of the Declaration of Philadelphia, whether referring to such matters as freedom of expression and of association, promotion of full employment, the raising of living standards, wages and conditions of work, social security measures, or protection of the life and health of workers, all serve to direct the ILO's actions toward the realization of human rights.

A major part of ILO action to attain these objectives consists of the adoption of international labour standards in the form of conventions and recommendations. The international labour convention is the main way to deal with essential issues, especially of basic human rights, about which sustained or energetic action by member states appears to be needed. It enables ratifying states to take on formal obligations and to secure international recognition of the status of their law and practice. The role of an international labour recommendation is less formal. Sometimes it is used to deal with subjects which do not lend themselves to precise obligations, as in cases in which the diversity of

---

* © Francis Wolf 1983.
[1] This chapter was prepared with the collaboration of Ebere Osieke, a staff member of the Office of the Legal Adviser, International Labour Office, Geneva. It is a revised version of Wolf, *ILO Experience in the Implementation of Human Rights*, 10 J. Int'l L. & Econ. 599 (1975) [hereinafter cited as Wolf, *ILO Experience*], brought up to date to March 1982.
[2] 62 Stat. 3485, T.I.A.S. No. 1868, 15 U.N.T.S. 35; *amended* 7 U.S.T. 245, T.I.A.S. No. 3500, 191 U.N.T.S. 143 (1953); 14 U.S.T. 1039, T.I.A.S. No. 5401, 466 U.N.T.S. 323 (1962); 25 U.S.T. 3253, T.I.A.S. No. 7987 (1972).

national conditions prevents the establishment of rules which can be universally and fully accepted, but in which it is useful to have a set of guidelines for governments. In a great number of cases, an international labour recommendation supplements an international labour convention—the former deals with questions of detail and means of implementation while the latter deals with basic questions—and may sometimes lay down a higher standard than that contained in the corresponding convention.

Most ILO conventions and recommendations concern the promotion and protection of human rights in a broad sense, since they deal with questions such as a safe working environment, the protection of children and young persons, working hours and other conditions of work, and other aspects of the economic, social, cultural, and civil rights enunciated in the International Covenant on Economic, Social and Cultural Rights[3] and the International Covenant on Civil and Political Rights.[4] However, a number of ILO instruments deal more specifically with certain fundamental rights and freedoms, such as freedom of association,[5] freedom from forced labour,[6] and equality of opportunity and treatment in employment.[7]

[3] G.A. Res. 2200, 21 U.N. GAOR, Supp. (No. 16) 49, U.N. Doc. A/6316 (1966).

[4] G.A. Res. 2200, 21 U.N. GAOR, Supp. (No. 16) 52, U.N. Doc. A/6316 (1966). *See generally Comparative analysis of the International Covenants on Human Rights and International Labour Conventions and Recommendations*, 52 (No. 2) ILO O. Bull. 188 (1969); Valticos, *The Place of Human Rights in the Constitution and the Various Instruments of the ILO and the Legal Framework for Their Protection*, in The International Dimensions of Human Rights 407–08 (K. Vasak ed. 1979).

[5] On the subject of freedom of association, the ILO has adopted the following instruments: Right of Association (Agriculture) Convention, 1921 (No. 11); Right of Association (Non-Metropolitan Territories) Convention, 1947 (No. 84); Freedom of Association and Protection of the Right to Organise Convention, 1948 (No. 87); Right to Organise and Collective Bargaining Convention, 1949 (No. 98); Workers' Representatives Convention, 1971 (No. 135), and Recommendation, 1971 (No. 143); Rural Workers' Organisations Convention, 1975 (No. 141), and Recommendation, 1975 (No. 149); and Labour Relations (Public Service) Convention, 1978 (No. 151), and Recommendation, 1978 (No. 159).

[6] On the subject of forced labour, the ILO has adopted the following instruments: Forced Labour Convention, 1930 (No. 29); Abolition of Forced Labour Convention, 1957 (No. 105); Forced Labour (Indirect Compulsion) Recommendation, 1930 (No. 35); and Forced Labour (Regulation) Recommendation, 1930 (No. 36).

[7] On the subject of equality of opportunity and treatment in employment, the ILO has adopted the following instruments: Equal Remuneration Convention, 1951 (No. 100), and Recommendation, 1951 (No. 90); Discrimination (Employment and Occupation) Convention, 1958 (No. 111), and Recommendation, 1958 (No. 111); and Workers with Family Responsibilities Convention, 1981 (No. 156), and Recommendation, 1981 (No. 165). It should be mentioned also that during the 60th Session of the International Labour Conference in June 1975, the Conference adopted a Declaration on Equality of Opportunity and Treatment of Women Workers.

The list of instruments adopted by the ILO dealing with basic human rights may be completed by referring to the ILO's instruments concerning migrant workers including Migrant Workers' (Supplementary Provisions) Convention, 1975 (No. 143), and Migrant Workers' Recommendation, 1975 (No. 151).

These conventions and recommendations clearly demonstrate the ILO's commitment to give effect to the basic human rights principles recognized in its constitutional documents. However, the framing of instruments and their formal acceptance by member states are only the first stages of the standard-setting work of the ILO. What matters is that the instruments result in effective measures at the national level for the benefit of those whose well-being they are intended to protect and promote and, more generally, that they help to shape the social policies of member States. Thus, the utility of these instruments lies in the availability of machinery for their acceptance by States and their effective implementation.

From its inception, the ILO established precise and original rules which, as supplemented over the years, presently constitute the most developed system for securing the effective application of international standards. The component parts of this system interlock to ensure, in the vast majority of cases, that when obligations are contracted, they are respected.

The system for ensuring the implementation of ILO conventions and recommendations applies to all such instruments, but it acquires special significance when they are concerned with human rights and the 'dignity inborn in the entire human family' is at stake.[8] In his opening address to the Abidjan World Peace through Law Conference in 1973, the Honorable Earl Warren, former Chief Justice of the United States Supreme Court, emphasized the importance of the machinery of the International Labour Organisation in the implementation of human rights.[9]

Standing before us also is the basic fact that a body of international law on human rights now exists. And because it exists we can now turn our attention to the means by which it can be implemented. . . . For the past three years, I have had the good fortune to be associated with a judicial review panel of the ILO. I have been impressed at the extent to which the basic features of effective implementation are built into the constitutional structure of the ILO—fact-finding, exposure, conciliation and adjudication. The handling of complaints, which is the heart of meaningful enforcement of human rights, has been carefully structured in a precise procedural manner. What is more important, there is a record demonstrating that these arrangements have produced concrete results . . . The ILO experience can be applied to the entire range of human rights concerns.[10]

---

[8] C. Jenks, The International Protection of Trade Union Freedom 37–38 (1957); *see* Jenks, *The International Protection of Trade Union Rights*, in The International Protection of Human Rights (E. Luard ed. 1957).

[9] Chief Justice Warren was a member of the ILO Committee of Experts on the Application of Conventions and Recommendations from 1970 to the time of his death in 1974.

[10] Quoted in Wolf, *ILO Experience, supra* note 1, at 601–02 (footnote omitted).

The machinery of the ILO for the implementation of human rights has also been favorably cited in a report submitted to the United States House of Representatives Committee on Foreign Affairs by its Subcommittee on International Organizations and Movements.[11] In testimony before the Subcommittee, it was noted that 'ILO procedures for inquiring into alleged breaches of their Conventions are probably the most sophisticated and most effective in the international sphere',[12] and that the methods of the ILO 'for the protection of human rights should be emulated by other international organizations'.[13]

The methods and procedures for the protection of human rights which exist in the ILO may be grouped under two headings. The first, that of *permanent supervision*, acts as a catalyst to obtain the widest possible application of the instruments concerned, and seeks to detect or prevent any derogation from conventions that have been ratified. Under this heading fall the submission by governments of reports on the implementation of conventions and recommendations; the examination of these reports by a committee of independent experts; and the discussion of problems of application and compliance with constitutional provisions relating to conventions and recommendations by a tripartite committee of the International Labour Conference.[14] The advantages of these methods are that they help states in the proper discharge of their obligations and that they permit the ILO to secure the application of universally valid legal rules formulated in pursuit of its aims.

In addition to reporting procedures, there exists another form of supervision based on *contentious proceedings*, following the presentation of representations and complaints.[15]

These methods and procedures—some of which are constitutional in character, while others have been progressively developed and adopted on an empirical basis—constitute the main stay of ILO experience in the implementation of standards relating to human rights. It may be useful, therefore, to examine briefly the manner in which they operate.

B. PERMANENT SUPERVISION OF THE APPLICATION OF ILO STANDARDS

1. *Information and reports*

a. *Information on the submission of conventions and recommendations to the competent authorities.* The ILO Constitution requires

[11] Human Rights in the World Community: A Call for U.S. Leadership (1974).
[12] *Id.* at 44.
[13] *Id.* at 45.
[14] For further details of this type of procedure, *see* section I.B, *infra*.
[15] For further details of this type of procedure and the cases involved, *see* section I.C. *infra*.

member States to bring any convention or recommendation adopted by the International Labour Conference before the competent authority —in most cases the national parliament[16]—for the enactment of legislation or other action. The obligation arises for each member whatever the attitude of its delegates at the Conference or the opinion of the government about ultimate ratification. The submission to the competent authority should generally be made within one year, and in no case later than eighteen months from the closing of the session of the Conference at which the convention[17] or recommendation[18] was adopted. In federal States, when a convention or recommendation contains elements on which action by the constituent units would be appropriate, arrangements must be made so that questions within the competence of the constituent units may be submitted to their proper authorities within the eighteen month period.[19]

The ILO Constitution also requires members to inform the Director-General of the International Labour Office of the measures they have taken to bring conventions and recommendations before the competent authorities, with particulars of such authorities and of the action those authorities have taken. This obligation is reinforced by the provisions of article 30 of the ILO Constitution, which authorizes a member to report to the Governing Body the failure of any other member to bring a convention or recommendation before its competent authorities.[20] If the Governing Body finds that there has been such a breach, it must report the matter to the Conference which may take whatever action it deems fit on the matter.

For purposes of convenience and uniformity, the information to be provided by members is indicated in a memorandum approved by the Governing Body of the International Labour Office in accordance with a decision by the International Labour Conference in 1953,[21] and last revised in 1980.[22]

b. *Reports on ratified conventions.* Since ratification is the act through which a convention creates binding legal obligations for member states, one of the main purposes of the system of international

[16] On the nature of the competent authority, *see* Memorandum of the Legal Adviser of the ILO, annexed to Report 1, Principles of Action, Programme and Statute of the ILO, 26th Sess. of the International Labour Conference 178 (1944); Minutes of the Governing Body of the International Labour Office 140th Sess. (Nov. 1958) at 96; ILO Doc. Appl. 19 S (Rev. 3) entitled 'Memorandum concerning the obligation to submit Conventions and Recommendations to the competent authorities' (1980).

[17] ILO Const. art 19(5)(b).

[18] *Id.* art. 19(6)(b).

[19] *Id.* art. 19(7)(b)(i).

[20] *See id.* art. 19(5)(c), 19(6)(c), 19(7)(b)(iii).

[21] 36th Sess., Proc. International Labour Conference, 393 (1953).

[22] *See* ILO Doc. Appl. 19S (Rev. 3) (1980).

labour standards is their ultimate ratification. The total number of ratifications in 1982 was over 5,000. This represents an impressive network of international commitments in the field of labour and human rights.

The constitutional obligation of a member state with respect to a convention does not terminate with ratification of the convention and the state's undertaking to make the convention effective. Members are required to submit annual reports on ratified conventions, in such form and containing such particulars as the Governing Body may request, to the International Labour Office.[23]

At the present time, detailed reports may be requested at one-year, two-year, or four-year intervals.[24] A government's first report on a ratified convention is due in the year following the date of its entry into force for the country concerned. The next two reports are then due at two-year intervals. After that, while for the majority of technical conventions reporting is at four-year intervals, reports relating to basic human rights (freedom of association, abolition of forced labour, equality of opportunity and treatment in employment, and migrant workers, among others) continue at least at two-year intervals.[25] In order to comply with the constitutional requirement that states report annually on the measures taken to give effect to ratified conventions, governments are required to supply a general report each year on those conventions for which detailed reports are not required that year.

c. *Reports on unratified conventions and recommendations.* The non-ratification of a convention is not a license for a member to ignore it. According to article 19(5)(e) of the ILO Constitution, if the competent authority fails to consent to the ratification of a convention, the government concerned must report to the Director-General of the International Labour Office, at appropriate intervals as requested by the Governing Body, the position of its law and practice in regard to the matters dealt with in the convention, and the effect which has been given, or is proposed to be given, to the instrument. Members are required to submit similar reports with respect to recommendations.[26] The practice in the application of these provisions is that every year the Governing Body chooses the conventions or recommendations for which such reports are to be requested, taking into account the importance of current interest of the instruments concerned. In doing so, the

[23] ILO Const. art. 22.
[24] For a full statement of the rules governing the reporting system, *see* 60 (No. 2) ILO O. Bull. (Ser. A) 45–46 (1977).
[25] For more detailed information on the operation of the system, *see* Samson, *The Changing Pattern of ILO Supervision*, 118 Int'l Labour Rev. 569, 570–71 [hereinafter cited as Samson].
[26] ILO Const. art. 19(6)(d).

Governing Body has in the past given a preponderant place to conventions and recommendations relating to human rights.

For instance, those governments which had not ratified the conventions dealing with forced labour were requested to supply reports in 1978 indicating the position of their law and practice in regard to the standards contained in those conventions. The receipt of these reports provided an opportunity for the Committee of Experts on the Application of Conventions and Recommendations[27] to make a general survey of the situation of the field covered by forced labour conventions in both ratifying and non-ratifying states.[28]

On the basis of a resolution adopted by the International Labour Conference at its 63rd session in June 1977, the Governing Body decided in 1979 to request member states which had not ratified the Discrimination (Employment and Occupation) Convention, 1958 (No. 111), to report at four-year intervals on their position with respect to that Convention, particularly as regards difficulty giving rise to non-ratification, steps being considered to overcome them, and prospects of ratification. The Conference resolution had stated that non-discrimination, like freedom of association, was a basic principle of the ILO and a constitutional obligation on all member states, and it requested the Governing Body to study ways and means of establishing or strengthening procedures for the supervision of this constitutional obligation.

In 1982, governments were required to report on the Freedom of Association and Protection of the Right to Organise Convention, 1948 (No. 87), on the Right to Organise and Collective Bargaining Convention, 1949 (No. 98), and on the Rural Workers' Organisations Convention, 1975 (No. 141), and Recommendation, 1975 (No. 149).

d. *Involvement of employers' and workers' organizations in the supervisory procedures.* Every year, the supervisory bodies of the ILO draw special attention to the role which employers' and workers' organizations may and should play, in the context of the supervisory procedures, in assessing whether conventions and recommendations are being satisfactorily implemented within their countries. One aspect of this role is based on article 23(2) of the ILO Constitution, which requires governments to send copies of their reports to the most representative employers' and workers' organizations in their countries. This procedure enables those organizations to submit observations concerning the measures taken by their governments to meet their obligations, particularly as regards the practical application of

[27] *See* section I.B.2a *infra*.
[28] *See* Abolition of Forced Labour, General Survey by the Committee of Experts, 65th Sess., International Labour Conference (1979).

ratified conventions. The supervisory bodies have always encouraged
the submission of such observations, and there has been a steady
increase in the number of observations received by the International
Labour Office following the introduction of various practical
measures to assist organizations in this field.[29]

The nature of these observations and the importance of the issues
which they raise vary considerably from case to case. However, experience has shown that observations from employers' and workers'
organizations which call for greater compliance with ratified conventions are frequently followed up by the governments concerned.[30]

In recent years, further action has been taken to strengthen tripartism in the ILO's activities. In 1971, the International Labour Conference adopted a resolution concerning the strengthening of tripartism in the overall activities of the ILO. This resolution led, on the
one hand, to closer attention being paid by the supervisory bodies to
observance of requirements in conventions regarding the association
or consultation of employers' and workers' organizations in the
implementation of ILO standards and, on the other hand, to the
placing on the agenda of the conference of the question of establishing
national tripartite machinery to improve the implementation of ILO
standards. The latter action resulted in the adoption in 1976 of the
Tripartite Consultation (International Labour Standards) Convention
(No. 144) and the Tripartite Consultation (Activities of the Institutional Labour Organization Recommendation (No. 152).[31]

2. *Supervisory bodies*

The reporting system can only be used to advantage if the information and reports submitted by members are properly scrutinized in
order to ascertain that conventions and recommendations are sub-

[29] Prior to 1973 when these measures were introduced, the number of observations received
from employers' and workers' organizations each year was well under 20, whereas in recent
years it has not fallen below 50 and has been considerably higher in some years. *See* Reports of
the Committee of Experts, Report III, Part 4A, of each session of the International Labour
Conference.

[30] In the year from Apr. 1974 to Mar. 1975, for example, legislative and other measures were
taken, as a consequence of such observations, by the government of Barbados in respect of the
Freedom of Association and Protection of the Right to Organise Convention, 1948 (No. 87), and
the Right to Organise and Collective Bargaining Convention, 1949 (No. 98); and by the
governments of Dahomey and the Republic of Viet-Nam in regard to the Minimum Wage-Fixing
Machinery Convention, 1928 (No. 26). In other cases—relating to the application of conventions nos. 87 and 98 by Japan, and the Placing of Seamen Convention, 1921 (No. 9) by The
Netherlands—measures were also taken by the governments concerned. *See also* Report of the
Committee of Experts, Report III, Part 4A, at 28–29, 65 Sess., International Labour Conference
(1979).

[31] As of Mar. 1982, the Convention had been ratified by 26 member states and some 13 others
had indicated their intention of ratifying it. *See* Report of the Committee of Experts, Report III,
Part 4B, 68th Sess., International Labour Conference (1982). *See also* Samson, *supra* note 25, at
574–75.

mitted to the competent authorities, that ratified conventions are duly complied with, and what difficulties prevent or delay ratification or implementation.

A few years after the establishment of the ILO, certain delegates to the International Labour Conference expressed concern that the reports submitted by members did not receive sufficient consideration from the Conference.[32] As a result, the Conference adopted at its 8th session in 1926 a resolution which authorized the Governing Body to appoint a Committee of Experts to make a preliminary report on the annual reports submitted by governments. The resolution also provided that every future session of the Conference should set up a special committee to consider the annual reports.[33]

a. *The Committee of Experts on the Application of Conventions and Recommendations.*[34] In accordance with the decision of the Conference in 1926, the Committee of Experts on the Application of Conventions and Recommendations was established by the Governing Body in the interval between the 1926 and 1927 sessions of the Conference. It is now composed of nineteen members appointed by the Governing Body on the proposal of the Director-General of the International Labour Office. These members are appointed in their personal capacity and not as representatives of their governments, and are chosen from among persons of recognized technical competence and complete independence—they are normally drawn from the judiciary or from academia but occasionally persons with considerable experience in public administration are appointed. Appointments are for periods of three years, which are renewable.

The primary function of the Committee of Experts is to examine the information and reports submitted by governments, in order to establish the extent to which each state has complied with its obligations under ratified conventions and under the provisions of the ILO Constitution relating to conventions and recommendations.[35] In the discharge of this task, the Committee of Experts is guided by the fundamental principles of supervision: independence, impartiality, and objectivity.

The Committee of Experts holds an annual session of about three

[32] *See, e.g.,* 7th Sess., International Labour Conference, Rec. Proc. 156–57 (1925).
[33] 8th Sess., International Labour Conference, Rec. Proc. 429, 238–44 (1926).
[34] For further details on this Committee, *see* Wolf, *Aspects Judiciaires de la Protection Internationale des Droits de l'Homme par l'O.I.T.*, 4 Revue des Droits de l'Homme, 781–87 (1971) [hereinafter cited as Wolf, *Aspects Judiciaires*].
[35] On the function of the Committee of Experts, *see generally* Valticos, *Un système de contrôle international: La mise en œuvre des Conventions internationales de Travail*, Recueil des Cours de l'Académie de Droit Internationale 311 (1968–I).

282 *Francis Wolf*

weeks on dates fixed by the Governing Body.[36] It organizes its work by assigning each of its members initial responsibility for a group of conventions; government reports and relevant documentation are sent to the expert concerned for examination prior to the Committee's session. Each member responsible for a group of conventions or a given subject submits his or her conclusions to the Committee of Experts as a whole. In addition, the Committee appoints working groups from among its members to deal with questions of principle or questions of a particularly complex nature. These working groups generally meet for a few days before the Committee's session and sometimes during the session as well. Their conclusions also are submitted to the Committee of Experts as a whole.[37] The Committee of Experts has kept its general working methods under review and in 1969, in 1971, and most recently on the occasion of its fiftieth anniversary in 1977 has set out in its report a detailed description of its principles and working methods. In the 1977 review, the Committee of Experts re-affirmed that its function is to determine whether the requirements of a given convention are being met, whatever the economic and social conditions in a given country. Subject only to any derogations which are expressly permitted by the convention itself, a convention's requirements remain constant and uniform for all countries. In carrying out this work, the Committee of Experts is guided by the standards laid down in the convention alone, mindful, however, of the fact that the modes of implementation may differ in different states.[38]

The comments of the Committee of Experts on ratified conventions take the form of observations which are incorporated in a printed report which is communicated to the member states and presented to the Conference for discussion. On points of secondary importance or calling for clarification, the Committee of Experts sends direct requests to the government involved, which are not published. The Committee of Experts also reports on and lists any specific improvements which have resulted from its previous comments.

The Committee of Experts also deals with unratified conventions and with recommendations. Basing itself on the reports submitted by

[36] The Committee elects its Chairman and Reporter at the beginning of each session and decides its procedure. It meets *in camera* and its deliberations and documents remain confidential. *See* Wolf, *Aspects Judiciaires, supra* note 34, at 281.

[37] Traditionally the conclusions of the Committee of Experts are unanimous. However, any minority views are recorded in its report, if the members concerned so request. The Report of the Committee of Experts is submitted to the Governing Body and presented to the following session of the Conference. *See* Report III, Part 4, at 6–15, 63d Sess., International Labour Conference (1977) (Description of the methods and procedures relating to the work of the Committee of Experts on the Application of Conventions and Recommendations).

[38] Report of the Committee of Experts, Report III, Part 4A, at 10–11, 63d Sess., International Labour Conference (1979).

governments on the instruments selected for reporting by the Governing Body, the Committee of Experts presents an overall survey of the way in which, and the extent to which, the relevant instruments are applied together with an indication of any prospects for the ratification of the conventions concerned. The Committee of Experts also explains how obstacles to full implementation of the instruments might be overcome.

The effect of the comments of the Committee of Experts depends on the kind of response they evoke from governments. With this essential purpose in mind, the Committee of Experts has endeavored not only to draw attention to any lack of conformity with a ratified convention, but also to focus on the positive steps needed to ensure better implementation. The results which have been achieved in this respect are encouraging.[39] Since 1964, over 1,400 discrepancies have been rectified by governments as a result of observations and direct requests made by the Committee of Experts, with many of these related to conventions on basic human rights.[40]

In addition to its supervisory functions with respect to ILO instruments, the Committee of Experts has assumed new responsibilities in the wider context of co-operation between international organizations in supervising the implementation of the International Covenant on Economic, Social and Cultural Rights. In November 1976, the Governing Body of the ILO decided to accede to the request of ECOSOC[41] that specialized agencies report to it on the progress made in achieving observance of the provisions of that Covenant falling within the scope of their activities, including the particulars of decisions and recommendations on implementation adopted by their competent organs. The Governing Body decided at the same time that the Committee of Experts should undertake this new task.[42] The Committee of Experts has examined these matters during each of its sessions since 1978 and has submitted reports to ECOSOC[43] relating to the implementation of articles 6 to 12 of the Economic Covenant by states parties whose reports were transmitted to the ILO by the United Nations.

[39] In 60% of cases in which divergencies were established, governments took the measures necessary to correct the situation and to eliminate, at least in part, the divergencies which had been brought to light. *See* E. Landy, The Effectiveness of International Supervision—30 Years of ILO Experience (1966). *See also* Landy, *The Influence of International Labour Conventions: Possibilities and Performance*, 101 Int'l Labour Rev. 555 (1970).

[40] *See* Report of the Committee of Experts, Report III, Part 4A, at 22–23, 68th Sess., International Labour Conference (1982).

[41] *See* ECOSOC Res. 1988 (LX) (1976).

[42] *See* 201st Sess., Minutes of the Governing Body of the International Labour Office, Agenda Item 15, § 26 (Nov. 1976).

[43] These ECOSOC reports were issued as U.N. documents E/1978/27, E/1979/33, E/1980/35, E/1981/41, and E/1982/41.

b. *The Conference Committee on the Application of Conventions and Recommendations.* During each of its annual sessions, the International Labour Conference establishes a tripartite Committee to consider and report on information and reports given by members of the ILO on the application of conventions and recommendations.[44] The Conference Committee on the Application of Conventions and Recommendations commences its work with a general discussion of questions arising out of the application of conventions and recommendations and the discharge by member states of their obligations under the ILO Constitution, based mainly on the information contained in the report of the Committee of Experts. It next discusses the general survey made by the Committee of Experts of the effect given to selected unratified conventions and recommendations. It concludes its work by examining individual cases concerning the application of ratified conventions and compliance with the constitutional obligations concerning conventions and recommendations, drawing mainly on the observations made by the Committee of Experts. In view of time constraints, the Conference Committee confines its discussion to a limited number of cases chosen from among those which have been the subject of observations by the Committee of Experts.

Over the past twenty years, the Conference Committee has adopted the practice of drawing the attention of the Conference to cases in which governments appeared to encounter serious difficulties in discharging obligations under the ILO Constitution or under conventions which they have ratified. In recent years, the Conference Committee has drawn attention to certain important cases by means of special paragraphs. In 1979 and 1980 it undertook a thorough re-examination of its methods of work and introduced certain changes in the presentation of its report. Although the form has changed—formerly attention was drawn to particular cases by means of a 'Special List'— the Conference Committee continues in its report to identify the cases of serious failure to comply with obligations relating to conventions and recommendations; to include a brief reference to special cases among those which it has discussed and to which it considers it appropriate to draw the attention of the Conference; and to list in its report any cases of continuing failure over several years to eliminate serious deficiencies in the application of ratified conventions which it has discussed in previous reports.[45]

[44] The Committee set up by the 67th Session of the Conference in June 1981 was composed of 168 members: 93 Government members, 21 Employers' members, and 54 Workers' members. It also included 11 Government deputy members, 26 Employers' deputy members, and 58 Workers' deputy members. As in the case of all the committees of the Conference, each of the three groups possesses the same number of votes and where the number of the representatives from the groups is not the same, the votes are weighted to maintain equality between the groups. *See* art. 65, Standing Orders of the Conference.

c. *The system of direct contacts.* In 1967, the Committee of Experts raised the question of whether more varied procedures might not make possible a fuller examination of certain questions and a more fruitful dialogue with governments. It then put forward a general suggestion for direct contacts with governments for the purpose of enabling it to reach its conclusions with due regard to all relevant considerations and of finding positive solutions to problems encountered in the application of conventions. The Conference Committee on the Application of Conventions and Recommendations agreed that the suggestion merited further exploration and requested the Committee of Experts to submit more precise and detailed proposals on the matter. In 1968, the Committee of Experts formulated principles and methods to be applied in initiating direct contacts with governments.[46]

According to these principles, the Committee of Experts, the Conference Committee, or the government concerned may take the initiative in suggesting such contacts. However, in the majority of cases in which direct contacts have taken place, the initiative has come from the government concerned. It sends a written communication to the Director-General of the International Labour Office, from whom an affirmative reply, also in the form of a written communication, is needed before direct contacts can be established.[47]

These contacts are intended to supplement and not to replace or limit the responsibilities of the established supervisory bodies of the ILO. Indeed, direct contacts appear to have fulfilled three essential functions. They have been used, as a form of technical assistance, to provide advice to states concerning the nature of action to be taken to meet their obligations under the ILO Constitution and international labour conventions; they have been used for fact-finding in cases where the practical application of national and international standards was at issue; and, in cases where there has been major problems or conflicting views between a government and the ILO supervisory bodies, especially in the field of basic human rights, direct contacts have provided an opportunity for fuller explanation of the positions of the parties and for the exploration of possible ways to eliminate the differences which existed.

In general, direct contacts take the form of detailed discussions between a representative of the Director-General of the International Labour Office, who visits the country in question with the consent of the government concerned, and representatives of the relevant govern-

45 *See* Prov. Rec. No. 37, at 4–7, 12–13, 19–22, 66th Sess., International Labour Conference (June 1980). For further details on the operation of the former 'special list', *see* Wolf, *ILO Experience, supra* note 1, at 611–12.

46 Report III, Part 4A, at 13–17, 65th Sess., International Labour Conference (1979).

47 Report III, Part 4A, at 13, 58th Sess., International Labour Conference (1973).

ment agencies who have sufficient responsibility and experience to speak with authority about the situation in their country and about their government's attitudes and intentions in the matter and to explain all the elements of the case. Contact is also made with the employers' and workers' organizations in the course of the visit. The Committee of Experts and the Conference Committee have been able to note in many cases that governments have taken action to improve compliance with their obligations in the cases that had been the subject of these contacts.[48]

C. CONTENTIOUS PROCEDURES

Two types of contentious procedure, *i.e.*, representations and complaints, round out this discussion of methods of supervision of the application of ratified conventions. These procedures are of general application, are regulated by the ILO Constitution, and have been resorted to particularly with respect to the application of the basic human rights conventions.

1. *Representations against members*

In accordance with the provisions of article 24 of the ILO Constitution, an industrial association of employers or of workers may submit a representation to the International Labour Office that any of the members of the ILO has failed to secure in any respect the effective observation within its jurisdiction of any convention to which it is a party. After the receipt of the representation, the Governing Body may communicate it to the government concerned and may invite that government to make a statement. If no statement is received within a reasonable time from the government, or if the statement, when received, is not deemed to be satisfactory by the Governing Body, the latter can publish the representation and the statement, if any, made in reply.[49] A fundamental feature of this procedure is that it allows employers' and workers' organizations to initiate procedures to examine the implementation by members of the ILO of conventions which those states have ratified.

Very little use was made of the representations procedure for many years, but the situation appears to be changing. There has been a growing tendency to resort to the procedure in recent years, particularly with respect to the implementation of the basic human rights

[48] In the first ten years, direct contacts took place in 28 countries (15 in Latin America, 7 in Africa, 4 in Asia, and 2 in Europe). They involved discussion of some 222 cases of shortcomings in the application of ratified conventions. In 115 cases, affecting 23 countries, the Committee of Experts subsequently noted improvements. Other results have included improved compliance with various constitutional obligations and additional ratifications. *See* Report of the Committee of Experts, Report III, Part 4A, at 13–27, 65th Sess., International Labour Conference (1979).

[49] ILO Const. art. 25.

conventions. In recent years, four representations have been received by the International Labour Office alleging the non-observance of the Discrimination (Employment and Occupation) Convention, 1958 (No. 111). The first representation was submitted by the World Federation of Trade Unions (WFTU) against the countries belonging to the European Economic Community (EEC) alleging that the 'political policing' inquiry conducted by EEC authorities constituted discrimination in respect of employment against the officials affected on the grounds of political opinion, directly involving the responsibility of the then nine EEC governments both from the point of view of the international labour standards they had ratified and because of moral responsibility. The tripartite committee set up by the Governing Body to examine this representation recommended that it should be declared irreceivable.[50] The second representation was submitted by the International Confederation of Free Trade Unions (ICFTU) against Czechoslovakia alleging that it had taken repressive measures affecting the employment of authors or signatories of documents which brought to public attention criticisms of that government's policy in the field of human rights. The Governing Body concluded in this case that the government's reply was not satisfactory and decided that the representation and the reply should be published together with the report of the tripartite committee.[51] The third representation was submitted by the WFTU against the Federal Republic of Germany alleging that the many cases arising from the application of the so-called 'work ban' (*Berufsverbot*)—in particular since the adoption by the Länder Prime Ministers' Conference in January 1972 of the Anti-Radical Decree (*Radikalererlass*) which bars citizens from access to employment or exercise of their occupation, particularly in the civil service, on the grounds of their political beliefs—amounted to a gross breach of the Convention. After examining the representation, the tripartite committee recommended to the Governing Body that it declare the case closed. Lastly, in 1982 the Norwegian Federation of Trade Unions submitted a representation against the Government of Norway alleging that amendments to labour legislation adopted in 1982 contravened Convention No. 111 by permitting employers to inquire into the political, religious or cultural views of job applicants even in circumstances where such inquiry was not justified by the nature of the job. This case is still under examination.[52]

---

[50] *See* 205th Sess., Governing Body Feb. 28–Mar. 3, 1978), ILO. Doc. GB.205/8/17, at 4 (1978).

[51] *See* 61 (No. 3) ILO O. Bull. (Ser. A) (Supp.) 5–6 (1978).

[52] 63 (No. 1) ILO O. Bull. (Ser. A) (1980); 210th Sess., Governing Body (May–June 1979), ILO Doc. GB.210/16/27, at 8 (1979). Regarding the 1982 Norwegian representation, *see* ILO Doc. GB.220/16/28 (1982).

2. *Complaints against members*

The complaint procedure is the most far-reaching of the supervisory procedures of the ILO. Its operation is based on the provisions of articles 26 to 29 and 31 to 34 of the ILO Constitution. Any member of the ILO has a right to file a complaint with the International Labour Office that it is not satisfied that another member is securing the effective observance of any convention which both have ratified.[53] Once a complaint has been received, the Governing Body may follow several courses. It may communicate the complaint to the government against which it is made—in the same manner as a representation under article 24[54]—and may invite that government to make such statement as it thinks fit on the matter.[55] If the Governing Body does not think it necessary to communicate the complaint or if, after such communication, a satisfactory response is not received within a reasonable time, the Governing Body may appoint a Commission of Inquiry to consider the complaint and to report thereon.[56] The Governing Body may also adopt these procedures on its own motion or on receipt of a complaint from a delegate to the Conference.[57] In this way, employers and workers who are represented on the Conference delegations may make a complaint leading to the establishment of a Commission of Inquiry.

In practice, when a complaint results in the creation of a Commission of Inquiry, the Commission is composed of three independent, highly qualified persons appointed by the Governing Body on the proposal of the Director-General of the International Labour Office.[58] This practice stems from the need to ensure that matters which are often very complex and controversial are examined in a completely impartial and objective manner.[59] The procedure followed by these Commissions (assembly of documentation, hearing of parties and of witnesses, and on-the-spot visits where necessary) is carried out in a judicial and impartial manner.[60]

When the Commission of Inquiry has fully considered the com-

---

[53] ILO Const. art 26(1).

[54] *See* section C.1 *supra.*

[55] ILO Const. art. 26(2).

[56] *Id.* art. 26(3).

[57] *Id.* art. 26(4).

[58] These normally include at least one person who has held high judicial office. Indeed, the Chairman of the Commission of Inquiry on the complaint against Chile was José Luis Bustamante i Rivero, a former President of the International Court of Justice.

[59] The members of a commission make a declaration that they will perform their duties and exercise their powers 'honourably, faithfully, impartially, and conscientiously'—a solemn declaration which corresponds to that made by judges of the International Court of Justice. *See* Wolf, *Aspects Judiciaires, supra* note 34, at 809.

[60] *See* Osieke, *The Exercise of Judicial Function with Respect to the International Labour Organisation*, 47 Brit. Y.B. Int'l L. 315, 330–38 (1974–1975) [hereinafter cited as Osieke].

plaint, it prepares a report embodying its findings on all questions of fact relevant to determining the issue between the parties and containing such recommendations as it may think proper as to the steps which should be taken to meet the complaint and the time within which they should be taken.[61] The Director-General communicates the report to the Governing Body and to each of the governments concerned and arranges for its publication.[62] Each of these governments is required to inform the Director-General within three months of whether it accepts the recommendations contained in the report of the Commission and, if not, whether it proposes to refer the complaint to the International Court of Justice (ICJ).[63] The ICJ may affirm, vary, or reverse any of the findings or recommendations of the Commission of Inquiry,[64] and its decision in this respect is final.[65] If any member of the ILO fails to carry out within the time specified the recommendations contained in the report of the Commission of Inquiry or in the decision of the ICJ, the Governing Body may recommend to the Conference such action as it may deem wise and expedient to secure compliance.[66]

The complaint procedure has been used mostly in the last two decades, during which time thirteen complaints have been received, as compared to one complaint during the first forty years of the ILO's existence. It is interesting, moreover, that many of these complaints were made in connection with the observance of the basic human rights conventions. The instruments on forced labour have been the subject of four complaints;[67] seven complaints concerned the freedom of association conventions;[68] and one complaint was made with re-

[61] ILO Const. art. 28.
[62] *Id.* art. 29(1).
[63] *Id.* art. 29(2).
[64] *Id.* art. 32.
[65] *Id.* art. 31.
[66] *Id.* art. 33.
[67] *See* the complaint filed by Ghana against Portugal in 1961 concerning the observance of the Abolition of Forced Labour Convention, 1957 (No. 105); and the complaint by Portugal against Liberia in 1961 with respect to the application of the Forced Labour Convention, 1930 (No. 29). 45 (No. 2) ILO O. Bull. (Supp. 2) (1962); ILO, Report of the Portugal v. Liberia Commission of Inquiry 46 (No. 2) ILO O. Bull. (Supp. 2) (1963). *See also* Osieke, *supra* note 60, at 327–29. Complaints against the Dominican Republic and Haiti concerning the observance of several Conventions, including the two Conventions on forced labour (Nos. 29 and 105) were filed in 1981 and are at present being examined by a Commission of Inquiry; ILO Doc. GB.217/4/8, GB.217/4/9 and GB.218/6/10.
[68] All the complaints were made by worker delegates to the Conference, as follows: (a) in 1968 against Greece for the non-observance of the Freedom of Association and Protection of the Rights to Organise Convention, 1948 (No. 87); and the Right to Organise and Collective Bargaining Convention, 1949 (No. 98); 54 (No. 2) ILO O. Bull. (1972); (b) in 1975 against Bolivia for the non-observance of Convention No. 87; ILO Doc. GB.198/6/4; (c) in 1976 against Uruguay concerning the non-observance of Conventions Nos. 87 and 98; ILO Doc. GB.200/17/44; (d) in 1977 against Argentina concerning the non-observance of Convention No. 87; ILO Doc. GB.203/19/42; (e) in 1981 against the Dominican Republic and against Haiti

spect to the Discrimination (Employment and Occupation) Convention, (No. 111).[69] Several of these cases were referred to Commissions of Inquiry for examination.[70] When the Commission finds that there has been non-observance of the convention in question, it makes recommendations as to the measures that should be taken by the government concerned to fulfill its obligations under the convention. It is normally left to the regular supervisory bodies to follow-up the implementation of these recommendations.

D.   SPECIAL FREEDOM OF ASSOCIATION PROCEDURES

The general procedures described above apply to the conventions on freedom of association as they do to all the others, but in view of the importance of freedom of association, the ILO has established additional machinery for its protection. This involves the examination of complaints by the Governing Body's Committee on Freedom of Association and by the Fact-Finding and Conciliation Commission on Freedom of Association. The complaints may even concern states which have not ratified the freedom of association conventions. For such states, the application of this machinery is based on their membership in the ILO and on the fact that the ILO Constitution has affirmed the principle of freedom of association; the ILO can accordingly promote the realization of this principle through procedures of investigation and conciliation.

1.   *The Committee on Freedom of Association*

This Committee, which was established by the Governing Body at its 117th session in November 1951 from among its members on a tripartite basis, in the first instance examines all complaints received and reports to the Governing Body on whether the complaints appear substantiated. It also determines whether recommendations should be addressed to the governments concerned or whether, in appropriate cases, a complaint should be referred to the Fact-Finding and Concilia-

for the non-observance of Conventions Nos. 87 and 98; *see* note 67 *supra*; and (f) in 1982 against Poland for non-observance of Conventions Nos. 87 and 98; ILO Doc. GB.220/16/26.

[69] *See* the complaint initiated by the Governing Body against Chile concerning the observance of the Hours of Work Convention, 1919 (No. 1); and the Discrimination (Employment and Occupation) Convention, 1958 (No. 111). International Labour Office Report of the Commission of Inquiry in the Case of Chile (1975).

[70] In three of the cases relating to conventions on freedom of association, the Governing Body decided to refer the complaints first to its Committee on Freedom of Association prior to any decision as to the establishment of a Commission of Inquiry. *See* Samson, *supra* note 25, at 578. In some of the cases referred to a Commission of Inquiry, the members of the Commission visited the territories of the state against which the complaint was made in order to ascertain whether reasonably specific allegations were supported by current or recent facts. *See* Osieke, *supra* note 60, at 332.

tion Commission. Wide recourse has been had to this special machinery. Since its establishment in 1951, the Committee on Freedom of Association has considered about 1,100 cases, with the number of complaints increasing considerably in recent years. Whereas the Committee used to receive about 30 new complaints each year, the numbers for 1980 and 1981 were 66 and 88 respectively.[71]

In trying first to establish the facts, the Committee on Freedom of Association follows the basic rule of all contentious procedures, namely, that of giving the opposing parties an opportunity to put forward their points of view. Accordingly, the complaints are communicated to the governments against which they are made so that they may submit their observations. In a case where a doubt or contradiction exists, or if it appears useful to inform the complainants of the observations of the government, the substance of these observations is communicated to them for their comments, and questions may be put to them. The Committee on Freedom of Association has frequently reviewed its procedure to introduce improvements, expedite the examination of cases, and ensure the follow-up of its recommendations. Over the years, a number of measures have been adopted by the Committee, and approved by the Governing Body, in order to achieve this purpose. Most recently, the Committee has started in certain cases to invite the government concerned to send a representative to provide oral information at its meetings. Increasing use has also been made of the procedure of direct contacts, described above, in order to permit an on-the-spot examination and discussion of certain cases.[72]

The influence of the Committee on Freedom of Association is primarily a moral one, deriving from the objectivity of its procedures, the persuasive effect and authority of its unanimous conclusions, and the publicity given its work. The Committee has succeeded—and this is in fact one of its main achievements—in gaining wider recognition for the international value of the principles of freedom of association. A substantial proportion of the cases examined by the Committee have raised issues relating to fundamental human rights, particularly in connection with the arrest, detention, or exile of trade unionists. In many of these cases, including in particular cases where the measures complained of had not been taken within the context of judicial proceedings, the governments concerned have finally released the persons in question or allowed their return from exile. There is no

---

[71] *See* von Potobsky, *Protection of Trade Union Rights: Twenty Years Work by the Committee on Freedom of Association*, Int'l Labour Rev. 69 (1972). *See generally* International Labour Office, Digest of the decisions of the Freedom of Association Committee of the Governing Body of the ILO (1974); Samson, *supra* note 25, at 579.

[72] On the Committee on Freedom of Association's procedures *see* Comm. on Freedom of Association, 193d Report, 62 (No. 1) ILO O. Bull (Ser. B) 155 (1979).

doubt that the action and efforts of the Committee on Freedom of Association in these matters have contributed to a large extent in obtaining the desired results from governments.

2. *The Fact-Finding and Conciliation Commission on Freedom of Association*

This Commission was established in 1950 by an agreement between the ILO and the United Nations. Its function is to examine such cases of alleged infringements of trade union rights as may be referred to it, to ascertain the facts, and to discuss the situation with the government concerned with a view to securing by agreement the adjustment of difficulties.

The Fact-Finding and Conciliation Commission is composed of independent persons appointed by the Governing Body on the proposal of the Director-General of the International Labour Office. The Governing Body refers cases to the Commission on the recommendation of the Committee on Freedom of Association. Complaints may also be referred to the Fact-Finding and Conciliation Commission at the request of the United Nations when the complaints concern member states of the United Nations which are not members of the ILO. In principle, no complaint may be referred to the Commission without the consent of the government concerned, except in cases covered by article 26 of the ILO Constitution.[73]

Four cases have so far been referred to the Fact-Finding and Conciliation Commission. These concerned respectively Japan,[74] Greece,[75] Lesotho,[76] and Chile.[77] The procedure followed by the Commission in dealing with these cases has been analogous to the procedure of the Commissions of Inquiry which are responsible for examining complaints with respect to ratified conventions.[78]

After examining the allegations, the Fact-Finding and Conciliation Commission normally recommends the measures to be adopted by the government concerned in order to ensure observance of the principles of freedom of association enshrined in the ILO Constitution. In certain cases, the implementation of the recommendations of the Commission may not be sufficient to restore confidence and trust between the parties, or even to ensure free trade union rights, and the government may be expected to take other measures beyond the field of trade

[73] *See* section C.2 *supra*
[74] 54 (No. 1) ILO O. Bull. (Spec. Supp.) (1966).
[75] 54 (No. 3) ILO O. Bull. (Spec. Supp.) (1966).
[76] *See* ILO Doc. GB.197/3/5 (1975).
[77] International Labour Office, The Trade Union Situation in Chile: Report of the Fact-Finding and Conciliation Commission on Freedom of Association (1975) [hereinafter cited as Trade Union Situation in Chile].
[78] *See* section C.2 *supra*.

union rights as such in order to fully meet the situation. This appeared to be the situation in the case concerning Chile, where the Fact-Finding and Conciliation Commission stated that while the implementation of its recommendations

will contribute towards the normalisation of the trade union movement . . . [it] will not suffice to ensure the free exercise of trade union rights. Many trade unionists will continue to be pursued by a feeling of constraint, and even of fear, until they are assured that there will be respect for the human rights which are essential to the normal pursuit of trade union activities, and in particular the right to freedom and personal safety, and to protection from arrest and arbitrary imprisonment, the right to a proper trial before an independent and impartial court, and freedom of opinion and expression.[79]

E.   NON-CONTENTIOUS PROCEDURES

This chapter would not be complete without reference to some of the non-contentious methods by which the ILO promotes the implementation of its standards. These methods, which are less spectacular than, but supplementary to, the supervisory procedures, include regional discussions and reviews;[80] *ad hoc* investigations at the request of government and assistance to governments, and employers' and workers' organizations;[81] collaboration with other international organizations as well as nongovernmental organizations and institutions of higher learning;[82] research and promotional activities;[83] and technical cooperation with member states in the field of human rights.[84] These forms of action are designed to deal with situations and problems which prevent or delay the application of conventions and recommendations, and to make the standards and procedures of the ILO better known to those they are intended to serve. Thus, they play an essential supporting role in bringing about the implementation of the standards adopted by the ILO.

F.   CONCLUDING REMARKS

An attempt has been made in this chapter to highlight the contribution which the ILO has been making in the promotion of human

[79] *See* Trade Union Situation in Chile, *supra* note 77 at 121. For the recommendations of the Fact-Finding and Conciliation Commission, *see id.* at 118–21.

[80] *See, e.g.*, Report of the Committee of Experts, Report III, Part 4A, at 8, 61st Sess., International Labour Conference (1975).

[81] *See* Rossillion, *ILO Examination of Human Rights Situation*, Rev. Int'l Comm'n Jurists (No. 12, June 1974) [hereinafter cited as Rossillion].

[82] *See* Report of the Committee of Experts, Report III, Part 4A, at 7, 61st Sess., International Labour Conference (1975). For a detailed examination of the collaboration between the ILO and all other specialized agencies in the U.N. system, *see* Samson, *supra* note 25, at 580–82.

[83] *See* In-Depth Review of International Labour Standards, 194th Sess., Governing Body, ILO Doc. GB.194/PFA/12/5, at 41 (Nov. 1974) [hereinafter cited as In-Depth Review].

[84] *See* Rossillion, *supra* note 81, at 41.

rights. The basis of this contribution is the adoption of international labour conventions and recommendations in the areas of basic human rights and the effective implementation of these instruments by decision-making and executing agencies at both the national and international levels. The ILO has adopted important instruments on forced labour, freedom of association, and discrimination; the machinery for the supervision of the implementation of these standards is contentious in some cases and non-contentious in others.

Although credit cannot be given to the instruments adopted by the ILO for all measures at the national level, there has been ample evidence of the direct influence of these standards. It is known that in addition to the influence of ratified conventions, certain conventions which have been relatively sparsely ratified and recommendations have had considerable influence on the law and practice of many countries and have acted as the inspiration for the formulation of national policies.[85] Furthermore, it has been pointed out recently that

the mere existence of a standard has led to universal recognition of the legitimacy and validity of certain fundamental principles which, in spite of many difficulties of application, have come to constitute a kind of common law whose effective application is sought through continuous action on both the national and international levels. Freedom of association standards are the most obvious example.[86]

Despite their undoubted influence, international labour standards have not always been as decisive as desired in reducing inequality, improving working and living conditions, and increasing respect for human rights. No one can expect these standards to provide a universal remedy, but in order to ensure that they fulfill their role, it is essential to examine their limitations and ways to overcome those limitations. Standards are proposed to states for their acceptance and can be effective only to the extent that they secure the interest, support, and action needed at the state level for their implementation. To provide a continuing stimulus to that end is the justification for the various supervisory procedures and the range of supplementary measures of advice and assistance developed by the ILO.

II. Teaching Suggestions

A.   PURPOSE OF THE COURSE

The purpose of a course on the ILO should be to examine its activities in the field of human rights in order to evaluate its contri-

[85] *See* International Labour Office, The Impact of International Labour Conventions and Recommendations (1976), and the extensive number of monographs cited therein.
[86] *See* In-Depth Review, *supra* note 83, at 2.

bution to the protection of fundamental human rights. As such, the course should cover the ILO's area of competence; the nature of its rules and standards; the machinery for supervising the implementation of the rules; and the results achieved. The course could be taught at undergraduate or postgraduate level. For the undergraduate programme, it would be sufficient to study the subject in a general way, but a detailed analysis and evaluation would be necessary in the postgraduate programme.

B.   THE MAIN ORGANS OF THE ILO

It would be useful to begin the course with a brief study of the main organs of the ILO in order to understand fully the basis of ILO activities in the field of human rights. There are three main organs in the ILO, namely the International Labour Office, the Governing Body of the International Labour Office, and the International Labour Conference.[87] The International Labour Office is the administrative organ, the Governing Body the main executive body, and the International Labour Conference the legislative organ. The International Labour Office is composed of international public officials, with a Director-General as the administrative head; the Governing Body is composed of a total of 56 regular members made up of 28 government, 14 employer, and 14 worker representatives; each state member of the ILO is entitled to nominate four delegates to the International Labour Conference, two government delegates, one representing the employers, and one representing the workers of the member. The tripartite structure of the ILO is one of its fundamental features and distinguishes it from the other international organizations and specialized agencies of the United Nations which are purely governmental.

C.   AREA OF ILO ACTIVITY

Since the primary purpose of the ILO is to promote social welfare, its contribution to the field of human rights should necessarily be related to the area of its general competence. Although most of the instruments adopted by the ILO relate to human rights in general, particular attention has been given to the areas of freedom of assocation, freedom from forced labour, and freedom from discrimination in employment. In discussing this subejct, it would be important to establish the meaning of each of these basic freedoms and its relationship to the other freedoms. For instance, what does 'freedom of association' mean, and what place should be given to this freedom in the general hierarchy of fundamental freedoms?

[87] *See* ILO Const. arts, 3, 7, 10.

It would be important also to examine the relationship between these freedoms and other norms or principles in national society, *e.g.*, national security and the general national interest. In other words, the question of the extent to which these basic freedoms should be given primacy over other rules and principles in the national society may be examined.

D.   ILO METHODS FOR THE PROMOTION OF HUMAN RIGHTS: INTERNATIONAL LABOUR STANDARDS

The ILO's primary method to promote basic human rights is the adoption of international labour standards in the form of conventions and recommendations. While examining this question it would be important to establish the circumstances which call for the adoption of a convention and/or recommendation. Similarly, when is it more appropriate to adopt a convention than a recommendation?

It would also be essential to examine the nature of the obligations which arise for members of the ILO as a result of the adoption of these instruments. A convention is open to ratification and ratifying members are under an obligation to implement its provisions.[88] On the other hand, a recommendation is not open to ratification and its adoption does not create any legal obligation to implement its provisions, but does give rise to some constitutional obligations for members.[89]

Finally, the legal character of conventions and recommendations could be compared to that of other international agreements. In doing so, it should be noted that a 'reservation' cannot be made to ILO conventions[90] and that they create legal obligations for members whether or not those members voted for their adoption.

E.   THE NATURE AND SCOPE OF ILO INSTRUMENTS

The ILO has adopted a large number of conventions and recommendations in the fields of freedom of association, forced labour, and discrimination in employment.[91] It would be useful to examine the provisions of some of these instruments in order to determine how adequately they deal with the problems which they were designed to resolve. Particular attention could be paid in this respect to Conventions Nos. 87 and 98 on freedom of association; Conventions Nos. 29

[88] *See id.* art. 19(5).
[89] *See id.* art. 19(6).
[90] *See* Valticos & Wolf, *L'OIT et les pays en voie de développement; technique d'élaboration et mise en œuvre des normes universelles*, in Pays en Voie de Développement et Transformation du Droit International 127, 131 (Société Française pour le Droit International 1974).
[91] *See* notes, 8, 9, & 10 *supra*.

and 105 on forced labour; and Convention No. 111 on discrimination in employment.

In appropriate cases, the provisions of these instruments could be compared with those of national legislation on the same subject. In such cases, it would be appropriate to determine the influence, if any, of the ILO Convention on the national legislation.

F.   THE SUPERVISORY MACHINERY

The activities of the ILO do not end with the adoption of conventions and recommendations. The ILO has highly developed machinery for the supervision of observance by member states of their obligations under international labour conventions and recommendations as well as under the ILO Constitution. In examining this machinery, it would be important to distinguish the contentious from the non-contentious procedures.

1.   *The contentious procedures*

The contentious procedures are normally applied in cases where there is an alleged breach by a member state of a convention which it had ratified. In examining this subject, special attention should be paid to three different procedures, namely representations and complaints under the ILO Constitution and the special freedom of association procedure.

a. *Representations procedure.* A representation is the main action that can be taken by employers' and workers' organizations against a member of the ILO for the non-observance of a convention which it has ratified. In examining this very important procedure, particular attention should be paid to the manner in which a representation can be initiated, the procedure for the examination of a representation, and the sanction available under the procedure. It should be noted that under this procedure, employers' and workers' organizations have been given a right to seek enforcement of a convention to which they are not parties. This situation could be compared with the general situation in the law of treaties, and even in the municipal law of contracts.

The main sanction available under this procedure is the publication of the representation and the statement, if any, made in reply to it.[92] It should be considered whether 'publication' constitutes an effective sanction for the non-observance of a convention by a member state, or whether another form of sanction could be envisaged. The case of Czechoslovakia in 1977 should be examined in this respect.

[92] *See* ILO Const. art. 25.

b. *Complaint procedure.* The complaint procedure is another method by which the non-observance of a convention can be investigated. In examining the procedure, it would be important to consider the circumstances that could give rise to a complaint and the entities that may initiate the procedure.

Over the years, the ILO has established very effective machinery for the examination of complaints, *i.e.*, the Commission of Inquiry. It would be important to examine the composition and procedure of a Commission of Inquiry, its role in the determination of disputes, and its contribution to the development of international jurisprudence.[93]

c. *Special freedom of association procedure.* The ILO has established a special freedom of association procedure to supplement the procedures provided for under the ILO Constitution. It involves the examination of complaints by the Governing Body Committee on Freedom of Association and by the Fact-Finding and Conciliation Commission on Freedom of Association. It would be necessary to examine the origins, terms of reference, and working methods of these two bodies, as well as the results that have been achieved. In the latter respect, a number of recent cases handled by the Committee and Commision could be examined and analyzed.

2. *Non-contentious procedures*

Various procedures which are non-contentious also exist for the supervision of the observance of conventions and recommendations. Special mention should be made of the Committee of Experts on the Application of Conventions and Recommendations; the Conference Committee on the Application of Conventions and Recommendations; the system of reporting on ratified and unratified conventions and on recommendations; direct contacts; and the special role of employers' and workers' organizations.

In the teaching of this section, emphasis should be placed on the origin, composition, methods of work, and powers of the Committee of Experts and the Conference Committee on the Application of Conventions and Recommendations. These two Committees could be compared and evaluated. It would be useful also to examine the methods of work of the Conference Committee before and after the changes introduced in 1980 with regard to the 'special list'. The role of the Governing Body in the 'reporting system' should also be examined, as should the nature of the response from member states to requests from the Governing Body.

The usefulness of the direct contacts procedure should be considered and, wherever possible, the results achieved under this system

[93] *See* Osieke, *supra* note 60.

should be evaluated. Some attention should be paid to the role of employers' and workers' organizations and the utility of the 'observations' which they submit to the International Labour Office.

Finally, the other non-contentious procedures could also be examined and evaluated on the basis of the results that have been achieved in recent years.

III. Syllabus

1. Purpose of the course.
2. The main organs of the ILO: the International Labour Office; the Governing Body of the International Labour Office; the International Labour Conference.
3. The tripartite structure of the ILO: Representation of employers and workers in the main organs of the ILO such as the Conference, the Governing Body, and important committees. The role of the nongovernmental bodies in the adoption of conventions and recommendations. (The text of the ILO Constitution should be consulted.)
4. ILO's competence in the field of human rights as defined in the ILO Constitution and the Declaration of Philadelphia.
5. ILO's area of activity in the field of human rights: particularly freedom of association; freedom from forced labour; freedom from discrimination in employment; the meaning of these freedoms and their relationship to other fundamental freedoms.
6. ILO methods for the promotion of basic human rights: international labour conventions and recommendations; essential characteristics of these instruments.
7. Nature and scope of ILO instruments on human rights, particularly on freedom of association, forced labour, and discrimination in employment.
8. The ILO machinery for the supervision of international labour standards.
   a. Contentious procedures: representations and complaints—the special freedom of association procedures.
   b. Non-contentious procedures: Committee of Experts and the Conference Committee on the Application of Conventions and Recommendations—direct contacts, role of employers' and workers' organizations, reports on ratified and unratified conventions and on recommendations.

Case Studies

1. Ghana v. Portugal, *in re* Observance of the Abolition of Forced Labour Convention, 1957 (No. 105); 45 (No. 2) ILO O. Bull. (Supp. 2) (Apr. 1962).

2. Portugal v. Liberia, *in re* Application of the Forced Labour Convention, 1930 (No. 29); International Labour Office Report of Commission of Inquiry, 46 (No. 2) ILO O. Bull. (Supp. 2) (1963).

3. Complaint against Chile, *in re* Observance of the Hours of Work Convention, 1919 (No. 1), and the Discrimination (Employment and Occupation) Convention, 1958 (No. 111); International Labour Office Report of the Commission of Inquiry (1975).

4. Representation by ICFTU v. Czechoslovakia, *in re* Observance of the Discrimination (Employment and Occupation) Convention, 1958 (No. 111); 61 (No. 3) ILO O. Bull. (Ser. A) (Supp.) (1978).

Suggested Subjects for Discussion

1. What is the basis of the competence of the ILO in the field of human rights?

2. What is the principle of tripartism and how does it affect the structure and decision-making process in the ILO?

3. What is the scope and content of ILO activities in the field of fundamental human rights?

4. The ILO Constitution contains provisions for (a) submission of newly adopted conventions and recommendations to the competent authorities, and (b) reporting by governments in respect of unratified conventions and of recommendations. Discuss the scope and nature of these obligations. What purpose do they serve? To what extent are workers' organizations involved?

5. What is meant by 'ratification' and what are the effects of ratification?

6. Discuss the respective roles of (a) the Committee of Experts, and (b) the Conference Committee on the Application of Conventions and Recommendations.

7. Describe the procedures for 'direct contacts'.

8. Discuss the role of workers' and employers' organizations within the framework of the ILO's regular supervisory procedures.

9. The ILO has established special procedures for the protection of freedom of association: (a) the Fact-Finding and Conciliation Commission on Freedom of Association, and (b) the Governing Body Committee on Freedom of Association. Discuss the origins, terms of reference, and working methods of these two bodies. What results have they achieved?

10. Representations and complaints procedures supplement the

regular supervisory procedures of the ILO. Discuss the workings of these procedures. Why are they useful? What is the role of workers and their organizations in initiating or contributing to action under these procedures?

IV. Minisyllabus

The following syllabus may be used for a two-hour lecture:
1. The competence of the ILO in the field of human rights—ILO Constitution, the Declaration of Philadelphia.
2. The structure of the ILO, including tripartism.
3. The measures adopted by the ILO for the promotion of human rights.
   a. International labour conventions—nature and legal character.
   b. International labour recommendations—nature and legal character.
   c. Declarations, such as 1964 Declaration on Apartheid, revised in 1980.
4. The main areas of activities of the ILO.
   a. Freedom of association.
   b. Freedom from discrimination in employment.
   c. Freedom from forced labour.
   d. Co-ordination with other international organizations.
5. Implementation of basic human rights conventions.
   a. Permanent supervisory machinery.
      (i) Reports on ratified and unratified conventions and on recommendations.
      (ii) Committee of Experts on the Application of Conventions and Recommendations.
      (iii) Conference Committee on the Application of Conventions and Recommendations.
   b. Contentious procedures.
      (i) Representations and complaints under articles 24–26 of the ILO Constitution.
      (ii) Special human rights procedures—the Governing Body Committee on Freedom of Association, and the Fact-Finding and Conciliation Commission.

V. Bibliography

A. ILO INSTRUMENTS ON BASIC HUMAN RIGHTS

Freedom of association
   Freedom of Association and Protection of the Right to Organise Convention, 1948 (No. 87).

302   *Francis Wolf*

Right to Organise and Collective Bargaining Convention, 1949
(No. 98).
Workers' Representatives Convention (No. 135), and Recom-
mendation (No. 143), 1971.
Rural Workers' Organisations Convention (No. 141), and Re-
commendation (No. 149), 1975.
Right of Association (Agriculture) Convention, 1921 (No. 11).
Right of Association (Non-Metropolitan Territories) Conven-
tion, 1947 (No. 84).
Labour Relations (Public Service) Convention (No. 151), and
Recommendation (No. 159), 1978.

Forced labour
Forced Labour Convention, 1930 (No. 29).
Abolition of Forced Labour Convention, 1957 (No. 105).

Discrimination and employment
Equal Remuneration Convention (No. 100), and Recommendation (No. 90), 1951.
Discrimination (Employment and Occupation) Convention (No.
111), and Recommendation (No. 111), 1958.
Employment Policy Convention (No. 122), and Recommendation (No. 122), 1964.

B.   ILO PUBLICATIONS

Freedom by dialogue: Economic development by social progress—
The ILO contribution. Report of the Director-General, Part 1,
56th Sess., International Labour Conference, (1971).
Freedom of association: Digest of decisions of the Freedom of
Association Committee of the Governing Body of the ILO (2d ed.
1976).
International Labour Office, International Labour Conventions and
Recommendations, 1919–1981 (1982).
The ILO and human rights. Report of the Director-General, Part 1,
52d Sess., International Labour Conference (1968); report pre-
sented by the International Labour Organisation to the International Conference on Human Rights.
The ratification and implementation of international labour conventions by American countries, with special reference to conventions relating to freedom of association, minimum wages, labour
inspection and indigenous populations. Report of the Director-
General, Report I, Part 2, Tenth Conference of American States
Members of the International Labour Organisation (Nov.–Dec.
1974).
The ratification and implementation of international labour con-

ventions in Africa, with special reference to conventions relating to employment policy, forced labour, social policy and labour inspection. Report of the Director-General, Report I, Part 2, Fourth African Regional Conference (Nov.–Dec. 1973).

International Labour Standards: A Workers' Educational Manual (1978).

The Impact of International Labour Conventions and Recommendations (1976).

Manual on Procedures Relating to International Labour Conventions and Recommendations (1980).

C. OTHER PUBLICATIONS

E. Haas, Human Rights and International Action: The Case of Freedom of Association (1970).

C. Jenks, The International Protection of Trade Union Freedom (1957).

—— Human Rights and International Labour Standards (1960).

—— Social Justice in the Law of Nations: The ILO Impact after Fifty Years (1970).

G. Johnston, The International Labour Organisation: Its Work for Social and Economic Progress (1970).

E. Landy, The Effectiveness of International Supervision: Thirty Years of ILO Experience (1966).

—— *The Influence of International Labour Conventions: Possibilities and Performance*, 101 Int'l Labour Rev. 555 (1970).

Osieke, *The Exercise of Judicial Function with Respect to the International Labour Organisation*, 47 Brit. Y.B. Int'l L. 315 (1974–1975).

Rossillion, *ILO Examination of Human Rights Situation*, Rev. Int'l Comm'n Jurists 40 (No. 12, June 1974).

Samson, *The Changing Pattern of ILO Supervision*, 118 Int'l Labour Rev. 569.

Valticos, *The International Labour Organisation: Its Contribution to the Rule of Law and the International Protection of Human Rights*, 9 J. Int'l Comm'n Jurists 3 (1968).

—— *The Place of Human Rights in the Constitution and Various Instruments of the ILO and the Legal Framework for their Protection*, in The International Dimension of Human Rights 407 (K. Vasak ed. 1979).

—— *La Commission d'Investigation et de Conciliation en Matière de Liberté Syndicale et le Mécanisme de Protection Internationale des Droits Syndicaux*, 13 Annuaire Français de Droit International 445 (1967).

—— *Une Nouvelle Expérience de Protection des Droits de*

l'Homme: Le Groupe d'Étude, de l'OIT Chargé d'Examiner la Situation en Espagne, 16 Annuaire Français de Droit International 567 (1970).

—— *Les Normes de l'Organisation Internationale de Travail en Matière de Protection des Droits de l'Homme*, 4 Revue des Droits de l'Homme 691 (1971).

—— *La Protection Internationale de la Liberté Syndicale Vingt-Cinq ans Après*, 7 Revue des Droits de l'Homme 5 (1974).

—— *Les Méthodes de la Protection Internationale de la Liberté Syndicale*, Recueil des Cours 79 (1975-I).

—— *The Role of the ILO: Present Action and Future Perspectives*, in Human Rights Thirty Years After the Universal Declaration 211 (B. Ramcharan ed. 1979).

—— International Labour Law (1979).

—— *The Future Prospects for International Labour Standards*, Int'l Labour Rev. 679 (1979).

—— & Wolf, *L'Organisation Internationale du Travail et les Pays en Voie de Développement: Techniques d'Élaboration et Mise en Oeuvre des Normes Universelles*, in Pays en voie de Développement et Transformation du Droit International 127 (Société Française pour le Droit International 1974).

Vincent-Davis, *Human Rights Law: A research Guide to the Literature—ILO and UNESCO*, 15 N.Y.U. J. Int'l L. & Pol. 000 (1982).

Wolf, *Les Conventions Internationales du Travail et La Succession d'États*, 7 Annuaire Français de Droit International 742 (1961).

—— *L'Interdépendance des Conventions Internationales du Travail*, 121 Recueil des Cours 114 (1967-II).

—— *Aspects Judiciaires de la Protection Internationale des Droits de l'Homme par l'OIT*, 4 Revue des Droits de l'Homme 773 (1971).

—— *L'Application des Conventions Internationale du Travail par Voie de Conventions Collectives*, 20 Annuaire Français de Droit International 103 (1974).

—— *ILO Experience in the Implementation of Human Rights*, 10 J. Int'l L. & Econ. 599 (1975).

—— *At the Apex of the Value Hierarchy: An International Organization's Contribution*, 24 N.Y.L.S. L. Rev. 179 (1978).

VI. Minibibliography

ILO, International Labour Standards: A Workers' Educational Manual (1978).

—— The Impact of International Labour Conventions and Recommendations (1976).

C. Jenks, Human Rights and International Labour Standards (1960).

E. Landy. *The Influence of International Labour Conventions: Possibilities and Performance*, 101 Int'l Labour Rev. 555 (1970).

N. Valticos, International Labour Law (1979).

—— *The International Labour Organisation: Its Contribution to the Role of Law and the International Protection of Human Rights*, 9 J. Int'l Comm'n Jurists 3 (1968).

F. Wolf, *Aspects judiciaires de la protection internationale des droits de l'homme par l'OIT*, 4 Revue des Droits de l'Homme 773 (1971).

—— *Human Rights and the International Labour Organisation*, in this volume.

Chapter 8

Race, Sex, and Religious Discrimination in International Law*

Jack Greenberg[1]

A U.S. civil rights lawyer in 1982, surveying the international human rights vista, experiences mixed feelings of despair (at how little can be achieved through employing international means) and *déjà vu* (at how international human rights resembles our domestic scene of the not too distant past). The U.S. law of race relations today is complex and rich, articulated in a superstructure of leading U.S. Supreme Court decisions, like *Brown v. Board of Education*,[2] which held unconstitutional racial segregation in education, and an infrastructure of thousands of high and low court pronouncements on what constitutes discrimination and what does not, as well as what are appropriate or necessary means of uprooting it. The explication in education alone continues in national legislation, such as Title VI of the Civil Rights Act of 1964,[3] and in regulations of the Department of Education, secretarial decisions, administrative law judge determinations, state and local implementing legislation, and local school board rules. Similar proliferation of law, in its various modes of expression, is replicated in employment, health care, housing, voting, prison conditions, capital punishment, and almost every conceivable area of human activity.[4] The most important legal issues, moreover, continue to change in form and substance.

Contrast this with the body of international human rights law. It is somewhat, but not a great deal, more detailed than basic U.S. constitutional texts. Confining ourselves for the moment to the Universal Declaration of Human Rights,[5] it consists principally of declarations like those of article 1 ('All human beings are born free and equal in dignity and rights.') and article 16 ('Men and women of full age,

---

[1] I am grateful to Linda Poon, New York University School of Law, Class of 1981, for her able research assistance in the preparation of this chapter.

[2] 347 U.S. 483 (1954).

[3] 28 U.S.C. §§ 2000d–2000d–3.

[4] Citation of various cases, statutes, rules, etc. for these propositions could be endless and not very edifying. But it may be noted that subspecialities of American civil rights law, *e.g.*, housing, employment, today are reported in multivolume services and the number of volumes in such services steadily increases.

[5] G. A. Res. 217A, U.N. Doc. A/810, at 71 (1948).

without any limitations due to race, nationality or religion, have the right to marry and to found a family.'). The international covenants[6] explicate these great principles somewhat, but as to detail only remotely resemble the corpus of U.S. civil rights law. A U.S. civil rights lawyer who would like to employ international human rights principles, for example, to assist black South Africans, Soviet Jews, or blacks in the United States must naturally wonder whether it is possible to convert the majestic international accords into concrete relief for victims of discrimination. The problem is partly one of means of implementation,[7] but also one of the jurist's task of translating general principles into precise application. With this there has been scant experience in the international human rights domain.

Similarly, teachers must wonder how to teach about general principles which have been relatively little applied and whose exegesis appears mostly in scholarly articles, which usually have none of the interest of concrete cases. Too often those articles resemble philosophical disputation more than conventional legal materials.

But if we look a quarter century back into U.S. law we find it was then little more developed than international human rights law today. Indeed, the U.S. law slightly over a century ago was not even nominally as advanced as the international documents we shall discuss. Only in 1868 did the fourteenth amendment pronounce that no state shall 'deny to any person within its jurisdiction the equal protection of the laws'. That provision and others of like purpose adopted after the Civil War were at best enforced in desultory fashion until the mid-twentieth century. Up to that time the country showed considerable disposition *against* according racial equality. Such landmark decisions as *Plessy v. Ferguson*[8] and the *Civil Rights Cases*,[9] which denied to blacks basic civil rights by restrictively interpreting the reconstruction amendments, were the norm. Great jurists like Holmes, Brandeis, and Stone joined in decisions denying rights which today the amendments are held to grant.[10]

Domestic civil rights law was virtually not taught at all until the 1960s. This author's *Race Relations and American Law*, published in 1959, stood alone as a text in its area; Emerson and Haber's *Political and Civil Rights in the United States* (1952) was the only case book in that field for many years. Now books and articles on civil rights are

[6] International Covenant on Economic, Social and Cultural Rights, G. A. Res. 2200, 21 U.N. GAOR, Supp. (No. 16) 49, U.N. Doc. A/6316 (1966); International Covenant on Civil and Political Rights, G. A. Res. 2200, 21 U.N. GAOR, Supp. (No. 16) 52, U.N. Doc. A/6316 (1966).

[7] Discussed in detail in ch. 10 *infra* and elsewhere in this volume.

[8] 163 U.S. 537 (1896).

[9] 109 U.S. 3 (1883).

[10] *See, e.g.*, Gong Lum v. Rice, 275 U.S. 78 (1927); Berea College v. Kentucky, 211 U.S. 45 (1908).

numerous, reflecting greater activity by human rights proponents. Teaching of international human rights law, similarly, will capture more interest as activity in this area increases.

The application, interpretation, and teaching of domestic human rights law developed in the United States when underlying political, economic, and social relations in the country changed. The new rules in turn permitted institutionalization of change and helped bring about further growth. Similarly, it seems not unreasonable to hope for change in international human rights doctrine and, particularly, in implementation as underlying conditions develop. As Professor Sohn has pointed out: 'We must measure the accomplishments of the last thirty years not against utopian dreams but against the accomplishments of the last 3,000 years of recorded history.'[11]

I. Legal and Policy Considerations

A. THE IMPORTANCE OF THE STRICTURES AGAINST DISCRIMINATION

Mere inspection of the basic international human rights documents demonstrates that racial, sexual, and religious discrimination are, certainly in terms of attention paid on the face of the agreements, the overarching human rights concern of the international community. If one only considers the outlook of the United States, where coping with racial discrimination has been central to our constitutional development, and former colonial peoples' preoccupation with racial domination, it becomes clear why the U.N. Charter, the Universal Declaration, the international covenants, and the various conventions[12] devote more attention to preventing discrimination than to any other single category of human rights. The paragraphs that follow describe those antidiscrimination principles in some detail and reflect on their meaning and efficacy, particularly in U.S. law.

B. THE UNITED NATIONS CHARTER AND UNIVERSAL DECLARATION OF HUMAN RIGHTS

The basic provisions of international human rights law are the U.N. Charter and the Universal Declaration of Human Rights. Both ensure freedom from racial, sexual, and religious discrimination in a variety of ways.

Detailed explication of the general principles of the Charter and the

---

[11] Sohn, *The Human Rights Law of the Charter*, 12 Tex. Int'l L.J. 129, 138 (1977).

[12] *See, e.g.*, International Convention on the Elimination of All Forms of Racial Discrimination, 660 U.N.T.S. 195; Convention on the Elimination of All Forms of Discrimination Against Women, *opened for signature* Mar. 1, 1980, G. A. Res. 180, 34 U.N. GAOR, Supp. (No. 46) 193, U.N. Doc. A/34/46 (1979).

Universal Declaration has been made in the International Covenant on Civil and Political Rights,[13] the International Covenant on Economic, Social, and Cultural Rights,[14] the International Convention on the Elimination of All Forms of Racial Discrimination,[15] and the Convention on the Elimination of All Forms of Discrimination Against Women,[16] while certain aspects have been provisionally defined in preliminary efforts to draft a Convention on the Elimination of All Forms of Religious Intolerance.[17] Other agreements deal with slavery,[18] genocide,[19] *apartheid*,[20] and various practices which are peculiar manifestations of discrimination. Specialized agencies, such as the International Labour Organisation (ILO) and the United Nations Educational, Scientific, and Cultural Organization (UNESCO) have promulgated strictures against discrimination.[21] Regional, *e.g.*, European[22] and inter-American,[23] and other applications of the same principles, *e.g.*, the Helsinki Accords,[24] adopt the U.N. standards or formulate them somewhat differently. In these pages, however, we shall consider the substantive rules of only the principal documents, their applicability, and perhaps useful means of teaching about them.

1. *U.N. Charter*

The keystone international legal document, the U.N. Charter,

[13] *See* note 6 *supra.*

[14] *See* note 6 *supra.*

[15] *See* note 12 *supra.*

[16] *See* note 12 *supra.*

[17] *See* text accompanying notes 161–72 *infra.*

[18] Slavery Convention, 46 Stat. 2183, T.S. No. 778, 60 L.N.T.S. 253; Protocol Amending the Slavery Convention, 7 U.S.T. 479, T.I.A.S. No. 3532, 182 U.N.T.S. 51; Supplementary Convention on the Abolition of Slavery, the Slave Trade, and Institutions and Practices Similar to Slavery, 18 U.S.T. 3201, T.I.A.S. No. 6418, 266 U.N.T.S. 3; Forced Labour Convention, 1930 (ILO No. 29), *reprinted in* Basic Documents on Human Rights 176 (2d ed. I. Brownlie 1981) [hereinafter cited as Brownlie]; Abolition of Forced Labour Convention, 1957 (ILO No. 105), *reprinted in* Brownlie, *supra*, at 187.

[19] Convention on the Prevention and Punishment of the Crime of Genocide, 78 U.N.T.S. 277, *reprinted in* Brownlie, *supra* note 18, at 31.

[20] International Convention on the Suppression and Punishment of the Crime of *Apartheid*, *opened for signature* Nov. 30, 1973, G.A. Res. 3068, 28 U.N. GAOR, Supp. (No. 30) 75, U.N. Doc. A/9030 (1973), *reprinted in* Brownlie, *supra* note 18, at 164.

[21] Discrimination (Employment and Discrimination) Convention, 1958 (ILO No. 111), *reprinted in* Brownlie, *supra* note 18, at 204; [UNESCO] Convention Against Discrimination in Education, 429 U.N.T.S. 93, *reprinted in* Brownlie, *supra* note 18, at 234.

[22] Convention for the Protection of Human Rights and Fundamental Freedoms, 213 U.N.T.S. 221, *reprinted in* Brownlie, *supra* note 18, at 242. *See* arts. 4, 9, 12, and 14.

[23] *See* art. 43, Charter of the Organization of American States, 2 U.S.T. 2394, T.I.A.S. No. 2361, 119 U.N.T.S. 3; Protocol of Amendment, 21 U.S.T. 607, 721 U.N.T.S. 324; American Convention on Human Rights, O.A.S. T.S. No. 36, *reprinted in* Brownlie, *supra* note 18, at 391.

[24] *See* arts. I(a) & VII of the Final Act of the Conference on Security and Co-operation in Europe, *signed* Aug. 1, 1975, 73 Dep't State Bull. 323, 325 (1975), *reprinted in* Brownlie, *supra* note 18, at 320.

makes clear at its outset the international community's basic commitment to equality. Its preamble asserts a reaffirmation of faith 'in the equal rights of men and women. . .' Among the purposes of the United Nations, it states, are 'develop[ing] friendly relations among nations based on respect for the principle of equal rights and self-determination of peoples'[25] and 'promoting and encouraging respect for human rights and fundamental freedoms for all without distinction as to race, sex, language, or religion'.[26] 'The United Nations shall place no restrictions on eligibility of men and women to participate in any capacity and under conditions of equality in its principal and subsidiary organs.'[27]

Among the powers of the General Assembly are initiating studies and making 'recommendations for the purpose of . . . assisting in the realization of human rights and fundamental freedoms for all without distinction as to race, sex, language, or religion'.[28] The United Nations shall 'promote . . . universal respect for, and observance of, human rights and fundamental freedoms for all without distinction as to race, sex, language, or religion'.[29] Similarly, the Economic and Social Council 'may make recommendations for the purpose of promoting respect for, and observance of, human rights and fundamental freedoms for all.[30] Furthermore, the basic objectives of the international trusteeship system include assuring 'equal treatment in social, economic, and commercial matters for all Members of the United Nations and their nationals, and also equal treatment for the latter in the administration of justice . . .'[31] In connection with *apartheid* in South Africa, this provision, and the feelings underlying it, have been the basis of a great deal of international expression and activity.

2. *Universal Declaration*

The Universal Declaration of Human Rights elaborates the Charter's equal rights prescriptions and, indeed, is suffused with the notion of equality. The preamble recognizes the inherent dignity and 'the equal and inalienable rights of all members of the human family' as the 'foundation of freedom, justice and peace in the world',[32] and reaffirms 'faith . . . in the equal rights of men and women'.[33] Ten of the thirty articles which constitute the International Bill of Human Rights

[25] U.N. Charter art. 1(2).
[26] *Id.* art. 1(3).
[27] *Id.* art. 8.
[28] *Id.* art. 13(1)(b).
[29] *Id.* art. 55(c).
[30] *Id.* art. 62(2).
[31] *Id.* art. 76(d).
[32] Universal Declaration, preamble, para. 1.
[33] *Id.* para. 5.

are in one way or another explicitly concerned with equality, and others implicitly so. Following is a summary of the specific references:

Article 1. All human beings are born free and equal in dignity and rights.

Article 2. Everyone is entitled to all the rights and freedoms set forth in the Universal Declaration without distinction of any kind, such as race, color, sex, language, religion, political or other opinion, national or social origin, property, birth, or other status.

Article 4. No one shall be held in slavery or servitude.

Article 7. All are equal before the law and are entitled without any discrimination to equal protection of the law.[34]

Article 10. Everyone is entitled in full equality to a fair and public hearing in the determination of rights and of any criminal charges.

Article 16. Men and women of full age, without any limitation due to race, nationality, or religion, have the right to marry and to found a family and are entitled to equal rights as to marriage, during marriage, and at its dissolution.

Article 18. Everyone has the right to freedom of thought, conscience, and religion.

Article 21. Everyone has the right of equal access to public service. The will of the people shall be expressed by universal and equal suffrage.

Article 23. Everyone, without any discrimination, has the right to equal pay for equal work.

Article 26. Higher education shall be equally accessible to all on the basis of merit.

In addition to these numerous explicit references to equality, the concept is implicit in repeated references to 'everyone' having the right to liberty,[35] to effective remedies before competent tribunals,[36] to freedom of movement,[37] to nationality,[38] and other rights.

As a component of an international human rights law curriculum it would be interesting to reflect briefly on the requirement of article 26 that higher education be 'equally accessible to all on the basis of merit'. 'Merit' is not defined; but, at the least, this standard would prohibit exclusion from higher education because of the inability to pay for it. At a minimum, 'merit' would seem to preclude admissions policies based on wealth, social standing, race, or similar factors. But the use of the term awakens interest today in the United States in what is referred

---

[34] *Compare* Universal Declaration, art. 7 *with* Political Covenant, art. 26, *discussed in* Lillich, ch. 4 *supra*, text accompanying notes 93, 96–102.

[35] Universal Declaration, art. 3.

[36] *Id*. art. 8.

[37] *Id*. art. 13.

[38] *Id*. art. 15.

to as the *Bakke*[39] issue. That subject is now of high interest on American campuses, but in 1948 the provision obviously was adopted without reference to a future U.S. dispute over affirmative action. Although 'merit' may be interpreted variously, and it would not be incompatible with affirmative action policies to admit minorities with grades and scores below those of white competitors, the word *today* has been captured by opponents of such admissions. Today in the United States, admission on 'merit' ordinarily means admission on the basis of superior tests and scores. Perhaps reflecting changing perceptions, the Economic Covenant, adopted a generation later, uses different language to deal with higher education.[40] The tension between a view of nondiscrimination which prohibits any distinctions and a view which permits discrimination in favor of disadvantaged groups for the purpose, for example, of compensating them for past discrimination pervades a number of the documents we are considering,[41] just as it does U.S. civil rights law.

3. *Enforceability of the Charter and the Universal Declaration*

What is the legal effect of these equal rights provisions of the Charter and the Universal Declaration? That is a question of particular interest to U.S. lawyers because the Charter is the only one of the U.N. human rights instruments which the United States has ratified, and many scholars argue persuasively that the Universal Declaration has the force of customary international law because of its universal recognition. The contending positions have been marshalled by Professor Schachter in a comprehensive article published in 1978,[42] which echoes positions that he had taken as early as 1951.[43]

Professor Schachter describes the 'long standing controversy, dating

[39] Bakke v. Regents of the Univ. of Calif., 438 U.S. 265 (1978).

[40] Economic Covenant, art. 13(2)(c) provides: 'Higher education shall be made equally accessible to all, on the basis of *capacity* . . .' (emphasis added). Those with adequate or superior 'capacity' may not have demonstrated 'merit', at least as some have used that term.

See text accompanying note 77 *infra*.

Many countries incorporate affirmative action policies in their basic law. *See, e.g.,* Constitution of India, pt. III, § 15(4) ('Nothing in this article . . . shall prevent the State from making any special provision for the advancement of any socially and educationally backward classes of citizens or for the scheduled castes and the scheduled tribes.'). *See also* Karpem, *University Admission Criteria: Some German–American Comparative Observations*, Int'l Rev. Educ. 203, 204–05 (1976); Hahn, *West German Higher Education*, 58 Educ. 403, 408 (1977). (Quotas required for different groups in German universities; no one who has qualifications may be excluded, although admission may be deferred.) Comparative treatment of this issue may be of interest in arriving at the meaning of art. 26 of the Universal Declaration, art. 13 of the Economic Covenant, and cognate provisions.

[41] *See* text following note 96 *infra*; text accompanying notes 130–32 *infra*.

[42] Schachter, *International Law Implications of U.S. Human Rights Policies*, 24 N.Y.L.S. L. Rev. 63 (1978) [hereinafter cited as Schachter, *International Law Implications*].

[43] Schachter, *The Charter and The Constitution, The Human Rights Provisions in American Law*, 4 Vand. L. Rev. 643 (1951).

back to the beginnings of the United Nations, as to the legal effect of
these articles.[44] The United States, he writes, for many years, 'tended to
avoid characterizing those Charter provisions as obligatory on states,
preferring instead to treat them as statements of general purposes
. . .'[45] Some scholars, he continues, characterized them as too vague to
be enforceable.[46] This position, of course, coincided with the basic
political stance, dominant in Congress in the 1950's and quite powerful even today, opposed to undertaking international obligations
which would supersede domestic jurisdiction. But, Schachter argues,
at least since 1977 when President Carter addressed the United
Nations General Assembly, 'the U.S. Government now acknowledges
both the obligatory character of the human rights articles of the
Charter and its corollary that member states are internationally
accountable for the observance of human rights in their countries'.[47]
He traces the evolution from the period of non-acknowledgement
through the present, including acceptance of such international
declarations as the Helsinki Accords of 1975, which specify rights and
freedoms embraced by the Charter. He concludes that 'the American
policy on the rights of states to censure violations of human rights by
other states rests on a well-founded premise that all states are under an
international obligation to observe and promote human rights.[48]
Furthermore, he asserts:

[T]he American position is also in keeping with, and lends support to, the
legal conclusion that the obligations relating to human rights are obligations
erga omnes (in the sense expressed by the International Court) and that, in
consequence, every state has a legal interest in the protection of such rights
everywhere and a corresponding right to raise the matter of non-observance
and to censure grave violations by other governments.[49].

The Universal Declaration has been universally approved, and
scholars seem to agree that it is valid international law. Saario and Cass
point out that 'even the small number of member states which
abstained from voting for the Universal Declaration have apparently
reconsidered their position, since all have voted affirmatively on many
subsequent resolutions making reference to the Universal Declaration.'[50] They write:

[A]s new nations have referred to it or incorporated it into their constitutions or fundamental law; as national judicial decisions have cited it approv-

[44] Schachter, *International Law Implications, supra* note 42, at 66.
[45] *Id.*
[46] *Id.* at 67.
[47] *Id.*
[48] *Id.* at 74.
[49] *Id.*
[50] Saario & Cass, *The United Nations and the International Protection of Human Rights: A Legal Analysis and Interpretation*, 7 Calif. W. Int'l L.J. 591, 596 (1977).

ingly; and as it has been acknowledged by or incorporated into a wide range of international conventions, declarations, and recommendations; its justifiable principles at least have been elevated with considerable authority to the status of customary international law.[51]

Professor Humphrey concurs: '[W]hatever its drafters may have intended in 1948', the Universal Declaration 'is now part of the customary law of nations' and therefore binding on all states.[52] The Universal Declaration and the principles enunciated in it have been officially invoked on many occasions both inside and outside the United Nations.[53]

For the U.S. civil rights practitioner, the Charter's obligatory nature and the Universal Declaration's legal validity raise the question of the means by which they may be applied to particular instances of abuse. Of course, as Professor Schachter points out, states may raise the matter of non-observance by other states and may censure each other.[54] And, as Professor Sohn discusses in chapter 10 of this volume, international bodies established to implement the various conventions and covenants may receive and, in a variety of ways, respond to complaints. But are there more direct remedies capable of application to discrete cases utilizing legal means which are ordinarily employed within domestic legal orders? In a study of the relationship of the human rights provisions of the Charter to domestic legal orders of member states, Bernard Schlüter has concluded that '[s]elf execution of the human rights clauses is . . . a *possibility* in almost all civil law member states, the United States, the socialist countries and some Third World countries'.[55] But, in an intricate analysis of particular provisions, potential modes of enforcement, legal doctrines in a variety of nations, and other factors, he seems to conclude no more than that 'human rights clauses, or at least some of their parts, are likely to have some domestic legal effect in *many* states'.[56]

There have been attempts to apply domestically the Universal Declaration or the Charter's human rights provisions. Those aspects which deal with racial discrimination, particularly, have been urged upon U.S. courts from shortly after the Charter's adoption to the present. The results have been uniformly discouraging, except to those who find hope in a fragment of affirmative dictum, the occasional less

[51] *Id.* at 607 (footnotes omitted).

[52] Humphrey, *The Implementation of International Human Rights Law*, 24 N.Y.L.S. L. Rev. 31, 32 (1978).

[53] *Id.* 33. On the question of the status under customary international law of particular provisions of the Universal Declaration dealing with civil rights, *see* Lillich, ch. 2 *supra*.

[54] Schachter, *International Law Implications, supra* note 42.

[55] Schlüter, *The Domestic Status of the Human Rights Clauses of the United Nations Charter*, 61 Calif. L. Rev. 110, 114 (1973) (emphasis added).

[56] *Id.* at 162 (emphasis added).

than conclusive scope of rejection, and the mere fact that the provisions have been advocated at all.

The case with which most discussion begins is *Sei Fujii v. California*,[57] as decided by a California intermediate appellate court in 1950. It involves the validity of the California Alien Land Law, which denied to plaintiff the right to own land in California because he had been born in Japan. Among the grounds of invalidity urged against the statute was that it was 'inconsistent with the declared principles and spirit of the United Nations Charter'.[58] The court agreed and held that '[t]he Charter has become the "Supreme Law of the Land; and the Judges in every State shall be bound thereby, any Thing in the Constitution or laws of any State to the Contrary notwithstanding". U.S Const., Art. VI, sec. 2'.[59] Citing various provisions of the Charter and the Universal Declaration, the court stated that 'restrictions contained in the Alien Land Law are in direct conflict with the plain terms of the Charter . . . [and] with Article 17 of the Declaration of Human Rights which proclaims the right of everyone to own property'.[60] The opinion concluded that 'The Alien Land Law must therefore yield to the treaty as superior authority. The restrictions of the statute based on eligibility to citizenship, but which ultimately and actually are referable to race or color, must be and are therefore declared untenable and unenforceable.'[61]

If this had remained the law, international human rights jurisprudence would have been off to a good start in the United States. But the California Supreme Court took a contrary view, holding that 'the provisions of the preamble and of Article 1 of the charter which are claimed to be in conflict with the alien land law are not self-executing'.[62] It also held that '[t]he language used in Articles 55 and 56 is not the type customarily employed in treaties which have been held to be self-executing and to create rights and duties to individuals'.[63] The Court concluded:

> The charter represents a moral commitment of foremost importance, and we must not permit the spirit of our pledge to be compromised or disparaged in either our domestic or foreign affairs. We are satisfied, however, that the charter provisions relied on by plaintiff were not intended to supersede existing domestic legislation, and we cannot hold that they operate to invalidate the alien land law.[64]

[57] 217 P.2d 481 (Cal. Dist. Ct. App. 1950).
[58] *Id*. at 483.
[59] *Id*. at 486.
[60] *Id*. at 488.
[61] *Id*.
[62] Sei Fujii v. California, 38 Cal. 2d 718, 722–23, 242 P.2d 617, 620 (1952).
[63] *Id*.
[64] *Id*. at 724–25, 242, P.2d at 622.

But, it would be incorrect to conclude that the requirements of the Charter, as invoked in that case, were not honored in U.S. Law. The opinion held that the Alien Land Law, as an instrument effectuating racial discrimination, violated the fourteenth amendment. In a sense, therefore, the Charter was observed, arguably in the way preferred above all others: by a domestic prohibition of such discrimination embodied in the national constitution.[65]

The interesting question is: what would have been the obligation of the United States under international law as a signatory of the Charter if the California Supreme Court or the U.S. Supreme Court had concluded that domestic constitutional law tolerated racial discrimination? Or what if the *School Segregation Cases*,[66] for example, had been decided in a way which validated racial segregation? Would the United States have owed a Charter-imposed obligation to the international community to correct the condition? How would it have been enforced? Would the world's response have been the same as it is to *apartheid* in South Africa, with the same international expressions of disapproval?

The Charter and the Universal Declaration remain theoretically applicable to other issues which arise in U.S. courts, not only with regard to conditions in the United States, but with regard to situations in other countries which are claimed to be adjudicable in U.S. courts. Nevertheless, efforts to employ them have been unsuccessful. Professor Lillich has observed that while it is not often today that courts refer to efforts to employ the Charter and other international human rights doctrine as 'tommyrot' or 'junk and gobbledygook',[67] cases regularly have been resolved 'on as narrow and technical a basis as possible. As a consequence, the possibility for a legitimate, innovative role for United States domestic courts in the area of human rights has been ignored.'[68]

One problem in applying the basic provisions of the Charter and the

[65] *See* Bitker, *Application of the United Nations Universal Declaration of Human Rights Within the United States*, 21 De Paul L. Rev. 337 (1971). For an analysis of U.S. obligations, national and international, with regard to school desegregation, *see* Yudof, *International Human Rights and School Desegregation in the United States*, 15 Tex. Int'l L.J. (1980).

[66] *See, e.g.,* Brown v. Board of Education, 347 U.S. 483 (1959). Subsidiary arguments made by plaintiffs and *amici* in this and related cases referred to the Charter and the Universal Declaration, but evoked no response from the Court.

[67] Lillich, *The Role of Domestic Courts in Promoting International Human Rights Norms*, 24 N.Y.L.S. L. Rev. 153, 154 (1978).

[68] *Id.* at 176. Among cases which declined to apply U.N. human rights standards to claims in the nature of racial discrimination are Kemp v. Rubin, 188 Misc. 310, 69 N.Y.S. 2d 680 (1947); Sipes v. McGhee, 316 Mich. 614, 25 N.W. 2d 638 (1947); Namba v. McCourt, 185 Ore. 579, 204 P.2d 569 (1949); Boyer v. Garrett, 183 F.2d 582 (4th Cir. 1950); Camp v. Recreation Board, 104 F. Supp. 10 (D.D.C. 1952); Rice v. Sioux City Cemetery, Inc., 245 Iowa 147, 60 N.W.2d 110 (1953), *aff'd* 348 U.S. 880 (1954); Hitai v. Immigration and Naturalization Service, 343 F.2d 466 (2d Cir. 1965); Diggs v. Richardson, 555 F.2d 848 (D.C. Cir. 1976). These and related cases

Universal Declaration to contemporary U.S. racial, sexual, or religious discrimination issues is that at this stage the issues in the United States have transcended generality and deal mostly with particulars of implementation. The Charter and the Universal Declaration were relevant to the 1954 *School Segregation Cases* issues and to California's Alien Land Law prohibitions. However, they offer no help with whether busing children to promote school integration and whether reassigning blacks to formerly forbidden lines of seniority in an industrial plant rights past wrongs or inflicts unjustifiable present harm on whites. Of course, women's rights issues in the United States today are more open than racial ones, but even as to these the treaties offer no guidance on how to eliminate sex discrimination in pension systems or the armed forces, for example, two subjects with which the country is grappling. As discussed below, the covenants and conventions spell out some guidance. But it is harder (if not impossible) to argue their applicability to domestic disputes in view of the United States' failure to ratify the international covenants and the Discrimination Against Women Convention. Moreover, should ratification occur, proposed reservations would purport[69] to make ratification meaningless if it would require changes in U.S. law.

C. THE INTERNATIONAL COVENANTS AND THE RACIAL DISCRIMINATION CONVENTION

Just beneath the Charter and the Universal Declaration in importance are the two international covenants which unfold their general terms into some detail and provide means of implementation. The Economic Covenant entered into force 3 January 1976 and the Political Covenant entered into force 23 March 1976, both having been

---

are discussed in R. Lillich & F. Newman, International Human Rights: Problems of Law and Policy 100–22 (1979).

One recent case which points in the direction of enforceability is Filartiga v. Peña-Irala, 630 F.2d 876 (2d Cir. 1980). *Filartiga* held that United States district courts have jurisdiction under the Alien Tort Statute, 28 U.S.C. § 1350, of civil actions by aliens for torts committed in violation of the law of nations, even though the torts occurred in another country. In *Filartiga*, torture was held to be such a tort. The case poses interesting questions concerning racial discrimination which might give rise to similar conclusions and questions regarding jurisdiction and choice of law issues. For example, could a South African black bring suit in a U.S. court for redress against a South African official or private person who injured her by racial discrimination in South Africa? The injury probably woud be irremediable under South African law, but could have been in violation of international standards which are not recognized in South Africa (or quite possibly in the United States, at least as enforceable international obligations). The theoretical exercise is intriguing, but at least at this point in history probably without practical utility.

[69] It may be, however, that these reservations are ineffectual, or that ratification subject to such reservation is ineffectual. *See* Schachter, *The Obligation of the Parties to Give Effect to the Covenant on Civil and Political Rights*, 73 Am. J. Int'l L. 462, 464–65 (1979), [hereinafter cited as Schachter, *Obligations of the Parties*].

opened for signature ten years earlier. On 13 May 1968, the International Conference on Human Rights announced the Proclamation of Teheran which reiterated the basic precepts of both covenants, the Racial Discrimination Convention, and the Universal Declaration, and urged all peoples and governments to redouble their efforts to 'provide for all human beings a life consonant with freedom and dignity and conducive to physical, mental, social and spiritual welfare'.[70]

1. *Economic Covenant*

The Economic Covenant recognizes that political and civil rights can be exercised effectively only under conditions of material, social, and cultural security.[71] For example, if one is poor and illiterate, the right to vote is relatively uninformed, and power to persuade others in the political process relatively ineffective. A pauper charged with a crime cannot afford to employ effective counsel. For the poor, the right to own property, as asserted in the Universal Declaration, is as empty as the right to participate in the cultural life of the community, also affirmed in the Universal Declaration. Hence while the economic rights are asserted for their own sake and for the material security they would afford, they have been guaranteed also to give real meaning to civil and political rights.

Like the Charter and Universal Declaration, the Economic Covenant repeatedly asserts a right to racial, sexual, and religious equality. The preamble commences, '*Considering* that . . . recognition of the inherent dignity and of the equal and inalienable rights of all members of the human family is the foundation of freedom, justice and peace . . .'[72] and the Covenant continues 'the rights enunciated in the present Covenant will be exercised without discrimination of any kind as to race, colour, sex, language, religion, political or other opinion, national or social origin, property, birth or other status'.[73] The parties 'undertake to ensure the equal right of men and women to the enjoyment of all economic, social and cultural rights' set forth in the Covenant.[74] Fair and equal remuneration for work is assured and 'in particular women [are] guaranteed conditions of work not inferior to those enjoyed by men, with equal pay for equal work'.[75]

Equal opportunity to be promoted is also assured. But this particular provision evokes, as did a provision in the Universal Declaration,[76]

---

[70] U.N. Doc. A/CONF.32/41 (1968).
[71] Economic Covenant, preamble, para. 3.
[72] *Id*. para. 1 (emphasis in original).
[73] *Id*. art. 2(2).
[74] *Id*. art. 3.
[75] *Id*. art. 7(a)(1).
[76] *See* text accompanying notes 39–41 *supra*.

the U.S. dispute over affirmative action: promotion is ensured 'subject to no considerations other than those of *seniority* and *competence*'.[77] International human rights law is a long way from grappling with the details of implementation, but were it doing so, two contending camps would exist on this point of the Economic Covenant. One, like its counterparts among many U.S. labour unions, would argue that blacks (or other disadvantaged groups) are not entitled to compensation for past discrimination and must move from the end of the line into promotional opportunities, even if that long delays their rise to equality. The opposing group would argue the case of affirmative action advocates, that if conventional seniority rules result in perpetuating discrimination, they must be overruled.

It is perhaps interesting while considering affirmative action to observe that article 13(2)(c) of the Economic Covenant, which deals with higher education, uses a different formula than does the Universal Declaration to describe the basis of access to higher education. Article 13(2)(c) prescribes that '[h]igher education shall be made equally accessible to all, on the basis of *capacity*,[78] by every appropriate means, and in particular by the progressive introduction of free education' (emphasis added). As has been observed,[79] 'capacity', 'merit', and 'competence' are terms susceptible to various meanings. How they are employed reflects—in these contexts—policies which may advance, retard, or exclude disadvantaged groups in connection with opportunities they seek. The U.S. controversy over 'quotas' and 'affirmative action' expresses these differences.

As with the Universal Declaration, various designated rights under the Economic Covenant shall be afforded 'everyone', thereby prohibiting race, sex, and religion as criteria to be used to discriminate. For example, cultural life, the benefits resulting from scientific progress, and other gains of civilization must be afforded to 'everyone'.[80]

2. *Political Covenant*

The Political Covenant also elaborates in various ways the prohibitions against racial, sexual, and religious discrimination. The parties undertake to ensure to all individuals the rights recognized in the Political Covenant 'without distinction of any kind, such as race, colour, sex, language, religion, political or other opinion, national or

---

[77] Economic Covenant, art. 7(c) (emphasis added).

[78] Art. 26(1). Universal Declaration reads in part: 'Technical and professional education shall be made generally available and higher education shall be equally accessible to all on the basis of *merit*.' (Emphasis added.)

[79] *See* text accompanying notes 39–41 *supra*.

[80] Economic Covenant, art. 15.

social origin, property, birth or other status',[81] the precise language also found in the Economic Covenant. Furthermore, '[t]he States Parties . . . undertake to ensure the equal right of men and women to the enjoyment of all civil and political rights . . .'[82] Even when the life of the nation is threatened by public emergency, although the parties may take steps derogating from certain obligations under the Political Covenant, such measures may 'not involve discrimination solely on the ground of race, colour, sex, language, religion or social origin'.[83] One wonders how the Japanese relocation cases[84] would have been decided if this provision had been applicable. Without doubt, the word 'solely' would have been a principal focus of dispute. Were the Japanese Americans evacuated from the West Coast *solely* because of ancestry or because of a belief that in case of invasion they would have aided the invaders? Was that belief reasonable? How would that be decided under wartime conditions?

The Political Covenant contains other relevant provisions. Article 8 forbids slavery. Article 14(1) states: 'All persons shall be equal before the courts and tribunals.' In the determination of criminal charges, 'everyone shall be entitled to . . . minimum guarantees, in full equality'.[85] 'Everyone shall have the right to recognition everywhere as a person before the law.'[86] 'Everyone', the treaty continues, 'shall have the right to freedom of thought, conscience and religion.'[87] Article 20 provides that '[a]ny advocacy of national, racial or religious hatred that constitutes incitement to discrimination, hostility or violence shall be prohibited by law', thereby raising serious issues under the first amendment to the U.S. Constitution.[88]

The states parties to the Political Covenant undertake to take 'appropriate steps to ensure equality of rights and responsibilities of spouses as to marriage . . .'[89] 'Each child shall have without any discrimination as to race, colour, sex, language, religion, national or social origin, property or birth, the right to such measures of protection as required by his status as a minor . . .'[90] The factors mentioned in article 2, *viz.*, race, color, sex, etc., may not bar persons from participating in public affairs.[91] Adverting to U.S. constitutional language,

[81] Political Covenant, art. 2(1).
[82] *Id.* art. 3.
[83] *Id.* art 4(1).
[84] *See, e.g.*, Korematsu v. United States, 323 U.S. 214 (1944).
[85] Political Covenant, art. 14(3).
[86] *Id.* art. 16.
[87] *Id.* art 18(1).
[88] *See, e.g.*, National Socialist Party v. Skokie, 432 U.S. 43 (1977); Terminiello v. Chicago, 337 U.S. 1 (1949).
[89] Political Covenant, art. 23(4).
[90] *Id.* art. 24(1).
[91] *Id.* art. 25.

the Political Covenant provides that '[a]ll persons are equal before the law and are entitled without any discrimination to the equal protection of the law'.[92] The treaty further provides that the law must prohibit and effectively protect against 'discrimination on any ground such as race, colour, sex, language, religion', and so forth.[93] Ethnic, religious, and linguistic minorities are assured the right to enjoy their own culture, religion, and language.[94]

3. *The Racial Discrimination Convention*

The Racial Discrimination Convention entered into force on January 4, 1969, well in advance of the international covenants. Although it largely repeats the discrimination provisions of the covenants, its existence as a separate instrument underscores the vast importance which the nations of the world place on non-discrimination. The preambular paragraphs of the Racial Discrimination Convention reiterate basic concepts of the Charter: 'dignity and equality', 'fundamental freedoms for all, without distinction as to race, sex, language or religion', 'all human beings are born free and equal in dignity and rights', 'all human beings are equal before the law and are entitled to equal protection of the law'. Note, once again, the incorporation of language reminiscent of the fourteenth amendment to the U.S. Constitution.

Article I commences with a definition of racial discrimination as 'any distinction, exclusion, restriction or preference based on race, colour, descent, or national or ethnic origin which has the *purpose* or *effect* of nullifying or impairing the recognition, enjoyment or exercise, on an equal footing, of human rights . . .' (emphasis added). The use of the standards of 'purpose' and 'effect' anticipated the full-blown controversy in the U.S. law of racial discrimination which became important after the U.S. Supreme Court decision in *Washington v. Davis*,[95] that mere discriminatory effect without the *purpose* of discriminating does not violate the Constitution. Some *statutes*, however, have been held to forbid discriminatory *effect*.[96] One may speculate whether the Racial Discrimination Convention, had it been in force in the United States at the time *Washington v. Davis* was decided, would have brought about a different result.

Article 1 of that Convention concludes by addressing affirmative action, referred to above several times:

---

[92] *Id*. art. 26; *cf*. U.S. Const. amend. XIV, § 1.

[93] Political Covenant, art. 26.

[94] *Id*. art. 27.

[95] 426 U.S. 229 (1978). *See also* Village of Arlington Heights v. Metropolitan Housing Development Corp., 429 U.S. 252 (1977).

[96] *See, e.g.*, Board of Education of the City of New York v. Harris, 444 U.S. 130 (1979).

Special measures taken for the sole purpose of securing adequate advancement of certain racial or ethnic groups . . . shall not be deemed racial discrimination, provided, however, that such measures do not, as a consequence, lead to the maintenance of separate rights for different racial groups and that they shall not be continued after the objectives for which they were taken have been achieved.

While this provision authorizes, but does not require, affirmative action, article 2(2) goes further:

States Parties *shall*, when the circumstances so warrant, take, in the social, economic, cultural and other fields, special and concrete measures to ensure the adequate development and protection of certain racial groups or individuals belonging to them, for the purpose of guaranteeing them the full and equal enjoyment of human rights and fundamental freedoms. (emphasis added)

However, such separate rights may not be continued after the objectives for which they were taken have been achieved.[97]

The Racial Discrimination Convention not only condemns racial discrimination, but its states parties undertake to pursue, by all appropriate means, and without delay, a policy of eliminating it in all of its forms.[98] The affirmative steps set forth in article 2 include repeal of laws and regulations which have the effect of creating or perpetuating discrimination,[99] and prohibition by all appropriate means, including legislation, of racial discrimination by persons, groups, and organizations.[100]

A commentary is suggested by U.S. experience. Article 2(1)(e) of the Racial Discrimination Convention, which looks away from ethnocentricity and towards integration, provides that the states parties to the Convention undertake to encourage 'integrationist multiracial organizations and movements and other means of eliminating barriers between races . . .' The provision therefore looks with favor on the policies of such U.S. organizations as the National Association for the Advancement of Colored People (which believes in integration) as compared to, for example, CORE (now a black nationalist group). Clearly, the terms 'where appropriate' and 'other means of eliminating barriers between races' in article 2(1)(e) could arguably include nationalist organizations which have integration as an ultimate purpose.

Article 4 poses the contradiction between international human rights concepts and U.S. constitutional principles of free expression,

[97] Racial Discrimination Convention, art. 2(2).
[98] *Id.* art. 2(1).
[99] *Id.* art. 2(1)(c).
[100] *Id.* art. 2(1)(d).

even for groups which preach race hatred, which frequently arises. Article 4 provides that the parties to the Convention 'condemn all propaganda and all organizations which are based on ideas or theories of superiority of one race or group of persons of one colour or ethnic origin, or which attempt to justify or promote racial hatred . . .' Parties shall declare it an offense punishable by law to disseminate 'ideas based on racial superiority . . . as well as all acts of violence or incitement to such acts against any race or group of persons of another colour or ethnic origin . . .'[101] In addition, they are required to 'declare illegal and prohibit organizations, and also organized and all other propaganda activities, which promote and incite racial discrimination . . .'[102] Combating racial discrimination in these ways would contradict U.S. first amendment doctrine in many situations. With some regularity, cases of Ku Klux Klansmen or Nazis or similar groups reach U.S. courts, and, nearly uniformly, their activities based on racial, ethnic, or religious hatred are permitted to continue.[103] This is not the place to pursue the dichotomy further, except to note that in other parts of the world, legal and political traditions are different than in the United States. Activities based on racial hatred are viewed with greater alarm by states which fear the inability of society to contain their evil consequences. Perhaps in many circumstances in the United States such activities present no clear and present danger, whereas elsewhere they may.

The most comprehensive provision of the Racial Discrimination Convention is article 5. It provides that 'States Parties undertake to prohibit and to eliminate racial discrimination in all its forms and to guarantee the right of everyone, without distinction as to race, colour, or national or ethnic origin, to equality before the law, notably in the enjoyment of . . .' a long catalog of rights. These include the 'right to equal treatment before . . . tribunals',[104] '[t]he right to security of person',[105] and '[p]olitical rights'.[106] Other civil rights which the article includes are freedom of movement and residence, the right to leave any country, the right to nationality, the right to marriage, to own property, to inherit, to freedom of thought, conscience, and religion, to freedom of opinion and expression, and to peaceful assembly and association.[107] Article 5 also lists '[e]conomic, social and cultural rights' whose enjoyment parties are to protect without dis-

---

[101] *Id*. art. 4(a).
[102] *Id*. art. 4(b).
[103] *See, e.g.*, cases cited in note 88 *supra*.
[104] Racial Discrimination Convention, art. 5(a).
[105] *Id*. art. 5(b).
[106] *Id*. art. 5(c).
[107] *Id*. art. 5(d).

crimination, including the right to work, to form and join trade unions, to housing, public health, education, and training, and to participation in cultural activities.[108] Finally, article 5 protects equal access to public accommodations.[109] As Partsch has written,

[t]he unresolved question is whether the States Parties, in ratifying this treaty, become obligated to positively enact legislative measures which guarantee the rights listed in Article 5, or whether States Parties agree only to bar racial discrimination in the enjoyment of these rights to the extent that these rights are safeguarded by a particular State Party.[110]

To make these rights meaningful, article 6 requires states parties to assure everyone within their jurisdiction effective remedies against human rights violations and article 7 requires states parties to undertake affirmative measures of teaching and education to combat racial prejudice.

4. *Enforceability*

The Political Covenant, the Economic Covenant, and the Racial Discrimination Convention are all in force. The United States has not ratified any of them, and the proposal of ratification which President Carter submitted to the Senate[111] contains reservations providing that ratification would require no modification of U.S. Law.[112] Ratification subject to such limitations, however, raises the question of why the United States, or any state making similar reservations, should ratify at all. In addition, there may be a question of whether such wholesale reservation is valid, or whether ratification subject to such reservation is valid.[113] After all, the most oppressive and racist government could ratify any international human rights instrument if it contained reservations which would not require it to make any changes in its policies. Moreover, the United States proposes to make a declaration accompanying ratification which would deny to the treaties self-executing effect, so that they will not in and of themselves become effective as domestic law.[114]

On the other hand, ratification would forbid regression which, in the United States, is unlikely anyway. Furthermore, while reservations could perhaps be repealed one by one, a step by step method of

[108] *Id*. art. 5(e).

[109] *Id*. art. 5(f).

[110] Partsch, *Elimination of Racial Discrimination in the Enjoyment of Civil and Political Rights*, 14 Tex. Int'l L.J. 191, 193 (1979). His answer is very complex.

[111] *See* Message of the President Transmitting Four Treaties Pertaining to Human Rights, S. Exec. Doc. No. 95–C, D, E, and F, 95th Cong., 2d Sess. (1978) [hereinafter cited as Message of the President].

[112] *See* relevant discussions in Henkin, ch. 2 *supra*.

[113] *See* Schachter, *Obligation of the Parties, supra* note 69, at 464–65.

[114] *See* Message of the President, *supra* note 111.

ratification does not seem to exist. Given the history of the United States' reluctance to join in international human rights compacts, ratification with wholesale reservations was apparently fastened upon as the most feasible political means of securing any U.S. acquiescence at all.

In the United States today, the foregoing three treaties are no more enforceable in domestic law than the Charter (which the United States has ratified) and the Universal Declaration. But what if the treaties were ratified? What would their effect be on domestic law? That, of course, would depend upon the particular provisions in question. In response to questions posed by Senator Jacob K. Javits concerning the effect of the human rights treaties, Professor Schachter replied that while certain provisions of the Economic Covenant, *e.g.*, the right 'to the continuous improvement of living conditions',[115] necessarily require legislative attention, prohibition of racial and related discrimination would be capable of judicial application without new legislation. In support of his conclusion, Professor Schachter cited provisions of the Political Covenant[116] which also need not be implemented legislatively before judicial application would become possible. In contrast, he argued that articles 20 and 23(1) of the Political Covenant would require further legislation because they are too general. Similarly, with respect to the Racial Discrimination Convention, articles 5 and 6 would be self-executing, but 3, 4, and 7 would not. Nevertheless, he concluded that the State Department's proposed declaration would render the treaties non-self-executing, although the United States would not thereby immunize itself from the international obligation to adopt legislation permitting implementation of the treaties. Although in that situation U.S. courts could not enforce the treaties, they could use the treaties as standards for interpreting domestic constitutional and statutory provisions.[117]

Given the paucity of international enforcement and the practical limitations on effecting change through international bodies, the U.N. Commission on Human Rights' Sub-Commission on Prevention of Discrimination and Protection of Minorities decided in 1977 'to consider, as a major part of its own contribution to the Decade for Action to Combat Racism and Racial Discrimination, ways and means of using domestic forums, including legislative forums, to help implement United Nations resolutions on racism, racial discrimination, *apartheid*, decolonization and self-determination and related

[115] Economic Covenant, art. 11.
[116] Political Covenant, arts. 6, 7, 9, 10, 11, 14, & 15.
[117] *International Human Rights Treaties: Hearings Before the Senate Comm. on Foreign Relations*, 96th Cong., 1st Sess. 84 (1979) (statement of Oscar Schachter).

matters'.[118] The report contains replies by a number of countries listing a variety of measures available in domestic forums.

The Committee on the Elimination of Racial Discrimination was established pursuant to article 8 of the Racial Discrimination Convention. Among the functions assigned to the Committee by the Convention is the review of reports which states parties to the Convention are required to submit on the measures they have taken to implement the Convention.[119] The Committee has found that although many of the principles contained in the Racial Discrimination Convention are reflected in the constitution and laws of a great many countries, some countries have failed to adequately report on the measures they have adopted to give effect to the Convention's provisions because they have had no problems of racial discrimination.[120] The Committee has maintained that the absence of discrimination in a state does not absolve the latter of the obligation to enact and report on anti-discrimination legislation. In a formal ruling in 1972, the Committee stated that its request for information, made pursuant to article 9 of the Convention, was 'addressed to all States Parties without distinction, whether or not racial discrimination exists in their respective territories'.[121]

D.   CONVENTION ON THE ELIMINATION OF ALL FORMS OF DISCRIMINATION AGAINST WOMEN

The most recent addition to the body of United Nations equal rights jurisprudence is the Discrimination Against Women Convention, opened for signature March 1, 1980. The states parties commenced by noting that the Charter and the Universal Declaration proclaim that 'all human beings are born free and equal in dignity and rights',[122] but that despite these instruments and various U.N. resolutions, discrimination against women continues.[123] The Convention defines 'discrimination against women' as 'any distinction, exclusion or restriction made on the basis of sex which has the effect or purpose of impairing or nullifying the recognition, enjoyment or exercise by women, irrespective of their marital status, on a basis of equality of men and women, of human rights and fundamental freedoms'.[124]

[118] Sub-Commission on Prevention of Discrimination and Protection of Minorities (Prov. Agenda Item 4), U.N. Doc. E/CN.4/Sub.2/L.679 (1978).
[119] Racial Discrimination Convention, art. 9.
[120] *See* Report of the Committee on the Elimination of Racial Discrimination, 27 U.N. GAOR, Supp. (No. 18) 22–23, U.N. Doc. A/8718 (1972).
[121] *Id.* at 38; Buergenthal, *Implementing the UN Racial Convention*, 12 Tex. Int'l L.J. 187, 190–91 (1977). On the practice of the Committee, *see generally id.*
[122] Discrimination Against Women Convention, preamble, para. 2.
[123] *Id.* para. 6.
[124] *See* text accompanying notes 95–96 *supra*.

The states parties agree to pursue immediately 'all appropriate means' to eliminate all discrimination against women.[125] They undertake, among other things, to 'embody the principle of equality of men and women in their national constitutions',[126] to 'adopt appropriate legislation and other measures ... prohibiting all discrimination against women',[127] to 'establish legal protection of the rights of women on an equal basis with men' through the country's national tribunals or other public institutions,[128] as well as to 'take all appropriate measures ... to modify or abolish existing laws, regulations, customs and practices', which, in effect, discriminate against women.[129]

Just as other international human rights agreements have, the Discrimination Against Women Convention addresses the affirmative action question. The '[a]doption by State Parties of temporary special measures aimed at accelerating *de facto* equality between men and women shall not be considered discrimination as defined in the Convention ...'[130] These steps, it continues, will be discontinued when equality of opportunity and treatment have been achieved. But, special measures 'aimed at protecting maternity shall not be considered discrimination'.[131]

To change 'social and cultural patterns', states parties will take appropriate measures to eliminate all prejudices and practices which are grounded upon ideas of 'inferiority or the superiority of either of the sexes ...'[132] 'States Parties shall take appropriate measures ... to suppress all forms of traffic in women ...'[133] Women must be assured the right of suffrage on equal terms with men[134] and equal opportunity to represent their governments at the international level.[135]

Discrimination against women in education must be eliminated and women must be provided 'the same conditions for career ... guidance, for access to studies',[136] 'the same curricula, the same examinations,'[137] 'the same opportunities to benefit from scholarships',[138] and

[125] Discrimination Against Women Convention, art. 2.
[126] *Id*. art. 2(a).
[127] *Id*. art. 2(b).
[128] *Id*. art. 2(c).
[129] *Id*. art. 2(f).
[130] *Id*. art. 4(1). *See* text accompanying notes 39–41 and 77–79 *supra*.
[131] Discrimination Against Women Convention, art. 4(2).
[132] *Id*. art. 5(a).
[133] *Id*. art. 6.
[134] *Id*. art. 7(a).
[135] *Id*. art. 8.
[136] *Id*. art. 10(a).
[137] *Id*. art. 10(b).
[138] *Id*. art. 10(d).

the same opportunities to participate in sports activities.[139] Moreover, nations must take steps to eliminate 'any stereotyped concept of the roles of men and women' through education, reduce female drop-out rates and organize programs for females who have left school prematurely.[140]

Since the right to work is 'an inalienable right of all human beings',[141] the states parties must strive to eliminate discrimination in the workplace by ensuring women the 'same employment opportunities,'[142] '[t]he right to free choice of profession and employment,'[143] 'equal remuneration,'[144] 'social security,'[145] and 'protection of health and . . . safety'.[146] Most importantly, in order to 'prevent discrimination against women on the grounds of marriage or maternity',[147] parties shall act to 'prohibit, subject to the imposition of sanctions, dismissal on the grounds of pregnancy or of maternity leave and discrimination in dismissals on the basis of marital status',[148] to 'introduce maternity leave with pay . . . without loss of former employment, seniority or social allowances',[149] and to 'provide special protection to women during pregnancy in types of work proved to be harmful to them'.[150]

Women shall be treated equally with men in the economic world, with the same right to family benefits, bank loans, mortgages, and other forms of financial credit,[151] and shall be accorded equality with men before the law and exercise a legal capacity identical to men.[152] The parties shall ensure that women have the same rights as men 'to enter into marriage',[153] 'freely to choose a spouse',[154] and to acquire the 'same rights and responsibilities during marriage and at its dissolution'.[155] Change of nationality by a husband during marriage shall not automatically change the nationality of the wife.[156]

The Discrimination Against Women Convention came into force on

[139] *Id.* art. 10(g).
[140] *Id.* art. 10.
[141] *Id.* art. 11(1)(a).
[142] *Id.* art. 11(1)(b).
[143] *Id.* art. 11(1)(c).
[144] *Id.* art. 11(1)(d).
[145] *Id.* art. 11(1)(e).
[146] *Id.* art. 11(1)(f).
[147] *Id.* art. 11(2).
[148] *Id.* art. 11(2)(a).
[149] *Id.* art. 11(2)(b).
[150] *Id.* art. 11(2)(d).
[151] *Id.* art. 13.
[152] *Id.* art. 15.
[153] *Id.* art. 16(1)(a).
[154] *Id.* art. 16(1)(b).
[155] *Id.* art. 16(1)(c).
[156] *Id.* art. 9(1).

September 3, 1981. Like all fundamental instruments written in general terms, it leaves unanswered many questions which will be resolved only when concrete applications are attempted. For example, at some point there will have to be resolved conflict between the Discrimination Against Women Convention and the declaration on religious discrimination.[157] If a religion relegates women to a certain societal or familial status which otherwise would be deemed discrimination on the basis of sex, which convention governs? Or, as with the Racial Discrimination Convention, how does one ascertain whether equality has been achieved so that affirmative action must be discontinued? The equality in sports provision[158] has its counterpart in U.S. law and has there given rise to questions of implementation such as whether girls and boys must play on the same teams or whether the same amount of money must be spent on men's and women's sports? If men and women are to have 'equality' in deciding spacing of children,[159] may a man require his pregnant spouse to undergo, or may a father-to-be prohibit the woman who is pregnant by him from undergoing, an abortion?

Some of these questions may be fanciful. Others will surely arise. When the Discrimination Against Women Convention is implemented the world community will find some guidance in the U.S. cases which have addressed sex discrimination issues. It will be some time, however, before U.S. lawyers can find guidance in international sex discrimination norms.[160]

E. DECLARATION ON RELIGIOUS DISCRIMINATION

As with racial discrimination and women's rights, existing international accords secure the right to be free from religious discrimination. Nevertheless, a further, more detailed charter of religious equality has been adopted. On November 25, 1981, the General Assembly adopted the Declaration on the Elimination of All Forms of Intolerance and of Discrimination Based on Religion or Belief.[161] The Declaration provides that everyone shall have the right to freedom of thought, conscience, and religion;[162] that no one shall be subject to

---

[157] See text accompanying notes 161–72 infra.
[158] Discrimination Against Women Convention, art. 10(g).
[159] Id. art. 16(1)(e).
[160] Counsel in Reed v. Reed, 404 U.S. 71 (1971), arguing discrimination against women, cited the U.N. Charter preamble, para. 2, in a footnote. Brief for Petitioner at 55 n.52. The U.S. Supreme Court in its decision made no reference to this argument. See also Guggenheim, Implementation of Human Rights by the U.N. Commission on the Status of Women, 12 Tex. Int'l L.J. 239 (1977); Taubenfeld & Taubenfeld, Achieving the Human Rights of Women: The Base Line, The Challenge, The Search for a Strategy, 4 Human Rights 125 (1975).
[161] G.A. Res. 36/55, U.N. Doc. A/RES/36/55 (1981).
[162] Id. art. 1(1).

coercion which would impair his or her freedom to have a religion or belief of his or her choice;[163] and that freedom to manifest one's religion or beliefs may be subject only to such limitations as are prescribed by law and are necessary to protect public safety, order, health, or morals, or the fundamental rights and freedoms of others.[164]

The Religious Discrimination Declaration asserts also that parents shall have the right to organize family life in accordance with their religion or belief[165] and that every child shall enjoy the right to have access to religious education[166] and, conversely, no child may be compelled to receive religious teaching if it would be against the wishes of his or her parents.[167] However, adopting a phrase which has currency in the U.S. law of domestic relations, the Declaration states that 'the best interests of the child' shall be the guiding principle in determining the kind of religious education the child receives.

The Declaration lists a number of freedoms, including the right to worship, to maintain charitable or humanitarian institutions, to acquire materials related to religious rights, to issue publications, to teach, to solicit financial contributions, to train leaders, to observe holidays, and to communicate with others regarding religion.[169] It calls for national legislation which would enable persons to avail themselves of such freedoms.[170]

In recognition of potential conflict between this Declaration and other human rights instruments, the Declaration states that nothing in it shall derogate from or restrict any right declared in the Universal Declaration and the international covenants.[171] We have already seen such conflict in U.S. law, for example, in the case of educational institutions with religious affiliations which discriminate on the basis of race. Undoubtedly, similar conflicts in other states involving religious requirements will have an effect on race, national origin, and sex discrimination issues. The international community, probably at some time well in the future, will be called upon to resolve such differences.[172]

---

[163] *Id.* art. 1(2).
[164] *Id.* art. 1(3).
[165] *Id.* art. 5(1).
[166] *Id.* art. 5(2).
[167] *Id.*
[168] *Id.*
[169] *Id.* art. 6.
[170] *Id.* art. 7.
[171] *Id.* art. 8.
[172] For material on earlier drafts of the Religious Discrimination Declaration, *see* Commission on Human Rights, 1979 U.N. ESCOR, Supp. (No. 6) 125, U.N. Doc. E/1979/36, E/CN.4/1347 (1979); Draft Report of the Commission on Human Rights, U.N. Doc. E/CN.4/L. 1500/Add.20 (1980).

F.   INTERPRETATION AND APPLICATIONS OF THE BASIC
INSTRUMENTS

We already have observed the scarcity of material bearing on the
application and interpretation of the basic documents on equality,
apart from scholarly exegesis. In this lies the greatest difficulty in
understanding what the documents may require in particular circumstances. Of course, international agreements may be implemented
differently from domestic law and some flesh may be observed on the
bare bones of the texts by looking beyond judicial determinations or
decisions by international bodies at, for example, unilateral censure by
one government of another. But extrapolating from text alone has its
limits. As any lawyer knows, general language, particularly that which
deals with moral or social questions, is susceptible of various meanings
which may change with circumstances. Witness the evolution in U.S.
law from 'separate but equal' to the prohibition of segregation to the
development of questions arising from affirmative action.

Nevertheless, there are a few opinions which should be noted.
Perhaps the most important is Judge Tanaka's dissenting opinion in
the *South West Africa Cases (Second Phase)*.[173] In his conclusion he
stated:

> The principle of equality does not mean absolute equality, but recognizes
> relative equality, namely different treatment proportionate to concrete indi-
> vidual circumstances. Different treatment must not be given arbitrarily; it
> requires reasonableness, or must be in conformity with justice, as in the
> treatment of minorities, different treatment of the sexes regarding public
> conveniences, etc. In these cases the differentiation is aimed at the protection
> of those concerned, and it is not detrimental and therefore against their
> will.[174]

Along with racial discrimination, discrimination on the basis of
language is forbidden by the international guarantees. The *Belgian
Linguistic Case*,[175] therefore, may illuminate other prohibitions of
discrimination. While that case involved application of the European
Convention on Human Rights and not the treaties discussed above, the
European Convention does stem from the resolve of 'European
countries which are like-minded and have a common heritage of
political traditions, ideals, freedom and the rule of law, to take the first
steps for the collective enforcement of certain of the Rights stated in
the Universal Declaration'.[176]

Belgian law had divided the country into a Dutch-speaking region,

[173] [1966] I.C.J. 4.
[174] *Id.* at 311.
[175] [1967] Y.B. Eur. Conv. on Human Rights 594 (Eur. Ct. of Human Rights).
[176] European Convention on Human Rights, preamble, para. 5.

Flanders, and a French-speaking area, Wallonia. Those who spoke French, but lived mainly in Dutch speaking areas, were required to send their children to nearby schools where they were taught in Dutch. To attend French-speaking schools required travelling a considerable distance. A case was submitted to the European Commission on Human Rights from which it went to the European Court of Human Rights. The European Court held that distinctions based on language are illegal if they do not have objective and reasonable justification in relation to the aims and effects of the measures concerned. But, as in U.S. courts making constitutional decisions bearing on state legislation, considerable deference would be given to national authority. Accordingly, the Court held that dividing the country into linguistic regions did not violate the European Convention.

Yet, while the European Commission and Court are virtually unique as international bodies which have explicated judicially the elements of substantive international equal rights jurisprudence, they have not issued a great many decisions on the subject. Most have been decided on technical or procedural grounds.[177]

Even though they rarely result in clear cut decisions, unilateral

[177] Following are some of the issues and cases before the European Court and Commission which have treated race, sex, religion, and similar discrimination: Bruggeman v. Federal Republic of Germany, [1978] Y.B. Eur. Conv. on Human Rights 638 (Comm. of Ministers) (A German statute regulating when and whether abortions may be performed did not violate the European Convention; it is cited here because in U.S. law the question of abortion is a species of women's rights litigation, although it may be characterized in other ways.); X v. United Kingdom, [1978] Y.B. Eur. Conv. on Human Rights 354 (Eur. Comm'n of Human Rights) (Applicant was sentenced to two and a half years imprisonment for homosexual relationships. The Commission accepted the application, framing the issue as to whether the view that eighteen to twenty-one year olds ought to be protected, expressed twenty years ago by the Wolfenden Commission, remains valid in a significantly changed moral climate.); X v. Netherlands, [1971] Y.B. Eur. Conv. on Human Rights 224 (Eur. Comm'n of Human Rights) (Applicant disputed a pension law which differentiated between married and unmarried women. The Commission found the legislation appreciates the difference of situation between single persons and married couples and was not out of proportion to the general purpose of the legislation. Accordingly, the application was dismissed.); X v. United Kingdom, [1967] Y.B. Eur. Conv. on Human Rights (Eur. Comm'n of Human Rights) (Because the right to be admitted to a particular country is not guaranteed by the Convention, discrimination with regard to admission does not violate the Convention; inadmissible).

There are various cases claiming denial of religious rights and/or religious discrimination by adherents of groups which refuse to comply with health, taxation, pension, or military requirements of national legislation. These claims have been rejected. *See, e.g.*, X. v. Netherlands, [1967] Y.B. Eur. Conv. on Human Rights 472 (Eur. Comm'n of Human Rights) (compulsory automobile insurance program allegedly violative of Convention; inadmissible); Grandath v. Federal Republic of Germany, [1967] Y.B. Eur. Conv. on Human Rights 626 (Eur. Comm'n of Human Rights) (legislation concerned exempted members of certain religious groups from military or alternative service; held refusal to grant same exemptions to Jehovah's Witnesses not violative of Convention); X v. Netherlands, [1962] Y.B. Eur. Conv. on Human Rights 278 (Eur. Comm'n of Human Rights) (farmer contesting health regulations pertaining to cattle; application inadmissible); Reformed Church of X v. Netherlands, [1960] Y.B. Eur. Conv. on Human Rights 648 (Eur. Comm'n of Human Rights) (contested pension program; application inadmissible).

efforts at human rights implementation also deserve a brief review. Some involve governmental action, *e.g.*, the Jackson–Vanik Amendments[178] which restrict United States trade with the Soviet Union for the purpose of influencing Jewish emigration, or the Country Reports[179] prepared by the U.S. State Department.[180]

NGO activities are discussed elsewhere in this volume.[181] However, private agencies which do not have formal NGO status may have influence. For example, the Helsinki Watch, a U.S. group which corresponds to similar bodies in other countries, including the Soviet Union, reports on domestic and Eastern European compliance with the human rights standards of the Helsinki accords. The Lawyers Committee for International Rights has participated in domestic litigation in the United States seeking to secure human rights and has appeared before international bodies. The Association of the Bar of the City of New York has sent a mission to study human rights in Argentina.[182] The National Conference on Soviet Jewry has sent missions to the Soviet Union on behalf of the Soviet Jews who seek to emigrate and has made representations in domestic and international forums around the world. A study of such groups, whose number is growing, and of what they have accomplished or failed to accomplish would be useful. There is good reason to believe that they have had some influence; how much and under what circumstances is difficult to say.

II. Teaching Suggestions

The following discussion contemplates devoting perhaps a semester to the subject matter of this chapter. If, however, an instructor has only two or three hours, it would seem best to focus on racial discrimination to the exclusion of sex and religious issues, which are not as maturely developed either in international or domestic law. And perhaps only one of the domestic aspects of the subject, such as affirmative action, might be treated when comparisons are being made. Moreover, the class could be limited to only U.S. enforcement of international standards, omitting other materials. The minisyllabus and minibiblio-

[178] 19 U.S.C. § 2432 (Countries which deny their citizens the right to emigrate or deter exercise of such rights are ineligible for most-favored-nation treatment.) Increase in Jewish emigration from the Soviet Union is thought by many to be attributable to Jackson-Vanik and like efforts.

[179] *See, e.g.*, Country Reports on Human Rights Practices for 1981, Report Submitted to the House Comm. on Foreign Affairs and the Senate Comm. on Foreign Relations, 97th Cong., 2d Sess. (1982) (status reports which examine the human rights policies of various countries for the purpose of aiding in determining their eligibility for assistance from the United States).

[180] On U.S. policy and its influence on other countries' human rights practices, *see* Derian, *Human Rights in American Foreign Policy*, 55 Notre Dame Law. 264 (1979).

[181] *See* ch. 11 *infra*.

[182] Mission of Lawyers to Argentina, *Report*, 34 Rec. A.B. City N.Y. 473 (1979).

graphy at the end of this chapter indicate materials which may be favored for brief consideration.

The basic international law of racial, sexual, and religious equality is set forth in the texts of the U.N. Charter, the Universal Declaration, the international covenants, both conventions, and the Religious Discrimination Declaration, all discussed in the foregoing pages. Interpretive materials, as noted above, may be found principally in scholarly commentary, a few committee or commission reports, and opinions of the European Commission and Court of Human Rights. Ordinarily, one would not consider an advocate's assertion of what the law requires to be an authoritative interpretation, but unilateral censure, criticism, or imposition of conditions (for example, as prerequisite to trade) sometimes are as effective as judicial or political decisions. Therefore, it is instructive to consider these sources as well.

The manner of teaching the subject, of course, is largely determined by the available sources and time which the instructor has to allocate. The bare rules should be mentioned, but, in this instance, they are relatively straightforward and with a few exceptions consist of what one might expect to find in a catalog of equal rights prescriptions. Of particular interest are rules which conflict with or are controversial in U.S. law. For example, affirmative action in employment and education merits discussion, not only in comparison to U.S. law, but with regard to the practice of other countries. So, too, does conflict between first amendment law and the international prohibition of activity or propaganda to incite racial hatred. The prohibition of discriminatory 'purpose' and 'effect' also bears comparison to U.S. law which in some situations only forbids conduct with discriminatory purpose, and other times may only prohibit discriminatory 'effect', and at yet other times combines 'purpose' and 'effect'.

For teaching purposes, a catalog of rights secured under the international accords might be drawn up and compared to protections of domestic law in order to ascertain the extent to which the United States in fact complies with international norms. This exercise would provide a useful background discussion of the United States' reluctance to ratify or its inclination to make reservations to international instruments on human rights. Specifically assigned projects might call for research into similar compliance issues in other countries. While U.S. constitutional law offers useful, highly articulated standards for comparison and guidance, so does the jurisprudence of the European Commission and Court of Human Rights. The law of other nations, *e.g.*, Great Britain and other English- or partially English-speaking countries such as Australia, Canada, South Africa, and India, may be readily accessible even at U.S. law schools with only modest library facilities. Students with language skills may possibly be able to venture further afield, as into German law, where there is a considerable human rights jurisprudence.

Finally, instruction may benefit from a clinical or quasi-clinical component—or at least a simulated one. Students might establish relationships with NGOs or private organizations and prepare complaints, briefs, memoranda, or other documents dealing with actual or alleged violations of human rights accords. Such techniques tend to reduce abstract propositions to concrete reality.

After reviewing the rules, domestic and international, and the judicial, political, and private activities which may achieve redress, it might be interesting and instructive to put them to use in simulated cases. One might select a number of issues of race, sex, or religious discrimination which have been decided by the U.S. Supreme Court and consider the means by which international human rights law could be brought to bear on them if they were to occur under various hypothetical circumstances. For example, one might consider what could be done if a particular situation were to occur in the United States and it had ratified the relevant conventions and covenants. There might be additional assumptions concerning whether ratification had occurred without qualification or whether the proposed reservations and declarations concerning non-self-execution had been adopted—and of course what weight, if any, domestic or international bodies would accord ratification hedged in this manner. The same cases might be viewed from a different perspective, as having occurred somewhere in the world other than the United States.

The range of cases which might be specimens for such exercises is vast. A teacher might engage classroom interest by using as the subject cases which are in the news as the semester develops. Or one might refer back to famous classic cases of U.S. equal rights law, *e.g.*, the School Segregation Cases, the Flag Salute Cases, the Abortion Cases, and so forth. All are available in any law library and in most general libraries. Moreover, most undergraduates constitutional law casebooks and, of course, law school casebooks contain much grist for this mill.

Cases

As an example of what might be done for an exercise of this sort, brief descriptions follow of three cases—race, sex, and religion—susceptible to such analysis, followed by reference to standards and procedures which might be brought to bear.

The first case is *Mclaughlin v. Florida*[183] in which defendants had been convicted of having violated a Florida statute which made it a

[183] 379 U.S. 184 (1964).

criminal offense for a white person and a black person of different sexes, not married to each other, to habitually live in and occupy in the night-time the same room. Florida sought to justify the law as a means of preventing breaches of the basic concepts of sexual decency. But the Supreme Court held that there was nothing in the suggested legislative purpose which made it essential to punish promiscuity between members of different racial groups and not that between members of the same group. The Court asserted that there was no suggestion that a white person and a black person are any more likely habitually to occupy the same room together than a white couple or a black couple, or to engage in illicit intercourse if they do. The Court concluded that Florida had trenched upon the constitutionally protected freedom from invidious official discrimination based on race. In the course of the opinion the Court expressed no view on the validity of laws prohibiting racial intermarriage, although several years later it declared them unconstitutional. It is interesting also that the Court implicitly upheld the notion of general state laws, which do not mention race, which punish sexual intercourse out of marriage.

The international ramifications will be discussed below, after posing some additional cases for consideration. But, for the moment, several general observations are in order: first, one might note the gingerly fashion in which the Court approached the issue in 1964. Today, a U.S. court and most judicial bodies with which this author is acquainted at least in the Western world, would have rejected the Florida law out of hand. But inter-racial sex was vastly more controversial in 1964 than it is today, although even today the subject can stir up rancorous argument.

McLaughlin might also be looked at for issues of sexual autonomy. Implicit in the decision is acceptance of the state's right to make sexual intercourse among nonmarried persons illegal. It is not clear whether most Americans would reject such a law today. Anti-fornication laws remain on the books and are enforced only very rarely. Nevertheless, they have not been held unconstitutional by the Supreme Court. In any event, it is worth noting that the subject matter of the *McLaughlin* case will lead to lively classroom discussion.

The second case for consideration is *Dothard v. Rawlinson*,[184] which involved an Alabama law specifying a minimum height of 5'2" and a minimum weight of 120 pounds for eligibility for employment as a state prison guard. At issue also was a state regulation prohibiting the hiring of women as prison guards at maximum security male penitentiaries in 'contact positions', *i.e.*, those which require close physical proximity to inmates. These rules made it impossible for a great many

[184] 433 U.S. 321 (1977).

women to become prison guards and excluded them from many such jobs even if they were able to meet the height and weight requirements. The U.S. Supreme Court held the height and weight regulations invalid under the Equal Employment Opportunity Act of 1964, but upheld the exclusion from contact positions.

In the course of the opinions, a majority of Justices observed that the height–weight rule excluded 41% of women from prison guard jobs, but only 1% of men. Moreover, it had not been established that the height–weight requirements bore any relationship to ability to do the job. There had not been proof that some small women did not have the strength to do what was required of them. But a majority also held that the contact position exclusion bore a reasonable relationship to security problems in view of the fact that there was a great deal of violence in the prisons and that many prisoners were sex offenders.

Dissenting views included the observation that appearance of strength is often necessary to maintain discipline and that small women were therefore properly excluded. On the other hand, Justices who dissented from the contact position determination argued that general violence was unrelated to the sex of the guards and that women ought not to be required to pay the price for the depraved conduct of some prisoners which should be controlled in other ways.

Finally, the class could look at *Trans World Airlines v. Hardison*[185] which dealt with religious discrimination. In that case, an employee whose religion required him to observe his Sabbath on Saturday was discharged when he refused to work on Saturdays. He charged religious discrimination in violation of the 1964 Civil Rights Act. A majority of the U.S. Supreme Court held that the employer had made reasonable efforts to accommodate the religious needs of the employee, that the employer was not required to violate its collective bargaining contract with the union to accommodate the employee by breaching the seniority system, and that alternative plans, which would have permitted the employee to work only four days a week, would have unduly burdened the employer.

As a teaching exercise, consider these cases in terms of the U.N. Charter, the Universal Declaration, the international covenants, the two conventions, and the Religious Discrimination Declaration.

What provisions of these instruments would one invoke against laws prohibiting inter-racial sex as in *McLaughlin v. Florida*, unduly limiting employment of women in circumstances detailed in *Dothard v. Rawlinson*, or discriminating on the basis of religion as asserted in *Trans World Airlines v. Hardison*?

How would those rules be advanced in U.S. courts if the United

[185] 432 U.S. 63 (1977).

States were to ratify various international instruments? What difference would it make if there were reservations and requirements of further execution?

What if the cases arose in some other country which had ratified? What would be the domestic law consequences there?

How would the cases be presented to the international bodies discussed in chapter 10? What sort of evidentiary presentation would be persuasive? What would the likely outcome be?

Consider chapter 13 on the European Convention: what does its jurisprudence suggest concerning possible outcomes?

What unilateral means might there be of achieving the complainant's goals? Could censure of one country's practice by another (consider Jackson-Vanik) make a difference?

Which of the three cases summarized above is likely to muster sufficient national sentiment in one country to move it to criticize another?

Are there not probably only a handful of highly egregious, universally or near universally condemned practices which could form the basis of unilateral international action? In the area of discrimination, what are they?

What sort of unilateral NGO or private action is likely to have an effect? Again, what are likely to be the subjects which might evoke such expressions?

These exercises, of course, need not be limited to issues of discrimination. Other fundamental freedoms are apt specimens. Out of such specific case studies is likely to come an appreciation of how the international rules may be applied in particular circumstances, which techniques or combination of techniques may be productive, and, unfortunately, how limited the utility of international standards is at present. But from that realism may stem further resolve to devise remedies and, better, develop political consensus.

III. Syllabus

The following syllabus contemplates moderately thorough consideration of the subject matter of this chapter, perhaps as much as 10 to 15 hours.

  1. The basic accords' provisions dealing with race, sex, and religious discrimination
     a. Charter.
     b. Universal Declaration.
     c. Political Covenant.
     d. Economic Covenant.

    e. Racial Discrimination Convention.
    f. Discrimination Against Women Convention.
    g. Religious Discrimination Declaration.
2. Other agreements concerned with the same issues.
    a. Slavery, genocide, *apartheid*.
    b. ILO, UNESCO.
    c. European Convention on Human Rights.
    d. Organization of American States.
    e. Helsinki Final Act.
3. Analogous provisions in U.S. law, their interpretation and application: a passing view of the fourteenth amendment, Title VII of the 1964 Civil Rights Act.
    a. Text of fourteenth amendment.
    b. Summaries of selected cases on race, sex, religion (*see, e.g.*, cases cited in text).
    c. Summary of substantive provisions of Title VII.
4. Analogies and conflicts in U.S. and international human rights law.
    a. Affirmative action.
    b. 'Purpose' and 'effect'.
    c. First amendment vs. prohibitions against racist propaganda.
5. Efforts to employ international standards in domestic law.
    a. U.S. experience; *Sei Fujii* and other cases cited in text.
    b. Other national experience, to the extent such materials are available.
6. Consideration of selected U.S. Supreme Court cases on the assumption of their presentation to an international forum.
    a. *McLaughlin* (*see* text).
    b. *Dothard* (*see* text).
    c. *Hardison* (*see* text).

IV. Minisyllabus

The following minisyllabus indicates priorities for teachers who devote only 2 or 3 hours to the subject.
1. The basic accords' provisions dealing with race, sex, and religious discrimination.
    a. Charter.
    b. Universal Declaration.
    c. Political Covenant.
    d. Racial Discrimination Convention.
2. Analogous provisions in U.S. law, their interpretation and application: a passing view of the fourteenth amendment.

    a. Text of fourteenth amendment.

    b. Summaries of selected cases on race, sex, and religion (*see, e.g.*, cases cited in text).

3. Analogies and conflicts in U.S. and international human rights law: affirmative action.

V. Bibliography

The following are extensive bibliographies on the subject matter of this book and chapter:

Reynolds, *Highest Aspiration or Barbarous Acts . . . The Explosion in Human Rights Documentation: A Bibliographic Survey*, 71 L. Lib. J. 1 (1978).

Vincent-Daviss, *Human Rights Law: A Research Guide to the Literature—Part I: International Law and the United Nations*, 14 N.Y.U. J. Int'l L. & Pol. 209 (1981); *Part II: International Protection of Refugees, and Humanitarian Law*, 14 N.Y.U. J. Int'l L. & Pol. 487 (1981); *Part III: Protection of Human Rights by the ILO and UNESCO*, 15 N.Y.U. J. Int'l L. & Pol. 000 (1982).

Books

Consult pertinent chapters of the following:

T. Buergenthal, Human Rights, International Law (1977).

J. Carey, International Protection of Human Rights (1968).

A. Henkin, Human Dignity (1978).

R. Lillich & F. Newman, International Human Rights: Problems of Law and Policy (1979).

M. McDougal, H. Lasswell & L. Chen, Human Rights and World Public Order (1980).

Articles

Bitker, *Application of the United Nations Universal Declaration of Human Rights Within the United States*, 21 De Paul L. Rev. 337 (1971).

Clark, *The United Nations and Religious Freedom*, 11 N.Y.U. J. Int'l L. & Pol. 264 (1979).

Guggenheim, *Implementation of Human Rights by the U.N. Commission on the Status of Women*, 12 Tex. Int'l L.J. 239 (1977).

Krishnaswami, *Study of Discrimination in the Matter of Religious Rights and Practices*, 11 N.Y.U. J. Int'l L. & Pol. 227 (1978).

Lillich, *The Role of Domestic Courts in Promoting International Human Rights Norms*, 24 N.Y.L.S. L. Rev. 153 (1978).

Mission of Lawyers to Argentina, *Report*, 34 Rec. A.B. City N.Y. 473 (1979).

Partsch, *Elimination of Racial Discrimination in the Enjoyment of Civil and Political Rights*, 14, Tex. Int'l L. J. 191 (1979).

Saario & Cass, *The United Nations and the International Protection of Human Rights: A Legal Analysis and Interpretation*, 7 Calif. W. Int'l L.J. 591 (1977).

Schachter, *International Law Implications of U.S. Human Rights Policies*, 24 N.Y.L.S. L. Rev. 63 (1978).

Schachter, *The Charter and the Constitution: The Human Rights Provision in American Law*, 4 Vand. L. Rev. 643 (1951).

Schachter, *The Obligation of the Parties to Give Effect to the Covenant on Civil and Political Rights*, 73 Am. J. Int'l L. 462 (1979).

Schlüter, *The Domestic Status of the Human Rights Clauses of the United Nations Charter*, 61 Calif. L. Rev. 110 (1973).

Sohn, *The Human Rights Law of the Charter*, 12 Tex. Int'l L.J. (1977).

Taubenfeld & Taubenfeld, *Achieving the Human Rights of Women: The Baseline, The Challenge, The Search for a Strategy*, 4 Human Rights 125 (1975).

Principal Texts and their Articles

United Nations Charter
    Articles: preamble, 1, 8, 13, 55, 62, and 76.

Universal Declaration of Human Rights, G.A. Res. 217A U.N. Doc. A/810, at 71 (1948)
    Articles: preamble, 1, 2, 3, 4, 7, 8, 10, 13, 15, 16, 17, 18, 21, 23, and 26.

International Convention on the Elimination of All Forms of Racial Discrimination, 660 U.N.T.S. 195.
    Articles: preamble, 1, 2, 4, 5, and 6.

International Covenant on Economic, Social and Cultural Rights, G. A. Res. 2200, 21 U.N. GAOR, Supp. (No. 16) 49, U.N. Doc. A/6316 (1966).
    Articles: preamble, 2, 3, 7, and 13.

International Covenant on Civil and Political Rights, G.A. Res. 2200, 21 U.N. GAOR, Supp. (No. 16) 52, U.N. Doc. A/6316 (1966).
    Articles: 2, 3, 4, 8, 14, 16, 20, 23, 24, 25, 26, and 27.

Convention on the Elimination of All Forms of Discrimination Against Women, U.N. Doc. A/RES/34/180 (1979).
    Articles: 2–10, 13, 15, and 16.

Declaration on the Elimination of All Forms of Intolerance and of Discrimination Based on Religion or Belief, G.A. Res. 36/55, U.N. Doc. A/RES/36/55 (1981).
    Articles: 1, 5, 6, 7, and 8.

[European] Convention for the Protection of Human Rights and Fundamental Freedoms, 213 U.N.T.S. 221.
    Articles: preamble, 4, 9, 12, and 14.

VI. Minibibliography

Bitker, *Application of the United Nations Universal Declaration of Human Rights Within the United States*, 21 De Paul L. Rev. 337 (1971).

Lillich, *The Role of Domestic Courts in Promoting International Human Rights Norms*, 24 N.Y.L.S. L. Rev. 153 (1978).

M. McDougal, H. Lasswell, & L. Chen, Human Rights and World Public Order (1980) (pertinent chapters).

Schachter, *International Law Implications of U.S. Human Rights Policies*, 24 N.Y.L.S. L. Rev. 63 (1978).

Schachter, *The Obligation of the Parties to Give Effect to the Covenant on Civil and Political Rights*, 73 Am. J. Int'l. L. 462 (1979).

Chapter 9

Human Rights in Armed Conflict: International Humanitarian Law*

Yoram Dinstein

I. Legal and Policy Considerations

A. INTRODUCTION

International law is primarily an inter-state legal system. That is to say, the rights and the duties that it creates devolve mainly on states. In this cardinal respect, there is very little difference between the special rules governing the law of armed conflict and the international legal norms applicable in general in peacetime. Nevertheless, more and more rights are being conferred by modern international law directly on individual human beings *per se*. Again, this is equally true in general as in the particular case of armed conflict. In other words, both in peacetime and in wartime, international law creates human rights.

The laws of armed conflict, like the rest of the international legal system, are partly customary and partly conventional. Many of the customary norms have been codified and now form parts of declaratory conventions. But there are still quite a few customary rules which are not reflected in any *jus scriptum*. Thus, for instance, the right of angary[1] is based on customary rather than conventional international law.[2]

As far as conventions are concerned, whether declaratory or constitutive by nature, there are two main sets of treaties. One consists of more than fifteen conventions adopted by the Hague Peace Conferences of 1899 and 1907.[3] The other comprises the four Conventions for the Protection of War Victims concluded in Geneva in 1949,[4] and two Additional Protocols done in 1977 also in Geneva.[5]

It is common practice to refer to the Geneva Conventions and Protocols as international humanitarian law. This appellation underlines the humanitarian motives that impelled the international com-

---

* © Yoram Dinstein 1983.

[1] Angary is the right of a belligerent, when in imperative need, to requisition neutral ships in its territory or in an occupied territory against full compensation. *See* G. Schwarzenberger, The Law of Armed Conflict 636 (1968).

[2] *See* G. von Glahn, Law Among Nations 753 (4th ed. 1981).

[3] The Hague Conventions of 1899 and 1907 are *reprinted in* 1 The Law of War: A Documentary History 204, 270 (L. Friedman ed. 1972) [hereinafter cited as Documents].

[4] The Geneva Conventions of 1949 are *reprinted in id.* at 525.

[5] *Reprinted in* 16 Int'l Legal Materials 1391 (1977).

munity to adopt them. It must be observed, however, that all the laws of war—whether formulated in Geneva, The Hague, or elsewhere—are an outcome of a realistic compromise between humanitarian considerations, on the one hand, and the requirements of military necessity, on the other. It is arguable that the Geneva Conventions reflect the tilting of the scales in favor of humanitarian considerations, whereas in other instances (principally, the Hague Conventions) there is a more balanced equilibrium between such considerations and the demands of military necessity. But, historically, many of the provisions of the Geneva Conventions are derived from the Hague Conventions. This is particularly true of the Geneva Convention for the Amelioration of the Condition of Wounded, Sick, and Shipwrecked Members of the Armed Forces at Sea of 12 August 1949 (Second Geneva Convention).[6] It replaces the Tenth Hague Convention of 1907,[7] which for its part was an adaptation to maritime warfare of the principles of the Geneva Convention for the Amelioration of the Condition of the Wounded and Sick in Armies in the Field of 6 July 1906.[8] The latter is the precursor of the Geneva Convention for the Amelioration of the Condition of the Wounded and Sick in Armed Forces in the Field of 12 August 1949 (First Geneva Convention).[9] Needless to say, the mere transposition of stipulations from one instrument drafted at The Hague to another formulated in Geneva does not by itself modify their nature. Legal norms do not acquire a humanitarian nature simply because they are incorporated in one series of conventions rather than another. Their character must be determined by substance and not by purely technical criteria.

In any event, international humanitarian law must not be confused with international human rights. First, it must be borne in mind that some wartime international human rights exist not as part of international humanitarian law but as a component of the ordinary (Hague-type) law of armed conflict. For instance, the protection of private property in occupied territories is governed, for the most part, not by the Geneva Conventions or Protocols but by the Hague Regulations (annexed to the Second Convention of 1899[10] and the Fourth Convention of 1907)[11] Respecting the Laws and Customs of War on Land.[12]

Secondly, international humanitarian law bestows rights not only

---

[6] 6 U.S.T. 3217, T.I.A.S. No. 3363, 75 U.N.T.S. 85.
[7] 36 Stat. 2371, T.S. No. 543.
[8] *Reprinted in* 1 Documents, *supra* note 3, at 257.
[9] 6 U.S.T. 3114, T.I.A.S. No. 3362, 75 U.N.T.S. 31.
[10] 32 Stat. 1803, T.S. No. 403.
[11] 36 Stat. 2277, T.S. No. 539.
[12] *See* G. Von Glahn, The Occupation of Enemy Territory 185–91 (1957).

on human beings as such, but also (and chiefly) on states. The adjective 'humanitarian' describes the contents of the norms and not the subject bound by them. There is one segment of international humanitarian law that applies directly to individuals, but there is another that applies only to states. Thus, article 7 of the First, Second, and Third Geneva Conventions,[13] as well as article 8 of the Fourth Convention,[14] explicitly refer to rights secured to persons protected by the Geneva Conventions. These are obviously human rights. On the other hand, many provisions in the four Geneva Conventions clearly create rights of states. By way of illustration, under article 16 of the First Convention and article 19 of the Second Convention, each belligerent is obligated to keep a record of particulars identifying wounded, sick, shipwrecked, or dead persons of the adverse party falling into its hands, and forward the information to the adverse party through the medium of a central Bureau. The corresponding right is accorded not to the individual victim of war (who may not even be alive), but to his or her state.

To the extent that international humanitarian law—and even more so the Hague Conventions—engender human rights, it is interesting to note the dates when the central instruments were formulated. Whereas the development of the international human rights of peacetime began in earnest only after World War II, some fundamental freedoms of wartime had a seminal existence even before World War I. Insofar as many peacetime human rights are concerned, 1948—the year in which the U.N. General Assembly adopted the Universal Declaration of Human Rights[15]—was the *dies a quo* from which they first started to crystallize in international law. By contrast, as regards numerous wartime human rights, 1949—the year in which the Geneva Conventions were opened for ratification—was the *dies ad quem* which finalized their consolidation as binding legal norms. It is thus safe to state that, generally speaking, wartime human rights preceded those of peacetime in the international arena. This should not be surprising, given the fact that historically the law of war is the most ancient part of international law.

For the most part, international humanitarian law deals with problems generated by inter-state wars. Thus, most of the stipulations of the four Geneva Conventions (some 400 articles) and the entire Protocol Additional to the Geneva Conventions of 12 August 1949, and Relating to the Protection of Victims of International Armed Conflicts

[13] Geneva Convention relative to the Treatment of Prisoners of War of 12 August 1949, 6 U.S.T. 3316, T.I.A.S. No. 3364, 75 U.N.T.S. 135.

[14] Geneva Convention relative to the Protection of Civilian Persons in Time of War of 12 August 1949, 6 U.S.T. 3516, T.I.A.S. No. 3365, 75 U.N.T.S. 287.

[15] G.A. Res. 217A, U.N. Doc. A/810, at 71 (1948).

(Protocol I)[16] (more than 100 articles) are devoted to international armed conflicts. However, to some extent intra-state, *i.e.*, internal, armed conflicts are also regulated by international humanitarian law. The subject is covered by article 3 common to the four Geneva Conventions and by the entire Protocol Additional to the General Conventions of 12 August 1949, and Relating to the Protection of Victims of Non-International Armed Conflicts (Protocol II).[17] Protocol II augments the protection afforded to the victims of internal wars, but it has a narrower scope of application than common article 3.[18] The human rights which are in force during internal armed conflicts raise a number of legal, psychological, and practical problems because of the unique circumstances of a conflict in which one of the parties is not a government but a group of rebels.[19] Yet, civil wars can be as devastating as inter-state wars, and the challenge that they pose to human rights must not be underrated.

B.　THE ESSENCE OF HUMAN RIGHTS IN ARMED CONFLICTS

Broadly speaking, wartime human rights can be divided into two categories: (i) rights granted to lawful or privileged combatants, *i.e.*, combatants respecting the laws of war and meeting the conditions which that body of law establishes;[20] and (ii) rights accorded to civilians.

In essence, the human rights of lawful combatants are two-fold:

(a) They have the right to the status of prisoners of war once they are placed *hors de combat* by force of circumstances (being wounded, sick, or shipwrecked) or by choice (laying down their arms). A series of specific subrights relating to the humane treatment of wounded, sick, and shipwrecked combatants is incorporated in the First and Second Geneva Conventions. However, it is primarily the Third Geneva Convention which details the protection that must be rendered to all prisoners of war, the injured as well as the able-bodied.

(b) Lawful combatants also have the right not to be targets of

---

[16] *Reprinted in* 16 Int'l Legal Materials 1391 (1977).

[17] *Reprinted in* 16 Int'l Legal Materials 1442 (1977).

[18] *See* Dinstein, *The New Geneva Protocols: A Step Forward or Backward?*, 33 Y.B. World Aff. 265, 279–80 (1979) [hereinafter cited as Dinstein]. *Cf.* Boyd, Digest of United States Practice in International Law 1977, at 924–30 (while the 'scope of application of the Protocol' is 'its Achilles heel' the 'Protocol nevertheless accomplishes much in developing the law . . .').

[19] *See* Dinstein, *The International Law of Civil War and Human Rights*, 6 Isr. Y.B. on Human Rights 62, 66–69 (1976).

[20] On the conditions laid down by the Geneva Conventions, *see* Meron, *Some Legal Aspects of Arab Terrorists' Claims to Privileged Combatancy*, in Of Law and Man 225 (S. Shoham ed. 1971), *reprinted in* 40 Acta Scandinavica Juris Gentium 47 (1970). On the changes introduced by the Additional Protocols, *see* Dinstein, *supra* note 18, at 269–73.

biological, bacteriological, or chemical weapons, poison, and several types of bullets or projectiles. Each forbidden item entails a separate subright and the *corpus juris* is to be found in instruments such as the 1868 St. Petersburg Declaration Renouncing the Use in War of Certain Explosive Projectiles,[21] the Hague Regulations,[22] and the 1925 Geneva Protocol for the Prohibition of Poisonous Gases and Bacteriological Methods of Warfare.[23]

The human rights of civilians in time of war relate to (a) the civilian population anywhere; (b) civilian enemy aliens in the territory of a belligerent state; and (c) the civilian population in occupied territories. The main legal provisions on which the protection of civilians is based are articles 42–56 of the Hague Regulations,[24] which relate to occupied territories, the Fourth Geneva Convention, pertaining to civilians generally but especially to enemy aliens and occupied territories, and Part IV of Protocol I, relevant to the civilian population as a whole. Under Protocol I, the civilian population as such, as well as individual civilians, enjoy the right to general protection against dangers arising from military operations.[25] Specifically, they are granted subrights against indiscriminate attacks,[26] reprisals,[27] destruction of cultural objects and places of worship,[28] starvation,[29] and so forth.[30] A Convention on Prohibitions or Restrictions on the Use of Certain Conventional Weapons which May Be Deemed to Be Excessively Injurious or to Have Indiscriminate Effects, concluded in 1980, protects civilians against incendiary weapons and mines.[31]

Traditionally, the rights of civilians are especially safeguarded under belligerent occupation. The laws of war establish a minimum international standard of due process of law for securing life, liberty, and property of civilians in occupied territories.[32] But it must be understood that civilians in occupied territories are not absolutely protected. Indeed, in certain circumstances, they may be deprived of their lives, liberty, and property. However, due process of law is a *conditio sine qua non* to such deprivation. Hence, the taking of hostages, an arbitrary measure *par excellence*, is prohibited,[33] whereas capital punish-

---

[21] *Reprinted in* 1 Documents, *supra* note 3, at 192.

[22] *See* notes 10 & 11 *supra.*

[23] *Reprinted in* 1 Documents, *supra* note 3, at 454.

[24] *See* notes 10 & 11 *supra.*

[25] *See* Protocol I, art. 51(1).

[26] *Id.* art. 51(4).

[27] *Id.* arts. 51(6) & 52(1).

[28] *Id.* art. 53.   [29] *Id.* art. 54(1).

[30] *See generally id.* arts. 51–56.

[31] Int'l Rev. Red Cross No. 220, Jan.–Feb. 1981, at 42.

[32] *See* Dinstein, *The International Law of Belligerent Occupation and Human Rights*, 8 Isr. Y.B. on Human Rights 104 (1978).

[33] *See* Fourth Geneva Convention, art. 34.

ment (if not abolished prior to the war within a territory subsequently occupied) may be pronounced by a competent court of the occupying state.[34] Civilians in occupied territories may be detained, even as a preventive-administrative measure, but a required procedure must be followed.[35] 'Contributions', which are involuntary, can be levied from the inhabitants of occupied territories provided that prescribed conditions are met.[36] Numerous other examples could be cited.

As for intra-state wars, the aforementioned article 3 common to the four Geneva Conventions establishes certain minimal human rights for persons taking no active part in the hostilities and for members of armed forces who are *hors de combat*. They are protected against murder, mutilation, cruel treatment, torture, taking of hostages, and the like. Nevertheless, humane treatment in the case of prisoners does not mean that they can only be kept captive and may not be executed. The execution of a prisoner on a charge of treason is perfectly permissible, provided that it follows a fair trial. What is disallowed is execution without due process of law. Protocol II supplements the human rights applicable during civil wars by detailed provisions relating to the protection of civilians in general,[37] children,[38] detainees,[39] the wounded, sick, and shipwrecked,[40] and persons facing penal prosecution.[41]

C. THE INTERPLAY OF HUMAN RIGHTS IN PEACETIME AND WARTIME

To appreciate the precise nature and the full complexity of the manifold human rights which are in force under international law in time of armed conflict, it is useful to compare them to the ordinary human rights that exist in peacetime. With such a comparison as a yardstick, six variations come into focus. These can be schematically presented as follows, with X representing a human right and O representing its absence (see table opposite).

Variation 1

This is the typical position of most human rights: they exist in peacetime, but may *disappear completely* in wartime. Thus, the fact that an armed conflict exists has a crucial significance for the average

[34] *See id.* art. 68.
[35] *See id.* art. 78.
[36] *See* Hague Regulations, *supra* notes 10 & 11, art. 49.
[37] Protocol II, arts. 4, 13–17.
[38] *Id.* art. 4(3).
[39] *Id.* art. 5.
[40] *Id.* arts. 7–12.
[41] *Id.* art. 6.

	Human Rights Applicable	
	In Peacetime	*In Wartime*
1	X	O
2	X	X
3	O	X
4	O	O
5	X	X minus
6	X	X plus

human right, which is suspended for the duration of the conflict. The suspension is not however automatic, but is left to the discretion of the involved state. For example, the [European] Convention for the Protection of Human Rights and Fundamental Freedoms states:

> In time of war or other public emergency threatening the life of the nation any High Contracting Party may take measures derogating from its obligations under this Convention to the extent strictly required by the exigencies of the situation, provided that such measures are not inconsistent with its other obligations under international law.[42]

A similar provision appears in article 30 of the European Social Charter,[43] article 4 of the International Covenant on Civil and Political Rights[44] (although it avoids the explicit term 'war'), and article 27 of the American Convention on Human Rights.[45]

The impact of an emergency situation on human rights was elucidated in the first judgment of the European Court of Human Rights, delivered in 1961, in the *Lawless Case*.[46] Lawless was a member of the Irish Republican Army (IRA) which employs terrorist methods with a view to joining the Northern Ireland part of the United Kingdom to the independent Republic of Ireland. Lawless was arrested by the Irish authorities and held for several months in administrative detention without trial in accordance with a special statute which vested in those authorities emergency powers for the suppression of acts of terrorism. Lawless petitioned the European Commission of Human Rights, which brought the case before the European Court of Human Rights. Even though the European Court held that, in general, administrative detentions are incompatible with the human rights guaranteed by the European Convention, it decided that in this

[42] 213 U.N.T.S. 221, art. 159(1), *reprinted in* Basic Documents on Human Rights 242 (2d ed. I. Brownlie 1981) [hereinafter cited as Brownlie].

[43] Europ. T.S. No. 35, *reprinted in* Brownlie, *supra* note 42, at 301.

[44] G.A. Res. 2200, 21 U.N. GAOR, Supp. (No. 16) 52, U.N. Doc. A/6316 (1966).

[45] O.A.S. T.S. No. 36, *reprinted in* Brownlie, *supra* note 42, at 391.

[46] Lawless Case (Merits), 3 Judgments Europ. Ct. of Human Rights 27 (1961).

instance Ireland had acted lawfully in view of the emergency and in the light of article 15 of the European Convention.[47] The result would of course be the same in wartime. Thus, if freedom from arbitrary detention in peacetime is represented by X, in time of armed conflict a government may suspend X and the individual is faced with O.

Variation 2

Exceptionally, some human rights are not subject to suspension even in wartime. That is, despite the fact that an armed conflict is being waged, the human rights in question are left intact. Each of the four derogation clauses mentioned under variation 1 lists a number of human rights which are excepted from its applicability. Foremost among the rights which cannot be suspended in wartime is freedom from torture. Indeed, the existence of this specific freedom in wartime is derived not merely from its not being subject to derogation; it is also, and independently, guaranteed under international humanitarian law. Thus, in noninternational armed conflicts, torture is expressly forbidden in the common article 3 of the four Geneva Conventions, as well as in article 4 of Protocol II. In international conflicts, torture is proscribed in articles 12 of the First and Second Geneva Conventions, article 17 of the Third Convention, and article 32 of the Fourth Convention.[48] It is also prohibited by article 75(2) of Protocol I. Consequently, if freedom from torture is represented by X, X is equally valid in wartime as in peacetime.

Variation 3

It is important to take into account the fact that the scope of wartime human rights is not limited to a partial list of peacetime human rights which cannot be or have not been suspended. In some instances, the special circumstances of an armed conflict engender new human rights which are valid in particular *vis-à-vis* an enemy state or an occupying power where no such rights existed before in the peaceful relationship between a person and the state of nationality or residence. For example, in peacetime there is no human right to avoid military service or alternative national service in the state of residence. Admittedly, freedom from forced or compulsory labour is recognized in article 4 of the European Convention, article 8 of the Political Covenant, and article 6 of the American Convention. Yet, all three clauses exclude from that freedom compulsory military service or, in the case of conscientious objectors, alternative national service. By contrast, in occupied terri-

---

[47] *Id.* at 54–62.

[48] Torture is a grave breach of the Geneva Conventions. *See* First Convention, art. 50; Second Convention, art. 51; Third Convention, art. 130; Fourth Convention, art. 147.

tories in wartime article 51 of the Fourth Geneva Convention bans compulsion of civilians to serve in the armed or auxiliary forces of the Occupying Power. If freedom from military service under belligerent occupation in wartime is represented by X, in peacetime there is no counterpart human right.

Variation 4

For the sake of the completion of the analysis, it should be noted that certain rights advocated by humanitarian activists and lawyers have not attained the status of recognized human rights either in peacetime or in wartime. They must, therefore, be represented by O on both sides of the diagram.

A case in point is that of freedom of immigration. Whereas international law vouchsafes to every person freedom of emigration, *i.e.*, the right to leave any country, including his or her own, on a permanent basis,[49] there is no parallel rule of general international law sanctioning freedom of immigration, *i.e.*, the right to enter a foreign country with a view to settling there.[50] This freedom is equally nonexistent in peacetime as in wartime.

Variation 5

Often a human right which is full-fledged in peacetime continues to exist in wartime, but due to the exigencies of the armed conflict its scope of application is *severely limited*. Let us take as an illustration freedom of assembly. This right is enshrined in article 20 of the Universal Declaration, article 11 of the European Convention, article 5(d)(ix) of the International Convention on the Elimination of All Forms of Racial Discrimination,[51] article 21 of the Political Covenant, and article 15 of the American Convention. Freedom of assembly is admittedly subject to the derogation clauses referred to above, and may, therefore, be suspended altogether in wartime.

However, as indicated above, suspension of human rights in the course of an armed conflict is a right and not a duty. Suppose, for the sake of argument, that freedom of assembly is not suspended altogether by a belligerent state. Freedom of assembly is not an absolute right even in peacetime. As the provisions of the Political Covenant, the European Convention, and the American Convention enunciate in no uncertain terms, restrictions may be placed on the exercise of freedom of assembly if imposed in conformity with the law and where necessary

[49] *See* Dinstein, *Freedom of Emigration and Soviet Jewry*, 4 Isr. Y.B. on Human Rights 266 (1974).

[50] *See* G. Goodwin-Gill, International Law and the Movement of Persons between States 196–97 (1978).

[51] 660 U.N.T.S. 195, *reprinted in* Brownlie, *supra* note 42, at 150.

in the interests of, *inter alia*, national security. National security considerations in the course of an armed conflict could legitimately dictate a severe curtailment of freedom of assembly, in terms of the nature of the gathering, its size, etc., even where a similar limitation is peacetime would be viewed as unjustifiable. It follows that if freedom of assembly in peacetime is represented by X, in wartime (assuming that it does not go down to O) we are confronted with X minus.

Variation 6

The reverse also happens in some cases so that the position in wartime of a human right is X plus. Freedom from medical experimentation may exemplify this. In peacetime, there is only a general provision in article 7 of the Political Covenant which provides that no one shall be subjected without free consent to medical or scientific experimentation. In wartime there are also general injunctions against biological experiments[52] as well as medical or scientific experiments of any kind which are not necessitated by the medical treatment of the protected person and carried out in his interest.[53] But, moreover, article 11 of Protocol I incorporates a much more detailed provision which rules out removal of tissue or organs for transplantation even with the consent of the donor, though an exception is made for voluntary donations of blood for transfusion or of skin for grafting. In peacetime, too, there is a grave problem of 'engineering of consent', particularly by exploiting the condition of necessitous men.[54] Nevertheless, there is no peacetime counterpart to the sophisticated stipulation of Protocol I.

D. THE INTERPLAY OF HUMAN RIGHTS AND CORRESPONDING DUTIES IN ARMED CONFLICT

The concept of a right connotes the existence of a corresponding obligation. When international human rights are involved, the rights are bestowed directly on individuals, but the corresponding obligations are generally incurred by states. From the viewpoint of those corresponding obligations, human rights may be subsumed under three headings depending on the states implicated. The duties corresponding to human rights may be imposed (a) on all the states of the world; (b) only on the state of which the individual is a national; or (c) solely on the states of which the individual is not a national. Most peacetime human rights, whether or not suspended in wartime, come within the bounds of the first two categories. On the other hand,

[52] First Geneva Convention, art. 12; Second Geneva Convention, art. 12.
[53] Third Geneva Convention, art. 12; Fourth Geneva Convention, art. 32. Biological experiments are grave breaches of the Convention. *See* note 48 *supra*.
[54] *See* E. Cahn, Confronting Injustice 366–67 (1966).

wartime human rights afforded to lawful combatants and to the civilian population belong primarily to the third category. In fact, the obligations corresponding to these human rights are incumbent not on an ordinary foreign state but on a very special one, an enemy state.

It goes without saying that the relationship between an individual and an enemy state in wartime is entirely different from the relationship between an individual and his or her state (or any other state) in peacetime. If in peacetime one may presume that a certain degree of goodwill characterizes the relations between the state and at least many of the individuals to which it owes certain obligations, in wartime no such presumption is valid *vis-à-vis* enemy subjects. The situation is abnormal and it calls for a special legal mechanism.

This special legal mechanism is based on a duality of rights. The obligations are binding on the enemy state. The dual rights, which exist simultaneously, are granted to the individual, as lawful combatant or civilian, as well as to the state to which he or she owes allegiance. The human right, of the lawful combatant or civilian, and the state right, of his or her state of nationality, consequently correspond to a single obligation imposed on the enemy state. This duality of rights has beneficial results from both a practical and a theoretical standpoint.

From a practical angle, since the state right and the human right exist contemporaneously yet independently, a more effective protection of the individual is made feasible. The lawful combatant or civilian may stand on his or her right without having to rely on the goodwill of the state of nationality and, by the same token, the state of nationality may stand on its right without depending on a call for help from the individual. If, for instance, a prisoner of war is tortured, the right of the prisoner and the right of the state of nationality are violated at one and the same time. Each is entitled to take whatever steps are available and deemed appropriate by virtue of their separate rights. Moreover, neither one of them is capable of waiving the other's independent right. The fact that the prisoner may not be willing to take action on the basis of his or her human right does not restrict the state of nationality. Similarly, the fact that the state of nationality is prepared to forgive and forget the incident does not bind the prisoner.

From a theoretical perspective, the fact that the state of nationality is waging a war of aggression, constituting a crime against peace,[55] does not detract from human rights which are not its own rights. This is particularly significant in the light of the fundamental principle *ex*

---

[55] For a definition of crimes against peace, *see* art. 6(a), Charter of the International Military Tribunal, annexed to the Agreement for the Prosecution and Punishment of Major War Criminals of the European Axis, *reprinted in* 1 Documents, *supra* note 3, at 885, 886–87 [hereinafter cited as Nuremberg Charter].

injuria jus non oritur. In accordance with that principle, it is possible to argue that the offending state, having perpetrated a crime against international law, cannot reap the benefits which ordinarily accrue to belligerents under the laws of war, and that a distinction must be made between it and the state which was the victim of aggression.[56] But, even if the argument is plausible, it would not affect the human rights of lawful combatants and civilians who were not accomplices to the crime.[57] Crimes against peace can be committed only by high-ranking persons (organs of the state) responsible for the formulation and execution of state policies.[58] Other individuals, below policy level, may not be regarded as criminals against peace. As a result, they are entitled to enjoy the human rights which are granted to them directly by the laws of war irrespective of the criminal conduct of their state.

In some instances, the special legal structure of wartime human rights produces not only a duality of rights, but also a duality of corresponding duties. Thus, if soldier *X* of state *A* tortures prisoner of war *Y* from state *B*, not only has state *A* violated an international legal obligation corresponding to the human right of *Y* and the state right of *B* but *X* himself concurrently contravenes a duty which devolves directly on him under international law. By torturing a prisoner of war, *X* commits a war crime,[59] and he is personally liable to prosecution and punishment regardless of the sanctions which may or may not be applied to state *A*.

E.   PROBLEMS OF IMPLEMENTATION AND SUPERVISION

The problem of implementation and supervision plagues international law as a whole because of the absence of a permanent international police force and an international court with universal compulsory jurisdiction. The problem is particularly acute where violations of human rights are concerned inasmuch as the relations between an individual victim of such violations and the state are characterized by enormous inequality. If this is true generally of human rights, it is especially true of wartime human rights.

There is no time like wartime in which passions are inflamed and even civilized persons, steeped in humanitarian values which appear to be self-evident in peacetime, are apt to show no restraint and to defend the indefensible out of devotion to the national cause and a conviction that the end (victory over the enemy) justifies the means. The extreme

---

[56] *See* Lauterpacht, *The Limits of the Operation of the Law of War*, 30 Brit. Y.B. Int'l L. 206, 212 (1953); Wright, *The Outlawry of War and the Law of War*, 47 Am. J. Int'l L. 365, 370–71 (1953).

[57] *See id.* at 373.

[58] *See* Dinstein, *International Criminal Law*, 5 Isr. Y.B. on Human Rights 55, 58 (1975).

[59] For a definition of war crimes, *see* art. 6(b), Nuremberg Charter, *supra* note 55, at 887.

barbarism of World War II, epitomized by the Holocaust, was admittedly unprecedented in the modern age, but violations of human rights occur in every war.

When such violations take place, it is not only the victim of the violation and its perpetrator who are involved. The whole international community has a definite interest that the legal structure of human rights should not crumble. The interest of the world at large in the observance of human rights in wartime is reflected in the fact that many of these rights are now viewed as emanating from peremptory norms of general international law, *i.e., jus cogens.* Under article 53 of the Vienna Convention on the Law of Treaties,[60] any conflicting treaty will therefore be void. In other words no 'contracting out' from imperative human rights is possible. As pointed out by Sir Gerald Fitzmaurice:

> If two countries were to agree that, in any future hostilities between them, neither side would be bound to take any prisoners of war, and all captured personnel would be liable for execution, it is clear that even though this was intended only for application as between the parties, and not *vis-à-vis* any other country that might be involved in hostilities with either of them, such an arrangement would be illegal and void.[61]

It is noteworthy that a common provision of the Geneva Convention[62] expressly provides that parties may not conclude special agreements adversely affecting the situation of protected persons. This prohibition follows primarily from the duality of rights referred to above: protected persons are entitled to human rights independently of state rights, and states may not renounce rights which do not belong to them. Under the aforementioned common provision, protected persons, for their part, may in no circumstances renounce in part or in whole the rights secured to them.

Another result of the duality of rights in wartime is that reprisals cannot be freely used with a view to safeguarding the observance of legal norms. Ordinarily, the implementation of the law of armed conflict hinges, to a very large degree, on practical considerations of reciprocity and the fear of reprisals. That is to say, whereas in peacetime states are often prepared to sleep on their infringed rights, wartime is marked by an absence of moderation with retaliation following swiftly. The prospect of reprisals serves as a sobering and inhibiting factor on a state which contemplates a departure from accepted norms of behavior. However, when state *A* commits an

---

[60] U.N. Doc. A/CONF.39/27 (1969), *reprinted in* 8 Int'l Legal Materials 679 (1969).

[61] Fitzmaurice, Third Report on Law of Treaties, U.N. Doc. A/CN.4/115, *reprinted in* [1958] 2 Y.B. Int'l L. Comm'n 20, 40, U.N. Doc. A/CN.4/SER.A/1958/Add. 1.

[62] Arts. 6 of the First, Second, and Third Geneva Conventions; art. 7 of the Fourth Geneva Convention.

illegal act against state *B* warranting reprisals, state *B* is not allowed to retaliate by performing an act which constitutes a violation of the independent human rights of persons who had nothing to do with the original illegality. Thus, if state *A* kills prisoners of war of state *B*, state *B* (while entitled to retaliate in other ways) may not kill prisoners of war of state *A*. Article 13 of the Third Geneva Convention expressly proclaims: 'Measures of reprisal against prisoners of war are prohibited.' Similar prohibitions of reprisals against protected persons appear in the other Geneva Conventions[63] and in Protocol I.[64]

Should wartime human rights be violated by a belligerent state or persons forming part of its armed forces, that state bears full international responsibility for the violation. If the case demands, the state must pay compensation in accordance with article 3 of the Fourth Hague Convention of 1907[65] and article 91 of Protocol I. The State may not absolve itself from international responsibility on the grounds that it has already punished the persons who committed the violation.[66]

On the other hand, the person who committed the violation may be punished by the state of his or her own nationality, under its domestic legal system, or even by any other state, under international law. As far as the state of nationality is concerned, it is required to ensure observance of the laws of war by issuing appropriate instructions to its armed forces and supervising their execution.[67] It must also enact any legislation necessary to provide effective penal sanctions for grave breaches of the Geneva Conventions.[68]

If the violation of wartime human rights constitutes a crime under international law, *i.e.*, a war crime or a crime against humanity,[69] so that there is a duality of duties corresponding to the duality of rights, the offender may be prosecuted and punished by any state, particularly, though not necessarily, by the enemy state. Jurisdiction over such crimes is universal.[70] Moreover, as the judgments of the International Military Tribunals in *Nuremberg*[71] and *Tokyo*[72] palpably demon-

[63] *See* art. 46, First Geneva Conventions art. 47, Second Geneva Convention; art. 33, Fourth Geneva Convention.

[64] Arts. 20 & 51(6).

[65] *Reprinted in* 1 Documents, *supra* note 3, at 310.

[66] *See* Third Geneva Convention: Commentary 630 (J. Preux ed. 1960).

[67] *See, e.g.*, art. 1, Fourth Hague Convention; art. 80, Protocol I.

[68] *See* art. 49, First Geneva Convention; art. 50, Second Geneva Convention; art. 129, Third Geneva Convention; art. 146, Fourth Geneva Convention.

[69] For a definition of crimes against humanity, *see* art. 6(c), Nuremberg Charter, *supra* note 55, at 887.

[70] *See* Baxter, *The Municipal and International Law Basis of Jurisdiction over War Crimes*, 28 Brit. Y.B. Int'l L. 382, 392 (1951).

[71] *Reprinted in* 2 Documents, *supra* note 3, at 922.

[72] *Reprinted in* 2 Documents, *supra* note 3, at 1029.

strate, war criminals (in the broad sense of the term) can be brought to justice even before an international criminal court. As the *Nuremberg* judgment proclaims:

Crimes against international law are committed by men, not by abstract entities, and only by punishing individuals who commit such crimes can the provisions of international law be enforced.[73]

The trouble is that no permanent international criminal court has yet been established. National proceedings against enemy war criminals are often tainted with lack of objectivity and, more often than not, take place only at the end of war when they are usually limited to trials of the vanquished by the victors.

Can something be done during an armed conflict to prevent violations of human rights, instead of simply waiting and punishing violators after the end of the conflict? The solution furnished by international law lies in the appointment of a Protecting Power, *i.e.*, a neutral country which undertakes to protect the interests of one party to the conflict and its nationals *vis-à-vis* another party. A common provision of the Geneva Conventions[74] stipulates that the Conventions shall be applied with the cooperation and under the scrutiny of Protecting Powers. Article 5 of Protocol I declares that it is the duty of parties to the conflict to secure the supervision and implementation of international humanitarian law by the application of the system of Protecting Powers.

However, the appointment of a Protecting Power is unfortunately contingent on acquiring the trilateral consent of all concerned, both belligerents as well as the neutral country selected, and in practice such consent proves elusive. In order to facilitate the process, article 5 of Protocol I provides that if the required consent has not been attained, the International Committee of the Red Cross (ICRC) shall, and any other impartial humanitarian organization may, offer its good offices in order to designate a Protecting Power. The ICRC may, *inter alia*, ask each party to the conflict to proffer a list of at least five states considered acceptable to act as Protecting Powers on its behalf and another five which it would accept as Protecting Powers of the adverse party, the assumption being that a comparison of the two lists will reveal some overlap.

Another common provision of the Geneva Conventions[75] declares that the appointment of a Protecting Power does not constitute an obstacle to the humanitarian activities which the ICRC or any other

---

[73] *Supra* note 71, at 940.

[74] Arts. 8 of the First, Second, and Third Geneva Conventions; art. 9 of the Fourth Geneva Convention.

[75] Arts. 9 of the First, Second, and Third Geneva Conventions; art. 10 of the Fourth Geneva Convention.

impartial humanitarian organization may undertake, subject to the consent of the parties to the conflict, for the benefit of protected persons.

The ICRC (which consists exclusively of Swiss citizens and must be distinguished from national Red Cross societies) plays a major role in the implementation of international humanitarian law. It has numerous specific functions under the Geneva Conventions and Protocol I which are independent of the operation of Protecting Powers. For instance, under article 126 of the Third Convention, whether or not there is a Protecting Power, ICRC delegates are allowed to visit all places in which there are prisoners of war, including places of internment, imprisonment, and labour, and to interview the prisoners without witnesses.

Moreover, another common provision of the Geneva Conventions[76] creates a legal edifice of protection with three layers. According to the first paragraph of the common article, parties to the conflict may, by mutual consent, entrust to an impartial and efficacious organization the duties incumbent on Protecting Powers by virtue of the Geneva Conventions. The correct interpretation of this vague paragraph is not that the organization in question substitutes for a Protecting Power, but rather that they share responsibility. The organization will concentrate on discharging the protective duties imposed by the Geneva Conventions, while the Protecting Power will perform the traditional functions which exist under customary international law irrespective of the Conventions.[77]

The second paragraph of the common article sets up a substitute for a Protecting Power. It states that, when protected persons do not or cease to benefit from the services of a Protecting Power or an organization as provided for in the first paragraph (services which require the consent of the two adversaries), the Detaining Power shall unilaterally request a neutral state or such an organization to undertake the functions performed by a Protecting Power under the Geneva Conventions. It must be stressed again that a Protecting Power in the full sense of the term can only be appointed on the basis of the consent of both adverse parties. Here only one party is involved in the process. Consequently, the state or organization appointed is not a genuine Protecting Power, although it carries out the tasks of one in conformity with the Geneva Conventions. Such duties are distinct from other duties under customary international law.[78]

If no protection can be arranged even on this basis, the third para-

[76] Arts. 10 of the First, Second, and Third Geneva Conventions; art. 11 of the Fourth Geneva Convention.
[77] *See* First Geneva Convention: Commentary 118–19 (J. Pictet ed. 1952).
[78] *See id.* at 120–21.

graph of the common article requires that the Detaining Power request on its own initiative, or accept the offer of, the services of a humanitarian organization such as the ICRC to assume the humanitarian functions performed by Protecting Powers under the Geneva Conventions. In this case only a humanitarian organization, rather than a neutral state, may be selected. The Detaining Power has freedom of choice as regards the organization: it need not accept the services offered by one organization if it prefers those of another. On the other hand, the paragraph resorts to binding language as far as the appointment of some (unspecified) organization is concerned. However, the binding nature of this language has not been borne out by the practice of states.[79] While article 5 of Protocol I reiterates that parties to the conflict shall accept without delay an offer which may be made by the ICRC or any other impartial organization to act as a substitute for a Protecting Power, it unequivocally adds that the functioning of such a substitute is subject to the consent of all parties to the conflict.

The Geneva Conventions stipulate that every party to the conflict may request an inquiry concerning any alleged violation of the Conventions' terms, but the parties must reach an agreement regarding the procedure for the inquiry.[80] In the absence of an agreement, it is recommended that the parties appoint an umpire who will decide upon the procedure to be followed.[81] Needless to say, as there is no clear legal obligation in the matter, a party which so desires may frustrate the inquiry. Article 90 of Protocol I lays the ground for the creation of a permanent International Fact-Finding Commission consisting of fifteen members serving in their personal capacity, provided that at least twenty High Contracting Parties have agreed in special declarations to accept the competence of this Commission on a reciprocal basis. The Commission is competent to inquire into any facts alleged to constitute a 'grave breach' as defined in the Geneva Conventions or Protocol I, or any other serious violation of those instruments, and to offer its good offices to restore an attitude of respect for those instruments. Unless otherwise agreed, inquiries are to be undertaken by a Chamber consisting of seven members, and the Commission must submit to the parties a report on the findings of fact of the Chamber, with such recommendations as it may deem appropriate.

The implementation of human rights is even less satisfactory for internal conflicts. All that article 3 common to the four Geneva Conventions provides is that an impartial humanitarian body, such as the ICRC,

---

[79] *See* Forsythe, *Who Guards the Guardians: Third Parties and the Law of Armed Conflict*, 70 Am. J. Int'l L. 41, 45–48 (1976).

[80] *See* art. 52, First Convention; art. 53, Second Convention; art. 132, Third Convention; art. 149, Fourth Convention.

[81] *Id.*

may offer its services to the parties to the conflict. The parties are not bound to accept these services,[82] and there is no place for the functioning of a Protecting Power. Article 18 of Protocol II also permits local relief organizations, *e.g.*, national Red Cross societies, to offer services for the peformance of traditional functions on behalf of the victims of the armed conflict. But, again, no obligation is imposed on the parties to accept those services and, in any case, the services to be rendered have nothing to do with supervision.

II. Teaching Suggestions

A.   A FULL COURSE

The teaching of a special course on the subject of human rights in armed conflict is not an easy undertaking if conducted without any basic knowledge on the part of the students of international law, the laws of war and human rights. As a matter of fact, even if students have already studied the last three subjects, it is desirable to refresh their memory by a brief résumé of fundamentals with an emphasis on the sources of international law (particularly, the relationship between customary and conventional law), the unique features of the law of war (especially, the quintessential distinction between combatants and civilians), and the singular nature of international human rights (as rights established directly for individuals without the interposition of the legal personality of the state).

It is preferable to incorporate into the course specific problems relating to concrete armed conflicts occurring at the time of teaching. This enables students to view legal norms not *in abstracto* but in their application to real events. Background materials should be selected from the abundant legal literature in the field. Of the many authorities cited in the footnotes and listed in the selected bibliography, it is recommended to use three treatises as general guides: 2 L. Oppenheim, *International Law* (H. Lauterpacht ed. 1952); G. Schwarzenberger, *The Law of Armed Conflict* (1968); and J. Stone, *Legal Controls of International Conflict* (1954). Other books and articles should be consulted in relation to specific themes of discussion. It is also useful to resort to the two principal military manuals: U.S. Army, Field Manual 27–10, *The Law of Land Warfare* (1956); and the U.K. War Office, *Manual of Military Law*, Pt. III: The Law of War on Land (1958).

The foremost pedagogic problem faced by instructors in the sphere of wartime human rights is the need to uphold the inarticulate major premise that such rights have a meaning not only in the classroom but also in the world of reality and, more specifically, in the battlefield.

---

[82] *See* Draper, *The Geneva Conventions of 1949*, 114 Recueil des Cours 63, 91 (1965).

Instructors usually have to contend with no less than five prevalent preconceptions which are, in fact, popular misconceptions. It is frequently maintained that: (i) In time of war there is no room for the application of legal norms, or, as Cicero put it, *silent enim leges inter arma*.[83] (ii) The laws of war, such as they are, are all in a 'chaotic' state.[84] (iii) In an era of 'total war', the basic distinction between civilians and combatants is more apparent than real.[85] (iv) With the threat of a thermonuclear disaster looming large on mankind's horizons, attempts to deal with the conduct of warfare are inconsequential. (v) Efforts to develop a workable *jus in bello* are inconsistent with the prohibition of war under the present *jus ad bellum*.

These are all psychological hurdles which must be surmounted if wartime human rights are to be taken seriously. It is necessary to impress upon students that:

(a) Far from resting dormant, international law is very active in the midst of arms. Unlike natural disasters, such as earthquakes or floods, war is a man-made cataclysm: it is a manifestation of human behavior.[86] All human behavior is subject to regulation by legal norms. The international community has always tried to check the basic human urge to brutalize war. In fact, historically, the laws of war were the most important component of international law.

(b) The laws of war, like all law, require constant revision: law reform is a perennial problem. Law almost always lags behind reality. After every major war, the modification of the laws of war appears to be more urgent than ever. Nevertheless, numerous provisions of international humanitarian law have survived many wars. In some respects, the first three Geneva Conventions are better entrenched today—more widely respected and more generally recognized—than quite a few legal instruments pertaining to the law of peace. They are actually viewed, by and large, as declaratory of customary international law.

(c) The distinction between civilians and combatants is still the cornerstone of the law of armed conflict. Even those who deny the existence of many juridical principles in this sphere are compelled to concede that civilians are entitled to some protection.[87] To be sure, the phenomenon of 'total war' creates profound problems affecting the

[83] Cicero, Pro Milone, IV, 11, at 16 (Loeb Classical Library ed.).

[84] This misconception is often perpetuated by well-intentioned jurists advocating the revision of the *lex lata*. See, e.g., Kunz, *The Chaotic Status of the Laws of War and the Urgent Necessity for their Revision*, 45 Am. J. Int'l L. 37 (1951).

[85] This thesis is developed in an erudite paper which, however, carries a partly valid point to exaggerated lengths. See Nurick, *The Distinction between Combatant and Noncombatant in the Law of War*, 39 Am. J. Int'l L. 680 (1945).

[86] See Tucker, *The Interpretation of War under Present International Law*, 4 Int'l L.Q. 11, 13 (1951).

[87] See Lauterpacht, *The Problem of the Revision of the Law of War*, 29 Brit. Y.B. Int'l L. 360, 364, 368 (1952).

protection of the civilian population. Some solutions have been found in Protocol I, though there still are many unresolved or poorly resolved questions.[88] The imperfections and shortcomings should not overshadow the tangible fact that, at least in part, the law is clear.

(d) The argument that thermonuclear devices, if used in a future world war, may bring about the annihilation of the human race commands efforts to ban such weapons. But the balance of terror, which has so far safeguarded humanity from a repetition on a larger scale of the experience of Hiroshima and Nagasaki, has not proved effective when it comes to the use of conventional weapons in conventional warfare. Our era is characterized by little wars in which much blood is shed and in which even Big Powers are occasionally embroiled. All in all, millions of human beings have lost their lives in a large number of conventional wars since the end of World War II. It is incongruous to overlook this present evil merely because of the much greater potential of the thermonuclear menace.

(e) The prohibition of war (except in cases of self-defense or collective security) under current international law does not mean that humanity can ignore with impunity its incidence. Even if war breaks out in flagrant violation of fundamental precepts, international law must cope with problems generated by such a violation. In point of fact, there has not been a single year of outright peace since the legal interdiction of war. While efforts 'to save succeeding generations from the scourge of war'[89] must continue, the present generation cannot escape from the reality of war.

B.   A MODULE WITHIN A GENERAL COURSE

When a special course on the subject of human rights in armed conflict is not offered, it is desirable to incorporate the topic as a two or three hour module within a broader course devoted to human rights in general. The brief time frame will not permit more than a short discussion covering some elements of the subject. Since no serious exposition of the topic is possible, it is recommended that instructors concentrate on a single issue encapsulating the main aspects of interaction between human rights and armed conflict. While one can conceive of several such issues, the one which may illuminate the salient points best is the protection of prisoners of war. Prisoners of war benefit from a number of human rights (the right to life, freedom from torture, etc.), yet are denied other fundamental freedoms which are taken for granted in peacetime (freedom from detention without trial, freedom from forced labour, etc.). The whole matter is now

---

[88] *See* Dinstein, *supra* note 18, at 273–75.
[89] U.N. Charter preamble, para. 1.

thoroughly covered by Levie's study, *Prisoners of War in International Armed Conflict*, consisting of one volume of text and another of source materials.

III. Syllabus

It is proposed that an elective (one term) course on human rights in armed conflict should cover the following elements.

1. Introduction A: international law.
   a. Definition.
   b. The interrelationship between customary and conventional international law.
   c. The distinction between the laws of peace and the laws of war.
2. Introduction B: the laws of war.
   a. The nature of war.
   b. The Hague Conventions, 1899–1907.
   c. The Geneva Conventions, 1949–1977.
   d. The distinction between combatants and civilians.
   e. Prohibited weapons and legitimate methods of warfare.
3. Introduction C: international human rights.
   a. The Universal Declaration of Human Rights, 1948.
   b. The [European] Convention for the Protection of Human Rights and Fundamental Freedoms, 1950.
   c. The International Covenant on Civil and Political Rights; the International Covenant on Economic, Social, and Cultural Rights, 1966.
   d. The American Convention on Human Rights, 1966.
   e. The unique nature of rights conferred directly on individuals under international law.
4. The suspension of ordinary (peacetime) human rights in time of armed conflict.
5. Human rights which are not subject to derogation in armed conflict.
6. International and internal armed conflicts.
   a. The distinction between inter-state and intra-state wars.
   b. Article 3 common to the Geneva Conventions.
   c. Protocol II.
   d. The special problems affecting the protection of human rights in the course of a civil war.
7. The meaning of international humanitarian law and its differentiation from the law of human rights.
8. The special (wartime) human rights of lawful combatants and the status of prisoners of war.

9. The special (wartime) human rights of civilians.
   a. The protection of the civilian population in general.
   b. The protection of enemy aliens.
   c. The protection of the civilian population in occupied territories.
10. The simultaneous coexistence of human rights and state rights.
11. Measures of supervision and implementation.
    a. State responsibility.
    b. Individual responsibility (war crimes).
    c. The Protecting Power.
    d. The ICRC.
    e. Fact-finding inquiries.
12. Conclusion.

IV. Minisyllabus

1. Introduction: the laws of war.
   a. The Hague Conventions, 1899–1907.
   b. The Geneva Conventions and Protocols, 1949–1977.
2. Protection of prisoners of war.
   a. Human rights protected.
   b. Fundamental freedoms denied.
   c. Implementation and supervision.

V. Bibliography

In addition to the sources referred to in the footnotes accompanying the text of this chapter, the following authorities should be consulted as background reading.

Books

G. Draper, The Red Cross Conventions (1958).
L. Greenspan, The Modern Law of Land Warfare (1959).
F. Kalshoven, The Law of Warfare (1973).
H. Levie, Prisoners of War in International Armed Conflict (Naval War College, 59 International Law Studies, 1978).
—— Documents on Prisoners of War (Naval War College, 60 International Law Studies, 1979).
L. Oppenheim, International Law (7th ed. H. Lauterpacht 1952).
E. Rosenblad, International Humanitarian Law of Armed Conflict (1979).
J. Stone, Legal Controls of International Conflict (1954).

Articles

Aldrich, *Remarks: Human Rights and Armed Conflict*, 67 Proc. Am. Soc'y, Int'l L. 141 (1973).

—— *New Life for the Laws of War*, 75 Am. J. Int'l L. 764 (1981).

Baxter, *So-Called 'Unprivileged Belligerency': Spies, Guerrillas, and Saboteurs*, 28 Brit. Y.B. Int'l L. 323 (1951).

—— *Ius in Bello Interno: The Present and Future Law*, in Law and Civil War in the Modern World 518 (J.N. Moore ed. 1974).

—— *Humanitarian Law or Humanitarian Politics? The 1974 Diplomatic Conference on Humanitarian Law*, 16 Harv. Int'l L.J. 1 (1975).

Bindschedler-Robert, *Problems of the Law of Armed Conflicts*, in 1 International Criminal law 295 (M. Bassiouni & V. Nanda eds. 1973).

Blix, *Remarks: Human Rights and Armed Conflict*, 67 Proc. Am. Soc'y Int'l L. 149 (1973).

Burwell, *Civilian Protection in Modern Warfare: A Critical Analysis of the Geneva Civilian Convention of 1949*, 14 Va. J. Int'l L. 123 (1973).

Dinstein, *Another Step in Codifying the Laws of War*, 28 Y.B. World Aff. 278 (1974).

—— *The International Law of Inter-State Wars and Human Rights*, 7 Isr. Y.B. on Human Rights 139 (1977).

Draper, *The Relationship between the Human Rights Regime and the Law of Armed Conflicts*, 1 Isr. Y.B. on Human Rights 191 (1971).

—— *The Status of Combatants and the Question of Guerilla Warfare*, 45 Brit. Y.B. Int'l L. 173 (1971).

Forsythe, *The 1974 Diplomatic Conference on Humanitarian Law: Some Observations*, 69 Am. J. Int'l L. 77 (1975).

Green, *The Geneva Humanitarian Law Conference 1975*, 13 Can. Y.B. Int'l L. 295 (1975).

—— *Humanitarian Law and the Man in the Field*, 14 Can. Y.B. Int'l L. 96 (1976).

—— *The New Law of Armed Conflict*, 15 Can. Y.B. Int'l L. 3 (1977).

—— *Derogation of Human Rights in Emergency Situations*, 16 Can. Y.B. Int'l L. 92 (1978). ←

Greenspan, *The Protection of Human Rights in Time of Warfare*, 1 Isr. Y.B. on Human Rights 228 (1971).

Gutteridge, *The Geneva Conventions of 1949*, 26 Brit. Y.B. Int'l L. 294 (1949).

Krafft, *The Present Position of the Red Cross Geneva Conventions*, 37 Trans. Grotius Soc'y 131 (1951).

Kunz, *The Geneva Conventions of August 12, 1949*, in Law and Politics in the World Community 279, 368, (G. Lipsky ed. 1953).

Pictet, *The New Geneva Conventions for the Protection of War*

Victims, 45 Am. J. Int'l L. 462 (1951).

Rubin, *The Status of Rebels under the Geneva Conventions of 1949*, 21 Int'l & Comp. L.Q. 472 (1972).

Schwarzenberger, *Human Rights and Guerrilla Warfare*, 1 Isr. Y.B. on Human Rights 246 (1971).

—— *The Law of Armed Conflict: A Civilized Interlude?*, 28 Y.B. World Aff. 293 (1974).

Smith, *The Geneva Prisoner of War Convention: An Appraisal*, 42 N.Y.U. L. Rev. 880 (1967).

Von Glahn, *The Protection of Human Rights in Time of Armed Conflicts*, 1 Isr. Y.B. on Human Rights 208 (1971).

Yingling & Ginnane, *The Geneva Conventions of 1949*, 46 Am. J. Int'l. L. 393 (1952).

*   *   *

Bibliography of International Humanitarian Law Applicable in Armed Conflicts (T. Huynh ed. 1980).

Vincent-Daviss, *Human Rights Law: A Research Guide to the Literature—Part II: International Protection of Refugees, and Humanitarian Law*, 14 N.Y.U. J. Int'l L. & Pol. 487, 517 (1981).

VI. Minibibliography

Aldrich, *New Life for the Laws of War*, 75 Am. J. Int'l L. 764 (1981).

Dinstein, *Human Rights in Armed Conflict: International Humanitarian Law*, in this volume.

H. Levie, *Prisoners of War in International Armed Conflict* (Naval War College, 59 International Law Studies, 1978).

—— *Documents on Prisoners of War* (Naval War College, 60 International Law Studies, 1979).

Chapter 10

Human Rights: Their Implementation and Supervision by the United Nations[*]

Louis B. Sohn

International protection of human rights implies at least two differ-ent processes. In the first place, it is necessary to achieve an inter-national agreement on the human rights standards to be applied throughout the world (or in a particular region); in the second place, methods of implementation and supervision need to be developed.

The United Nations has been successful in constantly broadening the number and increasing the depth of international instruments containing general and specific international human rights standards. By 1978 some fifty such instruments had been adopted by the United Nations and its specialized agencies,[1] and several additional ones have been adopted since or are in various stages of completion. In addition, parallel instruments on particular human rights have been adopted by regional organizations in Europe, the Americas, and Africa.[2] Similar instruments are being prepared by the League of Arab States.[3]

But standards are not enough. One cannot expect an automatic respect of these standards by all governments, authorities, public and private entities, and, most importantly, individuals. In fact most vio-lations of human rights are committed by individuals, whether acting in their official or private capacity. It is important, therefore, to make sure, as far as possible, that human rights are actually respected by all concerned. In order to achieve this result, most of the instruments mentioned above provide for measures of implementation and super-vision. Some measures are national, others are international.

I. Legal and Policy Considerations

A. NATIONAL MEASURES OF IMPLEMENTATION AND SUPERVISION

In principle, most international agreements on human rights leave

---

[*] © Louis B. Sohn 1983.

[1] For their texts, *see* United Nations, Human Rights: A Compilation of International Instru-ments, U.N. Doc. ST/HR/1/Rev. 2 (1978) [hereinafter cited as U.N. Compilation]. Some of these documents are discussed in chs. 4, 5, 6, 7, & 8 *supra*.

[2] Some of these documents are discussed in chs. 12 & 13 *infra*. For the African Charter on Human Rights and Peoples' Rights, *see* Rev. Int'l Comm'n Jurists 76–86 (No. 27, Dec. 1981).

[3] *See, e.g.,* U.N. Doc. E/CN.4/1229, at 29 (1976).

the question of implementation to states parties, which are supposed to enact the necessary legislative and other measures.

For instance, article 2 of the International Covenant on Civil and Political Rights[4] imposes on states parties several obligations of this kind. First, if a state party does not already have sufficient legislative or other measures for the implementation of the Political Covenant in its domestic law, it must take the necessary steps to adopt such measures in order to give effect to the rights recognized therein. Second, a state party has the duty to ensure that any person whose rights or freedoms are violated shall have an effective remedy, even when the violation has been committed by a government official. Third, while a state party has the option to make these remedies available through judicial, administrative, legislative, or other competent authorities, it shall provide a judicial remedy as soon as possible. Fourth, a state party shall ensure that the competent authorities shall enforce such remedies when granted.

As soon as the Political Covenant came into effect states parties were asked, pursuant to article 40 of that treaty, to submit reports on the measures they had adopted to give effect to their obligations under Article 2. These reports have been carefully scrutinized by the Human Rights Committee which is in charge of supervision of the implementation of the Political Covenant. For instance, the government of Denmark reported that before ratifying the Covenant it introduced the necessary legislation, but where it was not possible at that time to remove the discrepancies between the Political Covenant and Danish legislation, it had submitted appropriate reservations when ratifying the Covenant. It also noted that in Denmark there is a rule allowing the administrative authorities to interpret domestic law in such a way as to comply to the maximum extent possible with existing treaty obligations. Similarly, the Danish courts, when faced with a discrepancy between the Political Covenant and subsequent Danish legislation, apply the presumption that it has not been the intention of the Parliament to pass legislation contrary to Denmark's international obligations. The Danish representative before the Human Rights Committee pointed out that it was possible to invoke before a court the provisions of a treaty that were relevant to the case and that this has been done on some occasions. Nevertheless, the Human Rights Committee raised various questions about the implications of these general Danish statements and requested further information on several specific issues where some discrepancies between the Political Covenant and the provisions of Danish legislation were detected by some members of the Committee.[5]

[4] G. A. Res. 2200, U.N. GAOR, Supp. (No. 16) 52, U.N. Doc. A/6316 (1966).
[5] Report of the Human Rights Committee, 33 U.N. GAOR, Supp. (No. 40) 16–19, U.N. Doc. A/33/40 (1978).

Similarly, the Constitution of the International Labour Organisation (ILO)[6] contains both an obligation of member states to bring each convention adopted by the International Labour Conference before the competent authority for the enactment of legislation or other action and an obligation to report on the measures taken to give effect to the provisions of the conventions which they have ratified. The implementation of these obligations is carefully scrutinized not only by the Committee of Experts on the Application of Conventions and Recommendations but also by a Committee on the Application of Conventions and Recommendations, which is set up by the International Labour Conference at each session and which is a more political body, composed of representatives of governments and of organizations of employers and workers. In many cases the observations of these two Committees have led to important changes in national legislation.[7]

Some international human rights instruments are rather detailed with respect to national measures to be taken with respect to the ratified convention. Thus, the International Convention on the Elimination of All Forms of Racial Discrimination[8] obliges each state party: to 'take effective measures to review governmental, national and local policies, and to amend, rescind or nullify any laws and regulations which have the effect of creating or perpetuating racial discrimination wherever it exists';[9] and to 'prohibit and bring to an end, by all appropriate means, including legislation as required by circumstances, racial discrimination by any persons, group or organization'.[10] In addition, any state party which accepts the jurisdiction of the Committee on the Elimination of Racial Discrimination to receive communications from individuals or groups of individuals,[11] may establish or indicate a domestic body to which petitions must be submitted prior to their reference to the Committee.[12] Thus, in addition to the exhaustion of other local remedies, the individual or group concerned would be required to try to obtain satisfaction from the domestic body, and only in the event of failure to obtain

---

[6] 62 Stat. 3485, T.I.A.S. No. 1868, 15 U.N.T.S. 35; *amended* 7 U.S.T. 245, T.I.A.S. No. 3500, 191 U.N.T.S. 143 (1953); 14 U.S.T. 1039, T.I.A.S. No. 5401, 466 U.N.T.S. 323 (1962); 25 U.S.T. 3253, T.I.A.S. No. 7987 (1972).

[7] ILO Const. arts. 19(5) & 22. For ILO practice, *see, e.g.*, International Labour Office, The Impact of International Labour Conventions and Recommendations 37–56 (1976); N. Valticos, International Labour Law 234–38, 240–45 (1979). *See also* E. Landy, The Effectiveness of International Supervision: Thirty Years of ILO Experience (1967) [hereinafter cited as Landy]; ch. 7 *supra*.

[8] 660 U.N.T.S. 195, *reprinted in* U.N. Compilation, *supra* note 1, at 24 (hereinafter cited as Racial Discrimination Convention).

[9] *Id*. art. 2(c).

[10] *Id*. art. 2(d).

[11] *Id*. art. 14(1).

[12] *Id*. art. 14(2).

such satisfaction would it be permissible to move into the international plane.[13]

A seminar organized by the United Nations in Geneva in 1978 considered reports on various national and local institutions for the promotion and protection of human rights, and recommended a set of guidelines for the functioning and structure of such institutions. For instance, the seminar recommended that such institutions: should be authorized to receive complaints from individuals and groups concerning human rights violations; should possess independent factfinding facilities for the investigation of complaints alleging deprivations of human rights; and should provide appropriate remedies through conciliation or other means of redress. In particular, the seminar noted that the ombudsman system is being increasingly adopted in developing countries, with modifications to suit local needs. It was pointed out that an ombudsman is a most useful official, often selected by and answerable only to the national parliament; that he or she usually has extensive powers to investigate complaints of individuals whose rights may have been infringed by a public authority; and that he or she may even be authorized to institute criminal proceedings against public officials for breach or abuse of governmental functions entrusted to them. Similar officials function in other countries under various names, such as Procurator, Protector of the People, or Mediator, or such investigatory powers are vested in a national committee on human rights or civil rights.[14]

While national means of implementation are often commanded by international instruments, they also have another role to play on the international plane. Several international instruments require exhaustion of local remedies before a complaint, petition, or communication can be submitted to an international institution. Only when there are no effective local remedies or they are unreasonably prolonged can a complainant approach an international institution without exhausting such remedies.[15]

[13] *Id.* art. 14(5).

[14] United Nations, Seminar on National and Local Institutions for the Promotion and Protection of Human Rights, Geneva, 18–29 Sept. 1978, reported in U.N. Doc. ST/HR/SER.A/2 (1978). *See also* United Nations, Seminar on the Effective Realization of Civil and Political Rights at the National Level, Kingston, Jamaica, 25 Apr.–8 May 1967, U.N. Doc. ST/TAO/HR/29 (1967).

[15] For a study of the subject of exhaustion of local remedies by the International Law Commission, *see* Report of the International Law Commission, 32 U.N. GAOR, Supp. (No. 10) 67–116, U.N. Doc. A/32/10 (1977), *reprinted in* [1977] 2(2) Y.B. Int'l L. Comm'n 67–116, U.N. Doc. A/CN.4/Ser.A/1977/Add.1 (Part 2). *See also* Law, The Local Remedies Rule in International Law (1961); Hoesler, The Exhaustion of Local Remedies in the Case Law of International Courts and Tribunals (1968); Amerasinghe, *The Rule of Exhaustion of Local Remedies in the Framework of International Systems for the Protection of Human Rights*, 28 Zeischrift für ausländisches öffentlisches Recht und Völkerrecht 257 (1968); Chappez, La règle de l' epuisement des voies de recours internes (1972); Adede, *A Survey of Treaty Provisions on the Rule of Exhaustion of Local Remedies*, 18 Harv. Int'l L. J. 1 (1977).

B. INTERNATIONAL MEASURES OF IMPLEMENTATION AND SUPERVISION

The Charter of the United Nations requires the United Nations not only to promote human rights and their universal respect, but also to promote their observance.[16] For this purpose, the Economic and Social Council was empowered by the Charter to set up a commission for the protection of human rights,[17] and in fact established a Commission on Human Rights in 1946 in one of its first decisions.[18] The Commission, which is composed of representatives of member states, in turn established a group of experts to assist it, the Sub-Commission on the Prevention of Discrimination and Protection of Minorities.[19] A separate Commission on the Status of Women was established simultaneously to deal with problems of sex discrimination and the rights of women.[20] In addition, many special committees have been established by the United Nations to deal with special problems (such as *apartheid* or the violations of human rights in Chile or in Israeli-occupied territories) or with the implementation of particular conventions (*e.g.*, the Committee on the Elimination of Racial Discrimination). Various international supervisory organs have also been established by specialized agencies and regional organizations.[21] Some roles may also be played in international supervision by judicial organs such as the International Court of Justice, the European Court of Human Rights, and the Inter-American Court of Human Rights.[22]

Shifting from organs of supervision to international supervisory procedures, there seem to be three main methods of securing universal observance of human rights: various systems of periodic reports, procedures for dealing with complaints by one state against another state, and procedures for the consideration of communications by individuals and private organizations (national and international).

1. *Periodic Reporting Systems*

Article 64 of the U.N. Charter provides that the Economic and Social Council may make arrangements with the members of the

[16] U.N. Charter arts. 1(3), 55(c), & 62(2).

[17] *Id*. art. 68.

[18] E.S.C. Res. 5(I), 1 U.N. ESCOR 163 (1946).

[19] Commission on Human Rights, Report on the First Session, 4 U.N. ESCOR, Supp. (No. 3) 4, U.N. Doc. E/259 (1947).

[20] At first the Economic and Social Council established a Sub-Commission on the Status of Women, by Res. 5(I), *supra* note 18; but soon, by Res. 11(II), the Council changed that Sub-Commission to a full Commission. *See* 2 U.N. ESCOR 405 (1946).

[21] With respect to the ILO and the inter-American and European organizations, *see* ch. 7 *supra* and chs. 12 & 13 *infra* respectively. Concerning the Conciliation and Good Offices Commission established by UNESCO in 1962 to implement the Convention against Discrimination in Education, *see* U.N. Compilation, *supra* note 1, at 37.

[22] The last two courts are considered in chs. 12 & 13, respectively *infra*; the treaties providing for a reference to the International Court of Justice are discussed in subsection B.2.a *infra*.

United Nations or with the specialized agencies 'to obtain reports on the steps taken to give effect to its own recommendations and to recommendations on matters falling within its competence made by the General Assembly'. On October 31, 1947, the General Assembly called upon all member states 'to carry out all recommendations of the General Assembly passed on economic and social matters', and recommended that:

in fulfilment of Article 64 of the Charter of the United Nations the Secretary-General report annually to the Economic and Social Council and that the latter report to the General Assembly on steps taken by the Member Governments to give effect to the recommendations of the Economic and Social Council as well as to the recommendations made by the General Assembly on matters falling within the Council's competence.[23]

Various steps were taken by the Economic and Social Council to implement this resolution, but the general biennial reporting procedure was discontinued in 1952 and the Council decided instead 'to include in the future, wherever practicable, in its resolutions specific indications of the timing of the report expected from governments in implementation of the resolutions concerned'.[24]

In 1953 the United States suggested that, taking into consideration the obligations under articles 55 and 56 of the Charter, 'each Member [should] transmit each year to the Secretary-General a report on developments and achievements in the field of human rights in its country'.[25] After considerable discussion, the Commission on Human Rights decided in 1956 to recommend to the Economic and Social Council that it request 'each State Member of the United Nations and of the specialized agencies to transmit annually to the Secretary-General a report describing developments and progress achieved in the field of human rights and measures taken to safeguard human liberty' in its territories dealing with the rights enumerated in the Universal Declaration of Human Rights[26] and with the right of peoples to self-determination.[27] The Council approved this recommendation, but decided that annual reports would impose too great a burden upon the governments and the U.N. Secretariat and that, therefore, they should be transmitted 'every three years', describing developments and the progress achieved during the preceding three years.[28] In 1965 the Council approved a staggered three-year system of reporting, request-

[23] G.A. Res. 119, U.N. Doc. A/519, at 24–25 (1947).
[24] 3 Repertory of United Nations Practice 388–91 (1955); 14 U.N. ESCOR, Supp. (No. 1) 48–49, U.N. Doc. E/2332 (1952).
[25] U.N. Doc. E/CN.4/L.266 (1953).
[26] G.A. Res. 217A, U.N. Doc. A/810, at 71 (1948).
[27] 22 U.N. ESCOR, Supp. (No. 3) 4, U.N. Doc. E/2844 (1956).
[28] E.S.C. Res. 624B, 22 U.N. ESCOR, Supp. (No. 1) 12, U.N. Doc. E/2929 (1956).

ing states to report in the first year of each cycle on civil and political rights, in the second year on economic and social rights, and in the third year on freedom of information.[29] In 1971, the length of the cycle was increased to six years, the three reports being submitted at two-year intervals rather than annually.[30]

In its consideration of the periodic reports, the Commission on Human Rights had to proceed slowly, as some states considered that the reporting procedure violated the Charter's prohibition of intervention in matters which are essentially within the domestic jurisdiction of a state,[31] while others simply did not present any reports. The Commission has tried a variety of procedures and has limited its conclusions to general statements. Nevertheless, the Commission and its *Ad Hoc* Committee on Periodic Reports over the years have developed considerable expertise in this field and have found what are the positive functions and the limits of this process.[32]

In addition to these general reports, various United Nations resolutions provide for reports on special subjects. For instance, the Recommendations of the General Assembly on Consent to Marriage, Minimum Age for Marriage and Registration of Marriages asked Member States to report to the Commission on the Status of Women at the end of three years, and thereafter at intervals of five years, on their law and practice with regard to the matters dealt with in the Recommendations; in particular they were to report on 'the extent to which effect has been given or is proposed to be given to the provisions of the Recommendation and such modifications as have been found or may be found necessary in adapting or applying it'.[33]

Reporting requirements are also contained in several conventions on human rights. For instance, the Supplementary Convention on the Abolition of Slavery, the Slave Trade, and Institutions and Practices Similar to Slavery obliges the parties to the Convention 'to communicate to the Secretary-General of the United Nations copies of any laws, regulations and administrative measures enacted or put into effect to implement the provisions of this Convention'; and this documentation is to be used by the Economic and Social Council as a basis for further recommendations on this subject.[34]

---

[29] E.S.C. Res. 1074C, 39 U.N. ESCOR, Supp. (No. 1) 24, para. 6, U.N. Doc. E/4117 (1965).

[30] E.S.C. Res. 1596, 50 U.N. ESCOR, Supp. (No. 1) 20, U.N. Doc. E/5044 (1971).

[31] U.N. Charter art. 2(7).

[32] For a summary of the work of the Commission in this area, *see* Sohn, *A Short History of UN Documents on Human Rights*, in Commision to Study the Organization of Peace, The United Nations and Human Rights 39, 74–94 (1968); United Nations, United Nations Action in the Field of Human Rights, U.N. Doc. ST/HR/2/Rev.6, at 169–71 (1980) [hereinafter cited as U.N. Action].

[33] G.A. Res. 2018, 20 U.N. GAOR, Supp. (No. 14) 36–37, U.N. Doc. A/6014 (1965).

[34] Art. 8, 18 U.S.T. 3201, T.I.A.S. No. 6418, 266 U.N.T.S. 3.

The International Convention on the Elimination of All Forms of Racial Discrimination provides a more elaborate system of reporting. The states parties undertake to submit to the U.N. Secretary-General for consideration by the Committee on the Elimination of Racial Discrimination 'a report on the legislative, judicial, administrative or other measures which they have adopted and which give effect to the provisions of this Convention: (*a*) within one year after the entry into force of the Convention for the State concerned; and (*b*) thereafter every two years and whenever the Committee so requests'.[35] The Convention provides further that the Committee 'may make suggestions and general recommendations based on the examination of the reports and information received from the States Parties'; and that these 'suggestions and general recommendations shall be reported to the General Assembly together with comments, if any, from States Parties'.[36]

Detailed provisions on reporting are contained as well in the two international covenants. Under the International Covenant on Economic, Social and Cultural Rights,[37] the states parties undertake to submit to the Economic and Social Council 'reports on the measures which they have adopted and the progress made in achieving the observance of the rights recognized' in that Covenant.[38] These reports 'may indicate factors and difficulties affecting the degree of fulfilment of obligations' under the Economic Covenant.[39] When the Economic Covenant entered into force, the Economic and Social Council established a system of biennial reports for various parts of the Covenant, and decided to establish a sessional working group of the Council to assist it in the consideration of the reports.[40] The Council also decided that the states parties to the Economic Covenant will be henceforth excused from submitting, with respect to issues covered by that Covenant, parallel reports under the 1965 reporting system.[41] At the same time, the Council decided to rely on the cooperation of the specialized agencies in the implementation of the reporting procedure, avoiding thereby possible duplication of efforts in this area.[42]

---

[35] Racial Discrimination Convention, art. 9(1).
[36] *Id*. art 9(2).
[37] G.A. Res. 2200, U.N. GAOR, Supp. (No. 16) 49, U.N. Doc. A/6316 (1966).
[38] *Id*. art. 16.
[39] *Id*. art. 17.
[40] E.S.C. Res. 1988, 60 U.N. ESCOR, Supp. (No. 1) 11, U.N. Doc. E/5850 (1976); E.S.C. Dec. 1978/10, U.N. Doc. E/DEC/1978/6–40, at 5 (1978); 33 U.N. GAOR, Supp. (No. 3) 34–36, U.N. Doc. A/33/3 (1978).
[41] E.S.C. Res. 1988, *supra* note 40, para. 7.
[42] *Id*., para. 6. For the reports of the International Labour Organisation, *see, e.g.*, U.N. Docs. E/1978/27 (1978); E/1979/33 (1979); E/1980/35 (1980).

A different system exists under the Political Covenant. The states parties to that Covenant undertake to submit 'reports on the measures they have adopted which give effect to the rights recognized [therein] and on the progress made in the enjoyment of those rights'.[43] These reports are to indicate the factors and difficulties, if any, affecting the implementation of the Political Covenant.[44] They are considered by a special Human Rights Committee, which can make general comments thereon to the states parties and can transmit them also to the Economic and Social Council.[45] Once this system of reporting came into effect, the Economic and Social Council decided to exempt states parties to the Political Covenant from submitting reports on subjects covered by that Covenant under the 1965 reporting system.[46] Finally, the Economic and Social Council decided in 1981 to terminate the 1965 reporting system.[47]

As a result of the decisions taken by the Economic and Social Council in 1976, 1978, and 1981 there are now two basic reporting systems under the international covenants. In addition there are various reporting systems relating to particular conventions or declarations, some dealing with civil and political rights, others dealing with economic, social, and cultural rights.

It would seem desirable to simplify these reporting systems and to consolidate them into one or two overall systems. Until the international covenants can be amended, it will be difficult to combine their two parallel, but slightly different, reporting systems. It might be more feasible to consolidate all the reporting in the economic, social, and cultural field in the new sessional working group of the Economic and Social Council. As the reporting system for non-parties to the Economic Covenant on these subjects is the creature of the Council, and as the Council has already changed that system several times, it could authorize the sessional working group under the Covenant to also consider reports from non-parties to the Covenant. Consequently, the Economic and Social Council would have its own sphere of action in the human rights field, encompassing all the economic, social, and cultural rights, and would be able to bring into this area the perspective gained from its work on other aspects of these fields; and all the reports on economic, social, and cultural rights would be given a uniform treatment, regardless of whether or not the

---

[43] Political Covenant, art. 40(1).

[44] *Id.* art. 40(2).

[45] *Id.* art. 40(2), 40(3), 40(4).

[46] E.S.C. Res. 1978/20, U.N. Doc. E/RES/1978/235, at 37 (1978); 33 U.N. GAOR, Supp. (No. 3) 65–66, 68, U.N. Doc. A/33/3 (1978).

[47] 18 U.N. Chronicle (No. 7) 21 (1981).

reporting state is a party to the Economic Covenant. To enable the
sessional working group to accomplish this enlarged task, it may be
necessary to provide for pre-sessional meetings of that group or even
for intersessional meetings of sufficient duration.

It might be more difficult to streamline the system for civil and
political rights, as the Human Rights Committee under the Political
Covenant is an autonomous body established by the states parties to
that Covenant. But its expenses are paid by the United Nations and its
staff is provided by the U.N. Secretariat.[48] Consequently, it might be
possible for the Economic and Social Council to propose to the states
parties to the Political Covenant that they authorize the Committee to
consider also reports from states non-parties dealing with subjects
covered by the Political Covenant. The rules of the Committee already
provide that a representative of a state party may be present at the
meetings of the Committee at which the reports of that state are being
examined.[49] The Committee could be encouraged to revise its rules to
enable states non-parties to participate in the meetings on the same
terms as those provided for states parties, *i.e.*, appear when their
reports are being examined.

While theoretically the substance of reports based on the covenants
may differ from that of the reports based on other human rights
instruments, these differences are not crucial.

As far as various U.N. declarations are concerned, it would be easy
for the Economic and Social Council to transfer the reporting functions to its sessional working group on the Economic Covenant, or to
encourage the consideration of reports which pertain to civil and
political rights by the Human Rights Committee. The situation is more
difficult with respect to the reporting systems under various human
rights conventions. Nevertheless, it should be possible for the Economic and Social Council to recommend to the parties to these conventions that they transfer the consideration of the reports under these
conventions to the two principal bodies mentioned above. In some
cases the parties may be willing to do this by an informal decision; in
other cases a protocol to a particular convention may be necessary. By
using an analogy to article 37 of the Statute of the International Court
of Justice,[50] one might even envisage the possibility of drafting a
general protocol to the effect that whenever a convention provides for

---

[48] Political Covenant, arts. 35 & 36.
[49] Rule 68, 32 U.N. GAOR, Supp. (No. 44) 48, 60, U.N. Doc. A/32/44 (1977).
[50] Arts. 37 provides:
    Whenever a treaty or convention in force provides for reference of a matter to a tribunal to
    have been instituted by the League of Nations, or to the Permanent Court of International
    Justice, the matter shall, as between the parties to the present Statute, be referred to the
    International Court of Justice.

a system of reporting on human rights, the reports under that convention shall be submitted to the appropriate system of reporting established under the international covenants.

A step of a similar character has been taken in the International Convention on the Suppression and Punishment of the Crime of *Apartheid*,[51] which provides for reports on the legislative, judicial, administrative, or other measures that the parties to the Convention have adopted and that give effect to its provisions.[52] These reports are to be submitted to a group consisting of three members of the Commission on Human Rights to be appointed by its Chairman from among those members who are representatives of states parties to the *Apartheid* Convention.[53]

It should be noted, finally, that reporting systems exist also in other international organizations dealing with human rights. The most sophisticated system exists in the International Labour Organisation, which uses its system to effectively monitor the implementation of human rights conventions.[54]

2. Procedures for Dealing with Inter-State Complaints

a. *Reference to International Court of Justice.* A few conventions on human rights provide for the submission of disputes between the parties to the International Court of Justice. For instance, according to the Convention on the Prevention and Punishment of the Crime of Genocide[55] disputes between the parties relating to the interpretation, application, or fulfilment of that Convention 'shall be submitted to the International Court of Justice at the request of any of the parties to the dispute'.[56] Less clearly, some conventions provide that any such dispute 'which is not settled by negotiation shall be referred to the International Court of Justice for decision unless the Contracting

---

[51] G.A. Res. 3068, 28 U.N. GAOR, Supp. (No. 30) 75, U.N. Doc. A/9030 (1973).

[52] *Id*. art. 7.

[53] *Id*. art. 9(1). This article provides also for other appointments if there are not enough representatives of states parties on the Commission on Human Rights. *Id*. art. 9(2).

[54] *See* Landy, *supra* note 7, at 15–211. *See also* ch. 7 *supra*.

[55] 78 U.N.T.S. 277, *reprinted in* U.N. Compilation, *supra* note 1, at 45.

[56] *Id*. art 9. Similar provisions are contained in: art. 22, Convention for the Suppression of the Traffic in Persons and of the Exploitation of the Prostitution of Others, 96 U.N.T.S. 271, *reprinted in* U.N. Compilation, *supra* note 1, at 60; art. 38, Convention relating to the Status of Refugees, 189 U.N.T.S. 137, *reprinted in* U.N. Compilation, *supra* note 1, at 86; art. 10, Supplementary Convention on the Abolition of Slavery, *supra* note 34; art. 10, Convention on the Nationality of Married Women, 309 U.N.T.S. 65, *reprinted in* U.N. Compilation, *supra* note 1, at 75; art. 34, Convention relating to the Status of Stateless Persons, 360 U.N.T.S. 117, *reprinted in* U.N. Compilation, *supra* note 1, at 80; art. 8, Convention against Discrimination in Education, 429 U.N.T.S. 93, *reprinted in* U.N. Compilation, *supra* note 1, at 35; art. 14, Convention on the Reduction of Statelessness, U.N. Doc. A/CONF. 9/15 (1961), *reprinted in* U.N. Compilation, *supra* note 1, at 76; art. 4, Protocol relating to the Status of Refugees, 19 U.S.T. 6223, T.I.A.S. No. 6577, 606 U.N.T.S. 267.

Parties agree to another mode of settlement'.[57] It is probably understood, however, that also in this case the dispute can be submitted to the International Court of Justice at the request of any of the parties. On the other hand, the consent of all the parties to the dispute seems to be required when a convention provides that any dispute concerning its interpretation or application 'shall, at the request of all the parties to the dispute, be referred to the International Court of Justice for decision, unless the parties agree to another mode of settlement'.[58]

A more elaborate procedure for dealing with inter-state complaints operates within the framework of the International Labour Organisation. Its constitution, as revised in 1946, gives each member of the ILO the right to file a complaint that another member is not effectively observing an international labour convention which both members have ratified.[59] The Governing Body of the ILO may refer the complaint to a Commission of Inquiry,[60] which prepares a report embodying its findings on questions of fact as well as its recommendations on the steps to be taken to meet the complaint.[61] A member which does not accept the report may refer the matter to the International Court of Justice[62] which may affirm, vary, or reverse any of the findings or recommendations of the Commission of Inquiry.[63] If a member fails to carry out the recommendations of the Commission or of the Court, the Governing Body may recommend to the International Labour Conference 'such action as it may deem wise and expedient to secure compliance therewith'.[64] In addition, the ILO Constitution provides that any question or dispute relating to the interpretation of any convention concluded in pursuance to the provisions of that constitution shall be referred for decision to the International Court of Justice.[65] While several cases have been submitted to Commissions of Inquiry, no case has yet been referred to the International Court of Justice.[66]

---

[57] Art. 5, Convention on the International Right of Correction, 435 U.N.T.S. 191, *reprinted in* U.N. Compilation, *supra* note 1, at 98. A similar provision can be found in art. 9, Convention on the Political Rights of Women, 27 U.S.T. 1909, T.I.A.S. No. 8289, 193 U.N.T.S. 135.

[58] Art. 8, Convention on Consent to Marriage, Minimum Age for Marriage and Registration of Marriages, 521 U.N.T.S. 231, *reprinted in* U.N. Compilation, *supra* note 1, at 112.

[59] ILO Const. art. 26(1).

[60] *Id.* art. 26(3).

[61] *Id.* art. 28.

[62] *Id.* art. 29(2).

[63] *Id.* art. 32.

[64] *Id.* art. 33.

[65] *Id.* art. 37(1).

[66] *See, e.g.*, report of the complaint filed by Ghana against Portugal, 45 (No. 2) ILO O. Bull. (Supp. 2) (1962); report of the complaint filed by Portugal against Liberia, 46 (No. 2) ILO O. Bull. (Supp. 2) (1963).

b. *References to the European and Inter-American Courts of Human Rights.* The [European] Convention for the Protection of Human Rights and Fundamental Freedoms[67] contains an optional clause[68] under which a state party may recognize as compulsory the jurisdiction of the European Court of Human Rights with respect to all matters concerning the interpretation and application of the European Convention. In addition, any state party may refer to the European Commission of Human Rights any alleged breach of the provisions of the European Convention by another state party.[69] If a state has accepted the jurisdiction of the European Court of Human Rights, a case can be brought before the Court by either the European Commission or one of the states concerned (the state which referred the case to the Commission, the state against which a complaint has been lodged before the Commission, or the state whose national is alleged to be a victim). While more than ten inter-state cases have been considered by the Commission, only one inter-state case—a complaint by Ireland against the United Kingdom concerning alleged violations of the European Convention which occurred in Northern Ireland—has been submitted to the European Court of Human Rights.[70]

The American Convention on Human Rights[71] also contains an optional clause under which a state party may accept the jurisdiction of the Inter-American Court of Human Rights with respect to all matters relating to the interpretation or application of that Convention.[72] Once this jurisdiction has been accepted by a state party, a case can be submitted to the Inter-American Court either by the Inter-American Commission on Human Rights or by another state party. In addition the Court has broad jurisdiction to render advisory opinions on request of any state member of the Organization of American States or an organ of that Organization.[73]

c. *Fact-Finding and Conciliation.* The UNESCO Convention against Discrimination in Education provides for reference of inter-state disputes about its interpretation or application to the International Court of Justice, 'failing other means of settling the dispute'.[74] In 1962 the

---

[67] 213 U.N.T.S. 221, *reprinted in* Basic Documents on Human Rights 242 (2d ed. I. Brownlie 1981) [hereinafter cited as Brownlie].

[68] *Id.* art. 46.

[69] *Id.* art. 24.

[70] For further discussion of these European cases, *see* ch. 13 *infra*.

[71] O.A.S. T.S. No. 36, *reprinted in* Brownlie, *supra* note 67, at 391.

[72] *Id.* art. 62. Under art. 62, other modalities of acceptance of jurisdiction are also possible.

[73] For further discussion of the Inter-American Court of Human Rights and the Inter-American Commission on Human Rights, *see* ch. 12 *infra*. On the Inter-American Court, *see generally* Buergenthal, *The Inter-American Court of Human Rights*, 76 Am. J. Int'l L. 231 (1982).

[74] Art. 8.

Twelfth General Conference of UNESCO decided to supplement this provision by a protocol instituting an eleven-member Conciliation and Good Offices Commission which was to be responsible for seeking an amicable settlement of disputes relating to the application or interpretation of the Convention against Discrimination in Education.[75] If a state party considers that another state party is not giving effect to a provision of the Convention, and the matter cannot be adjusted by bilateral negotiations, either state has the right to refer the matter to the Commission.[76] The Commission will ascertain the facts and make available its good offices to the states concerned.[77] The Commission may recommend that the Executive Board (or, in some circumstances, the General Conference) of UNESCO request the International Court of Justice to give an advisory opinion on any legal question connected with a matter laid before the Commission.[78] If an amicable solution is not reached 'on the basis of respect for the Convention',[79] the Commission shall draw up a report on the facts and indicate the recommendations which it made with a view to conciliation.[80]

The Racial Discrimination Convention allows a state party which considers that another state party is not giving effect thereto to bring the matter to the attention of the eighteen-member Committee on the Elimination of Racial Discrimination established under that Convention.[81] After certain preliminary proceedings, the Chairman of the Committee shall, with the unanimous consent of the parties to the dispute, appoint an *ad hoc* Conciliation Commission of five persons (who may or may not be members of the Committee);[82] or, if the parties fail to agree on the composition of that Commission, its members will be elected by secret ballot by a two-thirds majority vote of the Committee from among its own members.[83] The *ad hoc* Conciliation Commission shall prepare a report embodying its findings on all questions of fact and containing recommendations for the amicable solution of the dispute.[84] The declarations of the parties to the dispute as to whether or not they accept the recommendations contained in the report[85] are communicated by the Chairman of the Committee to all the states parties to the Convention.[86]

[75] Protocol Instituting a Conciliation and Good Offices Commission, 651 U.N.T.S. 362, *reprinted in* U.N. Compilation, *supra* note 1, at 37.
[76] *Id.* art. 12.
[77] *Id.* art. 17(1).
[78] *Id.* art. 18.
[79] *Id.* art. 17(1).
[80] *Id.* art. 17(3).
[81] Racial Discrimination Convention, art. 11.
[82] *Id.* art. 12(1)(a).
[83] *Id.* art. 12(1)(b).
[84] *Id.* art. 13(1).
[85] *Id.* art. 13(2).
[86] *Id.* art. 13(3).

While the Economic Covenant contains no provisions concerning complaints, the Political Covenant includes an optional provision enabling a party to declare that it recognizes the competence of the Human Rights Committee established by the Political Covenant to receive and consider communications to the effect that this party is not fulfilling its obligations under the Political Covenant.[87] But no such communication shall be accepted by the Committee if it has been made by a party which has not made a similar declaration recognizing the competence of the Committee in regard to itself.[88] In each case submitted to it, the Committee shall make available its good offices to the parties to the dispute with a view to a friendly solution of the matter 'on the basis of respect for human rights and fundamental freedoms as recognized in the present Covenant'.[89] If no solution is reached, the Committee shall prepare a report limited to a brief statement of the facts and the text of the written and oral submissions of the parties.[90] The Covenant provides further that, with the consent of the parties, a matter which has not been thus resolved by the Committee may be referred to an *ad hoc* Conciliation Commission similar to the one envisaged by the Racial Discrimination Convention.[91] Unlike the very limited report of the Human Rights Committee, the report of the Conciliation Commission in a case in which no solution is reached shall embody not only its findings on questions of fact but also its views on the possibilities of an amicable solution of the matter.[92] These provisions came into force on 28 March, 1979 when ten states parties accepted this optional clause.[93]

From the point of view of the new international law of human rights, it would be extremely important to have some methods for dealing with inter-state human rights complaints. As a minimum there should be provisions for fact-finding and conciliation of the kind embodied in the widely ratified Racial Discrimination Convention.[94] The General Assembly might adopt a protocol applicable to all existing human rights instruments which do not contain a more effective system for the settlement of inter-state disputes. It would provide for the establishment of a fact-finding and conciliation commission, with powers

---

[87] Political Covenant, art. 41(1).

[88] *Id.*

[89] *Id.* art. 41(1)(e).

[90] *Id.* art. 41(1)(h)(ii).

[91] *Id.* art. 42(1)(a).

[92] *Id.* art. 42(7)(c).

[93] *See* U.N. Doc. A/34/440 (1979). As of Dec. 31, 1981, the following 14 states had made declarations under art. 41 of the Political Covenant: Austria, Canada, Denmark, Finland, Federal Republic of Germany, Iceland, Italy, the Netherlands, New Zealand, Norway, Senegal, Sri Lanka, Sweden, and the United Kingdom. U.N. Doc. E/CN.4/1511 (1981).

[94] As of July 1, 1982, 115 states were parties to the Racial Discrimination Convention. U.N. Doc. ST/4R/4/Rev. 4 (1982).

similar to the *ad hoc* Conciliation Commission established under the Racial Discrimination Convention. In ratifying such a protocol, a state might accept the Conciliation Commission's jurisdiction for disputes relating to the interpretation or application of all human rights instruments or might accept it only for some of them, or for all of them with the exception of certain ones.

3. *Procedures for the Consideration of Private Communications*

While the European and inter-American human rights systems,[95] as well as the International Labour Organisation,[96] include effective procedures for dealing with private complaints by individuals concerned or by national or international nongovernmental organizations (NGOs),[97] the record of the United Nations in this field is rather spotty.

The U.N. Charter provides for dealing with individual complaints in only one case. The General Assembly and the Trusteeship Council were authorized to accept 'petitions' relating to trust territories and to 'examine them in consultation with the administering authority'.[98] Under this provision large numbers of petitions have been considered by the Council, and in many cases the Council has made recommendations with respect to them to the administering authorities. Petitions have been also received and petitioners heard by the Fourth Committee of the General Assembly and in some cases recommendations have been made by the General Assembly to the administering authorities.[99] After considerable controversy, the Fourth Committee in 1961 also opened its doors to petitioners from non-self-governing territories other than trust territories.[100] That same year the General Assembly established a Special Committee on Territories under Portuguese Administration and authorized it to receive petitions and hear petitioners.[101] The United Nations Special Committee of Seventeen (later Twenty-Four) on decolonization, over the objections of some administering powers, agreed in 1962 to receive written petitions and to hear petitioners;[102] and since then it has considered more than a thousand

[95] *See generally* chs. 12 & 13 *infra.*

[96] *See generally* ch. 7 *supra.*

[97] *See generally* ch. 11 *infra.*

[98] U.N. Charter art. 87.

[99] 4 Repertory of United Nations Practice 340–61 (1955); *id.* Supp. (No. 1(2)) 279–82 (1958); *id.* Supp. (No. 2(3)) 336–41 (1963); *id.* Supp. (No. 3(3)) 208–10, 226–29 (1972). *See also* Murray, The United Nations Trusteeship System 150–74 (1957); Thullen, Problems of the Trusteeship System 75–81 (1964); Zonouzi, L'évolution du régime international de tutelle 147–53 (1967).

[100] 16 U.N. GAOR, C.4 (1208th mtg.) 322–26, U.N. Doc. A/C.4/SR.1208 (1961).

[101] G.A. Res. 1699, 16 U.N. GAOR, Supp. (No. 17) 38, U.N. Doc. A/5100 (1962).

[102] Report of the Special Committee on the Situation with regard to the Implementation of the Declaration on the Granting of Independence to Colonial Countries and Peoples, 17 U.N.

petitions.[103] It may be also noted that the Committee on the Elimination of Racial Discrimination has been authorized to consider petitions from non-self-governing territories transmitted to it by other United Nations bodies and to make recommendations with respect to them.[104]

However, since 1947 the Economic and Social Council has held the view that the Commission on Human Rights and the Commission on the Status of Women have 'no power to take any action in regard to any complaints' concerning, respectively, human rights or the status of women.[105] Despite many attempts to revise that rule, it is still in force today.[106] But when in 1965 the Special Committee on decolonization drew the attention of the Commission on Human Rights to evidence submitted by petitioners respecting violations of human rights in southern Africa,[107] the Economic and Social Council asked the Commission 'to consider as a matter of importance and urgency the question of the violation of human rights and fundamental freedoms, including policies of racial discrimination and segregation and of *apartheid* in all countries, with particular reference to colonial and other dependent countries and territories'.[108] Later the Council authorized the Commission to examine information relevant to 'gross violations of human rights and fundamental freedoms' (as exemplified by the policy of *apartheid* as practiced in southern Africa) contained in communications received by the Commission, and after thorough study of 'situations which reveal a consistent pattern of violations of human rights', to report with recommendations thereon to the Council.[109] The procedural proposals for dealing with this new assignment, which were prepared by the Commission on Human Rights and its Sub-Commission on Prevention of Discrimination and Protection

---

GAOR, Annexes (Add. Agenda Item 25) 18, U.N. Doc. A/5238 (1962). For comments on this decision, *see id.* at 6–17. Concerning the right of petition from non-self-governing territories, *see also* Repertory of United Nations Practice, Supp. (No. 3(3)) 62–65 (1972).

---

[103] For instance, with respect to petitions 1264 and 1265 (from the New Hebrides), *see* 31 U.N. GAOR, Supp. (No. 23, vol. III) 3, U.N. Doc. A/31/23/Rev. 1 (1977).

[104] Racial Discrimination Convention, art. 15. *See also* art. 7, Optional Protocol to the International Covenant on Civil and Political Rights, G.A. Res. 2200, U.N. GAOR, Supp. (No. 16) 59, U.N. Doc. A/6316 (1966), *reprinted in* U.N. Compilation, *supra* note 1, at 16.

[105] E.S.C. Res. 75 & Res. 76, 5 U.N. ESCOR, Supp. (No. 1) 20, 21, U.N. Doc. E/573 (1947). This decision was confirmed by the Economic and Social Council in Res. 728F, 28 U.N. ESCOR, Supp. (No. 1) 19, U.N. Doc. E/3290 (1959).

[106] For a short history of these attempts, *see* United Nations Action, *supra* note 32, at 177–81. *See also* L. Sohn & T. Buergenthal, International Protection of Human Rights 746–856 (1973) [hereinafter cited as Sohn & Buergenthal].

[107] 20 U.N. GAOR, Annexes (Add. Agenda Item 23), 58–59, U.N. Doc. A/6000/Rev.1 (1965).

[108] E.S.C. Res. 1102, 40 U.N. ESCOR, Supp. (No. 1) 6, U.N. Doc. E/4176 (1966).

[109] E.S.C. Res. 1235, 42 U.N. ESCOR, Supp. (No. 1) 17–18, U.N. Doc. E/4393 (1967).

of Minorities, were codified by the Economic and Social Council in
Resolution 1503.[110]

Resolution 1503 authorized a multi-step procedure, starting in a
Working Group of the Sub-Commission and proceeding through the
Sub-Commission to the Commission, whenever communications to
the Commission appear to reveal 'a consistent pattern of gross and
reliably attested violations of human rights'. The Commission can
consider the situation itself or, with the express consent of the state
concerned, it may refer it to an *ad hoc* committee for an investigation
and to endeavor to achieve a friendly solution. After considering over
20,000 individual communications in a number of years, the Working
Group drew some of the communications to the attention of the
Sub-Commission.[111] As all the bodies concerned are under an
injunction to keep all actions confidential until the Commission
decides to make recommendations to the Council, no information on
the subject has been forthcoming for several years. Starting in 1978,
the Commission began to announce at each session that it had taken
decisions in private sessions concerning certain specific countries;
for instance, in 1978 it listed Bolivia, Equatorial Guinea, Malawi,
the Republic of Korea, Uganda, Ethiopia, Indonesia, Paraguay, and
Uruguay, but the content of these decisions was not revealed.[112] In
1980, for the first time, the Commission concluded the examination
of a case under Resolution 1503 and recommended that the Economic
and Social Council should express its regret that the Government of
Malawi has failed 'to co-operate with the Commission on Human
Rights in the examination of a situation said to have deprived
thousands of Jehovah's Witnesses in Malawi of their basic human
rights and fundamental freedoms between 1972 and 1975, which
failure constrains the Economic and Social Council to publicize the
matter'; and also that the Council should express the hope that 'the
human rights of all citizens of Malawi have been fully restored and, in
particular, that adequate measures are being taken to provide remedy
to those who may have suffered injustices'.[113]

While the great expectations with respect to the procedure under
Resolution 1503 have not yet been fulfilled, the Commission on
Human Rights has been dealing with several cases of gross violations
of human rights without subjecting them to this complex procedure.
For instance, already in 1967, following an urgent request by the

[110] E.S.C. Res. 1503, 48 U.N. ESCOR, Supp. (No. 1A) 8–9, U.N. Doc. E/4832/Add.1 (1970).
[111] *See, e.g.*, U.N. Doc. E/CN.4/1101 (1972); E/CN.4/Sub.2/332, at 25 (1972).
[112] 1978 U.N. ESCOR, Supp. (No. 4) 47, U.N. Doc. E/1978/34, E/CN.4/1292 (1978). For a
comment on this decision, *see* Rev. Int'l Comm'n Jurists 33–35 (No. 20, June 1978).
[113] 1980 U.N. ESCOR, Supp. (No. 3) 3, U.N. Doc. E/1980/13, E/CN.4/1408 (1980); *id.* at
91–92, 202–03.

General Assembly's Special Committee on the Policies of *Apartheid*, the Commission on Human Rights established an *Ad Hoc* Working Group of Experts to investigate the charges of torture and ill-treatment of prisoners, detainees, or persons in police custody in South Africa; and the Commission authorized the Working Group to receive communications, to hear witnesses, and to recommend action to be taken in concrete cases.[114] The only authority cited for this decision was Resolution 9 of the Economic and Social Council which authorized the Commission 'to call in *ad hoc* working groups of non-governmental legal experts in specialized fields', with the approval of the President of the Economic and Social Council and the Secretary-General.[115] The Economic and Social Council welcomed this decision and extended the terms of reference of the Working Group to deal also with allegations regarding infringements of trade union rights in South Africa.[116] Later, the Economic and Social Council extended these terms of reference further, covering also violations of trade union rights in Namibia and Southern Rhodesia.[117]

Similar action was taken by the Commission on Human Rights in 1969 with respect to questions of human rights in the territories occupied as a result of the 1967 hostilities in the Middle East. The Commission established a Special Working Group of Experts 'to investigate allegations concerning Israel's violations of the Geneva Convention relative to the Protection of Civilian Persons in Time of War of 12 August 1949, in the territories occupied by Israel as a result of hostilities in the Middle East', and authorized the Working Group to 'receive communications, to hear witnesses, and to use such modalities of procedure as it may deem necessary'.[118] The Working Group seems to have been discontinued after the General Assembly established a Special Committee to Investigate Israeli Practices Affecting the Human Rights of the Population of the Occupied Territories[119] and that Committee presented its first report.[120]

[114] Comm'n on Human Rights Res. 2 (XXIII), 42 U.N. ESCOR, Supp. (No. 6) 76–78, U.N. Doc. E/4322, E/CN.4/940 (1967).

[115] E.S.C. Res. 9, para. 3, 2 U.N. ESCOR 400, 401 (1946).

[116] E.S.C. Res. 1216 & Res. 1236, 42 U.N. ESCOR, Supp. (No. 1) 12, 18, U.N. Doc. E/4393 (1967).

[117] E.S.C. Res. 1302, 44 U.N. ESCOR, Supp. (No. 1) 11, U.N. Doc. E/4548 (1968). Concerning the reports of the Working Group and the actions of the General Assembly based on its recommendations, *see* U.N. Action, *supra* note 32, at 84–87, 275.

[118] Comm'n on Human Rights Res. 6 (XXV), 46 U.N. ESCOR, Supp. (No. 6) 183–84, U.N. Doc. E/4621, E/CN.4/1007 (1969). For Israel's refusal to co-operate with the Working Group, *see id.* at 76. During its first year of operation the Working Group heard 103 witnesses. 48 U.N. ESCOR, Supp. (No. 5) 48, U.N. Doc. E/4816, E/CN.4/1039 (1970). *See also* Comm'n on Human Rights Res. 10 (XXVI), *id.* at 79–82.

[119] G.A. Res. 2443, 23 U.N. GAOR, Supp. (No. 18) 50, U.N. Doc. A/7218 (1969).

[120] U.N. Doc. A/8089 (1970). For the Commission's consideration of the question in 1971, *see* 50 U.N. ESCOR, Supp. (No. 4) 33–39, 79–82, U.N. Doc. E/4949, E/CN.4/1068 (1971). The

During the 1969 discussion in the Commission on Human Rights of the situation in Israeli-occupied territories a reference was made to the death sentences carried out in Iraq against a number of persons charged with spying for Israel. In reply it was stated that 'the question was a purely domestic one, coming within the exclusive jurisdiction of a sovereign State', and that the Commission had no right to deal with it.[121] In 1970, the attention of the Commission was drawn to several situations which, in the opinion of the speakers, might constitute situations revealing a consistent pattern of violations of human rights. Among them were: the situations of the Tibetans, of Soviet Jews wishing to emigrate to Israel, of citizens of Jewish faith living in some Arab countries, of Iranians resident in Iraq, of non-Russian nationalities in the Soviet Union, of political prisoners in Cuba, and of persons of African and Jewish origin living in the United States. Again the issue was raised whether article 2(7) of the U.N. Charter precluded consideration of these situations by the Commission.[122]

Some consideration was given in 1973 to the situations in Greece and in the South-Asian sub-continent (India, Pakistan, and Bangladesh);[123] in 1974 to the situation in Chile;[124] and in 1975 to the situations in Cyprus and Chile.[125] In the latter case, the Commission had before it information supplied by several NGOs as well as by the International Labour Office, UNESCO, and the Organization of American States.[126] It appointed an *Ad Hoc* Working Group 'to inquire into the present situation of human rights in Chile', and to prepare a report on the basis 'of a visit to Chile and of oral and written

---

question continued to be discussed by the Commission in later years. In 1977 its title was changed to 'Question of the violation of human rights in the occupied Arab Territories, including Palestine.' 62 U.N. ESCOR, Supp. (No. 6) 9, U.N. Doc. E/5927, E/CN.4/1257 (1977).

[121] Comm'n on Human Rights, Report on the Twenty-Fifth Session, 46 U.N. ESCOR, Supp. (No. 6) 73, U.N. Doc. E/4621, E/CN.4/1007 (1969).
[122] 48 U.N. ESCOR, Supp. (No. 5) 45, U.N. Doc. E/4816, E/CN.4/1039 (1970). Later reports of the Commission, while they refer to situations in some countries which were alleged to reveal a consistent pattern of violations of human rights, do not mention these countries by name. *See, e.g.*, 50 U.N. ESCOR, Supp. (No. 4) 51–52, U.N. Doc. E/4949, E/CN.4/1068 (1971); 52 U.N. ESCOR, Supp. (No. 7) 40–41, U.N. Doc. E/5113, E/CN.4/1097 (1972). Similar general statements are contained in later reports. However, in most cases the names of the countries concerned are mentioned in the summary records of the Commission.
[123] 54 U.N. ESCOR, Supp. (No. 6) 46, U.N. Doc. E/5265, E/CN.4/1127 (1973).
[124] 56 U.N. ESCOR, Supp. (No. 5) 30–31, U.N. Doc. E/5464, E/CN.4/1154 (1974). For the telegram sent by the Commission to Chile, *see id.* at 56–57.
[125] 58 U.N. ESCOR, Supp. (No. 4) 18–19, 23–26, U.N. Doc. E/5635, E/CN.4/1179 (1975). Concerning Cyprus, *see also* Comm'n on Human Rights Res. 4 (XXXII), 60 U.N. ESCOR, Supp. (No. 3) 59–60, U.N. Doc. E/5768, E/CN.4/1213 (1976); Res. 17 (XXXIV), 1978 U.N. ESCOR, Supp. (No. 4) 120–21, U.N. Doc. E/1978/34, E/CN.4/1292 (1978).
[126] U.N. Doc. E/CN.4/1166/Add.1–15 (1974–75). For comments by Chile, *see* U.N. Doc. E/CN.4/1158; U.N. Doc. E/CN.4/1174; U.N. Doc. E/CN.4/1174/Add.1 (1974–75).

evidence to be gathered from all relevant sources'.[127] The reports of the
Working Group were discussed not only in the Commission but also in
the General Assembly, and led to resolutions condemning 'constant
[and] flagrant violations of human rights' in Chile.[128] It may be noted
that in 1977 the observer for Chile had stated in the Commission that
'his Government agreed that the Commission had authority to deal
with all violations of human rights and had, therefore, never raised an
objection based on the argument of interference in domestic affairs';
his objections were limited to the objectivity of the Working Group's
report and the fairness of its procedure.[129] But a year later the observer
for Chile stated that his country strongly objected to a study by the
United Nations of the impact on human rights in Chile of foreign
economic aid, which constituted 'an unwarranted interference in the
internal affairs of his country', and considered the U.N. resolutions
and the inquiry of the *Ad Hoc* Working Group to be an infringement
of his country's sovereignty.[130] Nevertheless, after prolonged negotiation, the Working Group was allowed to visit Chile in July 1978.[131]

While no action was taken in 1977 on proposals relating to the
human rights situation in Uganda,[132] the Commission decided in 1978
at least to transmit to the government of Democratic Kampuchea for
comment a set of documents and the Commission's summary records
relating to the human rights situation in that country.[133] As noted
before, the Commission also disclosed in 1978 the names of nine
countries in which there were situations under consideration by the
Commission.[134]

In 1976 the procedures concerning communications became further
complicated by the entry into force of the Optional Protocol to the
International Covenant on Civil and Political Rights.[135] By the end of
1981, the Optional Protocol had been ratified by twenty-seven

---

[127] Comm'n on Human Rights Res. 8 (XXXI), 58 U.N. ESCOR, Supp. (No. 4) 66–67, U.N.
Doc. E/5635, E/CN.4/1179 (1975). The Working Group was not permitted to enter Chile in
1975. U.N. Doc. A/10285, at 21–28 (1975).

[128] G.A. Res. 3448, 30 U.N. GAOR, Supp. (No. 34) 89–90, U.N. Doc. A/10034 (1976);
Comm'n on Human Rights Res. 3 (XXXII), 60 U.N. ESCOR, Supp. (No. 3) 57–59, U.N. Doc.
E/5768, E/CN.4/1213 (1976). Similar decisions were adopted in later years. *See, e.g.,* G.A. Res.
31/124, 31 U.N. GAOR, Supp. (No. 39) 104–05, U.N. Doc. A/31/39 (1977).

[129] 62 U.N. ESCOR, Supp. (No. 6) 35, U.N. Doc. E/5927, E/CN.4/1257 (1977).

[130] 1978 U.N. ESCOR, Supp. (No. 4) 15, U.N. Doc. E/1978/34, E/CN.4/1292 (1978).

[131] *See* U.N. Doc. A/33/331, at 5–13 (1978). Similar steps were taken in 1981, on request of
the General Assembly, with respect to El Salvador and Bolivia. Comm'n on Human Rights Decs.
32 and 34 (XXXVII), 1981 U.N. ESCOR, Supp. (No. 5) 233, 235, U.N. Doc. E/1981/25,
E/CN.4/1475 (1981).

[132] 62 U.N. ESCOR, Supp. (No. 6) 17–18, U.N. Doc. E/5927, E/CN.4/1257 (1977).

[133] Comm'n on Human Rights Dec. 9 (XXXIV), 1978 U.N. ESCOR, Supp. (No. 4) 48, 137,
U.N. Doc. E/1978/34, E/CN.4/1292 (1978).

[134] *See* text preceding note 112 *supra.*

[135] *See* note 104 *supra.*

states;[136] and the Human Rights Committee established under the Political Covenant is therefore competent to deal with communications from individuals who are subject to the jurisdiction of a state party to the Optional Protocol and who claim to be victims of a violation by that state of any of the rights set forth in the Political Covenant.[137] After considering the communication in closed meetings,[138] the Committee shall forward its views to the state concerned and to the complaining individual.[139] The only additional publicity to be given these endeavors is by including in the annual report of the Committee a summary of its activities under the Optional Protocol.[140] In 1977 the Human Rights Committee decided to establish a Working Group to consider the communications in the light of all written information made available to it by the individual and by the state party concerned and to make recommendations to the Committee regarding the fulfilment of the conditions of admissibility laid down in the Optional Protocol.[141]

During 1977 and 1978 the Human Rights Committee considered forty communications. Seven of these were declared admissible, and another seven were declared inadmissible, while one was withdrawn by the author. The decision on admissibility was pending at the end of 1978 with respect to the remaining communications. Some of them were referred to the states concerned with a request for information and observations relevant to the question of admissibility; in some others the authors were asked to submit additional information.[142] In 1979 the Committee decided that two communications from Uruguay had disclosed violations of the Political Covenant, and expressed the view that Uruguay was under an obligation to provide effective remedies to the victims (including, in one case, compensation in accordance with article 9(5) of the Covenant).[143]

As soon as the Optional Protocol entered into force, the need to examine the relationship between the various procedures was recognized and suggestions were made for adopting a unified method for dealing with communications.[144] It was also noted, in another connec-

[136] As of 31 Dec. 1981, the following states were parties to the Optional Protocol: Barbados, Canada, Central African Republic, Colombia, Costa Rica, Denmark, Dominican Republic, Ecuador, Finland, Iceland, Italy, Jamaica, Madagascar, Mauritius, The Netherlands, Nicaragua, Norway, Panama, Peru, St. Vincent and the Grenadines, Senegal, Suriname, Sweden, Trinidad and Tobago, Uruguay, Venezuela, and Zaire. U.N. Doc. E/CN.4/1511 (1981).
[137] Optional Protocol, art. 1.
[138] *Id*. art. 5(3).
[139] *Id*. art. 5(4).
[140] *Id*. art. 6.
[141] Rules 89 & 94, 32 U.N. GAOR, Supp. (No. 44) 5, 64–65, U.N. Doc. A/32/44 (1977).
[142] 33 U.N. GAOR, Supp. (No. 40) 98, U.N. Doc. A/33/40 (1978).
[143] U.N. Press Releases HR/1854 & HR/1871 (1979).
[144] 62 U.N. ESCOR, Supp. (No. 6) 15–16, U.N. Doc. E/5927, E/CN.4/1257 (1977).

tion, that procedural difficulties have arisen as a result of the co-existence of public and confidential procedures for examining allegations of violations of human rights.[145]

It is too early to comment on the system established by the Optional Protocol, and perhaps some of its obvious limitations might be avoided in practice. It is clear, however, that the system established by the Economic and Social Council's Resolutions 1235 and 1503 [146] is not working satisfactorily. After more than ten years, this system has produced only one report for public scrutiny. At the same time, in several important instances the system has been bypassed by the Commission on Human Rights. The General Assembly itself has stepped into some of these cases with far-ranging recommendations.

One has to distinguish between those gross violations of human rights which contravene the Charter itself and the important, but more technical, violations of specific international instruments on human rights. The first ones can be considered effectively only in the glare of publicity, allowing public opinion to put pressure on the offending state. The present, mostly secret, procedure of the Commission on Human Rights is completely unsuitable for this purpose, and should be replaced by the procedure utilized by the General Assembly and the Commission on Human Rights in those cases which escaped the pitfalls of the procedure under Resolution 1503. There is no provision in the Charter prohibiting the General Assembly, the Economic and Social Council, or the Commission on Human Rights from considering communications received from individuals or organizations as a basis for public discussion and recommendation. The only thing required is a request by a state or a group of states that a particular case be considered in the light of the communications received and of other information which may become available.

When the Council of the League of Nations was faced with a similar problem in connection with petitions by members of minorities under the various treaties for their protection, it decided to appoint in each case a Committee of Three for the purpose of inquiring whether there had been a violation of a treaty. The rapporteur of each Committee presented the case to the Council, without involving the responsibility of his government, and some rapporteurs became specialists on certain areas or subjects.[147] Following this example, and building also on the recent practice of the Commission on Human Rights and of the General Assembly, the Commission on Human Rights might be authorized to appoint annually one or more pre-sessional working

[145] *Id.* at 18.

[146] *See* notes 109 and 110 *supra.*

[147] *See* the report of the Committee of Three of 6 June 1929. League of Nations O. J., Spec. Supp. 73, at 42–64 (1929), *reprinted in* Sohn & Buergenthal, *supra* note 106, at 213–50.

groups, composed either of experts acting in their private capacity or of representatives of five member states, one from each main geographic region, to consider whether any communications submitted to it relate to gross violations of human rights.[148] If the reply is positive, the rapporteur of the working group would, *ex officio*, be authorized to submit the case to the parent body for discussion. Each member of the working group might be assigned either a group of countries (in his or her region or some other region) or certain topics (*e.g.*, racial discrimination, treatment of prisoners, or equality of women) and would, after a while, become a specialist on the subject. The working group might also be authorized to submit to the parent body a draft recommendation for further action. The report of the working group and its recommendations would then be discussed in public and the pressure of public opinion could be mobilized to support the proposed action. Once this possibility is at the disposal of the working group, the state concerned might be more willing to discuss with it ways and means of settling the matter, thus avoiding exposure to public scrutiny. In such a case the working group would merely report that the case had been settled in conformity with the relevant international human rights instruments.

The procedure under the Political Covenant and its Optional Protocol is less likely to involve gross violations of human rights, and is probably destined to deal primarily with the difficulties caused by the imperfect introduction of international human rights provisions into domestic legal systems. As the European countries have realized, no legal system is flawless and the right to complain to an international institution helps to remove the blemishes. The changes which may be required by an international decision in such a case are not likely to interfere drastically with the domestic legal system and the decision can be easily, if sometimes reluctantly, obeyed.

Once it is shown that this is the case, one can hope that the Optional Protocol will be widely ratified and that it will not be necessary to devise some substitute system for states which are not bound by the Protocol. However, should such a substitute prove desirable it would not be too difficult for the General Assembly to come up with an adequate system. Alternatively, another optional protocol might be prepared allowing a state to accept the jurisdiction of the Human Rights Committee (or of another appropriate body) with respect to international instruments (other than the Political Covenant) to which it is a party which do not themselves provide for a system of handling communications relating to their violation.

[148] Alternatively, that function might be conferred upon the Bureau of the Commission on Human Rights. *See* 1978 U.N. ESCOR, Supp. (No. 4) 40, 42, U.N. Doc. E/1978/34, E/CN.4/1292 (1978).

4. *Conflicts between Various Implementation Procedures*

The entry into force of the Political and Economic Covenants has also raised the possibility of conflicts between their implementation provisions and the various procedures which already exist under instruments relating to specialized agencies or regional organizations. Both Covenants provide in general terms that nothing in them 'shall be interpreted as impairing the provisions of the Charter of the United Nations and of the constitutions of the specialized agencies which define the respective responsibilities of the various organs of the United Nations and of the specialized agencies in regard to matters dealt with' in these Covenants.[149] In addition, article 44 of the Political Covenant stipulates expressly that its provisions 'shall apply without prejudice to the procedures prescribed in the field of human rights by or under the constituent instruments and the conventions of the United Nations and of the specialized agencies'. More specifically, according to the same article, the Political Covenant's implementation procedures shall not prevent the states parties to it 'from having recourse to other procedures for settling a dispute in accordance with general or special international agreements in force between them'. Finally, the Optional Protocol, which relates to communications from individuals, prohibits the consideration by the Human Rights Committee of any communication when 'the same matter' is being examined under another 'procedure of international investigation or settlement'.[150]

This liberal attitude might be contrasted with the more exclusive approach of the European Convention, the states parties to which have agreed that 'they will not avail themselves of treaties, conventions or declarations in force between them for the purpose of submitting, by way of petition, a dispute arising out of the interpretation or application' of that Convention to 'a means of settlement' other than those provided in the European Convention.[151]

The provisions of the Political and Economic Covenants show clear preference for applying U.N. procedures only in cases where other procedures are not available. In particular, the procedures developed by the specialized agencies, such as the International Labour Organisation and UNESCO, are given triple protection. This seems to be justified when these procedures result in a settlement; but if no settlement has been reached under the procedure resorted to by the parties

---

[149] Political Covenant, art. 46; Economic Covenant, art. 24.

[150] Optional Protocol, art. 5(2)(a).

[151] European Convention, art. 62. For comments, *see* Eissen, *The European Convention on Human Rights and the United Nations Covenant on Civil and Political Rights: Problems of Coexistence*, 22 Buffalo L. Rev. 181 (1972); Tardu, *Quelques questions relatives à la coexistence des procédures universelles et régionales de plainte individuelle dans le domaine des droits de l'homme*, 4 Revue des Droits de l'Homme 589 (1971).

to the dispute, and if this procedure has not resulted in a final and binding decision, it should be possible to resort to the Human Rights Committee or some other available U.N. procedure. On the other hand, it would seem undesirable to provide for an appeal to the United Nations from a final and binding decision rendered under the auspices of a specialized agency.

As far as regional organizations are concerned, they are not mentioned expressly in the relevant articles of the Political and Economic Covenants. The Optional Protocol, however, may be interpreted as giving precedence to regional procedures. It is less clear whether the reference to examination under another procedure[152] is to be construed as an absolute prohibition of submission to the Human Rights Committee, or, more likely, a merely temporary restriction while the case is pending before another international body. Perhaps this provision might be treated similarly to the rule about exhaustion of local remedies;[153] regional remedies should also be exhausted unsatisfactorily before the matter can be submitted to the U.N. Human Rights Committee.

A clarification by the General Assembly or the Economic and Social Council of these relationships between the various U.N. procedures and the parallel procedures of specialized agencies and regional organizations would be desirable.

C. CONCLUSIONS

The preceding survey shows that important progress took place in the last thirty years with respect to the protection of human rights, and that a sometimes-bewildering variety of procedures has been devised for implementing those rights and for supervising that implementation.

The momentum achieved through the entry into force of the Political and Economic Covenants, the Optional Protocol, and the procedure under article 41 of the Political Covenant should not be lost. There are many constructive steps which the United Nations can take to improve the means available to it to promote and protect human rights. Where the desired results cannot be achieved by imaginative decisions of the General Assembly or of its subsidiary bodies, a variety of instruments and optional protocols might be preferred. The pessimists might again be confounded, and these new instruments might come into force sooner than expected and might bring the peoples of the world several steps further toward an effective system of international human rights law.

---

[152] Optional Protocol, art. 5(2)(a).
[153] *Id*. art. 5(2)(b).

II. Teaching Suggestions

It is necessary to distinguish at the outset between domestic implementation and international supervision. Domestic implementation in the United States (and some other countries) raises in the first place issues concerning the self-execution character of human rights treaties. It might be useful to discuss in this connection *Sei Fujii v. California*,[154] the proposed Bricker Amendment,[155] and the proposal of the Carter Administration that in ratifying four treaties on human rights the United States should declare that they are not self-executing.[156] Once these documents are ratified, various issues will arise as to their effect in the United States courts, especially as to their use in interpreting relevant United States legislation.[157]

It should also be noted that the United States may be internationally bound by a human rights treaty, but the courts may refuse to enforce it because it violates the Constitution, has been superseded by a later statute, or is not self-executing and the necessary implementing legislation has not been enacted. In such a case, the United States may nonetheless be internationally responsible for having violated its treaty obligations.[158] Whether the United States can be sued in such a case before an international court would depend on the existence of a jurisdictional clause encompassing the violation in question. In this connection, reference should be made to the so-called 'Connally reservation' to the United States declaration accepting the jurisdiction of the International Court of Justice, through which the United States exempted from the Court's jurisdiction any dispute which it has determined unilaterally to be essentially within the domestic jurisdiction of the United States. But that reservation does not apply where a particular treaty contains its own jurisdictional clause referring to the International Court of Justice any dispute relating to its interpretation or application.[159]

It should be easier to deal with international supervision. Most of

---

[154] 217 P.2d 481 (Cal. Dist. Ct. App. 1950), *rev'd* on the point concerning the self-executing character of the U.N. Charter, 38 Cal. 2d 718, 242 P.2d 617 (1952). For a summary of other U.S. cases on the subject, *see* Sohn & Buergenthal, *supra* note 106, at 944; for foreign cases, *see id.* at 992. *See also* R. Lillich & F. Newman, International Human Rights: Problems of Law and Policy 115 (1979) [hereinafter cited as Lillich & Newman]; 14 M. Whiteman, Digest of International Law 280 (1970) [hereinafter cited as Whiteman].

[155] Sohn & Buergenthal, *supra* note 106, at 948.

[156] Four Treaties Pertaining to Human Rights: Message from the President of the United States, S. Exec. Docs. C, D, E, and F, 95th Cong., 2d Sess. viii, xi, xv, xviii(1978).

[157] *See* 2 Hyde, International Law Chiefly as Interpreted and Applied by the United States 1463 (1945); 14 Whiteman, *supra* note 154, at 316.

[158] *See* 1 G. Schwarzenberger, International Law 69 (3d ed. 1957), summarizing the practice of international courts on the subject.

[159] *See* Bishop & Myers, *Unwarranted Extension of Connally-Amendment Thinking*, 55 Am. J. Int'l L. 135 (1961).

the internationally supervised treaties are of recent origin and practice under them is scant. In comparing various reporting procedures, it might be useful to take into account the experience of the International Labour Organisation discussed in chapter 7. Similarly, the experience of the European Commission of Human Rights, discussed in chapter 13, should be taken into account when discussing complaint procedures.

Discussion of U.N. reporting procedures might concentrate on the development of procedures under the Racial Discrimination Convention.[160] In considering the complaint procedures within the U.N. system, sharp distinction must be made between ordinary communications, to which little attention is paid despite their large numbers;[161] the special procedure in cases of gross violation which has been developed, especially under Resolution 1503 of the Economic and Social Council;[162] and the *ad hoc* procedure used in some cases of special concern to the United Nations (such as South Africa, Chile, and the Israeli-occupied territories).[163]

It is necessary to deal also with two recurrent, interconnected, general questions: is the international law of human rights really enforceable? and why are the existing procedures so ineffective? It is a common belief that since states are sovereign they can disregard international law with impunity. There are various possible answers to this. In the first place, most states comply with international law on most occasions as a matter of course or as a matter of convenience. They have found by experience that it is easier to live in the world community if everybody obeys certain basic rules. For example, domestically it proved to be important to have regulations governing road traffic; if everybody could drive as they pleased, very few people would survive a trip of even a few miles. Internationally, it proved equally important to observe the rules relating to air and sea navigation. If somebody disobeys, disasters similar to that of the *Andrea Doria* are likely to happen.

Secondly, once a state agrees that a rule is binding, it ordinarily follows it. Even those who are considered as arch-villains hesitate to

[160] *See, e.g.*, Sohn & Buergenthal, *supra* note 106, at 868; Buergenthal, *Implementing the Racial Convention*, 12 Tex. Int'l L.J. 187 (1977).

[161] *See* Sohn & Buergenthal, *supra* note 106, at 746.

[162] *See id.* at 772; Lillich & Newman, *supra* note 154, at 337.

[163] As to Chile, *see id.* at 292; Kirgis, International Organizations in Their Legal Setting 822 (1977); Bossuyt, *The United Nations and Civil and Political Rights in Chile*, 27 Int'l & Comp. L.Q. 462 (1978). *See also* Ermacora, *International Enquiry Commissions in the Field of Human Rights*, 1 Revue des Droits de l'Homme 180 (1968); Kaufman, *The Necessity for Rules of Procedure in Ad Hoc United Nations Investigations*, 18 Am. U. L. Rev. 739 (1969); Miller, *United Nations Fact-Finding Missions in the Field of Human Rights*, Austl. Y.B. Int'l L. 40 (1970–73).

imitate the German statement of 1914 that the treaty guaranteeing the neutrality of Belgium was a scrap of paper. Like domestic courts which do not want to apply a particular rule, international decision-makers seldom come out boldly and assert that their sovereign state is entitled to disregard a particular rule whenever it pleases; instead, they attempt to distinguish the case at hand from past precedents and try to present a legal argument for following a different path. Thus, even when a violation of international law is committed, the violator usually defends it as an allowed deviation from the rule. This is especially common in the field of human rights, where the violator often invokes the rule that matters of domestic jurisdiction are not subject to international law nor to international scrutiny through various implementation measures. Other common excuses are connected with the need to protect national security, public order, health, or morals.[164] If everything else fails, one can claim that there is a public emergency threatening the life of the nation.[165] While the international community cannot completely close these loopholes, there is a growing tendency to diminish the self-serving character of these exceptions by submitting them to the scrutiny of the competent international body, which may decide that their invocation was not justified in a particular instance.[166]

As far as outright disregard of human rights is concerned, it is true that some governments have grossly mistreated their peoples. It needs to be pointed out, however, that very few of the villains have avoided retribution. For instance, in 1979 the rule of three gross violators of human rights in Africa was terminated—in Uganda, the Central African Empire, and Guinea-Bissau. While some such violators have been punished by special international criminal courts after they lost a war, and others were punished when they were unable to escape after a revolution against them, there is as yet no general international criminal court able to punish such violations in peacetime. Nevertheless, this idea has been considered seriously from time to time, and is likely to be considered by the General Assembly again in the 1980s.[167]

The international legal system is constantly evolving and we have seen a great amount of progress in the field of human rights since 1945. It took a long time to develop a satisfactory system of human rights

[164] The Political Covenant allows the invocation of these exceptional circumstances in certain instances. *See* arts. 12(3), 14(1), 18(3), 19(3)(b), 21, & 22(2).

[165] *See id.* art. 4.

[166] For decisions of the European Commission of Human Rights and the European Court of Human Rights on this subject, *see* ch. 13 *infra*.

[167] For a detailed, well-documented summary of efforts to prepare a draft code of offenses against the peace and security of mankind and a statute of an international criminal court, *see* B. Ferencz, An International Criminal Court: A Step Toward World Peace: A Documentary History and Analysis (1980).

protection in the most developed countries; one cannot expect to develop it internationally overnight. But through teaching this subject to an ever growing community, one can expect that progress in this field will be expedited.[168]

III. Syllabus

    I. *Implementation*
       A. Differences between international and domestic implementation of human rights.
       B. Implementation in the United States: Special issues.
          1. Self-executing and non-self-executing human rights treaties.
          2. Conflicts with domestic legislation.
          3. International consequences of non-fulfillment of international obligations.
       C. Obligation to implement.
          1. Duties under article 2 of the International Covenant on Civil and Political Rights.
          2. Similar obligations under other human rights treaties.
          3. National and local institutions for the promotion and protection of human rights.
    II. *International Measures of Implementation and Supervision*
       A. International supervisory commissions.
       B. Methods of supervision.
          1. Periodic reporting systems.
             a. Under U.N. resolutions.
             b. Under various U.N. conventions.
             c. Under the International Convention on the Elimination of All Forms of Racial Discrimination.
             d. Under the Political Covenant and the International Covenant on Economic, Social and Cultural Rights.
       C. Procedures for dealing with inter-state complaints.
          1. Human rights treaties providing for reference to the International Court of Justice.
          2. Submission of complaints to other international courts.
          3. Submission of complaints to fact-finding and conciliation commissions.
       D. Procedures for the consideration of private communications.
          1. Comparison between U.N. procedures and procedures developed by the European Commission of Human

---

[168] *See* T. Buergenthal & J. Torney, International Human Rights and International Education (1976).

Rights and the Inter-American Commission on Human Rights.

2. Effective operation of the U.N. petition and communication systems in the areas of trusteeship and non-self-governing territories.
3. Unsuccessful efforts in the U.N. to establish a regular procedure for dealing with communications in other human rights areas.
4. Development of new procedures for dealing with 'gross violations' of human rights.
5. Other *ad hoc* procedures.
6. Entry into force of the Optional Protocol to the International Covenant on Civil and Political Rights, and development of procedures for dealing with communications relating to the Political Covenant.
7. Current difficulties and possible means of improving the system.

IV. Minisyllabus

Teachers who can only devote two or three hours to the teaching of the subject dealt with in this chapter should concentrate on dealing with individual complaints, as these are of special interest to both lawyers and private persons who may find it necessary some day to file a complaint.

After a short introduction explaining the existing institutions for implementation, the teacher may wish to concentrate on the European Convention as it has a vast jurisprudence on the subject, and on the inter-American system, as it is the only one now accessible to United States citizens. Thus the teacher may wish to combine the study of this chapter with chapters 12 and 13 relating to these two regional systems.

Consequently the short syllabus might be as follows:

I. Differences between international and domestic implementation of human rights.
II. International supervisory system: commissions and courts.
III. Procedures for the consideration of private communications.
   A. European system.
   B. Inter-American system.
   C. United Nations system.
      1. Gross violations.
      2. Communications under various special conventions and resolutions.
      3. Communications under the Optional Protocol to the International Covenant on Civil and Political Rights.

V. Bibliography

United Nations, United Nations Action in the Field of Human Rights, U.N. Doc. ST/HR/2/Rev.1 (1980).

—— Alternative Approaches and Ways and Means Within the United Nations System for Improving the Effective Enjoyment of Human Rights and Fundamental Freedoms: Report of the Secretary-General, U.N. Doc. A/10235 (1975).

—— Human Rights: A Compilation of International Instruments, U.N. Doc. ST/HR/1/Rev.1 (1978).

Aries, *International Human Rights and Their Implementation*, 19 Geo. Wash. L. Rev. 579 (1951).

Bilder, *The International Promotion of Human Rights: A Current Assessment*, 58 Am. J. Int'l L. 728 (1964).

—— *Rethinking International Human Rights: Some Basic Questions* 1969 Wis. L. Rev. 171.

Buergenthal, *Implementing the Racial Convention*, 12 Tex. Int'l L. J. 187 (1977).

J. Carey, UN Protection of Civil and Political Rights (1970).

R. Clark, A United Nations High Commissioner for Human Rights (1972).

A. Del Russo, International Protection of Human Rights (1970).

G. da Fonseca, How to File Complaints of Human Rights Violations: A Practical Guide to Inter-Governmental Procedures (1975).

Evans, *Self-Executing Treaties in the United States of America*, 30 Brit. Y.B. Int'l L. 178 (1953).

M. Ganji, International Protection of Human Rights (1962).

Golsong, *Implementation of International Protection of Human Rights*, 110 Recueil des Cours 1 (1963).

J. Green, The United Nations and Human Rights (1964).

Humphrey, *The Right of Petition in the United Nations*, 4 Revue des Droits de l'Homme 463 (1971).

—— *The International Bill of Rights: Scope and Implementation*, 17 Wm. & Mary L. Rev. 527 (1976).

Korey, *The Key to Human Rights—Implementation*, Int'l Conciliation, No. 570 (1968).

H. Lauterpacht, International Law and Human Rights (1950).

E. Luard, ed., The International Protection of Human Rights (1967).

Macdonald, *A United Nations High Commissioner for Human Rights: The Decline and Fall of an Initiative*, 10 Can. Y.B. Int'l L. 40 (1972).

McDougal, *et al., Human Rights and World Public Order*, 72 Nw. U. L. Rev. 227 (1977–78).

M. Moskowitz, International Concern with Human Rights (1974).

Mower, *The Implementation of the UN Covenant on Civil and Political Rights*, 10 Revue des Droits de l'Homme 271 (1977).

Nanda, *Implementation of Human Rights by the United Nations and Regional Organizations*, 21 De Paul L. Rev. 307 (1971).

A. Robertson, Human Rights in the World (1972).

Rodley, *Monitoring Human Rights Violations in the 1980s*, in J. Dominguez, *et al.*, Enhancing Global Rights (1979).

Schlüter, *The Domestic Status of the Human Rights Clauses of the United Nations Charter*, 61 Cal. L. Rev. 110 (1973).

Schwelb, *Civil and Political Rights: The International Measures of Implementation*, 62 Am. J. Int'l L. 827 (1968).

—— *Some Aspects of the Measures of Implementation of the International Covenant on Economic, Social and Cultural Rights*, 1 Revue des Droits de l'Homme 363 (1968).

—— *The International Measures of Implementation of the International Covenant on Civil and Political Rights and of the Optional Protocol*, 12 Tex. Int'l L. J. 141 (1977).

Sohn, *A Short History of United Nations Documents on Human Rights*, in Commission to Study the Organization of Peace, The United Nations and Human Rights 39 (1968).

V. Van Dyke, Human Rights, the United States, amd World Community (1970).

Weston, *et al.*, *International Procedures to Protect Human Rights: A Symposium*, 53 Iowa L. Rev. 268 (1967).

VI. Minibibliography

G. da Fonseca, How to File Complaints of Human Rights Violations: A Practical Guide to Inter-Governmental Procedures (1975).

Humphrey, *The International Bill of Rights: Scope and Implementation*, 17 Wm. & Mary L. Rev. 527 (1976).

Rodley, *Monitoring Human Rights Violations in the 1980s*, in J. Dominguez, *et al.*, Enhancing Global Rights (1979).

Schwelb, *The International Measures of Implementation of the International Covenant on Civil and Political Rights and of the Optional Protocol*, 12 Tex. Int'l L. J. 141 (1977).

Chapter 11

The Contribution of International Nongovernmental Organizations to the Protection of Human Rights*

David Weissbrodt[1]

There are a considerable number of nongovernmental organizations (NGOs) engaged in the protection of human rights.[2] Working at the international[3] and/or national levels,[4] these organizations function as

* © David Weissbrodt 1983.

[1] An earlier version of the substantive discussion appeared as Weissbrodt, *The Role of International Nongovernmental Organizations in the Implementation of Human Rights*, 12 Tex. Int'l L.J. 293 (1977), which is republished here in revised form with the permission of the editors of the Texas International Law Journal.

[2] *See* Shestack, *Sisyphus Endures: The International Human Rights NGO*, 24 N.Y.L.S. L. Rev. 89 (1978); Weissbrodt, *The Role of International Nongovernmental Organizations in the Implementation of Human Rights*, 12 Tex. Int'l L.J. 293 (1977) [hereinafter cited as *Role of International NGOs*]; Note, *Role of NGOs in Implementing Human Rights in Latin America*, 7 Ga. J. Int'l & Comp. L. 476 (1977). *See also* Green, *NGOs* in Human Rights and World Order 90 (A. Said ed. 1978). *See generally International Protection of Human Rights: The Work of International Organizations and the Role of U.S. Foreign Policy: Hearings Before the Subcomm. on Int'l Organizations and Movements of the House Comm. on Foreign Affairs*, 93d Cong., 1st Sess. (1973) [hereinafter cited as *House Hearings on International Protection of Human Rights*]; Rodley, *Monitoring Human Rights Violations in the 1930's*, in J. Dominguez, N. Rodley, B. Wood & R. Falk, Enhancing Global Human Rights 119 (1979) [hereinafter cited as Rodley]; Cassese, *How Could Non-Governmental Organizations Use U.N. Bodies More Effectively?*, 1 Universal Human Rights, 73 (No. 4, 1979). For current information on NGO human rights activities, *see* Human Rights Internat Newsletter (1976–present).

[3] Over 700 NGOs have accredited status with the U.N. Economic and Social Council. U.N. Doc. E/INF. 162 (1977). Among those organizations which have full-time international human rights programs are Amnesty International, Anti-Slavery Society, Commission of the Churches on International Affairs, International Association of Democratic Lawyers, International Commission of Jurists, International Committee of the Red Cross, International Confederation of Free Trade Unions, International Federation of Human Rights, International Indian Treaty Council, International League for Human Rights, Minority Rights Group, World Conference on Religion and Peace, and World Federation of Trade Unions. There are also numerous NGOs which devote part of their time and resources to human rights. *See* Shestack, *Sisyphus Endures: The International Human Rights NGO*, 24 N.Y.L.S. L. Rev. 89, 94–95 (1978).

[4] National Council of Churches of Christ in the U.S.A., *Human Rights in North America*, in 2 Human Rights and Christian Responsibility 80 (Commission of the Churches on International Affairs 1974). In the United States, a number of national NGOs have been in the forefront of protecting civil rights and civil liberties: American Civil Liberties Union Center for Constitutional Rights, National Association for the Advancement of Colored People, NAACP Legal Defense and Educational Fund, American Jewish Committee, and Lawyer's Committee for Civil Rights Under Law. For a description of the activities of Amnesty International national sections, *see* T. Claudius & F. Stepan, Amnesty International Portrait Einer Organisation 214–78 (3d ed: 1978). *See generally* Human Rights Periodicals (D. Christiano ed. 1977) (lists organizations and agencies active in civil liberties in the United States and Canada); Weissbrodt, *Deciding United States Policy in Regard to International Human Rights: The Role of Interest Groups*, in Dynamics of Human Rights in U.S. Foreign Policy (N. Hevener ed. 1981) [hereinafter cited as *Interest Groups*].

unofficial ombudsmen safeguarding human rights against governmental infringement, by such techniques as diplomatic initiatives,[5] reports,[6] public statements,[7] efforts to influence the deliberations of human rights bodies established by intergovernmental organizations,[8] campaigns to mobilize public opinion,[9] and attempts to affect the foreign policy of some countries with respect to their relations to states which are regularly responsible for human rights violations.[10]

These NGOs share the same basic purpose, that is, to gather information which can be effectively mustered—either directly or indirectly—to influence the implementation of human rights by governments. While the great bulk of the organizations' information may be gathered at their central offices from reading relevant laws, reviewing periodicals, studying submitted appeals or documents, interviewing occasional visitors, and corresponding with informants, the organizations may also pursue on-site investigations of human rights prob-

---

[5] *See, e.g.*, International Committee of the Red Cross, Annual Report 1977 (1978). The report contains, *inter alia*, accounts of diplomatic initiatives in Rhodesia/Zimbabwe, at 15, South Africa, at 17, and Indo-China, at 19.

[6] *See, e.g.*, Amnesty International, An Amnesty International Report: Political Imprisonment in the People's Republic of China (1978); A. Cook, South Africa: The Imprisoned Society (1974) (a publication of the International Defence and Aid Fund); S. Cronje, Equatorial Guinea: The Forgotten Dictatorship (1976) (Research Report No. 2 of the Anti-Slavery Society); International Commission of Jurists, Final Report of Mission to Chile, April 1974, to Study the Legal System and the Protection of Human Rights (1974); Minority Rights Group, The Sahrawis of Western Sahara: Report No. 40 (1979).

[7] For example, Amnesty International [hereinafter cited as AI] issued 76 news releases on 38 countries during the period July 1, 1977–June 30, 1978. AI, Amnesty International Report 1978 at 319 (1979); International Commission of Jurists, ICJ Protests Against the Bukovsky Trial, Jan. 11, 1972.

[8] *See, e.g.*, AI, Allegations of Human Rights Violations in Democratic Kampuchea: UN Sub-Commission on Prevention of Discrimination and Protection of Minorities: Statement Submitted by Amnesty International, a Non-governmental Organization in Consultative Status (1978); International League for Human Rights, Communication to the United Nations on a Consistent Pattern of Violations of Human Rights in the Republic of Guinea (1977).

[9] For example, Amnesty International conducted an El Salvador campaign during Oct.–Dec. 1978. It is documented by many mimeo materials. A year long campaign on specific aspects of political imprisonment in Uruguay began in Aug. 1979.

[10] Representatives from NGOs frequently appear before foreign policy committees of the U.S. Congress, *see, e.g., Human Rights in the Philippines: Report by Amnesty International: Hearing Before Subcomm. on Int'l Organizations of the House Comm. on Int'l Relations*, 94th Cong., 2d Sess. (1976); *Human Rights in Uruguay and Paraguay: Hearings Before Subcomm. on Int'l Organizations of House Comm. on Int'l Relations*, 94th Cong., 2d Sess. 66–104, 154–218 (1976); *Human Rights in Iran; Hearings Before the Subcomm. on Int'l Organizations of the House Comm. on Int'l Relations*, 94th Cong, 2d Sess. 1–16, 63–69 (1976); *Chile: The Status of Human Rights and its Relationship to U.S. Economic Assistance Programs: Hearings Before the Subcomm. on Int'l Organizations of the House Comm. on Int'l Relations*, 94th Cong., 2d Sess. 3–13, 196–97; *Human Rights in South Korea: Implications for U.S. Policy: Hearings Before Subcomms. on Asian and Pacific Affairs and Int'l Organizations and Movements of the House Comm. on Foreign Affairs*, 93d Cong., 2d Sess. 28–50, 54–69, 104–11 (1974); Lawyers Committee for International Human Rights, Violations of Human Rights in Uganda 1971–1978: Testimony prepared for the Subcommittee on Foreign Economic Policy of the United States Senate Committee on Foreign Relations (1978).

lems.[11] Over the past twenty years, NGOs have developed a fairly substantial practice of sending fact-finding missions.[12]

Among the most prominent international NGOs in the field of human rights are Amnesty International,[13] the Anti-Slavery Society,[14] the Commission of the Churches on International Affairs,[15] the International Association of Democratic Lawyers,[16] the International Commission of Jurists,[17] the International Committee of the Red Cross,[18] the International Defense and Aid Fund,[19] the International

[11] *See, e.g.,* AI, Report on Allegations of Torture in Brazil (1972); Judicial Sub-Commission of the International Commission of Enquiry into the Crimes of the Military Junta in Chile, The Crimes of the Chilean Military Junta in the Light of Chilean Law and International Law (Sept. 1974); AI, Amnesty International Briefing: Guatemala (Dec. 1976); AI, Political Imprisonment in the People's Republic of China (1978); Minority Rights Group, The Mexican Americans: Report No. 39 (1979); *Indonesia,* Rev. Int'l Comm'n Jurists 9 (No. 15, Dec. 1973).

[12] *See, e.g., Continued Absence of Democracy in Indonesia,* 27 Bull. Int'l Comm'n Jurists (Sept. 1966); AI, Report of an Amnesty International Mission to the Republic of the Philippines (2d ed. Mar. 1977); AI, The Republic of Nicaragua: An Amnesty International Report (July 1977). *See generally Role of International NGO's, supra* note 1, at 300–04; Wiseberg & Scoble, *The International League for Human Rights: The Strategy of a Human Rights NGO,* 7 Ga. J. Int'l & Comp. L. 289, 309–10 (1977) [hereinafter cited as *Int'l League for Human Rights*].

[13] *See* AI, Handbook (1977); T. Claudius & F. Stepan, Amnesty International Portrait Einer Organisation (3d ed. 1978); [1974] Y.B. Int'l Org. 29 (Union of International Associations). *See generally* E. Larsen, A Flame in Barbed Wire (1978); J. Moreillon, Le Comité International de la Croix-Rouge et la protection des detenus politiques 199–218 (1973) [hereinafter cited as Moreillon]; Scoble & Wiseberg, *Amnesty International: Evaluating Effectiveness in the Human Rights Arena,* Intellect, Sept.–Oct. 1976; Scoble & Wiseberg, *Human Rights & Amnesty International,* 413 Annals 11 (1974).

[14] *See* Anti-Slavery Society, Human Rights and Development, A 3-year research and action programme, 1978–1981 (unpublished manuscript, 1977).

[15] *See generally* Commission of the Churches on International Affairs, Human Rights and Christian Responsibility 2–12 (May 1974); N. MacDermot, Human Rights and the Churches (1976).

[16] *See generally* International Association of Democratic Lawyers, IXth Congress of the International Association of Democratic Lawyers (1970). *XXth Anniversary of the I.A.D.L.,* Int'l Assoc. Democratic Law. Bull. (1967). The IADL also publishes a journal, Revue de Droit Contemporain.

[17] *See generally* International Commission of Jurists, Objectives, Organizations, Activities (1972); MacDermot, *The Work of the International Commission of Jurists,* 1 Index on Censorship 15 (1972). The general principles advocated by the ICJ are found in International Commission of Jurists, The Rule of Law and Human Rights (1966).

[18] *See* M. Veuthey, Red Cross; D. Tansley, Final Report: An Agenda for Red Cross (1975); International Committee of the Red Cross, Le CICR, La Ligue et Le Rapport Tansley (1977); D. Forsythe, Humanitarian Politics: The International Committee of the Red Cross (1977) [hereinafter cited as Forsythe, Humanitarian Politics]; J. Freymond, Guerres, Revolutions, Croix-Rouge, Reflexions sur le rôle du Comité International de la Croix-Rouge (1976); M. Vauthey, Guerilla et droit humanitaire 48–61, 262–64, 319–33 (1976); Bissell, *The International Commission of the Red Cross and the Protection of Human Rights,* 1 Revue des Droits de l'Homme 255 (1968).

[19] The International Defense and Aid Fund (IDAF), headquartered in London, has regularly issued reports about human rights violations in South Africa and other African countries. *See, e.g.,* R. Ainslie, Masters and Serfs: Farm Labour in South Africa (rev. ed. 1977); IDAF, The Sun Will Rise (M. Benson ed. 1976); IDAF, Boss: The First 5 Years (1975); A. Hepple, Press Under Apartheid (1974); A. Cook, South Africa: The Imprisoned Society (1974); IDAF, South African Prisons and the Red Cross Investigation (1967) [hereinafter cited as IDAF, Prisons].

406

David Weissbrodt

Federation of Human Rights,[20] the International League for Human Rights,[21] the Minority Rights Group,[22] Survival International,[23] and the World Peace Council.[24]

Section I.A. of this chapter sketches the structure and characteristics of NGOs. The subject of section I.B. is the fact-finding techniques of NGOs, while I.C. considers their work, including diplomatic efforts, public discussions of human rights violations, contributions to international investigative procedures, aid to human rights victims, and local activities. Section I.D. discusses the contribution of NGOs to the development of human rights norms. Section II suggests an overall approach to the teaching of human rights through the work of NGOs with a description of two classes on how NGOs contribute to the protection of human rights, and includes a hypothetical which might serve as the basis for class discussion, as well as suggestions for issues which should be raised by the teacher. Section III contains a syllabus outlining the topics which a teacher might cover in dealing with NGOs. Section IV presents a bibliography on nongovernmental human rights organizations; the remaining two sections suggest a shorter syllabus and bibliography for more abbreviated treatment of the subject.

I. Legal and Policy Considerations

A. WHAT ARE INTERNATIONAL NONGOVERNMENTAL ORGANIZATIONS?

Most NGOs have consultative status with such intergovernmental bodies as the U.N. Economic and Social Council (ECOSOC),[25] the

[20] See Fédération Internationale des Droits de l'Homme Bull. No. 2 (Dec. 1977–Feb. 1978).

[21] See International League for Human Rights, Annual Review (1976–1977) (undated); [1974] Y.B. Int'l Org. 399 (Union of International Associations); Int'l League for Human Rights, supra note 12; Scoble & Wiseberg, Human Rights as an International League, in Human Rights and World Order 100 (A. Said ed. 1978).

[22] The Minority Rights Group is an international research and information group headquartered in London which publishes its research findings about minority groups suffering discrimination. See, e.g., Minority Rights Group, The Sahrawis of Western Sahara: Report No. 40 (1979); The Mexican Americans: Report No. 39 (1979); The Hungarians of Rumania: Report No. 37 (1978); Australia's Policy Towards Aborigines, 1967–1977: Report No. 35 (1978).

[23] See Survival International Rev. (Spring 1978).

[24] See [1974] Y.B. Int'l Org. 634 (Union of International Associations); see, e.g., World Peace Council, Violations of Human Rights in Haiti, El Salvador, and Nicaragua (undated).

[25] See note 3 supra. As of July 1974 there were over 600 NGOs with accredited relationships to the ECOSOC. Twenty held Consultative Status Category I; 192 held Consultative Status Category II. In addition, over 400 were listed on the Roster of the Office of Public Information by action of ECOSOC (86) or of the Secretary-General (27) or by virtue of their status with other U.N. bodies or specialized agencies. U.N. Doc. E/INF/144 (1974). The 1974 Yearbook of International Organizations lists over 4,000 international organizations, most of which are nongovernmental, and also suggests a definition, at 15, which supplements the distinctions

International Labour Organisation (ILO), the U.N. Educational, Scientific and Cultural Organization (UNESCO),[26] the Council of Europe,[27] and the Organization of American States (OAS).[28] Although they are founded upon a membership of people, rather than of governments, NGOs are most often structured so that there exists an international secretariat which more or less represents national sections in various countries.[29] The national sections often vary considerably. For example, the International League for Human Rights has its international secretariat in New York City near the U.N. building and counts among its sections the National Council for Civil Liberties in the United Kingdom, the Canadian Civil Liberties Association, the Moscow Human Rights Committee, the American Civil Liberties Union, and the New Zealand Democratic Rights Council,[30] P.E.N., which is an international association of poets, playwrights, essayists, editors, and novelists, and which possesses a total world membership of some 10,000, has its headquarters in London, and also has an American Center in New York City.[31] The International Commission of Jurists has national sections of lawyers and judges in over fifty countries.[32] The Commission itself is comprised of about forty dis-

between NGOs in Category I, Category II, and on the ECOSOC Roster, as set forth in E.S.C. Res. 1296, 44 U.N. ECOSOC, Supp. (No. 1), at 21, U.N. Doc. E/4548 (1968). *See also* note 71 *infra*.

  Nongovernmental organizations are specifically recognized by art. 71 of the U.N. Charter and frequently are called upon to help execute, publicize, or contribute to U.N. decisions. *See Preparatory Conference of Experts on the Role of Nongovernmental Organizations—Report*, 27 Int'l A. 35–36 (1975); U.N. Doc. E/C.2/603 (1963); E. Brock, Representation of Non-Governmental Organizations and the United Nations (1955); J. Robb, The Historical Background of Article 71, Charter Review Study Group, Sixth General Conference of Consultative NGOs, U.N. Doc. GC/SG/WP-NY/2/Rev. 1, at 2 (1955); U.N. Doc. E/43 (1946).

  [26] UNESCO, Directives Concerning UNESCO's Relations with International Non-Governmental Organizations (1960); *see* American Council of Learned Societies, The Role of Non-Governmental Organizations in International Intellectual Cooperation (1964).

  [27] *See* Council of Europe, The Consultative Assembly Procedure and Practice 372–81 (1969). *See also* notes 101–02 *infra*.

  [28] Organization of American States, Directory of Organizations with Which the OAS Has Agreements for Cooperative Relations (1973); Standards on Cooperative Relations Between the Organization of American States and the United Nations, its Specialized Agencies, and Other National and International Organizations, O.A.S. Doc. AG/Res. 57 (1971).

  The Organization of African Unity also grants observer status to NGOs. *See, e.g.*, O.A.U. Doc. CM/Res. 330 (XXII) (1972); O.A.U. Doc. CM/Res. 289 (XIX) (1974).

  [29] *See* B. Stosic, Les Organisations Non Gouvernmentales et Les Nations Unies 21–120 (1964); L. White, International Non-Governmental Organizations: Organizations; Their Purposes, Methods and Accomplishments (1968). *See also* Potter, *Non-Governmental Organizations Viewed by a Political Scientist*, 14 Int'l A. 403 (1962); *Draft Convention Aiming at Facilitating the Work of International Non-Governmental Organizations*, 11 Int'l A. 520 (1959).

  [30] International League for the Rights of Man, Annual Report 23 (1973); 15 Y.B. Int'l Org. 399 (1974); *Int'l League for Human Rights, supra* note 12.

  [31] *See* P.E.N. American Center, P.E.N., What it is—What it does 1 (1974).

  [32] International Commission of Jurists, Objectives, Organization, Activities (1972); *see* 15 Y.B. Int'l Org. 283–85 (1974).

tinguished jurists from many states in Africa, Asia, Western Europe, and the Americas, with a secretariat in Geneva and an office in New York City for its representatives to the United Nations.

One of the largest and newest of the NGOs concerned with human rights is Amnesty International.[33] There are Amnesty International sections in forty-one countries, but its main working arms are the international secretariat with its 50 researchers and other staff of 120 in London, as well as the approximately 2,700 groups principally located in Western Europe, the United States, Canada, Japan, and elsewhere—each group working for adopted prisoners of conscience, on country-oriented campaigns, or on urgent appeals for prisoners in imminent danger of torture or execution.

Considering what needs to be done, none of these organizations is very large. With rare exceptions the central offices are staffed by only a handful of people. Almost all the organizations rely heavily on voluntary work by members and subsist on meager budgets.

B.   SELECTION OF HUMAN RIGHTS VIOLATIONS AND FACT-FINDING

Amnesty International, the International Commission of Jurists, the International League for Human Rights, the Commission of the Churches on International Affairs of the World Council of Churches, the Pontifical Commission Justice and Peace, the International Committee of the Red Cross, and other international NGOs gather information in more or less the same way. At their international centers they collect information about human rights problems from newspapers, magazines, professional journals, U.N. publications, members, relatives of prisoners, escaped or freed victims, expatriot groups, disgruntled public officials, incidental travelers, and from each other. The reports are of widely varying reliability, though some care is taken to check sources and contradictions. The older organizations may have clipping files and dossiers about human rights violations going back ten or twenty years. For example, the treatment of Jehovah's Witnesses in Malawi; Kurds in Iraq, Iran, and Turkey; ministers and priests in Poland, Afghanistan, and China; and the indigenous peoples in Australia, New Zealand, Norway, Canada, Brazil, and the United States raise recurrent problems.[34] Often it is very useful to see the

[33] AI, Amnesty International Report 1982, at ii, 7 (1982).

[34] *See, e.g.,* Minority Rights Group, Jehovah's Witnesses in Central Africa (1976); The Kurds (1975); What Future for the Amerindians of South America (1973); Canada's Indians (1974). The Anti-Slavery Society—one of the oldest nongovernmental organizations, originally founded in 1823—has particularly concerned itself with the rights of indigenous peoples. So has Survival International, based in London. More recently, the Indian Treaty Council has obtained consultative status with ECOSOC and other North American Indian groups have become interested in activity at the United Nations.

newest outbreak of oppression or violence in the light of previous incidents and the governmental responses to them.

Quite frequently, the NGO must first determine whether it would be useful to intervene in a particular situation in which human rights are being violated. Might intervention help or hurt the victims? What sort of intervention would be most effective? Have interventions with this country or with respect to this type of problem been successful in the past? Are the officials of the country receptive to initiatives from outsiders? Are the facts sufficiently well established to permit diplomatic intervention or publicity? Which NGO would be most effective in raising the issue?

The standard of care of the various organizations differs considerably. Also, limited resources of the organizations require allocation of effort. There is sometimes a risk that an NGO will choose to investigate and pursue a particular violation only because the state concerned is an easy target. NGOs may avoid pursuing violations because that might upset influential friends, sources of financial support, friendly governments, etc. The possibilities for abuse in the selection of test cases are legion. It is a tribute to most of the organizations that they do remain remarkably independent despite their small size and impecunious position.

To a degree the nongovernmental organizations concerned with human rights remain subject to Cold War differences.[35] The International Association of Democratic Lawyers (IADL), the World Peace Council, and the World Federation of Democratic Youth find a large part of their members and support in socialist countries and in allied groups in nonsocialist nations. In the United States, for example, the National Conference of Black Lawyers and the National Lawyers Guild are affiliated with the International Association of Democratic Lawyers. The International Commission of Jurists and Amnesty International find most of their strength outside of the socialist countries. Accordingly, in the United States, the American Bar Association has a Committee of its International Law Section which cooperates with the International Commission of Jurists.

During periods of detente, joint action among the various organizations grows and differences are diminished.[36] The IADL is, however,

---

[35] *See* Epps, *Human Rights: General Reflection*, in 1 Human Rights and Christian Responsibility 13–14 (Commission of the Churches on International Affairs 1974).

[36] Governments may use friendly NGOs to test ideas in international discussion or to carry out political positions. For example, the representative of the People's Republic of China urged the expulsion of all NGOs with ties to Taiwan as a way of continuing political pressure on the Taiwan Government. U.N. Doc. E/SR.1944, at 3, 21–22 (1975); *cf.* E.S.C. Res. 2/3, 2 U.N. ESCOR, Annex 8a, at 360, para. 3, U.N. Doc. E/43/Rev. 2 (1946) (discredited fascist organizations excluded).

more restrained in its criticism of human rights violations in socialist countries than is the International Commission of Jurists.[37] Amnesty International, the Commission of the Churches on International Affairs, the Friends World Committee for Consultation, the Pontifical Commission Justice and Peace, Pax Romana, and the World Conference on Religion and Peace are far more willing to discuss such issues as conscientious objection and religious freedom[38] than are the World Peace Council and the World Federation of Democratic Youth.[39]

C. WHAT DO INTERNATIONAL NONGOVERNMENTAL ORGANIZATIONS DO TO IMPLEMENT HUMAN RIGHTS?

Most governments seem to be sensitive to any criticism by these organizations. The USSR has been very concerned about discussion concerning the emigration of Jews and the imprisonment of Ukrainians, Baptists, and Soviet human rights leaders. Guatemala has been at times highly sensitive to criticism of torture, imprisonment, and killing of *campesinos*, Indians, journalists, lawyers, and unionists.[40] The United States has considered its image in the world community to be very delicate with respect to the treatment of its black citizens and indigenous peoples.[41] Most countries are proud of the humanitarian ideals which form one basis for the legitimacy of the state. Almost every country's constitution prominently sets forth the fundamental rights of its citizens. If a government—whether democratic or dictatorial—acts tyranically towards its citizens, it violates the basic trust which permits it to continue ruling. It appears that even most dictatorships attempt to show at least a façade of democratic trappings or an appearance of enlightenment.

Governments do not wish to be reminded that they are ignoring the fundamental rights of their citizens. They particularly do not like to be

[37] *Le Congres de l'Association internationale des juristes democrates est marque par l'entre' enforce des pays du tiers-monde*, Le monde, Apr. 8, 1975, at 13, col. 3.

[38] *E.g.*, U.N. Doc. E/CN.4/NGO/176 (1974); U.N. Doc. E/CN.4/NGO/179 (1974); U.N. Doc. E/CN.4/NGO/181 (1974). *See also* Schaffer & Weissbrodt, *Conscientious Objection to Military Service as a Human Right*, Rev. Int'l Comm'n Jurists 33 (No. 9, 1972) [hereinafter cited as *Conscientious Objection*].

[39] Somewhat similar observations might be made about the Cold War origins and changing relations of the International Confederation of Free Trade Unions (ICFTU), on the one hand, and the World Federation of Trade Unions, on the other. *See* Boggs, *The ILO's Rocky Road*, Free Trade Union News, Sept. 1974, at 1, 11–12.

[40] AI, Briefing on Guatemala (1976); AI, Violence in Rural Guatemala (1979); AI, Repression of Journalists in Gautemala (1979); AI Repression of Lawyers in Guatemala (1979); AI, Repression of Trade Unions in Guatemala (1979).

[41] National Council of the Churches of Christ in the U.S.A., *Human Rights in North America*, in 2 Human Rights and Christian Responsibility 80–101 (Commission of the Churches on International Affairs 1974); National Conference of Black Lawyers, *et al.*, Petition to the United Nations Commission on Human Rights . . . Human Rights Violations in the United States, Dec. 17, 1978.

criticized in the openness of international debate.[42] Also, the International Bill of Human Rights[43] has attained such broad acceptance in the international community that a government cannot violate basic human rights without some fear of exposure. The pointed finger of shame, particularly when directed by an organization with some appearance of impartiality and political independence, has caused executions to be stayed, death sentences to be commuted, torture to be stopped, prison conditions to be ameliorated, prisoners to be released, and more attention to be paid to the fundamental rights of many citizens.[44]

Although some countries are not as sensitive as others and some resist pressure for many years, the pressure has some effect. For example, the racist government of South Africa is isolated from the world community.[45] It is not asked to participate in international

[42] For example, the Chilean Government considered it necessary to respond to criticism in International Commission of Jurists reports by paying for a series of half-page advertisements in the New York Times and the Washington Post. *See* McCarthy, *The Chilean Junta's Advertising Campaign*, Washington Post, Dec. 10, 1974, at A20, col. 3. *See also* U.N. Doc. E/SR.1944, at 8–9 (remarks of representative of Egypt), at 13–14 (remarks of representative of USSR) (1975). Sensitivity of countries to criticism caused UNESCO to ask AI not to hold its Paris Conference on Torture in UNESCO facilities in Dec. 1973 because of the issuance of a report which discussed allegations of torture in 65 countries. *UNESCO Ban Fails to Halt Conference*, AI Newsletter, Jan. 1974, at 2. *See also* Permanent Mission of India to the United Nations, *Groundless Charges Against India by League of Human Rights*, Press Release, June 7, 1976.

[43] *See* note 130 *infra*.

[44] For example, hesitant internal political liberalization and international human rights pressure apparently have combined to result in the release of some political detainees after others were executed. *Morocco*, Rev. Int'l Comm'n Jurists 19 (No. 13, 1974); AI, Morocco Background Paper (1974); AI, Recent Developments in Morocco (1974); H. Woesner, Report on Mission to Morocco (1973). Shortly after the International Commission of Jurists article, *Dents in the Image of Indonesia*, Rev. Int'l Comm. Jurists 16 (No. 13, 1974), appeared, the Indonesian government freed some of the 42 detainees mentioned in the article. *Cf. Amnesty Welcomes Commutation of Death Sentence of Pole*, AI News Release, Jan. 23, 1973. A Bulgarian economist was allowed to leave his country in Aug. 1974 after AI joined a worldwide campaign for his release from a death sentence. *Spetter Thanks Amnesty*, 1 AI Matchbox 26 (Winter 1975). *See also AI Appeals to India to Release 30,000 Detainees During Strike Crisis*, AI Newsletter, June 1974, at 2; *India Frees Rail Strike Leaders*, AI Newsletter, July 1974, at 2.

[45] Ndoh, *Violation of Human Rights in Africa* 8–11 (Commission of the Churches on International Affairs Background Information No. 3 1975); Carlson, *South Africa Today: The Security of the State vs. The Liberty of the Individual*, 2 Human Rights 125 (1972); U.N. Doc. A/8770 (1972); Davis, *Infringements of the Rule of Law in South Africa*, Rev. Int'l Comm'n Jurists 22 (No. 7, 1971); *A Vast Prison House*, Objective: Justice, Jan. 1970, at 15–16, U.N. Doc. ST/OPI/371 (1970); *The Lawless Laws of South Africa, id.* at 17–19; *Southern Africa*, Rev. Int'l Comm'n Jurists 19, 21–25 (No. 3, 1969); International Commission of Jurists, Erosion of the Rule of Law in South Africa (1968); U.N. Doc. ST/PSCA/SER.A/2 (1967); International Commission of Jurists, South Africa and the Rule of Law (1960), *Namibia: The United Nations and U.S. Policy, Hearings Before the Subcomm. on Int'l Organizations of the House Comm. on Int'l Relations*, 94th Cong., 2d Sess. (1976); AI, Annual Report 1975–76, at 67–68 (1976), AI, Annual Report 1974–75, at 49–50 (1975); U.N. Press Release HR/219 (Aug. 22, 1974) (report from International Student Movement for the United Nations concerning floggings in Namibia); *Freedom to Namibia*, International Defense and Aid Fund for Southern Africa News, Nov. 1974, at 7; Minority Rights Group, The Namibians of Southwest Africa (1974); *Military Interests and Decolonization*, Objective: Justice. Apr. 1970, at 34, U.N. Doc. ST/OPI/372 (1970).

sporting events. It is subjected to trade sanctions and arms embargoes. Its citizens often are shunned or questioned when they travel abroad. For a time Greece under the Colonels was morally, economically, and politically isolated from European allies because it tortured and illegally imprisoned its citizens. Both the isolated country and to a lesser extent its supporters suffer opprobrium in the eyes of world opinion—directed by the news media, international governmental organizations, and, to a considerable degree, international nongovernmental organizations.

In some ways, NGOs are far freer to criticize where criticism is due than are governments or international bodies. Most governments are concerned with keeping their bilateral relations on a friendly basis. Even where relations are quite close—or perhaps because they are close—governments hesitate to criticize one another.[46] Governments do occasionally make diplomatic interventions on issues relating to human rights (and should be doing much more in this respect), but presently they act on human rights questions infrequently and with exaggerated circumspection.

Although the setting of intergovernmental organizations permits somewhat greater scope for forthright discussion of human rights problems, governments remain reluctant to talk about such issues openly. When they do mention human rights issues, they are often accused of political bias. For example, the United States may mention violations of human rights in Eastern Europe, while the USSR and the Arab countries insist upon debates concerning human rights in Israel.

In most circumstances, NGOs are more independent of political forces and thus are able to identify and criticize human rights violations wherever they may occur. NGOs do not need to wait for the coming into force and active enforcement of international conventions or the development of acceptable implementation procedures in the U.N. Commission on Human Rights or other intergovernmental organizations. When those principles and procedures are available, the NGOs make use of them, but there is already an ample delineation of human rights standards in the International Bill of Human Rights for much NGO activity.

1. *Diplomatic Interventions and Missions by NGOs*

Having investigated and selected a case, the NGO may decide to seek a visit with representatives of the government concerned. Unless there is a need for immediate cessation of the human rights violations, *e.g.*, torture or impending execution, the initial contact may only

---

[46] *See generally* Weissbrodt, *Human Rights Legislation and U.S. Foreign Policy*, 7 Ga. J. Int'l & Comp. D. 231, 232–40, 281–83 (1977) [hereinafter cited as *Human Rights Legislation*].

apprise the government that a violation has been noted and the NGO may propose inquiry by appropriate officials. Such contacts generally are made discreetly, *i.e.*, with no publicity. Often the NGO functions as a much-needed intermediary between the highest officials in a government and human rights victims. In the absence of an effective right of *habeas corpus*, a free press, and/or an ombudsman, high officials may not know what is happening within their own prisons or may try to avoid knowing. But once an NGO brings a problem to the government's attention it becomes more difficult to ignore human rights violations. Also, interventions are made mostly with diplomatic personnel who have little to do with prisons or secret police and who are familiar with the governing international standards of conduct. When made aware of the problem and the possible risk of embarrassment, these diplomatic officers may take steps to help remedy the situation.

In addition, the NGO may offer or ask to send a mission to the country, to interview alleged victims, lawyers, and government officials, to witness trials, or to attempt to mediate disputes. Some countries are sufficiently concerned about their image (or sufficiently confident that the accusations are unfounded) that they accept NGO visits.[47] For example, Iran in 1972 received several visits from distinguished lawyers representing the IADL, the International Federation of Human Rights, and the International Commission of Jurists.[48] Chile received missions from Amnesty International and the International Commision of Jurists in 1973 and 1974.[49] The International League for Human Rights sent observers to trials in Yugoslavia during 1975 and in Spain during 1973. Amnesty International sent an observer

[47] *See, e.g.*, AI, Report of an Amnesty International Mission to Israel and the Syrian Arab Republic to Investigate Allegations of Ill-Treatment and Torture 10–24 October 1974 (1975). Sometimes an NGO is invited by a government to visit the country and to act as an impartial international fact-finding body on allegations of human rights violations. *See, e.g.*, W.C.C. *Team's Visit to Iraq*, Commission of the Churches on International Affairs, Newsletter No. 5 (1975); International Commission of Jurists, Report on the Events in Panama January 9–12, 1964 (1964); International Commission of Jurists, Report on the British Guiana Commission of Inquiry (1965).

[48] The International Federation for the Rights of Man, centered in Paris, has also sent numerous missions to Iran. *See also* AI, Briefing on Iran (1976); W. Butler & G. Levasseur, Human Rights and the Legal System in Iran (1976); *Iran*, Rev. Int'l Comm'n Jurists 5 (No. 8, 1972); AI, Iran: Trial Procedures for Political Prisoners (1972); Y. Baudelot, Prison Conditions for Political Detainees in Iran (1974). *See also* Simons, *Shah's 'Phobia' Pushes Iran*, Washington Post, 27 May 1974, at AI, col. 2; *More Executions in Iran*, 1 AI Matchbox 13 (Spring/Summer 1974).

[49] *See Human Rights in Chile, Hearings Before the Subcomm. on Inter-American Affairs of the House Comm. on Foreign Affairs*, 93d Cong., 2d Sess., at 1, 2–28, 51–84 (1974). The International Association of Democratic Lawyers, the International Association of Catholic Lawyers, and the International Federation for the Rights of Man also sent a combined mission to Chile in Fall 1973.

to a post-trial hearing in South Dakota in 1979,[50] and Afghanistan received an Amnesty International representative in 1979.[51] South Africa has accepted International Commission of Jurists observers for trials for over ten years.[52]

The International Committee of the Red Cross (ICRC), as one of the oldest and largest of the NGOs concerned with human rights, has the most extensive program of visiting places of detention with the permission of the respective governments.[53] The ICRC is composed almost exclusively of Swiss nationals; its international character is based on aims and activities which include visits to prisoner of war and civilian internment camps pursuant to the four Geneva Conventions of 1949 and the two Protocols of 1977.[54] For example, in 1978 the ICRC visited prisoners of war in Chad, Mauritania, Morocco, and Western Sahara.[55] In the same year, the ICRC also visited a number of persons detained for offenses or reasons of a political nature in Afghanistan, Argentina, Chile, Indonesia, Iran, Nicaragua, Paraguay, Portugal, Rhodesia, South Africa, Yemen Arab Republic, and Zaire.

The ICRC provides detailed findings of its missions only to host governments. Because of its considerable resources and reputation for independence it has less difficulty in obtaining permission to send missions than do other NGOs. In cases where governments misrepresent the findings, the ICRC reserves the right to release its results. Such was the situation with respect to the ICRC visits to Greek places of detention in 1969. Similarly, in 1980 the ICRC released full reports of earlier visits to Iranian prisons after the new Iranian régime released partial reports.[56] But the ICRC annual reports, monthly bulletins, occasional press releases, and the *ICRC Review* also reveal very significant information about the number of prisoners visited.

The recommendations of the NGO missions—particularly the ICRC missions—have substantial impact upon the treatment of political offenders. With the partial exception of the ICRC, most NGOs publicly report the results of their missions and thus provide invaluable first-hand information about violations of human rights.

[50] AI, Annual Report 1979, at 74 (1979).
[51] AI, Violations of Human Rights and Fundamental Freedoms in the Democratic Republic of Afghanistan (1979).
[52] *See* note 45 *supra*.
[53] *See* T. Bissell, The International Committee of the Red Cross and the Protection of Human Rights (1963); A. Milani, Les Organisations Non Gouvernmentales Des Nations Unies 63–73 (1952).
[54] International Committee of the Red Cross, Activities, Principles, Organization (1971); *see* Moreillon, *supra* note 13. *See also* ch. 9. *supra*.
[55] International Committee of the Red Cross, Annual Report 1978, at 20–23, 43 (1978).
[56] *Red Cross Found Jail Better in Shah's Last Year*, Washington Post, 10 Jan. 1980, at A23, cols. 1–4.

2. *Public Discussion of Human Rights Violations*

Publicity is clearly an important factor in the implementation of human rights law by NGOs. For example, in December 1971, the International Commission of Jurists issued an article entitled *Condemned without hope in California* on the use of indeterminate sentences in that state.[57] The article was the result of a visit by a representative of the Commission and was distributed to the justices of the California Supreme Court. They probably were a bit dismayed to find California discussed in the same journal with Guinea, Greece, Northern Ireland, Paraguay, Spain, Taiwan, and the USSR. Certainly the article drew international attention to California's sentencing practices and added to the growing criticism of the indeterminate sentence law and of the California Adult Authority which administered the law. The indeterminate sentence law has been repealed in California and questioned elsewhere. It is worthy of note also that the Supreme Court of California subsequently made at least one decision declaring the law cruel and unusual punishment as applied.[58]

Similarly, Amnesty International's 1972 report on allegations of torture in Brazil contained a listing of more than one thousand torture victims and demonstrated a consistent pattern of gross violations of human rights in Brazil.[59] P.E.N. has issued reports on the suppression of writers and intellectuals in Czechoslovakia.[60] The International Commission of Jurists has issued thoroughly researched reports on violations of human rights in Uganda,[61] Uruguay,[62] and Chile.[63] In addition, the Commission produces a *Review* twice each year which describes and comments upon human rights problems throughout the world. The International League for Human Rights and the Lawyers Committee for International Human Rights have produced reports on Argentina, Burundi, Greece, the USSR, Northern Ireland, and Yugoslavia. The ICRC and Amnesty International produce annual reports and some individual reports, which, taken together with the *Review of the International Commission of Jurists*, constitute an illuminating picture of human rights problems for each year.[64]

[57] Rev. Int'l Comm'n Jurists 17 (No. 7, 1971).

[58] *In re* Lynch, 8 Cal. 3d 410, 438–39, 503 P.2d 921, 940 (1973) (citing the International Commission of Jurists article). The California legislature has now abolished indeterminate sentencing in that state. Cal. Pen. Code §§ 667.5, 1168, 1170 *et seq.*, 12022 *et seq*; Oppenheim, *Computing a Determinate Sentence . . . New Math Hits the Courts*, 51 Cal. St. B.J. 604 (1976).

[59] AI, Report on Allegations of Torture in Brazil (1972).

[60] P.E.N. American Center, Czechoslovakia (Country Report No. 1, 1973).

[61] International Commission of Jurists, Violations of Human Rights and the Rule of Law in Uganda (1974, Supp. 1974).

[62] International Commission of Jurists, ICJ and Amnesty International Mission Report on Continuing Torture and Ill-Treatment of Political Suspects in Uruguay (1975).

[63] M. MacDermot, Final Report of International Commission of Jurists Mission to Chile (1974, Supp. 1975).

[64] Nevertheless, an NGO concerned with human rights might well consider the need for a

Often, press releases and other statements are issued jointly by NGOs. For example, in March 1971 Amnesty International, the Commission of the Churches on International Affairs, the Committee on Society, Development and Peace (SODEPAX, a joint organization of the World Council of Churches and the Pontifical Commission Justice and Peace), the International Federation of Human Rights, the International Association of Democratic Lawyers, the International Commission of Jurists, the International Youth and Student Movement for the United Nations, the Women's International League for Peace and Freedom, the World Federation of Trade Unions, the World Muslim Congress, and other NGOs made a united appeal to the Brazilian government to end the detention of political prisoners and the use of torture.[65] The U.S. Conference of Bishops[66] and the National Conference of Brazilian Bishops[67] made similar appeals to the Brazilian government.

In recent years the World Jewish Congress, the American Jewish Committee, and the American Israel Public Affairs Committee have mounted remarkably successful campaigns with respect to Jews in the Soviet Union, Iraq, and Syria.[68] In 1974, the International Commission of Jurists, the Women's International League for Peace and Freedom, and a number of other NGOs obtained the release of a lawyer from a South Vietnamese prison by convincing universities to invite her to teach and by fostering public discussion of her case by the press and by members of the U.S. Congress. The International League for Human Rights was successful in obtaining permission for Valery Chalidze to leave the USSR by similar methods. Despite the passing of International Women's Year in 1975, however, relatively few organizations have begun to work particularly and effectively for the release of women political prisoners or started to work in the

thorough annual or biannual review of the human rights situation in each country of the world. *See* Amnesty International, Report on Torture (2d ed. 1975); *Conscientious Objection, supra* note 38; International Commission of Jurists, *The Legal Protection of Privacy*, 24 Int'l Soc. Sci. J. 417 (1972). AI has begun to fill this need by issuing briefings on various countries. *See, e.g.*, AI, Briefing on Taiwan (Republic of China) (1976); AI Briefing on Malawi (1976). In addition, the U.S. State Department was initially required to publish reports on the human rights situation of all countries receiving U.S. aid and has begun to publish reports on all nations in the world. *See Human Rights Legislation, supra* note 46, at 263–74 (1977).

[65] *Study of the Situation in Brazil which Reveals a Consistent Pattern of Violations on Rights*, in *House Hearings on International Protection of Human Rights, supra* note 1, at 673–75. In order to promote cooperation and coordination among those NGOs particularly concerned with international human rights matters in the U.N. about 65 of these organizations meet and work regularly under the aegis of the Committees of NGOs on Human Rights in New York and Geneva.

[66] *Id.* at 671–73.

[67] *Id.* at 675–80; *see* Rev. Int'l Comm'n Jurists 15 (No. 11, 1973).

[68] *See, e.g.*, American Jewish Committees, Current Situation of Jews in Arab Lands (1973).

international arena to eradicate more structural discriminations against women.[69]

Reports, studies, bulletins, newsletters, and press releases of such NGOs as the Commission of the Churches on International Affairs, the International League for Human Rights, the Carnegie Endowment for International Peace, the American Committee on Africa, the International Press Institute, Writers and Scholars International, the Minority Rights Group, and P.E.N. are further disseminated by newspapers, magazines, and other media which may report upon human rights violations.[70]

Consultative status permits NGOs to contribute to the work of the U.N. Commission on Human Rights and its Sub-Commission on Prevention of Discrimination and Protection of Minorities.[71] Representatives of Amnesty International, the Anti-Slavery Society, the Commission of the Churches on International Affairs, the International Commission of Jurists, the International League for Human Rights, and the Minority Rights Group often make written

[69] *See, e.g.,* 2 ISIS Int'l Bull. 16 (Oct. 1976); 10 ISIS Int'l Bull. 17 (Winter 1978/79). *See also* U.N. Doc. E/CN.6/CR.25 (1980) (Non-confidential list of communications concerning the status of women from numerous individuals, as well as such organizations as the International Council of Social Democratic Women, the International Association of Democratic Lawyers, the World Council of Churches, ISIS, International Federation of University Women, International Alliance of Women, Socialist International, Lutheran World Federation, etc.).

[70] *See* J. Carey, UN Protection of Civil and Political Rights 130 (1970).

[71] Nongovernmental organizations in Consultative Status Category I may suggest items for the agenda of the Economic and Social Council and its appropriate subordinate bodies. E.S.C. Res. 1296, para. 23, 44 U.N. ESCOR, Supp. (No. 1), at 22. U.N. Doc. E/4548 (1968); U.N. Doc. E/5677, rule 83, at 28 (1975); *see* Prasad, *The Role of Non-Governmental Organizations in the New United Nations Procedures for Human Rights Complaints,* 5 Denver J. Int'l L. & Pol. 460 n.84 (1975). Representatives of NGOs in Category I or Category II may sit as observers at public meetings of the Economic and Social Council, its committees, and sessional bodies. NGOs on ECOSOC's Roster may send representatives when matters within their field of competence are being discussed. *See* Rules of Procedure of the Functional Commissions of the Economic and Social Council, U.N. Doc. E/4767, rule 75, at 16 (1970). Representatives of NGOs in Category I and Category II may submit communications to the Economic and Social Council and its subsidiary organs. U.N. Doc. E/5677, rules 82–83, at 27–28 (1975); E.S.C. Res. 1296, paras. 23–24, *supra;* Epps, *NGO Interventions at the ECOSOC Committee on NGO's,* 26 Int'l A. 454 (1974); White, *United Nations Consultation with Nongovernmental Organizations,* 24 Int'l A. 539 (1972). *See also* U.N. Doc. E/C.2/INF/2 (1971); G. Riegner, Consultative Status (1969); Brief History of the Consultative Relationship of Non-Governmental Organization with the Economic and Social Council, U.N. Doc. E/C.2/R.35 (1968). There has continued to be some controversy over the right of NGOs to mention individual countries during open sessions of the U.N. Commission on Human Rights or its Sub-Commission. *See, e.g.,* note 80 *infra.* While oral statements are subject to the government's right of reply, NGOs are relatively free to discuss human rights 'situations' around the world, so long as they do not overtly criticize governments. The U.N. Secretariat staff will not generally circulate written statements under E.S.C. Res. 1296, however, unless the NGOs purport to discuss general human rights phenomena or regional world-wide problems, mentioning country situations only by way of example. These unwritten rules of interpreting E.S.C. Res. 1296 are subject to political considerations, depending upon the countries mentioned.

and oral presentations during discussions of human rights issues.[72] Some of the NGO presentations add significantly to the debates.[73] At the 1974 session of the Commission on Human Rights, Mrs. Salvador Allende was able to speak as a special representative of two NGOs.[74] Her speech, along with reports of violations from other NGOs and from delegates,[75] prompted an extraordinary telegram from the Commission to the Chilean government.[76] This step then led the Sub-Commission, *inter alia*, to request NGOs in consultative status 'to submit reliable information on torture and other, cruel, inhuman or degrading treatment or punishment in Chile' so that additional information could be studied by the Commission as a basis for future action.[77] The great bulk of the documentary information on Chile that

[72] For example, all but one of the five NGO written statements circulated at the Commission Human Rights session in 1974 were made jointly. U.N. Doc. E/5464, E/CN.4/1154, at 89–90 (1974); *see, e.g.,* U.N. Doc. E/CN.4/NGO/176 (1974) (urging a declaration on the elimination of all forms of religious intolerance; twenty-two NGOs participated in the statement, including organizations from most of the world's major faiths). *See also* U.N. Doc. E/5265, E/CN.4/1127, at 140–43 (1973) (six of eight NGO statements were joint); 58 U.N. ESCOR Supp. (No. 4), Annex V, at 7, U.N. Doc. E/5635, E/CN.4/1179 (1975) (two of five NGO statements were joint). Since individual NGOs are limited by E.S.C. Res. 1296 to very brief statements (500 words for Category II organizations and 2,000 words for Category I organizations), joint statements are very useful.

[73] Nongovernmental organizations contributed significantly to the drafting of the human rights provisions of the U.N. Charter and the International Bill of Rights. *J. Marie*, La Commission Des Droits de l'Homme de L'ONU 23–27 (1975); O. Nolde, Free and Equal (1968); Humphrey, *The U.N. Charter and the Universal Declaration of Human Rights*, in The International Protection of Human Rights 39 (E. Luard ed. 1967); J. Blaustein, Human Rights— A Challenge to the United Nations and to Our Generation 6–7 (1963); D. Robins, United States Non-Governmental Organizations and the Educational Campaign from Dumbarton Oaks, 1944 Through the San Francisco Conference, 1945 (1960); J. De Groote, American Private Organizations and Human Rights—1940–1945 (1954); L. White, International Non-Governmental Organizations 10 (1951).

In 1968, U.N. Secretary-General U Thant addressed an NGO Conference convened to commemorate the twentieth anniversary of the Universal Declaration of Human Rights and observed:

This may be an appropriate moment for recalling once again the decisive role of non-governmental organizations in obtaining the inclusion in the United Nations Charter of appropriate references to the international obligation of States to promote respect for human rights through national measures supported and encouraged by the action of the international community, effectively organized for that purpose. Subsequently, during 1947 and 1948, non-governmental organizations participated at every stage in the strenuous process of preparing the Universal Declaration of Human Rights . . .

U.N. Doc. SG/SM/999, at 2 (1968).

[74] The International Association of Democratic Lawyers and the Women's International Democratic Federation. *See* U.N. Doc. E/CN.4/SR.1271 & 1274 (1974).

[75] *See* U.N. Doc. E/CN.4/SR.1274 & 1275 (1974).

[76] On 1 Mar. 1974, the U.N. Commission on Human Rights sent a telegram to the Government of Chile expressing concern about violations of human rights in that country and calling particular attention to the cases of five prominent detainees. E.S.C. Res. 1873, 56 U.N. ESCOR, Supp. (No. 5) 56–57, U.N. Doc. E/5464, E/CN.4/1154 (1974).

[77] Sub-Comm'n on Prevention of Discrimination and Protection of Minorities Res. 8 (XXVII), U.N. Doc. E/CN.4/1160, E/CN.4/Sub.2/354, at 53–54 (1974). *See also Protection of Human Rights in Chile*, G.A. Res. 3219, 29 U.N. GAOR, Supp. (No. 31) 83, U.N. Doc. A/9631 (1974).

was made available to the Commission in February 1975 came from NGOs.[78] Moreover, the Commission directed a working group of five members to mount an official inquiry into the human rights violations in Chile and to report the results of its inquiry.[79]

Indeed, because many national delegations lack the resources to do thorough human rights research, NGOs often provide delegates with information and even draft documentation for use in U.N. bodies. Hence, NGOs are not dependent entirely upon their rights to make oral and written interventions. Their influence may be felt even more strongly in informal cooperation with governmental representatives.

Because some of the NGOs tend to be activist and because the NGO's work is of uneven quality, some U.N. personnel and some delegates to the United Nations share a certain degree of suspicion about the motives and reliability of NGOs.[80] It is very difficult to

[78] U.N. Doc. E/5636, E/CN.4/1179, at 23 (1976). *See also* U.N. Doc. A/10295, at 11 (1975).

[79] Human Rights Comm'n Res. 8 (XXXI), 56 U.N. ESCOR, Supp. (No. 4) 66, U.N. Doc. E/5625, E/CN.4/1179 (1975). The first progress report of the *Ad Hoc* Working Group on the Situation of Human Rights in Chile was issued in Oct. 1975. U.N. Doc. A/10285 (1975). The second substantial report of the *Ad Hoc* Working Group was issued on Oct. 8, 1976. U.N. Doc. A/31/253 (1976). In an unsuccessful attempt to blunt U.N. criticism of its human rights practices, Chile released several hundred prisoners in Nov. 1976. Kandell, *Chile Trying to Better Image Abroad of Its Visible Repression*, Minneapolis Trib., Dec. 19, 1976, at 18A, cols. 1–6. Nevertheless, the U.N. General Assembly on Nov. 22, 1976, passed an extremely strong resolution condemning the constant and flagrant violations, deploring Chile's failure to cooperate with the Working Group, calling for further scrutiny by the Working Group, and raising the possibility of humanitarian or legal aid to victims. U.N. Doc. A/C.3/31/L.26/Rev. 1 (1976). *See also* U.N. Doc. A/C.3/31/6 (1976); U.N. Doc. A/C.3/31/6/Add. 1 (1976); U.N. E/CN.4/1221 (1977); U.N. Doc. A/33/331 (1978); U.N. Doc. A/34/583/Add. 1 (1979); U.N. Doc. A/34/829, at 23–30 (1979); U.N. Doc. A/C.3/34/L.61 (1979) (U.N. Trust Fund for Chile).

[80] For example, following a resolution by the Economic and Social Council, E.S.C. Res. 1225, 42 U.N. ESCOR, Supp. (No. 1) 24, U.N. Doc. E/4393 (1967), the Committee of Non-Governmental Organizations of ECOSOC initiated an investigation by questionnaire of NGOs, which focused on covert government financing of NGOs, involvement of NGOs in South Africa, relations of NGOs to Zionism, and criticism by NGOs of human rights violations in socialist countries. *See* U.N. Doc. E/C.2/ST.224 (1968); U.N. Doc. E/2361 (1968).

After the responses to the questionnaire were received, the ECOSOC Committee on Non-Governmental Organizations considered the responses and decided which organizations should be accorded consultative status. *See* U.N. Doc. E/C.2/R.38/Add. 1 & 2 (1968); U.N. Doc. E/C.2/R.39/Add. 1–11 (1968). AI, for example, was maintained as a Category II organization by a vote of eight for, none against, with four abstentions. U.N. Doc. E/4647 (1969). The consultative status of one organization—the Co-ordinating Board of Jewish Organizations—was particularly attacked for its relation to Israel, U.N. Doc. E/4799 (1970); U.N. Doc. E/SR.1691–92 (1970). No NGOs were deprived of their status as a result of this investigation, but several of the more active NGOs faced attempted exclusion by governments that had previously been criticized for human rights violations. S. Liskovsky, The U.N. Reviews its NGO System (unpublished manuscript 1970). *See also* Ascher, *The Economic and Social Council Reviews Consultative Status of Non-Governmental Organizations*, 20 Int'l A. 27 (1968).

Another eruption of suspicion about NGOs in the protection of human rights came at the 1975 session of the Commission on Human Rights, when governmental representatives expressed concern about supposed breaches by NGOs of the confidentiality requirements of E.S.C. Res. 1503, 48 U.N. ESCOR, Supp. (No. 1A) 8, para. 8, U.N. Doc. E/4832/Add. 1 (1970), which established a procedure for consideration of complaints about human rights violations. *See* U.N.

David Weissbrodt

discern the factual basis for these suspicions, and despite the undercurrent of doubt, the United Nations and its members constantly rely upon NGOs for information and for dissemination as well as implementation of U.N. decisions.[81] The doubts and political opposition to the work of NGOs have, however, created some limitations on the contributions NGOs may make to the consideration of issues in U.N. bodies.[82]

3. The NGO Contribution to International Investigative Procedures

Nongovernmental organizations also have used the developing procedures for individual communications about human rights violations in the U.N. Commission on Human Rights, the International Labour Organisation, the Inter-American Commission on Human Rights, and the European Commission of Human Rights.[83]

Doc. E/5635, E/CN.4/1179, at 19 (1975); Shestack & Cohen, *International Human Rights: A Role for the United States* 14 Va. J. Int'l L. 591 (1974). *See also* U.N. Doc. E/CN.4/1070, E/CN.4/Sub. 2/323, at 24 (1971). Also, an oral statement on February 11, 1975, by Dr. Homer A. Jack, Secretary-General of the World Conference on Religion and Peace, alleging violations of religious freedom in the Philippines, Northern Ireland, Pakistan, Syria, Cyprus, Egypt, Czechoslovakia, the USSR, and Zaire evoked a storm of criticism. *Id.; see* U.N. Doc. E/L.1652 (1975). *See also* U.N. Doc. E/SR.1944 and 1947 (1975). Liskofsy, *Coping with the Question of the Violation of Human Rights and Fundamental Freedoms*, 8 Revue des Droits de l'Homme 883, 896–900 (1975).

Yet another such episode occurred in 1978, when all NGOs were asked to submit quadrennial reports of their activities pursuant to E.S.C. Res. 1296, *supra* note 24. This request was aimed at the more activist human rights NGOs, but in the end only NGOs which failed to respond were placed in any real jeopardy.

[81] NGOs often are asked to disseminate views of the United Nations. *See, e.g.,* U.N. Doc. E/4476 (1968). The General Assembly has invited NGOs in consultative status to submit material on alternative approaches and ways and means for improving the effective enjoyment of human rights and fundamental freedoms. G.A. Res. 3221, 29 U.N. GAOR, Supp. (No. 31) 84, U.N. Doc. A/9631 (1974). It also has urged them to assist victims of *apartheid* and to help end military, economic, political, and other support for *apartheid*. G.A. Res. 3223, 29 U.N. GAOR, Supp. (No. 31) 85, U.N. Doc. A/9631 (1974). *See also Contribution of Non-Governmental Organizations to the Implementation of the Declaration of the Granting of Independence to Colonial Countries and Peoples,* E.S.C. Res. 1740, 54 U.N. ESCOR, Supp. (No. 1) 36, U.N. Doc. E/5367 (1973); G.A. Res. 2785, 26 U.N. GAOR, Supp. (No. 29) 8, U.N. Doc. A/8429 (1971) (NGOs' measures against racism and racial discrimination); G.A. Res. 2716, 25 U.N. GAOR, Supp. (No. 28) 81, U.N. Doc. A/8028 (1970) (NGOs called upon to consider ways and means to promote the status of women); G.A. Res. 2588, 24 U.N. GAOR, Supp. (No. 30) 60, U.N. Doc. A/7630 (1969) (NGOs' contribution to the International Year of Human Rights); Excerpts from General Assembly Resolutions Concerning Non-Governmental Organizations, U.N. Doc. SP/OPI (1972); U.N. Doc. E/5257/Add. 1 (1973).

[82] *See* E.S.C. Res. 1296, *supra* note 24, paras. 23, 24, & 36. When NGOs are asked to submit material on human rights issues they are frequently reminded not to submit anything which is 'politically motivated contrary to the principles of the Charter of the United Nations'. *See, e.g.,* G.A. Res. 3221, 29 U.N. GAOR, Supp. (No. 31) 84, U.N. Doc. A/9631 (1974); U.N. Doc. A/9767, Annex I, at 12 (1974).

[83] One of the challenges ahead for NGOs will be the determination of what role, if any, they might play in the enforcement of the two most recently activated safeguards for international human rights: the International Covenant on Civil and Political Rights, G.A. Res. 2200, 21 U.N. GAOR, Supp. (No. 16) 52, U.N. Doc. A/6316 (1966), and the International Covenant on

The procedures of the Sub-Commission on the Prevention of Discrimination and Protection of Minorities of the Commission on Human Rights state that communications may originate from:

a person or group of persons who, it can be reasonably presumed, are victims of the violations . . . , any person or group of persons who have direct and reliable knowledge of those violations, or non-governmental organizations acting in good faith in accordance with recognized principles of human rights not resorting to politically motivated stands contrary to the provisions of the Charter of the United Nations and having direct and reliable knowledge of such violations[84]

Economic, Social and Cultural Rights, G.A. Res. 2200, 21 U.N. GAOR, Supp. (No. 16) 49, U.N. Doc. A/6316 (1966). *See* AI, Memorandum NS 60/76 (9 Apr. 1976). *But see* U.N. Doc. W/5764 (1976). For example, art. 2 of the Optional Protocol to the International Covenant on Civil and Political Rights, G.A. Res. 2200, 21 U.N. GAOR, Supp. (No. 16) 59, U.N. Doc. A/6316 (1966), establishes procedures for the receipt of communications from 'individuals who claim that any of their rights enumerated in the [Political] Covenant have been violated . . .' Just as with the [European] Convention on Human Rights and Fundamental Freedoms, 213 U.N.T.S. 221, *reprinted in* Basic Documents on Human Rights (2d ed. I. Brownlie 1981), this language does not appear to allow for direct NGO communications. *See also* note 101 *infra*. But there does not appear to be any reason why the Human Rights Committee, established pursuant to the Political Covenant, could not utilize NGO information in considering communications under the Optional Protocol. NGOs have begun to represent and assist human rights victims in preparing communications. Furthermore, NGOs should have consultative status with the working group established by ECOSOC for reviewing reports filed pursuant to the Economic Covenant.

---

[84] Sub-Commission on Prevention of Discrimination and Protection of Minorities Res. 1 (XXIV), para. (2)(a), U.N. Doc. E/CN.4/1070, E/CN.4/Sub. 2/323, at 50–51 (1971); *see* E.S.C. Res. 1503, *supra* note 79. *See also* E.S.C. Res. 728F, 28 U.N. ESCOR, Supp. (No. 1) 19, U.N. Doc. E/3290 (1939); Commission on Human Rights Res. 8 (XXIII), 42 U.N. ESCOR, Supp. (No. 6) 131, U.N. Doc. E/4322, E/CN.4/940 (1967); E.S.C. Res. 1235, 42 U.N. ESCOR, Supp. (No. 1) 17, U.N. Doc. E/4393 (1967); Sub-Commission on Prevention of Discrimination and Protection of Minorities Res. 2 (XXIV), U.N. Doc. E/CN.4/1070, E/CN.4/Sub. 2/323, at 52–53 (1971). *See generally* United Nations Action in the Field of Human Rights, U.N. Doc. ST/HR/2/Rev.1, at 276–77.

More recently, in 1974 the Sub-Commission established yet another procedure whereby NGOs may submit 'reliably attested information' 'in good faith', 'not politically motivated', and not 'contrary to the principles of the Charter of the United Nations', concerning 'violations of the basic human rights of persons detained or imprisoned throughout the world'. Such information is to be reviewed annually by the Sub-Commission. Sub-Commission on Prevention of Discrimination and Protection of Minorities Res. 7 (XXVII), U.N. Doc. E/CN.4/1160, E/CN.4/Sub. 2/354, at 52–53 (1974); *see* Burke, *New United Nations Procedure to Protect Prisoners and Other Detainees*, 67 Cal. L. Rev. 201 (1976). The Sub-Commission, in a 1975 resolution, specifically requested that the U.N. Secretariat 'submit timely in advance of its next session . . . a synopsis of the materials received from non-governmental organizations'. Sub-Commission on Prevention of Discrimination and Protection of Minorities Res. 1 (XXVIII), U.N. Doc. E/CN.4/Sub. 2/CRP. 3/Add.8 at para. 5 (1975) (prov.); *see* U.N. Doc. E/CN.4/Sub.2/L.635 (1975). Similarly, the Sub-Commission created a working group to review and to report to the Sub-Commission concerning 'reliable information on slavery and slave trade in all their manifestations, the traffic in persons and the exploitation or the prostitution of others' as transmitted by NGOs, as well as governments, etc. Sub-Commission on Prevention of Discrimination and Protection of Minorities Res. 11 (XXVII), U.N. Doc. E/CN.4/1160, E/CN.4/Sub. 2/354, at 57–58 (1974); Sub-Commission on Prevention of Discrimination and Protection of Minorities Res. 5 (XXVIII), U.N. Doc. E/CN.4/1180, E/CN.4/Sub.2/364 (1975). *See generally* Ermacora, *Procedure to Deal with Human Rights Violations: A Hopeful Start in the United Nations*, 7 Revue des Droits de l'Homme 670 (1974); Moller *Petitioning the United*

In 1979, the Lawyers Committee for International Human Rights submitted a communication to the Sub-Commission on the widespread violations of human rights in Argentina.[85] In the same year the International Commission of Jurists submitted a communication on Uruguay. Similarly, in 1979, Amnesty International submitted communications on Afghanistan, Argentina, the Central African Empire, Ethiopia, Indonesia, Paraguay, and Uruguay. The International League for Human Rights presented a communication on Paraguay. The National Conference of Black Lawyers presented a petition complaining about the United States. The International Conference of Free Trade Unions submitted a communication concerning Tunisia and the International Human Rights Law Group submitted one concerning Romania.[86]

Nongovernmental organizations also have had the right to and sometimes do contribute to special studies on various human rights issues conducted by the United Nations, as well as to the periodic human rights reporting formerly established by the Commission on Human Rights.[87] In addition, NGOs are entitled to submit written or oral communications in other U.N. bodies:[88] the Trusteeship Council,[89] the Special Committee against *Apartheid*,[90] the Special

Nations, Universal Human Rights 57 (No. 4, 1979); U.N. Doc. E/CN.4/1317 (1979). In 1980 the U.N. Commission on Human Rights also established a working group for disappearances, which could receive all reliable information. Much of such information will undoubtedly come from NGOs. *See* Comm'n on Human Rights Res. 20, U.N. Doc. E/CN.4/L.1501/Add.5 (1980).

[85] Lawyers Committee for International Human Rights, Violations of Human Rights in Argentina: 1976–1979 (1979).

[86] Since the Commission on Human Rights has not yet initiated even one thorough study or investigation as a result of a E.S.C. Res. 1503 communication, the effort of NGOs to utilize this procedure may not have been worthwhile. Furthermore, the secrecy of these procedures lessens their impact. In 1979 the Commission did remove the case of Equatorial Guinea from the Res. 1503 procedure and appointed a special rapporteur to make a thorough study, because the country refused even to respond to the Res. 1503 communication. U.N. Doc. E/1979/36, E/CN.4/1347, at 57 (1979). Accused nations seem to have usually taken the communications quite seriously and sufficient information has informally been revealed about communications to have had some incremental impact on human rights violations. *See U.N. Commission on Human Rights*, Rev. Int'l Comm'n Jurists 23 (No. 16, 1976); Newman, *The New United Nations Procedure for Human Rights Complaints: Reform, Status Quo, or Chamber of Horrors?*, 34 Annales de Droit 129 (1974). In addition, some prisoners may have been released.

[87] *E.g.*, Rannat, Study of Equality in Administration of Justice, U.N. Doc. E/CN.4/Sub.2/296/Rev.1, at 246 (1972); Study of the Right of Everyone to be Free From Arbitrary Arrest, Detention and Exile, U.N. Doc. E/CN.4/Sub. 2/200/Rev.1, at 74 (1960).

[88] The many U.N. procedures dealing with communications concerning human rights and the utilization of these procedures by NGOs are discussed in T. van Boven, Partners in the Promotion and Protection of Human Rights (unpublished manuscript 1976). *See also* G. da Foneseca, How to File Complaints of Human Rights Violations: A Practical Guide to Intergovernmental Procedures (1975); M. Tardu, Human Rights, The International Petition System (1980); U.N. Doc. E/5628 (1975); U.N. Doc. E/NGO/30 (1975).

[89] *See* U.N. Charter art. 87. An example of such a communication is Communication from Mr. Jerome J. Shestack, Chairman of the International League for the Rights of Man, Concerning the Trust Territory of the Pacific Islands, U.N. Doc. T/PET.10/101/Add.1 (1976).

[90] *See* G.A. Res. 1761, 17 U.N. GAOR, Supp. (No. 17) 9, U.N. Doc. A/5217 (1962); G.A. Res.

Committee on the Situation with regard to the Implementation of the Declaration on the Granting of Independence to Colonial Countries and Peoples,[91] the Commission on Human Rights *Ad Hoc* Working Group of Experts on Human Rights in Southern Africa,[92] and the Special Committee to Investigate Israeli Practices Affecting the Human Rights of the Population of the Occupied Territories.[93]

The International Labour Organisation provides the most formal role for nongovernmental organizations of employers and employees.[94] They are entitled to receive and to comment upon governmental reports and the measures taken to comply with the many conventions and recommendations which comprise the international law administered by the ILO.[95] The ILO has also established a special procedure for receiving complaints alleging infringements of trade union rights; these complaints may be submitted by workers' or employers' organizations or by governments to the ILO Governing Body's Committee on Freedom of Association—a tripartite group of representatives of employers, employees, and governments.[96] The

2396, 23 U.N. GAOR, Supp. (No. 18) 19, U.N. Doc. A/7218 (1968); G.A. Res. 2775C, 26 U.N. GAOR, Supp. (No. 29) 42, U.N. Doc. A/8429 (1971) (authorizing Special Committee to hold consultations with experts and representatives of the oppressed people of South Africa as well as anti-*apartheid* movements and NGOs concerned with the campaign against *apartheid*). *See also*, *e.g.*, U.N. Press Release GA/AP/501 (Sept. 17, 1975) (letter from Lawyers' Committee for Civil Rights Under Law concerning detentions in South Africa); Report of Special Committee on Apartheid, 28 U.N. GAOR, Supp. (No. 22) 56, para. 278, U.N. Doc. A/9022 (1973). *See generally* United Nations Action in the Field of Human Rights, U.N. Dc. ST/HR/2/Rev.1, at 349–50 (1980).

[91] *See* 17 U.N. GAOR, Annexes (Add. Agenda Item 25) paras. 16–111, U.N. Doc. A/5238. *See also*, *e.g.*, U.N. Doc. A/10156, at 22 (1975) (paper outlining violations of human rights in South Africa presented by the International Defense and Aid Fund for Southern Africa).

[92] *See* Comm'n on Human Rights Res. 2 (XXIII), U.N. Doc. E/CN.4/L.908 (1967), 42 U.N. ESCOR, Supp. (No. 6) 76, U.N. Doc. E/4822 (1967). The *Ad Hoc* Working Group reported to the Commission on Human Rights in 1970 that letters were sent to various NGOs and African liberation movements requesting 'relevant information, including the names and addresses of witnesses' and that 'the names of most of the witnesses who were heard by the Group or sent written information were communicated by several of these organizations'. U.N. Doc. E/CN.4/1020 (1970).

[93] *See* Report of the Special Committee, 25 U.N. GAOR, Annexes (Agenda Item 101) 19, para. 45, U.N. Doc. A/8039 (1971). *See also*, *e.g.*, *id.* Annex VI, at 103 (Memorandum Received by the Special Committee from the Israeli League for Human and Civil Rights).

[94] Fischer, *Les organisations nongouvernmentales et les institutions internationales*, in 2 Les Nations Unies, Chantier De L'Avenir 113–28 (1961).

[95] *See* ILO Const. art. 24 *et seq.*, Morse, *Note on ILO Procedures for Supervising the Observance of International Labor Standards and Related Constitutional Obligations*, in *House Hearings on International Protection of Human Rights*, *supra* note 2, at 574–76.

[96] *See generally* E. Hass, Human Rights and International Action (1970); G. Weaver, The International Labor Organization and Human Rights 2 (1968); International Labour Office, Freedom of Association (1972). For a description of the procedure to be followed by the Committee on Freedom of Association in examining complaints of alleged infringements of trade union rights, *see* 34 (No. 3) ILO O. Bull. 207–10 (1951). Doc. E/4144, at 20 (1965). Allegations may originate from national and international organizations of employers or workers enjoying consultative status with the ILO or having a direct interest in the subject matter of the allegation. *See* 29th Report of Governing Body Committee of Freedom of Association, 43 (No. 2) ILO O.

International Confederation of Free Trade Unions and the World Federation of Trade Unions have made use of these procedures.[97]

Beginning in 1970, several NGOs, principally the U.S. Conference of Bishops and the International Commission of Jurists, submitted communications to the Inter-American Commission on Human Rights with respect to allegations of torture, detention of political prisoners, and political executions in Brazil.[98] Brazil refused to permit an on-site investigation but did reply to the complaint. The Inter-American Commission concluded that 'evidence collected in this case leads to the persuasive presumption that in Brazil serious cases of torture, abuse and maltreatment have occurred to persons of both sexes while they were deprived of their liberty'.[99] In addition, Amnesty International and the International Commission of Jurists in 1973 called upon the Inter-American Commission to investigate allegations of mass arrests and political executions in Chile. Inter-American Commission experts visited Chile in the summer of 1974 and issued a report in October to the Permanent Council of the Organization of American States, thus providing a thorough documentation of the continuing pattern of human rights violations in that country.[100] Also

Bull. 79, para. 9 (1960); 1st Report of Governing Body Committee on Freedom of Association, *reprinted in* International Labour Organisation: Sixth Report of the International Labour Organisation to the United Nations, App. V, para. 14 (1952); Wolf, *supra* ch. 7, section I.D.1.

If the state gives its consent, a complaint may be submitted to an independent Fact-Finding and Conciliation Commission on Freedom of Association. Unlike a Commission of Enquiry established under ILO Const. art. 26 which can only deal with complaints arising under ratified conventions, the Fact-Finding and Conciliation Commission can deal with complaints that trade union rights have been infringed even apart from alleged failures to comply with ratified conventions. *See* Report on the Establishment of a Fact-Finding and Conciliation Committee on Freedom of Association, Submitted to the Conference by the Governing Body of the International Labour Office, 33 (No. 2) ILO O. Bull. 86 (App. VI) (1950). *See also, e.g.*, 57 (No. 1) ILO O. Bull. 40, 114 (1974) (appointment of Fact-Finding and Conciliation Committee panel to deal with violations of human and trade union rights in Chile); Wolf, *supra* ch. 7, section I.D.2.

[97] 129th Report of the Governing Body Committee on Freedom of Association, Case No. 666 (Portugal), 55 ILO O. Bull. 92 (1972).

[98] *See* Handbook of Existing Rules Pertaining to Human Rights, Inter-American Commission on Human Rights, O.A.S. Doc. OEA/Ser.L./V/II.13, Rev. 6, at 13–15, 27, 35–37, 44–47, 60–62 (1979).

[99] Inter-American Commission on Human Rights Res. on Case 1684 (Brazil), O.A.S. Doc. OEA/Ser.L./V/II.28, doc. 14 (1972); *see* Rev. Int'l Comm'n Jurists 4 (No. 8, 1972); Inter-American Commission on Human Rights Res. on Case 1684 (Brazil), O.A.S. Doc. OEA/Ser.L/V/II.30, doc. 36 (1973) (inserting observation in annual report). The case against Brazil, however, failed to proceed to full consideration by the O.A.S. General Assembly and was apparently concluded without definitive action. *See* Diuguid, *OAS Ministers Table Study of Brazil and the United States and OAS Response*, in *House Hearings on International Protection of Human Rights*, *supra* note 2; at 897–912 (1973); *cf.* O.A.S. Doc. OEA/Ser.P/AG/doc. 409/74, at 108–11 (1974); OAS. Doc. OEA/Ser.G/CP/doc. 399/75, at 38–42 (1975); B. Wood, International Organization and Human Rights with Special Reference to the Organization of American States 18, 20–22 (unpublished manuscript 1976).

[100] *See* O.A.S. Doc. OEA/Ser.L./V/II.34, doc. 21 (1974); Hauser, *Human Rights in Latin America*, Washington Post, Mar. 5, 1975, at A15, col. 1. Having received a second report, the

in 1974, the International League for Human Rights successfully urged the Inter-American Commission to take up the case of slavery and genocide in Paraguay.[101]

Nongovernmental organizations have not been particularly active in fostering individual applications to the European Commission of Human Rights.[102] Amnesty International and other NGOs have, however, been relatively active in lobbying for consideration of human rights issues by the Consultative Assembly of the Council of Europe.[103]

4. *Aid and Human Rights*

Nongovernmental organizations that have adequate financial resources provide much needed assistance to victims of human rights violations. The ICRC provides medical supplies, blankets, clothing and food to both prisoners and civilians. Both the Program to Combat Racism of the World Council of Churches and the ICRC have given medical and educational assistance and other types of aid to the liberation movements in southern Africa. The World Council of Churches, the League of Red Cross Societies, CARE, Catholic Relief Services, Caritas, and numerous other organizations provide development, training, educational, and humanitarian assistance. The International Defense and Aid Fund for Southern Africa and the Africa Legal Assistance Project of the Lawyers' Committee for Civil Rights Under Law have provided assistance to the families of prisoners, to the victims of oppression, and to the legal defense of persons accused under the racist laws of South Africa.

O.A.S. General Assembly at its June 1976 meeting in Santiago, Chile called upon the Chilean Government to ensure full respect for human rights in Chile. O.A.S. Doc. AG/Res. 243 (1976); *see* O.A.S. Doc. OEA/Ser.L./V/II.37, doc. 19 (1976).

[101] *Paraguay: Slavery & Genocidal Acts*, The Rights of Man Bull., Sept. 1974, at 6; *see* Inter-American Commission on Human Rights, Informe Anual, O.A.S. Doc. OEA/Ser.L./V/II.37, at 172 (1976); *cf.* U.N. Doc. E/CN.4/Sub.2, 353 (1974).

[102] It should be noted that, unlike most of the U.N. procedures discussed above, NGOs may submit petitions to the European Commission of Human Rights only if they claim to be themselves victims of human rights violations. *See* art. 25, European Convention. *See, e.g.,* X (Evangelical-Lutheran Church of Sweden) v. Sweden [1969], Y.B. Eur. Conv. on Human Rights 664, 674–76 (Eur. Comm'n of Human Rights). It should also be noted, however, that the European Commission may decide to hear as a witness, expert, or 'in any other capacity any person whose evidence or statements seem likely to assist it in the carrying out of its task'. European Commission of Human Rights, Rules of Procedure, Rule 54(1), at 24 (1971). In addition, although Rule 36 of the European Commission's Rules of Procedure provides only for representation of victims by lawyers and professors of law, it appears that NGOs might under some circumstances be permitted to represent victims of human rights violations or to appear as representatives or advisors for governments. European Commission of Human Rights, Rules of Procedure, Rule 36, at 16 (1971); *see* Council of Europe, Convention for the Protection of Human Rights and Fundamental Freedoms, Case-Law Topics, *Bringing an Application Before the European Commission of Human Rights* 7–10 (1972).

[103] *Cf.* Golsong, *Les organisations non gouvernmentales et le Conseil de l'Europe*, in Les Organisations non Gouvernmentales en Suisse 93–106 (1973); P. Rohn, Relations Between the Council of Europe and International Non-Governmental Organizations (1957).

It is sometimes possible for general aid programs to be coordinated to achieve human rights ends. The assistance and attention given to liberation movements in Portuguese-occupied territories probably helped achieve self-determination for Mozambique, Guinea Bissau, and Angola. During 1972 the African Conference of Churches and the World Council of Churches were successful in mediating and helping to bring to an end the civil war in Sudan because of the availability of assistance to salve the wounds of war and help foster development.[104]

5.   *Activities at Local Levels*

Because of greater resources, many national sections of international NGOs and, indeed, many NGOs without any direct international ties succeed in implementing international human rights law in ways unavailable to international NGOs.

In the United States there are innumerable organizations which deal with human rights on the domestic level. The American Civil Liberties Union, the National Association for the Advancement of Colored People, the NAACP Legal Defense and Educational Fund, the Lawyers' Committee for Civil Rights under Law, the American Jewish Committee, the Mexican-American Legal Defense and Educational Fund, and the Native American Rights Fund are a few of the more prominent. Very few of those organizations, however, have recognized international human rights law or have attempted to use it in dealing with domestic human rights problems.[105]

Since January 1975, about two dozen national and international organizations have become active in Washington, D.C., and have cooperated under the name of the Human Rights Working Group in promoting human rights concerns in the U.S. government.[106] One of

[104] *See Southern Sudan*, Rev. Int'l Comm'n Jurists 14–15 (No. 8, 1972); L. Niilus, Peace in the Sudan (mimeo, 12 Mar. 1973).

[105] The Africa Legal Assistance Project of the Lawyers' Committee for Civil Rights Under Law, in Washington, D.C., the Center for Constitutional Rights in New York City, the Center for Law and Social Policy in Washington, D.C., the International Human Rights Law Group in Washington, D.C., and the Lawyers Committee for International Human Rights are five U.S. NGOs which have undertaken domestic litigation to further international human rights objectives. For example, the Lawyers' Committee for Civil Rights Under Law and the Center for Constitutional Rights sought before the New York City Human Rights Commission to restrain the *New York Times* from advertising job positions in South Africa for which blacks would not be considered. Lawyers' Committee for Civil Rights Under Law, Africa Legal Assistance Project—Interim Report 36–39 (1974); Center for Constitutional Rights. Docket Report 18 (1974). *See* Lillich, *The Role of Domestic Courts in Promoting International Human Rights Norms*, 24 N.Y.L.S. L.Rev. 153 (1978); Stein, *Public Interest Litigation and United States Foreign Policy*, 18 Harv. Int'l L.J. 375 (1977); Weissbrodt, *Domestic Legal Activity in Further-ance of International Human Rights Goals*, in Implementing International Human Rights Through the Domestic Legal Process 10 (W. Raymond ed. 1976).

[106] *See Interest Groups, supra* note 3; Note, *Role of NGOs in Implementing Human Rights in Latin America*, 7 Ga. J. Int'l & Comp. L. 476 (1977); Coalition for a New Foreign and Military Policy, What is the Human Rights Working Group? (1976); Ottoway, *The Growing Lobby for Human Rights*, Washington Post, 12 Dec. 1976, at B1.

the most potent forms of international pressure may be exerted by professional groups such as doctors, lawyers, trade unionists, teachers, and scientists expressing their concern about the violation of the human rights of their fellow professionals or unionists.[107] In many countries such as South Africa, Namibia, and Zimbabwe, certain Christian churches have performed invaluable work for human rights, while receiving vital encouragement and support from their sister churches abroad, particularly through the World Council of Churches, Lutheran World Federation, and Pontifical Commission Justice and Peace.[108]

Amnesty International's success in recent years has been due considerably to its ability to mobilize the efforts of local groups who work for the human rights of named prisoners.[109] Normally, Amnesty groups are assigned prisoners of conscience (selected by the International Secretariat) from different countries. (Amnesty International defines prisoners of conscience as those who are imprisoned in violation of their human rights and who have neither used nor advocated violence.) Local Amnesty groups manifest a personal concern for the release of their prisoners and work toward that end by writing letters to prison officials, judges, and various government officers of the state involved, by visiting embassies, and by sending appeals to lawyers and other NGOs which might intervene. Also, groups attempt to write letters directly to their adopted prisoner or to his or her family thereby giving moral support, and to provide economic and other assistance where possible. Some Amnesty groups, in addition, send telegrams and letters to protest or prevent imminent torture or executions.

At times the groups give Amnesty International a rather amateurish image, but it cannot be doubted that its person-to-person and energetic approach can be effective when the more professional, sophisticated, better researched, and discreet efforts of its International Secretariat or of other international NGOs are not successful.[110] Since

[107] For example, a group of distinguished professors cabled a plea to the O.A.S. expressing deep concern over violations of human rights in Chile and raised particularly the case of a former head of the Technical University of Chile. *Venezuelan Minister Vows OAS Support*, Washington Post, 13 May 1975, at A3, col. 1. Similarly, the Arab Lawyers Union has worked for lawyers and judges whose rights are infringed. *See also* A.B.A. Comm. on Int'l Human Rights, Reports of the Working Group on Independence of Lawyers in Foreign Countries, June 30, 1976.

[108] *See* Pontifical Commission Justice and Peace, The Church and Human Rights (1975); F. Parakatil, Human Rights—A Summary of Actions (mimeo 1971); N. Malicky, Religious Groups at the United Nations (1971); N. MacDermot, Human Rights and the Churches 2–4 (1976); *Motu Proprio* of Pope Paul VI, *Instatiam et pacem* (1977).

[109] *See* AI, Handbook (1977).

[110] *Sole AI Adoptee in Libya is Released*, AI Newsletter, Feb. 1974, at 3; *Joint AI–ICJ Mission Visits Uruguay; Five 'Marcha' Journalists Released*, AI Newsletter, June 1974, at 2; *Freed Tanzanians Maulidi Mshangama and Ali Muhsin Barwani Thank Amnesty*, AI Newsletter, June 1974, at 3; *East German POC's Freed*, 1 AI Matchbox 25 (Winter 1975); *Two Released Rhodesian POC's Aided by AI Groups*, AI Newsletter, May 1974, at 3; *Mexico Releases Six After AI Pleas*, Amnesty Action, July–Aug. 1973, at 3.

the organization was formed in 1961, it has been estimated that Amnesty International has assisted in the release of thousands of prisoners of conscience.[111] Often, several NGOs work for the release of named prisoners and many political, military, economic, as well as human rights factors may combine to result in the release of prisoners.[112]

[111] Amnesty International has launched a campaign against the use of torture. *See* AI, Report on Torture. Two of the lastest steps in making torture an important issue of world concern came with the adoption of G.A. Res. 3218, 29 U.N. GAOR. Supp. (No. 31) 82, U.N. Doc. A/9631 (1974), and with the adoption of G.A. Res. 3453, 30 U.N. GAOR, Supp. (No. 34) 92, U.N. Doc. A/10034 (1976). *See also* U.N. Doc. A/9767 (1974); U.N. Doc. A/10158 (1975); U.N. Doc. 10260 (1975); *Torture as Policy: The Network of Evil*, Time, 16 Aug. 1976, at 31; notes 113–15 *infra* and accompanying text.

Amnesty International has similarly attempted since 1978 to make the death penalty a matter of international human rights concern. *See, e.g.,* AI, The Death Penalty (1979). But the results have been far less immediate. Several NGOs, including AI, the International Commission of Jurists, and the International League for Human Rights have also attempted to identify disappearances as another phenomenon worthy of international human rights attention. *See* AI U.S.A. 'Disappearances': A Workbook (1981). The U.N. General Assembly and Commission on Human Rights have responded promptly to this problem. G.A. Res. 33/173, 33 U.N. GAOR, Supp. (No. 45) 158, U.N. Doc. A/33/45 (1978); Comm'n on Human Rights Res. 20 (XXXVI), U.N. Doc. E/CN.4/L.1501/Add.5 (1980). *See also* U.N. Doc. E/CN.4/1362 (1980).

[112] Only very fragmentary and inconclusive data on prisoner releases are available. In 1973, *Time* magazine reported that AI had taken up the cases of some 13,000 prisoners of conscience and as a result of its efforts 7,500 had been released. *Time*, July 9, 1973, at 27. The figure of 7,500 is misleadingly high, because many of the prisoners would probably have been released in any case. In 1976 AI attempted to measure more systematically the effectiveness of its efforts, but the study failed to distinguish meaningfully between releases of adopted prisoners caused partially or wholly by AI pressure and those resulting from expiry of sentence, change of government, pardon, health reasons, acquittal at trial, successful appeal, exchange of prisoners, or other outside pressure. *See* Scoble & Wiseberg, *Amnesty International: Evaluating Effectiveness in the Human Rights Arena*, Intellect 79, 81–82 (Sept. 10, 1976).

Frequently there is an interaction between international human rights pressure and internal political sentiment to achieve the release of improperly detained persons. For example, Julio Augusto de Peña Valdez was arrested on Jan. 31, 1971, in an apartment in Santo Domingo, Dominican Republic. He was participating in a political discussion, but was accused of harboring weapons in the apartment, although he contended that no weapons were found. Afterward he was sentenced to three years in prison and served his sentence. Nevertheless, after the supreme court ordered his release the government refused to release him and the five other persons arrested at the same time. In response all 250 political prisoners at La Victoria Prison went on a hunger strike, which received considerable support among those who were opposing the re-election of the President. In retaliation, the government cut off water, light, and medical services to the prison.

AI volunteers in the United States who had been working for the release of Mr. de Peña were alerted by a telephone call from Mrs. de Peña. After a frantic day of telegrams by well-organized volunteers, a television station announced that water and light were being restored to the prison. The AI telegrams and letters gave international credence to the already existing pressure for the release of the prisoners. The relatively free press of the Dominican Republic made the Dominican people aware of the international public opinion expressed by Amnesty International. The President finally announced that the prisoners would be released, and they were released after the election. Some were later rearrested and AI has continued, where necessary, to work for the release of prisoners at La Victoria. *Dominican Prisoners Freed*, Amnesty Action, Nov.–Dec. 1974, at 3. *See also All AI-Adopted Prisoners in Metropolitan Portugal Freed After Coup*, AI Newsletter, May 1974, at 1; *AI Was 'Light of Hope' to Ex-Prisoners, Portuguese Relief Group Says*, AI Newsletter, June 1974, at 1.

D. CONTRIBUTIONS TO THE DEVELOPMENT OF HUMAN RIGHTS NORMS

In addition to their active role in implementing human rights, NGOs were instrumental in the drafting of the Universal Declaration of Human Rights.[113] The representatives of NGOs may have been influential in the drafting process as much for their personal expertise and prestige as for the importance of their organizations. By their presence in drafting sessions and by their individual contacts with national delegates or U.N. staff, NGO representatives can have even more impact than their more formal interventions in open sessions. Most diplomatic experts and staff are eager for the ideas and information which thoughtful and knowledgeable NGO representatives could provide to great advantage. Amnesty International has been credited with raising world consciousness about torture and assisting with the adoption of the U.N. Declaration on the Protection of All Persons from being Subjected to Torture and Other Cruel, Inhuman or Degrading Treatment or Punishment.[114] Amnesty International and the International Commission of Jurists have taken an active part in the preparation of the draft principles on the rights of detainees[115] and of the draft convention against torture.[116]

Similarly, eight NGOs joined in 1979 in urging the Sub-Commission on the Protection of Minorities and Prevention of Discrimination to establish a new mechanism for encouraging nations to ratify the principal human rights treaties.[117] The Sub-Commission established a working group to inquire about progress toward ratification and to offer advice to states encountering obstacles.[118]

It is clear that international NGOs provide one way by which individuals may become actively involved in the day-to-day protection of human rights. These organizations achieve so very much with their

---

[113] G.A. Res. 217A, U.N. Doc. A/810, at 71 (1948). *See Role of International NGOs, supra* note 2, at 306 n. 71.

[114] G.A. Res. 3452, 33 U.N. GOAR, Supp. (No. 34) 91, U.N. Doc. A/10034 (1978). *See* Cassese, *How could Nongovernmental Organizations Use U.N. Bodies More Effectively?* Universal Human Rights 73 (No. 4, 1979); Leary, *A New Role for Non-Governmental Organizations: A Case Study of Non-Governmental Participation in the Development of International Norms,* in U.N. Law/Fundamental Rights 197 (A. Cassese ed. 1979). *See also* Archer, *New Forms of NGO Participation in World Conferences,* in Non-Governmental Organizations in International Co-operation for Development (B. Andemicael ed. forthcoming).

[115] *See* U.N. Doc. E/CN.4/WG.1/WR.1 (1979); *U.N. Commission on Human Rights,* Rev. Int'l Comm'n Jurists 19 (No. 22, 1979).

[116] *See Report of the Sub-Commission,* Rev. Int'l Comm'n Jurists 21 (No. 21, 1978). *See also* G.A. Res. 36/60, U.N. Doc. A/RES/36/60 (1981).

[117] U.N. Doc. E/CN.4/Sub.2/NGO/80 (1979); U.N. Doc. E/CN.4/Sub.2/NGO/80/Add.1 (1979).

[118] *See* U.N. Doc. E/CN.4/Sub.2/L.716 (1979).

present minimal resources[119] that it is possible to foresee that they could do far more if there were adequate support.

II. Teaching Suggestions

Nongovernmental organizations are active in nearly every phase of international human rights. They have advocated and helped to draft international human rights norms in multilateral treaties and resolutions. They have assisted intergovernmental organizations and governments in the implementation of human rights norms. Nongovernmental organizations have also engaged in various measures which directly encourage improvements in human rights situations, including diplomatic approaches, publicity, letter-writing campaigns, mounting of trial observer and fact-finding missions, providing aid to human rights victims, etc.

Nongovernmental organizations are also very accessible to students and others who wish to become active in human rights work. Accordingly, a general human rights course could be taught from the perspective of how NGOs have contributed and could contribute to international human rights. Such a course would necessarily cover all the basic human rights treaties and other norms under which the NGOs work and to which the NGOs have contributed. Most of the principal intergovernmental procedures for implementing human rights permit NGOs to be petitioners directly, to represent victims, to inform decision-makers, or to otherwise influence the implementation process.

Such an approach might appear out of balance with the significance of NGOs in the human rights field.[120] But since very few students can expect to represent governments in human rights proceedings and since NGOs are quite accessible to interested students, an NGO-oriented human rights course can motivate students to learn the doctrines and procedures of human rights for possible use in real situations.[121]

Even without completely structuring a human rights course around NGOs, they are sufficiently important to justify at least a few classes. With this narrower focus, a student might be given a copy of an article describing the general role of NGOs in the implementation of human

[119] One of the most important developments in the work of human rights organizations during the period beginning in 1975 has been the increased support of the Ford Foundation and, to a lesser extent, the Rockefeller Brothers Foundation for many NGOs and for such efforts as Human Rights Internet Newsletter, *see* note 2 *supra*, and the International Human Rights Internship Program. R. Magat, Confronting Man's Inhumanity 10–14 (1978).

[120] *Cf.* L. Sohn & T. Buergenthal, International Protection of Human Rights (1973).

[121] *Cf.* R. Lillich & F. Newman, International Human Rights: Problems of Law and Policy (1979).

rights, such as provided in section I above. In addition, the student might be asked how to deal with a realistic hypothetical, such as, for example, the following problem which should be accompanied by background material about the human rights situation in Argentina:[122]

A. PROBLEM

Yesterday, Martin Johnson visited our office. He is terribly concerned about his daughter, Edna. She was expected to telephone the family on her mother's birthday, September 26th, but she did not call. Edna is 26 years old; she was born in Minneapolis, attended Minneapolis Lutheran High School, St. Olaf's College in Northfield, where she majored in history; and then entered the Ph.D. program in history at the University of Minnesota. She began a thesis on the history of the union movement in Argentina a year ago. After several months of preparation and learning Spanish, she left for Argentina six months ago. She is normally very conscientious about writing her parents and telephoning them on holidays.

Martin had been a client of ours for some time because he is the manager of the retail baking division of Peavey Company in Minneapolis. Mr. Johnson would like us to consider the steps which can be taken to find out what happened to his daughter. He does not know any of the people with whom she was working in Argentina and telephone calls and letters to her previous place of residence have been unavailing.

Your initial research has revealed that the Associated Press reporter in Cordoba had heard that Edna Johnson was visiting the office of four Argentinean lawyers on September 14. She was talking with the lawyers about their representation of the National Federation of Mine and Metallurgical Workers, when the police arrived. They arrested all the lawyers and Edna. Argentinean newspapers have reported that Edna is being held at the provincial police station in Cordoba.

How would you work for Edna's release?

The student should begin to analyze this hypothetical first as to the sort of protection Ms. Johnson might expect from her own government. The student should be given material about the State Department approach to such cases[123] and the statue which apparently requires State Department efforts in such cases,[124] but which does not, in fact, provide much aid.[125] The student should be invited to consider

---

[122] *See, e.g.*, Lawyers Committee for International Human Rights, Violations of Human Rights in Argentina: 1976–1979 (1979).

[123] *Protection of Americans Abroad: Hearings before the Subcomm. on Int'l Operations of the House Comm. on Int'l Relations*, 95th Cong., 1st Sess., 88–94 (1977) (testimony of Dep. Ass't Sec'y of State William P. Stedman, Jr.).

[124] 22 U.S.C. § 1732 (1979).

[125] Redpath v. Kissinger, 415 F. Supp. 566 (W.D. Tex. 1976).

what the U.S. government might or might not do for its nationals and what considerations motivate U.S. action. The student should also consider how the U.S. government can ethically request the release of its nationals, when Argentineans are incarcerated and tortured for similar 'offenses'.[126]

Having concluded that the U.S. government may be unwilling or unable to assist Ms. Johnson, the class might consider which NGOs might be motivated and well placed to help obtain Ms. Johnson's release. The students should consider what human rights provisions might provide support for any NGO activity for Ms. Johnson. The class would then consider what measures NGOs might take and compare their prospects of success with the efforts of governments or intergovernmental organizations. The class should also ponder whether Ms. Johnson's interests might in some circumstances conflict with the efforts of NGOs and how such conflicts might be resolved.

Another class on the role of NGOs might provide the student with a sample communication under ECOSOC resolution 1503,[127] such as the International League for Human Rights complaint on India,[128] or the Lawyers Committee for International Human Rights complaint on Argentina,[129] The students should then be asked to review the complaint in the light of the International Bill of Human Rights.[130] After identifying all the substantive violations arguably alleged by the complaint, students should consider each of the principal U.N.,[131] O.A.S.,[132] ILO,[133] or other procedures which are available for

[126] *See* J. Brierly, The Law of Nations 276–96 (6th ed. 1963); Murphy, *State Responsibility for Injury to Aliens*, 41 N.Y.U. L. Rev. 125 (1966).

[127] *See* note 80 *supra*.

[128] Communication from International League for Human Rights to U.N. Secretary-General Kurt Waldheim, May 31, 1976.

[129] *See* note 122 *supra*.

[130] The International Bill of Human Rights is comprised of four documents: (a) The Universal Declaration of Human Rights; (b) the Political Covenant; (c) the Economic Covenant; and (d) the Optional Protocol, 8 J. Int'l Comm'n Jurists 17 (1967); E. Schwelb, Human Rights and The International Community (1964); J. Carey, UN Protection of Civil and Political Rights 12–19 (1970); Newman, *Interpreting the Human Rights Clauses of the U.N. Charter*, 5 Revue des Droits de l'Homme 283, 285 n.7 (1972); Humphrey, *The International Law of Human Rights in the Middle Twentieth Century*, in The Present State of International Law and other Essays 75, 85 (M. Dos ed. 1973); E. Luard, The International Protection of Human Rights 53 (1967); T. Buergenthal & J. Torney, International Human Rights and International Education 163 (1976); Human Rights: A Compilation of International Instruments, U.N. Doc. ST/HR/1/Rev.1, at 1–17 (1978); American Association for the International Commission of Jurists, International Bill of Human Rights (undated); International Human Rights: Selected Declarations and Agreements, 94th Cong., 2d Sess. (1976).

[131] *See* Optional Protocol; E.S.C. Res. 1296, *supra* note 71; E.S.C. Res. 1503, *supra* note 80; E.S.C. Res. 728F, *supra* note 84; E.S.C. Res. 1235, *supra* note 84; Sub-Commission on Prevention of Discrimination and Protection of Minorities Res. 1 (XXIV), *supra* note 84.

[132] Handbook of Existing Rules Pertaining to Human Rights, Inter-American Commission on Human Rights, O.A.S. Doc. OEA/Ser.L/V/II.50, doc. 6 (1980).

[133] International Labour Office, ILO Principles, Standards and Procedures Concerning Freedom of Association (1978).

handling the complaint. Students should be given copies of the rules for each major international human rights procedure and be asked to evaluate the merits of each alternative procedure, from the standpoint of such considerations as (1) access of NGOs to the procedure, (2) prospects of success, (3) usefulness of the procedures for achieving concrete ends, (4) confidentiality and visibility problems, (5) procedural rights for complainants, etc. From this problem students should not only learn about applicable human rights doctrines and procedures, but should acquire a technique for construing U.N. resolutions.

B.   MATERIALS TO BE DISTRIBUTED TO THE CLASS

For the classes on the work of NGOs in the implementation of human rights, students should receive copies of the following materials.

1. The Johnson Case (1 class—2 hours).
   a. The Johnson Hypothetical.
   b. The International Bill of Human Rights[134].
   c. The Lawyers Committee for International Human Rights communication on Argentina[135].
   d. State Department testimony of the protection of Americans abroad[136].
   e. 22 U.S.C. § 1732[137].
   f. *Redpath v. Kissinger*[138].
   g. Section I of this chapter.

2. NGO Communications Procedures (2 classes—4 hours).
   a. The Lawyers Committee for International Human Rights communication on Argentina[139].
   b. The International Bill of Human Rights[140].
   c. Principal U.N. resolutions establishing procedures to which NGOs may have access[141].
   d. Selections from the Inter-American Commission's Handbook of Existing Rules Pertaining to Human Rights[142].
   e. International labour procedures[143].

[134] *See* note 130 *supra*.
[135] *See* note 122 *supra*.
[136] *See* note 123 *supra*.
[137] *See* note 124 *supra* and accompanying text.
[138] 415 F. Supp. 566.
[139] *See* note 122 *supra*.
[140] *See* note 130 *supra*.
[141] *See* note 131 *supra*.
[142] *See* note 132 *supra*.
[143] *See* note 133 *supra*; notes 94–97 *supra* and accompanying text.

III. Syllabus

Section I of this chapter provides an overview of the ways in which NGOs contribute to the promotion and implementation of human rights. Section II proposes an activist and concrete approach to teaching how NGOs help to implement human rights. In addition to or instead of using the approach suggested by section II, the teacher might follow the outline of section I in lecture format and/or class discussion covering the following topics:

A. Structure and Characteristics of International Nongovernmental Organizations in the Human Rights Field.
   1. Consultative status with the U.N. Economic and Social Council, etc.
   2. NGO Secretariat.
   3. National sections or affiliates.
   4. Membership and constituency.
   5. Sources of financial support.
B. Relationship of NGO Characteristics to Selection of Targets for Fact-Finding and Action; How NGOs Select Their Areas of Concern.
   1. Availability of information.
   2. Financial implications.
   3. Political tendencies.
   4. Interests of constituency.
C. NGO Implementation of Human Rights.
   1. Effectiveness of NGO criticism and the sensitivity of governments.
   2. NGOs can often be more forthright and more impartial than governments and intergovernmental bodies.
   3. Aspects of the implementation process.
     a. Fact-finding.
     b. Diplomatic initiatives.
     c. Missions for fact-finding and direct contacts.
     d. Public reports.
     e. Statements to the United Nations and other international bodies.
     f. Petitions to international bodies.
       (i) E.S.C. Res. 1503.
       (ii) Optional Protocol.
       (iii) Other U.N. procedures.
       (iv) International Labour Organisations.
       (v) UNESCO.
       (vi) Inter-American Commission on Human Rights.

        (vii) European Commission of Human Rights.
     g. Relationship of financial aid and human rights.
     h. NGOs as conciliators.
     i. Relationship of international and national human rights efforts.
  D. Contributions of NGOs to the Development and Elaboration of Human Rights Norms.
     1. Contribution of NGOs to the U.N. Charter, Universal Declaration, Torture Declaration, etc.
     2. Consultative status as a means of contributing to the formulation of norms.
     3. Direct NGO assistance in drafting and pressure from NGO constituencies on government delegates.

IV. Minisyllabus

  A. Structure and Characteristics of International NGOs in the Human Rights Field.
  B. Relationship of NGO Characteristics to Selection of Targets for Fact-Finding and Action. How NGOs Select Their Areas of Concern.
  C. NGO Implementation of Human Rights.
     1. Effectiveness of NGO criticism and the sensitivity of governments.
     2. NGOs can often be more forthright and more impartial than governments and intergovernmental bodies.
     3. Aspects of the implementation process.
        a. Fact-finding.
        b. Diplomatic initiatives.
        c. Missions for fact-finding and direct contacts.
        d. Public reports.
        e. Statements to the United Nations and other international bodies.
        f. Petitions to international bodies.
        g. Relationship of international and national human rights efforts.
  D. Contributions of NGOs to the Development and Elaboration of Human Rights Norms.

V. Bibliography

B. Andemicael, *Non-governmental Organizations in International Co-operation for Development* (forthcoming).

—— & E. Rees, Non-governmental Organizations in Economic and Social Development (1975).

Archer, *Action by Unofficial Organizations on Human Rights*, in The International Protection of Human Rights 160 (E. Luard ed. 1967).

J. Bissel, The International Committee of the Red Cross and the Protection of Human Rights (1968).

E. Bock, Representation of Non-Governmental Organizations and the United Nations (1955).

Cassese, *How could Nongovernmental Organizations Use U.N. Bodies More Effectively?* 1 Universal Human Rights 73 (No. 4, 1979).

Clark, *The International League for Human Rights and South West Africa 1947–1957: The International Human Rights NGO as Catalyst in the International Legal Process*, 1 Human Rights Q. 101 (1981).

T. Claudius & F. Stepan, Amnesty International Portrait Einer Organization (1978).

E.S.C. Res. 1296, 44 U.N. ESCOR, Supp. (No. 1) 21, U.N. Doc. E/4548 (1968).

D. Forsythe, Humanitarian Politics, The International Committee of the Red Cross (1977).

—— *The Red Cross a Transnational Movement: Conserving and Changing the National–State System*, 30 Int'l Organization 607 (1976).

—— & Weisberg, *Human Rights Protection: A Research Agenda*, 1 Universal Human Rights 1, 15–19 (No. 4, 1979).

Golsong, *Les Organisations non gouvernmentales et le Conseil de l'Europe*, in Les organisations non gouvernmentales en Suisse 93 (1973).

Green, *NGOs*, in Human Rights and World Order 90 (A. Said ed. 1978).

Gunter, *Towards a Consultative Relationship Between the United Nations and Non-Governmental Organizations?* 10 Vand. J. Transnat'l L. 557 (1977).

Human Rights Internet Newsletter (1976–present).

J. Lador-Lederer, International Nongovernmental Organization and Economic Entities (1963).

E. Larson, A Flame in Barbed Wire: The Story of Amnesty International (1979).

Leary, *A New Role for Non-governmental Organizations: A Case Study of Non-Governmental Participation in the Development of International Norms on Torture*, in U.N. Law/Fundamental Rights 197 (A. Cassese ed. 1979).

—— *The Implementation of the Human Rights Provisions of the Helsinki Final Act: A Preliminary Assessment 1975–1977*, in Human Rights International Law and the Helsinki Accord, 111, 121–27 (T. Buergenthal ed. 1977).

N. MacDermot, Human Rights and the Churches (1976).

MacDermot, *The Work of the International Commission of Jurists*, 1 Index on Censorship 15 (1972).

A. Milani, Les Organisations Non Gouvernmentales des Nations Unies (1952).

J. Moreillon, Le Comité International de la Croix Rouge et la protection des détenus politiques (1973).

Note, *Role of Nongovernmental Organizations in Implementing Human Rights in Latin America*, 7 Ga. J. Int'l & Comp. L. 476 (1977).

R. Perruchoud, Les Résolutions des Conferences Internationales de La Croix-Rouge (1979).

Potter, Non-Governmental Organizations Viewed by a Political Scientist, 14 Int'l A. 403 (1962).

J. Power, Against Oblivion, Amnesty International's Fight for Human Rights (1981).

Prasad, *The Role of Non-Governmental Organizations in the New United Nations Procedures for Human Rights Complaints*, 5 Denver J. Int'l L. & Pol'y 441 (1975).

Rees, *Exercises in Private Diplomacy*, in Unofficial Diplomats 111 (M. Berman & J. Johnson eds. 1977).

D. Robins, United States Non-Governmental Organizations and the Educational Campaign from Dumbarton Oaks, 1944 Through the San Francisco Conference, 1945 (1960).

Rodley, *Monitoring Human Rights by the U.N. System and Nongovernmental Organization*, in Human Rights and American Foreign Policy (D. Kommers & G. Loescher eds. 1979).

P. Rohn, Relations Between the Council of Europe and International Non-Governmental Organizations (1957).

Scoble & Weisberg, *Amnesty International: Evaluating Effectiveness in the Human Rights Area*, Intellect, Sept./Oct. 1976, at 79.

—— *The International League for Human Rights: The Strategy of a Human Rights NGO*, 7 Ga. J. Int'l & Comp. L. 289 (1977).

—— *Human Rights and Amnesty International*, 413 Annals 11 (1974).

—— *Human Rights NGOs: Notes Toward Comparative Analysis*, 9 Revue des Droits de L'Homme 611 (1976).

Sheperd, *Human Rights Theory and NGO Practice: Where Do We Go From Here*, in Global Human Rights (V. Nanda ed. 1981).

Shestack, *Sisyphus Endures: The International Human Rights NGO*, 24 N.Y.L.S. L. Rev. 89 (1978).

B. Stosic, Les Organisations non gouvernmentales et les Nations Unies (1964).

D. Tansley, Final Report: An Agenda for the Red Cross (1975).

United Nations, List of Non-Governmental Organizations in Consultative Status with the Economic and Social Council, pts. I & II (mimeo 1978).

Vincent-Daviss, *Human Rights Law: A Research Guide to the Literature—Part I: International Law and the United Nations*, 14 N.Y.J. Int'l L. & Politics 209, 313–19 (1980).

Weissbrodt, *International Trial Observers*, 18 Stanford J. Int'l L. 27 (1982).

—— *Strategies for the Selection and Pursuit of International Human Rights Objectives*, 8 Yale J. World Public Order 301 (1982).

—— *Deciding United States Policy in Regard to International Human Rights: The Role of Interest Groups*, in The Dynamics of Human Rights in U.S. Foreign Policy 229 (N. Hevener ed. 1981).

—— *The Role of International Nongovernmental Organizations in the Implementation of Human Rights*, 12 Tex J. Int'l L. 293 (1977).

—— & McCarthy, *Fact-finding by Non-governmental Human Rights Organizations*, 22 Va. J. Int'l L. 1 (1981).

L. White, International Non-Governmental Organizations: Their Purposes, Methods and Accomplishments (1968).

VI. Minibibliography

Weissbrodt, *The Contribution of International Nongovernmental Organizations to the Protection of Human Rights*, in this volume.

Leary, *A New Role for Nongovernmental Organizations: A Case Study of Nongovernmental Participation in the Development of International Norms on Torture*, in U.N. Law/Fundamental Rights 197 (A. Cassese ed. 1979).

Cassese, *How Could Nongovernmental Organizations Use U.N. Bodies More Effectively?*, 1 Universal Human Rights 73 (No. 4, 1979).

E.S.C. Res. 1296, 44 U.N. ESCOR Supp. (No. 1) 21, U.N. Doc. E/4548 (1968).

Shestack, *Sisyphus Endures: The International Human Rights NGO*, 24 N.Y.L.S. L. Rev. 89 (1978).

Part III: Regional Protection of Human Rights

Chapter 12

The Inter-American System for the Protection of Human Rights*[1]

Thomas Buergenthal

I. Legal and Policy Considerations

The inter-American system for the protection of human rights has two distinct legal sources, giving rise to a dual institutional structure of protection.[2] One has evolved directly from the Charter of the Organization of American States; the other was created by the American Convention on Human Rights. The two overlap to a certain extent and share various institutions. The Inter-American Commission on Human Rights, for example, is an organ both of the Charter-based regime and of the one derived from the American Convention. At times both regimes are applicable to one and the same case, strengthening the institutional pressures that can be brought to bear on governments charged with violating human rights.

To understand how the inter-American system for the protection of human rights functions, one has to have a very clear conception of the legal and political evolution of these two regimes. Here we shall therefore explore the manner in which these regimes have evolved, their practice, and how they interact.

A. THE AMERICAN CONVENTION ON HUMAN RIGHTS

1. *In General*

The American Convention on Human Rights[3] was adopted in 1969

---

* © Thomas Buergenthal 1983.
[1] This study was completed in 1981.

[2] On the inter-American system for the protection of human rights, *see generally* Gros Espiell, *L'Organisation des Etats Américains*, in Les Dimensions Internationales des Droits de l'Homme 600 (K. Vasak ed. 1978); Buergenthal, *The Revised OAS Charter and the Protection of Human Rights*, 69 Am. J. Int'l L. 828 (1975) [hereinafter cited as *Revised OAS Charter*]; R. Goldman, The Protection of Human Rights in the Americas: Past, Present and Future (5 N.Y.U. Center for International Studies Policy Papers No. 2 1972). *See also* L. Sohn & T. Buergenthal, International Protection of Human Rights, ch. 8 (1973) [hereinafter cited as Sohn & Buergenthal], which contains extensive bibliographic references and primary source materials bearing on this subject.

[3] For the legislative history of the American Convention on Human Rights, *see* Conferencia Especializada Interamericana Sobre Derechos Humanos, San José, Costa Rica, 7–22 de noviembre 1969, Actas y Documentos, O.A.S. Doc. OEA/Ser. K/XVI/1.2 (1973) [hereinafter cited as Conferencia Especializada]. Additional documents and draft texts bearing on the drafting history of the American Convention can be found in the first three volumes of the

at an inter-governmental conference convened by the Organization of American States (O.A.S.). The meeting took place in San José, Costa Rica, which explains why the American Convention is also known as the 'Pact of San José, Costa Rica'. The American Convention entered into force in July 1978, after the eleventh instrument of ratification had been deposited.[4] Thereafter four more O.A.S. member states ratified. By 1981, the following states had become parties to the American Convention: Bolivia, Colombia, Costa Rica, Dominican Republic, Ecuador, El Salvador, Grenada, Guatemala, Haiti, Honduras, Jamaica, Nicaragua, Panama, Peru, and Venezuela.

Only O.A.S. member states have the right to adhere to the American Convention,[5] and barely a majority of them has done so thus far. All major O.A.S. powers—United States, Mexico, Brazil, and Argentina— are absent from the list. So too are Chile, Paraguay, and Uruguay, as well as Barbados, Trinidad and Tobago, Surinam, Dominica, and St. Lucia. The United States signed the American Convention and President Carter transmitted it to the Senate for its advice and consent to ratification,[6] but the Senate has not as yet acted on the request. If the United States ratifies the American Convention, it will join Jamaica as the only common law country to have done so. The legal systems of the other states parties adhere to the Spanish civil law tradition, although it appears that Barbados, another common law country which has already signed the American Convention, will ratify in the very near future. For the time being, the smaller and medium-sized Latin American states predominate among the parties to the American Con-

Inter-American Yearbook of Human Rights, published by the Inter-American Commission on Human Rights. The three volumes cover the period from 1960 to 1970 inclusive.

For the American Convention, O.A.S. T.S. No. 36, and other major O.A.S. human rights texts, see the O.A.S. Handbook of Existing Rules Pertaining to Human Rights [hereinafter cited as Handbook], published and annually updated by the Inter-American Commission on Human Rights. All references in this chapter are to the July 1980 edition of the Handbook. The American Convention and other O.A.S. human rights documents are also reproduced in L. Sohn & T. Buergenthal, Basic Documents on International Protection of Human Rights (1973) [herein-after cited as Basic Documents].

On the American Convention generally, *see* Fox, *The American Convention on Human Rights and Prospects for United States Ratification*, 3 Human Rights 243 (1973) [hereinafter cited as Fox]; A. Robertson, Human Rights in the World 122–39 (1972) [hereinafter cited as Robertson]; Thomas & Thomas, *Human Rights and the Organization of American States*, 12 Santa Clara Law. 319, 349–74 (1972); Buergenthal, *The American Convention on Human Rights: Illusions and Hopes*, 21 Buffalo L. Rev. 121 (1971) [hereinafter cited as Buergenthal].

[4] See American Convention, art. 74(2).

[5] *Id.* art. 74(1).

[6] President Carter transmitted the American Convention to the U.S. Senate together with other human rights treaties. *See* Message from the President of the United States Transmitting Four Treaties Pertaining to Human Rights, S. Exec. Doc. C, D, E and F, 95th Cong., 2d Sess. (1978) [hereinafter cited as President's Message]. *See also International Human Rights Treaties: Hearings before the Comm. on Foreign Relations*, 96th Cong., 1st Sess. (1979).

vention. Within that group, Costa Rica, Venezuela, and Ecuador provide strong pro-human rights leadership.

The American Convention is patterned on the European Convention of Human Rights.[7] This is true, in particular, of the American Convention's institutional framework which is quite similar to its European counterpart.[8] But the American Convention also drew heavily on the American Declaration of the Rights and Duties of Man, adopted on 2 May 1948,[9] and on the International Covenant on Civil and Political Rights,[10] especially in formulating the catalog of rights that the American Convention incorporates.[11]

The American Convention is longer than most international human rights instruments. It contains eighty-two articles and codifies more than two dozen distinct rights, including the right to juridical personality, to life, to humane treatment, to personal liberty, to a fair trial, to privacy, to a name, to nationality, to participation in government, to equal protection of the law, and to judicial protection. The American Convention outlaws slavery; it proclaims freedom of conscience, religion, thought, and expression, as well as freedom of association, movement, and residence, besides prohibiting the application of *ex post facto* laws and penalties.

The states parties to the American Convention undertake 'to respect' and 'to ensure' the 'free and full exercise' of these rights 'to all persons subject to their jurisdiction'.[12] The American Convention defines 'person' as 'every human being',[13] which indicates that corporations and other legal persons are not protected as such. But to the extent that an injury to a corporation or association violates an individual's rights under the American Convention, it can be assumed to give rise to a cause of action under it. The outlawing of a labour union, for example, may amount to a denial of the right to freedom of association enjoyed by the union members. The union as such, as distinguished from the injured individual, does not, however, enjoy the protection of the American Convention.

The states parties to the American Convention have an obligation not only 'to respect' the rights guaranteed in the Convention, but also

---

[7] [European] Convention on Human Rights and Fundamental Freedoms, 213 U.N.T.S. 221, *reprinted in* Basic Documents on Human Rights (2d ed. I. Brownlie 1981) [hereinafter cited as Brownlie].

[8] *See* Buergenthal, *supra* note 2, at 122; Robertson, *supra* note 2, at 126–36.

[9] For the text of the American Declaration, *see* Basic Documents, *supra* note 3, at 187; Handbook, *supra* note 3, at 17.

[10] G.A. Res. 2200, 21 U.N. GAOR, Supp. (No. 16) 52, U.N. Doc. A/6316 (1966).

[11] Dunshee de Abranches, *Comparative Study of the United Nations Covenants on [Human Rights] and the Draft Inter-American Convention on Human Rights*, [1968] Inter-American Y.B. of Human Rights 169.

[12] American Convention, art. 1(1).

[13] *Id.* art. 1(2).

'to ensure' the free and full exercise of those rights.[14] A government consequently has both positive and negative duties under the American Convention. On the one hand, it has the obligation not to violate an individual's rights; for example, it has a duty not to torture an individual or to deprive him or her of a fair trial. But the state's obligation goes beyond this negative duty, and may require the adoption of affirmative measures necessary and reasonable under the circumstances 'to ensure' the full enjoyment of the rights the American Convention guarantees. Thus, for example, a government of a country in which individuals 'disappear' on a massive scale might be deemed to violate article 7(1) of the American Convention,[15] even if it cannot be shown that its agents are responsible for the disappearances, provided the government is able but fails to take measures reasonably calculated to protect individuals against such lawlessness.

The catalog of rights which the American Convention proclaims is longer than that of the European Convention, and many of its provisions establish more advanced and enlightened guarantees than does its European counterpart, or for that matter, the Political Covenant.[16] But some of the provisions of the American Convention are so advanced that it may be doubted whether there is a country in the Americas that is in full compliance with all of them. This fact has not prevented the American Convention from obtaining the necessary number of ratifications to bring it into force. Most of these ratifications were unaccompanied by any reservations,[17] notwithstanding the fact that the *de jure* and *de facto* conditions in at least some of the ratifying countries should have prompted a larger number of reservations.

2.   Some Problems of Interpretation

a. *The Self-Executing Character of the American Convention.* A number of provisions of the American Convention have a direct bearing on the manner in which this treaty will be applied on the domestic legal plane of the states that have ratified it. One of these provisions is article 2, which reads as follows:

Where the exercise of any of the rights or freedoms referred to in Article 1 is not already ensured by legislative or other provisions, the States Parties

[14] *Id.* art. 1(1).
[15] Art. 7(1) provides: 'Every person has the right to personal liberty and security.'
[16] *See, e.g., id.* arts. 4, 5, 17(5), & 23.
[17] The only dramatic exception is the reservation of El Salvador, which declares that its ratification is 'with the reservation that such ratification is understood [to be] without prejudice to those provisions of the Convention that might be in conflict with express precepts of the Political Constitution of the Republic.' For the texts of the instruments of ratification, *see* Handbook, *supra* note 3, at 59.

undertake to adopt, in accordance with their constitutional processes and the provisions of this Convention, such legislative or other measures as may be necessary to give effect to those rights or freedoms.

Treaty provisions such as article 2 can have very important domestic legal consequences in countries which apply the so-called self-executing-treaty doctrine. In these countries, the self-executing provisions of a duly ratified treaty have the status of directly applicable domestic law and, as such, supersede prior conflicting domestic law. Non-self-executing treaty provisions, on the other hand, require implementing legislation to create directly enforceable rights in national courts. It follows that if a human rights treaty is characterized as non-self-executing, individuals will not be able to rely on it in domestic courts to override conflicting national laws, which greatly reduces the utility of such treaties.[18] While the test for judging whether a treaty provision is self-executing or not varies somewhat from country to country, depending upon national constitutional traditions and peculiarities,[19] the courts in some countries proceed on the assumption that a treaty, containing a provision such as article 2 of the American Convention, was designed to be non-self-executing. (This is the case, for example, under the law of the United States.)[20] And although this presumption appears to be rebuttable, some national courts view provisions of this type as proof that the drafters, by calling for national implementing legislation, intended the treaty to be non-self-executing. It is therefore useful to review the history of article 2 to determine what function it was designed to perform.

No comparable clause appeared in the draft text of the American Convention which was used as a working document of the San José conference.[21] The addition of this provision, which draws on the language of article 2(2) of the Political Covenant, was proposed by the Chilean delegation to the San José conference.[22] The Chileans favored this clause because they thought it important that the treaty contain an express statement that all states parties had the obligation to adopt whatever domestic laws were necessary to implement fully the rights proclaimed in the American Convention. The opposing argument

---

[18] *See, e.g.,* Sei Fujii v. State, 38 Cal. 2d 713, 242 P.2d 617 (1952). *See generally*, R. Lillich & F. Newman, International Human Rights: Problems of Law and Policy 68–122 (1979).

[19] Schlüter, *The Domestic Status of the Human Rights Clauses of the United Nations Charter*, 61 Cal. L. Rev. 110 (1973); Buergenthal, *The Domestic Status of the European Convention on Human Rights: A Second Look*, 7 J. Int'l Comm'n Jurists 55 (1966).

[20] *See* Fox, *supra* note 3, at 259–60; Restatement (Second) of Foreign Relations Law § 141 (1965). This matter is more recently dealt with in Restatement of Foreign Relations Law (Rev.) § 131, Comments h & i, at 46–48 (Tent. Draft No. 1, 1980).

[21] The draft Convention is reproduced in [1968] Y.B. Inter-American Comm'n on Human Rights 389.

[22] *See* Conferencia Especializada, *supra* note 3, at 38.

advanced by some delegates, who submitted that the provision was not necessary because under international law all parties to a treaty already had the obligation to take whatever domestic legal action was needed to comply with the treaty, did not persuade the Chileans to withdraw their amendment. In responding to the contention that nothing need be said about implementation on the domestic plane since in many Latin American countries duly ratified treaties acquired the status of domestic law, Chilean delegates pointed to article 18 of the Convention, which reads as follows:

> Every person has the right to a given name and to the surnames of his parents or that of one of them. The law shall regulate the manner in which this right shall be ensured for all, by the use of assumed names if necessary.

It was obvious, the Chileans contended, that even if article 18 as such was deemed to be domestic law, the 'law' referred to in it had to be enacted separately in all those countries that did not already have it. An express stipulation in article 2 that such a 'law' had to be enacted thus created an unambiguous legal obligation to do so.[23]

The soundness of the arguments advanced by the Chileans is less important than the fact that in moving the text of article 2 it was never their aim to make the American Convention non-self-executing. This fact was recognized by the U.S. delegation, which supported the inclusion of article 2, but for the opposite reason, namely, to make the American Convention non-self-executing under U.S. law.

> The United States agrees that this article should be included in the . . . Convention since it helps to clarify the legal effect of ratification on the domestic law of the respective parties. The article is sufficiently flexible so that each country can best implement the treaty consistent with its domestic practice. Some countries may choose to make the articles of the treaty directly effective as domestic law and this article would permit them to do so. The comments made by Chile suggest that its own practice may vary depending on the text of each article. Others may prefer to rely solely on domestic law to implement the articles of the treaty. In the U.S. we would interpret this article as authorizing us to follow the last course in these cases of matters within Part I, the substantive portions, of the draft convention. That will permit us to refer, where appropriate, to our Constitution, to our domestic legislation already in existence, to our court decisions and to our administrative practice as carrying out the obligations of the Convention. It will also mean that we will be able to draft any new legislation that is needed in terms that can be readily and clearly assimilated into our domestic codes. In other words, it is not the intention of the U.S. to interpret the articles of the treaty in Part I as being self-executing.[24]

---

[23] *Id.*
[24] *Id.* at 146–47.

The U.S. statement recognized that article 2 left the states parties free to implement the American Convention on the domestic plane as they saw fit, either by treating it as self-executing or not. The United States thus acknowledged that it was not the purpose of article 2 to make the American Convention non-self-executing. At the same time, of course, the delegation went on record that the United States would treat the American Convention as being non-self-executing. Article 2 neither compels nor prohibits this result, and the U.S. statement acknowledged as much. Given the history of article 2, a national judge sitting in a country that adheres to the self-executing-treaty doctrine might well conclude that the presence of article 2 in the American Convention does not *ipso facto* make the treaty as a whole non-self-executing.[25] But such a ruling would not necessarily foreclose a holding in one or another country finding individual provisions of the American Convention to be non-self-executing in those instances where they cannot be applied by the courts without some additional legislative action.[26]

b. *The Federal-State Clause.* Article 28 affects the domestic application of the American Convention in those states that have a federal system of government. Known as the 'federal clause', article 28 reads in part as follows:

1. Where a State Party is constituted as a federal state, the national government of such State Party shall implement all the provisions of the Convention over whose subject matter it exercises legislative and judicial jurisdiction.
2. With respect to the provisions over whose subject matter the constituent units of the federal state have jurisdiction, the national government shall immediately take suitable measures, in accordance with its constitution and its laws, to the end that the competent authorities of the constituent units may adopt appropriate provisions for the fulfillment of this Convention.

Article 28 is an anachronism which harks back to the days of the League of Nations. Few modern international human rights instru-

[25] A. U.S. judge could also reasonably reach this conclusion, although he or she would next have to decide what effect to give to the statement of the U.S. delegation 'that it is not the intention of the U.S. to interpret the articles of the treaty in Part I as being self-executing'. *Id.* the answer to this question is not easy because there is no settled U.S. law on the extent to which the courts are bound by such a statement. *Compare* Power Authority v. Federal Power Commission, 247 F.2d 538 (D.C. Cir. 1957) *with* Charlton v. Kelley, 229 U.S. 447 (1913). A somewhat different question would arise if the U.S. were to ratify the American Convention with the specific declaration that Pres. Jimmy Carter proposed when he transmitted the treaty to the Senate. The proposed declaration reads as follows: 'The United States declares that the provisions of Articles 1 through 32 of this Convention are not self-executing.' President's Message, *supra* note 6, at XVIII.

[26] Art. 18 of the American Convention would be an example of a non-self-executing provision in the sense that it would require the adoption of the 'law' referred to in it before it could be applied in full.

ments contain comparable clauses. The Political Covenant adopts precisely the opposite principle by declaring in article 50 that '[t]he provisions of the present Covenant shall extend to all parts of federal states without any limitations or exceptions'. The European Convention of Human Rights, the Convention on the Prevention and Punishment of the Crime of Genocide,[27] and the International Convention on the Elimination of All Forms of Racial Discrimination[28] contain no federal clause; they apply with equal force in unitary as in federal states. Moreover, many states which have a strong federal tradition, including Canada and the Federal Republic of Germany, have been able to adhere to these instruments without federal-state reservations.

Article 28 of the American Convention found its way into the treaty because the United States insisted on it.[29] In explaining the meaning of this provision, the U.S. delegation to the San José conference reported to the Secretary of State that

The present Convention . . . does not obligate the U.S. Government to *exercise* jurisdiction over subject matter over which it would not exercise authority in the absence of the Convention. The U.S. is merely obligated to take suitable measures to the end that state and local authorities may adopt provisions for the fulfillment of this Convention. Suitable measures could consist of recommendations to the states, for example. The determination of what measures are suitable is a matter of internal decision. The Convention does not require enactment of legislation bringing new subject matter within the federal ambit.[30]

The U.S. delegation proposed article 28 in order to ensure that a federal state not be deemed to have assumed any international obligation to prevent violations of the American Convention involving rights or acts within the jurisdiction of any governmental entity other than the federal government. Moreover, by limiting the international obligations of the federal state to subject matter over which it *exercises* jurisdiction, the United States sought to indicate that such a state has no obligation under the American Convention in situations where the federal government, although having jurisdiction, has not previously exercised it.

Put in the context of U.S. constitutional law, the delegation believed that article 28 prevented the application of the *Missouri v. Holland*[31] principle to the American Convention. Under *Missouri v. Holland*, a

[27] 78 U.N.T.S. 277, *reprinted in* Brownlie, *supra* note 7, at 31.

[28] 660 U.N.T.S. 195, *reprinted in* Brownlie, *supra* note 7, at 150.

[29] *See* Report of the United States Delegation to the Inter-American Conference on Protection of Human Rights, San José, Costa Rica, November 9–22, 1969, at 37 (1970) [hereinafter cited as Report of the U.S. Delegation]; Fox, *supra* note 3, at 250–54.

[30] Report of the U.S. Delegation, *supra* note 29, at 37 (emphasis in original).

[31] 252 U.S. 416 (1920).

treaty concluded by the United States that is otherwise constitutional[32] gives the federal government jurisdiction over the subject matter of the treaty even if such jurisdiction previously resided in the states of the Union. Thus, in the absence of article 28, if the United States was to ratify the American Convention, the federal government would have jurisdiction under *Missouri v. Holland* to enforce the American Convention throughout the country, notwithstanding that prior to such ratification some or all subjects dealt with by the treaty were within the jurisdiction of the several states.[33] But if article 28 accomplishes the result sought by the U.S. delegation, U.S. ratification of the American Convention will not affect a shift in jurisdiction from the states to the federal government. All in all, given the purpose attributed to it by the U.S. delegation, article 28 allows federal states to ratify the American Convention without making its provisions applicable within its entire territory.

The ostensible simplicity of article 28 hides the legal complexities inherent in it. It raises difficult international and domestic law issues not fully perceived by its drafters. Whether a federal state, for example, 'exercises legislative and judicial jurisdiction' over a specific subject matter is an international law issue to the extent that it involves an interpretation of a treaty. But it can be decided in a given case only by reference to the domestic law of a particular country. This conclusion suggests the question whether and to what extent the Inter-American Court of Human Rights, which has jurisdiction to interpret and apply the American Convention,[34] is empowered to verify a defense of a state party based on article 28. Suppose, for example, that a state defends its failure to enforce the American Convention on the ground that under its domestic law it lacks jurisdiction over a specific subject matter at issue. Is the Inter-American Court in such a case bound by the *ipse dixit* of the federal authority or is it free to examine the relevant domestic law and practice and determine for itself what the domestic law provides on the subject? To illustrate the problem, let us assume that in a case involving State *X*, counsel for *X* asserts that the subject matter of the claim is one over which the federal government exercises neither legislative nor judicial jurisdiction. Assume further that the complainant points to a decision of the Supreme Court of *X*, rendered in another case a year earlier, that plainly contradicts the view of counsel for *X*. Is the Inter-American Court free to consider the effect of the Supreme Court decision and, if so, may it receive expert evidence on the subject, or is it bound by *X*'s statement as to what the law is?

[32] *See* Reid v. Covert, 354 U.S. 1 (1957).

[33] *See generally*, L. Henkin, Foreign Affairs and the Constitution 144–48 (1972). *Cf.* National League of Cities v. Usery, 426 U.S. 833 (1976).

[34] American Convention, art. 62(3).

The issues might be even more troublesome in a country which, in addition to being a federal state, determines that the Convention is non-self-executing. Here a domestic court might never get the oppor- tunity to interpret article 28 or to apply it by reference to other provisions of the American Convention, making it more difficult for the international tribunal to ascertain what the relevant domestic law is. Sight must also not be lost of the fact that in some federal systems it is by no means easy, even as a matter of domestic law, to determine what constitutes an 'exercise of jurisdiction' or what is meant by 'subject matter' as that term is used in article 28.

c. *The Right of Derogation*. Problems relating to the domestic appli- cation of the American Convention are also likely to arise from the application of article 27, which recognizes that in certain circum- stances the state parties may suspend some of the rights that the treaty proclaims. Article 27 provides:

1. In time of war, public danger, or other emergency that threatens the independence or security of a State Party, it may take measures derogating from its obligations under the present Convention to the extent and for the period of time strictly required by the exigencies of the situation, provided that such measures are not inconsistent with its other obligations under international law and do not involve discrimination on the ground of race, color, sex, language, religion, or social origin.

2. The foregoing provision does not authorize any suspension of the following articles: Article 3 (Right to Juridical Personality), Article 4 (Right to Life), Article 5 (Right to Humane Treatment), Article 6 (Freedom from Slavery), Article 9 (Freedom from *Ex Post Facto* Laws), Article 12 (Freedom of Conscience and Religion), Article 17 (Rights of the Family), Article 18 (Right to a Name), Article 19 (Rights of the Child), Article 20 (Right to Nationality), and Article 23 (Right to Participate in Government), or of the judicial guarantees essential for the protection of such rights.

3. Any State Party availing itself of the right of suspension shall immediately inform the other State Parties, through the Secretary General of the Organization of American States, of the provisions the application of which it has suspended, the reasons that gave rise to the suspension, and the date set for the termination of such suspension.

Although this provision resembles the derogation clauses found in the European Convention and the Political Covenant,[35] it differs from them in a number of important respects. The situations which justify derogation under the American Convention are 'war, public danger,

---

[35] *See* Higgins, *Derogation under Human Rights Treaties*, 48 Brit. Y.B. Int'l L. 281 (1975–76). *See also* Buergenthal, *International and Regional Human Rights Law and Institutions: Some Examples of their Interaction*, 12 Tex. Int'l L.J. 321, 324–25 (1977); Eissen, *The European Convention on Human Rights and the United Nations Covenant on Civil and Political Rights: Problems of Coexistence*, 22 Buffalo L. Rev. 181, 211 (1972) [hereinafter cited as Eissen].

or other emergency that threatens the independence or security of a State Party'. This language differs from that of article 4 of the Political Covenant which speaks of a 'time of public emergency which threatens the life of the nation'. Article 15 of the European Convention allows derogations during a 'time of war or other public emergency threatening the life of the nation'. The tests of the European Convention and the Political Covenant appear to be more stringent than that of the American Convention, which suggests that the emergency need merely threaten the 'independence or security of a State Party' to justify the derogation.

The concept of a 'threat to the security' of a state, besides being vague and subject to abuse,[36] embraces threats that are less serious than threats 'to the life of the nation' or its 'independence'. Here it is important to remember, however, that this provision, like all other provisions of the American Convention, must be interpreted consistent with the provisions of article 29, which provides:

> No provision of this Convention shall be interpreted as:
> a. permitting any State Party, group, or person to suppress the enjoyment or exercise of the rights and freedoms recognized in this Convention or to restrict them to a greater extent than is provided for herein;
> b. restricting the enjoyment or exercise of any right or freedom recognized by virtue of the laws of any State Party or by virtue of another convention to which one of the said states is a party;
> c. precluding other rights or guarantees that are inherent in the human personality or derived from representative democracy as a form of government; or
> d. excluding or limiting the effect that the American Declaration of the Rights and Duties of Man and other international acts of the same nature may have.

Of some relevance too is article 30 of the American Convention, which stipulates that '[t]he restrictions that, pursuant to this Convention, may be placed on the enjoyment or exercise of the rights or freedoms recognized herein may not be applied except in accordance with laws enacted for reasons of general interest and in accordance with the purpose for which such restrictions have been established'. Moreover, in the first preambular paragraph of the American Convention, the state parties reaffirm 'their intention to consolidate in this hemisphere, within the framework of democratic institutions, a system of personal liberty and social justice based on respect for the essential rights of man'. The concept, 'threat to the security of a state', found in article 27 of the American Convention, will therefore have to be interpreted by

---

[36] *See generally* H. Montealegre, La Seguridad del Estado y los Derechos Humanos (1979) [hereinafter cited as Montealegre].

reference to the values and criteria that the aforementioned provisions articulate.

Although article 27(1) appears to make derogation somewhat easier than do the corresponding provisions of other international instruments, the catalog of rights from which no derogation is permitted is much longer under article 27(2) than under the European Convention or the Political Covenant. The European Convention lists only four non-derogable rights—the right to life, freedom from torture, and the prohibitions of slavery and *ex post facto* laws.[37] The Political Covenant proclaims seven non-derogable rights: the four enumerated by the European Convention, plus the prohibition against imprisonment for nonfulfillment of contractual obligation, the right to be recognized as a person before the law, and freedom of thought, conscience, and religion.[38] By contrast, under the American Convention no derogation is permitted from eleven specific rights, including the right to nationality and the right to participate in government. The 'judicial guarantees essential for the protection' of these rights are also not derogable under article 27(2).

It might be argued that the 'long list' approach of the American Convention is unwise, because governments are unlikely to recognize all of these rights in times of national emergency. The American Convention, however, permits derogation in emergencies which are much less serious than those envisaged by the other instruments, and to that extent an expanded list of non-derogable rights is more justified. Given the political realities of the Western Hemisphere with its frequent national emergencies and states of siege,[39] it is not all that unreasonable to prohibit derogation from the right to participate in government, for example, whose suspensions for long periods of time have tended to make it easier for dictatorial regimes to remain in power.

The differences between the derogation provisions of the Political Covenant and the American Convention have some very interesting consequences. A state which is a party to both the American Convention and the Political Covenant must take account of the fact that these instruments permit a state party to take measures derogating from its obligations, provided that such measures are not inconsistent with its other obligations under international law.[40] Because of this proviso, a state which has adhered to both instruments would violate its obliga-

[37] European Convention, art. 15(2).

[38] Political Covenant, art. 4(2).

[39] *See, e.g.*, Inter-American Commission on Human Rights [hereinafter cited as IACHR]. Report on the Situation of Human Rights in Nicaragua, O.A.S. Doc. OEA/Ser. L/V/II.45, doc. 16, Rev. 1, at 29–30 (1978); Montealegre, *supra* note 36, at 3.

[40] American Convention, art. 27(1); Political Covenant, art. 4(1).

tions under the Political Covenant if, in a public emergency threatening the nation, it took measures suspending those rights that are non-derogable under article 27(2) of the American Convention, even though the rights in question are otherwise subject to derogation under the Political Covenant. To the extent that the suspension of these rights would violate the American Convention, it would be inconsistent with the state's obligations under international law.

If this principle applies also to the test for determining the existence of the emergency that justifies the derogation, which is a more difficult question, a state party to the American Convention might be deemed to violate its obligations under the Political Covenant if, in a derogation based on article 27(1) of the American Convention and validly founded on a threat 'to the security' of the state, it took measures suspending any of the rights that the Political Covenant guarantees. Since a threat to a state's 'security' is not a valid ground for derogation under the Covenant, its validity under the American Convention might not be legitimate under the law of the Political Covenant.

B.   THE CONVENTION INSTITUTIONS

The American Convention establishes two organs to safeguard its implementation: the Inter-American Commission on Human Rights and the Inter-American Court of Human Rights. Each of these organs consists of seven experts, elected in their individual capacities and not as government representatives. The members of the Inter-American Commission are elected by the O.A.S. General Assembly with all O.A.S. member states, whether or not they are parties to the American Convention, participating in the nomination process and taking part in the vote.[41] The judges of the Inter-American Court, on the other hand, may only be nominated and elected by the states parties to the American Convention.[42] However, the judges need not be nationals of state parties. The only condition relating to nationality—and it applies equally to the members of the Inter-American Commission as to the judges—is that they must be nationals of an O.A.S. member state.[43]

The difference in the election process of the members of the Inter-American Commission and the judges may be attributed, in part at least, to the dual functions that the Commission performs. As will be

[41] The members of the Inter-American Commission are elected from a list of candidates nominated by the O.A.S. member states, with each state being allowed to nominate no more than three candidates. A state nominating three individuals must propose at least one candidate who is not its own national. American Convention, art. 36.

[42] The election of the judges must also take place in the O.A.S. General Assembly, but only the states parties to the American Convention may participate in the vote. American Convention, art. 53.

[43] *Id.* arts. 52(1) & 36(2). Of the judges now serving on the Inter-American Court, one of them—the present author—is a U.S. national who was nominated by Costa Rica.

explained in greater detail later, the Inter-American Commission is not only an institution created by the American Convention, it is also an O.A.S. Charter organ[44] with jurisdiction over all O.A.S. member states. The Inter-American Court, on the other hand, is not expressly mentioned in the O.A.S. Charter, and the functions assigned to it in relation to states not parties to the American Convention are much more limited than those of the Inter-American Commission.

The first elections of the members of the Inter-American Commission and the judges of the Inter-American Court took place in May 1979, almost a year after the entry into force of the American Convention. In the interim, the functions of the Commission were performed by its predecessor organ, the old Inter-American Commission on Human Rights, which had been established in 1960.[45] The Inter-American Court, an entirely new institution, was installed in June 1979.

1. *The Inter-American Commission on Human Rights*

a. *Its Functions.* Article 41 of the American Convention describes the functions of the Commission as follows:

The main function of the Commission shall be to promote respect for and defense of human rights. In the exercise of its mandate, it shall have the following functions and powers:

a. to develop an awareness of human rights among the peoples of America;

b. to make recommendations to the governments of the member states, when it considers such action advisable, for the adoption of progressive measures in favor of human rights within the framework of their domestic law and constitutional provisions as well as appropriate measures to further the observance of those rights;

c. to prepare such studies or reports as it considers advisable in the performance of its duties;

d. to request the governments of the member states to supply it with information on the measures adopted by them in matters of human rights;

e. to respond, through the General Secretariat of the Organization of American States, to inquiries made by the member states on matters related to human rights and, within the limits of its possibilities, to provide those states with the advisory services they request;

[44] *See* O.A.S. Charter, art. 51; Farer & Rowles, *The Inter-American Commission on Human Rights*, in J. Tuttle, International Human Rights Law and Practice 47 (1978) [hereinafter cited as Farer & Rowles].

[45] The authority of the Inter-American Commission to exercise the interim function was provided by a resolution of the O.A.S. Permanent Council, entitled 'Transition from the Present Inter-American Commission on Human Rights to the Commission Provided for in the American Convention on Human Rights.' Permanent Council Res. 253 (343/78), O.A.S. Doc. OEA/Ser.G (Sept. 20, 1978). For the debate on this resolution, *see* O.A.S. Doc. OEA/Ser.G., CP/ACTA 343/78 (Sept. 20, 1978).

f. to take action on petitions and other communications pursuant to its
authority under the provisions of Articles 44 through 51 of this Convention; and

g. to submit an annual report to the General Assembly of the Organization
of American States.

The first sentence of the Spanish text of this provision—the American
Convention was drafted in Spanish—declares that the Inter-American
Commission's main function is to promote 'la observancia y la defensa
de los derechos humanos', which should have been translated as 'the
observance and protection of human rights'. This is not only a more
felicitous rendition of the Spanish text, it also corresponds to the
English text of article 112 of the O.A.S. Charter whose Spanish version
is identical to the Spanish text of article 41 of the American Convention.[46] It follows that the principal function of the Inter-American
Commission is to 'promote the observance and protection' of human
rights in the Americas.

In sub-paragraphs (a) through (g) of article 41, the American Convention assigns the Inter-American Commission a number of different
tasks. First, article 41(a) gives the Commission very extensive promotional powers which, when supplemented by the authority granted
in sub-paragraphs (c) and (e), require it to support hemisphere-wide
education and research programs devoted to human rights. Secondly,
the provisions of article 41(b), (c), (d), and (g), read together, empower
the Inter-American Commission to take a variety of general and specific measures designed to prevent violations of human rights by any
O.A.S. member state, whether or not it has ratified the American
Convention. Such measures might include country studies, 'on-the-
spot' investigations, and the dispatch of 'observer' missions. The
exercise of these functions by the Inter-American Commission is not
tied to the complaint machinery established by the American Convention, and consequently enables the Commission to act on its own
motion without any specific request or petition. By giving it this
power, the American Convention preserves for the Inter-American
Commission the authority to perform the functions that the old Inter-
American Commission on Human Rights exercised under articles 9
and 9 *bis* of its Statute[47] and to comply with its O.A.S. Charter
mandate.[48] Finally, article 41(f) empowers the Commission to
examine petitions and communications charging the states parties
with violations of their obligations under the American Convention.

[46] Art. 112 of the O.A.S. Charter provides, in part, that 'there shall be an Inter-American
Commission on Human Rights, whose principal function shall be to promote the observance and
protection of human rights . . .'
[47] This topic is dealt with in section I.C. *infra.*
[48] *See* O.A.S. Charter, art. 112; section I.C. *infra.*

In performing this task, which will be described in detail in the next section, the Inter-American Commission exercises quasi-judicial functions similar to those of the European Commission of Human Rights.

In addition, the American Convention contains a very important grant of power spelled out in article 42, which stipulates:

> The States Parties shall transmit to the Commission a copy of each of the reports and studies that they submit annually to the Executive Committees of the Inter-American Economic and Social Council and the Inter-American Council for Education, Science, and Culture, in their respective fields, so that the Commission may watch over the promotion of the rights implicit in the economic, social, educational, scientific, and cultural standards set forth in the Charter of the Organization of American States as amended by the Protocol of Buenos Aires.

The O.A.S. Charter, as amended by the Protocol of Buenos Aires, proclaims a lengthy list of economic, social, and cultural principles.[49] By giving the Inter-American Commission a role in the implementation of these standards as they apply to the states parties to the American Convention, article 42 provides the legal foundation for an Inter-American system for the protection of economic, social, and cultural rights, which could have far-reaching consequences.[50] The Commission's new rules of procedure suggest that it is aware of these possibilities and that it intends to make use of its power in this area.[51]

b. *Individual and Inter-State Complaints.* The Inter-American Commission's power under article 41(f), which authorizes it to deal with complaints charging a state party with violations of human rights, differs in one important respect from the authority vested in other international human rights institutions. The American Convention stipulates that by becoming a party to it, a state has accepted *ipso facto* the jurisdiction of the Commission to deal with private complaints lodged against that state.[52] But the Inter-American Commission may only deal with so-called inter-state complaints—complaints filed by one state party against another—if both states, in addition to ratifying

---

[49] O.A.S. Charter, arts. 29–50.

[50] *See*, in this connection, the very interesting analysis of the Commision concerning the violation of economic and social rights in El Salvador. IACHR, Report on the Situation of Human Rights in El Salvador and Observations of the Government of El Salvador on the Report, O.A.S. Doc. OEA/Ser.P,AG/doc. 1086/79, at 162 (1979). Even though this report was prepared pursuant to the power the Inter-American Commission derives from the O.A.S. Charter, rather than from the American Convention, the analysis and approach is not likely to differ much in the future.

[51] *See* Regulations of the Inter-American Commission on Human Rights [hereinafter cited as Regulations], art. 60, *reprinted in* Handbook, *supra* note 3, at 117.

[52] American Convention, art. 44.

the American Convention, have made a further declaration recognizing the inter-state jurisdiction of the Commission.[53] The American Convention thus reverses the more traditional pattern utilized by the European Convention, for example, where the right of individual petition is optional[54] and the inter-state complaint procedure is mandatory.[55] The drafters of the American Convention apparently assumed that inter-state complaints might be used by some governments for political objectives or interventionist purposes, and that this risk existed to a much more limited extent with regard to private petitions. Whatever may be the soundness of these assumptions, it is undisputed that the availability of the right of private petition enhances the effectiveness of an international system for the protection of human rights. By enabling individuals to assert their own claims, the right of private petition makes the enforcement of human rights less dependent on the extraneous political considerations that tend to motivate governmental action and inaction.[56]

Unlike the European Convention, the American Convention does not provide that only victims of a violation may file private petitions.[57] It provides instead that:

Any person or group of persons, or any nongovernmental entity legally recognized in one or more member states of the Organization, may lodge petitions with the Commission containing denunciations or complaints of violation of this Convention by a State Party.[58]

Moreover, although the states parties must recognize the jurisdiction of the Inter-American Commission to deal with inter-state communications before they may institute them, the states need not prove any special interest in the case to file it. They are consequently free to submit complaints alleging violations committed against their own nationals, against stateless persons, or against nationals of any other state.[59]

The admissibility of a petition is conditioned on (a) the exhaustion of domestic remedies 'in accordance with the generally recognized principles of international law',[60] and (b) the requirement that the

[53] *Id.* art. 45.

[54] European Convention, art. 25(1).

[55] *Id.* art. 24.

[56] On this subject generally, *see* Schwelb, *Book Review*, 1 Revue des Droits de l'Homme 626, 630 (1968).

[57] *Compare* European Convention, art. 25(1) *with* American Convention, art. 44.

[58] American Convention, art. 44.

[59] *See id.* art. 45(1). The same principle has been consistently adhered to under the European Convention. *See*, e.g., the case law reproduced in Sohn & Buergenthal, *supra* note 1, at 1054–62. The 'special interest' doctrine enunciated by the International Court of Justice in the South West Africa cases, [1966] I.C.J. 6, consequently does not apply to inter-state complaints filed under the American Convention or the European Convention.

[60] American Convention, art. 46(1)(a).

petition be submitted to the Inter-American Commission within a period of six months from the date on which the victim of the alleged violation was notified of the final domestic judgment in his or her case.[61] But these requirements do not prevent the admissibility of a petition whenever it can be shown that:

a. the domestic legislation of the state concerned does not afford due process of law for the protection of the right or rights that have allegedly been violated;
b. the party alleging violation of his rights has been denied access to the remedies under domestic law or has been prevented from exhausting them; or
c. there has been unwarranted delay in rendering a final judgment under the aforementioned remedies.[62]

The Commission's rules of procedure provide, moreover, that the respondent government has the burden of demonstrating the non-exhaustion of available domestic remedies if the complainant alleges that it was impossible to comply with the exhaustion requirement.[63]

Article 47(d) of the American Convention provides that the Commission shall 'consider inadmissible any petition or communication . . . [that] is substantially the same as one previously studied by the Commission or by another international organization.'[64] Article 46(1)(c) conditions the admissibility of all complaints on the requirement 'that the subject of the petition or communication is not pending in another international proceeding for settlement'. The Inter-American Commission has clarified these provisions in article 36 of its rules of procedure. The rules indicate that a case pending in another international organization will be deemed inadmissible by the Inter-American Commission only if the respondent state is a party to the other proceeding and if an effective remedy is there available to dispose of the specific claim that was submitted to the Commission. What constitutes an effective remedy will presumably be determined by reference to the American Convention.[65] Furthermore, before a complaint will be deemed inadmissible on the ground that it is 'the same as one previously studied . . . by another international organization', the Inter-American Commission must ascertain, first, whether the

---

[61] *Id*. art. 46(1)(b).

[62] *Id*. art. 46(2).

[63] Regulations, *supra* note 51, art. 34(3). This rule is inapplicable only when petitioner's contention is manifestly contradicted by the information contained in the petition itself. *Id*.

[64] The Spanish text of art. 47(d) speaks of any petition or communication previously 'examinada', indicating that the English 'examined' would have been a more appropriate rendition instead of the more ambiguous 'studied'.

[65] For the petition to be inadmissible it must also appear, *inter alia*, that the victim or someone authorized by him instituted the proceedings in the other organ. Regulations, *supra* note 51, art. 36(2).

case was in fact finally resolved and, secondly, whether the solution addressed the specific claim of the complaint and provided an effective remedy.[66]

Article 36 of the Inter-American Commission's rules of procedure thus indicates that the mere fact that a complaint is simultaneously submitted to it and to another international organ is not an absolute bar to its examination by the Commission; the latter will be able to deal with the case as soon as it is no longer pending elsewhere. An individual who has filed the same complaint with a number of international human rights organs might therefore be informed by the Inter-American Commission that the case will be ruled inadmissible unless the other complaints are withdrawn. In other words, we are here dealing with relative or conditional inadmissibility. By contrast, a case is absolutely inadmissible if it was previously fully and effectively resolved by another international organ. Note that here the Inter-American Commission, drawing on the universally accepted principles of *res judicata*, very wisely makes absolute inadmissibility dependent, among other considerations, on the existence of a final decision or resolution of the dispute.[67]

A complaint which is not inadmissible for one of the reasons mentioned above and which contains allegations stating a *prima facie* violation of the American Convention, will advance to the next or second stage of the Inter-American Commission's proceedings.[68] Here the Commission examines the petitioner's allegations, seeks information from the government concerned, investigates the facts, and holds hearings in which both the government and the petitioners may participate.[69] Although a complaint ruled admissible may at this stage still be rejected as 'inadmissible or out of order',[70] this ruling must be based on a finding by the Inter-American Commission that it would have been obliged to reject the complaint at the admissibility stage if the relevant facts had been known to it at that time. If after investigating a complaint, the Commission concludes, for example, that the petitioner failed to exhaust all available domestic remedies, it has the power to rule the petition inadmissible. The same result would be indicated if the evidence deduced in the case left no reasonable doubt whatsoever that the complaint was without merit.[71] In other words, the authority

---

[66] *Id.* arts 36(1)(a) & 36(2)(a).

[67] On this problem generally, *see* Tardu, *The Protocol to the United Nations Covenant on Civil and Political Rights and the Inter-American System: A Study of Co-Existing Petition Procedures*, 70 Am. J. Int'l L. 778 (1976). *See also* Eissen, *supra* note 35.

[68] *See* American Convention, art. 47(b) & (c).

[69] *See id.* art. 48(1)(a), (d), & (e); Regulations, *supra* note 51, arts. 40–41, 61–63.

[70] American Convention, art. 48(1)(c).

[71] Under art. 47 of the American Convention, the Inter-American Commission must rule a complaint inadmissible if it plainly appears that 'the petition or communication is manifestly groundless or obviously out of order . . .'

granted to the Inter-American Commission at this stage enables it to dismiss cases which, in retrospect, should never have been admitted.[72] But this power is clearly not to be used by the Inter-American Commission to adjudicate on the merits.

During the second stage of the proceedings, the Inter-American Commission also has an obligation to 'place itself at the disposal of the parties concerned with a view to reaching a friendly settlement of the matter on the basis of respect for the human rights recognized' in the Convention.[73] If a friendly settlement is obtained, the Commission must prepare a report, describing the facts of the case and how it was resolved. This report is transmitted by the Commission to the Secretary General of the O.A.S. 'for publication'.[74]

A case moves into the third stage of the proceedings if the parties are unable to reach a friendly settlement. At this point, the Inter-American Commission must draw up a report setting out the facts that have emerged from its investigations and the conclusions it has reached about the case. This report, which may also include whatever recommendations the Commission wishes to make regarding the resolution of the dispute, is transmitted only to the states concerned and may not be published by them.[75] After receiving the report, the state has three months within which to act on it. During that period, the case may be either settled by the parties or referred to the Inter-American Court of Human Rights by the Inter-American Commission or a state; private parties have no standing to do so.

A case reaches the fourth stage of the proceeedings before the Inter-American Commission if it has been neither referred to the Inter-American Court nor otherwise settled by the parties. At this point 'the Commission may, by the vote of an absolute majority of its members, set forth its opinion and conclusions concerning the question submitted for its consideration'.[76] If the Commission decides to adopt this report—and it is obviously under no obligation to do so in all cases—it must set out its 'recommendations' and 'prescribe a period within which the state is to take the measures that are incumbent upon it to remedy the situation examined'.[77] Once this period has expired, and if the Commission in fact adopted the aforementioned report, it 'shall decide by the vote of an absolute

---

[72] The European Commission of Human Rights obtained a similar authority through an amendment to the European Convention. *See* Protocol No. 3 to the European Convention, art. 1, *reprinted in* Brownlie, *supra* note 7, at 260, art. 29, as amended. On this subject, *see* Sohn & Buergenthal, *supra* note 2, at 1091.

[73] American Convention, art. 48(1)(f).

[74] *Id.* art. 49.

[75] *Id.* art. 50; *see* Regulations, *supra* note 51, art. 43.

[76] American Convention, art. 51(1).

[77] *Id.* art. 51(2).

majority of its members whether the state has taken adequate measures and whether to publish its report'.[78] This last decision concludes the Inter-American Commission proceedings in the case.

It is obvious that the American Convention establishes a very cumbersome and ambiguous procedure for the resolution of cases by the Inter-American Commission. As we have seen, it provides for two Commission reports—one at the third stage of the proceedings and the other at the fourth. From the wording of the relevant provisions of the American Convention, it is by no means easy to ascertain how these reports differ in their contents and functions. It is important to note, however, that the report to be prepared by the Inter-American Commission at the third stage of the proceedings is mandatory; it does not require a vote of an absolute majority of the Commission members; and it has to contain the Commission's conclusions indicating whether the respondent state has or has not violated the American Convention.[79] If in this report the Inter-American Commission finds that no violation of the American Convention has been committed, it will in all likelihood not draw up the fourth-stage report. That report is not mandatory and appears to be designed for cases involving a breach of the American Convention which the state has failed to remedy in the manner suggested by the Inter-American Commission in its third-stage report. Although the American Convention does not say so expressly, it would appear that the fourth-stage report, if published, should also contain the Commission's decision on the question 'whether the state has taken adequate measures' to remedy the situation which gave rise to the case. That decision, after all, is an integral and indispensable part of the case and the proceedings relating to it. Interestingly enough, the Inter-American Commission's rules of procedure contain a specific provision enabling the Commission to include the fourth-stage report in its annual report to the O.A.S. General Assembly.[80] This approach, which does not prevent the report from also being published as a separate document, gets the case on the agenda of the O.A.S. General Assembly where the state's failure to comply with the Inter-American Commission's recommendations can then be discussed and acted upon. Since an O.A.S. General Assembly debate could subject a recalcitrant government to considerable adverse publicity, many governments will take seriously the threat of the publication of a critical report by the Inter-American Commission as well as any condemnatory resolution the O.A.S. Assembly might adopt in such a case.

Although the proceedings involving cases that have not been settled

---

[78] *Id.* art. 51(3); *see* Regulations, *supra* note 57, art. 45.
[79] *See* American Convention, art. 50.
[80] Regulations, *supra* note 51, art. 45(2).

or referred to the Inter-American Court end with the publication of the
Commission's fourth-stage report, the Commission can be deemed to
have the power under the American Convention and the O.A.S.
Charter to keep a serious situation 'under observation' beyond that
stage and to keep the O.A.S. Assembly informed. The Inter-American
Commission could provide this information on its own motion or at
the request of the Assembly. In due course the Commission probably
should develop appropriate formal procedures to monitor cases dealt
with in fourth-stage reports. Such an approach would be particularly
useful for dealing with situations requiring a substantial amount of
time to assess the extent of a government's compliance with the
recommendations of the Commission.

2.   *The Inter-American Court of Human Rights*[81]

The American Convention vests two distinct judicial functions in
the Inter-American Court of Human Rights. One involves the power
to adjudicate disputes relating to charges that a State Party has violated
the Convention. In performing this function, the Inter-American
Court exercises its so-called contentious jurisdiction.[82] The Court's
other power is to interpret the American Convention and certain
human rights treaties in proceedings that do not involve the adjudication of specific disputes.[83] This is the Inter-American Court's
advisory jurisdiction.

a.   *The Inter-American Court's Contentious Jurisdiction.* The contentious jurisdiction of the Inter-American Court is spelled out in article
62 of the American Convention, which reads as follows:

1. A State Party may, upon depositing its instrument of ratification or
adherence to this Convention, or at any subsequent time, declare that it
recognizes as binding, *ipso facto*, and not requiring special agreement, the
jurisdiction of the Court on all matters relating to the interpretation or
application of this Convention.

2. Such declaration may be made unconditionally, on the condition of
reciprocity, for a specified period, or for specific cases. It shall be presented to
the Secretary General of the Organization, who shall transmit copies thereof
to the other member states of the Organization and to the Secretary of the
Court.

3. The jurisdiction of the Court shall comprise all cases concerning the
interpretation and application of the provisions of this Convention that are
submitted to it, provided that the States Parties to the case recognize or have

---

[81] [Ed. note: On the Inter-American Court of Human Rights, *see generally* Buergenthal, *The
Inter-American Court of Human Rights*, 76 Am. J. Int'l L. 231 (1982).]

[82] American Convention, art. 62.

[83] *Id.* art. 64.

recognized such jurisdiction, whether by special declaration pursuant to the preceding paragraphs, or by special agreement.

This provision indicates that a state party does not subject itself to the contentious jurisdiction of the Inter-American Court by merely ratifying the American Convention. The Court acquires that jurisdiction with regard to a state party only when that state has either filed the declaration referred to in paragraphs 1 and 2 of article 62 or concluded the special agreement mentioned in paragraph 3. The declaration may be made when a state ratifies the American Convention or at any time thereafter; it may also be made for a specific case or a series of cases. To date only Costa Rica, Honduras, Peru, and Venezuela deposited the declaration for future cases. But since the states parties are free to accept the Inter-American Court's jurisdiction at any time in a specific case or in general, the Inter-American Commission's rules of procedure quite properly authorize it to invite states to permit cases being dealt with by the Inter-American Commission to be submitted to the Court.[84] It would probably make sense for the Inter-American Commission to extend that invitation in every case in which it has adopted its stage-three report.[85]

A case may also be referred to the Inter-American Court by 'special agreement'. In speaking of the 'special agreement', article 62(3) of the American Convention does not indicate who may conclude the agreement. While it is obvious that it may be concluded by and between states parties, it is less clear whether the Inter-American Commission could take the place of a state. A state might be willing, for example, to submit a case to the Inter-American Court by means of a special agreement concluded with the Commission, provided it and the Commission can agree to seek a Court judgment on only some, but not all, of the issues that the initial complaint presented. If it is assumed that the Court must adjudicate all the relevant issues raised by a case that was referred to it under a declaration accepting its jurisdiction, it would follow that the only way to obtain a more limited adjudication is to conclude a special agreement enumerating the issues to be decided. Whether the American Convention permits this solution is an issue which the Inter-American Court will no doubt have to decide one of these days.

In providing that '[o]nly the States Parties and the Commission shall have the right to submit a case to the Court', article 61(1) makes quite clear that private parties do not have standing to institute these

---

[84] Regulations, *supra* note 50, art. 47(3).

[85] It will be recalled that the decision whether to refer a case to the Inter-American Court must be made within a three-month period after the stage-three report has been transmitted to the states concerned.

proceedings. An individual who has filed a complaint with the Inter-American Commission cannot consequently bring that case to the Inter-American Court. A case arising out of an individual complaint can get to the Court, but it must be referred to it by the Commission or a state.

Although it is undisputed that the states parties to the American Convention have standing to submit cases to the Inter-American Court, it is less certain whether in a specific case only those states that participated in the prior proceedings before the Inter-American Commission may do so or whether all states parties have that right. Article 61(2) of the American Convention provides that a case may not be brought to the Inter-American Court until after the Inter-American Commission has dealt with it and adopted its stage-three report. But the Convention is silent on whether the standing of the states parties is otherwise restricted. In addition to various policy arguments that bear on the issue, two provisions of the American Convention appear to be relevant. One is article 50(2), which declares that the Commission's stage-three report 'shall be transmitted to the states concerned, which shall not be at liberty to publish it'. The other is article 61(1). It provides that '[o]nly the States Parties and the Commission shall have the right to submit a case to the Court'. If article 50(2) means that the stage-three report may be made available only to the 'states concerned' and if that reference embraces only states which have participated in the Inter-American Commission proceedings, then no other states will have access to the report. Other states will therefore lack the information necessary to take the case to the Inter-American Court. On the other hand, given the unambiguous language of article 61(1), it might be that 'states concerned', as used in article 50(2), refers to all states which have accepted the Inter-American Court's jurisdiction. Here it could be argued that these states must be deemed to be 'concerned' because they have standing to submit the case to the Court. The latter argument gains some support from the contention that, if the drafters had intended to limit the standing of states, they would have said so expressly in article 61(1) and they would have provided in article 50(2) that the report be transmitted only to 'the states parties to the dispute'.

As has been noted already, article 61(2) provides that '[i]n order for the Court to hear a case', the Inter-American Commission must first have dealt with it and a stage-three report must have been adopted. This provision raises at least two questions. The first is whether the states parties to a dispute may waive the proceedings before the Commission and go directly to the Court. Second, even assuming that the requirement relating to the role of the Commission cannot be waived, does it apply to all cases which might be brought to the

Court?[86] The answer to the first question will depend, in part at least, on a determination of the purpose of the requirement and whether it was designed solely for the benefit of the states parties to the dispute. The second question arises because, as will be recalled, the Inter-American Court may acquire jurisdiction either by declaration or special agreement. A case referred to the Court pursuant to a declaration will have originated in a complaint, whether inter-state or individual, charging a state with a violation of a human right proclaimed in the American Convention. That need not be true of disputes submitted to the Court under a special agreement. Such disputes might relate to any clause of the American Convention, in particular to those that are not human rights provisions as such. It is consequently entirely possible for State *X*, for example, to have a dispute with State *Y* regarding the application of article 70 of the American Convention, which accords members of the Inter-American Commission and judges of the Inter-American Court diplomatic immunity during their term of office. A hypothetical case might involve Judge *A*, who, while in *Y*, was denied the immunities to which *X* claims the judge is entitled under the Convention. If both *X* and *Y* are states parties to the American Convention, they could conclude a special agreement to submit the dispute to the Inter-American Court. Note that this would not be a dispute relating to a violation of 'a human right set forth in this Convention'.[87] For that reason, it would not be admissible if filed with the Inter-American Commission as a complaint,[88] and since the Commission has no jurisdiction to accept complaints by 'special agreement', it is clear that the dispute between *X* and *Y* could not be taken up by the Commission. This suggests that disputes between states might be referred directly to the Inter-American Court by special agreement without any intercession by the Commission, provided the disputes concern the interpretation or application of those provisions of the American Convention that do not concern individual human rights. Whether the same would be true of other disputes, that is a much more difficult question.

The judgment rendered by the Inter-American Court in any dispute submitted to it is 'final and not subject to appeal'.[89] Moreover, the 'States Parties to the Convention undertake to comply with the judgment of the Court in any case to which they are parties'.[90] The

[86] [Ed. note: The answers to these questions have been clarified by the Inter-American Court in its decision on Nov. 13, 1981, *In re* Viviana Gallardo, No. G. 101/81, *reprinted in* 20 Int'l Legal Materials 1424 (1981).]

[87] American Convention, art. 45(1).

[88] *Id.* art. 47(b).

[89] *Id.* art. 67.

[90] *Id.* art. 68(1).

American Convention does not specify that the Inter-American Commission is also bound by the judgments of the Inter-American Court. But this does not necessarily mean that the Commission is free to disregard the Court's rulings, which may be binding on it as *res judicata* or authoritative precedent. This conclusion follows from the fact that the Commission is a quasi-judicial body to which the Convention assigns a role that is hierarchically inferior to the Court for certain purposes and from the fact that the Commission participates in the proceedings before the Court.[91]

The American Convention, in article 63(1), contains the following stipulation relating to the judgments that the Court may render:

> If the Court finds that there has been a violation of a right or freedom protected by this Convention, the Court shall rule that the injured party be ensured the enjoyment of his right or freedom that was violated. It shall also rule, if appropriate, that the consequences of the measure or situation that constituted the breach of such right or freedom be remedied and that fair compensation be paid to the injured party.

This provision indicates that the Inter-American Court must decide whether there has been a breach of the American Convention and, if so, what rights the injured party should be accorded. Moreover, the Court may also determine the steps that should be taken to remedy the breach and the amount of damages to which the injured party is entitled. Let us assume, for example, that the Court finds that the trial of an individual violated the American Convention because he or she was denied various rights proclaimed in article 8 (Right to a Fair Trial) of the American Convention. After enumerating the specific rights to which the injured individual was and is entitled, the Court may also declare whether he or she should be granted a new trial and/or whether he or she should be awarded damages for the injuries sustained.

A separate provision of the American Convention deals with money damages. It provides that the 'part of a judgment that stipulates compensatory damages may be executed in the country concerned in accordance with domestic procedure governing the execution of judgments against the state'.[92] It is unclear what this provision means. If it means that an injured party is free to seek execution through the relevant domestic procedures, the provision has little significance and gives the individual no additional rights. It could also be interpreted to mean that, if there exist appropriate domestic procedures for judgments against the state, the Inter-American Court's judgment shall be

---

[91] On this problem generally, *see* Buergenthal, *The Effect of the European Convention on Human Rights on the Internal Law of Member States*, in The European Convention on Human Rights, Int'l & Comp. L.Q. Supp. No. 11, at 79, 94–95 (1965).

[92] American Convention, art. 68(2).

equated, for purposes of execution, to a domestic judgment. Thus interpreted, it might be a very useful remedy. Finally, the provision might be deemed to authorize a state to insist that the judgment be executed in the manner prescribed by domestic law for judgments against the state. The advantage or disadvantage of such an interpretation may well differ from country to country, depending on domestic legal procedures, including immunities, and the delays that are encountered in the execution of judgments. The provision, whatever its meaning, would have much greater significance if it expressly required full domestic law enforcement of the Court's judgment. That result could, of course, be achieved by appropriate domestic legislation.

In addition to regular judgments, the Inter-American Court also has the power to grant what might be described as temporary injunctions. This power is spelled out in article 63(2) of the American Convention, which reads as follows:

In cases of extreme gravity and urgency, and when necessary to avoid irreparable damage to persons, the Court shall adopt such provisional measures as it deems pertinent in matters it has under consideration. With respect to a case not yet submitted to the Court, it may act at the request of the Commission.

This extraordinary remedy is available in two distinct circumstances: the first consists of cases pending before the Inter-American Court; the second involves complaints being dealt with by the Inter-American Commission that have not yet been referred to the Court for adjudication.

In the first category of cases, the request for the temporary injunction can be made at any time during the proceedings before the Court, including simultaneously with the filing of the case. Of course, the requested relief may only be granted after the Court has determined, if only in a preliminary manner, that it has jurisdiction over the parties. Although article 63(2) does not say anything about jurisdiction, it is obvious that the Court can only deal with a case, whether it calls for provisional or permanent relief, in which the states parties have accepted its jurisdiction.[93] But since jurisdictional issues may at times be extremely complex and intertwined with matters bearing on the merits of the case, the Inter-American Court should not have to resolve fully all jurisdictional issues before ordering provisional measures, assuming, of course, that such measures are otherwise plainly indicated. Given the need for urgency and the extraordinary character of the relief, the Court would certainly be justified to follow the pre-

---

[93] *Id.* art. 62(3).

cedent of the International Court of Justice, which requires no more than a *prima facie* showing of jurisdiction before granting provisional measures in an otherwise appropriate case.[94]

The same principle should no doubt also apply to the second category of cases, that is, cases in which a preliminary injunction appears to be indicated even before the Inter-American Commission has had a chance either to complete its examination of the complaint or to refer it to the Inter-American Court. The Commission might receive a complaint, for example, in which it is asserted that State X, which has ratified the American Convention and accepted the jurisdiction of the Inter-American Court, plans within the next few days to execute Mr. B., who was convicted following a trial that is alleged to have violated various provisions of the Convention. The Inter-American Commission could take this type of case to the Court immediately on receipt of the complaint and seek the remedies provided for by article 63(2). The Court would here obtain jurisdiction only for purposes of dealing with the request for provisional measures. It would not acquire jurisdiction to decide the case on the merits until the proceedings before the Commission had been concluded and the complaint was thereafter referred to the Court for adjudication by the Commission or a state. But even if the case is subsequently not submitted to the Court, the provisional measures remain within its jurisdiction and can presumably be modified or revoked only by it.

Since the states parties to the American Convention are free at any time to accept the jurisdiction of the Inter-American Court for the adjudication of a specific case, the Inter-American Commission would appear to be entitled to seek provisional measures in a case in which the defendant state had not accepted the Court's jurisdiction. Of course, the Court could not comply with the demand until the state indicated, be it at the request of the Commission or the Court, that it would accept the Court's jurisdiction in the particular case. But until the state has unambiguously signaled its unwillingness to accept the Court's jurisdiction, it would be improper for the Court or the Commission to take it for granted.

Although the Inter-American Court lacks the power to enforce its judgments or preliminary rulings, one provision of the American Convention bears on this subject. It reads as follows:

To each regular session of the General Assembly of the Organization of American States the Court shall submit, for the Assembly's consideration, a

---

[94] *See* Case concerning United States Diplomatic and Consular Staff in Tehran, Provisional Measures, Order of Dec. 15, 1979, [1979] I.C.J. 7, 13, where the Court declared that provisional measures ought to be granted 'only if the provisions invoked by the Applicant appear, *prima facie*, to afford a basis on which the jurisdiction of the Court might be founded'.

report on its work during the previous year. It shall specify, in particular, the cases in which a state has not complied with its judgments, making any pertinent recommendations.[95]

This provision enables the Court to inform the O.A.S General Assembly of situations involving non-compliance with its decisions, and it permits the O.A.S. Assembly to discuss the matter and to adopt whatever political measures it deems appropriate. It should be noted, moreover, that the mere fact that article 65 speaks of 'regular sessions' of the Assembly does not mean that the matter of non-compliance by a state may not be raised at a special session of that body, either at the request of a member state or following consideration by the O.A.S. Permanent Council. Thus, since the Council acts for the Assembly when it is not in session,[96] the Inter-American Court would appear to be free to call the Council's attention to cases that might justify emergency measures such as, for example, threats of non-compliance with provisional measures adopted by the Court. This information might prompt the Council to convene a special session of the Assembly or to take some other measures it deems appropriate.[97]

b. *The Inter-American Court's Advisory Jurisdiction.* The jurisdiction of the Inter-American Court of Human Rights to render advisory opinions is more extensive than that of any other international tribunal in existence today. It is spelled out in article 64 of the American Convention, which reads as follows:

1. The member states of the Organization may consult the Court regarding the interpretation of this Convention or of other treaties concerning the protection of human rights in the American states. Within their spheres of competence, the organs listed in Chapter X of the Charter of the Organization of American States, as amended by the Protocol of Buenos Aires, may in like manner consult the Court.

2. The Court, at the request of a member state of the Organization, may provide that state with opinions regarding the compatibility of any of its domestic laws with the aforesaid international instruments.

Article 64 indicates, first, that standing to request an advisory opinion from the Court is not limited to the states parties to the American Convention; any O.A.S. member state may seek it. Second, the advisory jurisdiction is not limited to interpretations of the American Convention: it also extends to interpretations of any other treaty 'concerning the protection of human rights in the American states'. Third, all O.A.S. organs, including the Inter-American Commission on

[95] American Convention, art. 65.
[96] *See* O.A.S. Charter art. 91.
[97] *See id.* arts. 56, 59, & 60.

Human Rights, have standing to request advisory opinions.[98] Fourth, the member states of the O.A.S may also seek opinions from the Inter-American Court regarding the compatibility of their domestic laws with the American Convention or any of the aforementioned human rights treaties.

Article 64 leaves many questions unanswered, and the Inter-American Court has not as yet had an opportunity to deal with any of them. It is by no means clear, for example, what is meant by 'treaties concerning the protection of human rights in the American states'. This is not a concept that has an accepted juridical meaning within the inter-American system, and the *travaux préparatoires* of the American Convention do not help explain it. The phrase might have reference to human rights treaties concluded exclusively by American States or adopted within the framework of the inter-American system; it might also apply to human rights treaties, whether bilateral or multilateral, universal or regional, accepted by one or some American states. Despite the fact that the O.A.S. Charter deals with many different subjects, is it a 'treaty concerning the protection of human rights' to the extent that it also contains human rights provisions, thus enabling the Court to interpret those provisions? The answers to these questions are by no means self-evident. They are also very important, for they will determine *inter alia* whether the Court is deemed to have the power in appropriate cases to interpret a United Nations human rights treaty or the human rights provisions of a bilateral commercial treaty, for example, or whether its advisory jurisdiction applies only to treaties concluded within the framework of the O.A.S.

It is also not clear whether there are any limits on the scope of the Inter-American Court's power to render advisory opinions. Assume, for example, that a complaint has been filed with the Inter-American Commission against State X and that it has not accepted the jurisdiction of the Inter-American Court. If during the proceedings before the Commission a disagreement arises between State X and the Commission concerning the interpretation of a provision of the American Convention, may the Commission request the Court to render an advisory opinion on that legal issue even if State X objects? State X would presumably argue that this was not an advisory opinion but a

---

[98] In identifying the organs of the O.A.S. that have standing to seek an advisory opinion, art. 64 of the American Convention refers to Chapter X of the O.A.S. Charter. That chapter identifies the following organs: the General Assembly; the Meeting of Consultation of Ministers of Foreign Affairs; the Councils (consisting of the Permanent Council of the Organization, the Inter-American Economic and Social Council, and the Inter-American Council for Education, Science, and Culture); the Inter-American Juridical Committee; the Inter-American Commission on Human Rights; the General Secretariat; the Specialized Conferences; and the Specialized Organizations. *See* O.A.S. Charter art. 51.

disguised contentious case and that the Commission was resorting to it to get around *X*'s failure to recognize the Court's jurisdiction.[99] The strength of this contention may well depend on the weight that should be given to the claims that article 64 is unambiguous in imposing no limits whatsoever on the right to request advisory opinions; that such opinions may only deal with questions of law; that they are by definition not binding on any state; and that, consequently, they should not be equated with decisions rendered in contentious cases. It is not necessary to adopt one or the other of these arguments to recognize that the Court's advisory jurisdiction could significantly strengthen the Commission's capacity to deal with complex legal issues arising under the Convention. If it is recalled, moreover, that all O.A.S. organs, and not only the Commission, have standing to request advisory opinions from the Court, it is not unreasonable to assume that the political organs of the O.A.S. might find it politically useful in certain cases to resort to the Court.

Article 64(2) permits O.A.S. member states to seek an opinion from the Court on the extent to which their domestic laws are compatible with the Convention or with any other 'American' human rights treaty. This provision might have a number of important uses. Governments might resort to it to obtain the Court's opinion on pending legislation. States considering the ratification of the American Convention might invoke it to ascertain whether, given certain domestic laws, they should do so with specific reservations. National tribunals might use this provision to consult the Court before interpreting or applying the American Convention or the other human rights treaties covered by article 64. That approach, if adopted, would contribute very significantly to the uniform application of the Convention by national tribunals. This conclusion raises the question whether national courts may request an advisory opinion directly from the Inter-American Court or whether they have to go through their governments. The language of article 64(2) appears to suggest that the request must come from the state, *i.e.*, the government, rather than directly from national tribunals. If this interpretation is correct, governments should be encouraged to establish a domestic procedure, which would facilitate the transmittal of these requests and regulate the manner of their presentation to the Court. The matter could also be regulated by a special agreement between the Court and the govern-

---

[99] South Africa made a similar argument before the International Court of Justice in the *Namibia* case, but the Court rejected it. Advisory Opinion on Legal Consequences for States of the Continued Presence of South Africa in Namibia, [1971] I.C.J. 16. *See also* W. Bishop, International Law 74–76 (3d ed. 1971), where other precedents bearing on this subject are discussed.

ment. Article 27 of its Statute authorizes the Court to conclude such agreements.

Resort to the advisory jurisdiction of the Court, whether it be by the Inter-American Commission, the other O.A.S. organs, or the member states, has a number of advantages that its contentious jurisdiction does not provide. The latter can only be invoked by and against states that have recognized the Court's jurisdiction; no such requirement applies to its advisory jurisdiction. Although the Court's decision in a contentious case is binding, which is of course not true of an advisory opinion, that distinction may not be of great practical significance. Compliance and non-compliance by states with their international obligations depend less on the formal status of a judgment and its abstract enforceability. Much more important is its impact as a force capable of legitimating governmental conduct and the perception of governments about the political cost of non-compliance. States may find it as difficult in some cases to disregard an advisory opinion as a binding decision. The Inter-American Court may therefore be able to play an important role even if its contentious jurisdiction is not widely accepted by the states parties to the American Convention. Much will depend on the extent to which the advisory power is resorted to by O.A.S. organs and the member states; much will also depend on the wisdom and prestige of the Court.

C.   THE O.A.S. CHARTER AND HUMAN RIGHTS

A member state of the O.A.S. which has not ratified the American Convention on Human Rights is subject to the human rights regime that has its constitutional basis in the O.A.S. Charter.[100] This regime has evolved over the past three decades and achieved full constitutional legitimacy in 1970 with the entry into force of the 'Protocol of Buenos Aires', which amended the 1948 O.A.S. Charter in a number of important respects.[101] The entry into effect in 1978 of the American Convention on Human Rights resulted in some further institutional and legal modification in the Charter-based regime.

1.   *The Evolution of the Charter-Based Regime*

a. *Under the 1948 Charter.* The 1948 O.A.S. Charter contained very few provisions relating to human rights and all of them were phrased

[100] *See generally Revised OAS Charter, supra* note 2; Farer & Rowles, *supra* note 44.

[101] The Protocol of Buenos Aires was signed on Feb. 27, 1967, and entered into force on Feb. 27, 1970. 21 U.S.T. 607, T.I.A.S. No. 6847. The original O.A.S. Charter was signed at Bogotá in 1948, and entered into force in 1951. 2 U.S.T. 2394, T.I.A.S. No. 2361, 119 U.N.T.S. 3. On the Protocol of Buenos Aires, *see* Sepúlveda, *The Reform of the Charter of the Organization of American States,* 137 Recueil des Cours 83 (1972); Robertson, *Revision of the Charter of the Organization of American States,* 17 Int'l & Comp. L.O. 346 (1968).

in very general terms. The most important reference to human rights appeared in article 5(j), which has been retained in the amended Charter as article 3(j). In this provision the American States 'reaffirm' and 'proclaim' as a principle of the Organization 'the fundamental rights of the individual without distinction as to race, nationality, creed or sex'. But the 1948 Charter did not define the meaning of 'the fundamental rights of the individual', nor did it establish a mechanism to promote or protect them.[102] The American Declaration of the Rights and Duties of Man was proclaimed at the same Bogotá conference that produced the 1948 Charter but the American Declaration was adopted in the form of a simple conference resolution[103] and did not form part of the Charter itself. Moreover, whereas the American Declaration proclaimed that '[t]he international protection of the rights of man should be the principal guide of an evolving American law',[104] the Bogotá conference went on record with an understanding that the American Declaration had not been incorporated by reference into the Charter.[105] The Inter-American Juridical Committee reinforced this position with a 1949 ruling that the American Declaration 'does not create legal contractual obligations' and lacked the status of 'positive substantive law'.[106]

Following the Bogotá conference, sporadic attempts were made in the O.A.S. to establish some institutional mechanisms for dealing with human rights problems.[107] These efforts produced no tangible results until 1959, when the Fifth Meeting of Consultation of Ministers of Foreign Affairs, relying on article 5(j) of the O.A.S. Charter, adopted a resolution[108] mandating the creation of 'an Inter-American Commission on Human Rights, composed of seven members, elected, as individuals, by the [O.A.S.] Council . . .' The resolution provided further that 'the Commission, which shall be organized by the Council . . . and have the specific functions that the Council assigns to it, shall be

[102] For the drafting history of this provision, *see* A. Schreiber, The Inter-American Commission on Human Rights 13–20 (1970) [hereinafter cited as Schreiber].

[103] Res. XXX, Final Act of the Ninth International Conference of American States, Bogotá, Colombia, 30 Mar.–2 May 1948, at 48 (Pan American Union 1948), *reprinted in* Handbook, *supra* note 3, at 17.

[104] American Declaration, preambular para. 3.

[105] Department of State, Report of the Delegation of the United States of America to the Ninth International Conference of American States, Bogotá, Colombia, March 30–May 2, 1948, at 35–36 (Publ. No. 3263, 1948).

[106] Inter-American Juridicial Committee, Report of the Inter-American Council of Jurists Concerning Resolution XXXI of the Bogotá Conference September 26, 1949, *reprinted in* Pan American Union, Human Rights in the American States 163, 164–65 (prelim. ed. 1960).

[107] *See* Schreiber, *supra* note 102, at 22–27.

[108] Res. VII, Fifth Meeting of Consultation of Ministers of Foreign Affairs, Santiago, Chile, 12–18 Aug. 1959, Final Act, O.A.S. Doc. OEA/Ser.C/II.5, at 10–11 (1950); *reproduced in* Sohn & Buergenthal, *supra* note 2, at 1281–82.

charged with furthering respect for [human] rights'.\ The O.A.S.
Council adopted the Statute of the Commission and elected its
members in 1960, and the Commission began its activities that very
year.[109] The Statute described the Inter-American Commission as an
'autonomous entity' of the O.A.S. having the function 'to promote
respect for human rights'.[110] The definition was provided in article 2,
which declared that '[f]or the purpose of this Statute, human rights are
understood to be those set forth in the American Declaration of the
Rights and Duties of Man'. The 'non-binding' American Declaration
thus became the basic normative instrument of the Commission.

The Statute adopted by the Council in 1960 gave the Inter-American
Commission only very limited powers. These were spelled out in
article 9:

> In carrying out its assignments of promoting respect for human rights, the
> Commission shall have the following functions and powers:
> (a) to develop an awareness of human rights among the peoples of
>   America;
> (b) to make recommendations to the governments of the member states in
>   general, if it considers such action advisable, for the adoption of
>   progressive measures in favor of human rights within the framework
>   of their domestic legislation and, in accordance with their constitu-
>   tional precepts, appropriate measures to further the faithful obser-
>   vance of those rights;
> (c) to prepare such studies or reports as it considers advisable in the
>   performance of its duties;
> (d) to urge the governments of the member states to supply it with infor-
>   mation on the measures adopted by them in matters of human rights;
> (e) to serve the Organization of American States as an advisory body in
>   respect of human rights.

In a formal interpretation adopted at its first session, the Commission
determined that article 9(b) of its Statute empowered it 'to make
general recommendations to each individual member state, as well as
to all of them'.[111] This interpretation enabled the Inter-American
Commission to condemn, in general terms, violations of human rights
in specific countries and, for that purpose, to make use of the powers
granted it in paragraphs (c) and (d) of article 9. These powers would

---

[109] The 1960 Statute of the Inter-American Commission on Human Rights with subsequent amendments [hereinafter cited as Statute], is reproduced in Basic Documents, *supra* note 3, at 194. *See also* [1960] Annual Report of the [O.A.S.] Secretary General, O.A.S. Doc. OEA/Ser.D/III.12, at 19–20.

[110] Statute, art. 1.

[111] IACHR, Report on the Work Accomplished During its First Session, Oct. 3–28, 1960, O.A.S. Doc. OEA/Ser.L/V/II.1, doc. 32, at 10 (1961) [hereinafter cited as IACHR, First Report].

not have been of much use without article 9(b) and the interpretation placed on it by the Commission.

Relying on this interpretation, the Inter-American Commission embarked upon studies investigating 'situations relating to human rights' in various O.A.S. member states; it began to address recommendations to governments found to be engaging in large-scale violations of human rights; and it started to issue reports documenting violations of human rights in specific countries.[112] In order to prepare these country studies, the Commission examined complaints, heard witnesses, and, in some cases, carried out on-the-spot investigations in different countries. These 'visits' were based on article 11 of the Statute, which authorized the Commission to 'move to the territory of any American state when it so decides by an absolute majority of votes and with the consent of the government concerned'.[113]

At its first session in 1960, the Inter-American Commission also ruled, however, that its Statute did not authorize it 'to make any individual decisions regarding written communications . . . it receives involving the violation of human rights in American states, although, for the most effective fulfillment of its functions, the Commission shall take cognizance of them by way of information'.[114] This ruling prevented the Commission from examining and taking action on individual petitions. But it could rely and use these communications as a source of information in preparing country reports as well as in deciding whether to make a particular country the subject of an investigation.

The powers of the Inter-American Commission were expanded in 1965 by a resolution of the Second Special Inter-American Conference.[115] This resolution was restated in the Inter-American Commission's Statute as article 9(*bis*), which reads as follows:

The Commission shall have the following additional functions and powers:

(a) to give particular attention to observance of the human rights referred to in Articles I, II, III, IV, XVIII, XXV, and XXVI of the American Declaration of the Rights and Duties of Man;

(b) to examine communications submitted to it and any other available information; to address the government of any American state for information deemed pertinent by the Commission; and to make

[112] *See* Farer & Rowles, *supra* note 44, at 54–55; Thomas & Thomas, *The Inter-American Commission on Human Rights*, 20 Sw. L.J. 282, 287–305 (1966). *See also* Sohn & Buergenthal, *supra* note 2, at 1293–340, where some of the country studies are reproduced.

[113] *See, e.g.,* Schreiber & Schreiber, *The Inter-American Commission on Human Rights in the Dominican Crisis*, 22 Int'l Organization 508 (1968).

[114] IACHR, First Report, *supra* note 111, at 9.

[115] Res. XXII, Second Special Inter-American Conference, Rio de Janeiro, Brazil, Nov. 17–30, 1965, Final Act, O.A.S. Doc. OEA/Ser.C/I.13, at 32–34 (1965).

recommendations, when it deems this appropriate, with the objective of bringing about more effective observance of fundamental human rights;

(c) to submit a report annually to the Inter-American Conference or to the Meeting of Consultation of Ministers of Foreign Affairs, which should include: (i) a statement of progress achieved in realization of the goals set forth in the American Declaration; (ii) a statement of areas in which further steps are needed to give effect to the human rights set forth in the American Declaration; and (iii) such observations as the Commission may deem appropriate on matters covered in the communications submitted to it and in other information available to the Commission;

(d) to verify, as a condition precedent to the exercise of the powers set forth in paragraphs (b) and (c) of the present article, whether the internal legal procedures and remedies of each member state have been duly applied and exhausted.

The Inter-American Commission relied on this provision to devise an individual petition system that served to complement its other efforts, particularly the country studies and on-the-spot investigations which over the years have developed into its most important activities. The petition system applied only to the human rights that were singled out in article 9(a)(*bis*). It dealt with complaints alleging violations of the right to life, liberty, and personal security (article I); equality before the law (article II); freedom of religion (article III); freedom of expression (article XVIII); freedom from arbitrary arrest (article XXV); and due process of law (article XXVI).[116]

b. *Under the Revised O.A.S. Charter.* Until 1970, the human rights system of the O.A.S. was based on a very weak constitutional foundation. The Inter-American Commission's Statute lacked an express treaty basis and derived its existence from O.A.S. conference resolutions of uncertain legal force.[117] This situation changed dramatically with the entry into force of the Protocol of Buenos Aires, which effected extensive amendments of the O.A.S. Charter.[118] The newly revised Charter changed the status of the Inter-American Commission from an 'autonomous entity of the OAS' into one of the principal organs of the O.A.S.[119] Its functions were defined as follows in article 112 of the amended Charter:

[116] Some of the individual petitions considered by the Inter-American Commission are reproduced in Sohn & Buergenthal, *supra* note 2, at 1340–56. Additional ones are reproduced in the Commission's annual reports. *See*, *e.g.*, Annual Report of the Inter-American Commission on Human Rights to the General Assembly, O.E.A. Doc. OEA/Ser.P/AG/doc. 1101/79, at 28 (1979).

[117] *See generally Revised OAS Charter*, *supra* note 2, at 833–34.

[118] The text of the 1948 O.A.S. Charter together with the amended version are reproduced in L. Sohn, Basic Documents of the United Nations 125 & 140 (1968). Also *see* note 101 *supra*.

[119] O.A.S. Charter art. 52(e).

There shall be an Inter-American Commission on Human Rights, whose principal function shall be to promote the observance and protection of human rights and to serve as a consultative organ of the Organization in these matters.

An inter-American convention on human rights shall determine the structure, competence, and procedure of this Commission, as well as those of other organs responsible for these matters.

Although the Protocol of Buenos Aires entered into force in 1970— one year after the American Convention on Human Rights was adopted—it was drafted in 1967. At that time the American Convention was not yet in existence. The drafters of the Protocol consequently attached a transitory provision to the revised O.A.S. Charter, in which they provided that '[u]ntil the inter-American convention on human rights, referred to in [article 112], enters into force, the present Inter-American Commission on Human Rights shall keep vigilance over the observance of human rights'.[120]

These provisions of the revised O.A.S. Charter gave institutional legitimacy to the Inter-American Commission by recognizing it as a treaty-based O.A.S. organ. Moreover, through the transitory provision, the Commission's Statute became an inherent part of the O.A.S. Charter itself.[121] The revised Charter thus effectively legitimated the powers that the Commission exercised under article 9 and 9(*bis*) of its Statute and it recognized the normative character of the American Declaration of the Rights and Duties of Man as a standard by which to judge the human rights activities of all O.A.S. member states.[122]

c. *Effect of the American Convention.* The entry into force of the American Convention on Human Rights in 1978 also changed the status of the Inter-American Commission in relation to those O.A.S. member states that have not ratified the American Convention. To understand the post-1978 status of the Inter-American Commission as a Charter organ, it must be recalled, first, that article 112 of the O.A.S. Charter provides that 'the structure, competence, and procedure' of the Commission shall be determined by 'an inter-American convention on human rights', and second, that article 150 stipulates that until the American Convention enters into force 'the present Inter-American Commission on Human Rights shall keep vigilance over the obser-

---

[120] *Id.* art. 150.

[121] Farer & Rowles, *supra* note 44, at 49–50. *See also* Professor Farer's testimony supporting U.S. ratification of the American Convention on Human Rights, *Hearings before the Senate Foreign Relations Comm. on International Human Rights Treaties*, 96th Cong., 1st Sess., at 98 (1979).

[122] *See* Statute, art. 2.

vance of human rights'. By ratifying the O.A.S. Charter, all O.A.S. member states thus agreed, whether or not they ratified the American Convention, that 'the structure, competence, and procedure' of the Inter-American Commission *qua* O.A.S. Charter organ shall be determined by reference to the American Convention once it enters into force. It follows that as soon as the American Convention enters into effect, article 112 became fully applicable and the transitory arrangements envisaged in article 150 lapsed. The American Convention and the Statute of the Commission adopted pursuant to it now consequently determine 'the structure, competence, and procedure' of the Commission as a Charter organ.

To enable the new Inter-American Commission to perform the functions of a Convention organ as well as a Charter organ, the American Convention distinguishes, in defining the Commission's functions, between 'member states' and 'States Parties'.[123] Moreover, article 41 of the American Convention, which enumerates the powers of the Inter-American Commission, adopts verbatim most of the provisions of article 9 of the Commission's old Statute.[124] Although language comparable to that of article 9(*bis*) is not to be found in the American Convention, the omission does not appear to have been intended to deprive the new Commission of article 9(*bis*) power when dealing with states that have not ratified the American Convention. This conclusion finds support in the fact that there is one very important difference between the wording of article 41(b) of the American Convention and article 9(b) of the old Statute. The former gave the Inter-American Commission the power 'to make recommendations to the governments of the member states', whereas article 9(b) uses the same language but adds the phrase 'in general'. The old Commission interpreted the phrase 'in general' in article 9(b) to mean that it could address general recommendations to each O.A.S. member state or to all of them,[125] but the limitation concerning 'general recommendations' was understood to bar individual resolutions for specific cases. The omission of the phrase 'in general' from article 41(b) of the American Convention is thus very significant. Beyond codifying the previous interpretation of article 9(b) of the Statute and empowering the Inter-American Commission to adopt general and individual recommendations, it authorizes Commission action in the form of specific resolutions relating to individual cases.

The fact that article 41 is silent about communications, as is article

---

[123] *See, e.g.*, American Convention, arts. 41–44. Thus, for example, all functions of the Inter-American Commission enumerated in art. 41, except for art. 41(f), apply to 'member states'. Art. 41(f) applies only to states parties.

[124] *Compare* the texts of art. 41 of the American Convention *with* art. 9 of the Statute.

[125] *See* text accompanying note 111 *supra*.

9(*bis*), is of little significance. Although the Inter-American Commission recognized in 1960 that article 9 of the Statute did not empower it 'to make any individual decision regarding the written communications that it receives', it determined that it was authorized under article 9(b) and (c) 'to take cognizance of them by way of information'.[126] The Commission was prevented from doing more, that is, examining the communication and rendering a decision in an appropriate resolution, by its lack of power to adopt specific recommendations. Article 41(b) of the American Convention rectifies this omission and empowers the Commission *qua* O.A.S. Charter organ to do under article 41 what it was authorized to do under articles 9 and 9(*bis*) of its pre-Convention Statute.[127]

The new Statute of the Inter-American Commission on Human Rights, which was drafted by the Commission and approved by the O.A.S. General Assembly in 1979[128] following a thorough article-by-article review,[129] indicates that the O.A.S. General Assembly proceeded on the assumption that the new Commission, when acting as a Charter organ, possesses all of the powers that the old Commission had under its Statute. Three provisions of the new Statute—articles 18, 19, and 20—deal with the powers of the Commission. Article 18 enumerates the powers of the Commission 'with respect to the member states of the Organization of American States'. It restates the functions of the Inter-American Commission that are spelled out in article 41 of the American Convention and adds a stipulation authorizing the Commission 'to conduct on-site observations in a state, with the consent or at the invitation of the government in question.'[130] Article 19 of the new Statute applies only 'to the States Parties to the American Convention on Human Rights' and lists the functions that the Com-

---

[126] IACHR, First Report, *supra* note 111, at 13. The full text of the ruling is reproduced in Sohn & Buergenthal, *supra* note 2, at 1288–89.

[127] This conclusion is borne out by the *travaux préparatoires* of the American Convention. Art. 32 of the Draft Convention referred to the Statute of the Inter-American Commission and the resolution of the Second Special Inter-American Conference, *viz.*, to arts. 9 and 9(*bis*) of the Statute, in defining the functions of the Commission. This provision was deleted in favor of art. 41, not because the drafters wanted to limit the Commission's power, but because they thought it 'inappropriate for the Convention to establish the structure and functions of the Commission by reference to other instruments . . .' Conferencia Especializada, *supra* note 3, at 372.

[128] Statute of the Inter-American Commission on Human Rights, O.A.S. Doc. OEA/Ser.P, AG/doc. 1180 (1979), *reprinted in* Handbook, *supra* note 3, at 95 [hereinafter cited as 1979 Statute]. The O.A.S. General Assembly adopted this Statute in accordance with the provisions of art. 39 of the American Convention, which provides that '[t]he Commission shall prepare its Statute, which it shall submit to the General Assembly for approval'.

[129] *See* Informe del Relator de la Primera Comisión—Asuntos Jurídicos y Políticos, O.A.S. Doc. OEA/Ser.P, AG/doc. 1198/79, at 15–18 (1979).

[130] 1979 Statute, art. 18(g). Art. 11 of the old Statute of the Commission authorized such visits without denominating them 'on-site observations'.

mission exercises in relation to them. This provision is followed by article 20, which provides that:

In relation to those member states of the Organization that are not Parties to the American Convention on Human Rights, the Commission shall have the following powers, in addition to those designated in Article 18:
  a. to pay particular attention to the observance of the human rights referred to in Articles I, II, III, IV, XVIII, XXV, and XXVI of the American Declaration of the Rights and Duties of Man;
  b. to examine communications submitted to it and any other available information, to address the government of any member state not a Party to the Convention for information deemed pertinent by this Commission, and to make recommendations to it, when it finds this appropriate, in order to bring about more effective observance of fundamental human rights, and
  c. to verify, as a prior condition to the exercise of the powers granted under subparagraph b. above, whether the domestic legal procedures and remedies of each member state not a Party to the Convention have been duly applied and exhausted.

Note that the above quoted provision is virtually identical to the text of article 9(*bis*) of the old Statute from which only one paragraph has been omitted.[131] By incorporating the text of article 9(*bis*) into the new Statute, its drafters intended to put all states not parties to the Convention on notice that the new Commission had retained the powers that were conferred on it by article 9(*bis*).

The new Statute also declares in article 1(2) that

for the purpose of the present Statute, human rights are understood to be:
  (a) the rights set forth in the American Convention on Human Rights, in relation to the States parties thereto;
  (b) the rights set forth in the American Declaration of the Rights and Duties of Man, in relation to the other member states.

Paragraph (b) of this provision reaffirms the interpretation that the human rights referred to in various provisions of the O.A.S. Charter, notably in articles 3(j) and 112, must be defined by reference to the American Declaration, which thus establishes standards applicable to all O.A.S. member states. The American Convention on Human Rights recognizes this normative status of the American Declaration when it provides that 'no provision of this Convention shall be interpreted as ... excluding or limiting the effect that the American Declaration of the Rights and Duties of Man ... may have'.[132] It should be emphasized in this connection, that the Inter-American

[131] The omitted paragraph is art. 9(c)(*bis*), which dealt with the Commission's annual reporting requirement.
[132] American Convention, art. 29(d).

Commission may on occasion have to look to the American Convention for guidance in interpreting the American Declaration. This conclusion results from the fact that the American Declaration 'proclaims very general principles which are ill-suited for adjudicatory purposes. The Commission may find it useful, therefore, to draw on the language of the American Convention . . . to give juridical precision to the American Declaration.'[133]

2. *The Practice of the Commission as a Charter Organ*

The principal activities of the Inter-American Commission on Human Rights acting as an O.A.S. Charter organ have consisted of the preparation of country studies and the processing of individual complaints. Although the Commission also has broad promotional authority—article 41(a) of the American Convention requires the Commission 'to develop an awareness of human rights among the peoples of America'—it has thus far made very limited use of this power.[134] The Inter-American Commission has yet to undertake a systematic effort to promote human rights in the hemisphere by developing programs to encourage human rights education and research, for example. The neglect of its promotional activities may be attributed, in part at least, to its limited financial resources and its relatively small staff,[135] which appear to have forced it to make difficult choices in deciding upon which activities it should concentrate. Events in the hemisphere have also affected that choice because in recent years the Commission has been called upon with increasing frequency to investigate one human rights trouble spot after another. These so-called 'on-site' observations have left little time for other activities.

a. *Country Studies and 'On-Site' Observations.* As soon as it assumed office in 1960, the Inter-American Commission began to receive complaints charging violations of human rights in different O.A.S. member states. Although its Statute did not authorize specific action relating to these petitions, article 9 permitted the Commission to prepare

---

[133] Buergenthal, *supra* note 3, at 134. *See also* IACHR, Report on the Status of Human Rights in Chile: Findings of 'On the Spot' Observations in the Republic of Chile, O.A.S. Doc. OEA/Ser.L/II.34, doc. 21, Corr. 1 (1974), where the Commission looked to art. 27 of the American Convention—the derogation clause—to demonstrate that even a national emergency did not authorize the suspension by Chile of certain fundamental human rights guaranteed in the American Declaration. *Id.* at 2–3.

[134] The Inter-American Commission had the same power under art. 9(a) of its old Statute, but it never really developed a systematic plan or program to implement it.

[135] Farer & Rowles, *supra* note 44, at 52, reported in 1978 that 'until 1977 staffing had been frozen at four lawyers, despite a caseload that had increased nearly 1000% since 1973. The staff has recently expanded and there are now established slots for nine lawyers in addition to the Executive Secretary.' They also report that the budget of the Commission for 1978 represented slightly less than 2% of the regular O.A.S. budget for that year.

studies and reports, and to adopt general recommendations. Article 11 enabled it to hold meetings away from its headquarters. These two provisions of the Statute provided the Commission with the legislative authority to develop the system of country studies and 'on-site' observations.

A country study, that is, a report examining the human rights conditions in a specific country, was initiated, as a rule, if a large number of complaints began to be received by the Inter-American Commission charging that government with serious and large-scale violations of human rights. The first such reports were prepared in the early 1960s and dealt with Cuba, Haiti, and the Dominican Republic.[136] Both Cuba and Haiti refused to allow the Commission to visit their countries; the Dominican Republic permitted the Commission to enter, and it became the first country to be the subject of an 'on-site' investigation.[137]

In its initial country study of Cuba, the Commission established the precedent of hearing witnesses and receiving evidence. In that particular case, it held hearings in Miami and interviewed many refugees. During its visits to the Dominican Republic, the Commission travelled extensively in that country, held hearings, met with government and opposition leaders, with representatives of various church, business, and union groups, and with private individuals; it also set up temporary offices in the country where it accepted written and oral complaints. The *modus operandi* adopted by the Commission during its visits to the Dominican Republic in the 1960s became a model that is followed by the Commission to this day. Thus, during the more recent 'on-site' observations in Nicaragua,[138] El Salvador,[139] and Argentina,[140] the Commission employed basically the same fact-finding approach it had used in the Dominican Republic.

The 'on-site' investigations are usually arranged by an exchange of letters and cables between the chairman of the Inter-American Commission and the government concerned. As a rule, the Commission requests permission to visit a particular country,[141] but some govern-

---

[136] For information on these reports, *see* IACHR, The Organization of American States and Human Rights 1960–67, at 39–53 (1972). The Haitian and Dominican reports are reproduced in Sohn & Buergenthal, *supra* note 2, at 1293–1339.

[137] The first visit to the Dominican Republic took place in Oct. 1961.

[138] IACHR, Report on the Situation of Human Rights in Nicaragua: Findings of the 'on-site' Observations in the Republic of Nicaragua, Oct. 3–12, 1978, O.A.S. Doc. OEA/Ser.L/V/II.45, doc. 16, Rev. 1 (1978).

[139] IACHR, Report on the Situation of Human Rights in El Salvador and Observations of the Government of El Salvador in the Report, O.A.S. Doc. OEA/Ser.P, AG/doc. 1086/79 (1979).

[140] IACHR, Report on the Situation of Human Rights in Argentina, O.A.S. Doc. OEA/Ser.L/V/II.49, doc. 19 (1980).

[141] Art. 11 of the old Statute of the Commission plainly required such permission. Arts. 48(1)(d) and 48(2) of the American Convention, when read together, appear not to require

ments have lately begun to invite the Commission on their own initiative.[142] For many years, the Commission did not have a specific set of rules applicable to such visits. This meant that the ground rules had to be negotiated on an *ad hoc* basis. This situation changed in 1977 when the Commission adopted a 'Resolution on On-Site Observation',[143] which spelled out the undertaking a government had to give before the Inter-American Commission or one of its sub-committees would visit the country. These standards have been included, with some additions, in the Commission's new Rules of Procedure.[144] Article 54 of the rules of procedure requires the host government to put at the disposal of the Commission all facilities necessary for the accomplishment of its mission and to pledge that it will impose no punitive measures against individuals who cooperated with or supplied information to the Commission. The right of members of the Commission and its staff to travel freely in the host country, to meet with any individuals whatsoever, and to visit prisons are provided for in article 55 of the rules of procedure. This provision also establishes the government's obligation to assure the safety of the Commission and its staff, and to provide the Commission with whatever documents it may request.

The very presence of the Inter-American Commission in a country has at various times contributed to the improvement of conditions in it. The most dramatic example is provided by the role of the Commission performed during the Dominican civil war, when it saved hundreds of lives and obtained the release from detention camps and prisons of large numbers of political detainees.[145] A more recent example of the salutory effect of the presence of the Commission consists of its activities in Colombia in the spring of 1980, when it negotiated the release of various diplomats being held hostage in

permission in ordinary cases as far as states parties are concerned. However, art. 18(g) of the Commission's new Statute specifies that the Commission may 'conduct on-site observations in a state, with the consent or at the invitation of the government in question'. *See* text accompanying and note 130 *supra*.

[142] This was done, for example, by the Government of Panama. *See* IACHR, Report on the Situation of Human Rights in Panama, O.A.S. Doc. OEA/Ser.L/V/II.44, doc. 38, Rev. 1, at 1–3 (1978).

[143] The resolution was adopted at the 42d session of the Commission, held during Oct. 31–Nov. 12, 1977, and is reproduced in IACHR, Handbook of Existing Rules Pertaining to Human Rights, O.A.S. Doc. OEA/Ser.L/V/II.23, doc. 21, Rev. 6, at 40 (1978). The same publication also contains the Commission's 'Regulations Regarding On-Site Observations', adopted on 15 Oct. 1975. *Id.* at 39.

[144] *See* Regulations, *supra* note 51, arts. 51–55.

[145] *See* IACHR, Report of the Activities of the Commission on Human Rights in the Dominican Republic, June 1–Aug. 31, 1965, O.A.S. Doc. OEA/Ser.L/V/II.12, doc. 14, Rev. (1965). *See also* Sandifer, *The Inter-American Commission on Human Rights in the Dominican Republic, June 1965 to June 1966*, in J. Carey, The Dominican Republic Crisis, 1965, at 115 (1967); Sohn & Buergenthal, *supra* note 2, at 1325.

Colombia in return for the government's agreement, which was demanded by those holding the hostages, that the Commission be permitted to monitor the military trials of suspected terrorists.[146]

The impact of the Commission's country studies and 'on-site' investigations depends on various considerations, including the publication of the report and the action that the O.A.S. is willing to take after the report has been published. Governments like to prevent the publication of well-documented reports charging them with large-scale violations of human rights. They are also willing at times to stop the criticized practices if that will reduce the adverse impact of a report or stop its publication. That is why the Commission's power to publish its country studies and investigation reports can be a very effective method to promote compliance.

The procedure which the Inter-American Commission follows in these cases is to prepare a draft report,[147] which analyzes the conditions in the country by reference to the human rights that are proclaimed in the American Declaration and sets out the Commission's findings and recommendations. The draft report is then submitted to the government for its comments and a date is fixed within which the government is requested to present its observations. The government's response is analyzed by the Commission with a view to determining whether the report should be amended in light of the information brought to the Commission's attention by the government. After reassessing its findings, the Commission decides whether to publish the report. The rules of procedure of the Commission require the publication of the report if the government does not respond to the request for observations.[148] The Inter-American Commission need not publish it if the government replies and either agrees to comply with recommendations or demonstrates that it is not committing any violations. The reports that have been published by the Commission in the past few years have usually reproduced in full the observations of the governments. In most of these cases the governments disagreed with some or a majority of the findings of the Commission.[149]

In addition to the publication of the report, the Inter-American Commission may also transmit it for consideration by the O.A.S. General Assembly, which holds one regular session per year. The Commission may include the particular country study in whole or in part in its annual report to the Assembly or it may transmit it as a

[146] The Commission lawyers were still in Bogotá, Colombia, in the fall of 1980.
[147] *See* Regulations, *supra* note 51, art. 58.
[148] *Id.* art. 58(d).
[149] *But see* IACHR, Report on the Situation of Human Rights in Panama, *supra* note 142, at 119–22.

separate document. Because debates in the Assembly generally attract considerable public attention, reference to and discussion by the Assembly of a country report, followed by an appropriate resolution, can have a significant impact on the behavior of a government charged with violations of human rights and may lead to an improvement of conditions in the country. These considerations probably explain why for a number of years there seemed to be tacit agreement among O.A.S. member states not to discuss the annual report that the Inter-American Commission submitted to the Assembly. Instead, they would routinely and without debate adopt a resolution in which the General Assembly resolved 'to take note of the annual report of the Inter-American Commission on Human Rights and to thank the Commission for the important work it has been doing'.[150]

This situation began to change in the mid-1970s. The first break with tradition occurred in 1975 when the O.A.S. General Assembly had before it the Commission's annual report for the year 1974 as well as its report on 'The Status of Human Rights in Chile'. Although the Assembly once again passed its usual resolution on the annual report,[151] it also adopted a separate resolution dealing with the Chilean report,[152] which was preceded by a lengthy and well-publicized debate. The change was described as follows by William S. Mailliard, the U.S. Representative to the O.A.S.:

[T]his was the first occasion when the Inter-American Human Rights Commission reports were not merely noted and filed away. In the past the nations of the hemisphere strongly preferred not to point the finger at any one government, at least in part, for fear that they could be on the receiving end of accusations the next time. The real breakthrough then is this: We have now established a precedent which can insure that the status of human rights in the hemisphere receives full and frank airing at the annual OAS General Assembly.[153]

At the next annual O.A.S. General Assembly session, the Assembly adopted a much stronger resolution dealing with the Commission's report concerning violations of human rights in Chile,[154] besides passing another resolution dealing with various specific issues that the Commission had raised in its annual report for the year 1975.[155] This

[150] *See, e.g.,* O.A.S. General Assembly Res. 154 (IV-0/74); O.A.S. General Assembly Res. 83 (II-0/72).
[151] O.A.S. General Assembly Res. 192 (V-0/75).
[152] *Id.* 190 (V-O/75).
[153] *Hearings [on Human Rights Issues at the Sixth Regular Session of the Organization of American States General Assembly] before the Subcomm. on Int'l Organizations of the House Comm. on Int'l Relations,* 94th Cong., 2d Sess., at 3 (1976).
[154] O.A.S. General Assembly Res. 243 (VI-0/76).
[155] *Id.* 242 (VI-0/76).

practice has continued, and specific human rights issues raised by
annual reports of the Commission have been discussed and acted upon
in recent O.A.S. General Assembly sessions. Although O.A.S. General
Assembly resolutions, as a matter of law, are recommendations only,
they are acts emanating from the highest organ of the O.A.S. and
consequently carry considerable moral and political weight. Governments take these considerations into account when they have to decide
how to react to recommendations made by the Commission in one of
its country studies. Ultimately, as in all efforts to enforce internationally guaranteed human rights, the effectiveness of the Commission's
'country-study' practice depends on its prestige and credibility, on the
public opinion pressure that is likely to be exerted to support its
recommendations, and on the resolutions that the O.A.S. General
Assembly is willing to adopt to back the Commission.[156]

b. *Individual Communications.* Prior to the entry into force of the
American Convention, the Inter-American Commission examined and
acted on only those private communications that alleged a violation of
one of the 'preferred' freedoms enumerated in article 9(*bis*) of its
Statute.[157] This policy was based on the assumption that the power
which this provision conferred on the Commission with regard to
communications was intended to apply only to those fundamental
rights. Although it is debatable whether this restrictive interpretation
was in fact compelled by the text of article 9(*bis*), it is clear that the
Inter-American Commission today assumes that the entry into force of
the American Convention significantly expanded its powers for dealing with petitions concerning O.A.S. member states that have not
ratified the Convention. Its new rules of procedure, adopted after the
American Convention and the Commission's new Statute entered into
force, contain stipulations that allow the Commission to act on *all*
communications lodged against a non-state party, provided only that
the petitioner alleges the violation of a right that is proclaimed in the
American Declaration.[158] Moreover, for the purposes of examining
the admissibility of petitions, these rules make no distinction between

---

[156] At the session of the O.A.S General Assembly held in Nov. 1980, certain governments, led
by Argentina, successfully blocked the adoption of O.A.S. General Assembly resolutions, based
on thorough Commission reports, charging them with serious violations of human rights.
Eventually, a single watered-down resolution, applying to all states, was adopted. This action
amounted to a significant setback for the Inter-American Commission, in particular, and O.A.S.
human rights efforts, in general. For the text of the resolution, *see* O.A.S. General Assembly Res.
of 27 Nov. 1980 (Annual Report and Special Reports of the Inter-American Commission on
Human Rights), O.A.S. Doc. OEA/Ser.P, AG/doc. 1348/80, Rev. 1 (1980). It is too early to say
whether this development signals a weakening of the support for human rights that had
gradually built up in recent years in the O.A.S. General Assembly.

[157] *See* text accompanying notes 115–16 *supra*.

[158] *See* Regulations, *supra* note 51, art. 49.

complaints involving states that are parties to the American Convention and those that are not.[159] The admissibility requirements and the proceedings applicable to communications filed under the Convention consequently also govern complaints involving violations of the American Declaration, notwithstanding the fact that the latter complaints are dealt with by the Commission pursuant to the authority it derives from the O.A.S. Charter.

The Commission's new rules of procedure distinguish between complaints filed under the American Convention and those that are based on the American Declaration only when they have reached the post-admissibility stage.[160] A complaint filed against a state that is not a party to the American Convention, which has been ruled admissible and not resolved by means of a friendly settlement,[161] is not subject to the reporting stages applicable to petitions lodged under the Convention. Instead, after the Inter-American Commission has examined the complaint, it adopts a resolution containing the facts of the case, its conclusions, and whatever recommendations it deems appropriate.[162] The resolution, which must also specify by what date the recommendations are to be complied with, is transmitted to the defendant state and the petitioner.[163] Prior to the expiration of the date, the defendant state has an opportunity to request the Commission to re-examine its findings and recommendations.[164] It may also submit whatever additional evidence it deems relevant to support its motion.[165] The petitioner may be heard at this stage as well. If the Commission modifies the resolution after the rehearing, it may fix a new date for compliance. If the defendant state fails to comply with the recommendations by the date which the Commission fixed, it has the right to publish the resolution in its annual report to the O.A.S. General Assembly or in whatever other manner it deems advisable.[166]

Because a state that has not ratified the American Convention is not subject to the jurisdiction of the Inter-American Court of Human Rights, a complaint dealt with by the Commission acting exclusively as a Charter organ cannot be referred to the Inter-American Court for adjudication. But this is not to say that such cases can under no circumstances reach the Court. The Inter-American Court's advisory

---

[159] *See id*. arts. 29–40.

[160] *Id*. art. 50.

[161] *Id*. art. 42. Despite the fact that art. 42(1) refers to the American Convention, it appears also to apply to complaints involving the American Declaration. Judging from the context, the failure to refer to the Declaration seems to have been an oversight.

[162] *See* Regulations, *supra* note 51, art. 50(1).

[163] *Id*. art. 50(2).

[164] *Id*. art 50(3).

[165] *Id*.

[166] *Id*. arts. 50(4) & 50(5).

jurisdiction, for example, is not limited to states parties to the American Convention nor to questions regarding the interpretation of that Convention. Since any O.A.S. member state and any O.A.S. organ may seek advisory opinions from the Court and since the subject of the request may relate to treaties 'concerning the protection of human rights in the American states',[167] the Inter-American Commission, the O.A.S. General Assembly, or a member state might apply for an advisory opinion concerning legal issues arising in a case under consideration by the Commission acting as a Charter organ.[168] Here the Court might be asked to address questions about the powers of the Commission as a Charter organ, the human rights obligations of O.A.S member states that have not ratified the American Convention, and, possibly, the normative relationship between the American Declaration and the O.A.S. Charter.

Finally, it should be asked whether the procedures developed by the Inter-American Commission for dealing with individual complaints have been effective. The answer, regrettably, is that they have not proved very effective. For one thing, contrary to its practice involving country studies, the O.A.S. General Assembly has rarely considered the Commission's decisions in individual cases. Secondly, the Commission appears in the past few years to have devoted less and less time to individual complaints. It has no doubt been motivated by the realization that, given the attitude of the O.A.S. General Assembly, it can have much more significant impact by concentrating on country studies. Conditions in the hemisphere have also forced the Inter-American Commission to embark on an increasing number of country studies and on-site investigations, and these have been a drain on its staff resources. But whatever the reasons, there has been little institutional pressure on the Assembly to concern itself with individual cases. Therefore, since states know that they will rarely, if ever, be called to account for their actions in individual cases, it is easy for them to disregard the Commission's resolutions in such cases. One might consequently question the wisdom of the Commission's decision to make the petition system applicable to all rights proclaimed in the American Declaration. (Would it not make more sense to limit it only to violations of some of the most fundamental rights? This approach,

[167] American Convention, art. 64(1).

[168] *See*, in this connection, section I.B.2.b. *supra*. If such a request for an advisory opinion related exclusively to the American Declaration, the Inter-American Court would have to decide whether and under what circumstances, if any, the Declaration can be treated as a 'treaty' within the meaning of art. 64(1). A draft resolution sponsored by Costa Rica and a number of other states, which would have had the O.A.S. General Assembly request an advisory opinion from the Inter-American Court regarding the competence of the Inter-American Commission to prepare reports on the human rights situation in Cuba, failed to obtain the necessary number of affirmative votes during the 1980 O.A.S. General Assembly session.

which was reflected in article 9(*bis*) of the Commission's old Statute, enabled the Commission to concentrate on important cases.) The Commission's failure to be more selective in choosing the types of cases it deals with as a Charter organ weakens the entire O.A.S. petition system, including the petition machinery provided for under the American Convention. Both depend for their enforcement on the O.A.S. General Assembly, which has little interest in and patience for dealing with too many individual petitions. Of course, if the Assembly could be persuaded to establish, as one of its subsidiary organs, a special human rights committee to review the Commission's reports for each session of the Assembly and advise the Assembly on the measures it should adopt, the petition system might gradually acquire 'teeth'. Such a committee might also enhance the overall capacity of the Assembly to enforce decisions of the Inter-American Commission and the Inter-American Court and thus significantly strengthen the entire inter-American rights system.

D. CONCLUSIONS

This is not the best time to write about the inter-American system for the protection of human rights. The system is in a period of transition and so is the political milieu in which it operates. The new Convention-based regime is only now beginning to function and there is very little practice and no case law to draw on.[169] The extensive practice of the Charter-based regime, while still relevant and of value for purposes of analysis, is becoming increasingly less important because the regime's institutional framework has been modified with the entry into force of the American Convention, which more and more states are ratifying.

The political realities of the Americas and the fact that the region lacks political stability also quite obviously affect the protection of human rights in the hemisphere. The political instability of the region, whose causes are many and which is reflected in cyclical and often violent vacillations between representative democracy and military dictatorship, makes it hazardous to predict the future effectiveness of the inter-American human rights system.

The system depends for its effectiveness and survival on the member states of the Organization of American States and their willingness to support a strong regional machinery for the protection of human rights. The attitude of the major powers of the region, particularly the United States, is also very important. In the past few years, the United States has been the strong proponent of an effective inter-American human rights system, and that has helped to strengthen the system considerably. The mere fact, moreover, that the American Convention

---

[169] [Ed. note: *See* note 86 *supra*.].

has entered into force and that fifteen states have ratified it is an encouraging development. It is also evidence that the political transformation occurring in the region is bringing governments to power which are more responsive to demands for the enjoyment of basic human rights. If this trend continues, the American Convention and the institutions it has established could come to play a significant role in promoting and protecting human rights in the hemisphere. But whether it will remains to be seen.

II. Teaching Suggestions

In a general course on the international protection of human rights, it would be very helpful to discuss the two regional systems for the protection of human rights—the European and inter-American systems—as part of one teaching unit. By exploring the similarities and differences of these two systems, the instructor would have an opportunity to consider which of these two systems might be better suited for adaptation in other regions of the world. Here one may want to discuss the legal, political, economic, and linguistic prerequisites for effective regional systems.

A

The fact that the inter-American human rights system consists of two regimes—one based on the American Convention, the other derived from the O.A.S. Charter—must be a starting point of any discussion dealing with it. (In introducing this subject, it would be useful to provide a rudimentary description of the organizational structure of the O.A.S.) Which regime should be discussed first—the Convention or the Charter-based one—is a matter of personal preference. In this chapter, I started with the Convention-based regime because I wanted to focus on a number of important substantive and institutional problems arising under the American Convention and because it seemed to me that this approach might make it easier for students to understand how the two regimes interact. An instructor interested in exploring the process of international institution-building would probably want to start with the Charter-based regime and focus on its evolution.

In discussing the Convention-based system, it makes sense, after providing a general overview of the American Convention, to examine the powers and functions of the principal Convention institutions—the Inter-American Commission and the Inter-American Court—and to analyze a selected number of difficult substantive law problems that arise under the American Convention. (Almost every provision of the

American Convention presents one or more interesting analytic problems, and my recommendation would be that the criterion for their selection should be the students' and instructor's interest.) When dealing with the Inter-American Commission, it might be useful to explore, *inter alia*, the different functions the third-stage and fourth-stage reports perform and the problems this dual report procedure might create. In this connection, it might be asked whether the procedure favors the individual petitioner or the government and whether, given the voting requirements, the procedure is subject to political abuse. The fact that the American Convention makes private petitions obligatory and inter-state ones optional, thus reversing the traditional approach, also makes an interesting topic for comparative discussion and policy analysis.

When considering the role of the Inter-American Court, the differences between its contentious and advisory jurisdiction merit thorough discussion. Of particular importance, in this connection, are the functions the Court's advisory opinions might perform. The many legal ambiguities surrounding the Court's advisory jurisdiction are worthy of analysis. (What are the advantages and disadvantages of the ambiguities?) This topic leads easily into a discussion of the role international adjudication might play in the implementation of human rights.

B

The most interesting aspect of the Charter-based regime is its evolution and gradual transformation from a system of promotion to one of protection. Unlike most other human rights regimes, this one was not created by a human rights convention; it derived its normative standards from the American Declaration of the Rights and Duties of Man, which had been proclaimed as a 'mere' declaration. The manner in which the Inter-American Commission on Human Rights gradually achieved constitutional and institutional legitimacy is in and of itself an interesting lesson in international institution-building.

Despite the emphasis that has been placed in the literature on the individual petition system as it was developed by the Inter-American Commission on Human Rights, it is clear that its country studies and 'on-site' observations have been the backbone of the Charter-based regime. What factors would explain this situation is a topic worthy of discussion. Equally important is the question whether the 'on-site' observation model should be duplicated in other regional systems, particularly in regions that are likely to suffer large-scale violations of human rights similar to those that have victimized the Western Hemisphere. A related issue is whether the Charter-based system should concentrate on large-scale violations and/or on the more individual egregious violations of human rights instead of seeking to enforce, through individual complaints, all rights that are proclaimed in the American Declaration.

C

A topic that acquires special importance in assessing the effectiveness of the inter-American system for the protection of human rights concerns the role that the political organs of the O.A.S., particularly the O.A.S. General Assembly, play in the enforcement process. One might want to compare the O.A.S. General Assembly with the Committee of Ministers and Assembly of the Council of Europe, discuss the respective functions they perform, and consider to what extent they promote or hinder the enforcement of human rights decisions. It should also prove extremely interesting to explore the role that the Inter-American Court of Human Rights might play in the enforcement processes of the Charter-based system.

III. Syllabus

 I. *Introduction*
   A. The Organization of American States: General Introduction.
   B. Regional Systems for the Protection of Human Rights: An Overview.
 II. *The American Convention on Human Rights: Substantive Problems*
   A. In General.
   B. Selected Problems of Interpretation.
     (Topics choice of instructor.)
     1. The Self-Executing Character of the Convention.
     2. The Federal-State Clause.
     3. The Right of Derogation.
 III. *The American Convention on Human Rights: Institutions*
   A. The Inter-American Commission on Human Rights.
     1. Its Functions.
     2. Individual and Inter-State Complaints.
   B. The Inter-American Court of Human Rights.
     1. The Court's Contentious Jurisdiction.
     2. The Court's Advisory Jurisdiction.
 IV. *The O.A.S. Charter and Human Rights*
   A. Evolution of the Charter-Based Regime.
     1. Under the 1948 O.A.S. Charter.
     2. Under the Revised O.A.S. Charter.

      3. Effect of the American Convention.
  B. The Practice of the Inter-American Commission as a Charter-Based Organ.
      1. Country Studies and 'On-Site' Observations.
      2. Individual Communications.
V. *The Inter-American and European Systems Compared*
  A. Effectiveness and Political Realities.
  B. Models for Other Regional Systems.

IV. Minisyllabus

  I. *The Organization of American States: General Introduction*
  II. *The American Convention on Human Rights*
    A. In General.
    B. Selected Problems of Interpretation.
    (Topics choice of instructor.)
  III. *The American Convention on Human Rights: Institutions*
    A. The Inter-American Commission on Human Rights.
      1. Its Functions.
      2. Individual and Inter-State Complaints.
    B. The Inter-American Court of Human Rights.
      1. The Court's Contentious Jurisdiction.
      2. The Court's Advisory Jurisdiction.
  IV. *The O.A.S. Charter and Human Rights: The Practice of the Inter-American Commission as a Charter-Based Organ*
    A. Country Studies and 'On-Site' Observations.
    B. Individual Communications.

V. Bibliography

Buergenthal, *The American Convention on Human Rights: Illusions and Hopes*, 21 Buffalo L. Rev. 121 (1971).
—— *The Revised OAS Charter and the Protection of Human Rights*, 69 Am. J. Int'l L. 828 (1975).
—— *The Inter-American Court of Human Rights*, 76 Am. J. Int'l L. 231 (1982).
T. Buergenthal, R. Norris & D. Shelton, Protecting Human Rights in the Americas: Selected Problems (1982).
Cabranes, *Human Rights and Non-Intervention in the Inter-American System*, 65 Mich. L. Rev. 1147 (1967).
—— *The Protection of Human Rights by the Organization of American States*, 62 Am. J. Int'l L. 889 (1968).
Farer & Rowles, *The Inter-American Commission on Human Rights*,

in International Human Rights Law and Practice 48 (J. Tuttle ed. 1978).

Fox, *Doctrinal Development in the Americas: From Non-Intervention to Collective Support for Human Rights*, 1 N.Y.U. J. Int'l & Pol. 44 (1968).

—— *The American Convention on Human Rights and Prospects for United States Ratification*, 3 Human Rights 243 (1973).

Frowein, *The European and American Conventions on Human Rights—A Comparison*, 1 Human Rights L. J. 44 (1980).

Garcia-Bauer, *Protection of Human Rights in America*, in 1 René Cassin Amicorum Discipulorumque Liber 75 (1969).

R. Goldman, The Protection of Human Rights in the Americas: Past, Present and Future (5 N.Y.U. Center for International Studies Policy Papers No. 2, 1972).

Gros Espiell, *L'Organisation des Etats Americains*, in Les Dimensions Internationales des Droits de l'Homme 600 (K. Vasak ed. 1978).

Norris, *Bringing Human Rights Petitions before the Inter-American Commission*, 20 Santa Clara L. Rev. 733 (1980).

—— *Observations in Loco: Practice and Procedure of the Inter-American Commission on Human Rights*, 15 Texas Int'l L. J. 46 (1980).

Sandifer, *The Inter-American Commission on Human Rights in the Dominican Republic, June 1965 to June 1966*, in The Dominican Republic Crisis, 1965, at 115–41 (J. Carey ed. 1967).

—— *Human Rights in the Inter-American System*, 11 How. L. J. 508 (1965).

Scheman, *The Inter-American Commission on Human Rights*, 59 Am. J. Int'l L. (1965).

A. Schreiber, The Inter-American Commission on Human Rights (1970).

L. Sohn & T. Buergenthal, International Protection of Human Rights 1267–374 (1973).

Symposium [on] The American Convention on Human Rights 30 Am. U. L. Rev. 1–187 (1980).

Thomas & Thomas, *Human Rights and the Organization of American States*, 12 Santa Clara Law. 319 (1972).

—— —— *The Inter-American Commission on Human Rights*, 20 Sw. L. J. 282 (1966).

K. Vasak, La Commission Interamericaine des Droits de l'Homme (1968).

VI. Minibibliography

Buergenthal, *The Revised OAS Charter and the Protection of Human Rights*, 69 Am. J. Int'l L. 828 (1975).

—— *The American and European Conventions on Human Rights: Similarities and Differences*, 30 Am. U. L. Rev. 155 (1980).

—— *The Inter-American Court of Human Rights*, 76 Am. J. Int'l L. 231 (1982).

Farer & Rowles, *The Inter-American Commission on Human Rights*, in International Human Rights Law and Practice 48 (J. Tuttle ed. 1978).

Fox, *The American Convention on Human Rights and Prospects for United States Ratification*, 3 Human Rights 243 (1973).

Frowein, *The European and the American Conventions on Human Rights—A Comparison*, 1 Human Rights J. 44 (1980).

A. Schreiber, The Inter-American Commission on Human Rights (1970).

Thomas & Thomas, *Human Rights and the Organization of American States*, 12 Santa Clara Law. 319 (1972).

K. Vasak, La Commission Interamericaine des Droits de l'Homme (1968).

Chapter 13

The European Convention on Human Rights[*]

Rosalyn Higgins[1]

I. Legal and Policy Considerations

A. CONCEPTUAL ISSUES

The law of the European Convention on Human Rights[2] has to be understood at two levels: as an increasingly important body of procedural and substantive law, and as part of the wider fabric of international efforts for the promotion of human rights. It is both inward looking and outward looking. It is this dual facet (that which is special to Europe, and that which is of global significance) that must be reflected in a worthwhile course on the European Convention. Too often, university courses on the European Convention on Human Rights merely explain the structure of the institutions and then propel the students into a random study of some leading cases or a brief selection of case studies. There is no sense of the place of the European Convention in the global struggle for human rights.

The relationship between the precepts of the U.N. Universal Declaration of Human Rights[3] and the text of the European Convention is important. The Universal Declaration deals both with political and civil rights, and with economic and social rights. So far as the former are concerned, the Universal Declaration covers the right to life, liberty, and security of person;[4] slavery and servitude;[5] torture and cruel, inhuman, or degrading treatment or punishment;[6] entitlement to 'recognition everywhere as a person before the law';[7] effective remedies by competent national tribunals;[8] arbitrary arrest, detention, or exile;[9] fair trial and determination of rights and obligations;[10]

---

[*] © Rosalyn Higgins 1983.

[1] This study was completed in April 1981.

[2] European Convention for the Protection of Human Rights and Fundamental Freedoms, 213 U.N.T.S 221, *reprinted in* Basic Documents on Human Rights 242 (2d ed. I. Brownlie 1981) [hereinafter cited as Brownlie].

[3] G.A. Res. 217A. U.N. Doc. A/810, at 71 (1948).

[4] *Id*. art. 3.

[5] *Id*. art. 4.

[6] *Id*. art. 5.

[7] *Id*. art. 6.

[8] *Id*. art. 8.

[9] *Id*. art. 9.

[10] *Id*. art. 10.

privacy and protection of reputation;[11] freedom of movement;[12] asylum from persecution;[13] entitlement to nationality;[14] freedom to marry and found a family, based on consent;[15] the ownership of property and the prohibition against arbitrary deprivation of property;[16] freedom of thought, conscience, and religion;[17] freedom of assembly and association (including the right not to belong to an association);[18] the right to take part in government either directly or through representatives, and universal suffrage by secret ballot.[19] There is in penal matters a presumption of innocence.[20]

The European Convention includes many of these rights. The notions underlying articles 3, 4, 5, 6, 8, 9, 10, 18, and 20 of the Universal Declaration are also found in the European Convention. Sometimes the formulation of the right closely follows that used in the Universal Declaration: this is true, for example, of the prohibition of torture and cruel, inhuman, or degrading treatment or punishment. Sometimes there has been an alteration, or a change of emphasis. Thus article 8 of the European Convention drops the notion of protection of reputation and honor and uses the term 'respect' instead.[21] Again, the European Convention's clause on freedom of association[22] omits the provision found in the Universal Declaration which provides that no one may be compelled to belong to an association. This takes account of the existence of the 'closed shop' system of labour unions in certain European countries. Further, the European Convention's clause on the right to marry[23] is more limited than that of the Universal Declaration. The presumption of innocence in penal matters becomes part of the right to a fair trial.[24]

Certain Universal Declaration provisions, such as the ownership of property,[25] freedom of movement, asylum from persecution, the right

[11] *Id.* art. 12.
[12] *Id.* art. 13.
[13] *Id.* art. 14.
[14] *Id.* art. 15.
[15] *Id.* art. 16.
[16] *Id.* art. 17.
[17] *Id.* art. 18.
[18] *Id.* art. 20.
[19] *Id.* art. 21.
[20] *Id.* art. 11(1).
[21] *See* J. Fawcett, Application of the European Convention on Human Rights 186 (1969) [hereinafter cited as Fawcett] which finds the term 'respect' (for private and family life, home, and correspondence) tame, belonging to the world of manners rather than of law. 'Respect' contrasts with 'inviolability' or 'legal protection from', which could have been employed.
[22] Art. 11.
[23] Art. 12.
[24] Art. 6.
[25] *But see* First Protocol to the European Convention, art. 1, *reprinted in* Brownlie, *supra* note 2, at 257.

to participate in government and public life,[26] and the right to universal suffrage by secret ballot, find no mention in the European Convention.

Importantly, many of the rights that are repeated in the European Convention—whether in identical, similar, or somewhat different form—have qualifying clauses attached to them which limit their applicability. In particular, such clauses—which have figured prominently in the case law—are to be found in articles 5–11 of the European Convention.[27]

The Universal Declaration also contains an important list of economic and social rights.[28] These are not found at all in the European Convention, which limits itself to civil rights.[29] The International Covenant on Economic, Social and Cultural Rights[30] gives such matters the status of legal rights for the states parties.[31] Eastern Europe and much of the Third World regard economic and social aspirations as just as much of a human right as civil and political rights. These states charge that the West cynically disregards economic and social rights—and indeed that the capitalist political system makes 'the right to work', for example, or 'the right to housing' impossible to attain. The dilemma is that the full achievement of those economic and social rights entails a loss of individual liberties which is unacceptable to the western liberal democracies. The liberal democracies, knowing that these economic and social standards cannot be fully attained within their own political and economic structures, perceive them as 'aspirations' rather than legal rights. The developing countries further argue that the civil and political rights are 'secondary' to the economic and social rights—that the right of free expression, for example, means little to a man who is at starvation level—and, indeed, that the provision of these civil and political rights in a developing country is

[26] *But see* First Protocol, art. 3.

[27] These clauses are analyzed in Fawcett, *supra* note 21, at 57–227. For the difference between such qualifying clauses and derogation clauses, *see* Higgins, *Derogations Under Human Rights Treaties*, 48 Brit. Y.B. Int'l L. 281 (1976–77) [hereinafter cited as Higgins].

[28] *See* arts. 22, 23, 24, 25, 26, & 27 of the Universal Declaration, which cover such matters as social security, the rights to work, equal pay, just remuneration, holidays with pay, public assistance with housing and medical needs, etc. The non-discrimination clause of the Universal Declaration, art. 2, applies to both economic and social, and civil and political rights. The European Convention contains a clause, art. 14, which requires non-discrimination in respect of the rights contained therein, *i.e.*, civil rights.

[29] But there has been recent discussion and study on whether the European Convention should be amended to include social or economic rights. *See* Jacobs, *The extension of the European Convention to include Economic, Social and Cultural Rights*, 3 Human Rights Rev. 163 (1978); and draft Protocol to extend the rights, Doc. 5039, 7 Feb. 1983.

[30] G.A. Res. 2200, 21 U.N. GAOR, Supp. (No. 16) 49, U.N. Doc. A/6316 (1966).

[31] The Economic Covenant does not, however, have any enforcement or supervisory machinery, and is in that sense more cautious than the International Covenant on Civil and Political Rights, *id.* at 52.

counterproductive to the restructuring of society in a manner necessary to provide the 'more basic' economic and social rights.

In an ideal world, regional arrangements should buttress universal standards. In the field of human rights, however, the coexistence of the universal and the regional models is an uneasy one. The International Covenant on Civil and Political Rights embodies a considerable number of rights not found in the European Convention.[32] The European Convention contains a smaller number of rights not reflected in the Political Covenant.[33] Equally important, even where a right is embodied in both texts it may be couched in different terms.[34] Also significant is that the derogation clauses in each instrument, while they overlap to a certain extent, are differently drafted and not identical in the matters covered.[35] Other incompatibilities may be noted: the scope of the Political Covenant is narrower, being limited to individuals within the territory of a party and subject to its jurisdiction,[36] whereas the rights defined in the European Convention are secured by the contracting parties 'to everyone within their jurisdiction'.[37] Thus there are two sets of instruments whose texts do not fully coincide, and with very different implementing procedures. If the Political Covenant covers more rights, the implementing procedures of the European Convention are much stronger. It may further be noted that article 27(1)(b) of the European Convention would seem to preclude the European Commission of Human Rights from finding an application to it admissible if substantially the same matter has already been handled under the Political Covenant.

The parties to the European Convention have decided that, in respect of matters covered by the European Convention, they will use the regional rather than the universal machinery. Parties to the European Convention will be free to choose to use the procedure of the Political Covenant in respect of rights not covered by the European Convention.[38] For the moment, therefore, the possibility has receded

[32] *See* arts. 1, 6(4), 6(5), 10(1), 10(2)(b), 10(3), 14(4), 14(3)(a), 14(3)(g), 14(5), 14(6), 14(7), 16, 20, 23(3), 24, 25(b), 25(c), 26, & 27 of the Political Covenant.

[33] *See* European Conventions, arts. 2(2) & 16; First Protocol, art. 1; Fourth Protocol, arts. 3(1) & 4, *reprinted in* Brownlie, *supra* note 2, at 262.

[34] *Compare* art. 7 of the Political Covenant *with* art. 3 of the European Convention; art. 17 of the Political Covenant *with* art. 8 of the European Convention; art. 18(2) of the Political Covenant *with* art. 9 of the European Convention; art. 2(3) of the Political Covenant *with* art. 13 of the European Convention; art. 2 of the Political Covenant *with* art. 14 of the European Convention.

[35] *Compare* art. 4 of the Political Covenant *with* art. 15 of the European Convention.

[36] Political Covenant, art. 2(1).

[37] European Convention, art. 1. However, the Human Rights Committee can receive petitions from individuals subject to the jurisdiction of the state concerned, pursuant to art. 1 of the Optional Protocol to the International Covenant on Civil and Political Rights, G.A. Res. 2200, 21 U.N. GAOR, Supp. (No. 16) 59, U.N. Doc. A/6316 (1966).

[38] *See generally* Committee of Ministers Res. (70) 17, *reprinted in* Eissen, *The European*

of a state party to the European Convention using the procedure provided for in article 41 of the Political Covenant against another party to the European Convention, and the more obvious jurisdictional clashes seem to have been avoided. For the time being, the problems of coexistence remain theoretical.

Any course on human rights must make clear the areas in which the European Convention is modelled on the Universal Declaration; where they part company; and the extent to which the U.N. Covenants draw on or differ from the European Convention. This cannot be done by textual comparisons alone. An understanding of the philosophical, political, and economic background is also required.

The European Convention, then, covers the following rights, limited in scope but potentially effective in their enforcement: the right to life;[39] prohibition against torture and inhuman or degrading treatment or punishment;[40] prohibition against slavery, servitude, and forced or compulsory labour;[41] liberty and security of person;[42] fair and public hearings by an independent and impartial tribunal in the determination of civil rights and obligations or criminal charges;[43] prohibition of retrospective criminal liability;[44] respect for private and family life, home and correspondence;[45] freedom of thought, conscience, and religion;[46] freedom of expression;[47] freedom of peaceful assembly and association;[48] and the right to marry and found a family.[49] Other provisions serve to strengthen the efficacy of these rights, or to encourage governments (who are responsible for state security and who are anxious about frivolous litigation) to become parties to the European Convention. Thus article 13 speaks of the requirement of an effective remedy before a national authority.[50] Article 14 contains the

Convention on Human Rights and the United Nations Covenant on Civil and Political Rights: Problems of Coexistence, 22 Buffalo L. Rev. 181, 204–05 (1972); Directorate of Human Rights, Council of Europe, Proceedings of the Colloquy about the European Convention on Human Rights in Relation to other International Instruments for the Protection of Human Rights, Athens, Sept. 21–22, 1978 (Strasbourg 1979).

[39] Art. 2.
[40] Art. 3.
[41] Art. 4.
[42] Art. 5
[43] Art. 6.
[44] Art. 7.
[45] Art. 8.
[46] Art. 9.
[47] Art. 10.
[48] Art. 11.
[49] Art. 12.
[50] It is controversial whether this means that legal action *on the European Convention* should be available within the national legal systems of states parties. *See* 'Tyrer' Case [1978], Y.B. Eur. Conv. on Human Rights 612 (Eur. Ct. on Human Rights). *See also* Fawcett, *supra* note 21; A. Robertson, Human Rights in Europe 105–07 (2d ed. 1977) [hereinafter cited as Robertson].

vitally important provision that the enjoyment of the rights guaranteed by the European Convention shall be without discrimination as to sex, race, color, language, religion, political or other opinion, national or social origin, association with a national minority, property, birth, or other status. There is no right of non-discrimination *as such*, but rather non-discrimination in the securing of rights under the Convention. Article 15 provides, under carefully controlled conditions, for derogation from certain obligations in times of war or public emergency threatening the life of the nation.[51]

Article 17 warns that the European Convention may not be interpreted as implying for any state, group, or person any right to engage in any activity or perform any act aimed at the destruction or limitation of any of the rights or freedoms enumerated in the Convention.

There are various protocols to the European Convention. The First Protocol and the Fourth Protocol provide the opportunity for states to extend the rights guaranteed under the European Convention. The First Protocol protects a person from the deprivation of his or her possessions[52] 'except in the public interest and subject to the conditions provided for by law and by the general principles of international law.'[53] Article 2 provides that no person shall be denied the right to education, and that the state shall respect the right of parents to ensure education and teaching in conformity with their own religious and philosophical convictions.[54] Article 3 provides for the holding of free elections at reasonable intervals by secret ballot. However, there is no explicit reference to universal suffrage.[55] This Protocol, concluded in 1952, has been ratified by nineteen states to date.[56]

[51] No derogation may be made from art. 2 (except in respect of deaths resulting from lawful acts of war), or from arts. 3, 4(1), or 7. *See generally* Higgins, *supra* note 27.

[52] The text avoids reference to entitlement to own property. It is couched in terms of peaceful enjoyment of possessions. *Cf.* Universal Declaration, art. 17. For some case law under this clause, *see* Application 551/59, [1960] Y.B. Eur. Conv. on Human Rights 244 (Eur. Comm'n of Human Rights); Application 3039/67, [1967] Y.B. Eur. Conv. on Human Rights 506 (Eur. Comm'n of Human Rights); Application 5849/72, [1975] Y.B. Eur. Conv. on Human Rights 374 (Eur. Comm'n of Human Rights).

[53] First Protocol, art. 1.

[54] The leading case on art. 2 of the First Protocol is the 'Belgium Linguistics' Case [1968], 2 Y.B. Eur. Conv. on Human Rights 832 (Eur. Ct. of Human Rights). *See also* 'Case of Kjeldsen, Busk Madsen and Pedersen', [1976] Y.B. Eur. Conv. on Human Rights 502 (Eur. Ct. of Human Rights). It will readily be appreciated that claims under art. 2 of the First Protocol are often coupled with a claim under art. 14 of the European Convention, *i.e.*, non-discrimination.

[55] *Compare* art. 3 of the First Protocol *with* art. 21(3) of the Universal Declaration *and* art. 25 of the Political Covenant. There was a finding of a breach of art. 3 of the First Protocol in the 'Greek' Case, [1969] 1 Y.B. Eur. Conv. on Human Rights 175–80 (Eur. Comm'n of Human Rights).

[56] Austria, Belgium, Cyprus, Denmark, Federal Republic of Germany, France, Greece, Iceland, Ireland, Italy, Luxembourg, Malta, Netherlands, Norway, Portugal, Sweden, Turkey, and United Kingdom.

The Fourth Protocol[57] was concluded in 1963 and entered into effect in 1968. It provides for freedom from imprisonment for civil debts;[58] freedom of movement and of residence, and freedom to leave any country, including one's own;[59] freedom from exile and the right to enter the country of which one is a national;[60] and prohibition of a collective expulsion of aliens.[61] This Protocol has been ratified by eleven states to date.[62]

The Second Protocol[63] allows the European Court of Human Rights to give advisory opinions if certain conditions are fulfilled.[64] The Third Protocol[65] revised the original text of article 29 of the European Convention itself to deal with the grounds on which petitions already accepted may be rejected by the European Commission, and made small textual amendments to articles 30 and 34. The Fifth Protocol[66] amends the original articles 24 and 40 of the European Convention relating to terms of office for the European Commission, the Committee of Ministers, and the European Court. Thus the European Convention itself now exists with its text amended through the later Protocols.

In the European system it was decided to proceed with the serious promotion of a limited number of rights. For a proper understanding of the reasons for, and significance of, this decision the teacher will want a full discussion of the merits and demerits of a regional approach to human rights. There will also need to be some analysis of why the European Convention is limited to a small number of civil rights. The right to vote, for example, is not included in the Convention at all.[67] Freedom of movement only appears as a right in

---

[57] *See* note 33 *supra*.

[58] Fourth Protocol, art. 1.

[59] *Id*. art. 2.

[60] *Id*. art. 3.

[61] *Id*. art. 4.

[62] Austria, Belgium, Denmark, Federal Republic of Germany, France, Iceland, Ireland, Luxembourg, Norway, Portugal, and Sweden. The United Kingdom has not ratified the Fourth Protocol due to a lack of certainty as to the compatibility of its immigration policy with art. 3 of the Protocol.

[63] *Reprinted in* Brownlie, *supra* note 2, at 258.

[64] The Second Protocol has been ratified by eighteen states to date and came into effect in 1970, although its procedures have not yet been used.

[65] *Reprinted in* Brownlie, *supra* note 2, at 260.

[66] *Reprinted in id*. at 264.

[67] *But see* art. 3 of the First Protocol, whereby the parties 'undertake to hold free elections at reasonable intervals by secret ballot, under conditions which will ensure the free expression of the opinion of the people in the choice of the legislature.' This has been held to imply a right to vote. *See* Applications 6745/74 and 6746/74, W, X, Y, and Z v. Belgium, [1975] Y.B. Eur. Conv. on Human Rights 236, 244 (Eur. Comm'n of Human Rights); Application 6573/74, Decisions and Reports No. 6, at 87, 89.

an additional protocol to which not all Convention members are parties.[68] Why is this?

The question of the absolute or relative quality of human rights, referred to above in the context of civil/political and economic/social rights, arises in another context—namely whether certain human rights are applicable in times of war or other national emergency. It is possible to deal with this after dealing with the various substantive rights under the European Convention, but my own view is that it is better dealt with in the 'conceptual' part of the syllabus.

Necessarily, a discussion of derogation will focus on article 15 of the European Convention. Article 15 provides:

(1) In time of war or other public emergency threatening the life of the nation any High Contracting Party may take measures derogating from its obligations under this Convention to the extent strictly required by the exigencies of the situation, provided that such measures are not inconsistent with its other obligations under international law.

(2) No derogation from Article 2, except in respect of deaths resulting from lawful acts of war, or from Articles 3, 4 (paragraph 1) and 7 shall be made under this provision.

(3) Any High Contracting Party availing itself of this right of derogation shall keep the Secretary-General of the Council of Europe fully informed of the measures which it has taken and the reasons therefor. It shall also inform the Secretary-General of the Council of Europe when such reasons have ceased to operate and the provisions of the Convention are again being fully executed.

In principle, human rights may be derogated from if there is war or other major emergency, but the measures of derogation must be limited to those strictly necessary to meet the situation. The European Convention case law—especially the *'Lawless' Case*[69] and *Ireland v. United Kingdom*[70]—is illuminating on this point.

A contrast may be drawn between the reference to 'time of war' in article 15(1) and the total omission of that phrase in comparable article 4 of the Political Covenant.[71]

Article 15(2) makes it clear that there are certain human rights that are absolutely fundamental and that cannot be derogated from even in time of war or national emergency. These include the right to life (save for lawful wartime deaths), the prohibition against torture or degrading treatment (though compulsory labour, article 4(2), may per-

---

[68] Fourth Protocol, art. 2.

[69] [1961] Y.B. Eur. Conv. on Human Rights 430, 432 (Eur. Ct. of Human Rights) [hereinafter cited as *Lawless*].

[70] [1978] Y.B. Eur. Conv. on Human Rights 602, 608 (Eur. Ct. of Human Rights) [hereinafter cited as *Ireland*].

[71] *See* Higgins, *supra* note 27, at 289.

haps be permitted in wartime), and the prohibition against retrospective penalties. Again, this list of nonderogable human rights may be contrasted with the (wider) list in article 4(2) of the Political Covenant. The students will want to discuss why these particular rights, rather than others, can never be derogated from, and what the legal significance of that fact is. Is it indicative that these rights—and these alone—are *jus cogens*?

It is important that students get a feel for how the European institutions have handled the difficult question of derogations. Who determines whether the measures taken are those strictly needed to meet the exigencies of the situation? The practice indicates that while the European Court reserves the decision to itself, it will be prepared to leave the derogating state a 'margin of appreciation' in choosing between alternative methods compatible with the European Convention. This difficult question of margin of appreciation has come up (in the context of article 15) in the *'Lawless' Case*,[72] the *'Cyprus' Case*,[73] and the *Ireland v. United Kingdom*[74] case.

Attention can also be drawn to the way in which the procedural requirements of article 15(3) allow the European institutions to exercise a measure of control over derogations. The question of whether states can still avail themselves of article 15(1) if they have not done all that is required of them under article 15(3) is not wholly settled by the case law.[75]

This is an appropriate moment in the course to contrast the provisions of article 15 on derogations with the qualifying clauses that are attached to several of the substantive rights guaranteed by the European Convention. These will necessarily have to be analyzed in detail at a later stage of the course, but it should be clearly explained at this juncture that these qualifying clauses are available to governments at all times, and not just during war or national emergency and that therefore the questions of notification of appropriate measures and the reasons for them do not arise.

The class is now well prepared to turn to a very important topic: the relationship of the European Convention to the domestic law of the parties. In some of the member states the Convention has been made part of the local law. In yet others its terms are incorporated into constitutional laws; or constitutional laws contain terms that are similar.[76] Indeed in some states—for example Germany—there is both

---

[72] *Lawless, supra* note 69.

[73] [1958–1959] Y.B. Eur. Conv. on Human Rights 174 (Eur. Comm'n of Human Rights).

[74] *Ireland, supra* note 70, at 608.

[75] *See* Higgins, *supra* note 27, at 290.

[76] For an excellent survey, *see* Buergenthal, *The Effect of the European Convention on Human Rights on the International Law of Member States*, in The European Convention on Human Rights, Int'l & Comp. L.Q. Supp. No. 11, at 82 (1965).

a constitutional provision *and* the Convention is part of statute law. What is unique is for a country to have no written constitution and not to have incorporated the Convention into its national law. This is the situation with respect to the United Kingdom. Although the United Kingdom is party to the European Convention and accepts the two special procedures which gives states and individuals effective remedies, the Convention has not been made part of the law of the land. Accordingly, a person with a human rights claim against the United Kingdom may pursue it at the European institutions in Strasbourg, but not in English courts.[77] The United Kingdom government has been unhappy about the amount of adverse publicity generated by actions against it in Strasbourg; but it has resisted suggestions that the European Convention be made part of English law or that a Bill of Rights be enacted. There has, however, been keen debate on the issue of incorporation.[78]

At the same time, it should be said that the distinction between local law and European Convention law is not as rigid as it sometimes seems. In certain cases in the United Kingdom the courts have been willing to pay close attention to the European Convention, and they have offered their views as to whether a particular course of action on the part of the Executive would or would not be acceptable under the Convention. Thus in *Malone v. Metropolitan Police Commissioner*,[79] which concerned telephone tapping, the plaintiff claimed, *inter alia*, that interception of his phone calls violated article 8 of the European Convention. The judge found that as the European Convention was not justiciable in the English courts, the court could make no declaration in relation to it. But he was nonetheless prepared to say, referring to the leading European Convention case on the topic, 'I . . . find it impossible to see how English law could be said to satisfy the requirements of the Convention, as interpreted in the *Klass* case . . .' He

[77] It should be noted that it is possible for an applicant to pursue his or her case at Strasbourg even if there is no remedy available as a matter of law under the relevant domestic legal system. In the 'Amerkrane' Case, for example, [1973] Y.B. Eur. Conv. on Human Rights 356 (Eur. Comm'n of Human Rights), no remedy in any country would have been available. I am grateful to Mr. T. McNulty for pointing this out.

[78] *See, e.g.*, Draft Bill of Rights, H.L. Bill 100, 6 Dec. 1979; Hansard, 402 H.L. at col. 999 (1979); Hansard, 403 H.L. at cols. 287, 297 & 502 (1979).

[79] [1979] 2 W.L.R. 700.

[80] Art. 8 provides:
  1. Everyone has the right to respect for his private and family life, his home and his correspondence.
  2. There shall be no interference by a public authority with the exercise of this right except save as is in accordance with the law and is necessary in a democratic society in the interests of national security, public safety or the economic wellbeing of the country, for the prevention of disorder or crime, for the protection of health or morals, or for the protection of the rights and freedoms of others.

identified the requirements enunciated in the '*Klass*' *Case*[81] and thought that the English common law certainly fell short on one of those elements.

Students should be made aware that it is not correct to assume that the European Convention is ineffective if it is not incorporated into domestic law. This assumption is not true for a variety of reasons. First, as indicated above, domestic case law may often make reference to the requirements of the European Convention, even if the Convention may not—as in the United Kingdom—in formal terms be the basis of a cause of action. Second, the judgments of the European Court are binding, and that fact depends not at all upon the question of enforcement. Those countries accepting the jurisdiction of the Court are bound to give effect to its judgments. Third, countries will often amend their legislation or introduce new legislation during the course of proceedings before the European institutions so as to ensure that by the time the Court pronounces judgment there will be no grounds for complaint. However, the amendments may be claimed to be 'wholly independent' of any proceedings in which the institutions of the Convention are engaged.[82] Fourth, parties to the European Convention will have the European institutions very much in mind when drafting any new national legislation.

Before embarking on a study of the case law of the European Convention, it is necessary to have a clear understanding of the Convention's machinery and its operation.

B. THE MACHINERY

The European Commission of Human Rights has the same number of members as there are parties to the European Convention. The European Convention operates under its own Rules of Procedure and can deal with either inter-state cases or with individual petitions. Article 24 of the European Convention allows any state party to refer a case against another state party to the European Commission. Article 25—a crucial article—provides that the parties may recognize the competence of the European Commission to receive petitions 'from any person, non-governmental organization or group of individuals claiming to be the victim of a violation by one of the High Contracting Parties of the rights set forth in this Convention'. This operation of article 25 has been agreed to by the great majority of parties[83] to

---

[81] [1978] Eur. Conv. on Human Rights 622 (Eur. Ct. of Human Rights).

[82] *See, e.g.*, the legislation introduced by Belgium between the findings of the Commission and the judgment of the Court in the 'De Becker' Case, [1962] Y.B. Eur. Conv. on Human Rights 320 (Eur. Ct. of Human Rights).

[83] These do not include Cyprus, Greece, or Malta.

the Convention and is in many ways a test of a country's willingness to have its human rights commitments publicly examined. When a petition is received under article 25, the European Commission will not be able to deal with it if local remedies have not been exhausted.[84] Article 27 further directs that the Commission shall not deal with any petition which is anonymous, substantially the same as another already examined, 'manifestly ill founded', or an abuse to the right of petition.

There is interesting case law relevant to each of these requirements, and students will need to spend some time familiarizing themselves with the concept of abuse of petition.[85] It can also be difficult for students to understand when the European Commission rejects a claim upon examination of the merits rather than declaring it 'manifestly ill founded'.

When the Commission does declare a petition admissible, it investigates the facts and places itself at the disposal of the parties to secure a friendly settlement. Such friendly settlement must be on the basis of respect for the European Convention.[86] Thus the Commission has to act as guardian of the treaty, and the general practice is, for example, that money settlements are only to be regarded as an appropriate friendly settlement if there is no chance of a repetition of the alleged offense (*e.g.*, if new legislation or administrative directions are issued by the government concerned). If it succeeds in achieving a friendly settlement,[87] the Commission draws up a report and sends it to the states concerned and to the Committee of Ministers and the Secretary General of the Council of Europe. This brief report is published.[88] But if no friendly settlement is achieved, the Commission draws up a

---

[84] *See* art. 26. The local remedies requirement is not tied to art. 25, and could, as a matter of textual construction, relate also to inter-state actions under art. 24. It is now clear from the case law that the local remedies rule applies when the applicant state does no more than denounce a violation or violations allegedly suffered by 'individuals' whose place, as it were, is taken by the State. On the other hand and in principle, the rule does not apply where the applicant State complains of a practice as such, with the aim of preventing its continuation or recurrence, but does not ask the Commission or the Court to give a decision on each of the cases put forward as proof or illustrations of that practice. Ireland v. United Kingdom (Eur. Ct. of Human Rights 1978), *reprinted in* 17 Int'l Legal Materials 680, para. 159 (1978).

[85] 'Abuse of petition' turns not on who the applicant is, but on what he or she seeks to achieve. *See* Application 1270/61, [1962] Y.B. Eur. Conv. on Human Rights 126 (Eur. Comm'n of Human Rights). *See also* European Convention, art. 17.

[86] European Convention, art. 28(b).

[87] *See*, *e.g.*, Knechtl v. United Kingdom, [1970] Y.B. Eur. Conv. on Human Rights (Eur. Comm'n of Human Rights); Simon-Herold v. Austria, [1971] Y.B. Eur. Conv. on Human Rights 352 (Eur. Comm'n of Human Rights); 'Amerkrane' Case, [1973] Y.B. Eur. Conv. on Human Rights 356 (Eur. Comm'n of Human Rights). The last case is, in the view of the author, a settlement which is very hard to square with the requirement that it be in accordance with respect for the rights protected in the European Convention.

[88] European Convention, art. 30.

detailed report on the facts, and states whether or not it finds a breach of the Convention.[89] This is transmitted to the parties and to the Committee of Ministers, but is not published at that stage.[90] Publication is treated as a sanction.

Within three months after the transmittal of this report, the Commission, the state party whose national is alleged to be a victim, the state party which referred the case to the Commission (*i.e.*, in an inter-state dispute), or the state party against which the complaint has been lodged has the right to take the case on to the European Court of Human Rights.[91]

In an inter-state application, the decision to take the matter to the European Commission has already involved, for the applicant state concerned, political decisions at the highest level. A finding of admissibility by the Commission together with a failure to secure a friendly settlement is thus extremely likely to proceed to the European Court. The Commission itself will be inclined to refer a case that it regards as having important implications for the Convention; and the respondent state will choose to proceed to the Court when it regards the issue as one of principle and believes that it has good answers to the report of the Commission. States in this position will often choose to pre-empt the possibility that the Commission will refer the case by speedily referring it themselves.

If the question is *not* referred to the European Court within this time period, the Committee of Ministers of the Council of Europe decides whether there has been a violation of the Convention.[92] If the Committee considers that there has been a violation, it prescribes a time period during which measures required by its decision must be taken.[93] If satisfactory measures are not taken within this time period the Committee decides upon further measures and usually publishes the report of the Commission.[94] The decisions of the Committee are binding upon the parties.[95]

[89] *Id.* art. 31(1).

[90] *Id.* art. 31(2).

[91] *Id.* art. 48.

[92] *Id.* art. 32(1). The Committee of Ministers has adopted rules of procedure for the exercise of its responsibilities under art. 32 of the Convention. *See* Rules Adopted by the Committee of Ministers for the Application of Article 32 of the European Convention on Human Rights, *reprinted in* Appendix, Council of Europe, Collection of Resolutions Adopted by the Committee of Ministers in Application of Article 32 of the European Convention for the Protection of Human Rights and Fundamental Freedoms, 1959–1981, Council of Europe Doc. H. (81) 4 (1981) [hereinafter cited as Article 32 Resolutions]. For criticism of the role entrusted to the Committee of Ministers, *see* Higgins, *The Execution of Decisions of Organs Under the European Convention on Human Rights*, [1978] Revue Hellénique de Droit International 1 [hereinafter cited as Higgins, *Execution*].

[93] European Convention, art. 32(2).

[94] *Id.* art. 32(3).

[95] *Id.* art. 32(4).

If the case is to go to the Court, article 46 becomes crucial. This too, like article 25, is an 'optional clause', providing for jurisdiction in a manner comparable to article 36(2) of the Statute of the International Court of Justice, *i.e.*, parties may at any time declare that they recognize as compulsory *ipso facto* and without special agreement the jurisdiction of the European Court, such declarations being either unconditional or on condition of reciprocity.

If a basis for jurisdiction exists,[96] the Court will proceed to decide whether there has been a breach of the Convention.[97] The judgment of the Court is final and binding.[98] Two facts should particularly be pointed out. First, the judgment is binding whether or not the European Convention has been incorporated into domestic law. Second, the European Commission appears before the Court to present the applicant's case whether or not the Commission itself upheld the entirety of the applicant's case. The applicant's lawyer can assist the Commission if requested by the latter, and in respect of cases referred after January 1, 1983, can also directly represent the applicant.

The Court does not normally specify in any detail that amendments to national legislation or administrative regulations are needed. Rather, it identifies a breach, and the national authorities must then do whatever is necessary to bring themselves back into compliance with the Convention. It is for the Committee of Ministers to supervise the execution of the judgment, though in practice they have not rigorously inspected the compatibility of new legislation with the findings of the Court.[99]

The supervision of the execution of the judgments of the Court is carried out by the Committee of Ministers by virtue of article 54 of the European Convention and the special rules of procedure drawn up in relation thereto. The usual pattern has been for the Committee of Ministers to receive a report from the state adjudged by the Court to be in breach of the Convention. The rules of procedure allow the Committee to grant liberal extensions of time for the submission of such reports.[100] These reports will specify what action the state concerned

[96] Optional competence under art. 46 has been recognized by Austria, Belgium, Denmark, Federal Republic of Germany, France, Iceland, Ireland, Italy, Luxembourg, The Netherlands, Norway, Portugal, Sweden, Switzerland, and United Kingdom.
[97] European Convention, art. 50.
[98] *Id.* art. 52.
[99] *See* Robertson, *supra* note 50, at 236–67; Morgan, *Article 32: What Is Wrong?*, 1 Human Rights Rev. 157 (1976); Higgins, *Execution, supra* note 92.
[100] *See* Rule 2 & 3, Rules Adopted by the Committee of Ministers Concerning the Application of Article 54 of the European Convention on Human Rights, *reprinted in* Council of Europe, Collection of Resolutions Adopted by the Committee of Ministers in Application of Article 54 of the European Convention for the Protection of Human Rights and Fundamental Freedoms, 1976–1981, Council of Europe Doc. H (81) 5 (1981) [hereinafter cited as Article 54 Resolutions].

has taken in order to bring itself back into compliance with the Convention. The Committee of Ministers usually notes such reports and declares its duties under article 54 fulfilled. Disturbingly, it does not carry out (nor, being a political body, is it equipped to carry out) any quasi-judicial analysis as to whether the reported legislative changes do indeed achieve their stated purpose of terminating the breach found by the Court and making its repetition impossible in the future. In other words, there is an operational assumption that altered legislation equals compliance. The correctness of that assumption may have to be tested by subsequent litigants.

Notwithstanding this built-in inadequacy in the functioning of the Committee of Ministers, the judgments of the European Court are undeniably efficacious, in that states which are the subject of adverse findings by the Court have virtually without exception[101] been prepared to take the action necessary to bring themselves back into a position of compliance with the Convention. It should be emphasized to students that compliance does not always entail altering legislation as such. It may be that it is an administrative practice that is found to be contrary to the European Convention, and this may be remedied by a revision of administrative directives. Thus, after the adverse findings in the *'Golder' Case* the United Kingdom government altered prison regulations to remove the right of the prison authorities to control the communication of a prisoner with his or her lawyer.[102]

Certain cases call for particular comment so far as giving effect to the judgment of the Court is concerned. In the case of *Ireland v. United Kingdom*,[103] the latter state simply reported to the Committee of Ministers the measures that it had already taken before the case opened before the European Court. The United Kingdom had pointed out to the Court that these measures (to prohibit the use of the so-called 'five interrogation techniques') had already been put into effect before the case ever came before the Commission. Before the Court, the United Kingdom added weight to this fact by making a solemn declaration that these interrogation techniques would not be reintroduced in any circumstances. The Court declined to find that these events made the case 'moot' or that it was improper to proceed to judgment; but the Committee of Ministers found these same facts sufficient for a finding that the United Kingdom had given effect to the

---

[101] The exception is the implementation of the judgment in the 'Belgian Linguistics' Case [1968], 2 Y.B. Eur. Conv. on Human Rights 832 (Eur. Ct. of Human Rights). Some four years elapsed before Belgian constitutional reforms, and the effect of these reforms is not wholly clear in relation to the breach of art. 2 of the First Protocol and art. 14 of the European Convention.

[102] *See* Committee of Ministers Res. (79) 35, *reprinted in* Article 54 Resolutions, *supra* note 100. *See generally* text accompanying notes 171–72 *infra*.

[103] *Ireland, supra* note 70.

Court's conclusion that the 'five interrogation techniques' were contrary to article 3 of the European Convention.[104]

In the case of *Tyrer v. United Kingdom*,[105] where judicial birching of a minor in the Isle of Man was found to be contrary to article 3 of the European Convention, the government of the United Kingdom did not itself have the constitutional authority to prohibit judicial birching in the Isle of Man; nor was it able to persuade the Isle of Man legislature to take such action. Instead, it reported to the Committee of Ministers that it had notified all those who had the potential authority in the Isle of Man to order the punishment of a minor for a criminal offense by birching that this would be unlawful under the Convention. The Committee of Ministers declared that the judgment of the Court was to be regarded as executed.[106]

Notwithstanding the inadequacy of the execution mechanism, the judgments of the Court are very efficacious in securing human rights. While compliance with the judgments of the European Court is the norm, it must be stressed that compliance is only a small part of the efficacy of the European Convention system. Friendly settlement upon terms acceptable to the Commission[107] and what we may term 'anticipatory compliance' (alteration of legislative or administrative practice after a finding of admissibility and prior to a judgment of the Court) are an equally important part of the picture. Again, governments now have the European Convention very much in mind when drafting new legislation, and it will be a matter of self-interest for them to endeavor to ensure that new laws will not involve them in applications to the European Commission.

This survey of the institutions should leave the reader with a clear understanding of the following:

1. the criteria of admissibility of cases by the European Commission;
2. the optional procedures for individual petition and for jurisdiction of the European Court;
3. inter-state applications;
4. the friendly settlement procedure;
5. the interplay between the Commission, the Committee of Ministers, and the Court; and
6. the timing of publication of the Commission's reports and proposals.

The reader now has a sufficient conceptual understanding, and

---

[104] *Id.* at 606.
[105] *See* note 50 *supra*.
[106] Committee of Ministers Res. (78) 39, *reprinted in* Article 54 Resolution, *supra* note 100.
[107] European Convention, art. 28(b).

enough of an introduction to the institutions and source materials, to begin an examination of the substantive rights guaranteed by the European Convention. It is obviously a matter of choice as to whether one endeavors to cover them all (perhaps rather lightly), or whether, having briefly gone through articles 2–12, one selects certain articles for detailed examination. Certain rights seem to me to be central to an understanding of the European Convention—for example, protection against torture and degrading or inhuman treatment, the right to liberty and security of person, the entitlement to a fair trial, and the right to freedom of expression. It is also a useful technique to reserve a couple of seminars for rights that correspond to 'burning issues of the moment'.

In the ensuing sections, key issues and leading cases concerning those articles which would be an essential component of any course on the European system, *i.e.*, the rights protected in articles 3, 5, 6, and 10 of the European Convention, are discussed.

C. CASE STUDIES

1. *Case Study. Freedom from Torture and Inhuman or Degrading Treatment or Punishment*

Article 3 of the European Convention provides: 'No one shall be subjected to torture or to inhuman or degrading treatment or punishment.' There are no qualifying clauses at all and it is clear from article 15(2) that no derogations to article 3 are permissible. There are, as should be the case in liberal democracies, few applications under this article, but among the most important ones are the *'Greek' Case*, *Ireland v. United Kingdom*, and *Tyrer v. United Kingdom*, each of which merits detailed study.

There have been only a few cases where torture was directly in issue. In the early years of the European Convention, when Cyprus was still under British rule, Greece claimed that there were forty-nine cases of torture or maltreatment amounting to torture. The case was deemed admissible in respect of twenty-nine of those claimed.[108] However, when a political settlement was reached in Cyprus the parties requested that the proceedings be terminated. The Committee of Ministers decided that no further action was called for, and the Report of the European Commission has never been published.[109]

In 1967, Denmark, Norway, Sweden, and The Netherlands instituted proceedings against Greece. The Greek government had claimed to be able to derogate from many of the articles in the European

[108] [1958–1959] Y.B. Eur. Conv. on Human Rights 174–80 (Eur. Comm'n of Human Rights).
[109] *See* Committee of Ministers Res. (59) 32, *reprinted in* Article 32 Resolutions, *supra* note 92.

Convention by virtue of the provisions for a national emergency in article 15. The applicant governments claimed that Greece had violated articles 5, 6, 8, 9, 10, 11, 13, and 14 of the European Convention. After the applications had been declared admissible new allegations were added concerning article 3 and article 7 of the Convention. Irrespective of the complex arguments about the position of Greece with respect to article 15, and the question of the margin of appreciation,[110] it was clear that no derogations could be made from article 3. The European Commission engaged in the most extensive investigation of the facts it has ever undertaken, travelling to Greece, interviewing many witnesses, and visiting many localities. Professor A.H. Robertson writes of the Commission's Report:

> [M]ore than 300 pages of the report were devoted to the question of torture. It is impossible to read the report without being impressed by the objective manner in which the Commission required corroboration of the allegations made, offered the government every opportunity to rebut the evidence produced and even examined the possibility that (as alleged) many of the accounts of torture were deliberately fabricated as part of a plot to discredit the government.[111]

The Commission made detailed findings of torture (and thought there was strong *prima facie* evidence in respect of certain investigations which its investigatory sub-committee had not been allowed to complete). It further found that torture for political reasons was an administrative practice of the Athens security police, which the government had declined to control.[112]

The case was not referred to the European Court, but the Committee of Ministers, acting under article 32, found Greece in violation of various articles of the European Convention, including article 3.[113] The *'Greek' Case*, while reflecting appalling facts and while raising interesting points of law on derogations, gave rise to no particularly difficult points of law on the question of torture. But it seems salutary that charges of torture under the European Convention should merit the weightiest of investigations in respect of this most serious of offenses.

In *Ireland v. United Kingdom*,[114] Ireland submitted an application concerning the Northern Ireland situation, charging the United Kingdom with violations of articles 1, 2, 3, 5, 6, and 14. The European

---

[110] *See* Higgins, *supra* note 27, at 314.

[111] Robertson, *supra* note 50, at 41.

[112] [1969] 1 Y.B. Eur. Conv. on Human Rights 504–05 (Eur. Comm'n of Human Rights). This volume of the *Yearbook* is given over entirely to the *'Greek' Case*.

[113] *See* Committee of Ministers Res. DH (74) 2, *reprinted in* Article 32 Resolutions, *supra* note 92.

[114] *See* note 70 *supra*.

Commission, having declared the application admissible as regards articles 3, 5, and 14, endeavored to obtain a friendly settlement. It could not do this and therefore proceeded with a detailed investigation of the case—hearing witnesses *in camera* and providing them with anonymity, and security where necessary. In this report, the Commission found that derogations by the United Kingdom were properly applicable in respect of article 5 and that article 6 did not apply on the facts. Nor did it uphold the claim under article 14 that detention had been discriminatory. The focus of its attention was article 3. Here the main question was whether certain interrogation techniques constituted torture and an administrative practice. The Commission found they did and the case was submitted to the European Court.

Even by the time the European Commission pronounced on admissibility, the United Kingdom government had already issued an instruction to the Home Office that the practices complained of should cease. When the matter was referred to the European Court the United Kingdom did not contest the Commission's findings. Further, the Attorney General gave a solemn understanding before the Court that these 'five techniques' would not in any circumstances be reintroduced.

The Court was not, however, prepared to treat the issue as moot or disposed of.[115] It stated that the responsibilities assigned to it under the European Convention extended to pronouncing on non-contested allegations of violations under article 3. The Court then proceeded to find (although the United Kingdom had not itself contested the Commission's findings) that the five techniques did not amount to torture, although they did constitute a practice of inhuman and degrading treatment that was a breach of article 3.

The European Court was thus reserving a right to pronounce on all torture claims; but it still distinguished torture from inhuman and degrading treatment under article 3. Only the most appalling and dire acts of maltreatment would constitute the former.

The question still remains of how loosely or tightly 'inhuman or degrading treatment' will be interpreted. In the *'Tyrer' Case*,[116] the applicant, a resident of the Isle of Man, had pleaded guilty to assault occasioning actual bodily harm to a fellow pupil at his school. The Isle of Man Court ordered three strokes of the birch, under Isle of Man legislation. Tyrer complained, among other things, that the judicial birching contravened article 3 of the European Convention. He claimed damages and asked for repeal of the legislation concerned.

[115] *Compare* this *with* Northern Camerouns Case [1963], I.C.J. *and* Nuclear Tests Case [1974], I.C.J.

[116] [1978] Y.B. Eur. Conv. on Human Rights 612 (Eur. Ct. of Human Rights) [hereinafter cited as *Tyrer*].

514 *Rosalyn Higgins*

The Commission found in its Report of 14 December 1976 that the judicial corporal punishment inflicted on Tyrer was degrading and in breach of article 3. The European Court affirmed this view.[117] It agreed with the Commission that the corporal punishment did not amount to torture, as there was no suffering of the level inherent in this notion.[118] For the 'degrading' aspect of article 3 to apply, said the Court, the applicant must be humiliated not merely by virtue of the fact that he has been criminally convicted, but by the execution of the punishment. Notwithstanding that the Isle of Man legislation allowed for appeal against sentence and that there is a prior medical examination with the birching carried out in the presence of a doctor (who may order the punishment to be stopped) and of a parent, it offended article 3. Since there could be no derogation from article 3, even if law and order in the Isle of Man depended upon its retention (which the Court did not accept), birching would not be compatible with the European Convention.

The sole dissent was by Judge Sir Gerald Fitzmaurice. He said that torture and inhuman treatment do not have a monolithic and absolute character, and that the absence of a definition meant that in any particular case the tribunal must take account of all the circumstances. Quite simply, he was unable to accept the Court's proposition that the *very nature* of judicial corporal punishment was contrary to article 3, notwithstanding the adequacy of safeguards in its administration. Sir Gerald recognized that modern opinion had come to regard corporal punishment as an *undesirable* form of punishment, but pointed out that that does not automatically turn it into degrading punishment. He felt it did not degrade young offenders, although he was careful to reserve his position as to adult offenders.[119]

There are presently pending applications concerning the use of corporal punishment not as judicial punishment but as a disciplinary measure in Scottish schools.[120]

[117] The European Court has been asked by the Attorney General for the Isle of Man to strike the case off its list as Tyrer, when he acquired full age, had attested that he wished to withdraw the complaint. The Court decided that as the complaint raised questions of a general character under the European Convention, it could not accede to this request.

[118] *Tyrer, supra* note 116, at 614.

[119] The Isle of Man legislation, in respect of which the United Kingdom does not intervene because of constitutional convention, has not in fact been changed. Summary Jurisdiction Act, 1960, 8 Eliz., §§ 8, 10 (1960). The United Kingdom informed the Committee of Ministers that it had communicated the decision of the European Court to all persons on the Isle of Man authorized to pass a sentence of birching. The Committee of Ministers simply took note of the information. Committee of Ministers Res. (78) 39, *reprinted in* Article 54 Resolutions, *supra* note 100. *See* text accompanying notes 106–06 *supra*.

[120] Campbell and Cosans v. United Kingdom [1978], Y.B. Eur. Conv. on Human Rights 396 (Eur. Comm'n of Human Rights). [Ed. note: After this chapter was completed, the European Court unanimously held that the possible use of the tawse (a leather strap applied to the palm) in

The question of inhuman treatment has sometimes arisen in the context of expulsions. For example, in *Amerkrane v. United Kingdom*, Lt. Colonel Amerkrane was, without opportunity to contest it before the courts, transferred back to Morocco from Gibraltar, where he had fled after being convicted of attempting to kill the King of Morocco. It was claimed that the very fact of transferring him back to Morocco caused him to suffer inhuman treatment. Lt. Colonel Amerkrane was executed, and the claim, which was brought by his wife, was settled. She received a very large cash settlement.[121] The Commission had before it a similar claim by an African against Belgium. The applicant does not posses any documentation proving identity or nationality, and he claims that orders to leave Belgium amount to inhuman and degrading treatment under article 3 because he cannot legally go to any other country.[122]

A further group of article 3 applications center on claims by prisoners as to their conditions of imprisonment. In *Mahler v. Germany*,[123] the question of the compatibility of solitary confinement with article 3 was raised but not answered as it was found that the confinement had not actually been solitary. Friendly settlement ended *Simon-Herold v. Austria*[124] which had raised the question of whether it was inhuman and degrading treatment for a poliomyelitis sufferer, detained on remand, to be placed in a lunatic asylum. The government of Austria sent out a directive, of which the Commission took note, stating that there was a risk of violating article 3 if persons were put in institutions solely for security reasons.

2. *Case Study. Liberty of the Person*

A second central area of study has to be the question of liberty of the person. This concept has been particularly well-developed under the European Convention. Article 5 provides:

1. Everyone has the right to liberty and security of person. No one shall be deprived of his liberty save in the following cases and in accordance with a procedure prescribed by law:
    (a) the lawful detention of a person after conviction by a competent court;
    (b) the lawful arrest or detention of a person for non-compliance with

---

Scottish schools as a method of corporal punishment did not violate art.3. 15 Eur. Hum. Rts. Rep. 293 (1982).

[121] *See also* note 87 *supra*

[122] Application 5961/72, [1973] Y.B. Eur. Conv. on Human Rights 356 (Eur. Comm'n of Human Rights).

[123] Application 6038/73, 44 Recueil de Decisions 115 (1973).

[124] Application 4340/69, [1971] Y.B. Eur. Conv. on Human Rights 352 (Eur. Comm'n of Human Rights).

the lawful order of a court or in order to secure the fulfilment of any obligation prescribed by law;

(c) the lawful arrest or detention of a person effected for the purpose of bringing him before the competent legal authority on reasonable suspicion of having committed an offence or when it is reasonably considered necessary to prevent him committing an offence or fleeing after having done so;

(d) the detention of a minor by lawful order for the purpose of educational supervision or his lawful detention for the purpose of bringing him before the competent legal authority;

(e) the lawful detention of persons for the prevention of the spreading of infectious diseases, of persons of unsound mind, alcoholics or drug addicts, or vagrants;

(f) the lawful arrest or detention of a person to prevent his effecting an unauthorised entry into the country or of a person against whom action is being taken with a view to deportation or extradition.

2. Everyone who is arrested shall be informed promptly, in a language which he understands, of the reasons for his arrest and of any charge against him.

3. Everyone arrested or detained in accordance with the provisions of paragraph 1(c) of this article shall be brought promptly before a judge or other officer authorised by law to exercise judicial power and shall be entitled to trial within a reasonable time or to release pending trial. Release maybe conditioned by guarantees to appear for trial.

4. Everyone who is deprived of his liberty by arrest or detention shall be entitled to take proceedings by which the lawfulness of his detention shall be decided speedily by a court and his release ordered if the detention is not lawful.

5. Everyone who has been the victim of arrest or detention in contravention of the provisions of this article shall have an enforceable right to compensation.

Article 5(1)(a), (c), and (e) have received judicial attention. A considerable amount of case law now also exists on article 5(3), with the concepts of an 'officer authorized by law to exercise judicial power' and 'trial within a reasonable time' being particularly well-scrutinized. This is an area that merits detailed study since the right to liberty of the person is so fundamental and the built-in provisions for the exercise of judicial and other legitimate state functions so carefully worded. The issues that have arisen are basic to any democratic society. The interplay between article 5(3) and article 6(1) should also be considered.[125]

What does the phrase 'entitled to trial within a reasonable time or to release pending trial' found in article 5(3) mean? In the *'Neumeister'*

[125] *See* text accompanying notes 144–48 *infra*.

Case,[126] the European Court said that detention has to be reasonable and if it is not the accused must be released.[127]

What is a 'reasonable time' within which an accused must be brought to trial? In a series of cases, the answer to this question has been refined. There is no fixed period of time that one can designate as reasonable, no moment beyond which the time can be termed unreasonable.[128] What is reasonable depends upon all the circumstances. In the *'Wemhoff' Case*,[129] a German national, a broker, was arrested on November 9, 1961 for breaches of trust. He was ordered to be detained on remand. The reasons cited were the seriousness of the alleged crime, and fear that he might abscond and/or attempt to suppress evidence if left at liberty. The original warrant was succeeded by two detention orders of December 28, 1961 and January 8, 1962, which referred to suspicion of fraud as well as breach of trust. In the first half of 1963, two appeals were made to the Regional and Appeals Court respectively concerning the detention, the District Court having already turned down an application. These appeals were unsuccessful. The Court of Appeal thought that since Wemhoff would receive an appreciatively higher sentence if found guilty than had formerly been thought, the risk of absconding was even greater, notwithstanding that Wemhoff's lawyer had offered to deposit his client's identity papers. In January 1964, Wemhoff lodged an application with the European Commission of Human Rights.

A detailed indictment was filed in April 1964, and in July 1964 a new detention order was issued. Wemhoff's trial opened on November 9, 1964, by which time his application to the Commission had been declared admissible. The Commission was unable to secure a friendly settlement.

In April 1965, Wemhoff was found guilty and sentenced to six years and six months penal servitude, as well as a fine. The period of detention on remand was counted as part of the sentence. Pending appeal of his case, Wemhoff again several times sought his provisional release, and offered bank guarantees to be provided by his father. Release was not granted. In December 1965, his appeal was also rejected, and the time he had spent in detention since judgment at first instance was also counted towards his sentence. In November 1966, after serving two-thirds of his sentence, Wemhoff was conditionally released.

The European Commission found that Wemhoff had not been

---
[126] [1968] Y.B. Eur. Conv. on Human Rights 812 (Eur. Ct. of Human Rights).
[127] *See also* text accompanying notes 134–37 *infra*.
[128] *See* 'Matznetter' Case, [1969] Y.B. Eur. Conv. on Human Rights 406 (Eur. Ct. of Human Rights); *see* text accompanying notes 138–40 *infra*.
[129] [1968] Y.B. Eur. Conv. on Human Rights 796 (Eur. Ct. of Human Rights).

brought to trial 'within a reasonable time' and that this was so not-withstanding the fact that the period of detention was counted as part of the sentence. The detention on remand had been a lawful detention under article 5(1)(c), but contravened the 'reasonable time' require-ments of article 5(3).

The Commission suggested seven criteria for establishing whether a person lawfully detained was not being brought to trial within a reasonable time: (i) the actual length of the detention; (ii) the length of detention on remand in relation to the nature of the offense; (iii) the effects on the detained person; (iv) the conduct of the accused, with special reference to whether he contributed to delays, and to whether he requested bail; (v) the difficulties and complexity of the case; (vi) the manner in which the necessary investigation was conducted; and (vii) the conduct of the judicial authorities.

The matter proceeded to the European Court. The Court did not feel able to adopt the seven criteria of the Commission, saying that it 'must judge whether the reasons given by the national authorities to justify continued detention are relevant and sufficient to show that detention was not contrary to Article 5(3)'. It is hard to see how in making such a judgment the Court will not in fact (even if not in form) be mindful of the elements listed by the Commission. The Court thought that the anxiety of the German courts about suppression of evidence was justified. As to danger of flight, the Court found that the likelihood of a long sentence was not enough. Further, 'the effect of such fear diminishes as detention continues' and as the balance of such sentence which the accused may expect to have to serve is reduced.[130]

The Court found that where fear of flight is the only reason for detention, release pending trial must be ordered if financial guarantees were adequate. Therefore, there could only have been a breach of article 5(3) if the detention between November 1961 and April 1965 had been due to slowness of investigation, or too long a period between the end of investigation or the beginning of trial, or to the length of the trial. The Court found that no fault lay with the judicial authorities, and that '[t]he exceptional length of the investigation and of the trial are justified by the exceptional complexity of the case and by further unavoidable reasons for delay'.[131] The Court therefore overruled the Commission, and found by six votes to one that there was no breach of article 5(3).

Clearly, this case is an important clarification of the component elements of the notion of 'unreasonable time' under article 5(3), so far as questions relating to the conduct of the accused, fear of flight,

---

[130] *Id.* at 806.
[131] *Id.* at 808.

interference with evidence, adequacy of financial guarantees for bail, and slowness of investigation and/or of trial are concerned. But the Court also dealt with another important point of interpretation. The Commission had agreed with the German government that the period of detention in respect of which 'reasonable time' was to be judged ran from the date of arrest to the opening of the trial. The Court thought this too restrictive a view.[132] Emphasizing that it was giving interpretative priority to the aims and purposes of the European Convention rather than to minimizing the obligations of the parties, the Court decided that the protection against unduly long detention did not cease with the opening of the trial but continued up to the delivery of judgment. The Court further found that this meant judgment by a court of first instance, rather than a final judgment. Here the Court found article 5(1)(a) compelling, because a person convicted at first instance is lawfully deprived of liberty within the meaning of that clause. It was in principle lawful to hold such a person. The implication of the Court's findings is that conviction is *per se* enough for post-trial detention—there is no need to show, *e.g.*, fear of flight. The Court observed that if the post-trial detention became 'unreasonably long' a possible remedy would lie in article 6(1)[133] even if not in article 5(3).

The '*Neumeister*' Case[134] raised similar points. The applicant was an Austrian national suspected of defrauding the exchequer through customs fraud. He was arrested on August 11, 1959. In January 1960 his examination before an Investigating Judge began. He was provisionally released on parole in May 1961, and resumed work (though he had had to sell his previous company at a reduced price). In July 1961 he and his family went to Finland on holiday and in February 1962 he went to the Saar for several days on business. In 1962, however, he was denied permission to holiday again in Finland—though Neumeister claimed that permission *was* given to him by the Investigating Judge in spite of the wish of the Public Prosecutor that permission not be given. In July 1962 he was arrested on a warrant referring to the danger of flight. In a series of court cases Neumeister challenged his detention on remand, urging that he had had the

[132] The French and English texts lead to different conclusions—the latter refers to 'trial' while the former uses the word '*jugée*'. The European Court stated that the use of the term 'trial' referred to the whole of proceedings before the court, not just their beginning. In other words, 'entitled to trial' was not necessarily limited to 'entitled to be brought to trial'. The French text, which is of equal authority to the English one, permitted of only one interpretation. The obligation to release an accused person within a reasonable time continues until that person has been '*jugée*'—until the day of judgment. *Id.* at 798–99.

[133] Art. 6(1) refers to the right to a fair and public hearing 'within a reasonable time' for the determination of civil rights and liberties.

[134] [1968] Y.B. Eur. Conv. on Human Rights 812 (Eur. Ct. of Human Rights) [hereinafter cited as *Neumeister*].

opportunity to abscond, but had never done so. He also pointed out that his business interests were in Vienna, his wife had just opened a dress shop, and that he had already served nine months on remand, which fact argued against the dangers of flight. He offered to deposit with the court his identity papers and passport. The Austrian courts, however, noted the inadequacy of financial guarantees, and pointed to confessions incriminating Neumeister made by a fellow-accused.

Neumeister contended that statements made by a co-accused could not form the basis for detention on remand. He also urged that article 5(3) of the European Convention precluded the fixing of bail at such a high level that the prisoner's release became impossible in practice. The European Commission—once again using the 'seven criteria' as a guideline (the Commission handed down the decisions in *Wemhoff* and *Neumeister* on the same day)—found that several of the criteria pointed to the detention being unreasonably long, though on the seventh criterion (the conduct of the judicial authorities), the evidence was open to different evaluations. It found a violation of article 5(3).

On this case the Court agreed with the Commission. It was significant that while Neumeister's second period of detention was caused by the statements of his co-accused, he was not interrogated again during the fifteen month period that followed. And although the danger of flight had perhaps not decreased, the assessment of that danger still had to take account of other factors, such as his job, family ties, etc. Moreover, while the European Court declined to pronounce on whether the security offered by Neumeister was 'sufficient', it did note that article 5(3) made it inappropriate to fix the required security solely in relation to the amount of the loss imputed to him.[135] The Court therefore found that Neumeister's detention until September 16, 1964 constituted a violation of article 5(3).

The question of identifying the relevant period to be judged as reasonable or not arose also in this case, but in a somewhat different manner from *Wemhoff*. Neumeister had had two periods of detention. The European Court could not consider whether the first period as such was incompatible with the European Convention because, *inter alia*, Neumeister had not submitted an application to the European Commission until after the six month time limit laid down in article 26 of the Convention had expired.[136] This period of imprisonment had in any event been a fairly short period—two months and seventeen days. The second period lasted over two years and two months. However, the Austrian government argued that the European Court should not

---

[135] *Id.* at 822.
[136] Art. 26 provides that '[t]he Commission may only deal with the matter . . . within a period of six months from the date on which the final decision [of the domestic authorities] was taken.'

consider Neumeister's detention *subsequent* to the day on which he filed his application with the Commission, as the application could only relate to facts that had taken place before this date. Once again, the Court showed that in a human rights instrument strict rigidity was not a suitable canon of interpretation:

In his Application of 12th July 1963 Neumeister complained not of an isolated act but rather of a situation in which he had been for some time and which was to last until it was ended by a decision granting him provisional release, a decision which he sought in vain for a considerable time. It would be excessively formalistic to demand that an Applicant denouncing such a situation should file a new Application with the Commission after each final decision rejecting a request for release.[137]

The Court for these reasons found that it should examine the period of detention through to his provisional release.

The following year the Court had to deal with the *'Matznetter' Case*.[138] This concerned fraud charges against an Austrian tax consultant. Matznetter was arrested on May 15, 1963 and in December 1963 sought his release, noting that there was no real danger of absconding: he was an amputee with other severe disabilities, he had no funds abroad nor could transfer any, and he was of good record. The Austrian courts found a continued danger nonetheless—he had connections abroad, and a good financial position in spite of debts. There was also reference to the possibility of repeating the offenses. Matznetter continued his appeals on the question of provisional release, and by December 1964 was making the point that he had served the greater part, if not the whole, of any possible sentence because, as a first offender, he could reasonably expect an early release.

Matznetter had made his application to the European Commission on April 3, 1964. The Commision particularly noted that the preliminary investigation did not proceed at an adequate pace. Matznetter had to wait six months before appearing before the Investigating Judge (at his own request), who had to deal not only with this difficult case, but also with others. The Commission found a violation of article 5(3), but this was not upheld by the European Court. The Court confirmed its view in *Neumeister* that it could examine facts subsequent to the application; and that time in detention after the lodging of an application was to be taken into account in determining what delay was 'reasonable'. The Court thought the unusual length of the investigation was justified by the exceptional complexity of the case. Although there was significant delay in the investigatory procedure, the Court

---

[137] *Neumeister, supra* note 134, at 816.
[138] [1969] Y.B. Eur. Conv. on Human Rights 406 (Eur. Ct. of Human Rights).

declared itself satisfied that explanations given by the Austrian government were 'credible'.[139] The arguments of the Austrian government on
this point really related to the continued need to restrict Matznetter on
grounds of danger of absconding. Such justifications of the delay (in
contradistinction to the need to detain during such delay) turned on
the heavy work load of the Investigating Judge and the efforts made by
the Austrian government to provide assistance for him. The Court
said, '[W]hile an accused person held in custody is entitled to have his
case given priority and conducted with special diligence this must not
stand in the way of the proper administration of justice'.[140] But slow
investigation because of overwork is, in the view of this author not to
be assimilated to 'the proper administration of justice'. This judgment
provides a good teaching opportunity to discuss the relationship of
international obligations to the *bona fide* realities of domestic life.

On the same day, the European Court handed down its judgment in
the *'Stögmüller' Case*.[141] Stögmüller, an Austrian national, was
arrested on March 3, 1958 on suspicion of having committed offenses
under the Usury Act. His preliminary investigation began on March
10, 1958. On April 21, 1958 he was provisionally released. In June
1958 further information was laid against him alleging fraud and
related offenses. In the summer of 1959 Stögmüller changed his occupation and became a pilot. He sold his company. He flew to many
international airports, always returning. However, he did not attend a
regional examination by the Investigating Judge, going instead to
Greece, though Stögmüller did make sure that his whereabouts were
known and asked for an adjournment of the examination. When he
returned at the end of August he offered himself for examination, but
the Judge stated that he now would not have the time to examine him
until September. Three days later (August 24, 1961) his arrest was
ordered, on the grounds that he had gone abroad to Greece without
permission, thus breaking the conditions of his provisional release.
Stögmüller was detained from August 25, 1961 to August 26, 1963. In
July 1966 the preliminary investigation—in which hundreds of witnesses were interviewed and twenty thousand pages written—was
concluded. The interrogating judge conceded that when Stögmüller
changed his occupation, the likelihood of repetition of offenses ended,
but the danger of absconding increased.

The European Court found that while reasonable suspicion is a
relevant consideration for lawful arrest under article 5(1)(a), it was not

[139] *Id.* at 434.
[140] *Id.*
[141] [1969] Y.B. Eur. Conv. on Human Rights 364 (Eur. Ct. of Human Rights).
[142] [1971] Y.B. Eur. Conv. on Human Rights 838 (Eur. Ct. of Human Rights) [hereinafter
cited as *Ringeisen*].

of itself enough to prolong detention under article 5(3). It thought that there was little danger of the offenses being repeated and the fact that Stögmüller had always returned from his trips and had family left behind in Austria made the likelihood of absconding small. The mere opportunity to cross frontiers was not enough to make it likely that he would abscond. Austria was found in breach of article 5(3).

In July 1971 the Court handed down its decision in the *'Ringeisen' Case*.[142] Here an Austrian citizen was charged with certain real property frauds and with fraudulent bankruptcy. His first period of detention was from August 5, to December 23, 1963 and the second from March 15, 1965 to March 20, 1967. The first period alone fell outside of the European Court's review as Ringeisen's application to the European Commission in July 1965 was more than six months later. But, importantly, the Court said that 'these four and a half months of the first detention must be added to the period which followed for the purpose of assessing the reasonableness of the whole period of detention . . .'[143]

The Court found unpersuasive government arguments about the possibility of Ringeisen tampering with witnesses, noting that he had already been at liberty for five months since his arrest. Nor did it accept that he was likely to commit further offences. The Court held by five votes to two that his detention between May 14, 1965 to January 1966 was in violation of article 5(3).

On January 14, 1966 Ringeisen was convicted of fraud. His counsel requested that he be released pending appeals to this case. He again made a request for release in the fraudulent bankruptcy case. Both sets of requests were refused, and appeals were made in respect of each. He was eventually released in the fraudulent bankruptcy proceedings on March 20, 1967. The European Commission had asked the European Court to review its dictum in the *'Wemhoff' Case* that post adjudication detention is not covered by article 5(3) but only by article 6(1). Alternatively, the Court was asked to interpret its earlier dictum in such a way that 'reasonable delay' remains subject to article 5(3) until the conviction becomes final under the domestic law of the state concerned. The Court found it unnecessary to respond to this request because the detention from May 12, 1965 until March 15, 1967 (relating to the appeals procedure in the fraud conviction) fell within the limits of the remand in custody in the fraudulent bankruptcy case which ran from March 15, 1965 to March 2, 1967. The Court held by the narrower majority of four votes to three that the detention from January 1966 to March 1967 continued the breach of article 5(3).

The Court has given different meanings to 'reasonable time' in

[143] *Id.* at 856.

article 6(1) and article 5(3). It is therefore necessary to look at proceedings under the European Convention about the length of judicial
proceedings.

Article 6(1) provides:

In the determination of his civil rights and obligations or of any criminal
charge against him, everyone is entitled to a fair and public hearing within
a reasonable time by an independent and impartial tribunal established by
law . . .

In the *'Huber' Case*,[144] the applicant, who was a co-accused with
Neumeister, was arrested in February 1961 in Switzerland and released in May 1961 on grounds of ill health; he was re-arrested in
March 1962 and extradited to Austria in September 1962. He was
released from custody in July 1965. Various charges were dropped,
but he was convicted of one charge of fraud in July 1968. The European Commission declared his application inadmissible save as regards the length of the criminal proceedings. The case thus proceeded
forward with article 6(1) as the main issue. The Commission eventually adopted its report in February 1973.[145] Neither the Commission
nor Austria decided to take the case to the European Court; it therefore went to the Committee of Ministers. In spite of the Commission's
view that there had been a violation of article 6(1), the Committee of
Ministers found that no further action was called for.[146] The Committee of Ministers was no doubt greatly influenced by the fact that the
European Court had, in the *'Neumeister' Case*, found there was *no*
breach of article 6(1) (although it had found a breach of article 5(3)).

In 1978 the European Court gave its judgment in the *'König'
Case*.[147] König was the owner and director of a clinic in Germany, and
his licence to manage the clinic was withdrawn in 1967 on grounds of
professional misconduct. He appealed unsuccessfully to various
bodies and tribunals. He then claimed before the European Commission that proceedings before the Frankfurt Administrative Tribunal
were unreasonably lengthy. The Commission, and eventually the
European Court, upheld his claim. However, the Court rejected the
stated view of the German government and the Commission that time
starts to run from the date of filing of appeals with the court of first
instance. In this case the Court found that time began to run on the
day on which the applicant lodged an objection to the withdrawal of
his authorization to practise. Although Dr. König had himself to

---

[144] [1971] Y.B. Eur. Conv. on Human Rights 548 (Eur. Comm'n of Human Rights).
[145] *Reprinted in* [1975] Y.B. Eur. Conv. on Human Rights 324, 326 (Eur. Comm'n of Human
Rights).
[146] Committee of Ministers Res. DH (75) 2, *reprinted in* Article 32 Resolutions, *supra* note 92.
[147] [1978] Y.B. Eur. Conv. on Human Rights 618 (Eur. Ct. of Human Rights).

some extent contributed to the length of proceedings, the Court still found that the period was unreasonably long within the meaning of article 6(1).[148]

There have been other cases concerning article 5 of the European Convention that should be pointed out. It is the second part of article 5(3) which is concerned with the right to trial within a reasonable time. The first part of article 5(3) provides that '[e]veryone arrested or detained in accordance with the provisions of paragraph 1(c) of this article shall be brought promptly before a judge or other officer authorised by law to exercise judicial power. . . .'

Thus in the *'Schiesser' Case*,[149] the applicant had been placed in detention on remand by the District Attorney of Winterthur on suspicion of theft. Following earlier precedents, the European Court found that an 'officer' under article 5(3) was a person who was independent of the executive and the parties. He or she could still be subordinate to other judges or officers provided that they themselves enjoy similar independence. The 'officer' must also hear the individual concerned. As well as this procedural guarantee, the term also implies a substantive guarantee—that the 'officer' will employ legal criteria in deciding whether or not there are grounds for detention.

Comparable issues have arisen in relation to the meaning of the word 'court' in article 5(1)(a) of the European Convention.[150] Thus in the *'Engel' Case*,[151] which concerned detention by the Dutch military authorities under military disciplinary provisions, the term 'court' was held to apply to organs which had a judicial character, exemplified by their independence of the executive and the parties to the case, and which offered procedural guarantees. In this, the European Court was following its stated view in the *'Neumeister' Case*.[152] In the *'Eggs' Case*,[153] the European Commission's Report had to deal with the application of a Swiss national serviceman who received a disciplinary sanction of five days strict arrest for refusing to carry out certain orders. The penalty was confirmed by the Camp Commander and an appeal by Eggs to the Chief Military Prosecutor was unsuccessful. Eggs claimed that his deprivation of liberty had not been ordered by a trial court. The Commission found that the organization of military service

[148] *Id.* at 622. This case also raises difficult questions about whether a 'civil' right is involved in the withdrawal of a medical license by the state authorities. The present author has difficulty in following the logic of this part of the judgment. *See id.* at 620.

[149] [1979] Y.B. Eur. Conv. on Human Rights 432 (Eur. Ct. of Human Rights).

[150] Art. 5(1)(a) allows deprivation of liberty during 'the lawful detention of a person after conviction by a competent court'.

[151] [1976] Y.B. Eur. Conv. on Human Rights 490 (Eur. Ct. of Human Rights) [hereinafter cited as *Engel*].

[152] *See Neumeister, supra* note 134, at 828–30.

[153] Eggs v. Switzerland, Application 7431/76.

in Switzerland guaranteed the independence of military justice in general. Nonetheless, there was a merging of powers in the sense that the Chief Military Prosecutor could dismiss a case in his capacity as director of public prosecutions, but still be required to deal with it as the appeals authority in disciplinary proceedings. He therefore could *not* be likened to a court and the strict arrest was contrary to article 5(1). The matter went not to the European Court but to the Committee of Ministers. The Committee of Ministers noted that modifications to the Swiss Military Penal Code were to take effect in January 1980, the main aim of which was to substitute a judge for the Chief Military Prosecutor as the appeal authority. The Committee of Ministers therefore contented itself with noting[154] this fact, together with the report of the Commission.

When a person of unsound mind has committed an offense, his or her detention will also be considered under article 5(1)(a);[155] but the most directly relevant clause will be article 5(1)(e), which speaks of the permitted lawful detention of persons of unsound mind. The case law under article 5(1)(a) in this context has been growing.[156]

The first European Court decision in this area was the *'Winterwerp' Case*.[157] In May 1968 Winterwerp was committed to a psychiatric hospital for three weeks by order of the local Dutch burgomaster. This detention was extended by the public prosecutor, and was later renewed periodically on the application of his wife and at the request of the public prosecutor. Winterwerp was unaware of these proceedings and was not represented at them. He thus was unable to argue the law or to challenge the medical evidence. He did apply four times for release. The first request in 1969 was dismissed by the Regional Court. Later requests were dismissed by the public prosecutor, without reference to the Regional Court. Winterwerp claimed, *inter alia*, that his deprivation was not 'lawful' under article 5(1). The Commission found there was no breach of this article, and the European Court confirmed this. Both held that Winterwerp's detention fell under article 5(1)(e) (detention of persons of unsound mind), and that the deprivation of liberty had been carried out by a procedure prescribed by law. The Court also agreed with the Commission that a mental patient's right to treatment cannot be derived from article 5(1)(e).

[154] Committee of Ministers Res. DH (79) 7, *reprinted in* [1979] Y.B. Eur. Conv. on Human Rights 454.

[155] For an interesting criticism, *see* Muchlinski, *Mental Health Patients' Rights and the European Human Rights Convention*, 5 Human Rights Rev. 90 (1980), who argues that unless the offender was sane at the time of the offense but became insane in prison, there is a causal link between the illness and the detention.

[156] *See, e.g.* Application 4741/71, 43 Recueil de Decisions 14 (1973); Application 5624/72, 45 Recueil de Decisions 115 (1973) (two early cases).

[157] [1979] Y.B. Eur. Conv. on Human Rights 426 (Eur. Ct. of Human Rights).

The European Court and the Commission found that there had been a violation of article 5(4). This clause provides that a person deprived of liberty by arrest or detention 'shall be entitled to take proceedings by which the lawfulness of his detention shall be decided speedily by a court and his release ordered if the detention is not lawful'. The Court indicated that article 5(4) provides the right to have both the substantive and the formal lawfulness of detention verified by a court. Neither the burgomaster nor the public prosecutor could be regarded as having the characteristic of a 'court'.[158] The District Court and Regional Court clearly were 'courts' but the availability of procedural guarantees was still essential. A detained person should have access to a court, either personally or through representation.[159] Further, the later claims for discharge had not been referred by the public prosecutor to the courts. Accordingly, there was a violation of article 5(4).

There has been considerable current interest in the so-called United Kingdom Mental Health Case presently under consideration. In Application 6998/75, the applicant was ordered to be detained in a hospital for the criminally insane under the United Kingdom Mental Health Act, 1959, after pleading guilty to a charge of wounding with intent. He was subsequently conditionally discharged by the Home Secretary which meant that he could be recalled at any time on the decision of the Home Secretary and the responsible medical officer. Three years later he was recalled and returned to the hospital. He had committed no criminal offense but his probation officer said that his 'condition was giving cause for concern'. He applied unsuccessfully for habeas corpus.

The government contends that this is lawful detention under article 5(1)(a) of the European Convention. The applicant contends that article 5(1)(a) is inapplicable, and that the matter falls to be determined under article 5(1)(e)—that is to say, that his detention was related to his mental state rather than to the commission of any offense. It now remains to be seen whether the opinion of the applicant's probation officer is a sufficient basis for the Home Secretary to have exercised his discretion to recall the applicant. In short, the discretion that the Home Secretary possesses in these matters is probably in principle in conformity with the European Convention: what is at issue is whether its exercise is in the circumstances of this application in conformity with the European Convention.[160]

The interpretation of article 5(4) has arisen in various cases. Of

[158] *Id.* at 428.
[159] *Id.* at 430.
[160] [Ed. note: After this chapter was completed, the case, X v. United Kingdom, was decided on 5 Nov. 1981 by the European Court. *See* 14 Eur. Hum. Rts. Rep. 188 (1982). *annexed to* Eur. Comm'n of Human Rights Press Release B (81) 50 (1981).]

particular interest are the so-called *'Vagrancy' Cases*.[161] Three applicants had been detained under a Belgian Act of 1891 for the suppression of vagabondage and begging. They claimed that as their detention was ordered by a magistrate acting in an administrative capacity, their right to a court hearing in the lawfulness of their detention was denied. The European Court upheld this claim. Although the magistrate is a 'court', his functions in relation to vagrancy are administrative. Article 5(4) requires judicial supervision even in relation to vagrancy. There was found to be no breach of article 5(1)(e).[162]

A somewhat curious invocation of the notion of vagrancy occurred in *Guzzardi v. Italy*.[163] After being acquitted for lack of proof of charges of kidnapping, certain detention measures were ordered against Guzzardi under the Mafia Act of 1965. The Milan Regional Court ordered the applicant to reside in a specified locality (the island of Asinara) under supervision for three years. The Italian government claimed that there was no detention under article 5; but even if there were, it satisfied the conditions laid down in article 5(1)(e) on vagrancy. The European Commission was careful to point out that having to reside within a specified area did not necessarily amount to a deprivation of liberty.[164] But the nature of the restriction that applied to him did in fact amount to a deprivation of liberty under article 5(1) of the European Convention. Although the definition of 'vagrancy' offered in the *'Vagrancy' Cases* was not the only possible one, action had been taken against Guzzardi under the Mafia Act and he could not be described as a vagrant. His detention therefore did not fall under article 5(1)(e)—or indeed any of the categories in article 5.[165]

3. *Case Study. The Rights to a Fair Trial*

A further major area of the European Convention relates to the right to a fair trial guaranteed in article 6. This article provides:

1. In the determination of his civil rights and obligations or of any criminal charge against him, everyone is entitled to a fair and public hearing within a reasonable time by an independent and impartial tribunal

---

[161] 'De Wilde, Ooms and Versyp' Cases, [1971] Y.B. Eur. Conv. on Human Rights 788 (Eur. Ct. of Human Rights).

[162] Art. 5(3) was inapplicable because it refers back to art. 5(1)(c) with its mention of 'an offence' and vagrancy was not an 'offence' under Belgian law. The applicants were therefore not detained under art. 5(1)(c) but under art. 5(1)(e).

[163] Application 7367/76. Report of Eur. Comm'n, 7 Dec. 1978.

[164] But it might amount to a restriction upon movement under Fourth Protocol, art. 2. *See also* 'Engel' Case, [1976] Y.B. Eur. Conv. on Human Rights 490, 494 (Eur. Ct. of Human Rights); 'Greek' Case, [1969] 1 Y.B. Eur. Conv. on Human Rights 133 (Eur. Comm'n of Human Rights).

[165] On 6 Nov. 1980, the European Court delivered a decision in *Guzzardi v. Italy*. [Ed. note: On Apr. 30, 1981, the Committee of Ministers adopted Resolution DH (81) 6 on the 'Guzzardi' Case. Committee of Ministers Res. DH (81) 6, *reprinted in* Article 54 Resolution, *supra* note 100.

established by law. Judgment shall be pronounced publicly but the press and public may be excluded from all or part of the trial in the interests of morals, public order or national security in a democratic society, where the interests of juveniles or the protection of the private life of the parties so require, or to the extent strictly necessary in the opinion of the court in special circumstances where publicity would prejudice the interests of justice.

2. Everyone charged with a criminal offence shall be presumed innocent until proved guilty according to law.

3. Everyone charged with a criminal offence has the following minimum rights:
   (a) to be informed promptly, in a language which he understands and in detail, of the nature and cause of the accusation against him;
   (b) to have adequate time and facilities for the preparation of his defence ;
   (c) to defend himself in person or through legal assistance of his own choosing or, if he has not sufficient means to pay for legal assistance, to be given it free when the interests of justice so require;
   (d) to examine or have examined witnesses against him and to obtain the attendance and examination of witnesses on his behalf under the same conditions as witnesses against him;
   (e) to have the free assistance of an interpreter if he cannot understand or speak the language used in court.

It will be seen that a fair trial is guaranteed for both civil and criminal cases and that article 6(1) applies to each. Articles 6(2) and 6(3) provide procedural guarantees applicable to criminal proceedings—but even if these are met there may not be a fair trial under article 6(1). In other words, the guarantees of articles 6(2) and 6(3) are necessary but not exhaustive.[166] Qualifications on the right to a fair trial are limited only to the circumstances enumerated in article 6(1) as to when a trial need not be public. Otherwise no qualifications are permitted, save for such as could be justified under article 15, *i.e.*, derogations in times of war or national emergency.

The *'Ringeisen' Case*[167] is important not only in the context of article 5 but also for an understanding of article 6. It has been made clear in the jurisprudence of the European Convention that 'civil rights and obligations' as found in article 6(1) is a term with an autonomous meaning, and is not solely a reference to rights that are recognized under domestic law. In the *'Ringeisen' Case* it was made clear that a right could be a 'civil right' under article 6(1) even if it was a public law right rather than a private law right.[168] The European Court held that

---

[166] See 'Pfunders' Case (Austria v. Italy), [1963] Y.B. Eur. Conv. on Human Rights 790 (opinion of Eur. Comm'n of Human Rights) (before Committee of Ministers).

[167] *Ringeisen, supra* note 142. *See also* text accompanying and following notes 142–43 *supra*.

[168] *Ringeisen, supra* note 142, at 850. For a useful discussion, *see* F. Jacobs, The European

article 6(1) was applicable, but that it had not been violated. The test for the applicability of article 6(1) is not that both parties should be private parties, but that the pre-existing relations between individuals under private law are in some way affected. Thus, notwithstanding 'Ringeisen', the Commission has held that article 6(1) (the right to a fair hearing) is not applicable to proceedings regarding a pension claim to set aside a planning decision.[169]

The *'Delcourt' Case*[170] has made it clear that article 6(1) applies not only in proceedings at first instance, but also through the appeals process (and, indeed, in applications to appeal).

The question of the right of access to the courts has been fundamental. In *Knechtl v. United Kingdom*,[171] the United Kingdom government had contended that article 6(1) does not guarantee a right to initiate proceedings, but rather contains procedural rights before a court once those proceedings have been initiated. The applicant was a prisoner who had sought to commence legal action for the loss of his leg in prison, contending it was due to the negligence of the prison authorities. The United Kingdom argued that even if article 6(1) did provide a right to commence proceedings before a court, that right must necessarily be limited in the case of prisoners. The case reached a friendly settlement, so these issues were not resolved, though similar ones arose in the *'Golder' Case*.[172] In this case the applicant was in prison in the United Kingdom when rioting broke out. He was originally charged with participation in this, though the charges were not pursued. Golder, protesting that he had not been involved, wanted reference to the charge removed from his record book, and he also wanted to instigate libel charges against the prison officer who made the charge. He was particularly anxious that the reference to the riot and his alleged part in it might hinder his chances of parole. His letters were intercepted by prison authorities (in accordance with the Prison Rules, 1964) and the Home Secretary denied him permission to consult a solicitor. As to this last matter, Golder claimed a breach of article 6(1). As in *Knechtl*, the United Kingdom asserted that article 6(1) does not confer a right to access to the courts; and that even if it did, that right was not available to convicted prisoners. The government argued

Convention on Human Rights 79 (1975). The European Commission had held art. 6(1) to not be applicable to the situation in 'Ringeisen'—a view overturned by the European Court.

[169] *See, e.g.*, Application 5428/72, 44 Recueil de Decisions 49 (1973); 'König' Case, [1978] Y.B. Eur. Conv. on Human Rights 618 (Eur. Ct. of Human Rights). In the latter case, the European Court seems to have focused on the private, *i.e.*, commercial, nature of König's medical practice, rather than on the role of the public authorities in permitting medical practice. On the particular facts of the case, this is a curious choice of focus.

[170] [1970] Y.B. Eur. Conv. on Human Rights 1100 (Eur. Ct. of Human Rights).

[171] [1970] Y.B. Eur. Conv. on Human Rights 730 (Eur. Comm'n of Human Rights).

[172] [1975] Y.B. Eur. Conv. on Human Rights 290 (Eur. Ct. of Human Rights).

that article 5(4) explicitly provided for the right of access. If article 6(1) also provides access it would be expected to say so explicitly. To interpret article 6(1) as giving a right of access made article 5(4) redundant.

The European Court held that any ambiguity in article 6 had to be interpreted in such a way as to give effect to the purposes and objectives of the European Convention, rather than in a manner to limit the obligations of the parties. It thought that although article 6(1) does not specifically state the existence of a right of access to the courts, the right to institute proceedings in civil matters is one aspect of the right to a court,[173] Even without reference to the *travaux préparatoires*, the Court was prepared to find that article 6(1) secures to everyone the right to have any claim relating to civil rights and obligations brought before a court or tribunal. As to the 'implied limitation' argument, the Court was not prepared to advance a general theory. It merely said that Golder was entitled in the circumstances to consult a solicitor, and that it was not for the Home Secretary to appraise the prospects of the action contemplated. Article 6(1) thus applied and had been violated.

The 'implied limitation' question arose also in the *'Engel' Case*.[174] In this case, certain Dutch soldiers had been placed under arrest for certain actions of military indiscipline.[175] Was the military charge a 'criminal charge' under article 6(1)? The European Court thought it no more than a starting point to know whether the provisions determining the charge belonged to the criminal or disciplinary law of the state concerned. The nature of the offenses was the more important test. The Court agreed with the Dutch government that the offense was essentially disciplinary. But the Court then slid (through a process of logic that is not entirely clear to this author) into stating that the heavier punishment was of a sort associated with criminal offenses (*i.e.*, significant deprivations of liberty). Article 6 therefore applied to some of the applicants but not to Engel. As the hearing before the Supreme Military Court was *in camera*, in circumstances not justified in any way by the government as an exception to the general rule of public trial, there was a violation.

In a not dissimilar recent case, *Eggs v. Switzerland*,[176] the European Commission dealt with disciplinary measures imposed on a Swiss serviceman which were challenged under articles 5 and 6. The Commission held[177]—adopting the Court's tests in the *'Engel' Case*—that a

[173] *Id.* at 292.
[174] *Engel, supra* note 151.
[175] There were separate arguments raised about the freedom of members of the armed forces to print publications undermining military discipline. *See* text accompanying note 187 *infra*.
[176] Application 7431/76. *See* text accompanying notes 153–54 *supra*.
[177] Report of Eur. Comm'n, Mar. 4, 1978.

refusal to obey an order to perform fatigues did not affect the interests of society protected by criminal law, and that the severity of the penalty did not lead to the view that the offense was criminal. Article 6(1) was here found to be inapplicable.

In an interesting case, *Airey v. Ireland*,[178] the European Court held that the applicant was denied effective right of access to the courts to seek judicial separation by virtue of the fact that she could not afford the costs involved and no legal aid for separation proceedings was available. The Court was careful to confirm an earlier line of doctrine, *viz.* that the European Convention does not *per se* lay down a requirement for the provision of legal aid. But in these circumstances legal aid was essential if the applicant was to have access to the courts.

The *'Leudicke, Belkacem and Koç' Case*[179] raises pertinent questions relating to article 6(3). The applicants were non-Germans brought to trial for criminal offenses in Germany. They had each received interpreters for whom no charge had been made during the course of trial. But after conviction the applicants were ordered to pay for the interpreters. The German government argued that the entitlement under article 6(3)(e) to 'free assistance' was in respect of a person 'charged with a criminal offence'. After conviction they were no longer persons charged with criminal offenses,[180] and under German legislation became liable for costs. The European Court rejected this, holding that article 6(3)(e) guaranteed the right to free interpretation without having to repay the costs to persons who could not speak or understand the language of the court. Further, and importantly, that right extends also to all documentation or statements necessary for the accused to understand in order to have a fair trial.[181]

4. *Case Study. The Rights to Free Speech*

No course on the European Convention can reasonably omit special study of the right of freedom of speech under that instrument. Article 10 provides:

1. Everyone has the right to freedom of expression. This right shall include freedom to hold opinions and to receive and impart information and ideas without interference by public authority and regardless of frontiers. This article shall not prevent States from requiring the licensing of broadcasts, television or cinema enterprises.

[178] [1979] Y.B. Eur. Conv. on Human Rights 420 (Eur. Ct. of Human Rights).
[179] [1978] Y.B. Eur. Conv. on Human Rights 630 (Eur. Ct. of Human Rights).
[180] This argument would mean that an *acquitted* person would in principle equally have to pay, as that person too would no longer be 'charged with a criminal offence'.
[181] For an excellent analysis of this judgment, *see* Duffy, *The Luedicke, Belkacem and Koç Case*, 4 Human Rights Rev. 98 (1979).

2. The exercise of these freedoms, since it carries with it duties and responsibilities, may be subject to such formalities, conditions, restrictions or penalties as are prescribed by law and are necessary to a democratic society, in the interests of national security, territorial integrity or public safety, for the prevention of disorder or crime, for the protection of health or morals, for the protection of the reputation or rights of others, for preventing the disclosure of information received in confidence, or for maintaining the authority and impartiality of the judiciary.

As early as the *'De Becker' Case*[182] the European Commission had had to address itself to the compatibility of national legislation with the right to freedom of expression. It examined article 123 *sexies* of the Belgian Penal Code (which punished the applicant for wartime journalism in collaboration with the Nazis) by imposing upon him a prohibition against publishing or writing for publication. It was found that the breadth of this prohibition (which went beyond publication of political matters and continued in effect years after the end of the war) was contrary to article 10 of the European Convention. New legislation was introduced before the matter went to the European Court, and that body agreed, after reviewing the situation, to strike the case from its list.[183]

In *Pers N.V. v. Netherlands*,[184] a magazine publisher wanted to be able to include information on radio and TV programs but was prevented from doing so by the Copyright Act and the Broadcasting Act. The government pointed to the fact that there existed in The Netherlands seven broadcasting channels which jointly published details of broadcasting, and that even if there was a restriction on the applicant's freedom to publish, it was for the purpose of protecting the rights of others. The European Commission adopted a report[185] and the matter went to the Committee of Ministers. The Committee of Ministers agreed with the Commission[186] that there was no interference with the applicant's rights under article 10(1), as the freedom to impart information was limited to information produced, provided, or organized by the person claiming the right. In other words, article 10 does not cover information not yet in one's possession. The Committee of Ministers commented that article 10(1) was not directed to the protection of the commercial interests of particular newspapers.

In *'Engel'*,[187] Dutch soldiers claimed, *inter alia*, that in suffering

[182] [1962] Y.B. Eur. Conv. on Human Rights 320, 324–26 (Eur. Ct. of Human Rights).
[183] *Id.* at 336.
[184] *See* [1973] Y.B. Eur. Conv. on Human Rights 124 (Eur. Comm'n of Human Rights).
[185] Report of Eur. Comm'n, July 6, 1976.
[186] Committee of Ministers Res. DH (77) 1, *reprinted in* Article 32 Resolutions, *supra* note 92.
[187] *See* text accompanying notes 151 & 174–75 and note 151 *supra*.

disciplinary punishment for the publication of certain materials their freedom of expression had been denied. Was the restriction necessary in a democratic society for the protection of order? The European Court held that it must take into account the specific characteristics of military life, and also that The Netherlands goverment had a margin of appreciation in deciding how those characteristics should best be protected. It is in that context that one must read the otherwise curious dictum that 'there was no question of depriving them of their freedom of expression but only of punishing the abusive exercise of that discretion'. The European Court found there was no breach of article 10(2).

In the *'Handyside' Case*[188]—where the question of margin of appreciation was at issue again—the European Court was concerned with the reference to the limitation based on 'protection of morals' in article 10(2). Handyside was a publisher who planned to publish and distribute in the United Kingdom 'The Little Red Schoolbook'. It was seized prior to publication under the Obscene Publications Act and Handyside was convicted and fined. Handyside claimed before the European Commission that the action taken against the book and him was contrary to various articles of the European Convention, including article 10. The book—directed at schoolchildren—had in fact circulated without legal restraint in several other countries which were parties to the European Convention.

The United Kingdom claimed that its legislation was not in substance different from comparable legislation in other Western European states, that the legislation was necessary to protect the young, and that it fell within the limitation of article 10(2) which referred to the protection of morals. The Commission was narrowly divided in its findings, with the majority finding significant the fact that the book was intended for schoolchildren. It found that the interference had been necessary for the protection of morals of the young and was reasonably necessary in a democratic society. The dissenting members thought that their task was not to review the decision of the English court but rather to assess the book in the light of the Convention in order to ascertain whether an infringment fell under Article 10(2).

The European Court held that there was no violation of article 10. While the relevant national legislation did not reveal a uniform European concept of morals, the national authorities had a margin of appreciation (available alike to the domestic legislature, as to judicial and other bodies that have to interpret the law) in assessing pressing social needs. The European Court acknowledged that the very notion

[188] [1976] Y.B. Eur. Conv. on Human Rights 506 (Eur. Ct. of Human Rights).

of a 'democratic society' meant that there was freedom of expression for unpopular or shocking ideas as well as for ideas that were inoffensive: but the 'encouragement to indulge in precocious activities harmful for [children] or even to commit certain criminal offences' gave sufficient reason for the United Kingdom to rely on the limitation of article 10(2).

The *'Handyside' Case* introduced a range of issues that were also to be relevant in *'The Sunday Times' Case*.[189] In both cases there was at issue one of the limitations available under article 10, the question of 'margin of appreciation'[190] for the state in deciding that such a limitation needed to be relied on, and the particular difficulties that arise when the European Commission and the European Court deal with matters that arise out of judicial decisions at the national level. *'The Sunday Times' Case* arose out of legal actions against the Distillers Company, the manufacturers of thalidomide, by parents of thalidomide children. *The Sunday Times* had conducted a campaign supporting the thalidomide victims, a campaign critical to Distillers and the terms of settlement that it had eventually offered. Litigation was still pending when an injunction was granted by the High Court to prevent *The Sunday Times* from publishing an article which argued that Distillers showed insufficient concern about the dangers of the product at various stages. The Court of Appeal was prepared to allow publication, but the House of Lords unanimously affirmed the judgment of the High Court. The House of Lords addressed itself to the argument that the article constituted a contempt of court given that litigation was still outstanding. Their Lordships thought that public policy required a balancing of interests which might conflict—freedom of speech and the administration of justice. The latter required that citizens should have access to duly established courts, that they should be able to rely upon decisions free from bias, and that once a matter was submitted to a court of law the court's functions should not be usurped. The House of Lords felt that *The Sunday Times* was usurping the court's function and conveying a message to all who would read the article that an examination of the issues would show Distillers to have been negligent.[191]

The European Commission and the European Court were at pains to point out that they were not 'judging the House of Lords' but rather

---

[189] [1979] Y.B. Eur. Conv. on Human Rights 402 (Eur. Ct. of Human Rights).

[190] *See* Morrisson, *Margin of Appreciation in Human Rights Law*, 6 Revue des Droits de l'Homme 263 (1963).

[191] It might be thought that this was a less than robust attitude, given that the Distillers case was not to be heard before a jury, and the judges were presumably capable of ignoring articles in the press when weighing the evidence. This author also finds curious the suggestion of usurpation of the court's function.

scrutinizing whether the restriction imposed on *The Sunday Times*
could be justified under article 10(2). The law of contempt, though not
enshrined in a statute, was still a restriction 'prescribed by law'—albeit
a rather unclear case law. But given the professional training in impartiality that judges receive, *The Sunday Times* article would not
influence a competent judge. Nor did the newspaper's views purport to
be a legal assessment of the merits of the Distillers case under the laws
of England; it was journalism rather than a usurpation of the functions
of the court.[192]

II. Teaching Suggestions

Ideally, all courses on regional human rights machinery and jurisprudence should be prefaced by a general overview of human rights in
international law. There should be several classes devoted to what one
could term the conceptual aspects of human rights. Before embarking
on substantive materials the students should understand the classical
relationship of the individual to the state under international law—
whether his or her own state or another state. This is the moment for a
historical survey of the theory of individual/state relationships: Locke,
Mill, Rousseau, and Austin could be usefully explained and selected
readings assigned. Other more contemporary writings could also be
studied (see Bibliography).[193]

An appreciation is necessary of the limits of 'regular' international
law in advancing the rights of the individual against governments.
Why do we need a special body of law termed 'human rights'? In what
ways is international law unable to provide full protection for the
individual? General international law affords little direct assistance to
the individual in claims against his or her own government. And the
individual is still constrained in asserting direct benefits under a
treaty.[194] At best, the individual will be able in domestic courts to cite
international instruments to which his or her state is party, and which
have a bearing on the rights being asserted. If these international
treaties have not been transformed (through statutory instruments or

[192] *See also* Duffy, *The Sunday Times Case: Freedom of Expression, Contempt of Court and
the European Convention on Human Rights*, 5 Human Rights Rev. 17 (1980). This author has
also found it useful to compare the (still modest) views of the European Convention on freedom
of expression with the rather different case law in the United States on first amendment
questions.

[193] In addition, *see* ch. 3 *supra.*

[194] Where a treaty provides for rights *in rem*, it may be possible for an individual to directly
assert benefits, but he or she may still need to persuade the state of nationality to pursue the
matter on his or her behalf. The Permanent Court thought that the matter turned on the
intentions of the parties to the treaty. *See* Jurisdiction of the Courts of Danzig [1928], P.C.I.J.,
ser. B, No. 15. And even in the case of clearly expressed intentions, the treaty will need to be made
part of the law of the land before the individual will have direct municipal rights under it. The
direct applicability of certain parts of the EEC Rome Treaty affords an example.

constitutional equivalent) into part of the domestic law of the land, the courts may consider that relevant in deciding whether the plaintiff can rely on them.[195] Above all, classical international law does not provide the individual claimant with any access to an international court against his or her *own* government. The individual is treated as lacking the procedural capacity to pursue such a claim at the international level, and the international tribunals generally make no provision for individual claims.[196]

An individual who wishes to pursue a claim against a foreign government is hardly in a better position. If the complaint is actionable in the courts of the state against which the complaint lies, the claimant is likely to pursue the case there[197]—but if the state's action is lawful under its own laws it is unlikely the case will succeed. An individual claimant does not have the legal capacity to bring an action on the international level and the international law rule of nationality of-claims severely circumscribes the chances of finding someone else whose government would be willing to bring the claim. So the claimant must persuade his or her government of the rightness of the claim, and, through the link of nationality, the government must perceive the harm done to the individual as an international legal wrong done to it. The case will not be pursued unless the government finds it diplomatically and politically expedient to do so. And then, if all those hurdles are surmounted, there must be a sufficient basis of jurisdiction for the matter to proceed before an international tribunal.[198]

It is therefore useful for the student to be given some understanding of the question of international minimum standards in the treatment of aliens, as well as an outline of the law of state responsibility and the exhaustion of local remedies rule. The student will need to understand the operation of the nationality of claims rule and the way in which this combination of international legal precepts can leave the individual exposed.[199] This is also the time to introduce the notion of domestic

---

[195] *See generally* text accompanying notes 75–82 *supra.*

[196] Thus art. 34(1) of the Statute of the International Court of Justice provides: 'Only states may be parties in cases before the Court.'

[197] The ability of a person to pursue a claim against a state depends on a variety of factors including the jurisdictional rules of the forum and whether the state is exempt from legal action under domestic law.

[198] If the case is to go before the International Court of Justice, there must be jurisdiction on the basis of art. 36 of the Statute of the Court, either by virtue of both parties having made a declaration recognizing the Court's competence under art. 36(2), with no reciprocally applicable reservations, or by virtue of a jurisdictional clause in an applicable treaty, or by *ad hoc* reference to the Court.

[199] On the nationality of claims rule, *see* D. O'Connell, 2 International Law 734–46, 1116–24 (1965). For comments on the ways in which this rule leaves the individual vulnerable, *see* Higgins, *Conceptual Thinking About the Individual in International Law*, 4 Brit. J. Int'l Stud. 1, 7–8 (1978).

jurisdiction: in most claims by individuals against their own governments it will be beyond the reach of other governments to lend assistance, in part because of the nationality of claims rule, but also because
of the insistence by the allegedly offending government that the matter
is within its own jurisdiction. Most legal matters that concern the state
and its citizens will be regarded as within the domestic jurisdiction of
that state[200] and not a matter of legitimate international concern.

The great significance of the concept of human rights is that it
provides some prospects for mitigating this exposure of the individual
in the face of the state. Classical international law cannot fulfill this
function. Human rights law is a special branch of international law,
one of whose salient features is that it can provide an individual with
access to international institutions whether the complaint is against his
or her own state or against another state.[201] Human rights law imposes
obligations upon states in respect of their treatment of individuals,
whether nationals or not; and it gives those individuals procedural
capacity to defend their rights. The enormous significance of those acts
cannot be exaggerated. Herein lies the importance for an individual to
be able to classify a claim as a human rights claim. There are other
important psychological and political functions performed by desig-
nating a legal claim as a human rights claim; in the ordering process of
competing claims, the claim of entitlement as a human right assumes a
certain priority.[202] It not only becomes a matter of legitimate international concern, beyond the domestic jurisdiction of any one state,
but it assumes a special significance and weight.

One can, of course, simply define human rights as those legal rights
that have found their way into the major human rights instruments.
This may be pedagogically convenient, but it is hardly satisfactory
intellectually. It assumes that no human rights exist outside of treaty
law, and it ignores the important process of identifying what legal
rights have come to be codified as human rights, and why. A discussion
on this topic will give the student some understanding of the trans-
mutation of certain claims from political aspiration to perceived
human rights. The U.N. organs are a fruitful laboratory for this
process, as is the negotiating-conference material of the major international instruments. Such a discussion would provide the student

[200] This flows from the legal precept that states have jurisdiction over persons and events
within their territory as an attribute of state sovereignty. Thus questions of private law and
remedies will *prima facie* fall within this category, as will matters of constitutional and administrative law.
[201] The European Convention allows complaints against states parties to be filed with the
European Commission by persons of *any* nationality. *See* European Convention, art. 25(1).
[202] For an excellent analysis of this aspect of human rights claims, *see* Bilder, *Rethinking
International Human Rights: Some Basic Questions*, 2 Revue des Droits de l'Homme 557
(1969).

with a salutary survey of a range of U.N. materials and could lead to a look at some of the *travaux préparatoires* of the European Convention on Human Rights.[203] Of particular interest is the debate over the balance to be struck between civil and political rights on the one hand and economic and social rights on the other. Are the latter 'realistic'? Does the preference for political and civil rights in the West reflect inadequacies in the social structure of those states? How has the matter been handled in the various major international instruments? Where are the pressures for the alternative views?

There is one other important topic which is sometimes left to be dealt with as an incidental to the case law in which it arises, but which properly belongs among the conceptual issues which must be addressed before the student can begin to come to grips with the details of the European Convention. To what extent is the notion of human rights an absolute or a relative one? Are our views of human rights the product of our own culture? Do the rights that westerners regard as essential (right of liberty, right to a fair trial, freedom of expression) reflect a certain structure of society or are they witness to an objective truth? Do many of the designated rights require a certain stage of development to have been reached and are they in fact luxuries that only the developed world can afford? Is it realistic to expect adherence to these rights by states that are still seeking to make effective their nationhood, and that desperately fear all centrifugal tendencies? These questions obviously are not directly addressed in the case law of the European Convention, but there is no avoiding them. The student will need to understand why the global human rights picture is such a curious collage of different instruments (some universal, some regional) that attempts different things. The student will also need some explanation as to why the Universal Declaration found binding legal form in two, rather than one, Covenants—and why the enforcement and scrutinizing procedures of the Covenants differ.[204]

III. Syllabus

A. The Conceptual Issues
　　1. The emergence of the modern state. The place of the individual therein. The role of international law in delineating that relationship.

　　　　L. Sohn & T. Buergenthal, The International Protection of Human Rights 1–21 (1973).

---

[203] *See* 1–4 Collected Editions of the Travaux Préparatoires of the European Convention on Human Rights (1975–1977).
[204] *See* ch. 10 *supra*.

McDougal, *Human Rights and World Public Order*, 63
Am. J. Int'l L. 237 (1969).

L. Henkin, The Rights of Man Today, ch. 1 (1979).

Milne, *The Idea of Human Rights: A Critical Enquiry*, in
Human Rights: Problems, Perspectives and Texts, ch. 2
(F. Dowrick ed. 1979).

2. The extent to which the relationship between the state and
the individual is an unchanging or relative one. Are there
'absolute' rights? The process of specifying human rights.
Human rights and political ideology. Human rights and
diverse conditions. Human rights and economic development.

Bilder, *Rethinking International Human Rights: Some
Basic Questions*, 2 Revue des Droits de l'Homme 557
(1969).

McDougal, *Human Rights and World Public Order: Principles of Content and Procedure for Clarifying General
Community Policies*, 14 Va. J. Int'l L. 387 (1974).

F. Dowrick, Human Rights: Problems, Perspectives and
Texts, ch. 1, *supra*.

R. Higgins, Human Rights: Prospects and Problems
(1979).

Eze, *Les Droits de l'Homme et le Sous-developpement*, 12
Revue des Droits de l'Homme 5 (1979).

Mower, *Human Rights in Black Africa: A Double Standard?*, 9 Revue des Droits de l'Homme 39 (1976).

3. Nationality and the protection of human rights. Nationality
of claims. Minimum standards in the treatment of aliens.
Outlines of the law of state responsibility and local remedies
rule. Inadequacy of the traditional approach.

Sohn & Buergenthal, *supra*, 62–116, 124–36.

Weis, *Diplomatic Protection of Nationals and International Protection of Human Rights*, 4 Revue des
Droits de l'Homme 642 (1971).

McDougal, Lasswell & Chen, *Nationality and Human
Rights: The Protection of the Individual in External
Arenas*, 83 Yale L.J. 900 (1974).

CASES: Tunis and Morocco Nationality Decrees, [1923]
P.C.I.J., ser. B.

Nottebohm, [1955] I.C.J.

Barcelona Traction, [1970] I.C.J.

4. Derogations from accepted standards.

a. In peace.

Higgins, *Derogations Under Human Rights Treaties*, 48 Brit. Y.B. Int'l L. 281 (1976–1977).

Tremblay, *Les Situations d'Urgence qui Permittent en Droit International de Suspendre les Droits de l'Homme*, [1977] Cahiers de Droit 3.

Garibaldi, *General Limitations on Human Rights: The Principle of Legality*, 17 Harv. Int'l L.J. 503 (1976).

Warbrick, *The Protection of Human Rights in National Emergencies*, in Human Rights: Problems, Perspectives and Texts, ch. 7, *supra*.

Daes, *Restrictions and Limitations on Human Rights*, in 3 René Cassin Amicorum Discipulorumque Liber 79 (1971).

Jacobs, *The Restrictions on the Exercise of Rights and Freedom Guaranteed by the European Convention on Human Rights*, 4 International Colloquy on the European Convention on HumanRights, Council of Europe Doc. H/Coll (75) 5(1975).

CASES: 'Lawless' Case, [1961] Y.B. Eur. Conv. 14 (Eur. Comm'n).

Greece v. United Kingdom (First Cyrpus Case), [1958–1959] Y.B. Eur. Conv. 182 (Eur. Comm'n).

Greece v. United Kingdom (Second Cyprus Case), [1958–1959] Y.B. Eur. Conv. 186 (Eur. Comm'n).

'Greek' Case, [1969] 1 Y.B. Eur. Conv. (Eur. Comm'n).

b. In armed conflict.

Respect for human rights in armed conflict, Report of of the U.N. Secretary-General, U.N. Doc. A/7720 (1969).

S. Bailey, Prohibitions and Restraints in War, chs. 3 & 4 (1972).

Final Act, Diplomatic Conference on the Reaffirmation and Development of International Humanitarian Law Applicable in Armed Conflicts, Comnd. No. 6927 (1977).

Sandoz, *La Place des Protocols Additionnels aux Conventions de Guerre du 12 Aout 1945 dans le Droit Humanitaire*, 12 Revue des Droits de l'Homme 135 (1979).

B. The Machinery
  1. The optional clauses. Petitions. The organs.
      Sohn & Buergenthal, *supra*, at 1008–1238.
      Schwelb, *On the Operation of the European Convention of Human Rights*, 18 Int'l Organization 558 (1964).
      —— *Abuse of the Right of Petition*, 3 Revue des Droits de l'Homme 313 (1970).
      Fawcett, *Application of the European Convention on Human Rights*, World Today (Apr. 1972).
      —— *Spread of the Ombudsman System in Europe*, World Today (Oct. 1975).
  2. The European Convention and national law.
      Golsong, *The European Convention before Domestic Courts*, 38 Brit. Y.B. Int'l L. 445 (1962).
      Dale, *Human Rights in the United Kingdom: International Standards*, 25 Int'l & Comp. L.Q. 292 (1976).
      P. Merlens, Le Droit de Recours Effectif Devant les Instances Nationales en cas d'un Violation d'un Droit de l'Homme (1973).
      Bill of Rights, 6 Dec. 1979 (H.L. Bill 100); Hansard, 402 H.L. (8 Nov. 1979); Hansard, 403 H.L. (22 Nov., 29 Nov., 6 Dec. 1979).
      Fawcett. *A Bill of Rights for the United Kingdom*, 1 Human Rights Rev. 57 (1976).
      Mann, *Britain's Bill of Rights*, 94 L.Q. Rev. 512 (1978).
  3. Admissibility. Exhaustion of local remedies. 'Manifestly ill-founded'. Friendly settlement. Reports of the European Commission. Reference to the European Court. Execution of the decisions of the Court. 'Just satisfaction.' The notion of a 'victim'.
      Cancado Trinidade, *Exhaustion of Local Remedies in the Jurisprudence of the European Court of Human Rights: An Appraisal*, 10 Revue des Droits de l'Homme 141 (1977).
      —— *The Burdens of Proof with regard to the Exhaustion of Local Remedies*, 9 Revue des Droits de l'Homme 81 (1976).
      Higgins, *The Execution of Decisions of Organs. Under the European Convention on Human Rights*, [1978] Revue Hellénique de Droit International 1.
  4. The European Convention and other international instruments.
      a. The restriction of the European Convention to civil rights;

cf. the U.N. Covenants and the Universal Declaration of Human Rights.

> Jacobs, *The Extension of the European Convention on Human Rights to include Economic, Social and Cultural Rights*, 3 Human Rights Rev. 163 (1978).

b. Overlapping jurisdiction and liabilities.

> Tardu, *Coexistence des Procedures Universelles en Regionalles de Plainfe Individuelle dans la Domaine des Droits de l'Homme*, 4 Revue des Droits de l'Homme 585 (1971).
>
> Schermers, *The Communities Under the European Convention on Human Rights*, [1978] Legal Issues Eur. Integration 1.
>
> Robertson, Human Rights in Europe 286–91 (2d ed. 1977).
>
> Problems arising from the co-existence of the United Nations Covenants on Human Rights and the European Convention on Human Rights, Report of the Committee of Experts on Human Rights to the Committee of Ministers, Council of Europe Doc. H (70) 7 (1970).
>
> Proceedings of the Colloquy about the European Convention on Human Rights in Relation to other International Instruments for the Protection of Human Rights, Athens, Sept. 21–22, 1978 (Strasbourg 1979).

C. Case Studies: The Rights Protected

1. Torture or inhuman or degrading treatment or punishment (article 3).

> CASES: 'Greek' Case, [1969] 1 Y.B. Eur. Conv. (Eur. Comm'n).
>
> Ireland v. United Kingdom [1978] Y.B. Eur. Conv. 602 (Eur. Ct.).
>
> Tyrer v. United Kingdom, [1978] Y.B. Eur. Conv. 612 (Eur. Ct.).
>
> Amerkane v. United Kingdom, [1973] Y.B. Eur. Conv. 356 (Eur. Comm'n).
>
> Spjut, *Torture under the European Convention on Human Rights*, 73 Am. J. Int'l L. 267 (1979).
>
> O'Boyle, *Torture and Emergency Powers under the European Convention on Human Rights: Ireland v. the United Kingdom*, 71 Am. J. Int'l L. 674 (1977).

2. Liberty of the person (article 5).
   a. Mental health patients' rights.
   　　　CASES: Winterwerp v. Netherlands, [1979] Y.B. Eur. Conv. 426 (Eur. Ct.).
   　　　　　　X v. United Kingdom, Eur. Ct. Press Release C (81) 58 (Nov. 5, 1981).
   b. Pre-trial detention.
   　　　CASES: 'Wemhoff' Case, [1968] 2 Y.B. Eur. Conv. 796 (Eur. Ct.).
   　　　　　　'Neumeister' Case, [1968] 2 Y.B. Eur. Conv. 812 (Eur. Ct.).
   　　　　　　'Matznetter' Case, [1969] Y.B. Eur. Conv. 406 (Eur. Ct.).
   　　　　　　'Stögmüller' Case, [1969] Y.B. Eur. Conv. 364 (Eur. Ct.).
   　　　　　　'Ringeisen' Case, [1971] Y.B. Eur. Conv. 838 (Eur. Ct.).
   　　　　　　'Huber' Case, [1971] Y.B. Eur. Conv. 548 (Eur. Comm'n).
   　　　　　　'Schiesser' Case, [1979] Y.B. Eur. Conv. 432 (Eur. Ct.).
   　　　　　　'Engel' Case, [1976] Y.B. Eur. Conv. 490 (Eur. Ct.).
   　　　　　　'König' Case, [1978] Y.B. Eur. Conv. 618 (Eur. Ct.).
   　　　　　　'Vagrancy' Cases, [1971] Y.B. Eur. Conv. 788 (Eur. Ct.).

3. Fair trial and access to courts (article 6).
   　　　CASES: 'Ringeisen' Case, [1971] Y.B. Eur. Conv. 838 (Eur. Ct.).
   　　　　　　'Delcourt' Case, [1970] Y.B. Eur. Conv. 1100 (Eur. Ct.).
   　　　　　　Knechtl v. United Kingdom, [1970] Y.B. Eur. Conv. 730 (Eur. Comm'n).
   　　　　　　'Engel' Case, [1976] Y.B. Eur. Conv. 490 (Eur. Ct.).
   　　　　　　Eggs v. Switzerland, Report of Eur. Comm'n, 4 Mar. 1978.
   　　　　　　'Airey' Case, [1979] Y.B. Eur. Conv. 420 (Eur. Ct.).
   　　　　　　'Luedicke, Belkacem and Koç' Case, [1978] Y.B. Eur. Conv. 630 (Eur. Ct.).

'Golder' Case, [1975] Y.B. Eur. Conv. 290 (Eur. Ct.).

Harris, *The Application of Article 6(1) of the European Convention on Human Rights to Administrative Law*, 47 Brit. Y.B. Int'l L. 157 (1974–1975).

Duffy, *The Luedicke, Belkacem and Koç Case*, 4 Human Rights Rev. 98 (1979).

Del Russo, *Prisoners' Rights of Access to the Courts: A Comparative Analysis of Human Rights Jurisprudence in Europe and the U.S.*, 13 J. Int'l L. & Econ. 1 (1978).

4. Freedom of expression (article 10).
   CASES: 'De Becker' Case, [1962] Y.B. Eur. Conv. 320 (Eur. Ct.).
   Pers v. Netherlands, Report of Eur. Comm'n, 6 July 1976.
   'Engel' Case, [1976] Y.B. Eur. Conv. 490 (Eur. Ct.).
   'Handyside' Case, [1976] Y.B. Eur. Conv. 506 (Eur. Ct.).
   'The Sunday Times' Case, [1979] Y.B. Eur. Conv. 402 (Eur. Ct.).

Duffy, *The Sunday Times Case: Freedom of Expression, Contempt of Court and the European Convention on Human Rights*, 5 Human Rights Rev. 17 (1980).

Fiengold, *The Little Red Schoolbook and the European Convention on Human Rights*, 3 Human Rights Rev. 21 (1978).

5. Non-Discrimination/Protection of minorities (article 14).
   CASES: 'Belgian Linguistics' Case, [1968] 1 Y.B. Eur. Conv. 832 (Eur. Ct.).

International Convention on the Elimination of All Forms of Racial Discrimination, 660 U.N.T.S. 195.

Bruegel, *A Neglected Field: The Protection of Minorities*, 4 Revue des Droits de l'Homme 413 (1971).

Dinstein, *Collective Human Rights of Peoples and Minorities*, 25 Int'l & Comp. L.Q. 102 (1976).

6. Privacy and family life (article 8).
   CASES: 'Klass' Case, [1978] Y.B. Eur. Conv. 622 (Eur. Ct.).
   Malone v. Metropolitan Police Commissioner, [1979] 2 W.L.R. 700.
   Alam and Khan v. United Kingdom, [1967] Y.B. Eur. Conv. 478 (Eur. Comm'n) (admissibility);

[1968] 1 Y.B. Eur. Conv. 788 (Eur. Comm'n)
(friendly settlement).

East African Asians v. United Kingdom (unpublished). But see Joint Council for Welfare of
Immigrants, 'The Unpublished Report' (Dec.
1979).

Privacy and Human Rights (A. Robertson ed. 1973).

IV. Minisyllabus

In Europe it is now customary for human rights courses, while making due reference to the United Nations' role and human rights machinery, to focus primarily on the European Convention on Human Rights. There are two reasons for this. First, the European Convention now provides a case law in the field that is as yet unmatched for interest. Second, because of their impact on the domestic legal plane, the decisions of the European Commission and the European Court are widely reported in the European press, and thus attract the notice of students. The first reason is sufficiently objective and weighty that in this writer's view any serious course on human rights must include close study of the European Convention. But it is appreciated that outside of continental Europe the balance may be different, and the main emphasis may be on, for example, the U.N. instruments or the Inter-American system for human rights.

But even a severely curtailed course-module on the European Convention (say two or three two-hour sessions) must contain certain elements if it is to have even marginal value. The student must above all be made aware of the essential nature of the European model— of like-minded democratic states agreeing on effective machinery to protect a limited number of rights. The central place of individual petitions, the parallel role of inter-State applications, and the role of the European Commission in admissibility and friendly settlement also need clear explanation. Care should be taken to distinguish qualifications on protected rights from derogation, and the nature of the institutional control over each must be examined. The student must also appreciate that certain rights do not admit of derogation or qualification. The following is a suggested short syllabus.

1. The parties to the European Convention.
2. The rights protected therein.
3. The additional rights in the First Protocol and the Fourth Protocol, and the parties thereto.
4. The machinery.

    Optional clauses (articles 25 and 46).

Inter-state applications (article 24).

The European Commission.

Admissibility, with particular reference to the exhaustion of local remedies.

Articles 26 and 27 explained.

Investigation and friendly settlement (article 28).

The Committee of Ministers.

Its functions under articles 32 and 54.

The European Court.

Who may refer and when.

5. Jurisprudence—the rights protected (a brief selection).

Torture: *Ireland v. United Kingdom.*

Fair trial/access to courts: *'Engel' Case.*

'Golder' Case.

Freedom of expression: *'The Sunday Times' Case.*

Privacy: *'Klass' Case.*

(Inevitably, taking any one of these cases in isolation, without also dealing with the other case law on the topic, distorts and to that extent misleads.)

V. Bibliography

All students will require a copy of the European Convention and the Protocols. Extremely useful for teaching purposes is *Human Rights in International Law: Basic Texts*, Council of Europe Doc. H (79) 4 (1979), published by the European Commission Secretariat. It contains not only the European Convention and its six Protocols, but also other leading human rights instruments, thus greatly facilitating comparative examination. Students must rapidly learn to find their way around the *Yearbook of the European Convention on Human Rights* which contains general information and extracts from decisions of all the organs. Importantly, it also includes selected decisions of national courts on the European Convention and extracts from proceedings of national parliaments. It has a useful bibliography. So far twenty-two volumes have been published. (It should also be explained to students that a special volume exists on the *'Greek' Case.*) But not all decisions find their way into the *Yearbook*. The paperback series of *Decisions and Reports* will lead to lesser known materials. Other essential primary source materials are: *Collected Texts*, which includes the Rules of Procedure of the European Commission, of the European Court, and Rules of the Committee of Ministers, as well as the state of ratifications; the Explanatory Reports on the Second to Fifth Protocols, Council of Europe Doc. H (71) 11 (1971).

Finally, so far as fairly current materials are concerned, it is advisable for universities offering courses on the European Convention to receive the 'blue book' versions of Commission Reports and Court Judgments. These arrive *seriatim* from Strasbourg in speedy fashion, making it unnecessary to await the publication of Court Judgments in the *Series A* bound form, or the Commission's Reports in the *Yearbook*. (Students should also be aware that when a case goes on to the Court, the judgment will contain a fairly detailed resumé of the Commission's report.)

Students will find *Stocktaking*, which is a periodic survey of decisions and case law in respect of all the rights, invaluable. Two useful new publications are the *Collection of Resolutions Adopted by the Committee of Ministers in Application of Article 32, 1959–1981*, Council of Europe Doc. H (81) 4 (1981), and *Collection of Resolutions Adopted by the Committee of Ministers in Application of Article 54, 1976–1981*, Council of Europe Doc. H (81) 5 (1981).

Leading Textbooks

S. Castberg, The European Convention on Human Rights (1974).
The European Convention on Human Rights, Int'l & Comp. L.Q. Supp. No. 11 (1965).
J. Fawcett, The Application of the European Convention on Human Rights (1969).
F. Jacobs, The European Convention on Human Rights (1975).
Mélanges Offerts à Polys Modinos: Problèmes des droits de l'Homme et de l'implication européenne (1968).
L. Mikaelsen, European Protection of Human Rights (1980).
F. Monconduit, La Commission Européene des Droits de l'Homme (1965).
C. Morrisson, The Developing European Law of Human Rights (1976).
1–3 René Cassin Amicorum Discipulorumque Liber (1968–1971).
L. Sohn & T. Buergenthal, International Protection of Human Rights, ch. 7 (1973).
K. Vasak, La Convention Européene des Droits de l'Homme (1964).
G. Weil, The European Convention on Human Rights: Background, Development and Prospects (1963).

Source Materials

Collected texts.
[European Convention; 6 Protocols; Rules of Procedure of the European Commission and the European Court of Human

Rights; Rules of the Committee of Ministers for the Application of Articles 32 and 54; state of ratifications.]
Publications of the European Court of Human Rights.
   [Series A—decisions and judgments.
   Series B—pleadings, oral arguments, and documents.]
Yearbook of the European Convention on Human Rights.
   [General information; extracts from decisions of the European Commission and Court.]
1–5 Collected Edition of the Travaux Préparatoires of the European Convention on Human Rights.
Collection of Decisions of National Courts relating to the European Convention on Human Rights.
   [Plus 4 supplements to date.]
Activities of the Council of Europe in the field of Human Rights.
   [Annual survey.]
Stocktaking on the European Convention on Human Rights.
   [A periodic survey of the results achieved; invaluable.]

VI. Minibibliography

J. Fawcett, The Application of the European Convention on Human Rights (1975) [use when going through the listed rights and articles relating to admissibility].

A. Robertson, Human Rights in Europe (2d ed. 1977) [especially for an understanding of how the European Commission works].

F. Jacobs, The European Convention on Human Rights (1975).

Schwelb, *On the Operation of the European Convention on Human Rights*, 18 Int'l Organization 558 (1964).

Buergenthal, *The Effect of the European Convention on Human Rights on the International Law of Member States*, in the European Convention on Human Rights, Int'l & Comp. L.Q. Supp. No. 11, at 82 (1965).

Higgins, *Derogations Under Human Rights Treaties*, 48 Brit. Y.B. Int'l L. 281 (1976–1977).

Index